THE DELL CROSSWORD DICTIONARY

COMPILED AND EDITED BY KATHLEEN RAFFERTY

A DELL TRADE PAPERBACK BOOK
Published by
Dell Publishing Co., Inc.
1 Dag Hammarskjold Plaza
New York, New York 10017

ISBN: 0-440-56314-3

Printed in the United States of America

Third Dell Trade Paperback printing—June 1982

CW

ABOUT THIS BOOK

Looking for an "Assam silkworm"? Cannot remember the name of a
"Brazilian coin"? Do not know a "Candlenut tree"? You will with the
aid of this book.

The purpose of this dictionary is to give puzzlers the pleasure of
completing, down to the last three-letter word, every crossword they
begin. It is meant to eliminate the frustration of filling in "all but a few"
of those final puzzle squares. Here is a complete 384-page reference
book, including the exclusive cross-referenced Word-Finder, to be used
by puzzle-solvers to find all those little-known, but much-used, crossword words.

The Dell Crossword Dictionary is the result of many years of exhaus-
tive research and was prepared by the editor of the famous Dell crossword publications, all leaders in the puzzle world.

Kathleen Rafferty
Compiler and Editor

TABLE OF CONTENTS

CROSSWORD DEFINITIONS
WITH ANSWER WORDS
page 6 to page 186

All the important crossword puzzle words are listed alphabetically by definition.

Look under group headings for these special word listings:

SPECIAL SECTION
READY REFERENCE WORD LISTS

THE WORD-FINDER
starts page 218

Every essential two-, three- and four-letter word in the English language. Cross-referenced to Definition pages for utmost aid to solving. You can complete unfinished puzzle words with this section.

ABBREVIATIONS USED IN THIS BOOK

abbr. .... abbreviation
Abyssin. .... Abyssinia(n)
Afgh. .... Afghanistan
Afr. .... Africa(n)
Am. .... American
Arab. .... Arabia(n)
Arch. .... Architecture
A.-S. .... Anglo-Saxon
Austr. .... Austria(n)
Austral. .... Australia(n)
Babyl. .... Babylonian
Bibl. .... Biblical
biol. .... biology
bot. .... botany; botanical
Braz. .... Brazil(ian)
Cent. Am. ... Central America(n)
Chin. .... Chinese
comb. form .... combining form
Dan. .... Danish
Du. .... Dutch
Du. E. Ind. ... Dutch East Indies
E. .... East
Egyp. .... Egypt(ian)
E. Ind. .... East Indies
Eng. .... England; English
Eur., Europ. .... Europe(an)
fort. .... fortification
Fr. .... France; French
geol. ...... geology; geological
geom. .... geometry
Ger. .... German(y)
Goth. .... Gothic
govt. .... government
Gr. .... Greek
Hebr. .... Hebrew
Her. .... heraldry
Himal. .... Himalayan
Holl. .... Holland
Ind. .... India(n)
Indo-Chin. .... Indo-Chinese
Ir. .... Ireland; Irish
Is. .... Island

Ital. .... Italian; Italy
Jap. .... Japan(ese)
Lat. .... Latin
math. .... mathematics
med. .... medical
Medit. .... Mediterranean
Mex. .... Mexican; Mexico
milit. .... military
Min. .... Minor
mus. .... music; musical
myth. .. mythological; mythology
N., No. .... North
naut. .... nautical
N. Hebr. .... New Hebrides
N. T. .... New Testament
N. Z. .... New Zealand
Nor. .... Norway; Norwegian
O. Eng. .... Old English
P. I. .... Philippine Islands
P. R. .... Puerto Rico
Pacif. .... Pacific
Pers. .... Persian
pert. .... pertaining
pharm. .... pharmacy
philos. .... philosophical
poet. .... poetry
Polyn. .... Polynesia(n)
Port. ..... Portugal; Portuguese
Pruss. .... Prussian
R. C. .... Roman Catholic
Rom. .... Roman
Russ. .... Russian
S. .... South
S. Afr. .... South Africa(n)
Scot. .... Scottish
Sp. .... Spanish
Teut. .... Teutonic
Turk. .... Turkey; Turkish
W. .... West
W. Ind. .... West Indian
WW .... World War
zool. .... zoology

DEFINITIONS
SECTION

CROSSWORD DEFINITIONS
AND ANSWERS

HOW TO USE THIS SECTION:

Here are crossword DEFINITIONS, arranged alphabetically.

Look up the DEFINITION of a crossword word, and you will find, in bold-face type, the word you want.

There are two kinds of crossword definitions. One is the almost unvarying definition: "Bitter vetch" or "Vetch" is used to define ERS. If you look in this dictionary under "B" for "bitter vetch" or under "V" for "vetch" you will find it there.

The other kind of definition, far more common, is the more varied definition where the puzzle-maker can choose from among many descriptive words when he defines a puzzle word: "India nurse," "Oriental nurse," "Oriental maid," "Oriental nursemaid" are all used in crossword puzzles as definitions for AMAH. For efficiency's sake, crossword words with varying definitions are listed here under the ESSENTIAL definition word. In the case of AMAH, the listing is under "nurse," "maid," and "nursemaid".

So, if you don't find your wanted word under the first word of the definition given, look for it under the other words of the definition.

The length of a word is important to crossword solvers, and so, when a definition fits two or more words the words are arranged according to length. For example: adage .... SAW, MAXIM, PROVERB.

Remember to use also the efficiently-arranged reference word lists in the SPECIAL SECTION, beginning on page 187.

A

a
acquiesce, fully ..... ACCEDE
acquire .... WIN, GAIN, REAP
acrobat of India .... NAT
Acropolis of Thebes .. CADMEA
across: comb. form
TRAN, TRANS
acrostic, Hebrew .... AGLA
act ...... DEED, FEAT, EMOTE
act: Lat. ...... ACTU, ACTUS
action, put into .... ACTUATE
action word .... VERB
active ... SPRY, AGILE, BRISK,
LIVELY, NIMBLE
actor .... HISTRIO, HISTRION
actor's group .... TROUPE
actor's hint .... CUE
actor's valet .... DRESSER
actual .... REAL, TRUE
actual being .... ESSE
actuality .... FACT
adage .... SAW, MAXIM,
PROVERB
Adam's ale .... WATER
Adam's 1st mate: legend
LILITH
Adam's grandson .... ENOS
Adam's son . ABEL, CAIN, SETH
adapt .... FIT
adept .... ACE
add on .... AFFIX, ANNEX,
ATTACH

b
adder, common .... ASP
additions .... ADDENDA
addition, bill's .... RIDER
adequate .... DUE, FULL,
AMPLE, EQUAL
adhere .... CLING, STICK,
CLEAVE
adherent .... IST
adhesive .. GUM, GLUE, PASTE
ADJECTIVE ENDING, see SUF-
FIX, ADJECTIVE
adjust ...... FIX, SET, ADAPT,
ATTUNE, ORIENT
adjutant .... AIDE
adjutant bird .... ARGALA,
HURGILA, MARABOU
admonish .... WARN, EXHORT,
REPROVE
admonisher .... MONITOR
adolescence .... TEENS,
YOUTH, NONAGE
adopted son of Mohammed . ALI
Adriana's servant ...... LUCE
adroit ...... READY, HABILE,
SKILLFUL
adulterate .. DEBASE, DEFILE,
DENATURE
advance guard .... VAN
advantage .... USE, GAIN,
PROFIT, BENEFIT

c
adventitious lung sound .. RALE
adventure ...... GEST, GESTE
adviser, woman ...... EGERIA
Aeëtes' daughter ..... MEDEA
Aegir's wife .... RAN
Aeneas' wife .... CREUSA
Aeneid author VERGIL, VIRGIL
Aesir ... TIU, TYR, ULL, FREY,
LOKE, LOKI, ODIN, THOR,
VALE, VALI, DONAR,
FREYA, BRAGI, WODEN,
BALDER
affectionate ... FOND, WARM,
LOVING, TENDER
affirm .. AVER, POSIT, ASSERT
affirmative .... AY, AYE,
YEA, YES
affirmative vote .... AY, AYE,
YEA, YES
afflict ...... TRY, VEX, PAIN,
DISTRESS
affluence ...... EASE, RICHES,
WEALTH
affray .... BRAWL, FIGHT,
MELEE
Afghan prince .. AMIR, AMEER
Afghan title .... KHAN
afresh .... ANEW

d
afraid: obsolete .... REDDE
AFRICAN .... see also SOUTH
AFRICAN and AFRICAN in
SPECIAL SECTION
AFRICAN ANTELOPE
see ANTELOPE
Afr. bass .... IYO
Afr. bustard .... KORI
Afr. cotton garment .... TOBE
Afr. disease .... NENTA
Afr. worm .... LOA
Afr. grass, millet-like .. FUNDI
Afr. hornbill .... TOCK
Afr. plant .... ALOE
Afr. scrub .... BITO
Afr. soldier .... ASKARI
Afr. squirrel .... XERUS
Afr. stockade .... BOMA
Afr. tableland .... KAROO
Afrikaans ...... TAAL, BOERS
aft .... ABAFT, ASTERN
after awhile .... ANON
aftermath .... ROWEN
afterpart of ship's keel
SKAG, SKEG
afterpiece, comic ..... EXODE
aftersong .... EPODE
again .... ENCORE
against .... CON, ANTI,
CONTRA, VERSUS
agalloch wood .. AGAR, ALOE,
GAROO
Agamemnon's son .... ORESTES

Agate

a

agate stone .... **ACHATE**
age .... **EON, ERA, AERA, RIPEN, PERIOD**
aged ..... **OLD, ANILE, SENILE**
agave fiber .... **ISTLE**
agency, depression-era .. **N R A**
agency, govt. ... **E C A, F H A**
agency, wage, price .... **E S A**
agency, ration-book .... **O P A**
agency, World-War II .. **O P A**
agent .... **DOER, FACTOR, FACIENT**
agents acted through .. **MEDIA**
aggregate . **SUM, MASS, TOTAL**
agitate .... **STIR**
agitation .... **STIR, DITHER, TUMULT**
agitation, be in state of **SEETHE**
agnomen .... **NAME**
agree ..... **GIBE, JIBE, TALLY, ASSENT, CONCUR**
agreeable: old Eng. ... **AMENE**
agreeableness of letters **EUTONY**
agreement ...... **MISE, PACT, CONCORD, ENTENTE**
agriculture goddess .... **CERES, VACUNA, DEMETER**
Agrippina's son .... **NERO**
Ahasuerus' minister .. **HAMAN**

b

ahead . **ON, BEFORE, FORWARD**
Ahiam's father .... **SACAR**
aid ... **ABET, ASSIST, SUCCOR, FURTHER**
aim ...... **END, GOAL, ASPIRE**
aims, with the same ... **AKIN**
air .. **AER, ARIA, MIEN, TUNE**
air apparatus ...... **AERATOR**
air current, ascending **THERMAL**
air, fill with .... **AERATE**
air, fresh .... **OZONE**
air passage ...... **FLUE, VENT**
air spirit .... **SYLPH**
air, upper .... **ETHER, AETHER**
aircraft, motorless .... **GLIDER**
airplane .... **JET, AERO**
airplane: Fr. .... **AVION**
airport marker .... **PYLON**
airport, Paris .... **ORLY**
airship . **AERO, BLIMP, PLANE**
airy ...... **LIGHT, ETHEREAL**
ait .... **ISLE**
Ajax, tale about ...... **MYTH**
Ajax's father ...... **TELAMON**
akin .... **SIB**
along grass .... **LALANG**
alarm . **SCARE, SIREN, AROUSE**
alas! .. **ACH, HEU, OCH, OIME**
alas: Irish .. **OHONE, OCHONE**
alas: poetic .... **AY**
Alaska glacier .... **MUIR**

c

ALBANIAN see COINS, TRIBES, GAZETTEER in SPECIAL SECTION
Albanian dialect .. **GEG, CHAM, GHEG, TOSK**
albatross, sooty ...... **NELLY**
alchitran .... **TAR, PITCH**
alcohol radical .... **AL**
alcohol, solid . **STERIN, STEROL**
alcoholic drink .... **GIN, RUM, RHUM**
Alcott heroine ...... **JO, AMY, MEG, BETH**
alcove .... **BOWER, RECESS**
alder tree: Scot .... **ARN**
ale mug .... **TOBY**
ale, sour .... **ALEGAR**
alewife fish .... **POMPANO**
ALEUTIAN see TRIBES, GAZETTEER in SPECIAL SECTION
Alexandrian theologian . **ARIUS**
Alexander victory ... **ISSUS, ARBELA**
alfalfa .... **LUCERN, LUCERNE**
Alfonso's queen .... **ENA**
alga .... **NORI**
alga, one-cell .... **DIATOM**
algae genus, fan-shaped ... **PADINA**
algarroba tree ...... **CALDEN**

d

Algerian governor .... **DEY**
ALGERIA—see SPECIAL SECTION
ALGONQUIN .... see Page 192
Ali Baba's word ...... **SESAME**
Ali, caliph descendants **ALIDS**
Alien in Hebrew territory .. **GER**
alienate ... **WEAN, ESTRANGE**
align ... **TRUE, ALINE, RANGE**
alkali .... **LYE, REH, USAR**
alkaline solution .... **LYE**
alkaloid .. **CAFFEIN, CAFFEINE**
alkaloid, calabar bean ... **ESERINE**
all: Lat. .... **TOTO**
all religions, believer in ... **OMNIST**
all right .... **OKAY, OKEH**
allanite .... **CERINE**
allay .... **CALM, ASSUAGE, RELIEVE**
alleged force .... **OD**
allegory, religious ... **PARABLE**
Allepo native .... **SYRIAN**
alleviate .... **EASE, ALLAY, LESSEN**
alley .... **MIB, MIG**
alliance ...... **UNION, LEAGUE**
alliance, Western ...... **NATO**
alligator .... **LAGARTO**

8

a

alligator pear ..... **AVOCADO**
alligator, S.A. ...... **CAIMAN, CAYMAN**
allot .... **METE, GRANT, ASSIGN, PORTION**
allotment .... **QUOTA, RATION**
allow .... **LET**
allowance **TARE, TRET, RATION**
alloy .... **MOKUM, OROIDE**
alloy, aluminum ...... **DURAL**
alloy, copper .... **BRASS**
alloy, copper-tin ..... **BRONZE**
alloy, gold-silver: Egyp. . **ASEM**
alloy, lead-tin .. **CALIN, TERNE**
alloy, non-ferrous ...... **TULA**
alloy, yellow .... **AICH**
allspice .... **PIMENTO**
allure .... **TICE, TOLE, TEMPT, ENTICE**
allusion .... **HINT**
almond emulsion ..... **ORGEAT**
almost .... **ANEAR**
alms box or chest ...... **ARCA**
aloe .... **AGAVE**
aloe derivative .... **ALOIN**
aloes product .... **ALOIN**
alone, on stage .. **SOLA, SOLUS**
along .... **ON, BESIDE**
alp .... **PEAK**

b

alpaca .... **PACO**
alphabet letter, old .... **RUNE**
Alps, Austro-It.
     TIROL, TYROL, TIROLO
Alps, one of .... **BLANC**
Alps pass .... **CENIS**
Alps, river rising in .. **RHONE**
Altar constellation ...... **ARA**
altar end of church .... **APSE**
altar screen .... **REREDOS**
altar shelf . **GRADIN, RETABLE**
altar side curtain .... **RIDDEL**
altar top .... **MENSA**
alternate .... **ROTATE**
alternative ...... **OR, EITHER**
alumni .... **GRADS**
always ... **AY, AYE, EER, EVER**
amadou .... **PUNK**
amass ..... **HOARD, GATHER**
amateur **TIRO, TYRO, NOVICE**
Amazon cetacean ...... **INIA**
Amazon tributary .. **APA, ICA**
ambary .... **DA**
ambary hemp ...... **NALITA**
ambassador .. **ENVOY, LEGATE**
amber fish
     RUNNER, MEDREGAL
Amen-Ra's wife .... **MUT**
amend **ALTER, EMEND, REVISE**
amendment, document . **RIDER**
amends, make .... **ATONE**
ament .... **CHAT**

c

Am. artist ..... **WEST, HICKS, HOMER, MARIN, PEALE, BEN-TON, COPLEY, INNESS, COR-BINO, ALBRIGHT**
AMERICAN INDIAN ...... see **INDIANS, Page 192**
Am. aloe fiber .... **PITA, PITO**
Am. author . **ADE, POE, AMES, BAUM, HARTE, WYLIE, YERBY, CORWIN, FERBER, HERSEY, KANTOR, MORLEY**
Am. author, illustrator ... **PYLE**
Am. capitalist .... **ASTOR**
Am. caricaturist .. **REA, NAST**
Am. dramatist . **AKINS, BARRY, ODETS, CROUSE**
Am. editor .... **BOK**
Am. educator .... **MANN**
Am. explorer . **BYRD, FREMONT**
Am. general
     LEE, OTIS, GREENE
Am. humorist ..... **ADE, NYE, COBB, NASH, ROGERS**
Am. jurist .... **TANEY**
Am. inventor ... **IVES, MORSE, TESLA, EDISON**
American: Mex. ..... **GRINGO**
Am. nature writer **BEEBE, SETON**
Am. nighthawk .... **PISK**
AM. PAINTER see AM. ARTIST

d

Am. patriot ...... **HALE, OTIS, ALLEN, REVERE**
Am. philanthropist ..... **RIIS**
Am. philosopher ..... **EDMAN**
Am. pianist
     ARRAU, DUCHIN, LEVANT
Am. poet . **POE, AUDEN, BENET, FROST, GUEST, RILEY, STEIN, MILLAY**
Am. poetess ... **STEIN, LOWELL**
Am. sculptor .... **CALDER**
AM. SINGER ... see SOPRANO
Am. statesman
     CLAY, BARUCH, DULLES
Am. suffragist .... **CATT**
Am. surgeon .... **PARRAN**
AM. WRITER see AM. AUTHOR
AMERIND (means any American Indian) See pages 192, 193
amide, pert. to .... **AMIC**
a mine: Corn. .... **BAL**
ammonia compound .. **AMIN, AMIDE, AMINE**
ammoniac plant ...... **OSHAC**
ammunition . **SHOT, SHRAPNEL**
ammunition, short for: . **AMMO, AMMU**
ammunition wagon ... **CAISSON**
among ...... **IN, MID, AMID**
amorously, stare .. **LEER, OGLE**
amount assessed ...... **RATAL**

Amount

a amount staked in gambling .... **MISE**
amuse .... **DIVERT**
ampere .... **WEBER**
amphibian
FROG, TOAD, ANURAN
amphibian, order **HYLA, ANURA**
amphitheater .... **ARENA**
amphitheater, natural . **CIRQUE**
amplification factor ...... **MU**
amulet .... **CHARM, PERIAPT**
analyze .... **ASSAY, DISSECT**
analyze grammatically . **PARSE**
ancestor of Irish .... **IR, ITH, MIL, MILED**
ancestor of man, Hindu . **MANU**
ancestral spirit, P. I. .. **ANITO**
ancestral .... **AVITAL**
ancestral spirits **LARES, MANES**
anchor ..... **FIX, TIE, MOOR, KEDGE**
anchor part .... **FLUKE**
anchor, small, light ... **KEDGE**
anchor tackle .... **CAT**
ancient Asiatic .... **MEDE**
ancient Briton .... **CELT**
ancient Chinese .... **SERES**
anchovy sauce .... **ALEC**
ancient city, Asia Minor **MYRA, NICAEA**
ancient country ...... **GAUL**
Ancient Egyp. kingdom **SENNAR**
ancient flute .... **TIBIA**
ancient Greece division **AETOLIA**
ancient invader, India
SAKA, SACAE
b ancient people of Gaul .. **REMI**
ancient Persian .... **MEDE**
ancient Persian money .. **DARIC**
ancient philosophy .... **YOGA**
ancient race .... **MEDES**
ancient Slav
VEND, WEND, VENED
ancient times .... **ELD, YORE**
ancient tribe of Britons . **ICENI**
ancient weight .... **MINA**
and .. **TOO, ALSO, PLUS, WITH**
and: Lat. .... **ET**
and not .... **NOR**
and so on: abbr. .... **ETC.**
Andes cold higher region. **PUNA**
Andes grass .... **ICHU**
Andes mountain .... **SORATA**
andiron .... **DOG**
"Andronicus,—" ...... **TITUS**
anecdotage or anecdotes
ANA, TALES
anent .... **RE, ABOUT, BESIDE**
anent, close — .... **TO**
anesthetic ...... **GAS, ETHER**
Angel of Death .... **AZRAEL**
angel, Pers. .... **MAH**

c anger .... **IRE, RAGE RILE, CHOLER**
anger, fit of .. **PIQUE, TEMPER**
angle, 57 degrees .... **RADIAN**
angle of leaf and axis ... **AXIL**
angle of leafstalk ...... **AXIL**
angle of stem, pert. to . **AXILE**
Anglo-Saxon "G" . **YOK, YOGH**
A.-S. god of peace ...... **ING**
A.-S. lord's man **THANE, THEGN**
A.-S. king .... **INE**
A.-S. money (coin) ...... **ORA**
A.-S. slave .... **ESNE**
A.-S. warrior .. **THANE, THEGN**
Angora goat .... **CHAMAL**
angry .... **HOT, MAD, SORE, IRATE**
animal, Afr. .. **CIVET, GENET, POTTO, ZEBRA, GENETTE**
animal, ant-eating . **ECHIDNA**
animal, aquatic . **SEAL, OTTER, WHALE, DUGONG, WALRUS, MANATEE**
animal, arboreal .... **TARSIER**
animal, Austral. .... **ECHIDNA**
animal, badgerlike, Java
TELEDU
animal body .... **SOMA**
animal, draft ......**OX, OXEN**
d animal, fabulous .... **DRAGON**
animal, giraffelike .... **OKAPI**
animal, India .... **DHOLE**
animal, Madagascar
FOSSA, FOUSSA
animals of area ..... **FAUNA**
animal-plant life ...... **BIOTA**
animal, Peru .... **ALPACA**
animal, sea .... **SEAL, CORAL, WHALE, WALRUS, DUGONG, MANATEE**
animal, S. Afr. ...... **ZORIL**
animal, S. Am. .. **APARA, COATI**
animal trail .... **RUN, SLOT, SPUR, SPOOR**
animating principle .... **SOUL**
ankle **TALUS, TARSI, TARSUS**
ankle, pert. to ...... **TARSAL**
Annamese measure .... **TAO**
ANNAMESE..see also ANNAM
in SPECIAL SECTION
Annapolis student **PLEB, PLEBE**
anneal ... **TEMPER, TOUGHEN**
annex .... **ADD, ELL, WING, ATTACH**
annatto seeds: Sp. .. **ACHIOTE**
annihilate **DESTROY, DISCREATE**
ANNIVERSARY . see WEDDING
announce .... **HERALD**
annoy .. **IRK, TRY, VEX, RILE, PEEVE, TEASE, BOTHER, MOLEST, PESTER, DISTURB**

a annual, as winds .... **ETESIAN**
annuity, form of .... **TONTINE**
annul .... **UNDO, VOID,
CANCEL, REVOKE**
annular die .... **DOD**
annulet: Her. .... **VIRE**
anoint ... **OIL, ANELE, ENELE**
another ... **NEW, ADDITIONAL**
ant .... **EMMET, PISMIRE**
antarctic bird ...... **PENGUIN**
antarctic icebreaker .... **ATKA**
antecedent . **PRIOR, ANCESTOR**
antelope, Afr. .... **GNU, KOB,
BISA, GUIB, KOBA, KUDU,
ORYX, POKU, PUKU, TORA,
ADDAX, ELAND, ORIBI,
RHEBOK**
antelope, Afr., large .. **IMPALA**
antelope, Afr., small .. **DUIKER**
antelope, Ind.
SASIN, NILGAI, NILGAU
antelope, Siberian ..... **SAIGA**
antelope, tawny .... **ORIBI**
antenna **HORN, PALP, AERIAL
FEELER**
antenna, with nodose
NODICORN
anthracite, inferior ..... **CULM**
anti-aircraft shells ..... **FLAK**
anti-tank gun .... **PIAT**
b antic ... **DIDO, CAPER, PRANK**
antique red color .. **CHAUDRON**
antiseptic .... **EUPAD, EUSOL,
IODIN, SALOL, CRESOL,
IODINE**
antiseptic, mercury
EGOL, METAPHEN
antitoxin ...... **SERA, SERUM**
antler point .... **SNAG, TINE,
PRONG**
antler, unbranched ...... **DAG**
antlers, stag's .... **ATTIRE**
"Anthony and Cleopatra" character .... **IRAS**
anvil .... **INCUS, TEEST**
anxiety .... **CARE**
any: dialect .... **ONI**
any one .... **AN**
aoudad .... **ARUI**
apathy ... **ENNUI, DOLDRUMS**
ape .... **ORANG**
ape, long-tailed, India ... **KRA**
appelation ..... **NAME, TITLE**
APERTURE . see also OPENING
aperture .... **GAP, HOLE,
SLOT, VENT, ORIFICE**
apex, at the .... **APICAL**
aphasia, motor .... **ALALIA**
aphorism .. **SAW, RULE, SUTRA**
Aphrodite .... **VENUS**

c Aphrodite, got apple from
PARIS
Aphrodite, love of ... **ADONIS**
Aphrodite's mother .... **DIONE**
Aphrodite's son .... **EROS**
apocopate .... **ELIDE**
Apocrypha, book from . **ESDRAS**
Apollo's instrument ..... **BOW,
LUTE, LYRE**
Apollo's mother **LETO, LATONA**
Apollo's sister
DIANA, ARTEMIS
Apollo's son .... **ION**
Apollo's twin .... **ARTEMIS**
Apollo's vale, sacred ... **TEMPE**
apoplexy, plant .... **ESCA**
Apostle (12) .... **JOHN, JUDE
(THADDEUS), JAMES, JUDAS,
PETER (SIMON PETER), SI-
MON, ANDREW, PHILIP,
THOMAS (DIDYMUS), MAT-
THEW (LEVI), MATTHIAS,
BARTHOLOMEW**
Apostle, Capernaum **MATTHEW**
Apostles, teaching of . **DIDACHE**
apparent ..... **OVERT, PLAIN,
EVIDENT**
apparition .. **SPECTER, SPECTRE**
appear .... **LOOK, LOOM, SEEM**
appearance . **AIR, MIEN, GUISE**
d appease ...... **CALM, ALLAY
PLACATE**
appellation ..... **NAME, TITLE**
append .... **ADD, AFFIX,
ATTACH**
appendage, caudal ... .**TAIL**
appetizer . **CANAPE, APERITIF**
apple ... **POME, TREE, FRUIT,
PIPPIN**
apple acid .... **MALIC**
apple seed .... **PIP**
apple tree .... **SORB**
apple tree genus ...... **MALUS**
apple, winter .... **ESOPUS**
apples, crushed .... **POMACE**
apple-like fruit .... **POME**
appoint .. **SET, NAME, CHOOSE**
apportion **DEAL, METE, ALLOT**
appraise **RATE, VALUE, ASSESS**
apprise ...... **ADVISE, NOTIFY**
approach ...... **NEAR, ANEAR,
ACCESS**
appropriate, ... **APT, FIT, MEET**
appropriate, not **INAPT, UNFIT**
apricot, Jap. .... **UME**
apricot, Korean . **ANSU, ANZU**
apricots .... **MEBOS**
apropos .... **PAT, FITTING**
apteryx .... **KIWI**
aptitude ..... **FLAIR, ABILITY**

11

Aptitude

a
aptitude, natural
.... FLAIR, TALENT
aquamarine .... BERYL
AQUATIC . see SEA or MARINE
Arab ....GAMIN, SEMITE
Arab cloak, sleeveless .... ABA
Arab drink ...... BOSA, BOZA
.... BOZAH
Arab name .... ALI
Arab's state of bliss ..... KEF
Arabia, people of .... OMANI
ARABIAN . see ARAB, ARABIA,
.... SPECIAL SECTION
Arabian chief . SAYID, SAYYID
Arabian chieftain AMIR, EMIR,
.... AMEER, EMEER
Arabian chieftain's domain
.... EMIRATE
Arabian cloth .... ABA
Arabian district .... TEMA
Arabian garment .... ABA
Arabian jasmine .... BELA
Arabian judge .... CADI
"Arabian Nights" dervish . AGIB
Arabian noble .. AMIR, EMIR,
.... AMEER, EMEER
Arabian nomadic tribesman
.... SLEB
Arabian sailboat .. see VESSEL,
.... ARAB
Arabian sleeveless garment ABA
b
Arabian tambourine
.... TAAR, DAIRA, DAIRE
Arabic jinni, evil
.... AFRIT, AFREET, AFRITE
Arabic letter . GAF, KAF, MIM,
.... WAW, ALIF, DHAL
Arabic script .... NESKI
Arabic surname .... SAAD
arachnid . MITE, TICK, SPIDER
Arawakan language .... TAINO
arbitrator ... UMPIRE, REFEREE
arboreal .... DENDRAL
arc .... LINE, CURVE
arch of heaven .... COPE
arch, pointed .... OGIVE
archaeology, mound ..... TERP
archangel .... URIEL
archbishop .... PRIMATE
archbishop, Canterbury BECKET
archer in Eng. ballad
.... CLIM, CLYM
archetype ... MODEL, PATTERN
archfiend .... SATAN
architect's drawing ..... EPURE
architecture, school of
.... BAUHAUS
architecture, type
.... DORIC, IONIC
ARCTIC ..... see GAZETTEER
Arctic . NORTH, POLAR, FRIGID

c
arctic air force base .... THULE
arctic dog .... SAMOYED
arctic gull genus ...... XEMA
arctic plain .... TUNDRA
Arden .... FOREST
ardor ... ELAN, ZEAL, FERVOR
area measure .. RADII, RADIUS
area, small .... AREOLA
areca .... BETEL
arena .... FIELD
Ares' mother .... ENYO
Ares' sister .... ERIS
ares, 10 .... DECARE
Argonaut ... JASON, ACASTUS
Argonauts' leader ...... JASON
Argonauts' ship .... ARGO
argument .... AGON,
.... DEBATE, HASSLE
arhat .... LOHAN
aria ...... AIR, SOLO, SONG,
.... TUNE, MELODY
arias .... SOLI
aridity, having .... XERIC
arikara .... REE
arise .... REBEL, ACCRUE,
.... APPEAR
arista .... AWN
Arizona aborigine ...... HOPI
ARIZONA INDIAN see page 192
d
ARIZONA ... see also SPECIAL
.... SECTION
Ark, porter of: Bible ..... BEN
Ark's landing place .. ARARAT
arm .... LIMB, TENTACLE
arm, movable with verniers
.... ALIDADE
arm of sea . BAY, FIRTH, FRITH
armadillo ...... APAR, APARA
armadillo, Braz. . TATU, TATOU
armadillo, giant . TATU, TATOU
armadillo, large 12-banded
.... TATOUAY
armadillo, 6-banded .. PELUDO
armadillo, small .. PEBA, PEVA
armadillo, 3-banded .... APAR,
.... APARA, MATACO, MATICO
armed band .... POSSE
armed galley of old Northmen
.... AESC
ARMOR .... see also SPECIAL
.... SECTION, page 194
armor bearer .... ARMIGER
armor, body .... CUIRASS
armor, chain .... MAIL
armor, horse .. BARD, BARDE
armor, leg .... JAMB, JAMBE
armor, leg below knee GREAVE
armor, lower body ..... CULET

12

a
armor part .... LORICA
armor part, throat ... GORGET
armor, skirt .... TACE, TASSE, TASSET
armor, thigh ... CUISH, TUILE, CUISSE, TUILLE
armpit .... ALA
army .... HOST, TROOPS
army group .... CADRE
army provisioner ...... SUTLER
aroid, an .... ARAD, ARUM
aromatic herb
　　　　DILL, MINT, SAGE
aromatic herb, carrot genus
　　　　CARUM
aromatic herb-plant .... NARD
aromatic seed
　　　　CUMIN, CUMMIN
aromatic seed, plant ... ANISE
aromatic substance ... BALSAM
aromatic weed .... TANSY
around .... CIRCA
arouse .... FIRE, STIR, PIQUE
arpeggio .... ROULADE
arquebus support ...... CROC
arraign ..... ACCUSE, INDICT
arrange ...... FIX, SET, FILE, DISPOSE
arrangement: comb. form . TAX, TAXI, TAXO, TAXEO, TAXIS

b
arrangement, pert. to . . TACTIC
array .. DECK, ORDER, ATTIRE
arrest .... NAB, HALT
arrest writ .... CAPIAS
arris .... PIEN
arrow .... BOLT, DART
arrow, body of .... STELE
arrow, fit string to ..... NOCK
arrow, spinning .... VIRE
arrow wood .... WAHOO
arrowroot .... PIA, ARARU
arroyo .... HONDO
art: Lat. .... ARS
art style ...... DADA, GENRE
Artemis . UPIS, DELIA, PHOEBE
Artemis' twin .... APOLLO
Artemis' victim ...... ORION
artery, largest .... AORTA
artery of neck ..... CAROTID
artful .... SLY, WILY
arthritis aid ACTH, CORTISONE
Arthur's foster brother ... KAY
Arthurian lady
　　　ENID, ELAIN, ELAINE
article .... AN, THE, ITEM
article, Fr. ...... LA, LE, DES, - LES, UNE
article, Ger. .... DAS, DER
article, Sp. .. EL, LA, LAS, LOS
articulated joint ..... HINGE
artifice ... RUSE, WILE, TRICK

c
artificial language .... RO, IDO
ARTIST .... see also PAINTER
　　　　and under Country
　　　　of each artist
artist, primitive .... MOSES
artless .... NAIVE
arum family plant TARO, CALLA
arum plant ..... ARAD, AROID
Aryan .... MEDE, SLAV
as .. QUA, LIKE, SINCE, WHILE
as far as .... TO
as it stands: mus. .... STA
as written: mus. .... STA
asafetida .... HING
asbestos .... ABISTON
ascent .... UPGO, CLIMB
ascetic, ancient .... ESSENE
asceticism, Hindu ...... YOGA
ash, fruit, seed ..... SAMARA
ash key .... SAMARA
ashy pale .... LIVID
ASIA .. see also SPECIAL SEC-
　　　　TION
Asia Minor district, old IONIA
Asia Minor region, pert. to
　　　　EOLIC, AEOLIC
Asia native, S.E. ...... SHAN
Asiatic ancient people .. SERES

d
Asiatic country .. see page 210
Asiatic cow .... ZO, ZOH
Asiatic evergreen ...... BAGO
Asiatic fowl .... SAT
Asiatic gangster .... DACOIT
Asiatic sardine .... LOUR
Asiatic shrub .... TEA, TCHE
Asiatic tree .... ACLE, ASAK, ASOK, ASOKA
"— asinorum" .... PONS
askew .... WRY, AGEE, ALOP, AWRY
aspect ... SIDE, FACET, PHASE
asperse .... SLANDER
aspire .... HOPE
ass, wild
　KULAN, ONAGER, QUAGGA
assail .... BESET, ATTACK
ASSAM ..... see also SPECIAL
　　　　SECTION, Page 191
Assam hill tribe .... AKA
Assam mongol .... NAGA
Assam silkworm .... ERI, ERIA
Assam tribe, Naga Hills
　　　　AO, NAGA
assault .... ONSET, STORM
assault, prolonged ...... SIEGE
assayer .... TESTER
assaying cup .... CUPEL
assemble .... MEET, MUSTER, COLLECT

Assembly

a assembly .... **DIET, SYNOD SESSION, GATHERING**
assembly, A.-S. **GEMOT, GEMOTE**
assembly, China, Hawaii .. **HUI**
assembly, Dutch .... **RAAD**
assent, solemn .... **AMEN**
assert .... **AVER, POSIT, STATE**
assert formally .... **ALLEGATE**
assess ..... **TAX, LEVY, VALUE**
assessment **RATE, SCOT, RATAL**
asseverate .... **AVER**
assignor of property ... **CEDENT**
assimilate .. **ABSORB, DIGEST**
assistance **AID, HELP, SUPPORT**
assistant .... **AIDE**
associate .. **ALLY, COLLEAGUE**
association, trade **GILD, GUILD**
assuage .... **MITIGATE**
ASSYRIAN .. see also SPECIAL SECTION, Page 198
Assyrian king .... **PUL**
Assyrian queen, myth.
SEMIRAMIS
asterisk .... **STAR**
astern ..... **AFT, BAFT, ABAFT**
astringent .... **ALUM, STYPTIC**
astringent, black ...... **KATH**
astringent fruit .... **SLOE**
astrologer of India .... **JOSHI**
b astronomical .... **URANIC**
astron. luminous "cloud"
NEBULA
Aswan, ancient ...... **SYENE**
asylum ...... **HAVEN, REFUGE**
at all .... **ANY**
at any time .... **EVER**
at odds .... **OUT**
at the home of: Fr. ..... **CHEZ**
Atahualpa, king ... ... **INCA**
atap palm .... **NIPA**
atelier .... **STUDIO**
Athamas' wife .... **INO**
Athena ... **PALLAS, MINERVA**
Athena, appellation, title . **ALEA**
Athena, possession of ... **EGIS**
Athenian .... **ATTIC**
Athenian bronze coin **CHALCUS**
Athenian demagogue ... **CLEON**
Athens, last king of .. **CODRUS**
athlete, famous ...... **THORPE**
a-tiptoe .... **ATIP**
atmospheric pressure, of **BARIC**
at no time: poet. ...... **NEER**
atoll's pool .... **LAGOON**
atom part .... **PROTON**
atomic machine
BETATRON, RHEOTRON
atomic physicist .. **BOHR, RABI, UREY, FERMI, PAULI, COMPTON, MEITNER MILLIKAN**

c atomic submarine .... **SKATE, SARGO, TRITON, NAUTILUS**
atone for .... **REDEEM**
attach .... **ADD, FIX, TIE, APPEND**
attack .... **BESET, ONSET**
attack, mock .... **FEINT**
attar .... **OTTO**
attempt ... **TRY, STAB, ESSAY**
attendant, hunter's
GILLY, GILLIE
attention ... **EAR, CARE, HEED**
attest ..... **VOUCH, CERTIFY**
attic .... **LOFT, GARRET**
Attica resident .... **METIC**
Attila .... **ATLI, ETZEL**
attitudinize .... **POSE**
attribute .. **IMPUTE, ASCRIBE**
attune .... **KEY, ACCORD**
auction .... **SALE**
audience ...... **EAR, HEARING**
auditory .... **OTIC, AURAL**
auger .... **BORE, BORER**
augment .... **EKE**
augur .... **BODE, PORTEND**
augury ...... **OMEN, PORTENT**
auk genus .. **ALCA, ALLE, URIA**
auk, little ... **ROTCH, ROTCHE**
aura, pert. to .... **AURIC**
d aureola .... **HALO**
auric acid salt ...... **AURATE**
auricle .... **EAR**
auricular ...... **OTIC, EARED**
aurochs .. **TUR, URUS, AURUS**
aurora .... **EOS, DAWN**
auspices .... **EGIS, AEGIS**
Australasian harrier-hawk
KAHU
Australasian shrub genus
HOYA
AUSTRALIA . see also SPECIAL SECTION
Australian boomerang .. **KILEY**
Austral. food .... **KAI**
Austral. gum tree
KARI, TUART
Austral. hut .... **MIAM, MIMI**
Austral. marsupial
TAIT, KOALA
Austral. scaly-finned fish
MADO
Austral. tree, timber .. **PENDA**
Austrian folk dance .. **DREHER**
Austr. violinist .... **MORINI**
author .... **PARENT**
author, boys' .. **ALGER, HENTY**
author, nature stories .. **SETON**
authoritative .... **MAGISTRAL**
author unknown: abbr. .. **ANON**

14

a
authority, name as **CITE, QUOTE**
auto, old .. **JALOPY, JALOPPY**
automaton .... **ROBOT**
automaton: Jew. legend **GOLEM**
automobile "shoe" . **TIRE, TYRE**
ave .... **HAIL**
avena .... **OAT**
avenger: Hebr. .... **GOEL**
average .... **PAR, MEAN,**
   NORM, USUAL, MEDIAL
averse .... **LOTH, LOATH**
Avesta division
   YASNA, GATHAS, YASHTS
avid .... **KEEN, EAGER**
avifauna .... **ORNIS**
avocado, Mex. .... **COYO**
avoid .... **SHUN, ESCHEW**

c
avouch .... **AVER, ASSERT**
away .... **OFF, GONE, ABSENT**
aweather, opposed to .... **ALEE**
aweto .... **WERI**
awkward .... **INEPT**
awkward fellow .... **LOUT**
awn .... **ARISTA**
awned .... **ARISTATE**
awry .... **AGEE, AJEE, AGLEY**
axilla .... **ALA**
axilla, pert. to .... **ALAR**
axillary .... **ALAR**
axis deer .... **CHITAL**
Aztec god, sowing ...... **XIPE**
Aztec "Noah" (hero) ... **NATA**
Aztec "Noah's" wife .. **NANA**
Aztec spear .... **ATLATL**

B

b
babbler: Scot. .... **HAVEREL**
Babism, founder .... **BAB**
babul tree pods .... **GARAD**
baby animal: Fr. .... **TOTO**
baby carriage .... **PRAM**
BABYLONIAN GODS, DEITY,
   see also GODS and also SPE-
   CIAL SECTION on page 198
Babylonian abode of dead
   ARALU
Babylonian city .... **IS**
Babylonian chief gods ... **EA,**
   ANU, BEL, HEA, ENKI
Babylonian chief goddess
   ISTAR, ISHTAR
Babylonian chief priest of
   shrine .... **EN**
Babylonian division .... **SUMER**
Babylonian hero ...... **ETANA**
Babylonian lunar cycle
   SAROS
Babylonian neighbor
   ELAMITE
Babylonian numeral .... **SAROS**
Babylonian priestess .. **ENTUM**
Babylonian purgatory .. **ARALU**
Bacchanals' cry .... **EVOE**
bacchante .... **MAENAD**
Bacchus' follower ...... **SATYR**
Bacchus' son .... **COMUS**
back .. **AID, AFT, FRO, ABET,**
   HIND, REAR, SPONSOR
back, call .... **REVOKE**
back door .... **POSTERN**
back, flow ...... **EBB, RECEDE**
back, lying on ...... **SUPINE**
back of neck .... **NAPE**
back, pert. to ...... **DORSAL**

d
back, take .... **RETRACT**
back, thrust .... **REPEL**
back, toward .... **RETRAL**
back: Zool. **NOTA, NOTUM**
backbone ...... **CHINE, SPINE**
bacteria-free .... **ASEPTIC**
bacteriologist's wire ..... **OESE**
bacteriostatic subst. . **CITRININ**
badge, Jap. .... **MON**
badger .... **DAS, BAIT**
badgerlike animal
   PAHMI, RATEL
badgers, Old World .... **MELES**
baffle .... **FOIL, POSE, ELUDE**
bag .... **SAC**
bag net .... **FYKE**
bagatelle .... **TRIFLE**
bagpipe, hole in .... **LILL**
bagpipe sound .... **SKIRL**
bailiff, old Eng. .... **REEVE**
baize fabric .... **DOMETT**
baker bird .... **HORNERO**
baking chamber ... **OST, KILN,**
   OAST, OVEN
baking pit .... **IMU**
balance .. **REST, POISE, SCALE**
balance, sentence ... **PARISON**
Balance, The .... **LIBRA**
balancing weight ... **BALLAST**
Balder's killer **LOK, LOKE, LOKI**
Balder's wife .... **NANNA**
baldness .... **ACOMIA**
Balkan .... **SERB**
ball, low .... **LINER**
ball, to hit
   LOB, BUNT, SWAT

Ball

a ball, yarn thread ..... **CLEW**
ballad .... **LAY, DERRY**
ballet jump .... **JETE**
ballet skirt .... **TUTU**
ballet turn .... **FOUETTE**
balloon basket **CAR, NACELLE**
ball-rope missile
                BOLA, BOLAS
balm of Gilead ..... **BALSAM**
balsalike wood .... **BONGO**
balsam .... **FIR, TOLU, RESIN**
Balt .... **ESTH**
BALTIC ... see also SPECIAL
    SECTION
Baltic Finn .... **VOD**
Baltimore stove .... **LATROBE**
Balto-Slav .... **LETT**
Baluchistan tribe .... **REKI**
Baluchistan tribesman .. **MARI**
"Bambi" author ...... **SALTEN**
bamboo .... **REED**
bamboo shoots, pickled **ACHAR**
Bana's daughter: Hindu **USHA**
banal .... **STALE, TRITE**
banana genus .... **MUSA**
banana, kind of .. **PLANTAIN**
banana, Polyn. .... **FEI**
band .... **BELT, TAPE,**
             STRIP, FILLET
band: Arch. .. **FACIA, FASCIA**
band, muscle, nerve .. **TAENIA**
band, narrow .. **STRIA, STRIAE**
bandage ...... **STUPE, TAENIA**
bandicoot .... **RAT**
b bandmaster, Am. .... **SOUSA**
banish ..... **EXILE, RELEGATE**
bank .... **RELY, DEPEND**
bank, of a river ... **RIPARIAN**
bank, river .... **RIPA**
banker, India .. **SARAF, SHROFF**
banner .... **FLAG,**
     ENSIGN, BANDEROLE
banter ... **CHAFF, PERSIFLAGE**
BANTU   see also TRIBES in
   SPECIAL SECTION, Page 191
Bantu .... **KAFIR, KAFFIR**
Bantu, Congo ... **RUA, WARUA**
Bantu language .... **ILA**
Bantu nation .... **GOGO**
Bantu-speaking tribe
     RAVI, RORI, PONDO
Bantu tribesman ..... **DUALA**
baobab, dried .... **LALO**
baobab leaves, powdered .. **LALO**
baptism font .... **LAVER**
baptismal basin .... **FONT**
bar .... **RAIL, INGOT,**
        HINDER, STRIPE
bar legally .... **ESTOP**
bar, supporting .... **FID**
barb, feather .... **HARL, HERL**

c Barbados native .... **BIM**
barbarian .... **HUN, GOTH**
Barbary ape .... **MAGOT**
barber ..... **SHAVER, TONSOR**
bard, Goth. .... **RUNER**
bare ..... **BALD, MERE, NUDE**
bargain .... **DEAL, PALTER**
bargain: Dutch .... **KOOP**
barge .... **HOY**
bark .... **BAY, YAP, YIP**
bark, bitter .. **NIEPA, NIOTA**
bark, inner .... **CORTEX**
bark, lime tree .. **BAST, BASTE**
bark, medicinal .... **COTO**
bark, paper mulberry .. **TAPA**
bark, pert. to ..... **CORTICAL**
bark remover .... **ROSSER**
bark, rough exterior .... **ROSS**
barking .... **LATRANT**
barn owl genus .... **TYTO**
barometric line ...... **ISOBAR**
barony, Jap. .... **HAN**
barracuda, small **SPET, SENNET**
barrelmaker .... **COOPER**
barrel slat .... **STAVE**
barren land .... **USAR**
Barrie character ...... **ALICE**
barrow, Russ. .... **KURGAN**
base .... **LOW, VILE**
base, architectural
         SOCLE, PLINTH
d base, attached by .... **SESSILE**
baseball position: abbr. .... **LF,**
                 RF, SS
Bashan, king of .... **OG**
bashful .... **COY, SHY, TIMID**
basilica, Rome ..... **LATERAN**
basin: Geol. .... **TALA**
basis of argument ... **PREMISE**
basket .... **KISH, CABAS,**
       PANIER, PANNIER
basket, coarse .... **SKEP**
basket, Eng. ...... **PED, CAUL**
basket, fish ... **WEEL, CRAIL,**
       CREEL, WICKER
basket grass, Mex. ..... **OTATE**
basket, large .... **HAMPER**
basket strip .... **RAND**
basketball player ..... **CAGER**
basketry rod .... **OSIER**
Basra native .... **IRAQI**
bass, Europ. .... **BRASSE**
basswood .... **LINDEN**
bast fiber .... **RAMIE**
bat .... **RACKET**
batfish .... **DIABLO**
bathe .... **LAVE**
bathing-suit .... **MAILLOT**
baths, Roman ...... **THERMAE**
Bathsheba's husband
         URIA, URIAH

a baton .... ROD
batrachian ...... FROG, TOAD
batter .... RAM
battering machine ...... RAM
battery plate .... GRID
battle, Am. Rev. ... CONCORD
battle area .... SECTOR
battle, Arthur's last .. CAMLAN
battle ax ... TWIBIL, TWIBILL
battle, Civil War, Tenn. SHILOH
battle cry, Irish .. ABU, ABOO
battle, Eng.-Fr. CRECY, CRESSY
battle formation ...... HERSE
battle, Franco-Pruss. .. SEDAN
battle, 100 Years War
              CRECY, CRESSY
"Battle Hymn of Republic"
    author .... HOWE
battle, WWI .. MARNE, SOMME,
              YPRES, VERDUN
battlefield .... ARENA
bauble .... BEAD
bay .... COVE, BIGHT, INLET
bay, Orkney, Shetland ... VOE
bay tree .... LAUREL
bay window .... ORIEL
bazaar .... FAIR
be foolishly overfond ... DOAT,
                      DOTE
be silent: music ...... TACET
b be still .... SH, HUSH, QUIET
beach .... SHORE, STRAND
beach cabin .... CABANA
beads, prayer .... ROSARY
beak .... NEB, NIB, BILL
beam, supporting
        TEMPLET, TEMPLATE
bean .... SOY, URD, LIMA
bean, E. Ind. .... URD
bean, field .... PINTO
bean, green .... HARICOT
bean, poisonous ... CALABAR
bean, S. Am. .... TONKA
bean tree .... CAROB
bear .. STAND, YIELD, ENDURE
Bear constellation ...... URSA
bear, nymph changed to
                  CALLISTO
bear, Austral. .... KOALA
bear witness .. VOUCH, ATTEST
beard of grain .. AWN, ARISTA
bearded seal .... MAKLUK
bearer, Ind. .... SINDAR
bearing .... MIEN, ORLE
bearing plate .... GIB
bear's-ear .... ARICULA
beast of burden .... ASS,
              BURRO, LLAMA
beat .... WIN, CANE, DRUB,
        FLAP, POMMEL, PULSE
beat about: naut. ...... BUSK

c beater, mortar .... RAB
beauty, goddess of: Hindu
    SRI, SHRI, SHREE, LAKSHMI
beauty, Greek .... LAIS
beaver .... CASTOR
beaver skin .... PLEW
beche-de-mer ...... TREPANG
beckon .... NOD
bed .... KIP, PALLET
bed of dry stream .... DONGA
bed of press, handle .. ROUNCE
bed: slang .... DOSS
Bedouin headband cord .. AGAL
bee, honey, genus .... APIS
bee house ..... APIARY, HIVE
bee, male .... DRONE
bee tree .... LINDEN
bees, pert. to .... APIAN
bee's pollen brush ..... SCOPA
beech tree genus ...... FAGUS
beechnuts .... MAST
beefwood: Polyn. ...... TOA,
              TOOA, BELAH
beehive, straw .... SKEP
Beehive State .. see page 209
beer ...... ALE, BOCK, LAGER
beer, Afr. millet ..... POMBE
beer ingredient .. HOPS, MALT
beer mug .... STEIN
beer, P. I. rice ..... PANGASI
d beet variety .... CHARD
Beethoven's birthplace . BONN
beetle .... DOR, ELATER
beetle, burrowing ...... BORER
beetle, click .... ELATER
beetle, fruit-loving .... BORER
beetle genus, ground .. AMARA
beetle, ground .... CARAB
beetle, sacred Egyp. .. SCARAB
beetle, wood .... SAWYER
befall .... HAP
before .... ERE, PRE,
                  ANTERIOR
before: obs. .... ERER
before: naut. .... AFORE
beget .... EAN, SIRE
"Beggar's Opera" dramatist
                      GAY
beginner .... TIRO, TYRO,
        NOVICE, NEOPHYTE
beginning .... GERM, ONSET,
        ORIGIN, INITIAL
beginning .... NASCENCY
behave toward .... TREAT
behind .... AFT, AREAR,
                  ASTERN
behold ..... LO, ECCE, VOILA
behoove .... DOW
beige .... ECRU
being .... ENS, ENTITY

17

Being

being, abstract **ENS, ESSE, ENTIA**
being, essential .... **ENS**
Bela, son of .... **IRI**
beleaguerment .... **SIEGE**
Belem .... **PARA**
belief .... **CREED, FAITH, TENET**
believe .... **TROW, CREDO, CREDIT**
believer in god of reason **DEIST**
bell, alarm .... **TOCSIN**
bell, sacring .... **SQUILLA**
bell tower .... **BELFRY, CAMPANILE**
bell's tongue ...... **CLAPPER**
bellbird, N.Z. .... **MAKO**
bellowing .... **AROAR**
below: nautical .... **ALOW**
belt .... **CEST, SASH**
belt, sword .... **BALDRIC, BAWDRIC, BALDRICK**
ben .... **BENE**
bench ...... **EXEDRA, SETTLE**
bench, judge's .. see **JUDGE'S BENCH**
bench in a galley ..... **BANK**
bend .... **SNY, FLEX, GENU, STOOP, FLEXURE**
benediction .... **BENISON**
benefactor .... **PATRON**
beneficiary: Law ...... **USES**
benefit .... **BOON, AVAIL**
Bengal native .... **KOL**
Bengal singer .... **BAUL**
Benjamin's first born .. **BELA**
bent .... **PRONATE**
bequeath .... **WILL**
bequest .... **DOWER**
Berber .... **RIFF**
Bermuda arrowroot **ARARU, ARARAO**
Bermuda grass .. **DOOB, DOUB**
berserk .... **AMOK, AMUCK**
beseech .... **PRAY, OBTEST, ENTREAT**
beside .... **BY**
besides .. **TOO, YET, ALSO, ELSE**
bestow .... **AWARD, CONFER, IMPART**
bets, fail to pay **WELCH, WELSH**
betel leaf ...... **BUYO, PAUN**
betel nut .... **SERI, SIRI, BONGA, SIRIH**
betel palm .. **ARECA, PINANG**
betel pepper ..... **IKMO, ITMO**
Bethuel's son .... **LABAN**
betoken .... **DENOTE**
betroth .... **AFFY**
between: prefix .... **INTER**
Bevan's nickname .... **NYE**

bevel .... **BEZEL, SLANT**
bevel out .... **REAM**
bevel ship timber ..... **SNAPE**
bevel to join .. **MITER, MITRE**
BEVERAGE ... see also **DRINK**
beverage .... **ADE, ALE, TEA, BEER**
beverage, curdled .... **POSSET**
beverage, hot wine .... **NEGUS**
beverage, Polyn. **KAVA, KAWA**
beverage, S. Am. .... **MATE**
bewitch .... **HEX, SPELL**
beyond: comb. form .. **ULTRA**
Bhutan pine .... **KAIL**
biased person .... **BIGOT**
BIBLICAL .. see also SPECIAL SECTION
Biblical city .... **DAN, BABEL, EKRON**
Biblical character .. **ARA, IRA, ERI, ARAN, ATER, ONAN**
Biblical country . **EDOM, ENON SEBA, SHEBA**
Biblical driver .... **JEHU**
Biblical judge .... **ELI, ELON, GIDEON, SAMSON**
Biblical king **OG, ASA, AGAG, AHAB, ELAH, OMRI, SAUL, HEROD, NADAB**
Biblical kingdom ...... **ELAM, MOAB, SAMARIA**
Biblical land .... **NOD**
Biblical lion .... **ARI**
BIBLICAL MEASURE ...... see HEBREW MEASURE
BIBLICAL MOUNT see Page 197
Biblical name .... **ED, ER, IRI, ONO, REI, TOI, ABIA, ADER, ANER, ANIM, ASOM, DARA, ENOS, IRAD, IVAH, REBA, ABIAM, AHIRA, AMASA, ASEAS**
Biblical name for part of Arabia **SHEBA**
Biblical ornaments ..... **URIM**
Biblical priest, high ...... **ELI, AARON, ANNAS**
Biblical region .. **ARAM, EDAR**
Biblical ruler .... **IRA**
Biblical sacred objects .. **URIM**
Biblical serpent .. **NEHUSHTAN**
Biblical son .... **HAM**
Biblical spy .... **CALEB**
Biblical tower .... **EDAR**
Biblical town in Samaria **ENON**
BIBLICAL TRIBE .... see Page 197
Biblical weed .... **TARE**
Biblical well; spring . **AIN, ESEK**
Biblical wild ox .... **REEM**

Biblical witch's home .. **ENDOR**
Biblical woman **RAHAB, LEAH**
Biblical word .. **SELAH, MENE**
Biblical word of reproach **RACA**
bicarbonate .... **SODA**
bice blue .... **AZURITE**
bicker .... **CAVIL**
bicycle for two ...... **TANDEM**
biddy .... **HEN**
"— bien" .... **TRES**
big casino .... **TEN**
bile .... **GALL**
bill .... **DUN, NEB, BEAK**
bill of fare ..... **MENU, CARTE**
bill, part of .... **CERE**
billiard shot .. **CAROM, MASSE**
billow .... **SEA, WAVE**
bind .... **TAPE, SWATH**
biography ..... **LIFE, MEMOIR**
biological .. **BIOTIC, BIOTICAL**
biological reproductive body
.... **GAMETE**
biotic community ..... **BIOME**
bird .... **CLEE, COCK, CROW,**
DOVE, FINK, GLED, HUIA,
IIWI, JACU, KALA, KIWI,
KOEL, KORA, KUKU, KYAH,
LARK, LOON, LORO, LORY,
LOUN, LOWA, LULU, LUPE,
MAKO, MAMO, MIRO,
MOHO, MORO, MYNA,
NENE, PAPE, PEHO, PISK,
RAIL, RAYA, ROOK, RUFF,
RURU, RYPE, SKUA, SMEE,
SMEW, SORA, STIB, SWAN,
TEAL, TERN, TOCK, TOCO,
TODY, UTUM, WAEG,
WREN, YENI, YUTU,
DRAKE, ROBIN, SERIN, EL-
ANET, SHRIKE, SISKIN,
bird, Am. .... **TOWHEE**
bird, Arctic .. **BRANT, FULMAR**
bird, Austral. .... **EMU, KOEL,**
COOEE, COOEY
bird, black **ANI, ROOK, RAVEN**
bird, blue .... **JAY**
bird, C. & S. Am. ...... **COIN,**
CONDOR, CONDORES
bird cry .... **CAW, COO**
bird, diving ...... **AUK, LOON,**
LOUN, SMEW
bird, ducklike .... **COOT**
bird, extinct .... **MOA,**
DODO, MAMO
bird, Europ. .... **GLEDE, TEREK**
bird genus ...... **CRAX, RHEA**
bird, gull-like .... **TERN**
BIRD, HAWAIIAN .... see
HAWAIIAN BIRD
bird house .... **COTE**
bird, hunting .... **FALCON**

bird, India .... **SARUS**
SHAMA, ARGALA
bird, laughing .... **LOON**
bird life .... **ORNIS**
bird, long-legged
AGAMI, STILT
bird, marsh .... **RAIL,**
SORA, BITTERN
bird, mythical .... **ROC**
bird, national .... **EAGLE**
bird nest collector .. **OOLOGIST**
bird of prey ...... **ERN, ERNE,**
HAWK, KITE, EAGLE,
CORMORANT
bird, orange .... **ORIOLE**
bird order ..... **PICI, RASORES**
bird, oscine .. **CHAT, ORIOLE**
BIRD, OSTRICHLIKE ...... see
OSTRICHLIKE BIRD
bird, Persian .... **BULBUL**
BIRD, SEA ..... see SEA BIRD
bird, shore **RAIL, SORA, SNIPE,**
WADER, AVOCET, PLOVER
bird, small .... **TIT, PIPIT**
bird, small brown ...... **WREN**
BIRD, S. AM. .... see
S. AMER. BIRD
bird, swimming .. **LOON, GREBE**
bird, talking .. **MYNA, MYNAH**
bird, tropical ..... **ANI, ANO,**
TROGON, JACAMAR
bird, U. S.
COLIN, VEERY, TANAGER
BIRD, WADING .... see
..WADING BIRD
bird, wading, Afr.
UMBER, UMBRETTE
bird, water see WADING BIRD
BIRD, WEB-FOOTED .... see
WEB-FOOTED BIRD
bird, W. Ind. .... **TODY**
bird, white-plumed .... **EGRET**
bird, white-tailed .. **ERN, ERNE**
birds .... **AVES**
bird's beak .... **NEB, NIB**
bird's cry ...... **CAW, WEET**
birds of region .... **ORNIS**
birds' route .... **FLYWAY**
biretta .... **CAP**
birth, by .... **NEE**
birth, of one's .... **NATAL**
birthmark
MOLE, NEVUS, NAEVUS
birthplace, Apollo, Diana **DELOS**
birthplace, Constantine's
NIS, NISH
birthplace, Mohammed's **MECCA**
birthplace, Muses, Orpheus
PIERIA

19

Birthstone

a birthstone .... Jan., **GARNET;**
Feb., **AMETHYST;** March,
**JASPER, AQUAMARINE,
BLOODSTONE;** April, **DIA-
MOND;** May, **AGATE, EM-
ERALD;** June, **PEARL,
MOONSTONE;** July, **ONYX,
RUBY;** Aug., **CARNELIAN,
SARDONYX, PERIDOT;**
Sept., **SAPPHIRE;** Oct.,
OPAL; Nov., **TOPAZ;** Dec.,
TURQUOISE, ZIRCON
birthwort, Europ. .. **CLEMATITE**
bishop .... **PRELATE**
bishop of Róme .... **POPE**
bishopric .... **SEE**
bishop's attendant ... **VERGER**
bishop's hat
HURA, MITER, MITRE
bishop's office .... **LAWN**
bishop's seat ...... **SEE, APSE**
bishop's title, East ..... **ABBA**
bite .... **CHAM, MORSEL**
bite upon .... **GNAW**
biting .... **ACERB, ACRID**
bitter .... **ACERB, ACRID**
bitter almonds compound
AMARINE
bitter drug .... **ALOE**
bitter vetch .... **ERS**
b bittern .... **HERON**
bivalve .... **CLAM, MUSSEL**
bivalve genus .... **PINNA**
bizarre .... **OUTRE**
black .... **JET, EBON, INKY,
RAVEN, SABLE, TARRY,
NIGRINE**
black and blue .... **LIVID**
black buck .... **SASIN**
black gum tree genus **NYSSA**
black haw .... **SLOE**
black kelpie .... **BARB**
black nightshade .... **DUSCLE**
Black Sea arm ... **AZOF, AZOV**
blackbird
ANI, MERL, MERLE, RAVEN
blackbird, Europ.
OSSEL, OUSEL, OUZEL
blackbird: variant ...... **ANO**
blacken .... **INK, SOOT**
black-fin snapper .... **SESI**
blackfish .... **TAUTOG**
Blackmore heroine .... **LORNA**
blacksnake .... **RACER**
blacksmith's block .... **ANVIL**
blackthorn fruit .... **SLOE**
blackwood, India .... **BITI**
blade .... **OAR**
Blake's symbolic figure .. **ZOA**
Blake's symbolic figures **ZOAS**
blanch .... **ETIOLATE**

c blanket, cloak-like .. **PONCHO**
blanket, coarse wool .. **COTTA**
blanket, horse ...... **MANTA**
blanket, Sp.-Am. ..... **SERAPE**
blast furnace, stone in .. **TYMP**
blaubok, S. Afr. ...... **ETAAC**
blaze star .... **NOVA**
bleach .... **CHLORE**
bleaching vat .... **KEIR, KIER**
bleak .... **RAW**
blesbok .... **NUNNI**
bless .... **SAIN**
bless: Yiddish .... **BENSH**
blessing
BOON, GRACE, BENEFICE
blight .... **NIP**
blight of drought, India **SOKA**
blind, as hawks .... **SEEL**
blind dolphin .... **SUSU**
blind god, Teut. **HOTH, HODER**
blind impulse to ruin ... **ATE**
blindness .... **CECITY**
blister .. **BLEB, BULLA, BULLAE**
block, small arch
DENTEL, DENTIL
block, wood .... **NOG**
blockhead .... **ASS, DOLT**
blood factor .... **RH**
blood, lack of red
ANEMIA, ANAEMIA
d blood of gods .... **ICHOR**
blood, part of .... **SERUM**
blood, pert. to ...... **HEMAL,
HEMIC, HAEMAL, HAEMIC**
blood vessel .... **VEIN**
blood vessel, main .... **AORTA**
blood, watery part of
SERA, SERUM
blood sucker .... **LEECH**
blood-sucking parasite .. **TICK**
blouse, long .... **TUNIC**
blow..... **COUP, CRIG, ONER,
SWAT, WAFT**
blubber, piece of ..... **LIPPER**
blubber, to strip ..... **FLENSE**
blue .... **CADET, PERSE,
SMALT, COBALT**
blue-dye yielding herb **WOAD**
blue dyestuff .... **WOAD**
"Blue Eagle" .... **NRA**
blue-footed petrel ...... **TITI**
blue grass (genus) ...... **POA**
blue grape anthocyanin
ENIN, OÉNIN
blue gray
CHING, MERLE, SLATE
blue, greenish .... **BICE,
SAXE, TEAL, EMAIL**
blue mineral .... **IOLITE**
blue-pencil .... **EDIT**
blue pointer shark ..... **MAKO**

a
blue pine .... **LIM**
Bluebeard's wife ..... **FATIMA**
bluebonnet .... **LUPINE**
bluff .... **CRUSTY**
bluish-white metal ...... **ZINC**
blunder .... **ERR**
blunt .... **DULL**
blushing .... **ROSY**
boa, ringed .... **ABOMA**
boast .... **BRAG, VAUNT**
boastful air .... **PARADO**
BOAT . see also SHIP, CANOE, GALLEY, VESSEL,
boat .... **ARK, TUB, PUNT**
boat, assault .... **LST**
boat, Ceylon, India
DONI, DHONI
boat, collapsible
FALTBOAT, FOLDBOAT
boat, dispatch .... **AVISO**
boat, E. Ind. .... **DONI, DHONI**
boat, Egypt .... **BARIS**
boat, Eskimo .. **BIDAR, CAYAK, KAYAK, UMIAK, OOMIAC, OOMIAK, UMIACK**
boat, fishing
TROW, DOGGER, CORACLE
boat, fishing, North Sea **COBLE**
boat, flat-bottomed
SCOW, BARGE
b
boat, freight ...... **LIGHTER**
boat front ...... **BOW, PROW**
boat, Ind. landing .. **MASOOLA**
boat, landing .... **LCI, LST**
boat, Levantine .... **BUM**
boat, light .... **WHERRY**
boat, mail .... **PACKET**
boat, Malay .... **PAHI, PRAH, PRAO, PRAU, PROA, PRAHU, PRAHO**
boat, Manila Harbor .. **BILALO**
boat, military ..... **PONTOON**
boat, Nile 2-masted .. **SANDAL**
boat, P. I. .. **BANCA, BANKA**
boat, racing .. **SCULL, SHELL**
boat, river
BARGE, FERRY, PACKET
boat, river, Chin. ... **SAMPAN**
boat, small .... **DORY**
boat, 3-oar .... **RANDAN**
boat, used on Tigris
GUFA, KUFA
boat, with decks cut
RASEE, RAZEE
bob bait for fish .... **DIB**
bobbin .. **PIRN, REEL, SPOOL**
bobbins, frame for .... **CREEL**
bobwhite .... **COLIN**
Boche .... **HUN**
bodice, India .... **CHOLI**
bodily motion, pert. to **GESTIC**

c
body .... **SOMA, LICHAM**
body, heavenly . **STAR, COMET**
body of laws .... **CODE**
body of men .... **FORCE**
body of persons ...... **CORPS**
body of retainers .... **RETINUE**
body of writing .... **TEXT**
body, part of
THORAX, THORACES
body, pert. to **SOMAL, SOMATIC**
body, trunk of .. **TORSE, TORSO**
body: zool. .... **SOMA**
Boer general .... **BOTHA**
bog. **FEN, MIRE, QUAG, MARSH**
boggy .... **FENNY**
boil .... **STEW, SEETHE**
boil down .... **DECOCT**
boiled rice without salt: P. I.
CANIN
boiler, disk for hole in .. **SPUT**
"Bolero" composer .... **RAVEL**
boll weevil .... **PICUDO**
Bolshevik leader ...... **LENIN**
bolt .... **SCREEN**
bomb, defective .... **DUD**
bombardment, short, intense
RAFALE
bombast .... **ELA**
bombastic **TURGID, OROTUND**
Bombyx .... **ERI**
d
bond .... **NEXUS**
bond-stone .... **PERPEND**
bondman ...... **SERF, VASSAL**
bonds, chem. with 2 double
DIENE
bone .... **OS**
bone, ankle **TALUS, ASTRAGAL**
bone, arm .... **ULNA**
bone, arm, pert. to ... **ULNAR**
bone, breast
STERNA, STERNAL, STERNUM
bone, ear ..... **ANVIL, INCUS**
bone: Greek .... **OSTE**
bone, leg .... **FEMUR, TIBIA, FIBULA, TIBIAE**
bone, pelvic, hip ...... **ILIUM**
bone, pert. to .... **OSTEAL**
bone scraper .... **XYSTER**
bone, skull .... **VOMER**
bones .... **OSSA**
bones, dorsal .... **ILIA**
bones, end of spine .. **SACRA**
bones, hip .... **ILIA**
bonnet monkey **ZATI, MUNGA**
bonnyclabber .... **SKYR**
bony .... **OSTEAL**
book .... **MO, TOME, PRIMER**
book, case for **FOREL, FORREL**
book, largest .... **FOLIO**
book, manuscript
CODEX, CODICES

Book

a book, map .... **ATLAS**
book, Bible .. see SPECIAL SECTION, Page 196
book of devotions .... **MISSAL**
book of feasts, Catholic **ORDO**
book of hours .. **HORA, HORAE**
book palm, tree .... **TARA**
book, The .... **BIBLE**
books, Bible .... **GOSPEL**
bookbinding style ...... **YAPP**
bookkeeping entry **DEBIT, CREDIT**
booklet .... **BROCHURE**
boor **OAF, CLOD, LOUT, CHURL**
boot, Eskimo .... **KAMIK**
booth .... **STALL**
booth, Oriental market **SUQ, SOOK, SOUK**
bootlace .... **LACET**
booty ..... **LOOT, PELF, SWAG**
booty, take .... **REAVE**
borax, crude .... **TINCAL**
border ...... **HEM, RIM, EDGE, RAND, SIDE, MARGE**
border on .... **ABUT**
bore .... **TIRE, EAGRE, WEARY, CALIBER**
borecole ...... **KAIL, KALE**
boredom .... **ENNUI**
boric acid salts ...... **BORATE**
b born .... **NEE**
born, being .... **NASCENT**
born: old Eng. .... **NATE**
Bornean squirrel shrew **PENTAIL**
Borneo native .. **DYAK, DAYAK**
boron, pert. to .... **BORIC**
borough .... **BURG**
borrowed stock: Irish law **DAER**
bosh .... **ROT, POOH**
boss .... **STUD**
boss on shield .... **UMBO**
Bostonian .... **HUBBITE**
botanical suffix ...... **ACEAE**
botanist .... **MENDEL**
botch .... **FLUB, MESS**
both ears, involving use of **BINAURAL**
bother ... **ADO, FUSS, TODO, TEASE, MOLEST, PESTER**
bo-tree .... **PIPAL**
bottle, glass water .. **CARAFE**
bottle, oil, vinegar **CRUET, FLASK**
bottomless pit .... **ABADDON**
boundary ...... **LINE, MERE, METE, LIMIT**
boundaries, mark off **DEMARCATE**
bounder .... **CAD**
bounding line .... **SIDE**

c bounds .... **AMBIT**
bouquet .... **AROMA**
bovine .... **OX, COW**
bovine, male .... **STEER**
bow of ship .... **PROW**
bow, low Oriental **SALAM, SALAAM**
bow-shaped .... **ARCATE**
bower .... **ARBOR**
bowfin .... **AMIA**
bowl: cricket .... **YARK**
bowling term .... **SPARE**
bowstring hemp **IFE, PANGANE**
box .... **BIN, BINN, CASE, CIST, SPAR, CHEST**
box, ecclesiastic .... **ARCA**
box canyon: Sp. ...... **CAJON**
box, metal .... **CANISTER**
box opener .... **PANDORA**
box, papyrus rolls, Rom. **CAPSA**
box, sacred, ancient Rom. **CIST**
box sleigh .... **PUNG**
boxing glove, Rom. .... **CESTUS**
boxing term .... **KO, TKC**
BOY'S NAME .. see MAN'S NAME
boy ... **BUB, BUD, LAD, TAD**
boys in blue .... **ELI'S**
B.P.O.E. member .... **ELK**
d brace .... **PAIR, TRUSS**
braced aback: nautical **ABOX**
bracing .... **TONIC**
brag .... **BOAST, VAUNT**
Brahman rule .. **SUTRA, SUTTA**
Brahmany bull .... **ZEBU**
braid ... **PLAT, PLAIT, QUEUE**
braid, kind of .... **LACET**
brain canal-passage .... **ITER**
brain, layer in .... **OBEX**
brain opening .... **LURA, PYLA**
brain part .... **PIA**
brain: P. I. .... **UTAC**
brain ridges .... **GYRI**
brain tissue .... **TELA**
brain ventricle opening **PYLA**
branch .... **ARM, LIMB, RAMI, RAME, RAMUS, SPRIG**
branch-like **RAMOSE, RAMOUS**
branchia .... **GILL**
branch of learning ...... **ART**
brass, man of .. **TALOS, TALUS**
brassart .... **BRACER**
"Brave Bulls" author ... **LEA**
brawl .... **MELEE, FRACAS**
BRAZIL ..... see also SPECIAL SECTION
Brazil drink .... **ASSAI**
Brazil red .... **ROSET**
Brazil dance .... **SAMBA**
Brazil heron .... **SOCO**

22

a Brazil Negro .... MINA
Brazil plant ..... YAGE, YAJE
Brazil rubber tree ULE, HULE
Brazil tree ...... APA, ANDA
Brazil capital .... RIO
breach .... GAP
bread, hard-baked ...... RUSK
bread crumbs, dish with
               PANADA
breadfruit: P. I. .... RIMA
breadfruit: P. R. ... CASTANA
bread-tree seeds .... DIKA
break .... SNAP
break in .... STAVE
breakers .... SURF
breakwater ...... MOLE, PIER
breastbone, of ...... STERNAL
breastplate .... URIM
breastwork .... PARAPET
breastplate, Gr.
     THORAX, THORACES
breath of life .... PRANA
breathed .... SPIRATE
breathing, harsh
     RALE, STRIDOR
breech-cloth, Polyn. .. MALO
breeches: Scot. .... TREWS
breed .... REAR, RAISE
Bremen's river .... WESER
breviary .. PORTAS, PORTASS

b brewer's ferment .. LOB, LOBB
brewer's vat .... TUN
brewing .... MALTING
brewing, one
     GAAL, GAIL, GYLE
bribe .... SOP
brick carrier .... HOD
brick, sun-dried ...... ADOBE
bricklayer .... MASON
bricklayer's helper ..... CAD
bridal wreath .... SPIREA
bridge .... SPAN
bridge, floating .... PONTOON
bridge, maneuver .... FINESSE
bridge, Mississippi ..... EADS
bridge part TRESSEL, TRESTLE
brief .... SHORT, TERSE
brigand .... LATRON
Brigham Young U. site PROVO
bright .... APT, NITID
bright colored fish
     BOCE, OPAH, WRASSE
bright: music .... ANIME
brilliance .... ECLAT, ORIENCY
brilliant group .... PLEIAD
bring forth .... EAN
bring on oneself ...... INCUR
bring together ...... COMPILE
bring up .... REAR, RAISE
brisk: music .... ALLEGRO
bristle .... SETA

c bristles .... SETAE
bristle, pert. to .... SETAL
bristly .... SETOSE
Britain's ancient inhabitant
               PICT
BRITISH .. also see ENGLISH
British conservative ..... TORY
British king, legendary .. LUD,
  BELI, BRAN, BRUT, LUDD,
  NUDD
Britisher, early .... PICT
Brittany; city, ancient ...... IS
broach .... RIMER
broad band: Her. .... FESS
broadbill, E. Ind. ...... RAYA
broadbill duck .... SCAUP
broken glass to remelt .. CALX
broken seed coats ...... BRAN
broken spike of grain .. CHOB
broken stone, etc. ... RUBBLE
Bronte heroine .... EYRE
bronze, Rom. money ..... AES
brood ...... SET, NIDE, COVEY
brook, small ...... RUN, RILL
broom of twigs .... BESOM
broom-corn millet
     HIRSE, KADIKANE
brother .. FRA, FRIAR, FRATER
brought up .... BRED
brow of hill; Scot. ...... SNAB

d brown ..... TAN, SEAR, SEPIA,
  UMBER, BISTER, RUSSET,
  SIENNA, SORREL
brown kiwi .... ROA
brown, pale .... ECRU
brown, red-yellow ..... PABLO
brown, yellowish dull ... DRAB
brown-skinned race ... MALAY
brown sugar .... PANELA
browned .... RISSOLE
brownie ..... NIS, NIX, NISSE
Browning poem, girl in PIPPA
browse .... GRAZE
Brünnhilde's mother .... ERDA
brushwood .... TINET, TINNET
brusque ...... BLUNT, TERSE
Brythonic .... CORNISH
Brythonic sea god ...... LER
bubble .... BLEB
buck, 4th year .... SORE
Buddha .... FO
Buddha, Jap. AMIDA, AMITA
Buddha's foe .... MARA
Buddha's mother ...... MAYA
Buddha's tree .... PIPAL
Buddhist angel .... DEVA
Buddhist language ...... PALI
Buddhist church in Jap. .. TERA
Buddhist monastery, Jap. TERA
Buddhist Mongol ...... ELEUT
Buddhist monk .... BO, LAMA

Buddhist

Buddhist pillar .... **LAT**
Buddhist monument .. **STUPA**
Buddhist novice ...... **GOYIN**
Buddhist priest .... **LAMA**
Buddhist relic .... **STUPA**
Buddhist sacred city .. **LASSA**
Buddhist sacred dialect **PALI**
Buddhist sacred mountain **OMEI**
Buddhist saint **LOHAN, ARHAT**
Buddhist scripture **SUTRA, SUTTA**
Buddhist sect, Jap. ..... **ZEN**
Buddhist shrine **TOPE, STUPA, DAGABA, DAGOBA, DAG- HOBA, DHAGOBA**
Buddhist spirit of evil .. **MARA**
buds, pickled .... **CAPERS**
buffalo, India
    ARNA, ARNI, ARNEE
buffalo pea .... **VETCH**
buffalo, water, P. I. . **CARABAO**
buffet .... **SLAP, SMITE, TOSS**
buffoon .. **FOOL, MIME, ZANY, CLOWN, MUMMER, JESTER**
bug .... **BEETLE**
bugaboo: S. Afr. **GOGA, GOGO**
bugle call
    TATOO, TATTOO, TANTARA
bugle note .... **TIRALEE**
build .... **REAR, ERECT**
builder .... **ERECTOR**
builder, jetty-dam ...... **EADS**
building site .... **LOT**
building wing .... **ELL, ANNEX**
bulb, edible .... **SEGO**
bulb, Indian food
    CAMAS, CAMASS, CAMMAS
bulb-like stem .... **CORM**
BULGARIAN .. see also SPE-CIAL SECTION
Bulgarian czar .... **BORIS**
bulge, as eyes .... **BUG**
bulk .... **MASS**
bull, girl carried off on **EUROPA**
bull, sacred Egyp. .... **APIS**
bullet, size of
    CALIBER, CALIBRE
bullet sound ...... **ZIP, PHIT, PHUT, PIFF**
bullfight .... **CORRIDA**
bullfight cry .... **OLE**
bullfighter on foot .. **TORERO**
bullfighter's queue .... **COLETA**
bullfinch, Eng. .... **ALP**
bully .... **HECTOR**
bulrush .... **TULE**
Bulwer-Lytton heroine .. **IONE**
bumblebee .... **DOR**
bumpkin .... **LOUT**
bunch .... **TUFT, WISP**
bunch grass .... **STIPA**
bundle .... **BALE, PACK**

bundle, small .... **PACKET**
bundle, twig, stick .... **FAGOT**
bundling machine ...... **BALER**
bungle .... **BOTCH**
bunting .. **ESTAMIN, ETAMINE, ORTOLAN, ESTAMENE**
bunting bird .... **CIRL**
buoy, Eng. .... **DAN**
buoy, kind of. **CAN, NUN, NUT, BELL, SPAR, WHISTLING**
buoyancy .... **FLOTAGE**
burbot .... **LING**
burbot genus .... **LOTA, LOTE**
Burchell's zebra .... **DAUW**
burden ... **LADE, LOAD, ONUS**
burden bearer .... **ATLAS**
burglar .... **YEGG**
burial place, Polyn. ..... **AHU**
BURMA .. see also SPECIAL SECTION
Burma Buddhist (native) **MON**
Burma chief .... **BO, BOH**
Burmese capital, ancient **AVA**
Burmese demon (devil) .. **NAT**
Burmese gibbon .... **LAR**
Burmese governor **WUN, WOON**
Burmese hill-dweller ..... **LAI**
Burmese hills .... **NAGA**
Burmese knife .. **DAH, DHAO**
Burmese language .. **WA, PEGU**
Burmese mongoloid ...... **LAI**
Burmese native (s) **WA,LAI,WAS**
Burmese premier .... **UNU**
Burmese 3-string viol .. **TURR**
Burmese wood sprite .... **NAT**
burn incense .... **CENSE**
burn .... **ASH, CHAR, SERE**
Burnett, Frances, heroine **SARA**
burning bush .... **WAHOO**
burning, malicious .... **ARSON**
burnish .... **RUB**
burrowing animal **MOLE, RATEL**
burst asunder .... **SPLIT**
burst forth .... **ERUPT**
bury .... **INTER, INHUME**
bush or bushy clump .... **TOD**
bushel, fourth of .... **PECK**
Bushmen .... **SAN, SAAN**
bushy .... **DUMOSE**
business .... **TRADE**
business cartel .... **TRUST**
"Bus Stop" author ..... **INGE**
bustard genus .... **OTIS**
bustle .... **ADO, TODO**
bustle about .... **FISK**
busy, to be .... **HUM**
but .... **YET, ONLY, STILL**
butcher's hook .... **GAMBREL**
butter, illipe .... **MAHUA**
butter, India ...... **GHI, GHEE**
butter, liquid ..... **GHI, GHEE**

butter tree .... SHEA
butter tub .... FIRKIN
butterbur .... OXWORT
butterfly .... IO, SATYR
butterfly, large .... IDALIA
butterfly-lily .... SEGO
button .... STUD
button, part of ...... SHANK
buyer .... VENDEE
buyer: Law .... EMPTOR

buzzard .... BUTEO
buzzing sound .. WHIR, WHIZ
by .... AT, PER, PAST,
        ALONG, BESIDE
by birth .... NEE
by hand, bred .... CADE
by means of .... PER
bygone .... AGO
Byron poem .... LARA
Byzantine capital .... NICAEA

C

C, mark under ...... CEDILLA
caama .... ASSE
cab, Near East .... ARABA
cabal .... PLOT
cabbage .... COLE, KAIL,
        KALE, KEAL
cabbage type .... SAVOY
cabin, main .... SALOON
cabinet, open, bric-a-brac
        ETAGERE
cactus fruit, edible ... COCHAL
cactus, genus .... CEREUS
cactus-like .... CACTOID
caddis fly worm ..... CADEW
Caddoan Indian .... REE
cadet .... LAD
Cadmus' daughter .... INO
Caen's river .... ORNE
Caesar's conspirator-slayer
        CASCA, BRUTUS, CASSIUS
cafe .... CABARET
caffein in tea
        THEIN, THEINA, THEINE
caffein-rich nut .. COLA, KOLA
cage .... MEW
Cain's brother .... ABEL
Cain's land .... NOD
Cain's son .... ENOCH
Cain's wife, Byron poem
        ADAH
cake, rich ... TORTE, TORTEN
cake, small ..... BUN, BUNN
calabar bean alkaloid
        ESERIN, ESERINE
calamity ..... WOE, DISASTER
calcium oxide .... LIME
calf of leg, pert. to ... SURAL
calf's cry .... BLAT
caliber .... BORE, DIAMETER
calico colors, mix ..... TEER
calico horse .. PINTO, PIEBALD
calico-printing method .. LAPIS
California army base .... ORD
Calif. fish ...... RENA, REINA
Calif. fort .... ORD

Calif. herb .... AMOLE
Calif. motto .... EUREKA
Calif. shrub, berry ..... SALAL
Calif. wine valley .... NAPA
Caliph .... ALI, IMAM
call .. CRY, DUB, DIAL, NAME,
        ROUSE, WAKEN, MUSTER
call for hogs .... SOOK
call forth .. EVOKE, SUMMON,
        ELICIT, EVOCATE
call, to attract attention
        HEY, PST, HIST, PIST
calling ... METIER, VOCATION
Calliope's sister .... ERATO
calm .... LAY, COOL, LULL,
        QUIET, STILL, PLACID, SE-
RENE, SMOOTH, SOOTHE
calorie ..... THERM, THERME
columniate .... MALIGN
calumny .... SLANDER
Calvinists, Scotch .. BEREANS
calyx leaf .... SEPAL
cam .... TAPPET
cambric .... PERCALE
cambric grass .... RAMIE
CAME ....see COME
camel: Anglo-Ind. ...... OONT
camel hair cloth .... ABA
camel hair robe .... ABA
camel-like animal ..... LLAMA
Camelot lady .... ENID
cameo stone .... ONYX
camera platform ..... DOLLY
Cameroons tribe .... ABO
"Camille" author .... DUMAS
camlet .... PONCHO
camp, fortified ...... TABOR
camp, pert. to ...... CASTRAL
camphor, kind of ..... ALANT
campus, restrict. to Eng. GATED
Canaanite month .... BUL
Canada goose ...... OUTARDE
canal bank .... BERM, BERME
canal betw. N. and Balt. Seas
        KIEL

25

a
canary yellow ...... MELINE
canasta play .... MELD
cancel .. DELE, ANNUL, ERASE
candid .... OPEN, FRANK
candidates list .. LEET, SLATE
candle ..... DIP, TEST, TAPER
candle holder
    SCONCE, GIRANDOLE
candle wick .. SNAST, SNASTE
.... AMA
candlenut tree .... AMA
candlenut tree fiber ..... AEA
cane ... RATTAN, MALACCA
Canio's wife "I Pagliacci"
    NEDDA
canister, tea, alloy for .. CALIN
canna plant .... ACHIRA
cannabis .... HEMP
cannon .... MORTAR
cannon, old
    MOYENNE, ROBINET
CANOE .. see also BOAT
canoe, Afr. .. BONGO, BUNGO
canoe, Hawaii ...... WAAPA
canoe, Malabar ...... TONEE
canoe, Malay (South Seas) out-
    rigger ..... PAHI, PRAH,
    PRAO, PRAU, PROA,
    PRAHO, PRAHU
canoe, Maori .... WAKA

b
canoe, P. I. .. BANCA, BANKA
canon .... LAW, RULE
canonical hour .. SEXT (noon),
    LAUDS, NONES, PRIME,
    MATINS, TIERCE
canopy COPE, SHADE, TESTER
cant TIP, TILT, SLANG, CAREEN
cant-hook .... PEAVY, PEEVY,
    PEAVEY, PEEVEY
cantankerous command. . SCAT
cantata, pastoral .. SERENATA
canticle, Scripture ...... ODE
"Cantique de Noel" composer
    ADAM
CANTON .. see the country in
    SPECIAL SECTION
canvas .. DUCK, TUKE, SAILS
canvas, piece of .... TARP
canvas shelter .... TENT
canyon mouth .... ABRA
canyon, small .... CANADA
CAP .. see HEADGEAR
capable .... ABLE
cape .... NES, RAS,
    NASE, NAZE, NESS
cape, early .... COPE
cape, fur .... PALATINE
Cape Horn native .... ONA
cape, Pope's .. FANON, ORALE
Cape Verde native ..... SERER
Capek creature .... ROBOT

c
caper .... DIDO, LEAP, ANTIC
CAPITAL .. see SPECIAL SEC-
    TION
caprice WHIM, FANCY, VAGARY
captain, fiction .... AHAB
captain, Nile ...... RAIS, REIS
capture BAG, NAB, NET, SEIZE
car .... SEDAN
car, last CABOOSE, CAMBOOSE
car, old make .... REO
caracal .... LYNX
Caradoc .... BALA
caravan .... CAFILA
caravansary
    CHAN, KHAN, SERAI
caravel, Columbus NINA, PINTA
carbolic acid .... PHENOL
carbon, powdery .... SOOT
CARD .. see also GAME, CARD
card .. ACE, PAM, SIX, TEN,
    TWO, FOUR, JACK, KING,
    NINE, TREY, KNAVE,
    POSTAL
card game like bridge .. VINT
card game, 3-handed ... SKAT
card game, old ...... TAROT
card game, Sp. ...... OMBER,
    OMBRE
card holding .... TENACE
card in euchre .... BOWER
card, playing
    TAROC, TAROT, TAROCCO

d
card wool ...... TUM, TEASE
cards, highest ...... HONORS
care for .... RECK, TEND
care, heavy .... CARK
careen ...... TIP, LIST, TILT
caress .... PET
cargo .... LOAD, PORTAGE
cargo, put on .... LADE, LOAD
"Carmen" composer .... BIZET
carnation .... PINK
carnelian .... SARD
carnivore, Afr. .... RATEL
carol .... NOEL, SING
carol singer .... WAIT
carom .... RICOCHET
carousal ORGY, BINGE, SPREE
carouse .... REVEL
carp .... ID, CAVIL
carp, Jap. .... KOI
carp, red-eyed .... RUD, RUDD
carpet, Afgh.. HERAT, HERATI
carpet, Caucasian BAKU, KUBA
carpet, India .... AGRA
carpet, Pers. ... KALI, SENNA
carriage .. GIG, MIEN, POISE,
    CALASH, LANDAU, CARIOLE
carriage: Fr. .... FIACRE
carriage, India .... EKKA
carriage, Java, Oriental SADO

carried away .... **RAPT**
carrier, of Orient .... **HAMAL**
Carroll heroine .... **ALICE**
carrot-family plant .... **ANISE**
carrot-like herb genus .. **MEUM**
carrot ridges .... **JUGA**
carry ...... **LUG, BEAR, TOTE**
carry across water .... **FERRY**
carry on (a war) ...... **WAGE**
cart, heavy .... **DRAY**
carte .... **MENU**
Carthage, of .... **PUNIC**
Carthage queen .... **DIDO**
cartograph .... **MAP**
cartoonist
　　ARNO, CAPP, NAST, KIRBY
carve in itaglio .... **INCISE**
case, grammatical .... **DATIVE**
case of explosives .... **PETARD**
case, toilet, small
　　　　　ETUI, ETWEE
casing, bore-hole ...... **LINER**
cask .. **KEG, TUB, TUN, BUTT,**
　　CADE, TIERCE, PUNCHEON
cassava .. **AIPI, JUCA, YUCA**
cassia leaves .... **SENNA**
cast, founded .. **FUSIL, FUSILE**
cast metal mass .. **PIG, INGOT**
cast off **MOLT, SHED, MOULT**
caste **AHIR, BICE, GOLA, JATI**
caste, agricultural ...... **MEO**
caste, gardener .... **MALI**
caste, low **KOLI, KULI, PARIAH**
caste, Tamil merchant
　　　　　　CHETTY
caster ...... **CRUET, ROLLER**
casting mold .... **DIE**
castor-oil bean poison **RICIN**
castor-oil plant .... **KIKI**
Castor's killer .... **IDAS**
Castor's mother .... **LEDA**
cat .... **ANGORA**
cat, Afr.
　　CIVET, GENET, GENETTE
cat, Am.
　　PUMA, COUGAR, OCELET
cat cry .. **MEW, MIAU, MIAW,**
　　MIAOU, MIAOW, MIAUL
cat genus .... **FELIS**
cat-headed goddess, Egypt **BAST**
cat, spotted
　　PARD, MARGAY, OCELET
cat, tailless .... **MANX**
catalogue ..... **LIST, RECORD**
catamaran ...... **BOAT, RAFT**
catapult .... **ONAGER**
cataract .... **FALLS**
catch .... **NAB, HAUL, HOOK,**
　　SNAG, TRAP, DETENT
catchword ..... **CUE, SLOGAN**

catechu-like resin ...... **KINO**
category .... **GENRE, SPECIES**
cater ...... **PANDER, PURVEY**
caterpillar .... **LARVA**
caterpillar hair .... **SETA**
caterpillar, N. Z. .... **WERI**
catfish, Egypt ...... **DOCMAC**
catfish, S. Am. .... **DORAD**
cathedral .... **MINSTER**
cathedral city, Eng. ..... **ELY**
cathedral, famous .. **CHARTRES**
cathedral passage .. **SLYPE**
cathedral, Russian .... **SOBOR**
Catholic, Greek **UNIAT, UNIATA**
Catholic tribunal ...... **ROTA**
catkin ..... **AMENT, AMENTA**
catnip .... **NEP**
catspaw **DUPE, TOOL, STOOGE**
cattail ...... **TULE, MATREED**
cattail India, narrow .. **REREE**
cattail, N. Z. .... **RAUPO**
cattle, breed of .... **DEVON**
cattle dealer .... **DROVER**
cattle genus .... **BOS**
cattle stealing, crime of
　　　　　　ABIGEAT
CAUCASIAN .... see
　　　CAUCASUS NATIVE
Caucasian bharal ...... **TUR**
Caucasian goat .... **TUR, TEHR**
Caucasian ibex .... **ZAC**
Caucasian language
　　　　　ANDI, AVAR
Caucasion Moslem
　　　　　LAZ, LAZZI
Caucasian race in China
　　　　　LOLO, NOSU
Caucasus native
　　SVAN, SVANE, OSSET
caucho tree .... **ULE**
caudal appendage ...... **TAIL**
caulk lightly .... **CHINSE**
cause .... **CAUSA, REASON**
caustic ... **LYE, LIME, ACRID,**
　　ERODENT, MORDANT
caustic poison ...... **PHENOL**
cauterize .... **SEAR**
cautery plant .... **MOXA**
cautious **WARE, WARY, CHARY**
"Cavalleria Rusticana" heroine
　　　　　　LOLA
cavalryman .... **ULAN, UHLAN**
cavalryman, Turk., Alg.
　　　　　SPAHI, SPAHEE
cave: archaic .... **ANTRE**
cave explorer .... **SPELUNKER**
cave: poet. .... **GROT**
cavern .. **CAVE, GROT, GROTTO**
caviar .... **ROE, IKRA**
caviar fish .... **SHAD, STERLET**
cavil .... **CARP, OBJECT**

Cavity

a cavity .... **ATRIA, ANTRA, SINUS, ANTRUM**
cavity, ear, nose .... **ANTRUM**
cavity, in a rock .. **VUG, VOOG, VUGG, VUGH, GEODE**
cavy .... **APEREA**
cease! .... **HALT, AVAST**
Cecrops' daughter ...... **HERSE**
cedar, E. Ind. ...... **DEODAR**
Celebes ox .... **ANOA**
celebrated .... **EMINENT**
celery-like plant .... **UDO**
cella .... **NAOS**
cellulose acetate .... **ACETOSE**
cellulose: comb. form .. **CELLO**
Celt .... **ERSE, GAEL**
Celt, legendary **IR, ITH, MILED**
Celtic ... **ERSE, MANX, WELSH**
Celtic church early center **IONA**
Celtic dart .... **COLP**
Celtic god .... **TARANIS**
Celtic goddess
ANA, ANU, DANA, DANU
Celtic mother of gods
ANA, ANU, DANA, DANU
Celtic name meaning black
DHU
Celtic Neptune .... **LER**
b Celtic paradise ..... **AVALON**
Celtic sea god .... **LER**
Celtic sun god .... **LUG, LUGH**
cement..**LUTE, PUTTY, SOLDER**
cement well lining .... **STEEN**
cenobite .... **MONK**
censure.**BLAME, CHIDE, SLATE**
center .... **HUB, CORE, FOCI, FOCUS, HEART**
center, away from .... **DISTAL**
center, toward ...... **ENTAD**
centerpiece .... **EPERGNE**
centesimal unit..**GRAD, GRADE**
centesimi, 100 .... **LIRA**
centipede: Tahiti .... **VERI**
central .... **MID, FOCAL**
Cent. Am. gum tree
TUNO, TUNU
Cent. Am. tree .... **EBO, EBOE**
central line .... **AXIS**
central points .... **FOCI**
century plant .... **AGAVE**
century plant fiber..**PITA, PITO**
cere .... **WAX**
cereal .... **FARINA**
cereal grain .... **OAT, RYE**
cereal grass ...... **OAT, RYE, WHEAT, MILLET**
cereal grass, E. Ind. ... **MAND, RAGI, RAGGI, RAGGEE**

c cereal grass genus ... **SECALE**
cereal plant: obs. ...... **RIE**
cereal spike ...... **COB, EAR**
ceremonial chamber .... **KIVA**
Ceres' mother .... **OPS**
certificate, money ..... **SCRIP**
cerulean blue **COELIN, COELINE**
cervine animal .... **DEER**
cesspool .... **SUMP**
cetacean . **ORC, WHALE, NARWAL, NARWHAL, PORPOISE**
cetacean, dolphinlike, genus
INIA
Ceylon ape .... **MAHA**
Ceylon foot soldier ..... **PEON**
Ceylon governor .... **DISAWA**
Ceylon moss .... **AGAR**
Ceylon native
VEDDA, VEDDAH, WEDDAH
Ceylon sandstone ...... **PAAR**
Ceylon trading vessel .. **DONI**
chafe **RUB, FRET, FROT, GALL**
chaff .... **BANTER**
chaffinch ..... **CHINK, SPINK**
chain .... **CATENA**
chain, nautical .... **TYE**
chainlike .... **CATENATE**
chair .... **SEDAN**
chair part ...... **RUNG, SPLAT**
d chaise .... **GIG**
chalcedony .... **ONYX, AGATE**
chalcedony, red .... **SARD**
Chaldean astron. cycle .. **SAROS**
Chaldean city .... **UR**
chalice
AMA, AMULA, CALIX, GRAIL
chalice veil .... **AER**
chalky silicate .... **TALC**
challenge .. **DARE, DEFY, CAGE**
chamber .... **ROOM, CAMERA**
chamber, pert. to ... **CAMERAL**
champagne, Marne .... **AY**
chance .... **HAP, LOT, LUCK**
chances, excess of ..... **ODDS**
chanced upon .... **MET**
chancel part .... **BEMA**
chancel screen .... **JUBE**
chancel seat .. **SEDILE, SEDILIA**
change .... **FLUX, VARY, ALTER, AMEND**
change appearance .. **OBVERT**
change direction **CANT, KANT, TACK, TURN, VEER**
change: music .... **MUTA**
channel .... **GAT, MEDIA, STRIA, MEDIUM, STRIAL**
Channel Island .... **SARK**
channel marker .... **BUOY**
channels .... **MEDIA**

28

a chant .... INTONE
chanticleer .... COCK
chantry .... CHAPEL
chaos .... NU, NUN
chaos, Babyl. .... APSU
chaos, Egypt. ...... NU, NUN
chaos, Maori myth .... KORE
Chaos' son .... EREBUS
chap: S. Afr. .... KEREL
chapel, private .... ORATORY
chapel, sailor's ...... BETHEL
chaperon: Sp. DUENA, DUENNA
chaplain .... PADRE
chaplet .. ANADEM, WREATH
chapped .... KIBY
character .... NATURE
characteristic .... TRAIT
charcoal: Pharm. ...... CARBO
charge .... FEE, COST,
DEBIT, INDICT
charge solemnly ..... ADJURE
charged particle .... ION
charger .... STEED
chariot, ancient Briton
ESSED, ESSEDA, ESSEDE
chariot race site ...... CIRCUS
chariot, religious RATH, RATHA
charity .... ALMS
Charlemagne, race subdued by
AVARS
b Charlemagne's father ... PEPIN
Charlotte —, dessert .. RUSSE
charm .... JUJU,
SPELL, AMULET, GRIGRI
Charon, payment for .. OBOL
Charon, river of .... STYX
chart .... MAP
Charybdis, rock opp. .. SCYLLA
chasm GAP, ABYSS, CANYON
chaste .... PURE, VESTAL
chat, friendly .... COSE, COZE
Chateaubriand heroine, novel
ATALA
chatelaine bag .... ETUI
chatter GAB, GAS, YAP, PRATE
chatterbox .... PIET
cheat .... RENIG, RENEGE
cheat .... BAM,
CON, FOB, FUB, GIP, GYP,
BILK, MUMP, COZEN, SHARP
cheaters: slang ..... GLASSES
check ...... NIP, TAB, REIN,
STEM, BRAKE, STUNT
checking block .... SPRAG
cheek .... GENA, JOLE, JOWL
"cheek"..GALL, BRASS, NERVE
cheek, pert. to ...... MALAR
cheek-bone .... MALAR
cheer .... OLE, RAH,
BRAVO, ELATE, ENCORE
cheer pine .... CHIR

c cheer up .... LIVEN
cheerless .... SAD, DRAB
cheese ..... EDAM, STILTON
cheese, Dutch .... EDAM
cheese, hard brown .. MYSOST
cheese, soft .... BRIE
cheesy .... CASEOUS
cheetah, Ind. . YOUSE, YOUZE
chela .... CLAW
Chemical compound .. IMID,
AMIDE, AMINE, IMIDE,
IMINE, ESTER
CHEMICAL ELEMENT .... see
SPECIAL SECTION
chemical ending OL, INE, ENOL
chemical prefix .... ACI, OXA,
AMIDO, AMINO
chemical salt .... SAL, ESTER,
NITRE, BORATE
CHEMICAL SUFFIX .. see SUF-
FIX, CHEMICAL
chemical unit .... TITER
chemist's pot .... ALUDEL
cherish ... FOSTER, TREASURE
cherry .... GEAN
cherry red .... CERISE
chess piece .... MAN
chess term,—passant ..... EN
chessman .... KING, PAWN,
ROOK, QUEEN, BISHOP,
d CASTLE, KNIGHT
chest, acacia wood ...... ARK
chest, antique .... CIST, KIST
chest, sacred ARK, ARCA, CIST
chest sound .... RALE
chestnut, Eur. ...... MARRON
chestnut, Polyn. .... RATA
chevrotain . NAPU, MEMINNA
chew .... BITE, CHAM, GNAW
chew, leaf to .... COCA
chewink .... TOWHEE
Chibcha chief's title .... ZIPA
chick-pea .... GRAM
chicken snake .... BOBA
chide SCOLD, BERATE, REPROVE
chief ... ARCH, HEAD, MAIN
chief, Afr. tribe ...... KAID
chief, Am. Ind. ...... SACHEM
chief: Chinook .... TYEE
chief deity, Panopolis .... MIN
chief in Italy .... DUCE
chief, India .... SIRDAR
Chief Justice 1921-30 ... TAFT
Chief Justice 1941-46 .. STONE
chief, Moslem .... RAIS, REIS
chief officer, India .. DEWAN,
DIWAN
chief Norse god ...... ODIN,
WODAN, WODEN, WOTAN
chief, Pres. .... MIR
child .... TIKE, TYKE

Child

child of streets..**ARAB, GAMIN**
"Child of the Sun" ..... **INCA**
child, pert. to .... **FILIAL**
child: Scot. .... **BAIRN**
child: Tagalog, P. I. .... **BATA**
Chilean proletariat ..... **ROTO**
Chilean timber tree ..... **PELU**
Chilean volcano ..... **ANTUCO**
chill .... **ICE, AGUE**
chills and fever
　　　　　　AGUE, MALARIA
chimney: dialect .... **LUM**
chimney pipe .... **FLUE**
chin .... **MENTA, MENTUM**
China .... **CATHAY**
China blue .... **NIKKO**
China grass .... **BON**
Chinese .. **SERES, SERIC, SINIC**
Chinese aborigine . **YAO, MANS**
Chin. aboriginal population
　　division .... **MIAO**
Chin. are .... **MU**
Chin. boat .... **JUNK**
Chin. brick bed .... **K'ANG**
Chin. Causasian tribesman **LOLO**
Chin. characters in Jap. . **MANA**
Chin. club .... **TONG**
CHIN. COIN .. see also **COINS**
　　　　　　　　Page 190
Chin., coin, bronze .... **LI**
Chin., coin, early .... **PU**
Chin. Communist .. **MAO, CHOU**
Chin. cult .... **JOSS**
Chin. department .... **FU**
Chin. dialect .... **WU**
Chin. division .... **MIAO**
Chin. dynasty . **HAN, KIN, SUI,**
　　WEI, YIN, CH'IN, CHOU,
　　HSIA, T'ANG, MING, SUNG,
　　TS'IN, YUAN
Chin. factory .... **HONG**
Chin. feudal state .... **WEI**
Chin. flute .... **TCHE**
Chin. god .... **GHOS, JOSS**
Chin. govt. section
　　　　　　　HIEN, HSIEN
Chin. guild .... **HUI**
Chin. idol ...... **GHOS, JOSS**
Chin. instrument, stringed . **KIN**
Chin. kingdom, old
　　　　　　WU, SHU, WEI
CHIN. MEASURE.see also pages
　　　　　　　　188, 189
Chin. measure of length . **TSUN**
Chin. mile .... **LI**
Chin. monetary unit .... **YUAN**
CHIN, MONEY see also page 190
Chin. negative principle ... **YIN**
Chin. noodles .... **MEIN**
Chin. official .. **KUAN, KWAN**
Chin. philos. principle.**LI, YANG**

Chin. plant .... **UDO**
Chin. pottery .... **CHUN,**
　　　　KUAN, MING, TING
Chin. ruler .. **YAO, YAU, YAOU**
Chin. secret society ..... **TONG**
Chin. shop: Du. E. Ind. .. **TOKO**
Chin. silk .... **PONGEE**
Chin. wax, wax insect .. **PELA**
Chin. wormwood ...... **MOXA**
Chin. yellow .... **SIL**
chinin .... **COYO**
chink ...... **RIFT, RIMA, RIME**
chink-like .. **RIMAL, RIMATE**
chinky ...... **RIMAL, RIMOSE,**
　　　　　　　　RIMOUS
chip .... **NICK**
chip of stone .. **SPALL, GALLET**
chipmunk .... **HACKEE**
chirp **CHEEP, TWEET, TWITTER**
chisel, primitive .... **CELT**
chisel, very broad .... **TOOLER**
chocolate powder ..... **PINOLE**
chocolate source ...... **CACAO**
choice .... **CREAM, ELITE,**
　　　　　　PRIME, SELECT
choke up .... **DAM, CLOG**
choler .... **IRE, BILE, RAGE**
choose .... **OPT, ELECT**
chop ... **AXE, CUT, HEW, LOP**
chop fine .... **MINCE**
chopped .... **HEWN**
choral music
　　　　MOTET, CANTATA
chord, 3 tones .... **TRINE**
chore .... **JOB, CHARE**
Chosen ...... **COREA, KOREA**
Christ's thorn .. **NABK, NUBK**
Christmas ...... **NOEL, YULE**
Christmas crib ...... **CRECHE**
chromosome .... **IDANT**
chronicle .... **ANNAL, ANNALS**
chrysalis .... **PUPA**
chrysanthemum .. **MUM, KIKU**
chub, Europ. .... **CHEVIN**
chunk .... **GOBBET**
church .... **FANE**
church bench .... **PEW**
church, body of ...... **NAVE**
church calendar .... **ORDO**
church contribution .... **TITHE**
church council .... **SYNOD**
church court .... **ROTA**
church dignitary.**POPE, BISHOP,**
　　　　PRELATE, CARDINAL
church dish .... **PATEN**
church, India .... **SAMAJ**
church living .... **BENEFICE**
church maintenance, canon's
　　　　　　　　PREBEND
church officer .... **ELDER**

a church official ...... SEXTON, VERGER
church part ..... APSE, BEMA, NAVE, ALTAR
church, Pope's ..... LATERAN
church porch .... PARVIS
church property .... GLEBE
church reader .... LECTOR
church recess .... APSE
church, Scot. .... KIRK, KURK
church vessel .. AMA, PIX, PYX
churchman .... PRELATE
churl.CEORL, VILLAIN, VILLEIN
churl: var. .... CARLE
churn plunger .... DASHER
cibol .... ONION
cicatrix .... SCAR
cigar .... CLARO, SMOKE, CORONA, CHEROOT
cigar, cheap ... STOGY, STOGIE
cigarette, medicinal ... CUBEB
cigarfish .... SCAD
cincture .... BELT
cinnamon, kind of .... CASSIA
cion .... GRAFT
cipher .... ZERO, OUGHT
cipher system .... CODE
Circe's home .... AEAEA
circle .... CIRC, CIRQUE, RONDURE

b circle of light ... HALO, NIMB
circle, part of .... ARC
circle segment .... SECTOR
circuit .... LAP, TOUR, AMBIT, ORBIT
circuit judge, court ...... EYRE
circular motion .... GYRE
circular plate ...... DISC, DISK
circular turn .... LOOP
circular saw .... EDGER
cirque, geol. .... CWM
cistern .... BAC, VAT
citation .... CITAL
cite .... QUOTE, ADDUCE
citron ...... ETROG, CEDRAT, ETHROG
citrus fruit .... LIME, LEMON, ORANGE, SHADOCK, SHADDOCK
CITY .. see also TOWN and GAZETTEER
city, ancient, Asia Min. . MYRA, TYRE, SARDES, SARDIS
city, ancient Thessalian ...... LARISSA
city: Gr. .... POLIS
City of a Hundred Towers PAVIA
City of Bridges ...... BRUGES
City of God .... HEAVEN
City of Kings .... LIMA
City of Lights .... PARIS

c City of Luxury ...... SYBARIS
City of Masts .... LONDON
City of Rams .... CANTON
City of Refuge ...... MEDINA
City of Saints .... MONTREAL
City of the Prophet .. MEDINA
City of the Seven Hills .. ROME
City of the Violet Crown ...... ATHENS
City of Victory .... CAIRO
city, pert. to .. CIVIC, URBAN
city, Philistines' ...... EKRON
city political division ... WARD
civet, Chinese .... RASSE
civet, Indian .... ZIBET
civet, Java .... DEDES
civet, Madagascar .... FOSSA, FOUSSA
civetlike cat . GENET, GENETTE
civic goddess, Gr. ...... ALEA
Civil War commander ..... LEE, POPE, GRANT, EWELL, MEADE, SCOTT, SYKES, HOOKER, CUSTER, FORREST, JACKSON
civil wrong or injury .... TORT
claim ...... ASSERT, DEMAND
clam genus .... MYA
clam, giant .... CHAMA
clam, razor .... SOLEN
clamor .... DIN, NOISE

d clamp .... VICE, VISE
clan ...... GEN, SEPT, TRIBE
clan chieftain successor.TANIST
clan division: Gr. .... OBE
clan, Gr. .... GENOS
clan, head of .... ALDER
clarinet socket .... BIRN
clash .... JAR, COLLIDE
clasp . HASP, ENFOLD, INFOLD
clasp for a cope ..... MORSE
class .... ILK, CASTE, GENUS, GENERA, SPECIES
class leader, Eng. .... DUX
class, lowest Jap. .... HEIMIN
class, scientific ...... GENUS, GENERA
classic tongue .... LATIN
classification .... RATING
classification method . SYSTEM
classify .. RANK, RATE, SORT, TYPE, GRADE
claw .... NAIL, TALON, UNGUIS, UNGUES
claw, crustacean's ...... CHELA, CHELAE
claw ornament .... GRIFF
claw: zool. .... UNCI, UNCUS
clay ..... BOLE, ARGIL, LOESS
clay, baked .... TILE

a

clay bed .... GAULT
clay, building: Sp.
                  ADOBE, TAPIA
clay-covered .... LUTOSE
clay, friable .... BOLE
clay layer ..... SLOAM, SLOOM
clay, melting pot ..... TASCO
clay mineral .... NACRITE
clay molding plate ...... DOD
clay pigeon shooting ... SKEET
clay pipe .... TD
clay plug .... BOTT
clay, porcelain ...... KAOLIN
clay, potter's .... ARGIL
clayey .... BOLAR
clayey soil. BOLE, MALM, MARL
cleansing agent ...... BORAX
clear. NET, RID, LUCID, LIMPID,
     AUDIBLE, TRANSPARENT
clear, as anchor .... AWEIGH
clear of charges ..... ACQUIT
clearing of land, Eng. ... SART
cleave ... REND, RIVE, CLING
cleaving tool .... FROE
cleft ...... REFT, RIFT, RIMA
Clemenceau's nickname . TIGRE
clement .... MILD
Cleopatra's attendant ... IRAS
Cleopatra's handmaid ... IRAS

b

Cleopatra's needle ... OBELISK
Cleopatra's serpent ...... ASP
clergyman .... ABBE, CANON,
     VICAR, CURATE, PRIEST,
     RECTOR
cleric, Fr. .... ABBE
clerical cap .... BIRETTA
clerical, not .... LAIC, LAICAL
clever .... APT, HABILE
click beetle ...... DOR, DORR,
                      ELATER
climb .... GRIMP, SCALE
climbing plant ..... IVY, VINE,
                LIANA, LIANE
cling .... STICK, ADHERE
clingfish .... TESTAR
clinging, for .... TENENT
Clio, sister of .... ERATO
clip . CUT, MOW, SNIP, SHEAR
clique .... SET
CLOAK .... see also GARMENT
cloak ... ABA, WRAP, CAPOT,
          CAPOTE, MANTLE
cloak, Ind. .... CHOGA
cloak, Rom. . SAGUM, ABOLLA,
                ABOLLAE
cloak, woman's ..... DOLMAN
clock, ship-form .... NEF
clog-like shoe .... PATTEN
cloister .... MONASTERY
"Cloister-Hearth" author. READE

c

close eyes of .... SEEL
close, keep .... HUG
close: musical .... CODA
close to . AT, BY, NEAR, ANEAR
close, to fit ..... FAY, FADGE
closed, as wings .... PLIE
closing measure, music .. CODA
CLOTH .... see also SILK,
          COTTON, FABRIC
cloth, bark .... TAPA
cloth, figured old ..... TAPET
cloth measure .... ELL
cloth, old wool ..... CHEYNEY
cloth, stout .... BRIN
cloth strip, India .... PATA
cloth used in mourning . CRAPE
cloth, wrapping .... TILLOT
clothe .... GIRD, VEST, ENDUE
clothes moth .... TINEA
clothespress, old Dutch ... KAS
clothing .. DUDS, GARB, GEAR,
          TOGS, RAIMENT
cloud .... SMUR, CIRRI,
          NUBIA, CIRRUS
cloud dragon, Vedic ...... AHI
cloud, luminous ..... NIMBUS
clouds, broken .... RACK
clouds, wind-driven. RACK, SCUD
cloudberry .... MOLKA
cloudy .... DULL, LOWERY

d

clout .... HIT, SWAT
cloven-footed ...... FISSIPED
clover .... HUBAM,
          ALSIKE, MELILOT
clown .... APER, GOFF, ZANY
clown, Shakespearean . LAVACHE
cloy .... PALL, SATE, ACCLOY
club member, Gr. .... ERANIST
club, women's .... ZONTA
clubfoot ... TALIPED, TALIPES
clumsily, handle . PAW, BOTCH
clumsy ...... INEPT, OAFISH
cluster .... NEP, TUFT
cluster, grape .... RACEME
cluster pine .... PINASTER
coach dog ...... DALMATIAN
coach, Eastern .... ARABA
coagulate .... GEL, CLOT
coal dust ...... COOM, SMUT
coal, heat-treated ...... COKE
coal, live .... EMBER
coal, size of .. EGG, NUT, PEA
coal refuse .... CULM
coal scuttle .... HOD
coalfish .... CUDDY
coalition .... UNION, MERGER
coarse .... GROSS
coarse sugar, E. Ind. ..... RAAB
coast bird .... GULL, TERN
coast dweller ...... ORARIAN
coastal range, India .... GHAT

a COAT ..... see also GARMENT
coat .... LAYER
coat, animal .... PELAGE
coat, Arab .... ABA
coat, soldier's .... TUNIC
coat with alloy .... TERNE
cob .... SWAN
cobbler .... SUTOR
cobra ... HAJE, NAGA, MAMBA
cobra genus ..... NAIA, NAJA
cocaine source ... COCA, CUCA
cockatoo, Austral. .... GALAH
cockatoo, palm .. ARA, ARARA
cockboat .... COG
cockpit .... ARENA
coconut, dried .... COPRA
coconut fiber .... COIR, KOIR,
KYAR, COIRE
coconut, Ind. .... NARGIL
coconut palm, P. I. ..... NIOG
cocoon insect .... PUPA
cocoon, silkworm .... CLEW
cod genus .... GADUS
cod, pert. to .... GADOID
cod, young ... . SCROD
code .... LAW, CIPHER
codfish, Eur. .... POOR
coffee ... RIO, JAVA, MOCHA
coffee-chocolate flavor.MOCHA
coffer-dam, Egypt ...... SADD
b coffin stand .... BIER
cognizant .... AWARE
cognomen ... NAME, EPITHET
cohere .... BIND
coil .... WIND, TWINE
TWIST, WREATHE
COIN ...... see also SPECIAL
SECTION, Page 190
coin .... RIN, YEN, SPECIE
coin, cut edges of .... NIG
coin, edging .... REEDING
coin, gold .... LEV
coin, mill .... NURL
coin money .... MINT
coin, pewter .... TRA
coin, reverse side ...... VERSO
coin, silver .... SCEAT
coin tester, Orient
SARAF, SHROFF
coin, tin .... TRA
coincide .... JIBE, AGREE
colander .... .SIEVE
cold .... ALGID, GELID
cold, producing ...... ALGIFIC
cold tableland, Andes ... PUNA
collar .. ETON, FICHU, GORGET
collar, clerical ...... RABAT,
RABATO, REBATO
collar, deep .... BERTHA
collar, wheel-shaped .... RUFF
collect ...... AMASS, GARNER

c collection .... ANA, SET
collection .... SORTITE
collection, motley ...... RAFT
collection of facts .... ANA
collection of sayings .... ANA
COLLEGE DEGREE . see DEGREE
college, Iowa .... COE
college, N.J., East Orange
UPSALA
college official .... DEAN
college quadrangle ..... QUAD
colloquialism .... IDIOM
colonists greeting to Ind. NETOP
colonize .... SETTLE
colonizer .... OECIST
colonnade .... STOA
colony, Eng. ...... CAROLINA
colony, Fr. .... ALGERIA
color .... DYE, HUE, TINT
color .. ASH, BAY, RED, TAN,
BLUE, FAON, FAWN, GRAY,
GREY, HOPI, JADE, LIME,
NAVY, NILE, PINK, PUCE,
ROSE, SAXE, AMBER, BEIGE,
CORAL, CREAM, EBONY,
HENNA, IVORY, MAUVE,
MOCHA, SEPIA, UMBER,
CERISE, CITRON, COBALT,
MAROON, RESEDA, SEVRES,
SIENNA, SORREL, CAR-
MINE, CELESTE, CITRINE,
MAGENTA
d color brown sugar ... CARAIBE
color changer, photo ... TONER
color, neutral .. GREGE, GREIGE
color, purplish-brown ... PUCE
color, slightly .... TINT, TINGE
color, stripe of .... PLAGA
color, terrapin ...... FEUILLE
Colorado park .... ESTES
coloring agent .... RUDDLE
coloring matter in fustic.MORIN
colorless .... DRAB
colorless alkaloid ...... ESERIN
colorless oil .... CETANE
columbite, variety of.DIANITE
Columbus' birthplace .. GENOA
Columbus' city sailed from
PALOS
Columbus' ship .. NINA, PINTA
column, Buddhist-Hindu, building
LAT
column, Gr. .... DORIC, IONIC
column, memorial .... LAT
column, twisted . TORSE, TORSO
columns, arranged in TABULAR
coma .... TRANCE
comb horse .... CURRY
comb wool ..... CARD, TEASE
combat, field, place of . ARENA
combat, knight's ...... JOUST

Combat

a   combat, scene of ..... ARENA
combination .. UNION, CARTEL
combination, card .... TENACE
COMBINING FORMS:
above .... SUR
air ...... AER, AERI, AERO
all .... PAN, OMNI
ass .... ONO
bad .... MAL
bee .... API
beyond .... SUR
black .... MELA
blood .... HEMO
body ...... SOMA, SOMATO
bone .... OSTEO
both .... AMBI
boundary .... ORI
bread .... ARTO
bristle .... SETI
cetacean .... CETO
Chinese .... SINO
communications .... TEL
contemporary .... NEO
daybreak .... EO
dry .... XER
ear .... OTO, AURI
earth .... GEO
egg .... OO, OVI
eight .... OCT, OCTO
equal .... ISO, PARI

b   eye .... OCULO
far .... TEL, TELE
fat ... SEBI, STEAT, STEATO
fearful .... DINO
feast day .... MAS
female .... GYNE
firm .... STEREO
five .... PENTA
follower .... IST
food .... SITO
foot ...... PED, PEDI, PEDO
four-parted .... TETRA
fruit .... CARPO
gas .... AER, AERO
gate .... PYLE
glade .... NEMO
gland .... ADEN
gray .... POLIO
great .... MEGA
gums .... ULO
hair .... PIL, PILI
half .... DEMI, SEMI
heat ..... THERM, THERMO
hundred ..... CENTI, HECTO
idea .... IDEO
ill .... MAL
individual .... IDIO
inner .... ENTO
in zoology .... EAE
late, latest .... NEO
line .... STICH

c   many .... POLY
medicine .... IATRO
middle .... MEDI
milk .... LACT, LACTO
monster .... TERAT
mountain .... ORO
mouth ...... STOM, STOMO
moving .... KINO
narrow .... STENO
neck types .... DERA
needle .... ACU
nerve .... NEURO
new .... NEO
nine .... ENNE, ENNEA
nose .... NASI
not .... UN, NON
numerical .... UNI
numerous .... MULTI
oil .... OLEO
one .... UNI, MONO
on this side .... CIS
other .... HETER
outside .... ECTO
peculiar .... IDIO
power .... DYNA
powerful .... MEGA
quality .... ACY
recent .... NEO, CENE
reversal .... ALLO

d   ribbon .... TENE
round .... GYRO
sad .... TRAGI
seeds .... CARPO
seizure of illness .... AGRA
self .... AUT, AUTO
shoulder .... OMO
small .... STENO
solid .... STEREO
speak .... LALO
star .... ASTRO
stone .... LITH
strange .... XENO
sun .... HELIO
ten .... DECA
thin .... SERO
third .... TRIT
thread .... NEMA
threefold, thrice ...... TER
tooth .... ODONT
touch .... TAC
thought .... IDEO
thousand .... MILLE
up .... ANO
vapor .... ATMO
various .... VARI, VARIO
watery .... SERO
white .... ALBO
whole .... TOTO
wind .... ANEMO
within .... ENT, ESO,
ENDO, ENSO, ENTO

34

a
without .... ECT
wood .... XYLO
worker .... ERGATE
come . ENSUE, ACCRUE, ARRIVE
come back .... RECUR
come forth .... ISSUE,
EMERGE, EMERSE
come forth from .. JET, GUSH,
SPEW, EMANATE
comedian's foil .... STOOGE
comedy .... FARCE
"Comedy of Errors" servant
LUCE
comfort .... EASE, SOLACE
comfortable .... COSH, SNUG
comforter .... SCARF
command .... BID, FIAT,
ORDER, DICTATE
command: archaic ..... HEST
command to horse
GEE, HAW, HUP
commander, Egypt .... SIRDAR
commander, Moslem
AGA, AGHA
commander, fortress CAID, QAID
commentary: Hebrew .... BIUR
commission, milit. .... BREVET
commodity .... WARE, STAPLE
common ... VULGAR, GENERAL
common brant .... QUINK

b
common: Hawaiian ..... NOA
common man .... PLEB
commonplace .. BANAL, TRITE
commotion . ADO, STIR, TO-DO
commune, Dutch, Holland EDE
COMMUNE   see its country in
GAZETTEER
communion cup .... AMA
communion dish ...... PATEN
communion service ..... MASS
communion table ...... ALTAR
compact ...... DENSE, SOLID
companion .... PAL, MATE
comparative conjunction . THAN
comparative suffix ending . ER
compass point .... NE, SE, SW,
ENE, ESE, NNE, NNW, SSE,
SSW, WNW, WSW
compass point, mariner's RHUMB
compassion ...... PITY, RUTH
compel .... MAKE, FORCE,
COERCE
compendium .... SYLLABUS
compensate .... PAY
compensation, N. Z. ...... UTU
competent .... ABLE
complain .... FRET, FUSS,
GRIPE, REPINE
complainant .... RELATOR
complete ...... TOTAL, UTTER,
ENTIRE, PLENARY

c
completely .... ALL, QUITE
completely occupy ... ENGROSS
complication ..... NODE, NODI
comply .... OBEY, YIELD
composer, Am. . NEVIN, SOUSA,
FOSTER, COPLAND
composer, Eng. .... ARNE,
ELGAR, COATES
composer, Fr. .. LALO, AUBER
BIZET, IBERT, RAVEL
composer, Ger. .... ABT, BACH,
WEBER
composer, Roum. ..... ENESCO
COMPOSITION . see also MUSIC
composition ... ESSAY, THEME
composition, mus. ...... OPUS,
ETUDE, MOTET, RONDO,
SUITE, SONATA, CON-
CERTO, FANTASIA
composition of selections . CENTO
composition, operatic .. SCENA
composition, sacred ... MOTET
compositor .... TYPO
compound, organic .... AMIDE
compound with oxygen . OXIDE
comrade-in-arms .... ALLY
concave .... DISHED
conceal: law .... ELOIN
concealed ..... INNER, PERDU
concealed obstacle ...... SNAG
concede .... ADMIT,

d
GRANT, YIELD
conceive .... IDEATE
concern .... CARE
concerning .... RE. INRE,
ABOUT, ANENT
conch .... SHELL
conciliate .... ATONE
conciliatory gift .... SOP
concise .. BRIEF, SHORT, TERSE
concluding passage music CODA
concoct .... BREW
concrete mixer .... PAVER
concur .. JIBE, AGREE, ASSENT
condescend .... DEIGN, STOOP
condiment .... SALT,
CURRY, SPICE
condition .. IF, STATE, STATUS
condition in agreement PROVISO
conduct ...... LEAD, GUIDE
conductor .... MAESTRO
conductor's stick ..... BATON
conduit . MAIN, DRAIN, SEWER
cone ... STROBIL, STROBILE
cone of silver .... PINA
confection .... COMFIT
confection, nut ...... PRALINE
confederate .... ALLY
Confederate soldier .... REB
confederation .... LEAGUE
conference .... PALAVER

35

Confess

a confess .... AVOW, ADMIT
confession of faith .... CREDO
confidence .... FAITH, TRUST
confidences .... SECRETS
confident .... RELIANT
confidential .... ESOTERIC
confine ...... BOX, HEM, PEN,
              CAGE, CRAMP
confined .... PENT
confront .... MEET
confused, make .... ADDLE
confusion .... BABEL
congealed dew .... RIME
conger .... EEL
congregate .. MEET, GATHER
conical mass of thread ... COP
coniferous tree ..... FIR, YEW,
      PINE, CEDAR, SPRUCE
conjunction .... OR, AND,
              BUT, NOR
connect ... JOIN, LINK, UNITE
connecting strip of land
               ISTHMUS
connection
     NEXUS, CORRELATION
connective .... AND, NOR
connective tissue ..... FASCIA
connubial .... MARITAL
conquer .... MASTER
conqueror, Mex.
b   CORTES, CORTEZ
Conrad's "Victory" heroine
               LENA
conscript .... DRAFT
consecrate .... BLESS
consecrated .... OBLATE
consequence .... OUTCOME
conservative .... TORY
consider .... DEEM, RATE,
          TREAT, REGARD
consonant, hard ...... FORTIS
consonant, unaspirated .. LENE
conspire .... PLOT
Constantine VIII's daughter . ZOE
constellation ...... ARA, LEO,
    APUS, ARGO, LYNX, LYRA,
    PAVO, URSA, VELA, ARIES,
    CANIS, CETUS, DRACO,
    LIBRA, MENSA, ORION,
    VIRGO, AQUILA, GEMINI,
    PISCES, TAURUS
constellation, Altar ...... ARA
constellation, Aquila ... EAGLE
constellation, Ara .... ALTAR
constellation, Aries ..... RAM
constellation, Balance .. LIBRA
constellation, Bear ...... URSA
constellation, Bull .... TAURUS
constellation, Crab ... CANCER
constellation, Crane ..... GRUS
constellation, Crow ... CORVUS

c constellation, Dog .... CANIS
constellation, Dragon .. DRACO
constellation, Hunter ... ORION
constellation, Lion .... LEO
constellation near South Pole
               APUS
constellation, northern .... LEO
constellation, Peacock ... PAVO
constellation, Ram ..... ARIES
constellation, Southern .. ARA,
    APUS, ARGO, GRUS, PAVO,
    VELA, INDUS
constellation's main star .. COR
constitution supporter .CARTIST
constrictor ..... BOA, ABOMA
constructor .... ERECTOR
consume: obs. .... ETE
container .... BOX, CAN, TIN,
      TUB, VAT, URN, CASE
containing ore .... ORY
contempt, exclamation of .PISH
contempt, look of ..... SNEER
contend .... VIE, COPE,
         DEAL, COMPETE
contest .... AGON, BOUT
continent: abbr. ...... NA, SA,
             AFR, EUR
continue .... LAST,
      ENDURE, RESUME
contort . WARP, GNARL, TWIST
d contradict ..... DENY, REBUT,
              NEGATE
contrition .... REMORSE
contrive .... MAKE, DEVISE
control .... STEER
controversial .... ERISTIC
controversy .... DEBATE
conundrum .. ENIGMA, RIDDLE
convert to Judaism ...... GER
conveyance of estate .. DEMISE
convoy .... ESCORT
cony .. DAS, DAMAN, GANAM
cook in cream .... SHIR, SHIRR
cooking odor .... NIDOR
cooking pot .... OLLA
cooky .... SNAP
cool .... ICE
coolie woman ...... CHANGAR
Cooper novel .... PILOT
copal .... ANIME
copper .... CENT
Copperfield, Mrs. .... DORA
copse .... HOLT, COPPICE
Coptic bishop .... ANBA
copy .... APE, MODEL, ECTYPE
copy, court record ... ESTREAT
coral .... POLYP
cord .... LINE, RAIP,
          ROPE, WELT
cord, hat of Bedouin .... AGAL
cord, Hawaii .... AEA

a cordage fiber . **DA, COIR, ERUC,**
    FERU, HEMP, IMBE, JUTE,
    RHEA, ABACA, SISAL
cordage tree .... **SIDA**
Cordelia's father .... **LEAR**
"Cordiale, —" ...... **ENTENTE**
core ...... **AME, PITH, HEART**
core, casting mold .... **NOWEL**
core material of earth ... **NIFE**
core to fashion metal ... **AME**
core, wooden .... **AME**
cork .... **SPILE**
Cork County port .... **COBH**
cork, extract of .... **CERIN**
cork, flat .... **SHIVE**
cork helmet ..... **TOPI, TOPEE**
corkwood .... **BALSA**
corm .... **BULB**
corn crake bird .... **RAIL**
corn crake genus .... **CREX**
corn, hulled .... **HOMINY**
corn, India ... **RAGEE, RAGGEE**
corn lily .... **IXIA**
corn meal .... **MASA**
cornbread .... **PONE**
corner ... **NOOK, TREE, ANGLE**
cornerstone .... **COIN, COYN,**
    COIGN, QUOIN, COIGNE
cornice support ...... **ANCON**
b Cornish prefix: town .... **TRE**
Cornish prefix in names . **LAN,**
    ROS
cornu .... **HORN**
Cornwall mine .... **BAL**
corolla part .... **PETAL**
corona ... **AUREOLA, AUREOLE**
coronach, Scot. .... **DIRGE**
coronation stone ...... **SCONE**
corpulent .... **OBESE**
corral: Sp. .... **ATAJO**
correct .. **OKEH, TRUE, AMEND,**
    EMEND, REVISE
correct behaviour, Chin. ... **LI**
correlative .... **OR, NOR**
correspond **JIBE, AGREE, TALLY**
corridor .... **HALL**
corrie .... **CWM**
corrode .... **EAT, RUST, ERODE**
corrupt ...... **TAINT, VENAL,**
    VITIATE
corrupt with money .... **BRIBE**
corsair .... **PIRATE**
corset bone .... **BUSK**
cortege .... **RETINUE**
corundum .... **EMERY**
cos lettuce .... **ROMAINE**
Cos, pert. to .... **COAN**
cosmic cycle .... **EON**
cosmic order: Vedic ..... **RITA**
Cossack .... **TATAR**
Cossack chief ...... **ATAMAN**

c Cossack headman ... **HETMAN**
Cossack regiment . **POLK, PULK**
cosset .... **PET**
costa .... **RIB**
coterie .... **SET**
cottage, Ind. .... **BARI**
cotton batting .... **BATT**
cotton, Bengal .... **ADATI**
cotton, Egypt .... **SAK, PIMA,**
    SAKEL
cotton fabric ... **JEAN, LAWN,**
    LENO, DENIM, SURAT,
    MADRAS
cotton fabric, corded. **CANTOON**
cotton machine .... **GIN**
cotton, matted .... **BATT**
cotton tree .... **SIMAL**
cottonwood, Texas .... **ALAMO**
couch .... **LAIR**
cougar ..... **PUMA, PANTHER**
council .... **SOVIET**
council, ecclesiastical . **SYNOD**
council, king's .... **WITAN**
"Council of —" ...... **TRENT**
counsel .... **REDE**
counselor .... **MENTOR**
count .... **ENUMERATE**
count, Ger. .... **GRAF**
counter .... **BAR**
counter, in cards ...... **MILLE**
d countercurrent .... **EDDY**
countermand .... **REVOKE**
counterpart .... **LIKE**
countersink .... **REAM**
counting frame ...... **ABACUS**
COUNTRY see also GAZETTEER,
    beginning on Page 210
country, ancient .... **ELAM**
country, ancient, Asia Min., Gr.
    EOLIS, AEOLIA, AEOLIS
country, ancient, Bib. .. **SHEBA**
country, ancient Greek ... **ELIS**
country bumpkin
    RUBE, YOKEL, RUSTIC
country: law .... **PAIS**
COUNTY .see also GAZETTEER,
    beginning on Page 210
county: Dan. .... **AMT**
county: Eng. .... **SHIRE**
county: Nor. .... **AMT, FYLKE**
county: Swed. .... **LAN**
couple .... **TWO, PAIR**
courage .... **METTLE**
courier .. **ESTAFET, ESTAFETTE**
course .... **WAY, ROAD,**
    TACK, ROUTE
course, complete ...... **CYCLE**
course, meal . **SALAD, ENTREE**
course, part of ..... **LAP, LEG**
court .... **AREA**

court action .... SUIT
court, A.-S. .. GEMOT, GEMOTE
court, church .... ROTA
court cry .... OYES, OYEZ
court hearing .... OYER
court, inner .... PATIO
court, Jap. ..... DARI, DAIRO
court, old English .... LEET
court order .... ARRET
court panel .... JURY
court, pert. to church .. ROTAL
court proceeding ...... TRIAL
courtly .... AULIC
courtship strut, grouse's .. LAK
courtway .... AREA
courtyard .... PATIO
Covenant, — of the .... ARK
cover inner surface ..... LINE
covering .. TEGMEN, TEGUMEN
covey .... BEVY, BROOD
cow .... BOSSY, BOVINE
cow house .... BYRE
cows .... KINE, BOSSIES
coward .... CRAVEN
cowboy garment ...... CHAPS
cowboy, S. Am. ..... GAUCHO
cowfish .... RAY, TORO
cowl .... HOOD
cowlike .... COUS
coxcomb .... FOP
coy .... ARCH
coyotillo .... MARGARITA
coypu .... NUTRIA
cozy .... HOMY, SNUG
cozy place .... DEN, NEST
crab-eating mongoose .. URVA
crab, front of .... METOPE
crack . SNAP, CHINK, CREVICE
crackling .... CREPITANT
crackpot .... NUT
craft .... ART, TRADE
craftsman .... ARTISAN
crafty ...... SLY, FOXY, WILY
craggy hill .... TOR
cramp .... KINK
crane arm .... GIB, JIB
crane genus .... GRUS
crane, India .... SARUS
crane, pert. to .... GRUINE
crane, ship's .... DAVIT
cranelike bird ...... CHUNGA
cranelike bird, S. Amer.
.... SERIEMA
cranial nerve ... VAGI, VAGUS
cravat .... TIE
crave . ASK, BEG, LONG, DESIRE
craw .... MAW, CROP
crayon .... CHALK, PASTEL
craze .... FAD, MANIA
crazy .... LOCO, LUNY, WILD

cream .... ELITE
credit transfer system .. GIRO
creed .... CREDO, NICENE
creek .... RIA, KILL
creek: N.Y. .... VLEI
creeper .... IVY
creeping .. REPENT, REPTANT
Cremona .... AMATI
crescent moon's point ... CUSP
crescent-shaped ..... LUNATE
crescent-shaped figure .. LUNE
crescent-shaped mark . LUNULA
crest . TOP, COMB, PEAK, TUFT
crest, sharp rugged mountain
.... ARETE
crested as birds ..... PILEATE
Cretan princess .... ARIADNE
Cretan spikenard .... PHU
CRETE . see SPECIAL SECTION
crevice ... CREVAS, CREVASSE
crew .... MEN, GANG,
.... TEAM, EIGHT
cribbage pin or score ..... PEG
cribbage term .... NOB, NOBS
cricket .... GRIG
cricket, ball in .... EDGER
cricket, field parts ONS, OFFS
cricket, run in .... BYE
cricket term OVER, TICE, YORK
crime. Eccl. .... SIMONY
Crimean river .... ALMA
criminal .... FELON
crimp .... CURL, GOFFER
crimson ..... RED, CARMINE
crippled ...... HALT, LAME
criticize .... SLATE
criticize in a small way
.... CARP, CAVIL
crocodile, India ...... GAVIAL
crocodile-head god, Egyp.
.... SOBK, SEBEK
crocus .... IRID
crocus bulb .... CORM
Croesus' land .... LYDIA
crony .... PAL, CHUM, BUDDY
crony: old Eng. .... EME
crooked .... AGEE, AWRY
crooner, early .... VALLEE
crop .... MAW, CRAW
crop, spring, India ...... RABI
cross ...... IRATE, TRAVERSE
cross, church .... ROOD
cross-examine .... GRILL
cross of life, Egypt .... ANKH
cross oneself .... SAIN
cross out .... DELETE
cross-stroke .... SERIF
cross timber, ship ...... SPALE
crossbeam ..... TRAVE, TREVE
crossbill genus .... LOXIA
crossbow .... RODD

crossing, fence .... STILE
crosspiece . BAR, RUNG, CLEAT
crosspiece, vehicle ... EVENER
crossthreads ..... WEFT, WOOF
crosswise .... THWART
crossword champion, former
  COOPER
crow .. ROOK, CRAKE, CORVUS
crow: Eng. .... BRAN
crow, Guam .... AGA
crow, kind of .... DAW
crowd, common ... MOB, RUCK
crowd together .. HERD, SERRY
crowded .... SERRIED
crown .... CAP, PATE,
  TIARA, DIADEM
crown colony, Brit.
  ADEN, BAHAMAS
crown of Osiris or Egypt .. ATEF
crown: poetic .... TIAR
crown, Pope's triple TIAR, TIARA
crucial point .... CRUX, PIVOT
crucible .... CRUSET
crucifix .... ROOD
crude . RAW, ROUGH, COARSE
crude metal .... ORE
crude sugar-molasses MELADA
cruel person .... SADIST
cruet .... AMA, CASTER
cruising .... ASEA
crumbled easily ..... FRIABLE
Crusader's foe ...... SARACEN
Crusader's headquarters . ACRE
crush .... MASH, SUBDUE
crustacean .... CRAB, ISOPOD,
  SHRIMP, LOBSTER
crustacean order, one of
  DECAPOD
cry .... HO, HOA, SOB, HOWL,
  WAIL, WEEP, LAMENT
cry, Austral. ... COOEE, COOEY
cry for silence, court
  OYES, OYEZ
crystal-clear .... PELLUCID
ctenophores, no tentacle .NUDA
Cuban dance .... CONGA
Cuban rodent .... PILORI
Cuban secret police ... PORRA
Cuban timber tree ..... CUYA
cubic decimeter .... LITER
cubic measure .. CORD, STERE
cubic meter .... STERE
cubicle .... CELL
cubitus .... ULNA
Cuchulain's wife . EMER, EIMER
cuckoo, black, keel-billed ANI
cuckoo, Oriental .. COEL, KOEL
cuckoopint .... ARUM
cucumber .... CUKE, PEPO
cud .... QUID, RUMEN

cudgel .... BAT, CLUB, DRUB,
  BASTE, STAVE, STICK
cue .... HINT
cue, music .... PRESA
cuff fastener .... TAB
cuirass .... LORICA
cull .... SORT
culmination ..... ACME, APEX
cultivate land .... HOE, PLOW,
  TILL, HARROW
cultivation method, Bengal
  JUM, JOOM
cultivation, soil .... TILTH
culture medium .... AGAR
cunning ... ART, CUTE, FOXY,
  WILY, DEDAL, CALLID,
  DAEDAL
cup .... CRUSE
cup, assaying .... CUPEL
cup, ceremonial .... AMA
cup, gem cutting .... DOP
cup stand of metal .... ZARF
cup to hold gem .... DOP
cupbearer .... SAKI
cupbearer of gods ...... HEBE
cupboard .... AMBRY, CLOSET
Cupid .... AMOR, EROS
Cupid's title .... DAN
cupola .... DOME
cur .... MUT, MUTT
curare ...... URALI, OORALI
curassow .... MITU
curassow genus .... CRAX
curdling powder ..... RENNET
cure-all .... ELIXIR, PANACEA
cure by salting .... CORN
cure with salt grass ..... DUN
curfew .... BELL
curios .... VIRTU
curl COIL, FRIZ, WIND, FRIZZ
curl of hair ...... FEAK, TRESS,
  RINGLET
curling, mark aimed at ... TEE
currant genus .... RIBES
current .... AC, DC, EDDY,
  RIFE, TIDE, STREAM
curt ...... BRUSK, BRUSQUE
curve .... ARC, BOW, ESS,
  ARCH, BEND, SINUS
curve in a stream . HOEK, HOOK
curve, plane .... ELLIPSE,
  PARABOLA
curve, sigmoid or double .. ESS
curved handle .... BOOL
curved in .. ADUNC, CONCAVE
curved out .... CONVEX
curved plank, vessel's .... SNY
Cush, son of .... SEBA
cushion ...... PAD, HASSOCK
custard .... FLAN
custard apple ...... ANNONA

Custard

a
custard cake .... **ECLAIR**
custard dish .... **FLAN**
custody .... **CHARGE**
custom .... **LAW, WONT, HABIT, USAGE**
custom, India .... **DASTUR**
custom: Lat. .... **RITUS**
custom: obs. .... **URE**
customer .... **PATRON**
customs .... **MORES**
cut . **HEW, LOP, MOW, DOCK, GASH, HACK, KERF, REAP, SLIT, SNEE, SNIP, TRIM, SEVER, SHEAR, SLIVE, CLEAVE, TREPAN**
cut down .... **FELL**
cut edges of coins .... **NIG**
cut of meat .... **LOIN**
cut off ... **DOCK, SNIP, ELIDE**
cut off, as mane ..... **ROACH**
cut out .... **EXCISE**
cut: Shakespeare ...... **SLISH**
cut vertically
SCARP, ESCARP, ESCARPE
cutter .... **SLED**
cutting .... **SECANT, INCISAL**

c
cutting tool .. **AX, ADZ, AXE, HOB, SAW, SAX, SYE, ADZE**
cuttlefish ...... **SEPIA, SQUID**
cuttlefish fluid .... **INK**
Cyclades, one of, see **GAZET-TEER**
cycle, astronomical ..... **SAROS**
cyclorama .... **CYKE**
cylinder, moving ...... **PISTON**
cylindrical .... **TERETE**
cyma .... **GOLA**
cyma recta or reversa ... **OGEE**
cymbal, Orient .... **ZEL**
cymbals, India .... **TAL**
Cymbeline's daughter . **IMOGEN**
Cymric deity
GWYN, LLEU, LLEW
Cymry .... **WELSH**
cypher system .... **CODE**
cyprinoid fish .... **ID, IDE, CARP, CHUB**
Cyrus' daughter ..... **ATOSSA**
cyst .... **WEN**
Czar .... **IVAN, FEDOR**
Czech .... **SLAV**
Czech, Eastern .... **ZIPS**

D

b
Dadaist .... **ERNST**
dado, pedestal ...... **SOLIDUM**
Daedalus' son .... **ICARUS**
dagger .. **DIRK, SNEE, BODKIN**
dagger, ancient . **SKEAN, SKENE**
dagger, Ir. **DHU, SKENE, SKEAN**
dagger, Malay ... **CRIS, KRIS, CREES, KREES, CREESE, KREESE**
dagger: obs. .... **SNEE**
dagger, thin .... **STILETTO**
Dahomey Negro .. **FON, FONG**
daily .... **DIURNAL**
dais .... **ESTRADE**
daisy . **MOON, OXEYE, SHASTA**
Dallas school .... **SMU**
dam .... **WAER, WEIR**
dam, Egypt ...... **SADD, SUDD**
dam site .... **ASWAN**
damage . **MAR, HARM, IMPAIR**
Damascus river ...... **ABANA**
damp .... **DANK**
damselfish .... **PINTANO**
dance ...... **HOP, JIG, REEL, GALOP, GAVOT, POLKA, TANGO, RUMBA, REDOWA, RHUMBA, GAVOTTA, GAVOTTE**
dance, country . **REEL, ALTHEA**
dance, Gr. .... **HORMOS**
dance, Israeli .... **HORA**

d
dance, lively ..... **JIG, REEL, GALOP, POLKA, BOLERO**
dance, old Eng. ...... **MORRIS**
dance, Sp. ... **TANGO, BOLERO**
dance, stately, old
PAVAN, MINUET, PAVANE
dance step ..... **PAS, CHASSE, GLISSADE**
dancer .... **KELLY, SHAWN, BOLGER, ZORINA, ASTAIRE**
dancing girl, Egypt .... **ALMA, ALME, ALMEH**
dancing girl, Jap. ...... **GEISHA**
dandy **FOP, DUDE, JAKE, TOFF**
DANISH ... see also **DENMARK** in SPECIAL SECTION
Danish astronomer .... **BRAHE**
Dan. borough (in Eng.) .. **BORG**
Dan. chieftain .... **JARL, YARL**
Dan. division, territorial . **AMT**
Dan. fjord .... **ISE**
Dan. king ..... **CNUT, KNUT, CANUTE**
Dan. measure .... **ALEN**
Dan. money ..... **ORA, ORAS**
Dan. physicist .... **BOHR**
Dan. speech sound ...... **STOD**
dank .... **WET**
Dante's patron .... **SCALA**
Danube city ..... **ULM, LINZ**
Danube, old name of ... **ISTER**

a
Danube tributary
    INN, OLT, ISAR, PRUT
daring .... BOLD, NERVE
dark .... MIRKY, MURKY
dark horse .... ZAIN
dark rock .... CHERT
dark wood ...... TEAK, EBONY
darkness .... MIRK, MURK
darling: Ir. . ROON, ACUSHLA,
    ASTHORE
darnel .... TARE
dart along .... FLIT
"Das Rheingold" role ... ERDA
dash .... ELAN
date, pert. to .... DATAL
date plum .... SAPOTE
date, Roman .... IDES, NONES
"David Copperfield" character
    DORA, HEEP, DARTLE
David's captain .... JOAB
David's commander ... AMASA
David's daughter ..... TAMAR
David's father .... JESSE
David's nephew .... AMASA
David's ruler, one of ..... IRA
David's son .... SOLOMON
David's wife .... MICHAL
dawn .... DEW, EOS, AURORA
dawn, pert. to .... EOAN
day, Hebr. .... YOM

b
day, Rom. .... IDES, NONES
day-breeze, It. .... ORA
days: Lat. .... DIES
day's march .... ETAPE
daybreak .... DAWN
dazing larks, device for DARE
deacon's stole ...... ORARION
dead ... FLAT, AMORT, INERT
dead, abode of . HADES, SHEOL
dead, region of: Egypt AMENTI
dead trees .... DRIKI
deadly ...... FATAL, LETHAL
deadly carrot .... DRIAS
deadly sins, 7 ENVY, LUST, AN-
    GER, PRIDE, SLOTH, GLUT-
    TONY, COVETOUSNESS
dealer .... MONGER
dealer, cloth
    DRAPER, MERCER
dean ...... DOYEN, DOYENNE
dearth .... WANT
death .... MORT, DEMISE
death deity: Rom. ...... MORS
death note on hunter's horn
    MORT
death notice .... OBIT
death rattle .... RALE
debate—debatable
    AGON, MOOT
debauchee ...... RAKE, ROUE
debris, rocky .... SCREE

c
decade .... TEN
decamp ...... ELOPE, LEVANT
decay, dental .... CARIES
decay tree ...... CONK, KONK
deceit .... SHAM, WILE,
    FRAUD, GUILE
deceive .. BILK, DUPE, FOOL,
    GULL, TRICK, ILLUDE
decelerate .... RETARD
deception HOAX, STRATAGEM
decide: Rom. law .... CERN
decimal unit .... TEN
deck, ship's .... POOP
decks, cut away . RASEE, RAZEE
declaim .... RANT, RAVE,
    ORATE, RECITE
declaration in whist ... MISERE
declare .... AVER, AVOW,
    STATE, AVOUCH
declare, in cards .... MELD
decline .... EBB, SINK,
    WANE, REFUSE
declivity ...... SCARP, SLOPE
declivity in menage .. CALADE
decorate .... DECK, ADORN
decorated letter .... FAC
decorated wall part ..... DADO
decorous ..... STAID, DEMURE
decoy .... LURE, PLANT
decrease .... EBB, WANE,
    LESSEN, RECEDE

d
decree .... ACT, FIAT,
    CANON, EDICT, ORDAIN
decree, Fr. law .... ARRET
decree, Moslem .... IRADE
decree, Rom. law .... DECRETE
decree, Russian .... UKASE
deduce .... INFER
deed .... GEST, GESTE
deeds .... ACTA
deer, Asia ...... AHU, KAKAR,
    SAMBAR, SAMBUR,
    SAMBHAR, SAMBHUR
deer, barking .... KAKAR
deer, Chile, Andes ..... PUDU
deer, female . DOE, ROE, HIND
deer genus, E. Ind. ..... RUSA
deer, India .... AXIS
deer, Jap. .... SIKA
deer, Kashmir ...... HANGUL
deer, red .... ROE, HART
deer, S. Am. .... GEMUL,
    GUEMAL, GUEMUL
deer, spotted .... CHITAL
deer, Tibet .... SHOU
deer track .... SLOT
deerlet .... NAPUS
deerlike .... CERVINE
defamation .... LIBEL
defeat, chess .... MATE
defeat utterly ... BEST, ROUT

Defect

a
defect, weaving .... SCOB
defendant's plea .... NOLO
deference .... RESPECT
defraud .... GYP, BILK,
                    GULL, CHEAT
defy .... DARE
degrade ...... ABASE, LOWER,
                    DEBASE
degrading .... MENIAL
degree .... GRADE, STAGE
degree .. (dental) DDS, DDSC;
    (engineer) CE, EE; (divin-
    ity) DD; (science) BSC;
    (arts) BA, MA, MFA; (law)
    LLB, LLD
degree, extreme .... NTH
degree taken, Cambridge
                    INCEPTOR
degrees, angle of 57.30. RADIAN
deified sky, Rom. ..... CAELUS
DEITY . see also GOD, GODDESS
            and SPECIAL SECTION
deity .... GOD
deity, Buddhist ... DEV, DEVA
deity, Hindu ...... DEV, DEVA
deity, Jap. .. AMIDA, AMITA
deity, primeval .... TITAN
deity, Sumerian .... ABU
deity, Syrian .... EL

b
delay . WAIT, DETAIN, LINGER
delay, law .... MORA, MORAE
delicacy .... FINESSE
delight .... REVEL
delusion: Buddhism .... MOHA
demand . NEED, CLAIM, INSIST
demeanor .... AIR
Demeter's daughter CORA, KORE
demigod .... HERO
demolish .... RASE, RAZE
demon ... IMP, DEVIL, FIEND
demon, Arab, Moslem, Oriental
            JIN, JINN, GENIE,
        GENII, JINNI, JINNEE
demon, Hindu . ASURA, DAITYA
demon, sun-swallowing, Hindu
    myth .... RAHU
demon, Zoroastrian
            DEV, DIV, DEVA
demonstrative pronoun
        THAT, THIS, WHOM
den ...... DIVE, LAIR, HAUNT
denary .... TEN
denial .... NO, NAY
DENMARK .. see also DANISH
            and SPECIAL SECTION
denomination .... SECT
denote .... MEAN, SHOW,
                    INDICATE
denoting unfit ships in Lloyd's
    registry .... AE

c
dense . **CRASS, THICK, STUPID**
density .... DORD
dental tool .... SCALER
deny .... NEGATE
depart ..... BEGONE, DECAMP
depart fast VAMOSE, VAMOOSE
depart: Lat. .... VADE
departed ... GONE, LEFT, WENT
department, Chin. .. FU, FOO
departure .... EXODUS
dependent .... MINION
depict .... DRAW, PAINT,
                    DESCRIBE
deplore .... LAMENT
deposit, alluvial DELTA, GEEST
deposit, clayey .... MARL
deposit, geyser .... SINTER
deposit, mineral .... LODE
deposit, river
        ALLUVIA, ALLUVIUM
deposit, wine cask ... TARTAR
depressed .... SAD
depression ...... DENT, FOVEA
deprivation .... LOSS
deprived .... REFT
depute .... SEND
deputy .... AGENT, VICAR
derby .... BOWLER
deride .... GIBE, JIBE
derrick .... CRANE, STEEVE

d
dervish, "Arab. Nights" . AGIB
dervish, Moslem ..... SADITE
descendant .... SON, CION
descendant, Fatima's
        SAID, SEID, SAYID
descendants, male line .. GENS
descent, deep .... SCARP
descriptive term ..... EPITHET
desert dweller .... EREMITE
desert, Mongolia .... GOBI
desert plant .... AGAVE
deserter .... RAT
deserve .... EARN, MERIT
design .... AIM
desire .... YEN, URGE,
                WANT, WISH
desire eagerly .... ASPIRE
desirous .... FAIN
desolate .... LORN, BLEAK
despoil .... RUIN
despot .. CZAR, TSAR, TZAR,
        TYRANT, DICTATOR
dessert .... ICE, PIE, MOUSSE,
                    TRIFLE
destiny . DOOM, FATE, KARMA
destroy .... RASE, RAZE,
                DECIMATE
destruction .... RUIN
detach .... WEAN
detachable button ...... STUD
detail .... ITEM

a detain **CHECK, DELAY, ARREST**
detecting device ...... **SONAR**
detective .... **TEC, DICK**
detent .... **PAWL**
determination .... **WILL**
determine .... **FIX, DECIDE,**
RESOLVE
detest .... **HATE, LOATHE**
dethrone .... **DEPOSE**
detonator .... **CAP**
"— deum" .... **TE**
devaluate .... **DEBASE**
developed compound animal
ZOON
Devi .... **UMA**
deviate ... **ERR, YAW, DIVERGE**
deviation .... **LAPSE**
deviation from course .... **YAW**
devil .. **DEMON, DEUCE, SATAN**
devil: Gypsy .... **BENG**
devil, Moslem
SHAITAN, SHEITAN
devil, Russian folklore .. **CHORT**
devil worship ...... **SATANISM**
devilfish .... **MANTA**
Devon river .... **EXE**
devotee .... **FAN, IST**
devotion, nine-day .. **NOVENA**
devoutness .... **PIETY**
dewberry .... **MAYES**
b dewy .... **RORAL, RORIC**
dexterity .... **ART**
dexterous .... **CLEVER**
diadem .... **TIARA**
diagonal .... **BIAS**
DIALECT . see also **LANGUAGE**
dialect . **IDIOM, LINGO, PATOIS**
dialect, Chin. .... **CANTON**
dialect, Ethiopic .... **TIGRE**
dialect, Gr. .... **DORIC, IONIC**
diamond corner .... **BASE**
diamond fragments ..... **BORT**
diamond holder .... **DOP**
diamond, impure industrial **BORT**
diamond, perfect ... **PARAGON**
diamonds, low quality ... **BORT**
Diana .... **ARTEMIS**
Diana's grove .... **NEMUS**
Diana's mother ...... **LATONA**
diaphanous ..... **THIN, SHEER**
diaphragm, pert. to .. **PHRENIC**
diatonic note .... **MI**
diatribe .. **SCREED, HARANGUE**
dibble .... **DAP, DIB**
Dickens character .. **PIP, TIM,**
DORA, GAMP, HEEP,
FAGIN, DORRIT
Dickens' pseudonym ...... **BOZ**
"Die Fledermaus" girl .. **ADELE**
die for making drain pipe . **DOD**
die, gambling .. **TAT, TESSERA**

c "Dies —," "Day of Wrath" **IRAE**
diet .... **BANT, FARE**
differ ...... **VARY, DISAGREE**
difference between solar and
lunar year .... **EPACT**
different ..... **OTHER, DIVERS**
difficulty .... **RUB, KNOT**
dig ...... **GRUB, PION, DELVE**
digest .... **PANDECT**
digit, foot .... **TOE**
digraph **AE, EA, OA, OE, SH, TH**
dike .... **LEVEE**
dilation .... **ECTASIA**
dilatory ...... **SLOW, TARDY,**
REMISS
dilemma .... **FIX**
dill herb .... **ANET**
dilute .... **THIN, WATER**
dim, become .. **BLEAR, DARKLE**
diminish ... **EBB, BATE, SINK,**
WANE, ABATE, TAPER
diminish front: military **PLOY**
dingle ..... **DALE, DELL, GLEN**
dining room, ancient ... **OECUS**
diocese center .... **SEE**
Dioscuri .... **ANAX**
dip .... **DAP, DIB, DOPP,**
DUNK, LADE
dip out .... **BAIL**
diplomacy .... **TACT**
d diplomat .... **ENVOY, CONSUL,**
ATTACHE
diphthong ..... **AE, IA, OA, UO**
Dipper constellation ..... **URSA**
direct .... **AIM, LEAD**
direct attention .... **REFER**
direct steering of boat ... **CONN**
dirge .... **LINOS, LINUS**
dirigible .... **BLIMP**
dirk ....**SNY, SNEE**
dirty lock .... **FRIB**
disable .... **LAME, MAIM**
disagreeable .... **ILL**
disappear gradually . **EVANESCE**
disavow ...... **DENY, RECANT**
disbeliever .... **ATHEIST**
disburse ...... **SPEND, EXPEND**
discard . **DROP, SCRAP, REJECT**
discernment .... **TACT**
discharge .... **EMIT, FIRE,**
SACK, SHOOT
discharged .... **SHOT**
disciple .... **APOSTLE**
disciple: India .... **CHELA**
disciplinarian ..... **MARTINET**
disclaim .... **DENY**
disclose .... **BARE, REVEAL**
discolored ...... **DOTY, LIVID**
disconcert ...... **FAZE, ABASH**
discourse .. **HOMILY, DESCANT**
discourse, art of ... **RHETORIC**

43

Discover

discover . **SEE, SPY, ESPY, FIND**
discriminate .... **SECERN**
discuss ...... **TREAT, DEBATE**
discussion group ...... **FORUM**
disease ..... **MAL, POX, HIVES**
disease, Afr. .... **NENTA**
disease cause .... **VIRUS**
disease, diver's .... **BENDS**
disease, fowl ...... **PIP, ROUP, PEROSIS**
disease, fungus .... **ERGOT**
disease, grape-vine **ESCA, ERINOSE**
disease, plant ... **SMUT, SCALD**
disease, skin .... **ECZEMA**
disease spreader **VECTOR, CARRIER**
disease, tropical .... **SPRUE**
disembark .... **LAND**
disembodied spirit: Chin. **KUEI, KWEI**
disencumber .... **RID**
disengage .... **FREE**
disfigure .... **MAR, DEFACE**
disgrace .... **SCANDAL**
disguise .... **MASK**
disgust, word of .... **AW**
DISH .... also see **VESSEL**
dish .... **PLATE**
dish, Hawaiian .... **POI**
dish, highly seasoned **OLIO, OLLA**
dish, hominy .... **POSOLE**
dish, Hungarian .... **GOULASH**
dish, It. .... **RAVIOLI**
dish, main .... **ENTREE**
dish, meat .... **STEW, RAGOUT**
dish, Mex. .. **TAMAL, TAMALE, TAMALI**
dish, stemmed ..... **COMPOTE**
dishearten .... **DAUNT, DETER**
dishonor .... **SHAME, VIOLATE**
dishonorable .... **BASE**
disinclined .... **AVERSE**
disinfectant . **CRESOL, PHENOL, CRESSOL, CRESSYL**
disk, ice hockey ..... **PUCK**
disk, like a .. **DISCAL, DISCOID**
disk, metal .... **PATEN**
dislocate .... **LUXATE**
dismal .... **DREAR**
dismantle .... **STRIP**
dismay .... **APPAL, DAUNT**
dismiss .... **DEMIT, FIRE**
dismounted .... **ALIT**
disorder .... **MESS, DERAY, CLUTTER**
disorderly flight .... **ROUT**
disparaging .... **SNIDE**
disparaging remark ..... **SLUR**
dispatch .... **SEND, HASTE**

dispatch boat .... **AVISO**
dispelled .... **GONE**
display .... **AIR, SHEW, SHOW, ARRAY, EVINCE**
display proudly **VAUNT, OSTENT**
displease .... **VEX, MIFF, ANGER, ANNOY**
disposed .... **PRONE**
disposition .... **MOOD, TEMPER**
dispossess .... **OUST, EVICT**
disprove .... **REFUTE**
disputable .... **MOOT**
dissertation ... **THESES, THESIS**
dissolute person .. **RAKE, ROUE**
dissonant .... **ATONAL**
distance, at-from a . **OFF, AFAR**
distant ... **FAR, YON, REMOTE**
distilling vessel .... **MATRASS**
distinctive air ... **AURA, MIEN, CACHET**
distracted .... **DISTRAIT**
distraint: old Eng. law .. **NAAM**
distribute .. **DEAL, DOLE, METE**
DISTRICT .... see also **REGION**
district .... **AREA, ZONE**
district, old Eng. court **SOC, SOKE**
disturb .... **ROIL, MOLEST**
disturbance ...... **ROW, RIOT**
ditch .... **FOSS, RINE, FOSSE, TRENCH**
ditch, castle .... **MOAT**
ditch, fort. .... **RELAIS**
ditch millet .... **HUREEK**
ditto .... **SAME**
divan .... **SOFA**
dive .... **DEN, HEADER**
dive bomber .... **STUKA**
diverge .... **DEVIATE**
divers .... **SEVERAL**
divest .... **STRIP, DEPRIVE**
divide .... **PART, SHARE**
divide for study ..... **DISSECT**
divided .... **REFT, SPLIT**
divider .... **MERIST**
dividing wall, membrance, partition ..... **SEPTA, SEPTUM**
divination by lots: Lat. **SORS, SORTES**
"Divine Comedy" author **DANTE**
divine favor .... **GRACE**
divine law: Rom. .... **FAS**
divine revelation **TORA, TORAH**
divine utterance ..... **ORACLE**
divinity .... **DEITY**
divorce bill, Jewish law **GET, GETT**
divorce, Moslem ...... **TALAK**
"— dixit" .... **IPSE**
dizziness, pert. to ..... **DINIC**

a docile .... TAME
dockyard barge .... LUMP
doctor ..... INTERN, INTERNE
Dr. Brown's dog hero .... RAB
Dr. Jekyll's other self .. HYDE
doctrinaire .... ISMY
doctrine .. ISM, DOGMA, TENET
documents, box for .. HANAPER
dodder .... AMIL
dodo genus .... DIDUS
doe .... HIND
doe, young .... TAG, TEG
dog, ... CANIS, CANINE
dog ..... POM, CHOW, PEKE,
   BASSET, POODLE, SPANIEL
dog, chops of .... FLEWS
dog-faced ape .... AANI
dog-fisher .... OTTER
DOG, GUN see DOG, HUNTING
dog, Hungarian PULI, KUVASZ
dog, hunting (bird) .. ALAN,
   ALAND, ALANT, BASSET,
   BEAGLE, SETTER, COURSER,
   HARRIER, POINTER
dog, John Brown's ...... RAB
dog, large .... ALAN
dog, "Odyssey" .... ARGOS
dog salmon .... KETA
dog, small-toy ..... POM, PUG,
   PEKE
b dog snapper, fish ...... JOCU
dog, Sputnik's .... LAIKA
dog star .... SEPT, SOPT,
   SEPTI, SIRIUS
dog, tropical .... ALCO
dog, Welsh .... CORGI
dog, wild, Austral. ..... DINGO
dog, wild, India ...... DHOLE
doge, office of ...... DOGATE
dogfish .... SHARK
dogma .... TENET
dogwood ..... OSIER, CORNEL
dole .... METE
dolphin fish .... DORADO
dolphin genus .... INIA
dolphin-like cetacean .... INIA
dolt .... ASS, OAF, CLOD,
   LOUT, DUNCE
domain ..... BOURN, REALM,
   BOURNE, DEMENE, ESTATE,
   DEMESNE
dome .... CUPOLA
dome-shaped .... DOMOID
Domesday Book money ... ORA
domestic .... MAID, LOCAL
domestic animal .... ASS, CAT,
   COW, DOG, HOG, PIG,
   RAM, SOW, MULE
domestic slave .... ESNE
domesticated .... TAME
dominion .... REALM, EMPERY

c domino .... MASK
Don Juan's mother ...... INEZ
donkey .... ASS, MOKE,
   BURRO, NEDDY
doom .... CONDEMN, DESTINE
doom palm, Afr. .... DUM
door .... PORTAL
door: Lat. .... JANUA
door part ...... JAMB, SASH,
   SILL, LINTEL
door section .... PANEL
doorkeeper, Masonic .... TILER
dorado, color .... CUIR
Doric frieze slab ...... METOPE
dormant ..... ASLEEP, LATENT
dormouse .... LOIR
dormouse, garden ...... LEROT
dormouse genus .... GLIS
dorsal .... NOTAL
dote .... DRIVEL
dots, paint with ...... STIPPLE
dotted with figures ...... SEME
double . DUAL, TWIN, BINATE
double cocoon ...... DUPION
double dagger .... DIESIS
double, Egypt .... KA
double salt .... ALUM
double tooth .... MOLAR
doubletree .... EVENER
d dovekie ...... ROTCH, ROTGE,
   ROTCHE
Dovyalis .... ABERIA
dowel ..... PIN, COAG, COAK
dower, pert. to .... DOTAL
dower property .... DOS
down ..... FUZZ, PILE, EIDER
down, facing. PRONE, PRONATE
down quilt .... DUVET
"downunder" native clan .. ATI
downward, curve ...... DEFLEX
dowry .... DOS, DOT
drag ... LUG, TUG, HAUL, SNIG
dragnet .... TRAWL
dragon, like a ... DRACONTINE
dragon of darkness, Bibl. RAHAB
drain . SAP, DEPLETE, VITIATE
drain .... SUMP, SEWER
dram, small .... NIP
DRAMA ...... see also PLAY
Dravidian KOTA, MALE, NAIR,
   TODA, TULU, TAMIL
draw ...... TIE, TOW, LIMN,
   PULL, DEPICT
draw forth .... EDUCE
draw from .... DERIVE
draw out . EDUCE, ATTENUATE
draw tight: naut. .... FRAP
drawing curve .... SPLINE
drawing room .... SALON
dreadful .... DIRE
dream, day .... REVERIE

Dream

a "Dream Girl" playwright . **RICE**
dregs .... **FAEX, LEES,
DROSS, SEDIMENT**
drench .... **SOUSE, TOUSE**
drenched .... **WET, DEWED**
DRESS .... see also **GARMENT**
dress .... **GARB, CLOTHE,
ACCOUTER**
dress, as stone ...... **DAB, NIG**
dress feathers .... **PREEN**
dress leather ...... **DUB, TAN**
dress up .... **TOG, PREEN**
dressed .... **CLAD**
dressing wounds, material for
LINT, LINTS
dried berry: Sp. .... **PASA**
dried up .... **SERE**
drift .... **TREND**
drill .... **BORE, TRAIN**
drilling rod .... **BAR, BIT**
DRINK .... see also **BEVERAGE**
drink .... **GULP, SWIG,
QUAFF, IMBIBE**
drink, Christmas **NOG, WASSAIL**
drink, fermented ...... **MEAD**
drink, honey .... **MEAD**
drink, hot .... **TODDY**
drink, hot milk .... **POSSET**
drink of gods .... **NECTAR**
drink of liquor .. **NIP, BRACER**
b drink, old honey ...... **MORAT**
drink, palm .... **NIPA**
drink, rum-gin .... **BUMBO**
drink slowly .... **SIP, SUP**
drink, small .... **NIP, PEG,
DRAM, SLUG**
drink to excess .. **TOPE, BOUSE**
drink, whiskey .... **STINGER**
drinking bowl .... **MAZER**
drinking cup, Gr. .... **HOLMOS**
drinking vessel .... **CUP, MUG,
TIG, TYG, JORUM,
STEIN, TANKARD**
drive ..... **RIDE, URGE, IMPEL**
drive away ..... **SHOO, DISPEL**
drive back
ROUT, REPEL, REPULSE
drive in .... **TAMP**
drivel .... **DROOL, SLAVER**
driver, fast reckless ..... **JEHU**
drizzle .. **MIST, SMUR, SMURR**
droll .... **ODD**
dromedary, female .... **DELUL**
dromedary, swift .... **MEHARI**
drone .... **BEE, DOR, HUM**
droop .... **LOP, SAG, WILT**
drooping .... **ALOP**
drop ...... **DRIB, FALL, SINK,
GUTTA, GLOBULE**
drop a fish line or bait .. **DAP**
drop, one .... **MINIM**

c drop: Prov. Eng. ...... **SIE, SYE**
dropsy .... **EDEMA**
dross .. **SLAG, SPRUE, SCORIA**
drought-tolerant plant .. **GUAR**
drove .... **HERD, RODE**
drove of horses .... **ATAJO**
drowse .... **NOD**
drudge ... **MOIL, TOIL, LABOR**
drug ..... **DOPE, SINA, ALOES,
OPIATE, DILANTIN**
drug, Hippocrates' .... **MECON**
drugged bliss .... **KEF**
drum-call to arms .... **RAPPEL**
drum roll, reveille ...... **DIAN**
drum, small . **TABOR, TABOUR,
TABRET**
drum, W. Ind. .... **GUMBY**
drumbeat .... **DUB, TATOO,
TATTOO**
drunkard .... **SOT, SOAK,
SOUSE, TOPER**
dry .. as wine **SEC, ARID, SERE**
dry, as wine .... **SEC**
dry bed of river .... **WADI**
dry goods dealer ..... **DRAPER**
dub .... **NAME, KNIGHT**
duck .... **ANAS, SMEE,
TEAL, PEKIN**
duck, Arctic .... **EIDER**
d duck, breed of .... **ROUEN**
duck, diving .... **SMEW**
duck eggs, Chin. ...... **PIDAN**
duck, fresh water .... **TEAL**
duck genus .. **AEX, AIX, ANAS**
duck, like a .... **ANATINE**
duck lure .... **DECOY**
duck, male .... **DRAKE**
duck, Muscovy .... **PATO**
duck, pintail .... **SMEE**
duck, ring-necked ...... **DOGY**
duck, river ..... **TEAL, EIDER,
SHOVELER**
duck, sea ...... **COOT, SCAUP**
duck, sea, northern ... **SCOTER**
duck-shooting boat ..... **SKAG**
duck to cook: Fr. ... **CANETON**
duct: anat. .... **VAS, VASA**
dude .... **FOP, DANDY**
due, India .... **HAK, HAKH**
duet .... **DUI, DUO**
dugout canoe **BANCA, PIROGUE**
dugout, India . **DONGA, DUNGA**
duke's dominion ...... **DUCHY**
dulcimer .... **CITOLE**
dulcimer, Oriental ..... **SANTIR**
dull . **DRY, DUN, DRAB, LOGY,
BLUNT, PROSY, BORING**
dull color .. **DUN, MAT, DRAB,
MATTE, TERNE**
dull in finish .... **MAT, MATTE**

a
dull silk fabric .... **GROS**
dullard .... **BOOR**
Dumas hero
    ATHOS, ARAMIS, PORTHOS
dummy whist .... **MORT**
dung beetle .... **DOR**
dunlin bird .... **STIB**
dupe .... **USE, FOOL**
duration measure .... **TIME**
dusk .... **EVE**
dusky .... **DIM, DARK, SWART**
dusty: Scot. .... **MOTTY**
DUTCH see also NETHERLANDS,
            SPECIAL SECTION
Dutch: bit ....**DOIT**
    cupboard .... **KAS**
    donkey.......... **EZEL**
    "mister" .... **HEER**
    out .... **UIT**
    woman .... **FROW**
Dutch cheese .... **EDAM**
Dutch commune .... **EDE**
Dutch early geographer .. **AA**
Dutch fishing boat .. **DOGGER**
Dutch measure, old ..... **AAM**
Dutch meter .... **EL**
Dutch minor coin .... **DOIT**
Dutch news agency, old **ANETA**
Dutch painter
    LIS, HALS, LELY, STEEN
Dutch two-masted vessel **KOFF**
duty .... **CHORE, TARIFF**
dwarf .. **RUNT, STUNT, TROLL**

c
dwarf cattle, S. Am.
            NATA, NIATA
dwell ...... **BIDE, LIVE, ABIDE**
dwelling .... **ABODE**
dwindle .... **PETER**
Dyak knife .... **PARANG**
Dyak, sea .... **IBAN**
dye base .... **ANILINE**
dye, blue .... **WOAD**
dye, blue-red .... **ORSELLE**
dye gum .... **KINO**
dye, indigo .... **ANIL**
dye, lichen
    ARCHIL, ORCHAL, ORCHIL
dye plant .... **ANIL**
dye, red **AAL, ANATO, AURIN,**
    EOSIN, ANATTA, ANATTO,
    AURINE, EOSINE, ANNAT-
    TA, ANNATTO, ANNOTTO,
    ARNATTO
dye, red, poisonous
        AURIN, AURINE
dye stuff .. **EOSINE, MADDER**
dye, yellow .... **WELD,**
        WOLD, WOALD
dyeing apparatus ...... **AGER**
dyeing reagent .... **ALTERANT**
dyestuff from lichens .. **LITMUS**
dyewood tree .... **TUI**
dynamite inventor .... **NOBEL**
DYNASTY see CHIN. DYNASTY
dynasty, first Chin. ..... **HSIA**
dynasty, It. .... **SAVOY**

E

b
eager .. **AGOG, AVID, ARDENT**
eagle .... **ERN, ERNE**
eagle, Bible .... **GIER**
eagle, tried to mount to heaven
    on .... **ETANA**
eagle, sea .... **ERN, ERNE**
eagle's nest
    AERY, EYRY, AERIE, EYRIE
eaglestone ... **ETITE, AETITES**
ear .... **LUG, HANDLE**
ear canal .... **SCALA**
ear cavity .... **UTRICLE**
ear doctor .... **AURIST**
ear inflamation .... **OTITIS**
ear of wheat: archeol.
        SPICA, SPICAE
ear, pert. to .... **OTIC, AURAL**
ear, prominence **TRAGI, TRAGUS**
ear shell .. **ORMER, ABALONE**
ear stone .. **OTOLITE, OTOLITH**
earache ... **OTALGY, OTALGIA**
eared seal .... **OTARY**

d
early Britisher .... **PICT**
early Christian priest ... **ARIUS**
earnest
    ARDENT, INTENT, SINCERE
earnest money: law .... **ARRA,**
        ARLES, ARRHA
earth .... **GEO**
earth deposit in rocks .. **GUHR**
earth: dial. .... **ERD**
earth god, Egypt. **GEB, KEB, SEB**
earth goddess ..... **GE, ERDA,**
        GAEA, GAIA
earth goddess, Khonds' .. **TARI**
earth goddess, Rom.
        CERES, TERRA
earth, kind of .... **LOAM**
earth, pert. to .... **GEAL**
earth's surface, made on
        EPIGENE
earthenware maker ... **POTTER**
earthly .... **TERRENE**
earthquake .. **SEISM, TEMBLOR**

Earthquake

a earthquake, pert. to .. **SEISMIC**
earthquake, shock of. **TREMOR**
earthwork, Rom. ...... **AGGER**
East .. **ASIA, LEVANT, ORIENT**
E. African native ... **SOMALI**
E. Afr. spiritual power .. **NGAI**
E. Indian animal .... **TARSIER**
E. Ind. dye tree ...... **DHAK**
E. Ind. fruit **DURIAN, DURION**
E. Ind. grass .... **KASA**
E. Ind. herb .... **PIA, SESAME**
E. Ind. herb root **CHAY, CHOY**
E. Ind. palm .... **NIPA**
E. Ind. plant .. **JUTE, SESAME**
E. Ind. shrubby herb .... **SOLA**
E. Ind. tanning tree .. **AMLA, AMLI**
E. Ind. term of address **SAHIB**
E. Ind. timber tree..**ACH, SAJ, SAL, SAIN, SAUL, TEAK**
E. Ind. tree, large ..... **SIRIS**
E. Ind. vine ..... **AMIL, GILO, ODAL, ODEL, SOMA**
E. Ind. vine, milky ..... **SOMA**
E. Ind. weight .... **TOLA**
E. Ind. wood, strong, heavy **ENG**
E. Ind. woody vine **ODAL, GILO**
East Indies .... **INDONESIA**
east wind .... **EURUS**
east wind's opposite .... **AFER**
Easter ...... **PASCH, PASCHA**

b Eastern .... **ORTIVE**
Eastern Catholic ...... **UNIAT**
Eastern Church doxology **DOXA**
Eastern European ...... **SLAV**
Eastern garment .... **SARI**
Eastern name ..... **ALI, ABOU**
Eastern title ...... **AGA, RAS**
Eastern Turkey tribesman **KURD**
easy .... **SOFT**
easy gait .... **LOPE**
easy job **SNAP,CINCH,SINECURE**
eat away .... **ERODE**
eat voraciously **RAVEN, RAVIN, RAVINE**
eaten away .... **EROSE**
eating away **CAUSTIC, ERODENT**
eccentric person .... **GINK**
eccentric piece, rotating .. **CAM**
ecclesiastic .... **PRELATE**
ECCLESIASTICAL see **CHURCH**
eclipse .... **DIM**
eclipse demon, Hindu **KETU, RAHU**
ecru .... **BEIGE**
Ecuadorian extinct Indians **CARA**
edentate genus .... **MANIS**
edge .... **HEM, LIP, RIM, ARRIS, BRINK, MARGE**
edged unevenly .... **EROSE**
edging .... **PICOT**

c edging, make .... **TAT**
edible fungus .... **CEPE**
edible root ...... **OCA, YAM, TARO, CASAVA, CASSAVA**
edible shoot, Jap. .... **UDO**
edict .... **LAW, FIAT, DECREE**
Edinburgh: poet ...... **EDINA**
edit .... **REVISE, REDACT**
editorial "I" .... **WE**
Edom district .... **TEMAN**
Edomite .... **OMAR**
Edomite city .... **PAU**
Edomite duke **UZ, ARAN, IRAM**
Edomite king, ruler ..... **BELA**
educated .... **BRED, LETTERED**
educator, Am. .... **MANN**
educe .... **EVOKE, ELICIT**
Edward Bradley's pseudo. **BEDE**
eel, marine .... **CONGER**
eel: old Eng. .... **ELE**
eel-shaped amphibian ... **OLM**
eel, S. Am. .... **CARAPO**
eel, young .... **ELVER**
eelworm .... **NEMA**
Eghbal's land .... **IRAN**
effervescent, to make . **AERATE**
effigy .... **IDOL**
effluvium ... **MIASM, MIASMA**
effort .... **DINT, ASSAY, NISUS, TRIAL**

d effusive .... **GUSHING**
eft .... **EVET, NEWT**
egg .... **OVUM**
egg dish .. **OMELET, OMELETTE**
egg drink .... **NOG, NOGG**
egg, insect .... **NIT**
egg-shaped **OOID, OVAL, OVATE, OVOID**
egg-shaped ornaments ... **OVA**
egg white, raw .... **GLAIR**
eggs .... **OVA, ROE**
ego .... **SELF**
Egypt, pert. to ...... **COPTIC**
Egyptian bird .... **IBIS**
Egyp. Christian .... **COPT**
Egyp. city, ancient **SAIS, THEBES**
Egyp. cobra .... **HAJE**
Egyp. crown .... **ATEF**
Egyp. dog-headed ape, deity **AANI**
Egyp. gateway .... **PYLON**
Egyp. god of creation ... **PTAH**
EGYPTIAN GODS — GODDESSES —DEITY see also **GODS** and **SPECIAL SECTION**
Egyp. guard .... **GHAFIR**
Egyp. heaven **AALU, AARU, IALU, YARU**
Egyp. immortal heart **AB, HATI**
Egyp. king .. **MENES, RAMESES**
Egyp. lute .... **NABLA**

a Egyp. nationalist party . **WAFD**
Egyp. precious alloy .... **ASEM**
Egyp. primeval chaos ..... **NU**
Egyp. queen of gods .... **SATI**
Egyp. sacred bird .. **BENU, IBIS**
Egyp. sacred bull .... **APIS**
Egyp. season .... **AHET**
Egyp. tambourine ...... **RIKK**
Egyp. thorn .... **KIKAR**
Egyp. writing surfaces **PAPYRI**
eh?: obs. ....**ANAN**
eight days after feast .. **UTAS**
eight, group of
OCTAD, OCTET, OCTAVE
eight, set of .... **OGDOAD**
eighth day of feast .... **UTAS**
eighth day, on ...... **OCTAN**
eighth note .... **UNCA**
Eire legislature .... **DAIL**
ejaculation, mystic ...... **OM**
eject ...... **EMIT, OUST, SPEW**
elaborate .... **ORNATE**
Elam, capital of .... **SUSA**
eland .... **IMPOFO**
elanet .... **KITE**
elasmobranch fish **RAY, SHARK**
Elbe, river to ...... **EGER, ISER**
Elbe tributary .... **EGER, ISER**
elbow .... **ANCON**
elder .... **SENIOR**

b elder son of Zeus ...... **ARES**
elder statesmen, Jap. ... **GENRO**
eldest: law ..... **AINE, EIGNE**
electric catfish .... **RAAD**
electric force .... **ELOD**
electric force unit ...... **VOLT**
electric reluctance unit .. **REL**
electric unit .. **ES, AMP, MHO,**
OHM, REL, PERM, FARAD,
HENRY, AMPERE
electrified particle ...... **ION**
electrode .. **ANODE, CATHODE**
electromagnet .... **RELAY**
electron tube
TRIODE, KLYSTRON
elegance .... **GRACE**
elegant .... **FINE, POSH**
elegist .... **POET**
elegy .... **NENIA**
ELEMENT, non-metallic and metallic, gaseous on page 195
elemi .... **ANIME**
element, radioactive of **URANIC**
elephant goad .... **ANKUS**
elephant: India .... **HATHI**
elephant's cry .... **BARR**
elephant's ear .... **TARO**
elevated ground **MESA, RIDEAU**
elevation of mind .. **ANAGOGE**
elevator: Brit. .... **LIFT**

c elf .... **SPRITE**
elf, Egypt. .... **OUPHE**
elfin .... **FEY**
Elia .... **LAMB**
elicit .... **EDUCE**
elide .... **DELE, OMIT**
Elija .... **ELIAS**
eliminate ... **DELETE, REMOVE**
Elizabeth I, name for **ORIANA**
elk, Am. .... **WAPITI**
elk, Europ. .... **MOOSE**
elk, Europ. genus ...... **ALCES**
elliptical ...... **OVAL, OVOID**
elm .... **ULM, ULME**
elm fruit seed ...... **SAMARA**
elongated .... **PROLATE**
else .... **OTHER**
elude .... **DODGE, EVADE**
elver .... **EEL**
emaciation .... **TABES, MACIES**
emanation .... **AURA**
emanation, star .... **BLAS**
embankment ... **DAM, BUND,**
DIKE, DYKE, DIGUE, LEVEE
embellish
GILD, ADORN, DECORATE
embellished .... **ORNATE**
ember .... **ASH, COAL**
emblem ... **INSIGNE, INSIGNIA**

d emblem of authority .... **MACE**
emblem of U.S. .... **EAGLE**
embrace
HUG, CLASP, ENARM, INARM
embrocation ...... **LINIMENT**
embroidery frame
TABORET, TABOURET
emend .... **EDIT**
emerald .... **BERYL, SMARAGD**
emerge **RISE, ISSUE, EMANATE**
emetic .... **IPECAC**
eminent .... **NOTED**
emit .... **REEK, EXUDE**
emmer .... **SPELT**
emmet .... **ANT**
Emperor of Russia
CZAR, TSAR, TZAR
emphasis .... **ACCENT, STRESS**
empire .... **REALM**
employ .... **USE, HIRE, PLACE**
employed for wine, meas. **AAM**
employees ...... **PERSONNEL**
employer .... **BOSS, USER**
employment .... **PLACE**
emporium ...... **MART, STORE**
Empress, Byzant. ...... **IRENE**
Empress, Russian ... **CZARINA,**
TSARINA, TZARINA
empty .... **VOID, INANE,**
DEPLETE
emulate .... **RIVAL**
enamel ware .... **LIMOGES**

a enchantress .... **CIRCE, MEDEA**
encircle .... **ORB, GIRD, GIRT,
RING, EMBAY**
encircled
GIRT, RINGED, SURROUNDED
encircling band .... **ZONE**
enclose .... **MEW**
enclosure .... **MEW, PEN, REE,
STY, CORRAL**
enclosure, cattle ..... **ATAJO**
enclosure: Sp. Am. ... **CANCHA**
encomium .... **ELOGE**
encompass .. **GIRD, GIRT, RING**
encompassed by .... **AMID**
encore .... **BIS**
encounter .... **MEET**
encourage .... **ABET**
end **TIP, FINIS, LIMIT, OMEGA**
end: music .... **FINE**
end result .... **PRODUCT**
end, tending to an ..... **TELIC**
endeavor .. **TRY, ESSAY, NISUS**
ENDING ... see also SUFFIX or
type of ending
ending, comparative . **IER, IOR**
ENDING, NOUN see SUFFIX,
NOUN ENDING
ending, plural .... **EN, ES**
ending, superlative ...... **EST**
b endow ...... **DOWER, INVEST**
endue .... **ENDOW**
endure .... **BEAR, LAST, WEAR**
endure: dial. .... **BIDE**
energy .... **PEP, VIM, ZIP,
POWER, VIGOR, VIGOUR**
energy, potential ...... **ERGAL**
energy unit **ERG, RAD, ERGON**
enfeeble **WEAKEN, DEBILITATE**
engage **HIRE, ENTER, CHARTER**
engender .... **BEGET,
BREED, PROMOTE, GENERATE**
engine, donkey ...... **YARDER**
engine of war .... **RAM**
engine part .... **STATOR**
engine, rotary ...... **TURBINE**
engineer, Am. .... **EADS**
engineer, military .... **SAPPER**
English actor .... **EVANS**
Eng. actress .... (Nell) **GWYN,
TERRY, NEAGLE**
Eng. architect .... **WREN**
Eng. author .... **MORE, WEST,
ARLEN, BACON, CAINE,
DEFOE, DORAN, ELIOT,
HARDY, READE, SHUTE,
WAUGH, WELLS, AMBLER,
AUSTEN, BARRIE, BELLOC,
BRONTE, ORWELL, STERNE**
Eng. car .... **ROVER**
Eng. cathedral city **ELY, YORK**
Eng. city, historic **COVENTRY**

c Eng. college ... **ETON, BALIOL**
ENG. COMPOSER
see COMPOSER, ENG.
Eng. country festival .... **ALE**
Eng. dramatist
SHAW, PEELE, DRYDEN
Eng. emblem .... **ROSE**
Eng. essayist .... **SALA, STEELE**
Eng. explorer ... **ROSS, CABOT**
Eng. historian .... **BEDE**
Eng. king
BRAN, CNUT, KNUT, CANUTE
Eng. monk ..... **BEDE, BAEDA**
Eng. murderer .... **ARAM**
Eng. musician .... **ARNE**
ENG. NOVELIST .... see ENG.
AUTHOR
Eng. painter .... **OPIE, ORPEN**
Eng. philosopher ...... **HUME,
JOAD, BACON, SPENCER**
Eng. playwright .... **SHAW**
Eng. poet ..... **GRAY, AUDEN,
BLAKE, BYRON, CAREW,
DONNE, ELIOT**
Eng. queen ..... **ANNE, MARY**
Eng. rebel leader, 1450 .. **CADE**
Eng. royal house **YORK, TUDOR**
Eng. scholar, schoolmaster
ARAM
Eng. school, boys' ...... **ETON**
Eng. sculptor .... **EPSTEIN**
d Eng. spa .... **BATH, MARGATE**
Eng. spy .... **ANDRE**
Eng. statesman ... **EDEN, PITT**
Eng. theologian ..... **ALCUIN**
Eng. woman politician .. **ASTOR**
ENG. WRITER ..... see ENG.
AUTHOR and ENG. ESSAYIST
engraver ... **CHASER, ETCHER,
GRAVER**
engraver, famous .. **PYE, DORE**
engraver's tool .... **BURIN**
engrossed .... **RAPT**
enigma .... **RIDDLE**
enlarge
DILATE, EXPAND, INCREASE
enlarge a hole .... **REAM**
enlarging, as chimneys .. **EVASE**
enmity .... **ANIMUS**
Enoch's father .... **CAIN**
enough .... **ENOW**
enrol .... **ENTER, ENLIST**
ensign .... **FLAG**
ensnare .... **NET, WEB**
entangle .... **MAT, MESH**
enter .... **ENROL**
entertain
AMUSE, DIVERT, REGALE
enthusiasm
ELAN, ARDOR, VERVE, SPIRIT
enthusiastic .... **RABID**

a entice .... BAIT, LURE,
    TOLE, TEMPT, ALLURE
enticement .... TICE
entire man .... EGO
entity .... ENS, ENTIA
entomb .... INURN
entrance
    ADIT, DOOR, GATE, PORTAL
entrance halls .... ATRIA
entreat .... PRAY, PLEAD
entreaty .... PLEA
entry, separate .... ITEM
entwine
    WEAVE, ENLACE, WREATHE
enumerate .... COUNT
envelop WRAP, ENFOLD, INFOLD
environment .... MILIEU
envoy .... LEGATE
envy .... COVET
enzyme .... ASE, LOTASE,
    RENNIN, MALTASE
eon .... OLAM
ephah, 1/10 .... OMER
epic poetry .... EPOS, EPOPEE
epoch .... ERA
epochal .... ERAL
epode .... POEM
eponymous ancestor .... EBER
equal IS, ARE, TIE, EVEN, PEER
equality .... PAR, PARITY

b equally .... AS
equilibrium .... POISE
equine .... HORSE
equip .... FIT, RIG
equitable ... JUST, IMPARTIAL
equivalence .... PAR
equivocate .... EVADE
era .... EPOCH
eradicate .... ERASE, UPROOT
eral .... EPOCHAL
erase .... DELE, DELETE
erect .... REAR, RAISE
ergo .... HENCE
Eris' brother .... ARES
ermine, summer .... STOAT
Eros .... CUPID
errand boy .... PAGE
error, publication ...... TYPO,
    ERRATA, ERRATE, ERRATUM
Esau .... EDOM
Esau's brother .... JACOB
Esau's father-in-law ... ELON
Esau's grandson ...... OMAR
Esau's home .... SEIR
Esau's wife .... ADAH
escape .. LAM, ELUDE, EVADE
eschew .... SHUN
escutcheon band .... FESS
Esdra's angel .... URIEL
eskers .... OSAR
Eskimo .... ITA

c Eskimo boat
    KIAK, KYAK, KAYAK
Eskimo boot .... MUKLUK
Eskimo coat
    PARKA, NETCHA, TEMIAK
Eskimo curlew .... FUTE
Eskimo house
    IGLU, IGLOE, IGLOO, IGLOU
Eskimo settlement ..... ETAH
Eskimo summer hut .... TOPEK
Eskimos of Asia YUIT, INNUIT
esoteric .... INNER
espy .... SEE, SPY
esquire .... ARMIGER
essay ... TRY, TEST, ATTEMPT
essay, scholarly
    THESIS, TREATISE
essence: Hindu religion .. RASA
essence, rose .... ATTAR
essential oils fluid ..... NEROL
essential part .... CORE, PITH
"— est" (that is) .... ID
establish .... BASE, FOUND
established value .... PAR
estate, landed, large .. MANOR
estate manager .... STEWARD
estate, not held by feudal ten-
    ure ALOD, ALLOD, ALODIUM
esteem .... HONOR,
    PRIZE, ADMIRE, HONOUR

d ester, hydriodic acid ... IODIDE
ester, liquid .... ACETIN
ester, oleic acid ..... OLEATE
estimate .... RATE, APPRAISE
Estonian .... ESTH
estuary .... RIA
estuary, Brazil .... PARA
estuary, S. Am. .... PLATA
Eternal City .... ROME
eternity ..... AGE, EON, OLAM
ether compound .... ESTER
ethereal .... AERY, AERIAL
ETHIOPIA see also ABYSSINIA
Ethiopia .... CUSH
Ethiopian title .... RAS
Ethiopic .... GEEZ
ethos, opposed to .... PATHOS
Etruscan god .... LAR
Etruscan Juno .... UNI
Etruscan Minerva .... MENFRA
Etruscan title, peer LAR, LARS
eucalyptus secretion
    LAAP, LARP, LERP
eucalyptus tree .... YATE
Eucharist case ...... PIX, PYX
Eucharist cloth
    FANO, FANON, FANUM
Eucharist spoon .... LABIS
Eucharist wafer .... HOST
eulogy .... ELOGE
euphorbia .... SPURGE

a Eurasian dock plant .. **PARELLE**
eureka red .... **PUCE**
Euripides heroine ..... **MEDEA**
EUROPEAN see also specific
word, as FISH, ANIMAL,
etc.
European .... **POLE, SLAV**
Eur. colorful fish ...... **BOCE**
EUROP. FISH .. see FISH, EUR.
European, in Moslem East
FRANGI
Europ. iris .... **ORRIS**
Europ. kite ..... **GLED, GLEDE**
Europ. porgy .... **PARGO**
Eurytus' daughter ...... **IOLE**
evade
SHUN, DODGE, ELUDE, SHIRK
evaluate .... **RATE, ASSESS**
Evangelist ...... **LUKE, MARK**
Evans, Mary Ann ...... **ELIOT**
Eve's grandson .... **ENOS**
even ..... **EEN, LEVEL, PLANE**
even if .... **THO**
evening party .... **SOIREE**
evening prayer .... **VESPER**
eventual lot .... **FATE**
ever .... **EER**
evergreen .... **FIR, YEW, PINE,
CAROB, CEDAR, OLIVE,
SAVIN, LAUREL, SABINE,**
b **SAVINE, SPRUCE**
evergreen, bean ...... **CAROB**
evergreen genus
OLAX, ABIES, CATHA
evergreen, red-berry
YEW, WHORT
evergreen, tropical ... **CALABA**
everlasting ... **ETERN, ETERNE**
evict .... **OUST**
evident **CLEAR, PLAIN, PATENT**
evil .... **MAL**
evil god, Egypt. ... **SET, SETH**
evil intent: law .... **DOLUS**
evil spirit, Haiti **BAKA, BOKO**
evil spirit, Hindu ..... **ASURA**
evolve .... **EDUCE**
ewe, old .... **CRONE**
exact **BLEED, DEMAND, EXTORT**
exacerbate .... **IRE**
exact point .... **TEE**
examine ..... **PRY, SPY, SCAN**
excavate .. **DIG, PION, DREDGE**
excavation for extracting ore
STOPE
excavation, mine .. **PIT, STOPE**
exceed .... **TOP**
exceedingly: music .....**TRES**
excellence .... **VIRTU**
excellent .... **AONE**
except .... **BUT, SAVE**
excess ...... **LUXUS, NIMIETY**

c excess, fill to ... **GLUT, SATE**
excess of solar year ... **EPACT**
exchange medium, Chin. **SYCEE**
exchange premium, discount
AGIO
exchequer .... **FISC, FISK**
excite .... **ELATE, ROUSE**
excited .... **AGOG, MANIC**
excitement, public
FUROR, FURORE
exclamation .. **AH, EH, HA, HI,
MY, OH, OW, UM, ACH,
AHA, AUH, BAH, BAW, FIE,
FOH, GRR, HAH, HAW,
HAY, HEM, HEP, HEU, HEY,
HIC, HIP, HOI, HOY, HUH,
OHO, OUF, PAH, PEW, POH,
PUE, SOH, TCH, TCK, TUT,
UGH, WEE, WHY, WOW,
YAH, YOI, YOW, ALAS,
PHEW, ALACK**
exclamation, Fr. .... **HEIN**
exclamation, Ger. ..... **HOCH**
exclamation, Ir. .... **ADAD,
AHEY, ARAH, ARRA, ARRO,
BOOH, EHEU, OCHONE**
exclude ... **BAR, OMIT, DEBAR**
exclusive .... **SOLE**
exclusive set .... **ELECT, ELITE**
exclusively .... **ONLY**
d excoriate .... **ABRADE**
excrete from skin ...... **EGEST**
excuse .. **PLEA, ALIBI, REMIT**
excuse, court **ESSOIN, ESSOINE**
execrated ..... **CURST, SWORE**
exemplar ... **MODEL, PATTERN**
exhaust
SAP, TIRE, SPEND, DEPLETE
exhausted .... **EFFETE**
exhibits leaping ..... **SALTATE**
exigency .... **NEED**
exist .... **LIVE**
exist .. all forms of verb "BE"
exist, beginning to .. **NASCENT**
existence .... **ENS, ESSE**
existentialist leader ... **SARTRE**
existing **ALIVE, BEING, EXTANT**
exit .. **LEAVE, DEPART, EGRESS**
expand ..... **DILATE, DISTEND**
expanse .... **SEA**
expatriate .... **EXILE**
expectation .... **HOPE**
expedite .... **HURRY, HASTEN**
expedition .. **SAFARI, SUFFARI**
expert ... **ACE, ONER, ADEPT**
expiate .... **ATONE**
explain .... **DEFINE**
explode
POP, DETONATE, FULMINATE
exploit
DEED, FEAT, GEST, GESTE

a explosive
CAP, TNT, GAINE, TONITE
explosive sound ... POP, CHUG
expose .... AIR, DISPLAY
expression, elegant . ATTICISM
expression, local .... IDIOM
expressionless ..... WOODEN
expunge DELE, ERASE, DELETE
extend
JUT, LIE, REACH, BEETLE
extend the front ..... DEPLOY
extensive .... AMPLE
extent .... AREA
external .... EXOTERIC
external covering. HIDE, HUSK,
PEEL, PELT, RIND, SKIN
extinct wild ox .... URUS
extirpate .. ROOT, ERADICATE
extort .... BLEED, EXACT
extra .... ODD, SPARE
extra leaf .... INSERT
extra, theatrical .... SUPE
extract DRAW, ELICIT, EVULSE
extraneous .... EXOTIC
extraordinary person, thing
ONER

c extravagance .... ELA
extreme .... ULTRA
extreme unction, give
ANELE, ENELE
exudate, plant
GUM, LAC, RESIN
exude ..... EMIT, OOZE, REEK
exult .... ELATE
eye .... ORB, SEE, OGLE
eye cosmetic ... KOHL, KUHL
eye inflammation STY, IRITIS
eye, inner coat ...... RETINA
eye, layer .... UVEA
eye of bean .... HILA, HILUM
eye of insect .... STEMMA
eye, part of the .... IRIS,
UVEA, CORNEA, RETINA
eye, pert. to .... OPTIC
eye socket .... ORBIT
eye, symbolic .... UTA
eye-worm, Afr. .... LOA
eyelash .... CILIA, CILIUM
eyes: old Eng. .... NIE
eyestalk .... STIPE
eyewink ...... LOOK, GLANCE
eyot .... ISLE, ISLET

F

b Fabian .... SHAW
fable .... APOLOG, APOLOGUE
fable writer .... ESOP, AESOP
fabled bird .... ROC, RUKH
"Fables in Slang" author ADE
fabric .... REP, ACCA, BAFT,
DRAB, DUCK, IKAT,
LAWN, LENO, MOFF, REPP,
SILK, SUSI, TAPA, TUKE,
CRAPE, CREPE, MOIRE,
NINON, ORLON, RAYON,
CANVAS, COVERT, MAN-
TUA, MOHAIR
farbic, Angora ..... CAMLET,
MOHAIR
fabric, coarse cotton .. SURAT
fabric, coarse wool
TAMIN, TAMINE
fabric, corded REP, REPP, PIQUE
fabric, cotton ... LENO, MULL,
DENIM, MANTA, SCRIM,
CALICO, CRETON, NAN-
KIN, PENANG, NANKEEN,
CRETONNE
fabric, curtain ... NET, SCRIM
fabric, felt-like .... BAIZE
fabric, fig'd DAMASK, PAISLEY
fabric from remnants MUNGO
fabric, Ind. .. SHELA, SHELAH

d fabric, knitted .... TRICOT
fabric, light wool .... ALPACA
fabric, lustrous POPLIN, SATEEN
fabric, mourning ALMA, CRAPE
fabric, net .. TULLE, MALINE
fabric, plaid . MAUD, TARTAN
fabric, printed BATIK, BATTIK
FABRIC, RIBBED
see RIBBED FABRIC
fabric, satin .. PEKIN, ETOILE
fabric, satiny
SATINET, SATINETTE
fabric, sheer .... GAUZE,
BEMBERG, ORGANZA
fabric, short nap .... RAS
fabric, silk .... SURAH,
PONGEE, SAMITE, TOBINE
fabric, silk, gold, medieval ACCA
fabric, silk, thick ...... GROS
fabric, stiff .... WIGAN
fabric stretcher
TENTER, STENTER
fabric, striped .. SUSI, DOREA,
DORIA, DOOREA, MADRAS
fabric, thick .... DRAB
fabric, twilled .... REP
fabric, upholstery .. BROCATEL,
BROCATALL, BROCATELL
BROCATELLE

Fabric

a fabric, velvet-like .... PANNE
fabric, voile-like .... ETAMINE
fabric, wool .. SERGE, TAMIN,
TAMIS, MERINO, TAMINE,
TAMINY, TAMISE, TAM-
MIN, ESTAMIN, ETAMINE,
STAMMEL, ESTAMINE
fabric, worsted ...... ETAMINE
fabricate .... MAKE
fabulist .... ESOP, AESOP
fabulous bird ..... ROC, RUKH
face MAP, MUG, PHIZ, FACADE
face with stone ...... REVET
facet of gem .. BEZEL, BEZIL,
CULET, COLLET
facile .... EASY
facing glacier .... STOSS
fact .... DATUM
fact, by the: law ..... FACTO
facts .... DATA
faction .... SECT, SIDE, CABAL
factor .... GENE
factory .... PLANT
faculty .... SENSE
fade ...... DIE, DIM, WITHER
"Faerie Queene" iron man
TALUS
"Faerie Queene" lady .... UNA
failure .... DUD, FLOP
fainting: med. ..... SYNCOPE
b fair . BAZAR, FERIA, BAZAAR
KERMIS, KIRMES
fair JUST, CLEAR, IMPARTIAL
fair-haired .. BLOND, BLONDE
fair-lead, naut. .... WAPP
fairy .. ELF, FAY, PERI, SPRITE
fairy fort .... LIS, LISS
fairy king .... OBERON
fairy queen ... MAB, TITANIA
fairy, Serbo-Croat VILA, VILY
fairylike creature ...... PERI
faith, article of ...... TENET
faith, pert. to .... PISTIC
faithful .... LEAL,
TRUE, STANCH, STAUNCH
falcon .... SACER, SAKER,
LANNER, MERLIN, SAKERET
falcon, Asia LAGGAR, LUGGAR
falcon genus .... FALCO
falcon-headed god
MENT, MENTU
falcon, Ind. SHAHIN, SHAHEEN
falcon of sea ...... ERN, ERNE
falconer's bait .... LURE
fall DROP, PLAP, PLOP, SPILL
fall back .... RETREAT
fallacy ...... IDOLA, IDOLUM
fallow-deer, female ..... TEG
false excuse .... SUBTERFUGE
false friend .. IAGO, TRAITOR
false fruit of rose .... HIP

c false god .... IDOL
Falstaff's follower ...... NYM
fame .... ECLAT, KUDOS,
RENOWN, REPUTE
famed .... NOTED
familiar .... VERSANT
familiar saying .... SAW, TAG
family, Florentine .... MEDICI
family, Genoese ...... DORIA
family: Scot. .... ILK
famous .... NOTED
fan .... ROOTER
fan palm genus .... INODES
fan's stick .... BRIN
fanatical .... RABID
fancy ... IDEA, WHIM, IDEATE
fanfare .... TANTARA,
TANTARO, TANTARARA
fanning device
PUNKA, PUNKAH
fare .... DIET
farewell ... AVE, VALE, ADIEU
farinaceous .... MEALY
farinaceous food SAGO, SALEP
farm group .... GRANGE
farm, small, Sp. Am. CHACRA
farm, Sw. small leased .. TORP
farm: Swedish .... TORP
farm, tenant .... CROFT
farmer .... KULAK, GRANGER
d farmyard, S. Afr. ...... WERF
Faroe Is. wind .... OE
Faroe judge .... FOUD
Farouk's father .... FUAD
fashion .... FORM, MODE,
MOLD, MODEL, STYLE
fasten ... BOLT, LOCK, NAIL,
SEAL, SNIB, TACK, RIVET
fasten: naut BELAY, BATTEN
fastener .... NUT, PIN, BRAD,
CLIP, HASP, NAIL, SNAP,
STUD, CLASP, RIVET,
CLEVIS, COTTER
fastener, wire .... STAPLE
fastener, naut. .... BITT
fastener, wood
FID, NOG, PEG, PIN
fastening .... LATCH
fastidious .... NICE
fasting month .... RAMADAN
fasting period .... LENT
fat LARD, LIPA, SUET, OBESE
fat, animal .. ADEPS, TALLOW
fat: comb. form STEAT, STEATO
fat, liquid part ...... ELAIN,
OLEIN, ELAINE, OLEINE
fat, natural .... ESTER
fat, of .... SEBAIC
fat, solid part
STEARIN, STEARINE
fatal ...... FUNEST, LETHAL

a fate .... **LOT, DOOM, KISMET**
Fates, Gr. & Rom. .... **MOIRA,
MORTA, PARCA, CLOTHO,
DECUMA, MOIRAI, PAR-
CAE, ATROPOS, LÁCHESIS**
fateful .... **DIRE**
father .... **SIRE, BEGET**
father: Arab. .... **ABU, ABOU**
father: Hebr. .... **ABBA**
father of modern engraving **PYE**
father's side, kinship on
AGNAT, AGNATE
fathom .... **PROBE, SOUND**
fatigue .. **FAG, TIRE, WEARY**
Fatima's huband .... **ALI**
fatty .... **ADIPOSE**
fatty gland secretion **SEBUM**
fatuous .... **INANE**
faucet ... **TAP, COCK, SPIGOT**
fault find ...... **CARP, CAVIL**
faultfinder .. **MOMUS, CAVILER**
faulty .... **BAD**
faux pas ...... **ERROR, GAFFE**
favor .... **BOON**
favorable vote .. **AY, AYE, YES**
favorite .... **PET, IDOL**
fawn color .... **FAON**
fawning favorite .... **MINION**
fear .... **PHOBIA**
fearful .... **TREPID**
b feast .... **REGALE**
feast day: comb. form .... **MAS**
feather **PENNA, PINNA, PLUME**
feather grass .... **STIPA**
feather palms .... **EJOO, IROK**
feather: zool. .... **PLUMA**
feathers, cast .... **MEW**
feathers of o-o .... **HULU**
feathered scarf .... **BOA**
feeble .. **PUNY, WEAK, DEBILE**
feel .... **SENSE**
feel one's way .... **GROPE**
feeler **PALP, PALPI, ANTENNA**
feet, having .... **PEDATE**
feet, pert. to **PEDAL, PEDARY**
feign .... **ACT, SHAM**
feline .... **CAT, PUMA**
felis leo .... **LION**
fellow .... **GUY, LAD, BOZO,
CHAP, DICK, CHAPPY,
CHAPPIE**
felt .... **GROPED, SENSATE**
female animal, parent
DAM, DOE
female camel .... **NAGA**
female disciple at Joppa
DORCAS
female insect .... **GYNE**
fence of shrubs .... **HEDGE**
fence of stakes .... **PALISADE**
fence step .... **STILE**

c fence, sunken, hidden
AHA, HAHA
fence to restrain cattle .. **OXER**
fencer's cry .. **HAI, HAY, SASA**
fencing dummy .... **PEL**
fencing position **CARTE, SIXTE,
QUARTE, QUINTE, TIERCE,
SECONDE, SEPTIME**
fencing sword ...... **EPEE, FOIL**
fencing term .... **TOUCHE**
fencing thrust ...... **LUNGE,
PUNTO, REMISE, RIPOST,
RIPOSTE, REPRISE**
fend .... **WARD**
fennel: P. I. .... **ANIS**
"Ferdinand the Bull" author
LEAF
feria, pert. to .... **FERIAL**
ferment .... **YEAST**
ferment: med. .... **ZYME**
fermented milk dessert **LACTO**
fern, climbing, P. I. .... **NITO**
fern, Polyn., edible .... **TARA**
fern root, N. Z. .... **ROI**
fern "seed" .... **SPORE**
fern species .... **WEKI**
fern spore ...... **SORI, SORUS**
Ferrara ducal family .... **ESTE**
ferrum .... **IRON**
ferryboat .... **BAC**
d ferryboat, Afr. .... **PONT**
fertilizer ..... **MARL, GUANO**
fervent .... **ARDENT**
fervor ... **ZEAL, ZEST, ARDOR**
fester .... **RANKLE**
festival ... **ALE, FAIR, FETE,
GALA, FERIA, FIESTA, KER-
MIS, KIRMES**
festival, Creek Indian .. **BUSK**
festival, Gr.
AGON, DELIA, HALOA
fetid .... **OLID, RANK**
fetish ...... **OBI, JUJU, OBIA,
ZEME, ZEMI, CHARM,
OBEAH, GRIGRI**
fetish, P. I. .... **ANITO**
fetter .... **GYVE, IRON**
feud, opposed to ...... **ALOD,
ALLOD, ALODIUM, ALLODIUM**
feudal benefice .... **FEU**
feudal estate **FEOD, FEUD, FIEF**
feudal land .... **BENEFICE**
feudal service, form of **AVERA**
feudal tax
TAILAGE, TALLAGE, TAILLAGE
feudal tenant .... **VASSAL**
fever, intermittent
AGUE, TERTIAN
feverish .... **FEBRILE**
fez .... **TARBUSH,
TARBOOSH, TARBOUCHE**

Fiber

a fiber .... JUTE, PITA, RAFFIA, STAPLE, THREAD
fiber, bark
TAPA, OLONA, TERAP
fiber, coarse .... ADAD
fiber, cordage .... DA, COIR, FERU, HEMP, IMBE, JUTE, RHEA, ABACA, SISAL
fiber from palm .... ERUC
fiber, hat or basket .... DATIL
fiber knot .... NEP
fiber plant
ISTLE, IXTLE, IXLE, RAMIE
fiber plant, Brazil .... CAROA
fiber plant, E. Ind. SANA, SUNN
fiber, textile .... SABA
fiber, tropical
IXLE, ISTLE, IXTLE
fiber, woody .... BAST, BASTE
fictional submarine character
NEMO
fiddle, medieval .... GIGA
fiddler crab genus ...... UCA
field LEA, ACRE, WONG, CROFT
field deity .:... PAN, FAUN
field, enclosed: law ..... AGER
field, stubble .... ROWEN
fifth segment crustacean
CARPOS
b fig marigold, Afr. ..... SAMH
figs, Smyrna .. ELEME, ELEMI
fight
CLEM, FRAY, MELEE, AFFRAY
figurative use of word .. TROPE
figure .... SOLID
figure, equal angles
ISAGON, ISOGON
figure, 4-sided .... TETRAGON
figure, geom. .... SECTOR
figure of speech
TROPE, SIMILE, METAPHOR
figure, oval .... ELLIPSE
figure, 10-sided .... DECAGON
figwort .... MULLEIN
Fiji chestnut .... RATA
Fiji tree .... BURI
filament .... FIBER, HAIR
filament, flax ... HARL, HARLE
filament, plant
ELATER, THREAD
filch .... STEAL
file .... ROW
file, coarse .... RASP
file, three-square single-cut
CARLET
filled to capacity
SATED, REPLETE
fillet, architectural ORLE, ORLO
fillet, narrow heraldic
ORLE, ORLO, LISTEL
fillet, shaft's ..... ORLE, ORLO

c fillip .... SNAP
film, old green ..... PATINA
filthy .... VILE
filthy lucre .... PELF
finale: music .... CODA
finally: Fr. .... ENFIN
finback whale .... GRASO
finch .. MORO, LINNET, SISKIN
finch, Europ.
TARIN, TERIN, SERIN
finch, S. Afr. .... FINK
find fault ...... CARP, CAVIL
fine, as a line .... LEGER
fine, punish by ...... AMERCE
fine, record of ...... ESTREAT
finesse .... ART, SKILL
Fingal's kingdom .... MORVEN
finger .... DIGIT
finger cymbals ... CASTANETS
finger, 5th PINKIE, MINIMUS
finger inflammation ... FELON
finger nail half-moon
LUNULA, LUNULE
fingerless glove .... MIT, MITT
fingerprint pattern .... WHORL
finial ornament, slender .. EPI
finisher .... EDGER, ENDER
finishing tool .... REAMER
FINLAND, FINNISH
see also SPECIAL SECTION
d Finland .... SUOMI
Finn in Ingria ..... VOT, VOTE
Finns .... SUOMI
Finnish god .... JUMALA
Finnish poetry .... RUNES
Finnish steam bath ... SAUNA
fire basket .... CRESSET
fire bullet .... TRACER
fire god .... VULCAN
fire god, Hindu .. AGNI, AKAL, CIVA, DEVA, KAMA, SIVA
fire in heart: Buddhism RAGA
fire opal: Fr. ...... GIRASOL
fire, sacrificial, Hindu .. AGNI
fire worshipper PARSI, PARSEE
firearm . GUN, RIFLE, MAUSER, PISTOL, CARBINE, REVOLVER
firecracker .... PETARD
fired clay .... TILE
firedog .... ANDIRON
fireplace
GRATE, INGLE, HEARTH
fireplace side shelf .... HOB
firewood bundle BARIN, FAGOT
firewood, Tex. .... LENA
firework .... GERB
firm FAST, STANCH, STAUNCH
firm: Hawaii .... HUI
firmament .... SKY
firn .... NEVE
firs, true .... ABIES

a first **PRIME, INITIAL, ORIGINAL**
first American-born white
   child .... **DARE**
first appearance ...... **DEBUT**
first born: law .... **EIGNE**
first fruits of a benefice
   ANNATES
first miracle site ...... **CANA**
first mortal, Hindu ..... **YAMA**
first part in duet ..... **PRIMO**
first principles .... **ABCS**
first-rate .... **ACE**
firth: Scot. .... **KYLE**
fish .. **ANGLE, TRAWL, TROLL,**
fish ..... **ID, EEL, IDE, CARP,**
  DACE, HAKE, HIKU, JOCU,
  LIJA, LING, MADO, MASU,
  OPAH, ORFE, PEGA, PETO,
  PIKE, POGY, ROUD, RUDD,
  SCAD, SCUP, SESI, SHAD,
  SIER, SKIL, SOLE, SPET,
  TOPE, TUNA, ULUA, PAR-
  GO, POWAN, POWEN,
  ROACH, SKATE, CONGER,
  MULLET, SABALO, TOMCOD
fish, ancient .. **ELOPS, ELLOPS**
fish, Atlant. **TAUTOG, ESCOLAR**
fish, boneless .. **FILET, FILLET**
fish, bony .... **CARP, TELEOST**
fish, butterfly .... **PARU**
b fish by trolling .... **DRAIL**
fish, Calif. surf .... **SPRAT**
fish, carplike
  RUD, DACE, ROUD, RUDD
fish cleaner .... **SCALER**
fish, climbing ...... **ANABAS**
fish, cod-like **CUSK, HAKE, LING**
fish, colorful
  BOCE, OPAH, WRASSE
fish, Congo .... **LULU**
fish, Cuban .... **DIABLO**
fish, cyprinoid
  ID, IDE, ORF, ORFE
fish, edible .... **SPRAT**
fish eggs .... **ROE**
fish, Egypt. .... **SAIDE**
fish, elongated **EEL, GAR, PIKE**
fish, Europ. .. **ID, BOCE, DACE,**
  BREAM, SPRAT, UMBER,
  BARBEL, BRASSE, PLAICE,
  SENNET, WRASSE
fish, flat .. **DAB, RAY, SOLE,**
  BRILL, FLUKE, FLOUNDER
fish, Florida .... **TARPON**
fish, food .. **COD, CERO, HAAK,**
  HAIK, HAKE, LING, SHAD,
  TUNA, TUNNY, SARDINE
fish, food: Ind. .... **HILSA**
fish, fresh water
  IDE, BASS, DACE, ESOX
fish from boat .... **TROLL**

c fish, game .... **BASS,**
  MARLIN, TARPON, TARPUN
fish, gobeylike .... **DRAGONET**
fish, Gr. Lakes .. **CISCO, PERCH**
fish, Hawaiian .... **AKU**
fish, herringlike .... **SHAD**
fish, hook for **GIG, GAFF, DRAIL**
fish, lancet .... **SERRA**
fish line ...... **SNELL, TRAWL**
fish line cork .... **BOB**
fish, linglike .... **COD**
fish, long-nosed .... **GAR**
fish, mackerellike
  CERO, TUNNY, TINKER
fish, many .... **SHOAL**
fish, marine **BONITO, TARPON**
fish measure .... **MEASE**
fish, Medit. .... **NONNAT**
fish, nest-building .... **ACARA**
fish net
  SEINE, TRAWL, SPILLER
fish, N. Z. .... **IHI**
fish, No. Pacif. .... **INCONNU**
fish, parasitic .... **REMORA**
fish, perch-like ...... **DARTER**
fish, Pers. myth .... **MAH**
fish pickle .... **ALEC**
fish, piece of ... **FILET, FILLET**
fish, pikelike .... **GAR**
d fish-pitching prong . **PEW, GAFF**
fish-poison tree .... **BITO**
fish, predatory .... **GAR**
fish, river .... **BLAY**
fish, Russian .... **STERLET**
fish sauce .... **ALEC, GARUM**
fish sign .... **PISCES**
fish, silvery .... **MULLET**
fish, small .. **ID, IDE, DARTER**
fish, snouted .... **SAURY**
fish, S. Am. ...... **ARAPAIMA**
fish, sparoid .... **SAR, SARGO**
fish, spiny ..... **GOBY, PERCH**
fish, sucking .... **REMORA**
fish, trap .... **WEEL, WEIR**
fish, tropical
  SARGO, ROBALO, SALEMA
fish, warm sea
  GUASA, GROUPER
fish, W. Ind.
  BOGA, CERO, TESTAR
fish whisker .... **BARBEL**
fish with moving line .. **TROLL**
fish with net .. **SEINE, TRAWL**
fish, young .... **FRY**
fisherman's hut, Orkney
  SKEO, SKIO
fishhook line-leader. ... **SNELL**
fishhook part .... **BARB**
fishing expedition: Scot. **DRAVE**
fishing grounds, Shetlands **HAAF**

a fissure .... **RENT, RIFT, RIMA, RIME, CLEFT**
fissures, full of **RIMOSE, RIMOUS**
fist .... **NEAF**
fit .. **APT, RIPE, SUIT, ADAPT**
fit for cultivation .... **ARABLE**
fit for human consumption **POTABLE**
fit of sulks .... **HUFF**
five-dollar bill .... **VEE**
five-franc piece .... **ECU**
five, group of .... **PENTAD**
five in cards .... **PEDRO**
fix or fixed .... **SET**
fixed charge .... **FEE**
fixed income person .. **RENTIER**
fixed payment .... **KIST**
flaccid .... **LIMP**
flag. **JACK, ENSIGN, BANDEROLE**
flag, flower, blue .... **IRIS**
flag, military .... **GUIDON**
flag, pirate .... **ROGER**
flag, small **BANNERET, BANNERETTE**
flagellants .... **ALBI**
flag's corner .... **CANTON**
flank .... **SIDE**
flank: dialect .... **LEER**
flannel .... **LANA**
b flap .... **TAB, LOMA**
flap, as sails .... **SLAT**
flare .... **FUSEE, FUZEE**
flaring edge.. .. **LIP, FLANGE**
flashed lightning ... **LEVINED**
flask, drinking ..... **CANTEEN**
flat .... **EVEN, LEVEL, PLANE**
flat-bottomed boat **ARK, DORY, PUNT, SCOW**
flat, music ...... **MOL, MOLLE**
flatfish ..... **DAB, RAY, SOLE, BRILL, FLUKE, FLOUNDER**
flatten out .... **CLAP**
flattened .. **OBLATE, PLANATE**
flatter .... **PALP**
flattery .... **PALAVER**
flavor .... **LACE, TANG, AROMA, SAPOR, SEASON**
flavoring plant .. **HERB, LEEK, MINT, ANISE, BASIL**
flavoring root ...... **LICORICE**
flax fiber .... **TOW**
flax, like .... **TOWY**
flax, prepare .... **RET**
flee .... **LAM, BOLT**
fleece .... **FELL, WOOL**
fleece, poorest .... **ABB**
fleet .... **NAVY**
fleet, esp. Span. **ARMADA, ARMADO, ARMATA**
fleet, merchant ...... **ARGOSY**
fleur-de-lis .... **LIS, LYS, LISS**

c fleur-de-lis, obs. ...... **LUCE**
flexible .... **LITHE**
flexible wood: dial. ..... **EDDER**
flight ...... **HEGIRA, HEJIRA**
flight of ducks .... **SKEIN**
flight organ .... **WING**
flight, pert. to .... **AERO**
flightless bird **EMU, KIWI, WEKA, PENGUIN**
flip .... **SNAP**
flit .... **FLY, GAD**
float **BUOY, RAFT, SWIM, WAFT**
floating .... **NATANT**
floating vegetation on Nile **SADD, SUDD**
floating wreckage .. **FLOTSAM**
flock of quail .... **BEVY**
flock of swans .... **BANK**
flock, pert. to .... **GREGAL**
flock, small .... **COVEY**
flog **BEAT, LASH, WHIP, SWINGE**
flood .... **SEA, EAGRE, SPATE, FRESHET, TORRENT**
floodgate ..... **CLOW, SLUICE**
flora and fauna .... **BIOTA**
floral leaf ..... **BRACT, SEPAL**
Florentine family ..... **MEDICI**
d Florida tree .... **MABI**
flounder **DAB, SOLE, FLUKE, PLAICE**
flour sieve .... **BOLTER**
flour, unsorted Ind. **ATA, ATTA**
flourish, music ...... **ROULADE**
flourishing: dialect ..... **FRIM**
flow .... **RUN, FLUX**
flow out .... **EMIT, SPILL**
flow, to stop **STANCH, STAUNCH**
flower cluster **CYME, ANADEM, RACEME**
flower extract **ATAR, OTTO, ATTAR, OTTAR**
flower, fall **ASTER, COSMOS, SALVIA**
flower, field .... **GOWAN**
flower, genus of .... **ROSA**
flower-goddess, Norse **NANNA**
flower-goddess, Rom. .. **FLORA**
flower leaf ... **BRACT, SEPAL**
flower, Oriental ...... **LOTUS**
flower part .... **PETAL, SEPAL, CARPEL, SPADIX**
flower, showy .... **CALLA**
flower spike .... **AMENT**
flowering plant .... **ARUM**
fluctuate .... **WAVER**
fluent .... **GLIB**
fluff, yarn .... **LINT**

a fluid, aeriform .... GAS
fluid, medical ... SERA, SERUM
fluid, serous .... SERA, SERUM
fluidity unit .... RHE
flume .... SHUTE, SLUICE
flushed .... RED
flute, ancient Gr. .. HEMIOPE
flute, India ... BIN, MATALAN
flute, small .... FIFE
flutter .. FLAP, WAVE, HOVER
fly GNAT, SOAR, WING, AVIATE
fly agaric .... AMANITA
fly aloft .... SOAR
fly, artificial
HARL, HERL, CAHILL, CLARET
fly, kind of .... BOT
fly, small ...... GNAT, MIDGE
fly, S. Afr. .... TSETSE
flycatcher
TODY, ALDER, PEWEE, PHOEBE
flying .... VOLANT, VOLITANT
"Flying Dutchman" saver SENTA
flying fox .... KALONG
flying lemur .... COLUGO
flying, of .... AERO
flying saucer .... UFO
foam .... SUD, SUDS
focus .... CONCENTRATE
fodder pit .... SILO
fodder storage place .... SILO
b fodder, to store ...... ENSILE,
ENSILO, ENSILAGE, ENSILATE
fog .... MIST
fog horn .... SIRENE
fog: old Eng. .... RAG
foist .... FOB, PALM
fold .... LAP, PLY, PLIE,
RUGA, PLEAT, CREASE
fold of skin .... PLICA
folds, arrange in ...... DRAPE
folded .... PLICATE
folio .... PAGE
folk dance, Slavic ...... KOLO
folklore being .... TROLL
folkway .... MOS
folkways .... MORES
follow .... DOG, TAIL,
ENSUE, TRACE, SHADOW
follow suit, not RENIG, RENEGE
follower .. IST, ITE, ADHERENT
foment .... ABET
fondle .... PET, CARESS
fondness: Ir. .... GRA
font .... LAVER, STOUP
food .... FARE, MEAT,
MANNA, ALIMENT, PABULUM
food bit .... ORT
food, farinaceous ..... SAGO
food for animals .... FORAGE
food forbidden Israelites TEREFA

c food, Hawaii .... POI
food: Maori, N. Z. ...... KAI
food of gods
AMRITA, AMREETA, AMBROSIA
food: Polyn. .... KAI
food, provide .... CATER
food, soft invalid's ...... PAP
foods, choice .... CATES
fool..ASS, DOLT, GABY, RACA,
SIMP, IDIOT, NINNY
fool's bauble ...... MAROTTE
fool's gold .... PYRITE
foolish .. DAFT, ZANY, INANE,
SILLY, HARISH, ASININE
foot, animal's ..... PAD, PAW
foot, Chin. .... CHEK
foot, Gr. poet. .... IONIC
foot, having .... PEDATE
foot part, horse's .. PASTERN
foot, poet. ... IAMB, IAMBIC,
IAMBUS, ANAPEST, ANAPAEST
foot soldier .... PEON
foot soldier, Ir. KERN, KERNE
foot, two-syllable
SPONDEE, TROCHEE
foot, verse .... IAMB,
DACTYL, ANAPEST, ANAPAEST
football position: abbr. ... FB,
HB, LE, LT, QB, RE, RT
d footless .... APOD, APODAL
footless animal APOD, APODE
footless animal genus .. APODA
footlike .... PEDATE
footlike part .... PES
footpad .... WHYO
footstalk, leaf .... STRIG
footstool HASSOCK, OTTOMAN
for .... PRO
for example .... EG
for fear that .... LEST
for shame .... FIE
forage plant .. GUAR, ALSIKE,
LUCERN, ALFALFA, LUCERNE
foramen .... PORE
foray .... RAID
forbidden
TABU, TABOO, BANNED
Forbidden City .... LASSA
forbidding .... STERN
force ...... VIS, DINT, DRIVE,
IMPEL, POWER, ENERGY,
VIOLENCE
force, alleged
OD, BIOD, ELOD, ODYL
force, hypothetical .... OD
force, unit of .... DYNE
force, with .... AMAIN
foreboding .... OMEN
forefather .... SIRE
forefoot .... PUD
forefront .... VAN

Forehead

a forehead, of the .... **METOPIC**
forehead strap .... **TUMP**
foreign in origin ...... **EXOTIC**
foreign trade discount .. **AGIO**
foreigner: Hawaii ..... **HAOLE**
foreigners' quarter, Constanti-
nople .... **PERA**
foremost part
BOW, VAN, FRONT
foremost segment, insect's
ACRON
foreordain .... **DESTINE**
foreshadow .... **BODE**
forest: Brazil .... **MATTA**
forest clearing .... **GLADE**
forest: obsolete .... **WOLD**
forest ox .... **ANOA**
forest partly inundated **GAPO**
forest, pert. to
SILVAN, SYLVAN, NEMORAL
forest, P. I. .... **GUBAT**
forest warden ...... **RANGER**
forestall .... **AVERT, PREVENT**
foretell .... **AUGUR, INSEE**
foreteller .... **SEER**
foretoken .... **OMEN**
forever .... **AY, AYE**
forever: Maori .... **AKE**
forever: poet. **ETERN, ETERNE**
forfeit .... **LOSE, LAPSE**

b forfeits, Jap. .... **KEN**
forgetfulness fruit .... **LOTUS**
forgetfulness water ... **LETHE**
forgive .... **REMIT**
forgiving .... **CLEMENT**
forgo .... **WAIVE**
form a network .... **PLEX**
form: Buddhism .... **RUPA**
form into line **ALIGN, ALINE**
form, pert. to .... **MODAL**
form, philos. .... **EIDOS**
formal choice .... **VOTE**
formation, military .. **ECHELON**
former .... **ERST**
former ruler **CZAR, TSAR, TZAR**
formerly .... **NEE, ERST, ONCE**
formerly: pref. .... **EX**
formic acid source ...... **ANT**
formicid .... **ANT**
formula .... **LAW**
forsaken .... **LORN**
fort .... **DIX, ORD, REDAN,**
CITADEL, REDOUBT, RAVELIN
fort, N. Z. .... **PA, PAH**
forth .... **OUT**
forth, issuing ..... **EMANANT**
forthwith .... **NOW**
fortification ⸗
REDAN, RAVELIN, REDOUBT

c fortification, ditchside
SCARP, ESCARP, ESCARPE
fortification, felled trees
ABATIS
fortification, slope .... **TALUS**
fortified place ...... **LIS, LISS**
fortify .... **ARM, MAN**
fortunate (India) .... **SRI**
fortune: Gypsy .... **BAHI**
forty days fast ...... **CARENE**
forty: Gr. .... **MU**
forward .... **ON, AHEAD**
fossil, mollusk .... **DOLITE**
fossil resin .... **RETINITE**
fossil worm track ... **NEREITE**
foul smelling
OLID, FETID, REEKY
found .... **BASE**
found, thing .... **TROVE**
foundation .. **BED, BASE, BASIS**
fountain .... **FONS**
four, group of ...... **TETRAD**
four-inch measure ...... **HAND**
fourth calif (caliph) ..... **ALI**
fourth estate .... **PRESS**
fowl .... **HEN, CAPON, POULT**
fowl's gizzard, etc. .... **GIBLET**
fox .... **TOD**
fox, Afr. .... **FENNEC**
fox hunter's coat ...... **PINK**
d fox, S. Afr. ..... **ASSE, CAAMA**
"Fra Diavolo" composer **AUBER**
fraction ..... **PART, DECIMAL**
fragment, pottery
SHARD, SHERD, SHEARD
fragments .... **ANA, ORTS**
fragrant .... **OLENT**
frame, supporting
TRESSEL, TRESTLE
framework .... **TRUSS**
France .... **GAUL**
franchise .... **CHARTER**
Franciscan .... **MINORITE**
frank .... **OPEN, HONEST**
Franks, pert. to .... **SALIC**
frankincense ...... **OLIBANUM**
Frankish law .... **SALIC**
Frankish peasant .. **LITI, LITUS**
fraud .... **SHAM**
fraught .... **LADEN**
fray .... **MELEE**
free .... **RID, GRATIS**
free-for-all .... **FRAY, MELEE**
free from discount ..... **NET**
free from knots: obs. .. **ENODE**
freebooter .... **PIRATE**
freedman, Kentish law .. **LAET**
freehold land, Turkey .. **MULK**
freeman ...... **CEORL, THANE**
freight-boat .... **ARK**

a freight car .... **GONDOLA**
FRENCH WORDS: (accent marks
omitted throughout)
  according to ..... **ALA, AUX**
  after .... **APRES**
  again .... **ENCORE**
  airplane .... **AVION**
  alas .... **HELAS**
  all .... **TOUT**
  among .... **ENTRE**
  and .... **ET**
  angel .... **ANGE**
  annuity .... **RENTE**
  arm .... **BRAS**
  article .... **LA, LE, DE,**
  (plural) **DES, LAS, LES, UNE**
  at the home of ..... **CHEZ**
  aunt .... **TANTE**
  baby .... **BEBE**
  bacon .... **LARD**
  back .... **DOS**
  ball .... **BAL**
  bang! .... **PAN**
  bath .... **BAIN**
  beach .... **PLAGE**
  beast .... **BETE**
  before .... **AVANT**
  being .... **ETRE**
  bench .... **BANC**
  between .... **ENTRE**
b beware .... **GARE**
  bitter .... **AMER**
  black .... **NOIR, NOIRE**
  blue .... **BLEU**
  bread crumbs ...... **PANURE**
  bridge .... **PONT**
  business house .... **CIE**
  but .... **MAIS**
  cabbage .... **CHOU**
  cake .... **GATEAU**
  carefully groomed .. **SOIGNE**
  carriage .... **FIACRE**
  charmed .... **RAVI**
  chicken .... **POULE**
  child .... **ENFANT**
  clear .... **NET**
  climax, theatre .... **CLOY**
  cloth .... **DRAP**
  cloud .... **NUAGE**
  coarse cloth .... **BURE**
  connective .... **ET**
  cowardly .... **LACHE**
  cup .... **TASSE**
  dance, formal .... **BAL**
  dare .... **OSER**
  daughter .... **FILLE**
  deal .... **DONNE**
  dear .... **CHER, CHERI**
  deed .... **FAIT**
  defy .... **DEFI**

c department .... see SPECIAL
    SECTION, GAZETTEER
  depot .... **GARE**
  detective force .... **SURETE**
  devil .... **DIABLE**
  dirty .... **SALE**
  donkey .... **ANE**
  down with .... **ABAS**
  dream .... **REVE**
  duck to cook .... **CANETON**
  dugout .... **ABRI**
  duke .... **DUC**
  dungeon .... **CACHOT**
  ear of grain .... **EPI**
  east .... **EST**
  egg .... **OEUF**
  elegance .... **LUXE**
  enamel .... **EMAIL**
  equal .... **PAREIL**
  evening .... **SOIR**
  exaggerated .... **OUTRE**
  exclamation .... **HEIN**
  exist .... **ETRE**
  fabric .... **RAS, DRAP**
  father .... **PERE**
  fear .... **PEUR**
  finally .... **ENFIN**
  fingering .... **DOIGTE**
  fire .... **FEU**
d five .... **CINQ**
  for .... **CAR**
  friend .... **AMI, AMIE**
  froth .... **BAVE**
  full .... **PLEIN**
  game .... **JEU, JEUX**
  gift .... **CADEAU**
  god .... **DIEU**
  golden .... **DORE**
  good .... **BON**
  good-bye **ADIEU, AU REVOIR**
  grain ear .... **EPI**
  gray .... **GRIS**
  gravy .... **JUS**
  grimace .... **MOUE**
  ground .... **TERRE**
  half-mask .... **LOUP**
  hall .... **SALLE**
  handle .... **ANSE**
  head .... **TETE**
  health .... **SANTE**
  here .... **ICI**
  hill .... **PUY**
  his .... **SES**
  house .... **MAISON**
  hunting match .... **TIR**
  husband .... **MARI**
  idea .... **IDEE**

(French words continued on
pages 62 and 63)

French

a FRENCH:

impetuosity .... ELAN
in .... DANS
income, annual ..... RENTE
is .... EST
island .... ILE
kind .... SORTE
king .... ROI
lamb .... AGNEAU
land .... TERRE
laugh .... RIRE
laughter .... RISEE
law .... LOI, DROIT
leather .... CUIR
lift .... LEVE
lily .... LIS
little .... PEU
lively .... VIF
lodging place .... GITE
low .... BAS
maid .... BONNE
mail .... POSTE
mask, half .... LOUP
material .... DRAP
May .... MAI
meat dish .... SALMI
milk .... LAIT
mine .... AMOI
mother .... MERE

b mountain .... MONT
museum .... MUSEE
nail .... CLOU
name .... NOM
near .... PRES
network .... RESEAU
night .... NUIT
no .... NON
nose .... NEZ
nothing .... RIEN
number, one .... UNE
nursemaid .... BONNE
of .... DE
one .... UNE
our .... NOS, NOUS
out .... HORS
outbreak .... EMEUTE
over .... SUR
oyster farm .... PARC
petticoat ..... JUPE, COTTE
picnic spot .... BOIS
pinion .... AILE
poem .... DIT
pork .... SALE
pout .... MOUE
preposition .... DES
pretty .... JOLI, JOLIE
pronoun .... CES, ILS, MES,
             TOI, UNE, ELLE
queen .... REINE
quickly .... VITE

c rabbit .... LAPIN
railway station ...... GARE
read .... LIRE
rear .... ARRIERE
reception .... ACCUEIL
rent .... LOUER
river .... RIVIERE
roast .... ROTI
royal edict .... ARRET
saint: abbr. .... STE
salt .... SEL
salted .... SALE
school .... ECOLE, LYCEE
scow .... ACON
sea .... MER
security .... RENTE
senior .... AINE
servant .... BONNE
she .... ELLE
sheath .... ETUI
sheep .... MOUTON
shelter .... ABRI
shine .... LUSTRE
shooting match .... TIR
sickness .... MAL
silk .... SOIE
situated .... SISE
small .... PETIT
smitten .... EPRISE
soldier .... POILU

d some .... DES
son .... FILS
soul .... AME
spirit .... AME
star .... ETOILE
state .... ETAT
stocking .... BAS
storm .... ORAGE
summer .... ETE
superior quality ..... LUXE
superfluous .... DETROP
surnamed .... DIT
sweetmeat .... DRAGEE
that CE, CET, QUE, QUI, CELA
thee .... TE
there! .... VOILA
they .... ILS
thirty .... TRENTE
this .... CE
thou .... TOI
to be .... ETRE
to go .... ALLER
to love .... AIMER
too much .... TROP
under .... SOUS
upon .... SUR
us .... NOUS
verb .... ETRE
verse .... RONDEL

FRENCH:

very	TRES
vineyard	CRU
wall	MUR
water	EAU
wave	ONDE
weapon	ARME
well	BIEN
wine	VIN
wine, delicacy of	SEVE
wine-plant	CEP
with	AVEC
with the	AU
without	SANS
wing	AILE
wood	BOIS
yesterday	HIER
you	TOI
your	VOTRE

Fr., annuity .... RENTE
Fr. art group .... FAUVES
Fr. artist .. DORE, DUFY, GROS, COROT, DEGAS, MANET, MONET, BRAQUE, DERAIN, RENOIR, CHAGALL, CHIRICO, MATISSE, UTRILLO
Fr. artist cult .... DADA
Fr. author .. SUE, GIDE, HUGO, LOTI, ZOLA, CAMUS, DUMAS, RENAN, STAEL, VERNE, RACINE, SARTRE, COCTEAU
Fr. Calvinist .... CALAS
Fr. chalk .... TALC
Fr. coin, old .... SOU
Fr. commercial company .. CIE
FR. COMPOSER
                see COMPOSER, FR.
Fr. dramatist .... RACINE
Fr. ecclesiastic city ...... SENS
Fr. explorer .... CARTIER
Fr. fort, battle of Verdun VAUX
Fr. general .... FOCH, HOCHE GAMELIN
Fr.-Ger. river basin ...... SAAR
Fr. guerillas .... MAQUIS
Fr. Guiana tribesman .... BONI
Fr. historical area ..... ANJOU
Fr. honeysuckle .... SULLA
Fr. illustrator .... DORE
Fr. island .... ILE
Fr. lace-making town CLUNY
Fr. marshal ..... NEY, MURAT
FR. NOVELIST see FR. AUTHOR
FR. PAINTER see FR. ARTIST
Fr. philosopher ...... COMTE
Fr. premier, former .... LAVAL
Fr. priest .... ABBE, PERE
Fr. protectorate ...... TUNIS
Fr. psychologist .... BINET

Fr. Revolution month NIVOSE, FLOREAL, PRAIRAL, VENTOSE, BRUMAIRE, FERVIDOR, FRIMAIRE, MESSIDOR, PLUVIOSE, THERMIDOR
Fr. revolutionist ..... MARAT
Fr. sculptor .... RODIN
Fr. security .... RENTE
Fr. singer ..... PIAF, SABLON
Fr. soprano .... PONS, CALVE
Fr. statesman .... COTY
FR. WRITER .. see FR. AUTHOR
Frenchman .... GAUL
frenzied .... AMOK
frequently .... OFT
fresh .... NEW, SPICK
fresh supply .... RELAY
freshet .... FLOOD, SPATE
freshwater worm .. NAID, NAIS
fretted .... EROSE
Frey's wife .... GERD
friar .... FRA, MONK
friar, mendicant ..... SERVITE
friend: law .... AMY
friends .... KITH
Friendly Islands ...... TONGA
friendship .... AMITY
frigate bird, Hawaiian ... IWA
Frigg's brother-in-law ..... VE
Frigg's husband .... ODIN
fright .... FUNK, PANIC
frighten FLEY, ALARM, SCARE
frill, neck ...... RUFF, JABOT
fringe of curls ...... FRISETTE
fringe: zool. .... LOMA
frisk .... PLAY, ROMP
frisky .... PEART
FROCK see GARMENT
frog .... TOAD
frog genus .... RANA
frogs, order of .... ANURA
frogs, pert. to .... RANINE
frolic ... LARK, PLAY, ROMP, CAPER, SPORT, SPREE
from head to foot . CAP-A-PIE
from: Lat. .... DE
from: prefix .... AB
front ... VAN, FORE, FACADE
front page weather box .. EAR
front, to extend ...... DEPLOY
frontier post .... FORT
frontiersman BOONE, CARSON
frost .... ICE, HOAR, RIME
frosty .... RIMY
froth .... FOAM, SPUME
frothlike .... SPUMY, YEASTY
frown .... LOUR, GLOOM, LOWER, SCOWL, GLOWER
frugal .... CHARY
fruit .... BERRY, OLIVE
fruit, Afr. .... PECEGO

Fruit

a
fruit, aggregate ..... **ETAERIO**
fruit decay .... **BLET**
fruit dish
   COMPOTE, COMPOTIER
fruitdots, fern .... **SORI, SORUS**
fruit, dry .... **ACHENE**
fruit, fleshy ...... **PEAR, PEPO**
fruit, hard-shelled **NUT, GOURD**
fruit, India .... **BEL**
fruit-jelly .... **RHOB**
fruit, lemonlike ..... **CITRON**
fruit of maple ...... **SAMARA**
fruit pigeon, Polyn. ..... **LUPE**
fruit, plumlike .... **SLOE**
fruit, pulpy ..... **UVA, DRUPE**
fruit shrub, E. Ind. .... **CUBEB**
fruit, small, 1-seeded
  AKENE, ACHENE, ACHENIUM
fruit, southern .... **PAPAW**
fruit squeezer .... **REAMER**
fruit, tropical .. **DATE, MANGO**
fruit, vine .... **MELON**
fruit, yellow tropical
  PAPAW, PAPAYA, PAWPAW
fruiting spike .... **EAR**
frustrate ... **SCOTCH, THWART**
fry lightly .... **SAUTE**
Fuegan Indian .... **ONA**
fuel **LOG, COAL, COKE, PEAT**
fuel ship .... **OILER, TANKER**
fuel, turf .... **PEAT, PEET**
fugue theme .... **DUX**
fulcrum, oar .... **THOLE**
full .... **PLENARY**
full and clear ..... **OROTUND**
fullness .... **PLENUM**
fulmar .... **NELLY, MALDUCK**
fume .... **REEK, SMOKE**

c
fun .... **SPORT**
function ...... **GO, USE, WORK**
function, trig. ... **SINE, COSINE**
fundamental
  BASIC, ELEMENTAL
funeral bell **KNELL, MORTBELL**
funeral music .... **DIRGE**
funeral notice .... **OBIT**
funeral oration .... **ELOGE**
funeral pile .... **PYRE**
funeral song .... **NENIA**
fungi, tissue in .... **TRAMA**
fungus .... **AGARIC**
fungus, edible
  MOREL, MORIL, TRUFFLE
fungus, white-spored **AMANITA**
fur ...... **SEAL, VAIR, GENET**
  MARTEN, NUTRIA, MINIVER
fur cape .... **PELERINE**
fur: Her. **PEAN, VAIR, VAIRE**
furbelow ...... **FRILL, RUFFLE**
Furies, Gr. .... **ERINYS**
ERINNYS, ERINYES, ERINNYES
Furies, one of
 ALECTO, MEGAERA, TISIPHONE
Furies, Rom. .... **DIRAE**
furlongs, eight .... **MILE**
furnish crew .... **MAN**
furnish with .... **ENDOW**
furnishings, mode of .. **DECOR**
furrows, with **RIVOSE, RUTTED**
further .... **AID, YET**
furtive .... **SLY, SNEAKY**
fury .... **IRE**
furze .... **WHIN, WHUN,**
  GORSE, GORST, GORSTE
fuse partly .... **FRIT**
fuss .... **ADO, TO-DO**

G

b
gabi .... **TARO**
Gad, son of .... **ARELI**
gadget .... **GISMO**
Gael .... **SCOT**
Gaelic .. **ERSE, CELTIC, KELTIC**
Gaelic poem .... **DUAN**
Gaelic sea god .... **LER**
gaff .... **SPAR**
gain .... **GET, WIN, EARN**
gait .. **LOPE, CANTER, GALLOP**
gait, horse's ..... **PACE, RACK**
Galahad's mother ..... **ELAINE**
Galatea's beloved ..... **ACIS**
Galilee town .... **CANA**
galla ox ...... **SANGA, SANGU**
gallery, art .... **SALON**
gallery: hist. .... **ALURE**

d
gallery, open .... **LOGGIA**
gallery protecting troops
  ECOUTE
galley, armed, old Northmen's
  AESC
galley, fast
  DROMON, DROMOND
galley, 1 oar bank **UNIREME**
galley, 2 oar banks .. **BIREME**
galley, 3 oar banks **TRIREME**
gallop, rapid .... **TANTIVY**
gallop slowly .... **LOPE**
Galsworthy heroine .... **IRENE**
Galway Bay, isles in .... **ARAN**
gamble .... **GAME**
gambling place ...... **CASINO**

a gambol .... **DIDO, CAPER**
game ... **LOTO, BINGO, LOTTO**
game, Basque .... **PELOTA**
game, board ... **CHESS, HALMA**
game, card .... **LU, LOO, NAP, PAM, PUT, FARO, CINCH, MACAO, MONTE, OMBER, OMBRE, STUSS, TAROT, WHIST, BASSET, CASINO, ECARTÉ, ROUNCE, CANASTA**
game, child's .... **TAG**
game, dice .... **LUDO**
game, follow .... **STALK**
game, gambling **FARO, PICO, STUSS**
game, Hawaii .... **HEI**
game, Ind. guessing .. **CANUTE**
game, It. guessing .... **MORA**
game of skill .... **POOL, CHESS**
game piece ... **MAN, DOMINO**
gamecock .... **STAG**
gamekeeper .... **RANGER**
gaming cube .... **DIE, DICE**
Ganges boat .... **PUTELI**
gangplank .... **RAMP**
gangster .. **MUG, THUG, WHYO**
gannet, common ...... **SOLAN**
gannet genus .... **SULA**
gap .... **HIATUS, LACUNA**
gap in hedge

b **MUSE, MEUSE, MUSET**
gar fish .... **SNOOK**
garland .... **LEI, ANADEM**
GARMENT . see COAT, BLOUSE
garment .... **ROBE**
garment, Arab .... **ABA**
garment, bishop's **CHIMAR, CHIMER, CHIMERE**
garment, church ...... **COTTA**
GARMENT, CLERICAL OR ECCLESIASTIC, see GARMENT, PRIESTLY
garment, fitted .... **REEFER**
garment, India, Hindu .. **SARI, SAREE, BANIAN, BANYAN**
GARMENT, LITURGICAL see GARMENT, PRIESTLY
garment, loose .**CAMIS, CAMUS, CYMAR, SIMAR, CAMISE**
garment, Malay ..... **SARONG**
garment, Moslem ...... **IZAR**
garment, N. Afr. .... **HAIK**
garment, Old Ir. .... **INAR**
garment, outer **CAPOTE, PALETOT**
garment, Polyn. ...... **PAREU**
garment, priestly .. **ALB, COPE, AMICE, EPHOD, STOLE**
garment, rain ...... **PONCHO**
garment, scarflike .... **TIPPET**

c garment, Turk. .... **DOLMAN**
garment, woman's **BODICE, MANTUA**
garnishment .... **LIEN**
garret .... **ATTIC**
garter snake genus ..... **ELAPS**
gas .... **FUEL, NEON**
gas apparatus ...... **AERATOR**
gas, charge with ..... **AERATE**
gas, colorless .... **OXAN**
gas, inert .... **ARGON, XENON**
gas, radioactive **RADON, NITON**
GASEOUS ELEMENT see ELEMENTS, SPECIAL SECTION, Page 195
gaseous sky "cloud" . **NEBULA**
GASTROPOD see also MOLLUSK
gastropod ...... **WELK, WILK, WHELK, LIMPET**
gastropod, Haliotis .. **ABALONE**
gate .... **PORTAL**
gate, water .... **SLUICE**
gateway .... **PYLON**
gateway, Buddhist temple **TORAN, TORANA**
gateway, Pers. .... **DAR**
gateway, Shinto temple . **TORII**
gather .... **AMASS, GLEAN, GARNER, MUSTER**
gather, as grouse .... **LEK**

d gather in bundles .... **SHEAVE**
gathers, put in **SHER, SHIR, SHIRR**
gaunt .... **SPARE**
Gawain's father .... **LOT**
gazelle .... **ARIEL**
gazelle, Afr. .. **ADMI, DAMA, MOHR, KORIN, MHORR**
gazelle, Asia .... **AHU**
gazelle, black-tailed ..... **GOA**
gazelle, Pers. .... **CORA**
gazelle, Sudan .... **DAMA**
gazelle, Tibetan .... **GOA**
gear .... **CAM**
gear tooth .... **COG**
gear wheel, smallest .. **PINION**
Geb's consort .... **NUT**
Gelderland city .... **EDE**
gelid .... **ICY, COLD**
GEM .... see also STONE
gem ..... **JADE, ONYX, OPAL, RUBY, SARD, AGATE, PEARL, STONE, GARNET, SPINEL, EMERALD, PERIDOT**
gem-bearing earth, Burma **BYON**
gem, carved .... **CAMEO**
gem facet ..... **BEZEL, BEZIL, CULET, COLLET**
gem weight .... **CARAT**
Gemini's mortal half .. **CASTOR**

a gender, a .... NEUTER
genealogy .... TREE
GENERAL, CIVIL WAR
  see CIVIL WAR COMMANDER
general, Morocco .... KAID
general Sitting Bull defeated
                        CUSTER
generation .... AGE
Genesis matriarch ...... SARAI
genie, Egypt. .... HAPI
genip tree .... LANA
genipap wood .... LANA
gentle . MILD, TAME, TENDER
gentle breeze .... AURA
gentle heat .... TEPOR
genuflect .... KNEEL
GENUS . see PLANT or
              ANIMAL named
genus of plants .... ARUM
geode VUG, VOOG, VUGG, VUGH
geological division . LIAS, LYAS
geol. epoch BALA, ECCA, LIAS,
        MUAV, ERIAN, UINTA,
        PLIOCENE
geol. formation ..... TERRAIN,
        TERRANE, TERRENE
geol. period .... DYAS,
        EOCENE, MIOCENE
geol. stage ...... RISS, ACHEN
geol. vein angle .... HADE
b geometric ratio .... SINE
geometric solid
        CONE, CUBE, PRISM
geometrical lines ...... LOCI,
        LOCUS, SECANT
geometry rule ...... THEOREM
geometry term .... VERSOR
geophagy .... PICA
George Sand novel ..... LELIA
Geraint's wife .... ENID
geranium lake color . NACARAT
germ .. BUG, VIRUS, MICROBE
germ-free ASEPTIC, ANTISEPTIC
germs, produced by ... SEPTIC
GERMAN . see also TEUTONIC
GERMAN WORDS: (umlauts
omitted throughout)
  "A" .... EIN
  above .... UBER
  again .... UBER
  alas .... ACH
  article ...... DAS, DER, EIN
  ass .... ESEL
  beer .... BIER
  blood .... BLUT
  conjunction .... UND
  count .... GRAF
  donkey .... ESEL
  dumpling .... KNODEL
  eat .... ESSEN

c eight .... ACHT
evening .... ABEND
everything .... ALLES
exclamation .... HOCH
four .... VIER
gentleman .. HERR, HERREN
hall .... AULA, SAAL
heaven .... HIMMEL
hunter .... JAGER
"I" .... ICH
ice .... EIS
iron .... EISEN
is .... IST
it .... ES
league (s) .... BUND, BUNDE
love .... LIEBE
mister .... HERR
nation .... VOLK
never .... NIE
new .... NEUE
no .... NEIN
noble .... EDEL
old .... ALT
one .... EIN, EINE
out of .... AUS
pronoun .... ICH
people .... VOLK
school hall .... AULA
softly .... LEISE
d song .... LIED
spirit .... GEIST
state .... STAAT
steel .... STAHL
temperament ...... GEMUT
than .... ALS
the .... DAS, DER
three .... DREI
thunder .... DONNER
title .... VON, PRINZ
town .... STADT
us .... UNS
very .... SEHR
with .... MIT
without .... OHNE
yes .... JA
you .... SIE
your ...... IHR, DEIN, EUER

German .... BOCHE
Ger. admiral .... SPEE
Ger. bacteriologist ..... KOCH
Ger. camp, war ...... STALAG
GER. COMPOSER
        see COMPOSER, GER.
Ger.-Czech region ... SUDETEN
Ger. district, old .... GAU
Ger. dive bomber ...... STUKA
Ger. emperor .... OTTO
Ger. highway ..... AUTOBAHN
Ger. John .... HANS

a
Ger. king .... OTTO
Ger. landscape painter .. ROOS
Ger. name prefix .... VON
Ger. philosopher . KANT, HEGEL
Ger. physicist .. OHM, ERMAN
Ger. president .... EBERT
Ger. princely family ..... WELF
Ger. theologian .... ARND
Ger. title .. VON, GRAF, PRINZ
Ger. tribal region
GAU, GAUE, GAUS
Germanic deity .... DONAR
Germanic letter .... RUNE
gesture dance, Samoa; Fiji SIVA
get out! . SCAT, SHOO, SCRAM
ghastly .... LURID
ghost .... HANT, SPOOK,
SPECTER, SPECTRE
ghost, India .... BHUT
ghost-town state: abbrev.: UT
giant .... TITAN
giant, frightful .... OGRE
giant, Hindu myth ..... BANA
giant, killed by Apollo .. OTUS
giant, Norse, Scand. myth YMER,
YMIR, JOTUM, MIMIR
giant, Rom. .... CACA
giant, 1000-armed, Hindu BANA
giants, Bibl. .... ANAK, EMIM
gibbon, Malay .... LAR
gift, receiver of .... DONEE
b gig .... NAPPER
gigantic person ...... TITAN
"Gil —" LeSage novel .. BLAS
Gilead's descendant .... ULAM
Gilgit language, Kashmir SHINA
gills, four .... PINT
gilt .... DORE
gin .... TRAP
gingerbread tree .... DUM
ginkgo tree .... ICHO
GIPSY .... see GYPSY
giraffe-like animal .... OKAPI
girasol .... OPAL
girder .... TRUSS
girdle .... OBI, CEST, SASH
girl .... SIS, CHIT,
DAME, SKIRT
GIRL'S NAME
see WOMAN'S NAME
girth, saddle .... CINCH
gist .... NUB, PITH
give: law .... REMISE
give reluctantly ..... GRUDGE
give up .. CEDE, WAIVE, YIELD
give up wholly ...... DEVOTE
give way .... YIELD
glacial hill .... PAHA
glacial ice block, pinnacle SERAC
glacial ridge .. AS, OS, ASAR,
KAME, OSAR, ESCAR,
ESKAR, ESKER

c glacial snow field FIRN, NEVE
glacial stage .... WURM
glacier chasm
CREVAS, CREVASSE
glacier, facing a .... STOSS
gladiolus .... IRID
gladly .... FAIN
gland .... PINEAL, THYROID
gland, edible .... NOIX
glass .... LENS
glass, blue .... SMALT
glass bubble .... BLEB
glass defect .... TEAR
glass, flatten .... PLATTEN
glass furnace mouth .. BOCCA
glass ingredient ...... SILICON
glass-like material .. .. PLASS
glass maker .... GLAZIER
glass, molten .... PARISON
glass, partly fused FRIT, FRITT
glass, transparent ..... UVIOL
glass vial .. AMPULE, AMPOULE
glassmaker's oven . LEER, LEHR
glasswort .... KALI
glassy .... HYALINE
glazier's tack .... BRAD
gleam .... GLINT
glide .... SKIM, SLIP,
SKATE, SLIDE
d glittering piece .... SPANGLE
globe .... ORB, SPHERE
global .... ROUND, SPHERAL
gloom .... MIRK, MURK
gloomy .... DARK, DOUR,
DREAR, DREARY
"Gloomy Dean" .... INGE
glossy-surfaced .... GLACE
glottal stop: Dan. ...... STOD
glove leather ..... KID, NAPA,
MOCHA, SUEDE
glove shape, unstitched TRANK
glowing .... CANDENT
glucoside, root .... GEIN
glut ... SATE, GORGE, SATIATE
gnarl ..... NUR, KNUR, NURR
gnat, small .... MIDGE
gnome .... NIS, GREMLIN
go .... WEND
go astray .... ABERRATE
go astray slightly .... ERR
go back .... REVERT
go forth .... FARE
go hence: Lat. .... VADE
go on! .... GARN, SCAT
go shufflingly .. MOSY, MOSEY
goad .... PROD, SPUR, INCITE
goal .... AIM, END
goat, Alpine mountain .. IBEX
goat antelope .... GORAL
goat, Asian .... JAGLA

Goat

a goat, genus .... **CAPRIA**
goat god .... **PAN**
goat, wild .. **TUR, IBEX, TAHR,**
TAIR, TEHR, THAR
goatsucker .... **POTOO**
gob .... **TAR**
Gobi Desert .... **SHAMO**
goblet .... **HANAP**
goblin .... **POOK, PUCA, PUCK**
goblin, Egypt .... **OUPHE**
goblin, Norse **NIS,NISSE,KOBOLD**
goby, small .... **MAPO**
GOD . see also DEITY, and see
also SPECIAL SECTION
god, Babyl. **EA, ABU, ANU, BEL**
GOD, CHIEF see CHIEF NORSE
GOD, also BABYLONIAN
CHIEF GOD
god: Chin. .... **SHEN**
god: Hebrew .... **EL**
god: Jap .... **KAMI**
god: Lat. .... **DEUS**
god of alcoholic drinks, **SIRIS**
god of Arcadia .... **PAN**
GOD OF CHAOS ... see CHAOS
god of darkness—evil, Egyp.
SET, SETH
god of dead, Hindu .... **YAMA**
god of dead, Rom. .... **ORCUS**
b god of discord, Norse
LOK, LOKE, LOKI
god of earth, Babyl. .. **DAGAN**
GOD OF EARTH, Egyptian
see EARTH GOD
god of evil: Egyp. .. **SET, SETH**
god of evil, to ward off **BES,BESA**
god of fertility, Norse ... **FREY**
god of fields, flocks, forest
PAN, FAUN
god of fire ... **AGNI, VULCAN**
god of Hades ..... **DIS, PLUTO**
god of harvests ...... **CRONUS**
god of light, Norse
BALDR, BALDER, BALDUR
god of love, Gr. .... **EROS**
god of love, Rom. **AMOR, CUPID**
god of love, Vedic .... **BHAGA**
god of mirth .. **COMUS, KOMOS**
god (goddess) of mischief . **ATE**
god of michief, Norse
LOK, LOKE, LOKI
GOD OF MOON see MOON GOD
god of music .... **APOLLO**
god of north wind ... **BOREAS**
god of pleasure ..... **BES, BESA**
god of procreation, Egyp. **MIN**
god of prosperity, Teutonic **FREY**
god of revelry, Gr. ... **COMUS,**
KOMOS
god of ridicule .... **MOMUS**
GOD OF SEA .... see SEA GOD
GOD OF SKY .... see SKY GOD

c God of Southeast Wind: Gr.
EURUS
GOD OF STORMS
see STORM GOD
GOD OF SUN .... see SUN GOD
god of thunder **THOR, DONAR**
god of Tuesday **TIU, TIW, TYR**
GOD OF UNDERWORLD
see UNDERWORLD GOD
god of war, Assyrian
ASUR, ASSUR
god of war, Babyl. . **IRA, IRRA**
god of war, Gr. .... **ARES**
god of war, Norse
TY, TYR, TYRR
god of war, Rom. .... **MARS**
god of war, Teut. .... **ER**
god of wind, Norse ... **VAYU**
god of wind, storm, Babylonian
ZU, ADAD, ADDA, ADDU
god of winds, Gr. ..... **AEOLUS**
god of wisdom, Babyl.
NABU, NEBO
god of wisdom, Norse .. **ODIN**
god of youth .... **APOLLO**
god skilled with bow, Norse **ULL**
god, Sumerian .... **ABU**
god, unknown, Hindu ..... **KA**
gods, Chief Teut., Norse **AESIR**
gods: Lat. .... **DI**
d gods, mother of .... **RHEA**
gods, mother of: Ir. **ANA, ANU**
GODS, QUEEN OF
see QUEEN OF GODS
gods, the .... **DEI, DII**
GODDESS see also SPECIAL SECT.
GODDESS, CHIEF see BABY-
LONIAN CHIEF GODDESS
goddess, cow-headed ..... **ISIS**
goddess: Latin .... **DEA**
GODDESS, MOTHER
see MOTHER GODDESS
goddess of agriculture
CERES, DEMETER
goddess of art or science **MUSE**
goddess of astronomy **URANIA**
goddess of beauty: Norse **FREYA**
goddess of betrothal, Norse **VOR**
goddess of chase .**DIAN, DIANA**
goddess of crops, Rom. **ANNONA**
goddess of dawn, Gr. ..... **EOS**
goddess of dawn, Rom.
AURORA
goddess of dawn, Vedic .. **USAS**
goddess of dead ... **HEL, HELA**
goddess of deep, Babyl. . **NINA**
goddess of destiny, Norse
URD, URTH
goddess of destruction ... **ARA**
goddess of discord .. **ATE, ERIS**
goddess of earth, Teut. . **ERDA**

a goddess of earth ... GE, ERDA, GAEA, GAIA, TARI
goddess of earth: Rom. CERES, TERRA
goddess of faith, Rom. . FIDES
goddess of fate, Rom. NONA, PARCA
goddess of fate, Teutonic NORN
goddess of fertility ASTARTE
goddess of fertility, Anatolian MA
goddess of field, Rom. . FAUNA
goddess of flowers, Gr. CHLORIS
goddess of flowers, Norse NANNA
goddess of flowers, Rom. FLORA
goddess of grain CERES, DEMETER
goddess of harvest ...... OPS
goddess of harvest, Attica CARPO
goddess of healing .... EIR
goddess of hearth ..... VESTA
goddess of heavens, Egyp. . NUT
goddess of hope .... SPES
goddess of hunt . DIAN, DIANA
goddess of infatuation .. ATE
goddess of justice . MA, MAAT
b goddess of love ...... VENUS, ASTARTE, APHRODITE
goddess of love, Babylonian ISTAR, ISHTAR
goddess of love, Norse FREYA, FREYJA
goddess of magic .... HECATE
GODDESS OF MATERNITY see MATERNITY GODDESS
goddess of mischief .... ATE
GODDESS OF MOON see MOON GODDESS
goddess of nature CYBELE, ARTEMIS
GODDESS OF NIGHT, NORSE see NIGHT, NORSE
goddess of night: Rom.NOX,NYX
goddess of peace IRENE, EIRENE
goddess of plenty .... OPS
goddess of prosperity: Rom. SALUS
goddess of retribution .... ATE
goddess of retribution, Gr. ARA
goddess of revenge .. NEMESIS
GODDESS OF SEA see SEA GODDESS
goddess of seasons .... HORAE
goddess of splendor, Hindu UMA
goddess of truth, Egypt MA, MAAT
GODDESS OF UNDERWORLD see UNDERWORLD GODDESS

c goddess of vegetation .. CORA, KORE, CERES
goddess of vengeance .... ARA
goddess of victory ...... NIKE
goddess of volcanoes, Hawaii PELE
goddess of war, Gr. .... ENYO
goddess of wisdom ATHENA, PALLAS
goddess of woods ...... DIAN, DIANA, ARTEMIS
goddess of youth .... HEBE
goddess, Queen .. HERA, JUNO
goddesses of destiny ... FATES
goddesses of fate, Gr. MOERAE
goddesses of fate, Norse NORNS
Goethe drama .... FAUST
Goethe heroine ...... MIGNON
golconda .... MINE
gold .... AU, CYME, GILT
gold alloy, ancient ..... ASEM
Gold Coast Negro .... GA
Gold Coast tong. CHI, TWI, TSHI
gold-colored metal . ORMOLU
gold, cover with .... GILD
gold deposit .... PLACER
gold district-field, Afr. .. RAND
gold: Her. .... OR
gold, mosaic .... ORMOLU
gold, pert. to .... AURIC
golden .... AUREATE
d Golden Fleece keeper .. AEETES
Golden Fleece seeker .. JASON
golden in color .. DORE, DURRY
golden oriole .... PIROL
golden oriole, Eur. .... LORIOT
golden-touch king .... MIDAS
golf attendant .. CADY, CADDY
golf club ...... IRON, CLEEK, MASHIE, PUTTER
golf club, part .... TOE
golf club socket .... HOSEL
golf hole .... CUP
golf pro .... SNEAD
golf score .... PAR
golf stroke-shot .. PUT, BAFF, CHIP, LOFT, PUTT, DRIVE, SCLAFF
golf term ..... LIE, PAR, TEE
golfer .... TEER
gomuti .... ARENGA
gondolier's song BARCAROLE, BARCAROLLE
gone .... OUT, AWAY
gone by .... AGO, PAST, YORE
gonfalon .... BANNER
good-bye: Fr. ADIEU,AU REVOIR
good digestion ..... EUPEPSIA
good health, in .... PEART
"Good King" .... HAL
good news EVANGEL, EVANGILE

69

Good

"Good Queen Bess," name for ORIANA
good: Tagalog .... MABUTI
goods .... WARES
goods in sea .... JETSAM
goods sunk at sea
LAGAN, LIGAN
goose barnacle genus .. LEPAS
goose cry ...... HONK, YANG
goose genus .... ANSER
goose, male .... GANDER
goose, sea .... SOLAN
goose, wild .... BRANT
gooseberry .... FABES
gopher tortoise ... MUNGOFA
gorge .... GLUT, CHASM,
FLUME, RAVINE
Gorgons, one of ..... MEDUSA
gorse ... WHIN, WHUN, FURZE
goshawk genus . ASTUR, BUTEO
gospel ... EVANGEL, EVANGILE
gossamer .... WEB
gossip .... EME
gossip: India .... GUP
Gottfried's sister .... ELSA
gourd fruit .... PEPO
gourd rattle .... MARACA
gourmet .... EPICURE
gout of knee ...... GONAGRA
government .... STATE
government control .... REGIE
STATISM
governor .... REGENT
governor, Mecca
SHERIF, SHEREEF
governor, Persia ..... SATRAP
governor, Turkish .... BEY
GOWN .... see GARMENT
grace .... ADORN
Graces' mother ...... AEGLE
Graces, The . AGLAIA, THALIA
graceful .... GAINLY
grackle .... DAW, MINA,
MYNA, MYNAH
grade .... RANK, RATE,
SORT, STEP
gradient .... SLOPE
Graf —, ship .... SPEE
graft .... CION, SCION
grafted: Her. .... ENTE
Grail, Holy, finder of .... BORS
grain .... OAT, RYE, SEED,
WALE, SPELT, MILLET
grain beetle .... CADELLE
grain, chaff of .... BRAN
grain, coarse .... SAMP
grain given Romans . ANNONA
grain, sorghum, Ind., .. DARI,
DORA, DURR, MILO, CHENA,
DARRA, DARSO, DURRA,
DHURRA, DOURAH, HEGARI

grain, sorghum, U. S. FETERITA
grain, stalks of ...... HAULM
grain to grind .... GRIST
gram molecule .... MOL
grammatically, describe . PARSE
grampus .... ORC
granary, India
GOLA, GUNJ, GUNGE
grandparental .... AVAL
grandson, Adam's, Eve's. . ENOS
grant .... CEDE, MISE, REMISE
grant, India, Hindu .... ENAM
grant of rights
PATENT, CHARTER
granular snow .... FIRN, NEVE
grape .... UVA, MUSCAT,
CATAWBA, CONCORD
grape conserve .... UVATE
grape disease .... ESCA
grape genus .... VITIS
grape jelly .... SAPA
grape juice DIBS, MUST, STUM
grape juice sirup .... SAPA
grape-like .. UVA, UVAL, UVIC
grape-like fruit .... UVA
grape refuse .... MARC
grape, white .... MALAGA
grapefruit .. POMELO, PUMELO
graphite .... KISH
grasp .... SEIZE
grass .... POA, REED, DARNEL
grass, Andes .... ICHU
grass, blue .... POA
grass, coarse .... REED, SEDGE
grass genus ...... AIRA, COIX,
AVENA, STIPA
grass, kind of .... RIE
grass, marsh .... REED
SEDGE, FESCUE
grass, N. Afr. .... ALFA
grass, pasture .... GRAMA
grass rope: Sp. .... SOGA
grass, rope-making
MUNG, MUNJ
grass, sour .... SORREL
grass stem .... CULM
grass tuft .... HASSOCK
grass, yard, wire .... POA
grasshopper .... GRIG
grassland
SAVANNA, SAVANNAH
grassland, S. Afr. ..... VELDT
grasslands, Western ... RANGE
grate ...... JAR, RASP, GRIDE
gratify . SATE, ARRIDE, PLEASE
grating . GRID, GRILL, GRILLE
gratuitous .... FREE
gratuity .... FEE, TIP
gratuity, customer ..... PILON
grave .... SOBER

a gravestone, Gr. & Rom. **STELA,**
    STELE, STELAE, STELAÍ
graving tool .... **STYLET**
Gray, botanist .... **ASA**
gray .... **OLD, HOAR,**
    ASHEN, SLATE
gray kingbird .... **PIPIRI**
gray, mole .... **TAUPE**
gray parrot .... **JAKO**
gray plaid, gray shawl .. **MAUD**
grayish-brown ... **DUN, TAUPE**
graze .... **AGIST, BROWSE**
grease ... **OIL, LARD, AXUNGE**
great barracuda ..... **PICUDA**
Great Barrier Island, N. Z. **OTEA**
"Great Emancipator" .... **ABE**
great: Gypsy .... **BARO**
greater .... **MORE, MAJOR**
Greece, ancient name . **HELLAS**
Greece, modern .... **ELLAS**
greedy .... **AVID**
    Greek Letters, Numbers:
Greek A, One .... **ALPHA**
Greek B, Two .... **BETA**
Greek D, Four .... **DELTA**
Greek E, Eight .... **ETA**
Greek I, Ten .... **IOTA**
Greek M, Forty .... **MU**
b Greek N, Fifty .... **NU**
Greek O, 800 .... **OMEGA**
Greek P, Eighty .... **PI**
Greek R, 100 .... **RHO**
Greek T, 300 .... **TAU**
Greek Z, Seven .... **ZETA**
Greek 90 .... **KOPPA**
Greek 900 .... **SAMPI**
Gr. ancient .... **ATTIC**
Gr. assembly .... **AGORA**
Gr. athletic contest ..... **AGON**
Gr. authors .... **ZENO, AESOP,**
    HOMER, PLATO, TIMON,
    HESIOD, PINDAR, SAPPHO,
    STRABO, THALES, PLU-
    TARCH
Gr. city, ancient **ELIS, SPARTA**
Gr. city, word for ..... **POLIS**
Gr. colony, ancient .... **IONIA**
Gr. column ..... **DORIC, IONIC**
Gr. commonalty ...... **DEMOS**
Gr. community .... **DEME**
Gr. dialect ..... **EOLIC, AEOLIC**
Gr. district, ancient ... **ATTICA**
Gr. drama .... **MIME**
Gr. festival city .... **NEMEA**
Gr. galley **TRIREME, UNIREME**
Gr. garment .... **CHITON**
Gr. ghost .... **KER**
GREEK GODS, GODDESSES . see
    SPECIAL SECTION and see
    GODS, GODDESSES
Gr. hero ...... **AJAX, JASON**

c Gr. historian .... **CTESIAS**
Gr. January .... **GAMELION**
Gr. legendary hero ...... **IDAS**
Gr. market place ..... **AGORA**
Gr. meeting place of voters
    PNYX
Gr. musical term .. **MESE, NETE**
Gr. myth flier .... **ICARUS**
Gr. native .... **CRETAN**
Gr. patriarch .... **ARIUS**
Gr. philosopher **PLATO, THALES**
Gr. poet ..... **ARION, HOMER,**
    PINDAR
Gr. poetess ... **SAPHO, SAPPHO**
Gr. poetry, simple ..... **DORIC**
Gr. priest .... **MYST**
Gr. princess .... **IRENE**
Gr. province .... **NOME**
Gr. resistance group ..... **EDES**
Gr. rose .... **CAMPION**
Gr. sculptor .... **PHIDIAS**
Gr. shield .... **PELTA**
Gr. slave .... **PENEST**
Gr. statesman ..... **ARISTIDES**
Gr. temple .... **NAOS**
Gr. theologian .... **ARIUS**
Gr. township-commune .. **DEME**
Gr. underground .... **ELAS**
Gr. vase .... **PELIKE**
d Gr. weight, old .. **MNA, MINA**
green ..... **NILE, VERD, VERT,**
    OLIVE, RESEDA
green chalcedony ..... **JASPER**
green cheese .... **SAPSAGO**
green chrysolite ..... **PERIDOT**
green copper arsenate . **ERINITE**
green fly .... **APHID**
green: Her. .... **VERT**
Green Mountain hero ... **ALLEN**
green parrot: P. I. .... **CAGIT**
green stone ... **JADE, PERIDOT**
greenish yellow **OLIVE, RESEDA**
Greenland Eskimo .... **ITA**
Greenland geol. div. .... **KOME**
Greenland settlement, town,
    base .... **ETAH**
Greenland's colonizer ... **ERIC**
greeting .. **AVE, HAIL, SALUTE**
gridiron .... **GRILL**
grief .... **DOLOR, DOLOUR**
griffon genus .... **GYPS**
grimalkin .... **CAT**
grinding .... **MOLAR**
grindstone, Indian ..... **MANO**
grit .... **SAND**
grivet .... **WAAG**
grivet monkey .... **TOTA**
grommet, naut. ...... **BECKET**
groom, India . **SAIS, SICE, SYCE**
groove .... **RUT, SCARF**

a groove, pilaster **STRIA, STRIAE**
grooved ..... **LIRATE, STRIATE**
grope .... **FEEL**
gross .... **CRASS**
ground grain .... **MEAL**
ground wheat-husk ..... **BRAN**
groundhog .... **MARMOT**
group .... **BAND, BODY, CREW, TEAM**
group, animal ..... **NID, NYE, HERD, NIDE, COVEY, DROVE, CLUTCH**
grouper .... **MERO**
grouse .... **PTARMIGAN**
grouse, red: Scot. . **MUIRFOWL**
grove, small-tree ...... **COPSE**
grow .... **WAX, RAISE**
grow together ...... **ACCRETE**
growing out .... **ENATE**
growl .... **YAR, GNAR, YARR, SNARL**
growth, skin .... **WEN**
grub .... **LARVA**
grudge .... **SPITE**
gruel, maize .... **ATOLE**
gruesome .. **GRISLY, MACABRE**
guarantees .... **SURETIES**
b guard .... **SENTRY**
guard, as door .... **TILE**
guardhouse .... **BRIG**
guardian, alert **ARGUS, CERBERUS**
Guatemala fruit .... **ANAY**
guava .... **ARACA**
Gudrun's husband **ATLI, SIGURD**
Guenon monkey .... **MONA**
guest house .... **INN**
Guiana tree .... **MORA**
guide .... **LEAD, PILOT, STEER**
guiding .... **POLAR**
guiding rule .... **MOTTO**
Guido's note .... **UT, ELA**
guild, merchants' ..... **HANSE**
guillemot ...... **COOT, MURR, MURRE**
guilty .... **NOCENT**
guinea fowl's young ..... **KEET**
guinea pig .... **CAVY**
gulch: Sp. .... **ARROYO**
GULF, ... also see **GAZETTEER**
gulf, Ionia sea .... **ARTA**
gulf, Medit. .... **TUNIS**

c gull ..... **MEW, SKUA, TERN, WAEG, XEMA**
gull, fork-tailed .... **XEMA**
gull genus ...... **LARI, XEMA**
gulls, of, like .... **LARINE**
gullet .... **MAW, CRAW**
gullible person .. **DUPE, GULL**
"Gulliver's Travels," men **YAHOOS**
gully: Afr. .... **DONGA**
gulp .... **SWIG**
gum .... **RESIN, BALATA**
gum arabic **ACACIA, ACACIN, ACACINE**
gum, astringent .... **KINO**
gum resin .... **ELEMI, LOBAN, MYRRH**
gum resin, aromatic ... **MYRRH**
gum, Somaliland ..... **MATTI**
gums .... **ULA**
gumbo ... **OCRA, OKRA, OKRO**
gumbo limbo tree ... **GOMART**
gun .... **GAT**
gun, British .... **STEN**
gun fire, burst of ..... **SALVO**
gun, Ger. .... **BERTHA**
d gun, kind of .... **BREN**
gun lock catch .... **SEAR**
gun, P. I. .... **BARIL**
gun, slang ..... **ROD, HEATER ROSCOE**
gun: S. Afr. ..... **ROER, ROHR**
gunny cloth .... **TAT**
gusto .... **ZEST**
gutta mixture .... **SOH**
gutta, Sumatra .... **SIAK**
guy-rope .. **STAT, STAY, VANG**
gym feat .... **KIP**
gymnast .... **TURNER**
gypsum, kind of . **YESO, GESSO, YESSO, SELENITE**
gypsy .... **ROM, CALE, CALO, ROAMER, ROMANY**
gypsy boy .... **ROM**
gypsy gentleman .... **RYE**
gypsy girl .... **CHAI**
gypsy husband .... **ROM**
gypsy lady .... **RANI**
gypsy married woman .. **ROMI**
gypsy: Sp. .... **GITANO**
gypsy tent, camp .... **TAN**
gypsy village .... **GAV**
gypsy word .... **LAV**
gypsy word for paper, book .**LIL**

H

H .... **AITCH**
habit .... **RUT, WONT, USAGE**
habitat plant form ..... **ECAD**
habitation .... **ABODE**
habituate ..... **ENURE, INURE**
habituated .... **USED**
hackney coach, Fr. .... **FIACRE**
hackneyed ..... **STALE, TRITE**
Hades ... **DIS, ORCUS, PLUTO,**
 SHEOL, TARTARUS
Hades: Old Eng. .... **ADES**
Hades, place before .. **EREBUS**
Hades river
 STYX, LETHE, ACHERON
hag .... **CRONE**
haggard .... **DRAWN**
Haggard, H. Rider, novel .. **SHE**
hail .... **AVE, GREET**
hail: naut. .... **AVAST**
hair, arrange .... **COIF**
hair, caterpillar .... **SETA**
hair coat .... **MELOTE**
hair-do, old .... **TETE**
hair dressing .... **POMADE**
hair, false . **RAT, WIG, TOUPEE**
hair, head of .... **CRINE**
hair, knot of .. **BUN, CHIGNON**
hair, lock of .... **CURL, TRESS**
hair net .... **SNOOD**
hair, remove .... **EPILATE**
hair, rigid .... **SETA**
hair, rough, matted .... **SHAG**
hair shirt .... **CILICE**
hair, standing .... **ROACH**
hair unguent .... **POMADE**
hairless: Sp. Am. ...... **PELON**
hairlike process
 CILIA, CILIUM
hairy . **PILAR, COMOSE, PILOSE**
Haiti bandit .... **CACO**
Halcyone's husband .... **CEYX**
half .... **MOIETY**
half-boot .... **PAC**
half-breed ... **MESTEE, MUSTEE**
half-caste .... **METIS**
half-moon figure .... **LUNE**
half-way .... **MID**
halfway house .... **INN**
halfpenny: Brit. .... **MAG**
hall: Ger. .... **AULA, SAAL**
hallow .... **BLESS**
halo .... **NIMB, CORONA,**
 NIMBUS, AUREOLA, AUREOLE
halt .... **LAME, STOP**
halting place, troops' .. **ETAPE**
Hamilton's party .... **FEDERAL**

Hamite .... **SOMAL, BERBER,**
 SOMALI
Hamitic language **AGAO, AGAU**
hamlet ... **BURG, DORP, TOWN**
Hamlet's castle .... **ELSINORE**
hammer .... **KEVEL**
hammer head part ...... **PEEN**
hammer, heavy .... **MAUL**
hammer, large .... **SLEDGE**
hammer, lead .... **MADGE**
hammer, tilt .... **OLIVER**
hamper ..... **CRAMP, FETTER,**
 TRAMMEL
Ham's son .... **CUSH**
hand .... **PUD, NEAF, MANUS**
hand, pert. to .... **CHIRAL**
hand, whist .... **TENACE**
handbill .... **LEAF**
handcuff .... **MANACLE**
handle ... **EAR, LUG, PAW,**
 ANSA, HILT, KNOB,
 HELVE, TREAT
handle, bench plane .... **TOTE**
handle, having ...... **ANSATE**
handle roughly ... **PAW, MAUL**
handle, scythe .... **SNATH,**
 SNEAD, SNEED, SNATHE
handstone for grinding . **MANO**
handwriting .... **SCRIPT**
handwriting on the wall . **MENE,**
 MENE, TEKEL, UPHARSIN
hang .... **DRAPE, DROOP,**
 HOVER, IMPEND
hank of twine .... **RAN**
Hannibal's defeat ...... **ZAMA**
Hannibal's victory .... **CANNAE**
happen ...... **OCCUR, BEFALL,**
 BETIDE, CHANCE
happening .... **EVENT**
happiness god, Jap.
 EBISU, HOTEI
harangue .... **ORATE,**
 TIRADE, DIATRIBE
Haran's son .... **LOT**
harass .... **NAG, BESET**
harbinger .... **HERALD**
harbor .... **BAY, COVE,**
 PORT, HAVEN
hard cash .... **SPECIE**
harden .... **GEL, SET**
 ENURE, INURE, INDURATE
hardship .... **TRIAL**
hardtack .... **PANTILE**
hardwood .... **ASH, OAK**
Hardy novel heroine ..... **TESS**
hare: dialect .... **WAT**

a hare, genus .... **LEPUS**
hare, young, 1 year .. **LEVERET**
harem ... **ZENANA, SERAGLIO**
harem room .... **ODA**
harlot of Jericho, Bibl. . **RAHAB**
harm .**BANE, DAMAGE, INJURE**
harm: old Eng. .... **DERE**
harm: poetic .... **BALE**
harmful .... **NOCENT**
harmonize .... **ATTUNE**
harmony .. **UNISON, CONCORD**
harp, ancient .... **TRIGON**
Harp constellation ...... **LYRA**
harp guitar key .... **DITAL**
harp, kind of .... **EOLIC**
harp, Nubian .... **NANGA**
harpy, Gr. myth .... **AELLO**
harquebus projection .... **CROC**
harrow .... **DRAG**
harsh to taste .... **ACERB**
hartebeeste ..... **ASSE, TORA,**
CAAMA, KAAMA
harvest .... **REAP**
harvest festival, Rom. . **OPALIA**
harvest goddess .... **OPS**
harvest, India ... **RABI, RABBI**
has not: Old Eng. .... **NAS**
hashish .... **BHANG**
hasty pudding .... **SEPON**
HAT .... see HEADGEAR
b hat: Anglo-Ir. ...... **CAUBEEN**
hat plant .... **SOLA**
hat, straw .. **MILAN, PANAMA**
hatchet, archeol. ...... **HACHE**
hatchet, stone .... **MOGO**
hatred .... **ODIUM, AVERSION**
hatred: Buddhism ...... **DOSA**
hatter's mallet .... **BEATER**
haul tight, naut. . **BOUSE, TRICE**
haunt, low .. **DEN, DIVE, NEST**
hautboy .... **OBOE**
haven .... **LEE**
having buttery account:
Oxford .... **BATTEL**
having holes, as cheese **EYEY**
having true luster when uncut
NAIF
haw!: P.I. .... **MANO**
haw, as cattle .... **HOI**
Hawaiian bird .. **IO, O-O, IIWI**
Hawaiian bird, extinct . **MAMO**
Hawaiian bird, red-tailed **KOAE**
Hawaiian blueberry ... **OHELO**
Hawaiian chant .... **MELE**
Hawaiian cloth .. **TAPA, KAPA**
Hawaiian cudweed ... **ENAENA**
Hawaiian dance .... **HULA**
Hawaiian farewell, greeting
ALOHA
Hawaiian feather cloak . **MAMO**
Hawaiian fern .... **HEII**

c Hawaiian floral emblem **LEHUA**
Hawaiian food .... **POI**
Hawaiian food-game fish .**ULUA**
Hawaiian garland .... **LEI**
Hawaiian god .... **KANE**
Hawaiian goddess, fire .. **PELE**
Hawaiian goose .... **NENE**
Hawaiian gooseberry .... **POHA**
Hawaiian governor, 1st . **DOLE**
Hawaiian grass .... **HILO**
Hawaiian hawk .... **IO**
Hawaiian herb .... **HOLA**
Hawaiian loincloth .... **MALO**
Hawaiian musical instrument
PUA
Hawaiian porch .... **LANAI**
Hawaiian president, 1st .. **DOLE**
Hawaiian royal chief ... **ALII**
Hawaiian shrub .... **AKIA**
Hawaiian staple .... **POI**
Hawaiian starch .... **APII**
Hawaiian timber tree ... **OHIA**
Hawaiian tree
KOA, AULU, ALANI, ILIAHI
Hawaiian tree, dark .... **AALII**
Hawaiian tree fern ..... **PULU**
Hawaiian vine .... **IE**
Hawaiian volcano goddess.**PELE**
Hawaiian windstorm .... **KONA**
hawk .... **KITE**
d hawk, falconry .... **BATER**
hawk, fish .... **OSPREY**
hawk genus .... **BUTEO**
hawk-head god, Egypt .. **HORUS**
hawk, India .... **SHIKRA**
hawk-like bird .... **KITE**
hawk, Scot. .... **ALLAN**
hawk, young ..... **BRANCHER**
hawks .... **IOS**
hawk's cage .... **MEW**
hawk's leash .... **LUNE**
hawthorn .... **MAY**
hawthorn berry .... **HAW**
hay, spread to dry .... **TED**
haystack .... **RICK**
hazard .... **DARE, RISK, PERIL**
hazardous .... **CHANCY**
haze: Old Eng. .... **HASE**
hazelnut .... **FILBERT**
hazy, make ..... **DIM, BEDIM**
"he remains": Lat. .... **MANET**
head ..... **NOB, LEAD, PATE,**
POLL, TETE, CAPUT, CHIEF,
CAPITA, LEADER, NODDLE,
NOODLE
head covering .... **CAP, HAT,**
TAM, HOOD, VEIL, BERET
head covering, fleecy .. **NUBIA**
head, crown of .... **PATE**
head, having round ... **RETUSE**
head, membrane covering **CAUL**

a head, Moslem .... **RAIS, REIS**
head of Benjamin's clan .. **IRI**
head, shaved .... **TONSURE**
head: slang .... **NOGGIN**
head wrap .... **NUBIA, SHAWL**
headband, Gr. .... **TAENIA**
HEADDRESS
see also **HEADGEAR**
headdress, bishop's
MITER, MITRE
headgear, brimless ..... **TOQUE**
headgear, clerical
BERETTA, BIRETTA
headgear, dervish .... **TAJ**
headgear, kind of ... **PANAMA**
headgear, military .... **SHAKO**
headgear, Moslem .. **TARBUSH,**
TARBOOCH, TARBOOSH,
TARBOUCHE
headgear, poetic .... **TIAR**
headgear, priest's
BERETTA, BIRETTA
headgear, tropics
TOPI, TERAI, TOPEE
headgear, Turk. .... **FEZ**
headland .. **RAS, CAPE, NASE,**
NESS, NOZE
headless: Her. .... **ETETE**
headstrong .... **RASH**
healing goddess .... **EIR**
health, in good .... **FIT**
b health-drinking word
SALUD, PROSIT
health resort .... **SPA**
heap ...... **PILE, RAFF, RAFT**
hear ye! .... **OYES, OYEZ**
hearing: law .... **OYER**
hearken .. **HEAR, HEED, LIST,**
ATTEND, LISTEN
heart .... **COR, CORE**
heart auricle . **ATRIA, ATRIUM**
heart contraction .... **SYSTOLE**
heart, immortal, Egyp. .... **AB**
heart trouble .... **ANGINA**
heartleaf .... **MEDIC**
heartless ... **CRUEL, SARDONIC**
heat .... **WARM, CALOR**
heated to whiteness .**CANDENT**
heath .... **MOOR**
heath genus .... **ERICA**
heathen .... **PAGAN**
heathen god .... **IDOL**
heather .... **LING, ERICA**
heating apparatus, vessel.**ETNA**
heave upward .... **SCEND**
heaven .. **SION, ZION, URANO**
heaven, eagle-borne flier to
ETANA
heaven personified: Babyl.. **ANU**
heavens, pert. to .... **URANIC**
heavenly .... **EDENIC**

c heavenly being .... **ANGEL**
SERAPH, SERAPHIM
heavenly Jerusalem **SION, ZION**
heavy blow .... **ONER**
HEBREW see also **JEWISH**
and **BIBLICAL**
Hebr. Bible books .... **NEBIIM**
Hebr. Bible pronunciation aid
GRI, KRI, KERE, KERI,
QERE, QERI, QUERI
Hebr. drum .... **TOPH**
Hebr. dry measure .. **CAB, KAB**
Hebr. lyre .... **ASOR**
Hebr. measure .... **KOR, EPHA,**
OMER, EPHAH
Hebr. precept .... **TORA**
HEBREW PROPHETS . see
SPECIAL SECTION, Page 196
Hebr. proselyte .... **GER**
Hebr. reclaimer .... **GOEL**
Hebr. teacher ...... **RAB, REB**
Hebr. universe .... **OLAM**
Hebrews' ancestor, legend
EBER
Hector's mother ..... **HECUBA**
hedge plant .... **PRIVET**
hedgerow: Eng. .... **REW**
heed .... **HEAR, MIND,**
OBEY, RECK
heel .... **CAD, CALX**
d height .... **STATURE**
heir .... **SON, SCION,**
HERITOR, LEGATEE
held, able to be .... **TENABLE**
Helen: It. .... **ELENA**
Helen of Troy's mother . **LEDA**
Helen's lover .... **PARIS**
helical .... **SPIRAL**
Helios .... **SUN**
hell .... **HADES, SHEOL**
Hellespont swimmer . **LEANDER**
helm position .... **ALEE**
helmet, light .... **SALLET**
helmet, medieval
ARMET, HEAUME
helmet, Rom. .... **GALEA**
helmet-shaped ...... **GALEATE**
helmet-shaped part ... **GALEA**
helmsman .... **PILOT**
Heloise's husband ... **ABELARD**
help .. **AID, ABET, BACK, TIDE,**
ASSIST, SUCCOR, SUCCOUR
helper .... **AIDE**
Helvetic .... **SWISS**
hem in .... **BESET**
hemp .... **TOW, RINE, RAMIE**
hemp, Afr. .... **IFE**
hemp, India .... **KEF, BANG,**
KEEF, KEIF, KIEF, BHANG,
DAGGA, RAMIE
hemp, Manila .... **ABACA**

75

Hemp

hemp narcotic ...... **CHARAS**
hemp shrub, India
　　　　　　 PUA, POOA, POOAH
hen .... **LAYER**
hen harrier, Europ. .... **FALLER**
hence .... **SO, OFF, AWAY**
Hengist's brother ..... **HORSA**
Henry IV birthplace ...... **PAU**
"Henry IV" character ... **PETO**
"Henry V" knave ...... **NYM**
"Henry VI" character ... **IDEN**
hep .... **ONTO**
her: obs. .... **HIR**
Hera's son .... **ARES**
herald .... **USHER**
HERALDIC TERMS . see also
　　SPECIAL SECTION, Page 194
herald's coat .... **TABARD**
heraldic bearing **ORLE, FILLET**
heraldic cross .... **PATEE**
heraldic wreath .... **ORLE**
herb ..... **RUE, LEEK, MINT,
MOLY, WORT, ANISE, TANSY,
YARROW, OREGANO**
herb, aromatic **BASIL, DITTANY**
herb, bitter .... **RUE, ALOE**
herb, carrot family .... **ANISE**
herb eve .... **IVA**
herb, fabulous **MOLY, PANACE**
herb, forage .... **SULLA**
herb genus .... **ABFA
GEUM, RUTA, ALETRIS**
herb, medicinal .. **ALOE, SENNA**
herb of grace .... **RUE**
herb, snake-charm ... **MUNGO**
herb with aromatic root . **NONDO**
herb, wooly .... **POLY**
Hercules' captive .... **IOLE**
Hercules, monster slain by
　　　　　　　　 HYDRA
Hercules' mother .. **ALCMENE**
herd .... **DROVE**
herd of horses .... **CAVIYA**
herd of whales .... **GAM, POD**
herdsman, Swiss .... **SENN**
hereditary right .... **UDAL**
hereditary factor .. **GEN, GENE**
heretic, 4th cent.
　　　　　　 ARIAN, ARIUS
heretofore .... **ERENOW**
Hermes' mother .... **MAIA**
Hermes' son .... **PAN**
hermit . **EREMITE, ANCHORITE**
hero, legendary .... **PALADIN**
Hero's love .... **LEANDER**
heroic .... **EPIC, EPICAL**
heroic poem **EPIC, EPOS, WORK**
heroic song .... **EDDA**
heron .... **EGRET**
heron brood, flock .... **SEDGE**
heron, kind of ...... **BITTERN**

herring .... **ALEC, BRIT, SILL**
herring, grayback ..... **CISCO**
herring keg .... **CADE**
herring small Eur. ...... **SPRAT**
hesitate
　　 DEMUR, FALTER, TEETER
hesitation syllable .... **ER, UM**
Hesperides, one of .... **AEGLE**
Heyward, Du Bose, heroine. **BESS**
Hezekiah's mother .... **ABI**
hiatus .... **GAP, LACUNA**
hickory tree ...... **SHELLBARK**
hidden ..... **INNER, ARCANE,
　　　　 COVERT, LATENT**
hide .... **VEIL, CACHE**
hide of beast ..... **FELL, SKIN**
hide, thongs of .... **RIEM**
hide, undressed .... **KIP**
hides, Russian leather ... **JUFTI**
hiding in .... **PERDU**
high in pitch: mus. ...... **ALT**
high on scale .... **ELA**
high priest ...... **ELI, AARON,
　　　　　　　　 ANNAS**
highest note .... **ELA**
highest point .. **APEX, ZENITH**
highway .... **ITER, PIKE**
highway, Alaska-Canada **ALCAN**
highwayman .. **PAD, LADRONE**
hike .... **TRAMP**
hill .... **TOR**
hill, broad .... **LOMA, LOMITA**
hill dweller, Ceylon .... **TODA**
hill dweller, India ..... **DOGRA**
hill, flat-topped .... **MESA**
hill fort: Ir. .... **RATH**
hill, isolated .... **BUTTE**
hill, pointed .... **TOR**
hill, Rome
　　　 CAELIAN, PALATINE
hill, S. Afr. ...... **KOP, BULT**
hill: Turk. .... **DAGH**
hillock .... **TUMP**
hillside: Scot. .... **BRAE**
hilltop .... **KNAP**
hilt, sword .... **HAFT, HANDLE**
Himalayan animal .... **PANDA**
Himal. broadmouth ..... **RAYA**
Himal. ibex .... **KYL**
Himal. monkshood ...... **ATIS**
Himal. mountain .... **API**
Himal. wild goat . **KRAS, TAHR,
　　　　　　 TAIR, THAR**
hind ...... **ROE, BACK, REAR**
hinder by fear .... **DETER**
hindrance .... **BAR, LET**
Hindu age, cycle .... **YUGA**
Hindu ancestor .... **MANU**
Hindu ascetic .... **JOGI,
　　　　 YATI, YOGI, FAKIR,
　　　　 SADHU, FAKEER**

a
Hindu bible .... VEDA
Hindu charitable gift ... ENAM
Hindu cymbal .... TAL
Hindu deity .... DEVA, RAMA,
SIVA, SHIVA
HINDU DEITY . see also GOD
and see SPECIAL SECTION
Hindu divorce law ..... TALAK
Hindu female slave ..... DASI
Hindu festival .... HOLI
Hindu festival, religious . PUJA
Hindu gentlemen BABU, BABOO
HINDU GODS .... see SPECIAL
SECTION, Page 200, and
also GOD
Hindu guitar .... BINA,
VINA, SITAR
Hindu holy man .... SADH
Hindu laws, giver of ... MANU
Hindu legendary hero ... NALA
Hindu life energy .... JIVA
Hindu, low caste .... KORI
Hindu magic .... MAYA
Hindu mantra .... OM
Hindu mendicant ...... NAGA
Hindu monastery ...... MATH
Hindu "Olympus" ...... MERU
Hindu philosophy ...... YOGA
Hindu poet .... TAGORE
Hindu prince
RAJA, RANA, RAJAH
b Hindu progenitor, myth MANU
Hindu queen .... RANI, RANEE
Hindu religious adherent
JAIN, JAINA
Hindu rites .... ACHARA
Hindu sacred literature .. VEDA
Hindu sacred word .... OM
Hindu scripture ...... AGAMA
Hindu scriptures, pert. to VEDIC
Hindu sect, one of SEIK, SIKH
Hindu teacher .... GURU
Hindu temple .... DEUL
Hindu term of respect SAHIB
Hindu title .... AYA, SRI
Hindu trader
BANIAN, BANYAN
Hindu unknown god ...... KA
Hindu, unorthodox .... JAINA
Hindu widow, suicide .. SUTTEE
Hindu woman's garment
SARI, SAREE
Hindu word .... OM
Hindu writings .... VEDA
Hinduism, elixir
AMRITA, AMREETA
Hindustani .... URDU
hinge, kind of .... BUTT
hint .... TIP, CLEW, POINTER
hip .... COXA, ILIA, ILIAC
hipbone, of the .... ILIAC

c Hippocrates' birthplace ... KOS
Hippodrome .... ARENA
hire
LET, RENT, ENGAGE, CHARTER
hired carriage .... HACK
hired labor: S. Afr. ..... TOGT
history .... LORE
hitherto .... YET
Hittites ancestor .... HETH
hive for bees .... SKEP
hives .... UREDO
hoard .... AMASS, STORE
hoarder .... MISER
hoarfrost .... RIME
hoarfrost: Eng. .... RAG
hoary .... OLD, GRAY
hoax .... RUSE, CANARD
hobgoblin ..... PUCK, SPRITE
hock, horse's ..... GAMBREL
hockey ball .... ORR
hodgepodge ...... MESS, OLIO
hog cholera .... ROUGET
hog deer .... AXIS
hog, female .... GILT
hog plum, W. Ind. AMRA, JOBO
hog, wild .... BOAR, PECCARY
hog's heart, liver, etc. HASLET
Hogan, golfer .... BEN
hoist .... HEAVE
hold, as in war .... INTERN
d hold back .... DETER
hold fast: naut. ...... BELAY
holding .... TENURE
holding device .. VISE, TONGS
hole for molten metal .. SPRUE
hole in embankment .... GIME
hole in mold .... GEAT
hole-in-one .... ACE
holidays, Roman .... FERIA
HOLLAND see NETHERLANDS
SPECIAL SECTION
hollow .... DENT, HOWE
holly .... HOLM, ILEX
holly, U. S. .... ASSI,
YAPON, YUPON, YAUPON
holm oak .... ILEX
"Holy Hill," Gr. ...... ATHOS
Holy Land city .... DAN
holy orders, give .... ORDAIN
holy water font .... STOUP
homage .... HONOR
home .... ABODE
home of gods, Norse .. ASGARD
"Home Sweet Home" author
PAYNE
homeopath school-founder
HERING
Homer's epic .... ODYSSEY
hominy, Indian coarse .. SAMP
honey .... MEL
honey-badger .... RATEL

Honey

a honey buzzard .... **PERN**
honey drink .. **MEAD, MORAT**
honey eater bird
    IAO, MOHO, MANUAO
honeybee .... **DESERET**
honeycomb, like a ... **FAVOSE**
honor .... **EXALT, REVERE**
honorarium .... **TIP**
honorary commission .. **BREVET**
Honshu bay .... **ISE**
Honshu port .... **KOBE**
hooded garment ...... **PARKA**
hoodoo .... **JINX, JYNX**
hoof .... **UNGUES, UNGUIS**
hook, bent into ..... **HAMATE**
hook, double curve .... **ESS**
hook, engine .... **GAB**
hook for pot .... **CLEEK**
hook money .... **LARI, LARIN**
hooks .... **HAMI**
hookah .... **NARGILE**
hooked .... **HAMUS,**
   HAMATE, HAMOSE, FALCATE
Hoover Dam lake ...... **MEAD**
hop-picker's basket ...... **BIN**
hope goddess, Rom. ..... **SPES**
hop plant .... **LUPULUS**
hopscotch stone ...... **PEEVER**
Horae, one of .... **DIKE,**
     EIRENE, EUNOMIA
Horeb .... **SINAI**
b horizontal stripe .... **BAR**
horizontal timber ..... **LINTEL**
horn .... **CORNU**
horn, crescent-moon ..... **CUSP**
horn, Hebr. **SHOFAR, SHOPHAR**
horn quicksilver ..... **CALOMEL**
horn-shaped structure .. **CORNU**
horn sounded for kill .. **MORT**
horn tissue, bit of .... **SCUR**
horneblende .... **EDENITE**
hornless, Eng. dial. ...... **NOT**
hornless stag .... **POLLARD**
hors d'oeuvre .... **CANAPE**
horse .. **BAY, COB, NAG, ARAB,**
   MARE, MERE, ROAN,
   MOUNT, STEED, EQUINE,
   JENNET
horse, Austral. .... **WALER**
horse, Barbary native ... **BARB**
horse blanket .... **MANTA**
horse breed .... **MORGAN**
horse, brown
    BAY, ROAN, SORREL
horse color **BAY, ROAN, SORREL**
horse dealer, Eng. .... **COPER**
horse, disease of .... **SPAVIN**
horse, draft .... **SHIRE**
horse genus .... **EQUUS**
horse: gypsy .. **GRI, GRY, GRAS**
horse-mackerel .... **SCAD**

c horse-man, myth ... **CENTAUR**
horse, piebald .... **PINTO**
horse, race .... **PACER**
horse-radish, fruit of ... **BEN**
horse, saddle .... **MOUNT**
horse, small .... **GENET,**
   GENNET, JENNET, GENETTE
horse, Sp. Am. ...... **CABALLO**
horse, swift .. **ARAB, COURSER**
horse, talking, Gr. .... **ARION**
horse, war .... **CHARGER**
horse, white-flecked ... **ROAN**
horse, wild Asiatic ... **TARPAN**
horse, young .... **COLT, FOAL**
horses, goddess of ..... **EPONA**
horse's sideways tread ... **VOLT**
horsehair .... **SETON**
horsemanship, art of **MANEGE**
horseshoe gripper ...... **CALK**
horseshoeing stall
    TRAVE, TREVE
Horus' mother .... **ISIS**
Hosea's wife .... **GOMER**
host .... **ARMY, HORDE**
hostelry .... **INN**
hot air chamber .... **OVEN**
hot iron to sear ..... **CAUTER**
hot spring, eruptive .. **GEYSER**
Hottentot .... **NAMA**
hourly .... **HORAL**
d house **ROOF, VILLA, COTTAGE**
house, like a .... **DOMAL**
house, mud, Afr. ..... **TEMBE**
house urn: Rom. ... **CAPANNA**
housefly genus ...... **MUSCA**
housefly genus, lesser **FANNIA**
household **MENAGE, MAINPOST**
household god .... **LAR, LARES**
howl .... **ULULATE**
howling monkey **MONO, ARABA**
hub .. **NAVE, BOSTON, CENTER**
hubbub .. **ADO, STIR, TUMULT**
hue .... **COLOR, TINGE**
huge .... **VAST, ENORM**
Huguenot leader ..... **ADRETS**
hull .... **POD, HUSK**
humble .... **ABASE**
hummingbird
   AVA, TOPAZ, COLIBRI
humorist .... **WIT**
humpback salmon
    HADDO, HOLIA
Humphreys, Mrs. (pseudo.)
    RITA
hundred .... **CENTUM**
hundredweight ...... **CENTAL**
Hungarian dog .... **PULI**
Hungarian hero .... **NAGY**
Hungarian king .... **BELA**
Hungarian people ... **MAGYAR**
Hungarian pianist ... **SANDOR**

a
Hungarian playwright **MOLNAR**
Hungarian violinist .... **AUER**
Huns, king of
   ATLI, ETZEL, ATTILA
hunt, Ind. .... **SHIKAR**
hunter ...... **ORION, NIMROD**
hunter, India .... **SHIKARI**
hunting cry .. **HO, YOI, TOHO,**
   HALLOO, YOICKS, TALLY-
   HO
hunting hat .... **TERAI**
hunting hound .... **ALAN**
huntress .... **ATALANTA**
huntsman .... **JAGER**
HUNTSMAN'S CRY see **HUNT-**
   ING CRY
hup: army .... **ONE**
hurdy-gurdy ..... **LIRA, ROTA**
hurry .... **HIE, HASTEN**
hurt .... **MAR, ACHE, LESION**

c
hurt: old Eng. .... **DERE**
hurtful .... **MALEFIC**
husband's brother ...... **LEVIR**
hush .... **SH, HSH**
husk, cereal .... **BRAN**
hut, India .... **BARI**
hut, Mex. .... **JACAL**
hydrate, as lime ..... **SLAKE**
hydraulic pump .... **RAM**
hydrocarbon . **TOLAN, ETHANE,**
   OCTANE, RETENE, TERPENE
hydrogen compound .. **IMINE**
hydrogen isotope ... **PROTIUM**
hymn .... **ODE**
hymn of praise ..... **ANTHEM**
hypnotic state ...... **TRANCE**
hypothetical force
   OD, BIOD, ELOD, ODYL
hypothetical force of ... **ODIC**
hyson .... **TEA**

I

b
! .... **EGO**
"I have found it" .... **EUREKA**
"I love": Lat. .... **AMO**
Iago's wife .... **EMILIA**
Iberians .... **IBERI, IBERES**
ibex .... **KYL, TUR, KAIL**
Ibsen character ... **ASE, NORA**
ice block, glacial ...... **SERAC**
ice mass .... **BERG, FLOE**
ice, slushy ...... **SISH, LOLLY**
iced .... **GLACE**
Iceland epic, literature, tales
   EDDA
Icelandic narrative ..... **SAGA**
icy .... **GELID**
"id —" (that is) .... **EST**
idea, Plato .... **EIDOS**
ideal .... **UTOPIAN**
ideal republic, imaginary
   OCEANA
ideal state .... **UTOPIA**
identical .... **ONE, SAME**
ideology .... **ISM**
idiocy .... **ANOESIA**
idiot ...... **AMENT, CRETIN**
idle .... **OTIANT, OTIOSE**
idle, to be ...... **LAZE, LOAF**
idol: archaic .... **PAGOD**
idol: philos. .... **EIDOLON**
idolatrous .... **PAGAN**
ids, pert. to .... **IDIC**
Idumaea .... **EDOM**
if ever .... **ONCE**
if not .... **ELSE**
ignoble .... **BASE**

d
ignominy .... **SHAME**
ignorance, Hindu philos. **TAMAS**
ignorant .. **STUPID, UNAWARE**
ignore .... **ELIDE**
Igorot's neighbor tribesman **ATA**
ill .... **EVIL**
ill-will .... **SPITE, RANCOR**
illumination unit .... **LUX**
illusion .... **CHIMERA**
illusory riches .... **MINE**
image .... **IDOL,**
   IDOLON, IDOLUM, EIDOLON
image, pert. to ...... **ICONIC**
image, religious .. **ICON, IKON**
imagine: arch. .... **WIS**
imbecile .... **AMENT,**
   ANILE, CRETIN
imbibe .... **SIP, GULP, DRINK**
imitate ... **APE, MIME, MIMIC**
imitation .... **MIMESIS**
imitation gems .... **PASTE**
immature seed .... **OVULE**
immature: zool. ..... **NEANIC**
immeasurable .... **BOUNDLESS**
immediately ..... **NOW, ANON**
immense .... **VAST**
immerse .. **DIP, DUNK, DOUSE**
immigrant, Greek ..... **METIC**
immunizing substance
   SERUM, HAPTEN, HAPTENE
imou pine .... **RIMU**
impair .. **MAR, DAMAGE, SPOIL**
impart .... **GIVE, LEND**
impartial .... **EVEN**
impede ...... **ESTOP, HAMPER**
impel .... **URGE**

79

Impertinent

a

impertinent ..... **PERT, SAUCY**
IMPLEMENT ... see also TOOL
implement, pounding .. **PESTLE**
implement to skid logs .. **TODE**
implied .... **TACIT**
import .... **SENSE**
important, critically ... **VITAL**
importune .... **URGE**
impose .... **LAY**
impost .... **TAX**
imposture .... **SHAM**
impoverish .... **IMPOOR**
impressionist painter .. **DEGAS**
    MANET, MONET, RENOIR
imprison .... **IMMURE**
improve .... **AMEND**
improvise music .... **VAMP**
impudence .... **LIP,**
    BRASS, CHEEK, NERVE
impure metal product .. **MATTE**
in addition .. **TOO, ALSO, YET**
in agreement .... **UNITED**
in disagreement .... **OUT**
in half, in — .... **TWO**
"in medias —" .... **RES**
in name only ...... **NOMINAL**
in same place .... **IBID**
in so far as .... **QUA**
in the know .... **AWARE**
in the matter of .... **INRE**
in the past .... **OVER**

b

in the very near future. .**ANON**
in unison .... **ONE**
in very truth .... **AMEN**
inability to hear ..... **ASONIA**
inactive .... **INERT**
inadequate .... **SCANT**
inborn .... **NATIVE**
incarnation, Hindu .... **RAMA,**
    AVATAR
incense ingredient
    GUM, SPICE, STACTE
incense receptacle, Rom.**ACERRA**
incense, Somali .... **MATTI**
incentive .... **GOAD, MOTIVE**
incessantly .... **EVER**
inch, .001 of .... **MIL**
incidentally .... **OBITER**
incinerate .... **CREMATE**
incite ..... **EGG, PROD, URGE,**
    IMPEL, SET ON, SUBORN
inciter .... **EGGER**
inclination .... **BENT**
incline .. **TEND, SLOPE, TREND**
inclined .... **APT, PRONE**
inclined way .... **RAMP**
income, annual, Fr. .... **RENTE**
incompletely .... **SEMI**
inconsiderable ..... **NOMINAL**
increase .... **WAX, RISE**
incrustation .... **SCAB**

c

incursion, predatory .... **RAID**
indeed: Ir. ...... **ARU, AROO**
indentation
    CRENA, CRENAE, CRENELET
index mark .... **FIST**
INDIA, INDIAN ... see also
    SPECIAL SECTION and see
    also HINDU
India farmer .... **MEO**
India minstrel .... **BHAT**
India native chief .... **SIRDAR**
India native servant ... **MATY**
India: poet. .... **IND**
India, swamp belt of .. **TERAI**
INDIAN .. see also page 192
Indian .... **SAC**
INDIAN, ALGONQUIN .... see
    page 192
Indian, Arawak ...... **ARAUA**
Indian, Arikara .... **REE**
Indian, Athapasca ..... **TAKU**
Indian buzzard .... **TESA**
Indian corn .... **MAIZE**
Indian corn: N. Z. ... **KANGA**
Indian elk .... **SAMBAR**
Indian farmer, Fla. .. **CALUSA**
Indian in Chaco .... **TOBA**
Indian mahogany tree .. **TOON**
Indian mulberry **AL, AAL, ACH**
Indian of Jalisco ...... **CORA**
Indian of Keresan ...... **SIA**
Indian of Mex., scattered **CORA**

d

Indian ox .... **ZEBU**
Indian, Panamint .... **KOSO**
INDIAN, PLAINS . see page 193
Indian race .... **JAT**
Indian shell currency
    ULO, UHLLO
INDIAN, SIOUAN see page 193
Indian, S. Peru ..... **CHANCA**
INDIAN TREE.see TREE, INDIA
Indian, warlike ...... **APACHE**
Indian weight ..... **SER, TOLA**
Indian, whaler .... **HOH**
Indian yellow .... **PURI,**
    PIURI, PURREE
indicating succession **ORDINAL**
indict .... **ARRAIGN**
indifferent to pain
    STOIC, STOICAL
indigo plant .... **ANIL**
indistinct, make ...... **BEDIM**
indite .... **PEN, WRITE**
individual .... **ONE, SELF**
Indo-Chin. native **LAO,MRU,TAI**
Indo-Chin. tribe **TAI,LAOS,SHAN**
Indo-Chin. tribes .... **MOI**
Indo-European **ARYA, ARYAN**
Indo-Malayan animal .: **NAPU**
indolent ...... **OTIOSE, SUPINE**
Indonesian ..... **ATA, NESIOT**

a Induce .... **LEAD**
Indus tribesman .... **GOR**
ineffectual .... **VAIN**
inelastic .... **LIMP**
inert .... **SUPINE**
infatuation .... **ATE**
infertile moor .... **LANDE**
infinity .... **OLAM**
infirm .... **ANILE, SENILE**
inflamed, be .... **RANKLE**
inflammable liquid .. **ACETONE**
inflammation: med. .. **ANGINA**
inflexible .... **IRON, RIGID**
inflict .... **DEAL, IMPOSE**
inflorescence **RACEME, SPADIX**
inflorescence, racemose **AMENT**
influence .... **AFFECT**
informer: slang .... **NARK**
infusion .... **TEA**
ingenuous .... **NAIVE**
inhabitant .... **ITE**
inhabitant of a town ..... **CIT**
inheritance .... **ENTAIL**
inheritor .... **LEGATEE**
initiate .. **OPEN, BEGIN, START**
initiate, Gr. ... **EPOPT, EPOPTA**
injure ... **MAR, HARM, MAIM**
injury ..... **LESION, TRAUMA**
inlaid .... **MOSAIC**
inlaid decoration .... **BUHL**
b inlet .. **ARM, BAY, RIA, FIORD**
inlet: Dutch .... **ZEE**
inlet, Orkneys .... **VOE**
inn .... **KHAN,
   HOSTEL, POSADA, HOSPICE**
Inn, "Canterbury Tales" **TABARD**
inn, Oriental .... **SERAI**
inn, Turkish .... **IMARET**
inner .... **ENTAL**
inner meaning .. **CORE, HEART**
inner parlor: Scot. ...... **BEN**
innkeeper **PADRONE, BONIFACE**
insect ... **ANT, BEE, BUG, DOR,
   FLY, FLEA, GNAT, MITE,
   APHID, CADEW, EMESA,
   BEETLE, CADDIS, CICADA,
   CICALA, MANTIS**
insect, adult .... **IMAGO**
insect body
   THORAX, THORACES
insect, immature ...... **PUPA,
   LARVA, INSTAR**
insect mature .... **IMAGO**
insect order .... **DIPTERA**
insect, plant sucking .. **APHID**
insect, ruinous **APHID, BORER**
insertion mark .... **CARET**
inset .... **PANEL**
insidious .... **SLY**
insincere talk .... **CANT**
insipid, become .... **PALL**

c Insist .... **URGE, PRESS**
inspire .... **IMBUE**
install .... **INSTATE**
instance .... **CASE**
instant .... **MO, TRICE**
instar .. **PUPA, IMAGO, LARVA**
instigate .. **EGG, ABET, INCITE**
instruct ..... **BRIEF, EDUCATE**
INSTRUMENT .. see also MUS-
   ICAL INSTRUMENT
Instrument, Afr. reed
   GORA, GORAH, GOURA
instrument, Chin. ancient **KIN**
instrument, Hebr. ... **TIMBREL**
instrument, India ..... **RUANA**
instrument, Jap. .... **SAMISEN**
instrument, lutelike **BANDORE**
instrument, lyrelike ... **KISSAR**
instrument, math. .... **SECTOR**
instrument, medieval .. **ROCTA**
instrument, naut.
   PELORUS, SEXTANT
instrument, Sp. .... **CASTANET**
instrument, stringed ... **LYRE,
   NABLA, REBAB, REBEC,
   SAROD, SITAR, VIOLA,
   CITHER, CITHARA, CITH-
   ERN, CITTERN, GITTERN**
instrument, surveying **TRANSIT**
instrumentality **MEDIA, MEDIUM**
d insulate .... **ISLE**
insult .... **CAG**
insurgent .... **REBEL**
intact .... **WHOLE**
intellect .... **MIND,
   NOUS, MAHAT, REASON**
inter .... **BURY, INHUME**
intercharged ..... **PERMUTED**
interdict .... **BAN**
interferometer ...... **ETALON**
interior, ancient temple **CELLA**
interjection for silence .... **TST**
interlace .... **WEAVE**
interlock .... **LINK**
international language **RO, IDO**
inter. money unit .... **BANCOR**
international pact ... **ENTENTE**
interpret .... **REDE**
intersect .... **MEET**
interstice, small
   AREOLA, AREOLE
interstices, with .... **AREOLAR**
intervening: law ...... **MESNE**
interweave .. **TWINE, RADDLE**
intimidate **AWE, COW, DAUNT**
intone .... **CHANT**
intoxicant: India ...... **SOMA**
intoxicated .... **SOSH**
intricate .... **DEDAL, DAEDAL,
   GORDIAN**

Intrigue

a   intrigue .... CABAL
introduce
    BROACH, INSERT, PRESENT
introducer of jetties for deepen-
    ing .... EADS
inundation .... SPATE
inveigle ..... LURE, ENTICE
inventor, claim of rights PATENT
inventor, elevator .... OTIS
inventor, sewing machine HOWE
inventor, steam engine WATT
invest ..... ENDOW, ENDUE,
    INDUE, CLOTHE, ORDAIN
invested .... CLAD
investigate .... PROBE
investigator .... TRACER
invite .... ASK, BID
involve ENTAIL, ENTRAMMEL
Io butterfly .... KIHO
iodine source .... KELP
ion, negative .... ANION
ion, positive .... CATION
Ionian city .... TEOS
iota .... JOT, MITE
Iowa college town ...... AMES
ipecac source .... EVEA
IRAN .. see also PERSIAN
Iran, former part of .... ELAM
Iranian .... TAT, KURD
b   Iranian Turk .... SART
irascible .... TESTY
irate .... MAD
Ireland .... EIRE, ERIN
Ireland, old name ..... IERNE
Ireland personified .... IRENA
iridescent gem .... OPAL
iris .... FLAG
iris, Florentine, European ORRIS
iris, layer of .... UVEA
iris, of a layer .... UVEAL
iris root .... ORRIS
IRISH .. see also IRELAND
Irish .... ERSE
Ir. alphabet, early
    OGAM, OGUM
Ir. ancestor IR, MIL, ITH, MILED
Ir. assembly .... DAIL
Ir. church .... KIL
Ir. city, ancient .... TARA
Ir. clan, ancient .... SEPT
Ir. competitive meet .... FEIS
Ir. crowning stone, — Fail LIA
Ir. dramatist .... SYNGE
Ir. exclamation .... ARU,
    AROO, ARRA, WHIST, WURRA
Ir. fairies .... SHEE
Ir. family .... CINEL
Ir. Free State .... EIRE
Irish-Gaelic .... ERSE
Ir. goddess, battle BADB, BODB

c   IR. GODS' MOTHER see page 200
Ir. kings' home .... TARA
Ir. law, tribe .... CINEL
Ir. lower house parliament DAIL
Ir. nobleman .... AIRE
Ir. poet
    AE, COLUM, MOORE, YEATS
Ir. rebel group .... IRA
Ir. tribe .... SIOL
Ir. writing .... OGAM, OGHAM
Irishman .. AIRE, CELT, MICK
iron disulfide .... PYRITE
iron, pert. to .... FERRIC
ironwood ...... ACLE, COLIMA
irony .... SATIRE
Iroquoian .... ERIE
Iroquois demon .... OTKON
irrational number ...... SURD
irregularity .... JOG
irrigation ditch FLUME, SLUICE
irritate .... VEX, GALL, RILE,
    NETTLE, RANKLE
Isaac's son EDOM, ESAU, JACOB
Ishmael .... PARIAH
Ishmael, son of ...... DUMAH
Ishmael's mother ..... HAGAR
isinglass .... MICA
Isis, husband of .... OSIRIS
ISLAM .... see MOSLEM
d   island ... OE, AIT, CAY, KAY,
    KEY, EYOT, HOLM, ILOT,
    ISLE, ATOLL, ISLET, ISLOT
ISLAND, AEGEAN .... see
    GAZETTEER
island, Argyll .... IONA
island, coral .... ATOLL
island, Dodecanese . COO, KOS,
    CASO, LERO, SIMI
island, Great Barrier ... OTEA
island, Gr. (fine marble) PAROS
island, Gr., pert. to ... CRETAN
island, inhabiting an . NESIOTE
ISLAND, INNER HEBRIDES
    see HEBRIDES GAZETTEER
island, Ionian .... ZANTE
island, Micronesia ... PONAPE
island near Ireland ..... ARAN
island, near Italy ...... CAPRI
island off Scotland .... IONA,
    ARRAN
island, Riga Gulf ...... OESEL
island, river AIT, EYOT, HOLM
island, South Seas ...... ARU,
    TAITI, TAHITI, OTAHEITE
island, west of Sumatra .. NIAS
islands, Gulf of Bothnia ALAND
islands, Irish .... ARAN
islands, off Timor ...... LETI
Isle of Man, pert. to ... MANX
islet .... AIT, CAY, HOLM
isolate .... ENISLE

Israel .... **JACOB**
ISRAEL, KING OF ... see KING
OF ISRAEL
ISRAELITE .. see also HEBREW
and BIBLICAL
ISRAELITE JUDGE ...... see
BIBLICAL JUDGE
ISRAELITE KING .. see KING
OF ISRAEL
Israelite tribe .... **DAN**
Israelites .... **SION, ZION**
issue. **EMIT, EMERGE, EMANATE**
isthmus .... **NECK**
istle fiber .... **PITA, PITO**
it proceeds: music .... **VA**
ITALIAN WORDS: (accent marks
omitted throughout)
arts .... **ARTES**
article .... **LA**
canal (s) **CANALE, CANALI**
chest .... **CASSO**
custom house ..... **DOGANA**
day-breeze .... **ORA**
dear .... **CARA, CARO**
dough .... **PASTA**
drink .... **BEVERE**
enough .... **BASTA**
evening .... **SERA**
enthusiasm .... **ESTRO**
feast .... **FESTINO**
field .... **CAMPO**
food .... **PASTO**
from beginning .... **DACAPO**
gentleman .... **SER**
goodby .... **ADDIO**
gondola cabin ...... **FELZE**
hamlet .... **CASAL, CASALE**
hair .... **PELO**
hand .... **MANO**
harbor .... **PORTO**
harp .... **ARPA**
hatred .... **ODIO**
Helen .... **ELENA**
holiday .... **FESTA, FESTE**
host .... **OSTE**
Italy .... **ITALIA**
judge .... **PODESTA**
lady .... **DONNA, SIGNORA**
lake .... **LAGO**
little .... **POCO**
love .... **AMORE**
lover .... **AMOROSO**
mother .... **MADRE**
mountain peak ...... **CIMA**
nine .... **NOVE**
ninth .... **NONO**

one .... **UNO**
paste .... **PASTA**
peak .... **CIMA**
pronoun .... **MIA**
right .... **DESTRO**
Rome .... **ROMA**
sign .... **SEGNO**
somebody .... **UNO**
street .... **CALLE**
three .... **TRE**
time .... **TEMPO**
tour .... **GIRO**
town ..... **CASAL, CASALE**
you .... **TU**
voice .... **VOCE**
well .... **BENE**
with .... **CON**

Italian actress .... **DUSE**
It., ancient
ITALI, OSCAN, SABINE
It. astronomer ...... **GALILEO**
It. author .... **SILONE**
It. car .... **FIAT**
It. cathedral city .... **MILAN**
It. commune .... **ESTE**
It. composer .... **BOITO,**
GUIDO, VERDI, ROSSINI
It. day breeze .... **ORA**
It. family .... **ESTE,**
CENCI, DORIA, MEDICI
It. family royal name ... **ESTE**
It. gambling game ..... **MORA**
It. gentleman .... **SER**
It. guessing game ..... **MORA**
It. lady ..... **DONA, SIGNORA**
It. millet ...... **BUDA, MOHA**
It. painter .... **RENI,**
LIPPI, VINCI, ANDREA,
CRESPI, GIOTTO
It. poet
DANTE, TASSO, ARIOSTO
It. resort .... **LIDO**
It. rice dish .... **RISOTTO**
It.: Rome .... **ROMA**
It. sculptor .... **LEONI**
It. singer .... **AMATO**
It. title, early .... **SER**
It. university city **BARI, PADUA**
It. violin maker ...... **AMATI**
It. wine .... **ASTI**
Italy .... **ITALIA**
itch .... **PSORA**
itemize .... **LIST**
ivory nut ...... **ANTA, TAGUA**
ivy crowned .... **HEDERATED**
ivy thicket .... **TOD**

J

jack in cribbage .... NOB
jack-in-the-pulpit ARAD, AROID
jack tree .... JACA
jackal, Afr. .... THOS
jackal, India .... KOLA
jackal, N. Afr. .... DIEB
jackdaw .... DAW
jackdaw: Scot. .... KAE
JACKET .. see also GARMENT
jacket .. ETON, JUPE, BOLERO
jacket, armor .... ACTON
jacket, Malay .... BAJU
Jackson heroine ... RAMONA
Jacob's brother .. EDOM, ESAU
Jacob's son..DAN, GAD, ASER,
LEVI, ASHER
Jacob's twin brother .... ESAU
Jacob's wife .. LEAH, RACHEL
jaeger gull ..... SKUA, ALLAN
jagged line .... ZAG, ZIG
jai alai .... PELOTA
Jamashid .... YIMA
James II daughter ..... ANNE
Janizaries, Chief of ...... DEY
JAPANESE: . see also SPECIAL
SECTION
Jap. aborigine ... AINO, AINU
Jap. admiral .... ITO
Jap.-Am. .... ISSEI
KIBEI, NISEI, SANSEI
Jap. army reserve ..... HOJU
Jap. army second line ... KOBI
Jap. art of self-defense JUDO
Jap. badge, family ...... MON
Jap. badge, imperial KIRIMON
Jap. beer, rice .... SAKE, SAKI
Jap. beverage .... SAKE
Jap. box, girdle .... INRO
Jap. bush clover ...... HAGI
Jap. cedar .... SUGI
Jap. celery-like vegetable UDO
Jap. cherry .... FUJI
Jap. clogs .... GETA
Jap. deer .... SIKA
Jap. drama ..... NO, KABUKI
Jap. emperor's title ... TENNO
Jap. festival .... BON
Jap. fish .... TAI, FUGU
Jap. food, seaweed
KOBU, KOMBU
Jap. gods .... KAMI
Jap. happiness god
EBISU, HOTEI
Jap. harp .... KOTO
Jap. herb, stout .... UDO

Jap. immigrant .... ISSEI
Jap. mile measure .... RI
Jap. monastery .... TERA
Jap. national park ..... ASO
Jap. naval station ..... KURE
Jap. news agency ... DOMEI
Jap. nobleman .... KUGE
Jap. outcast
ETA, YETA, RONIN
Jap. outer garment
MINO, HAORI, KIMONO
Jap. parliament .... DIET
Jap. perfecture .... FU
Jap. persimmon .... KAKI
Jap. plant .... UDO
Jap. plane .... ZERO
Jap. primitive ... AINO, AINU
Jap. province, old ... ISE, KAI
Jap. receptacle .... INRO
Jap. salad plant .... UDO
Jap. salmon .... MASU
Jap. sash, kimono .... OBI
Jap. school of painting KANO
Jap. ship name .... MARU
Jap. sock .... TABI
Jap. statesman .... ITO
Jap. straw cape .... MINO
Jap. sword .. CATAN, CATTAN
Jap. vegetable ... UDO, GOBO
Jap. verse .... UTA
Jap. village .... MURA
Jap. volcano .... FUJI
Jap. writing .... KANA
Japheth, son of .... GOMER
jar ...... EWER, OLLA, CRUSE
jar ring .... LUTE
jar, wide-mouthed ...... OLLA
jargon CANT, ARGOT, PATOIS
Jason's father .... AESON
Jason's 2d wife ..... CREUSA
Jason's ship .... ARGO
Jason's wife .... MEDEA
jaunty .... PERK
Java plum: P. I. ..... DUHAT
Javanese carriage ...... SADO
Javanese language KAVI, KAWI
Javanese poison tree ... UPAS
javelin, Afr. ASSAGAI, ASSEGAI
javelin game .. JERID, JEREED
javelin, Rom. .... PILUM
jeer .... GIBE, SCOFF
jeer at .... TAUNT, DERIDE
Jehoshaphat, father of ... ASA
Jehovah .... GOD
Jehovah: Hebr. .... JAH,
JAVE, JAVEH, YAHWEH

jejune .. **DRY, ARID, BARREN**
jelly base .... **PECTIN**
jelly fruit .... **GUAVA**
jelly, meat .... **ASPIC**
jeopardize .... **ENDANGER**
Jericho, land opposite .. **MOAB**
jersey, woollen ..... **SINGLET**
Jerusalem, ancient name **SALEM**
Jerusalem: poet. ...... **ARIEL**
jest .... **JAPE**
jester ...... **MIME, BUFFOON**
jet, U.S. .... **SABRE, SCORPION**
Jether, son of .... **ARA**
jetty .... **MOLE**
Jew .... **SEMITE**
JEWEL ...... see **GEM, STONE**
jewelry setting .... **PAVE**
jewels, adorn with ..... **BEGEM**
JEWISH .. see also **HEBREW**
Jewish ascetic ...... **ESSENE**
Jewish benediction ... **SHEMA**
Jewish bride .... **KALLAH**
Jewish ceremony **SEDAR, SEDER**
Jewish feast of tabernacles
            SUCCOTH
Jewish festival **PURIM, SEDER**
Jewish law, body of .. **TALMUD**
Jewish marriage contract
            KETUBA
Jewish offering ..... **CORBAN**
Jewish prayer book . **MAHZOR**
Jewish scholar .... **RAB**
Jewish sect, ancient .. **ESSENES**
Jewish teacher ... **REB, RABBI**
Jewish title of honor
            RAB, GAON
Jezebel's husband ..... **AHAB**
Joan of Arc's victory **ORLEANS**
Job's-tears .... **COIX**
jog .... **TROT, NUDGE**
John: Gaelic, Scot. **IAN, EOAN**
John: Ir. .... **EOIN, SEAN**
John: Russ. .... **IVAN**
johnny-cake .... **PONE**
Johnson, Dr., hero .. **RASSELAS**
join ..... **LINK, PAIR, SEAM,
    WELD, YOKE, MERGE,
    UNITE, ATTACH**
join corners ... **MITER, MITRE**
join wood .... **RABBET**
joining bar .... **YOKE**
joint **HIP, KNEE, NODE, HINGE**
joint part **TENON, MORTISE**
joke with **KID, RIB, JAPE, JOSH**
joker .... **WAG, WIT**
Jordan city, ancient region
            PETRA
Joseph's father .... **JACOB**
Joseph's nephew .... **TOLA**

Joshua tree .... **YUCCA**
Joshua's father .... **NUN**
jostle .... **JOG, ELBOW**
jot .... **IOTA, TITTLE**
journey .... **ITER, RIDE, TOUR,
    TREK, TRIP, TRAVEL**
journey in circuit .... **EYRE**
joy ...... **DELIGHT, RAPTURE**
joyous .... **GLAD**
Judah, city in ... **ADAR, ENAM**
Judah's son .... **ER, ONAN**
Judaism scriptures
            TORA, TORAH
judge .. **DEEM, RATE, ARBITER**
JUDGE, BIB. ... see **BIBLICAL
            JUDGE**
Judge in Hades ...... **MINOS**
judge of dead, Egypt ... **OSIRIS**
judge's bench .... **BANC**
judge's chamber .... **CAMERA**
judges' rule, Israel **KRITARCHY**
judgment, Fr. law ..... **ARRET**
JUDICIAL see also **LEGAL, LAW**
judicial assembly ..... **COURT**
jug, large beer ..... **RANTER**
jug shaped like man ... **TOBY**
jug, wide-mouthed .... **EWER**
juice .... **SAP**
juice, thickened .... **RHOB**
jujitsu .... **JUDO**
jujube .... **BER, ELB**
Jules Verne character ... **NEMO**
Juliet's betrothed ...... **PARIS**
Juliet's father, family **CAPULET**
jumble .... **PI, PIE, MESS**
jump: music .... **SALTO**
jumping disease, Malay **LATA**
jumping rodent ..... **JERBOA**
juncture, line of .... **SEAM**
June bug .... **DOR**
Jungfrau's site .... **ALPS**
jungle clearing .... **MILPA**
juniper .... **GORSE,
    SAVIN, SABINE, SAVINE**
juniper, Europ. .... **CADE**
juniper tree, Bibl. **EZEL, RETEM**
Jupiter .... **JOVE**
Jupiter's moon, inner ..... **IO**
Jupiter's wife .... **HERA, JUNO**
jurisdiction .... **VENUE**
jurisdiction, old Eng. **SOC, SOKE**
jurisprudence .... **LAW**
jury list .... **PANEL**
jury, writ summoning **VENIRE**
just .... **MORAL**
justice, goddess of . **MA, MAAT**
jute .... **DESI**
Jutlander .... **DANE**
jutting rock .... **TOR**
juxtaposition, place in **APPOSE**
lynx .... **SPELL**

K

Kaffir language .... XOSA
Kaffir tribe .... ZULU
Kaffir war club .... KIRI
Kaffir warrior .... IMPI
Kalmuck ..... ELEUT, ELEUTH
Kandh language .... KUI
kangaroo, male ...... BOOMER
kangaroo, young .... JOEY
Katmandu's country ... NEPAL
kava .... AVA
kava bowl .... TANOA
Kaw .... AKHA
Keats poem-1820 .... LAMIA
keel .... CAREEN
keel, at right angle to ABEAM
keel block wedge ... TEMPLET
keel, having no ...... RATITE
keel, kind of .... FIN
keel, part of .... SKEG
keel-shaped part
        CARINA, CARINAE
keen ACUTE, SHARP, ASTUTE
keep account of .... TAB
keepsake .... TOKEN
keeve .... KIVER
Kentucky coffee tree . CHICOT
Kentucky college ..... BEREA
kerchief .... MADRAS
kernel .... NUT
ketch, Levant .... SAIC
ketone, liquid ...... ACETONE
ketone, oily .... CARONE
kettledrum .. NAKER, ATABAL,
    ATTABAL, TIMPANI, TIM-
    PANO, TYMPANO
key .... ISLE
key fruit .... SAMARA
key notch .... WARD
key part .... BIT
key-shaped ...... URDE, URDY
keyed up .... AGOG
Khedive's estate ...... DAIRA
kid, undressed .... SUEDE
kidney .... NEER
kidney bean .... BON
kidneys, pert. to ..... RENAL
killer whale .... ORCA
kiln ...... OST, OAST, OVEN
kiloliter .... STERE
kind
    ILK, SORT, GENRE, SPECIES
kind: Gr. .... GENOS
kindle: dialect .... TIND
kindly .... BENIGN
kindness .... LENITY
kindred .... SIB

king .... REX, REY, REGES
king —, cartoon character
                    AROO
King Alfred's city: abbr. .. LON
king, Amalekite .... AGAG
King Arthur's abode
    AVALON, AVALLON, CAMELOT
King Arthur's burial place
        AVALON, AVALLON
King Arthur's court CAMELOT
King Arthur's father .. UTHER
King Arthur's fool .. DAGONET
King Arthur's lance ..... RON
King Arthur's mother IGERNA,
    IGERNE, YGERNE, IGRAINE
King Arthur's queen
    GUINEVER, GUINEVERE
KING, BIBLICAL .... see
            BIBLICAL KING
King Ethelred "The —"
                  UNREADY
king, Gr. .... MINOS
King Gradlon's capital .... IS
king, Hebrew .... HEROD
king, Midianite .... REBA
king, mythical .... MIDAS
king of beasts .... LION
King of Colchis' daughter
                  MEDEA
king of Crete .... MINOS
king of elves ...... ERLKING
king of gods, Egypt
    AMEN, AMON, AMUN
king of Greece, ancient MINOS
king of Israel ... AHAB, ELAH,
    OMRI, SAUL, NADAB
king of Jews .... HEROD
king of Judah ... ASA, AHAZ,
    AMON, UZZIAH
king of Judea .... HEROD
king of Naples ...... MURAT
king of Persia .... CYRUS
king of Sodom .... BERA
king, pert. to .... REGNAL
king, Phrygian .... MIDAS
king, rich .... CROESUS
king, Spartan AGIS, LEONIDAS
king, Teut. Visigoth .. ALARIC
king's bodyguard ..... THANE
king's yellow ...... ORPIMENT
KINGDOM ..see also COUNTRY
kingdom, ancient ...... MOAB
KINGDOM, BIB. .. see page 197
kingfish .... HAKU, OPAH
kinkajou .... POTTO
kinship, Moslem law ... NASAB
Kipling hero .... KIM

a
kismet .... FATE
kiss .... BUSS, SMACK
kitchen, ship's ...... GALLEY
kitchen tool
    CORER, RICER, GRATER
kite, bird
    GLED, GLEDE, ELANET
kittiwake gull, Shetlands WAEG
kitty, feed the .... ANTE
kiwi .... ROA
knave .... ROGUE
knave, in cribbage ..... NOBS
knave of clubs .... PAM
knead .... ELT
knead, in massage .... PETRIE
knee: Lat. .... GENU
kneecap ... ROTULA, PATELLA
KNIFE .. see also DAGGER
knife .... CHIV, STAB,
    MACHETE, MACHETTE
knife, Burmese .... DAH, DOW
knife dealer .... CUTLER
knife, Eskimo .... ULU
knife, large ...... SNY, SNEE
knife, loop-cutting
    TREVAT, TRIVAT, TRIVET
knife, P. I. .... BOLO
knife, single-edge .... BOWIE
knife, surgical .... SCALPEL
knight SIR, RITTER, TEMPLAR
knight, heroic ...... PALADIN
knight, make .... DUB
knight, medieval ...... BEVIS
knight's mantel ..... TABARD

c
knight's wife .... DAME
knitting stitch .... PURL
knob: anat. .... CAPUT
knobbed .... TOROSE
knoblike .... NODAL
knobkerrie .... KIRI
knockout .... KO, KAYO
knot ..... MILE, NODE, NODI,
    SNAG, GNARL, KNURL,
    NODUS
knot, fiber .... NOIL, NOYL
knot in wood .... BURL,
    KNAR, KNOR, KNUR, NURL
knot, insecure ..... GRANNY
knot lace .... TAT, TATT
knot, like a .... NODAL
knot of thread .... BURL
knots, fiber .... NEP
knots, having .... NODED
know .... KEN, WIST
knowledge .... KEN, LORE
knowledge, pert. to .. GNOSTIC
knowledge, pure ..... NOESIS
known as milo maize, grain
    MILO
knucklebones, sheep ... DOLOS
kobold .... NIS, NISSE
Kol dialect .... HO
kopecks, 100 .... RUBLE
Koran chapter .... SURA
Koran interpreters .... ULEMA
Korea .... CHOSEN
Korean president ..... RHEE
Korean soldier .... ROK
Kronos' wife .... RHEA
kurrajong tree .... CALOOL

L

b
"La Boheme" heroine ... MIMI
Laban, daughter of .... LEAH
label .... TAG, PASTER
LABOR GROUP ... see UNION
laborer, China . COOLY, COOLIE
laborer, India .... TOTY
Labrador tea .... LEDUM
labyrinth .... MAZE
lac .... RESIN
lace .... BEAT, LASH
lace, barred GRILLE, GRILLEE
lace, Fr. ... CLUNY, ALENCON
lace, gold, silver .... ORRIS
lace, metal tip of
    AGLET, AIGLET
lace, square hole ...... FILET
lacerate .... RIP, TEAR
laceration .... RIP, TEAR
lack .... NEED, WANT
lack of power .... ATONY

d
Laconian clan group ..... OBE
Laconian subdivision ..... OBE
ladder, scale fort wall with
    SCALADE, SCALADO, ES-
    CALADE, ESCALADO
ladderlike .... SCALAR
lady, India .... BIBI
"Lady of the Lake" outlaw DHU
ladylove, in poetry .... DELIA
lagoon .... LIMAN
lake .... MERE
lake, Afr. salt .. SHAT, SHOTT
lake, Blue Nile source .. TANA
Lake Erie battle officer PERRY
Lake, Great (5) ERIE, HURON,
    ONTARIO, MICHIGAN, SU-
    PERIOR
lake, mountain .... TARN
lake near Galilee sea .. MEROM
lake, resort .... TAHOE

a lake: Scot. .... LOCH
Lake Tahoe trout ...... POGY
lake whitefish .... POLLAN
lama, head .... DALAI
lamb .... EAN, EWE, YEAN
lamb, holy .... AGNUS
lamb: Lat. .... AGNI, AGNUS
lamb, young .... COSSET
Lamb's pen name ...... ELIA
Lamech, ancestor of ... CAIN
Lamech's son
        NOAH, JABAL, JUBAL
lament .... KEEN, WAIL,
        WEEP, GRIEVE, PLAINT
lamentation .... LINOS
lamp black .... SOOT
lamprey .... EEL
lance head .... MORNE
lance, mythical .... RON
lance rest, breastplate FAUCRE
lance, short .... DART
Lancelot's beloved ... ELAINE
lancer, Ger. ... ULAN, UHLAN
lancewood .... CIGUA
land, absolute property ALOD,
    ALLOD, ALODIUM, ALLODIUM
land amid water .. ISLE, ISLET
land breeze .... TERRAL
land, church's .... GLEBE

b land held in fee simple
        ODAL, UDAL
land: law .... SOLUM
LAND MEASURE .. see also
    AREA in SPECIAL SECTION
land measure
    AR, ARE, ROD, ACRE, ROOD
land ownership, pert. to ODAL
land snail genus ...:. CERION
land spring .... LAVANT
land, tilled, plowed: Sp.
        ARADA, ARADO
land under tenure: Scot. .. FEU
landing place ..... KEY, PIER,
        QUAI, QUAY, LEVEE
landing place, India
        GAUT, GHAT
landing ship .... LST
landmark .... COPA
landmark: Sp. .... SENAL
lands .... ACRES
language, Aramaic ... SYRIAC
language, Assam .... AO, AKA
language, dead .... LATIN
language, early It. .... OSCAN
language, Egypt. ..... COPTIC
language, Finnish ..... UGRIC
language form, peculiarity
        IDIOM
language, Gilgit ...... SHINA
language, Hittite ...... PALA
language, Indic .... HINDI

c language, Indo-Chin. ..... AO,
    WA, AKA, ANU, LAI, LAO,
    MRO, MRU, PWO, SAK,
    AHOM, AKHA, AMOY,
    BODO, GARO, KAMI, NAGA,
    RONG, SGAU, SHAN
language, Ir. .. CELTIC, KELTIC
language, Kandh .... KUI
language, Kashmir .... SHINA
language, Mossi .... MO, MOLE
language, N. Afr. .... BERBER
language of Bible days
        ARAMAIC
language, P. I.
        TAGAL, TAGALOG
language, Scot. CELTIC, KELTIC
language, Semitic .... ARABIC
language, Siberian
        ENISEI, YENISEI
language, S. Afr. .... TAAL
language, Sudanic MO, MOLE
language, synthetic .. RO, IDO
language, Welsh CELTIC,KELTIC
languages, E. Europ. ... UGRIC
languish .... FLAG, PINE
languor, drug-induced
        KEF, KAIF, KIFF
langur .... MAHA
lantern feast .... BON

d Laomedon's father ...... ILUS
Laomedon's son
        PRIAM, TITHONUS
Laos aborigine ... KHA, YUN
lapel .... REVER
lapidate .... STONE
Lapp's sledge ... PULK, PULKA
larboard .... APORT
larch TAMARAC, TAMARACK
large amount .... SCAD
lariat .... LAZO, ROPE,
        LASSO, REATA, RIATA
lariat, metal eye of
    HONDA, HONDO, HONDOO
larva .... GRUB
larva of fly ...... BOT, BOTT
lash .... TIE, WHIP
lasso
    ROPE, REATA, RIATA, LARIAT
last .... FINAL, OMEGA
last but one .... PENULT
"Last Days of Pompeii" char-
    acter .... IONE
last Imam .... MAHDI
last section .... FINALE
Last Supper picture .... CENA
Last Supper room .. CENACLE
latching: naut. .... LASKET
late ... NEW, TARDY, RECENT
late, one at school ..... SERO
lateen-rigged boat ..... DOW,
    DHOW, SETEE, MISTIC

a latent .... DORMANT
lateral .... SIDE
lath .... SLAT
LATIN .... see also ROMAN
LATIN:
abbot .... ABBAS
above ...... SUPER, SUPRA
about .... CIRCITER
across .... TRANS
act .... ACTU, ACTUS
after .... POST
aged .... AET (abbr.)
all .... TOTO
alone .... SOLO, SOLUS
and .... ET
and others .... ETAL (abbr.)
around .... CIRCUM
art .... ARS
backward .... RETRO
before .... ANTE
behold .... ECCE
being .... ESSE
believe, I .... CREDO
beneath .... INERA
bird .... AVIS
book .... LIBER
blessed .... BEATA
bronze .... AES
but .... SED
cattle .... PECORA
b country .... RUS, RURIS
cup .... CALIX
custom .... RITUS
day .... DIEM
days .... DIES
depart! .... VADE
divination by lots .... SORS,
SORTES
door .... JANUA
earth .... TERRA
egg .... OVUM
eight .... OCTO
error .... LAPSUS
event .... REI
evil .... MALA, MALUM
fate .... NONA
field .... AGER
fields .... AGRI
fire .... IGNIS
first .... PRIMUS
fish .... PISCES
force .... VIS
from .... DE
go! .... VADE
god .... DEUS
goddess .... DEA
gods .... DI
gold .... AURUM
good ...... BONUM, BONUS
grandfather .... AVUS
he .... ILLE

c he remains .... MANET
he was .... ERAT
head .... CAPUT
high .... ALTA
himself .... IPSE
I love .... AMO
in so far as .... QUA
is .... EST
itself .... IPSO
ivory .... EBUR
journey .... ITER
knee .... GENU
lamb .... AGNI, AGNUS
land .... AGER
learned .... DOCTUS
life .... VITA, ANIMA
lo .... ECCE
man .... VIR
mass .... MISSA
mine .... MEUM
more than .... SUPER
mountain .... MONS
name .... NOMEN
nose, of the .... NAS
not .... NON
observe .... NOTA
offense ..... MALA, MALUM
d once .... SEMEL
or .... AUT
other .... ALIA
over .... SUPER
pardon .... VENIA
palm .... VOLA
part .... PARS
partly .... PARTIM
peace .... PAX
pin .... ACUS
pledge .... VAS
possessive .... SUA
power .... VIS
pronoun .... SUA
property .... BONA
quickly .... CITO
rate .... RATA
religious law .... FAS
right .... DEXTER
same .... IDEM
scarcely VIX
see .... VIDE
side .... LATUS
table .... MENSA
tail .... CAUDA
that is .... "ID EST"
that one .... ILLE
the same .... IDEM
thing .... RES

Latin

LATIN(continued from page 89)

this one .... HIC, HAEC
thus .... SIC
throat .... GULA
to be .... ESSE
to use .... UTOR
tooth .... DENS
toward .... AD
twice .... BIS
under .... SUB
unless .... NISI
vein .... VENA
voice .... VOX
water .... AQUA
we .... NOS
well .... BENE
where .... UBI
within .... INTRA
without .... SINE
wool .... LANA
wrong ...... MALA, MALUM

Latvia, native of .... LETT
laugh .... FLEER
laugh, able to .... RISIBLE
laughing .... RIANT
laughing, pert. to .. GELASTIC
laurel .... BAY, DAPHNE
laurel bark, medicinal .. COTO
lava .... AA, LATITE, SCORIA
lava, rough .... AA
lavender, Eur. .... ASPIC
lavish affection .... DOTE
law
    JURE, RULE, CANON, EDICT
law, abstract .... JUS
law, D. E. Ind. .... ADAT
law excluding women from
    reign .... SALIC
law of Moses .. TORA, TORAH
law, Rom. .... JUS, LEX
lawful .... LEGAL, LICIT
lawgiver, Gr.
    DRACO, MINOS, SOLON
lawgiver, Hebr. .... MOSES
lawmaker .... SOLON
lawyer .... LEGIST
lawyers' patron saint ... IVES
lay .... PUT, DITTY
layer .... PLY,
    LAMINA, STRATA, STRATUM
layer of a plant ..... PROVINE
layer, wood .... VENEER
layman .... LAIC
lazar .... LEPER
lazy .... OTIOSE
lead-colored .... LIVID
lead: music PRESA, PRECENT
lead, ore .... GALENA

lead, pellets of .... SHOT
lead, pencil ...... GRAPHITE
lead sulphide, native GALENA
lead telluride ...... ALTAITE
lead, white .... CERUSE
leaden color, having ... LIVID
leader, fishing .... SNELL
leader of movement .... VAN
leader, Rom. .... DUX
leaf appendage ...... STIPEL
leaf-cutting ant ...... ATTA
leaf division .... LOBE
leaf, fern .... FROND
leaf, flower .... BRACT, SEPAL
leaf-miner beetle ..... HISPA
leaf of book .... FOLIO
leaf vein .... RIB
league, Ger. .... BUND
league, trading .... HANSE
Leah's father .... LABAN
Leah's son .... LEVI
lean .. CANT, GAUNT, SPARE
lean-to .... SHED
Leander's love .... HERO
"Leaning Tower" city .... PISA
leap LUNGE, VAULT, CURVET
leap: music .... SALTO
leap: Scot. LOUP, LOWP, STEND
leaping .... SALTANT
learned .. ERUDITE, LETTERED
learning .... LORE
learning, man of
    SAGE, PEDANT, SAVANT
Lear's daughter ...... REGAN
Lear's faithful follower KENT
least bit .... RAP
leather bottle .... MATARA
leather flask, Gr. .... OLPE
leather, glove
    KID, NAPA, MOCHA, SUEDE
leather, kind of ... ELK, BOCK
leather, prepare—make into
    TAN, TAW
leather, soft
    NAPA, ALUTA, SUEDE
leather thong, hawk's .. BRAIL
leatherfish .... LIJA
"leatherneck" .... MARINE
leave
    GO, QUIT, EXEAT, DEPART
leave destitute ...... STRAND
leave of absence, school EXEAT
leave-taking .... CONGE
leaves, having: Her. .. POINTE
leaven .... YEAST
leaving .... ORT
leavings .... DREGS, RESIDUE
Lebanese port, old .... TYRE
ledge, fort .... BERM, BERME
ledger entry
    ITEM, DEBIT, CREDIT

a lee, opposed to .... STOSS
leeangle .. LEAWILL, LEEWILL
leer .... OGLE
Leeward Island .... NEVIS
left: comb. form ...... LEVO
left-hand .... LEVO
left-hand page ... VO, VERSO
left, to turn .... HAW
leftover .... ORT
leg, covering, ancient PEDULE
leg, front of .... SHIN
leg joint, animal .... HOCK
leg-like part .... CRUS
leg of mutton, lamb .. GIGOT
leg, part of .... SHIN, SHANK
leg, pert. to calf of ... SURAL
legal action suit .. RES, CASE
legal claim .... LIEN
legal delays .... MORAE
legal injury .... TORT
legal job .... CASE
legal matter .... RES
legal offense .. DELIT, DELICT
legal order .... WRIT
legal paper .... DEED
legal profession ... BAR, LAW
legal prosecution ...... SUIT
legend ... MYTH, SAGA, TALE
legion division, Rom. COHORT
legislate .... ENACT

b legislative assembly, Afr. RAAS
legislator ... SOLON, SENATOR
legislature ... DIET, SENATE
legislature: Sp. ...... CORTES
legume ..... PEA, POD, BEAN
leisure .... REST, OTIUM
lemur .... MAKI, INDRI,
    LORIS, AYE-AYE, SEMIAPE
lemur, Afr. .... GALAGO
lemur, Asia, Ceylon LORI, LORIS
lemur, Ceylonese .... LORI
lemur, flying .... COLUGO
lemur, ruffed .... VARI
lemuroid .... POTTO
lengthily, address .. PERORATE
Leningrad's river .... NEVA
lens, hand .... READER
lentil .... ERVUM
leopard .... PARD
Leporidae, one of the ... HARE
leprosy .... LEPRA
Lepus genus, one of ..... HARE
lerp .... LAAP
Lesbos, poet of ...... ARION
"Les Etats —" .... UNIS
less .... MINUS
lessen BATE, ABATE, MITIGATE
let HIRE, RENT, LEASE, PERMIT
let bait drop .... DAP
let it stand! .... STA, STET

c let up .... ABATE
lethal .... FATAL
lethargy
    COMA, STUPOR, TORPOR
letter .. AR (18), EF (6), EM
    (13), EN (14), EX (24),
    WY (25), BEE (2), CEE
    (3), DEE (4), ESS (19),
    GEE (7), JAY (10), PEE
    (16), TEE (20), VEE (22),
    WYE (25), ZED (26), ZEE
    (26), AITCH (8)
letter, according to .. LITERAL
letter, Ang.-Sax. .. EDH, ETH
letter, early Gr. .... SAN
LETTER, GR. and NUMBER . see
    also GREEK LETTER
letter, Gr. .. MU, NU, PI, XI,
    CHI, ETA, PHI, PSI, RHO,
    TAU, BETA, IOTA, ZETA,
    ALPHA, DELTA, GAMMA,
    KAPPA, OMEGA, SIGMA,
    THETA, LAMBDA, EPSILON,
    OMICRON, UPSILON
letter, Hebr. HE (5), PE (17),
    AIN (16), MEM (13),
    NUN (14), SIN (21), TAV
    (22), TAW (22), VAU
    (16), WAW (16), ALEF
    (11), AYIN (16), BETH
    (2), CAPH (11), ELEF (1),

d KAPH (11), KOPH (19),
    QOPH (19), RESH (20),
    SADE (18), SHIN (21),
    TETH (9), YODH, (10),
    ALEPH (13), GIMEL (3),
    LAMED (12), DALETH (4),
    LAMEDH (12)
letter of resignation .. DEMIT
letters, sloping ...... ITALICS
lettuce, kind of COS, ROMAINE
Levantine ketch .... SAIC
levee .... DIKE, DYKE
level EVEN, RASE, RAZE, PLANE
leveling slip .... SHIM
lever .... PRY, PEVY, PEAVY,
    PEEVY, PEAVEY, PEEVEY,
    TAPPET
levy .... TAX, CESS, IMPOST
Lew Wallace hero .... HUR
Lhasa holy man .... LAMA
Lhasa's country .... TIBET
liability .... DEBT
liana .... CIPO
liang .... TAEL
liar .... ANANIAS
Liberian native ..... VAI, VEI
Liberian tribes .. GI, KRA, KRU
license: slang .... READER
lichen .... MOSS
lichen genus USNEA, EVERNIA

a
lichen, kind **PARELLA, PARELLE**
lie in wait .... **LURK**
Liege, town near .... **ANS**
liegeman .... **VASSAL**
lieu .... **STEAD**
life .... **BIOS, BIOTA**
life: Lat. ...... **VITA, ANIMA**
life, of .... **VITAL**
life principle .... **PRANA**
life principle, Hindu .. **ATMAN**
life prolonger .... **ELIXIR**
life, relating to
         BIOTIC, BIOTICAL
life tenant .... **LIVIER**
lifeless **AMORT, AZOIC, INERT**
lifetime .... **AGE**
lifted with effort ...... **HOVE**
ligament .... **BOND**
light .... **LAMP, KLEIG,**
         KLIEG, TAPER, ILLUME
light and fine, as lines .. **LEGER**
light as a line .... **LEGER**
light bulb filler ...... **ARGON**
light, circle of
         HALO, NIMB, NIMBUS
light intensity unit ...... **PYR**
light, kind of .... **ARC**
light ring .... **CORONA**
light, science of ..... **OPTICS**
light, sun's **AUREOLA, AUREOLE**

b
light unit **PYR, LUMEN, HEFNER**
lighter, lamp .... **SPILL**
lighter, make .... **LEAVEN**
lighthouse .... **PHAROS**
lightning: poet. .... **LEVIN**
ligulate .... **LORATE**
like .... **AS, AKIN**
likely .... **APT**
likeness .... **ICON, IMAGE**
likewise not .... **NOR**
lily .... **LIS, LYS, ALOE,**
         ARUM, SEGO, CALLA
lily family plant ..... **CAMAS**
         CAMASS, CAMMAS
lily genus .... **ALOE**
lily genus, plantain .... **HOSTA**
Lily Maid of Astolat
         ELAIN, ELAINE
lily, palm .... **TI**
limb ...... **ARM, LEG, MANUS**
limber .... **LITHE**
lime, to hydrate ..... **SLAKE**
lime tree .... **TEIL, TEYL**
limestone, grainy ..... **OOLITE**
limestone, Irish .... **CALP**
limestone, soft **MALM, CHALK**
limicoline bird **SNIPE, PLOVER**
limit .... **TERM, BOURN,**
         STENT, STINT, BOURNE
limn.......... **DRAW, PAINT**
Lindbergh's book .... **WE**

c
linden .... **LIN, TEIL, TEYL**
line .... **ROW, RANK**
line, cutting .... **SECANT**
line, fine, on type letter **CERIF,**
         SERIF, CERIPH
line, fishing .... **SNELL**
line, in a .... **AROW**
line, intersecting ..... **SECANT**
line inside of .... **CEIL**
line, math. .... **VECTOR**
line, naut. . **EARING, MARLINE**
line not forming angle **AGONE**
line on a letter .... **SERIF**
line, pert. to .... **LINEAR**
line, thin ..... **STRIA, STRIAE**
line, waiting .... **CUE, QUEUE**
line with stone **STEAN, STEENE**
lines, marked with
         RULED, STRIATE, STRIATED
lines, telescope-lens .. **RETICLE**
linen .... **CREA**
linen, fine ..... **LAWN, TOILE**
linen, household, table **NAPERY**
linen, one caring for royal
         NAPERER
linen tape, braid ...... **INKLE**
linger .... **WAIT, TARRY**
lingo .... **ARGOT**
lingua .... **GLOSSA**
liniment .... **ARNICA**

d
link .... **YOKE, CATENATE**
links connected ..... **CATENAE**
linnet ...... **TWITE, LENARD**
lion .... **LEO, SIMBA**
lion group .... **PRIDE**
lion killed by Hercules **NEMEAN**
lion of God .... **ALI**
lionet .... **CUB**
lips, pert. to .... **LABIAL**
liqueur .... **CREME, NOYAU**
liqueur, sweet .... **GENEPI**
liquid element
         BROMIN, BROMINE
liquid, made ... **FUSIL, FUSILE**
liquid, without ..... **ANEROID**
liquor .. **GIN, RUM, RYE, GROG**
liquor, malt .... **ALE, PORTER**
liquor, oriental ..... **ARRACK**
liquor, P. I............ **VINO**
liquor, Russian **VODKA, VODKI**
liquor, sugar-cane
         TAFIA, TAFFIA
Lisbon's river .... **TAGUS**
lissome .... **SVELTE**
list .... **ROTA, SLATE,**
ROSTER, CATALOG, CATALOGUE
list of persons
         ROTA, PANEL, ROSTER
list, one of a .... **ITEM**
listen .... **HARK, HEAR**
listless, be .... **MOPE**

a listlessness .. ENNUI, APATHY
liter, Dutch .... AAM, KAN
literary collection .... ANA
literary extracts
    ANALECTA, ANALECTS
literary master ...... STYLIST
literary scraps, bits ANA, NOTES
literate .. LEARNED, LETTERED
lithograph .... CHROMO
Lithuanian .... BALT, LETT
litter, E. Ind. .. DOOLI, DOOLY,
    DOOLEE, DOOLEY, DOOLIE
"Little Boy Blue" poet .. FIELD
little casino .... TWO
little chief hare .... PIKA
little: music .... POCO
liturgy .... RITE
live .... all forms of verb "BE"
live oak, Calif. ...... ENCINA
lively .... PERT, BRISK, PEART
lively, make .... PERK
lively: music
    VIVO, DESTO, ANIMATO
lively person .... GRIG
lively song .... LILT
liver .... HEPAR
liver, pert. to .... HEPATIC
liverwort genus .... RICCIA
b livid .... BLAE
living in currents ...... LOTIC
Livonian LIV
lixivium .... LYE, LEACH
lizard .. GILA, GECKO, GUANA,
    SKINK, VARAN, IGUANA
lizard, Am. .... ANOLE, ANOLI
lizard, beaded .... GILA
lizard, changeable CHAMELEON
lizard genus .... UTA, AGAMA
lizard, large .. GILA, MONITOR
lizard, old world ...... SEPS
lizard, small ..... EFT, GECKO
lizard, starred .... AGAMA
lizard, tropical ...... AGAMA
lizardlike .... SAURIAN
llamalike animal ..... ALPACA
load .... LADE, ONUS
loadstone .... MAGNET
loaf, small: dial. .... BAP
loam .... LOESS
loam, India .... REGUR
loath .... AVERSE
loathe .... ABHOR
lobster box .... CAR
local .... TOPICAL
locale .... SITE
locality .... AREA,
    LOCUS, VENEW, VENUE
location ... SITE, SPOT, PLACE
lock .... CURL, TRESS

c locks, Panama Canal .. GATUN
lockjaw ... TETANUS, TRISMUS
locust .... ACACIA,
    CICADA, CICALA
locust, N. Z. .... WETA
lodge, soldier's .... BILLET
lofty dwelling .... AERIE
log birling contest .... ROLEO
log drive, escape work on SNIB
log, spin floating ...... BIRL
log splitter .... WEDGE
logarithm unit .... BEL
loge .... STALL
logger's implement ... PEAVY,
    PEAVEY
logic, omission of step in
    proof .... SALTUS
logician .... DIALECTOR
Lohengrin's wife .... ELSA
Loire, city on .... BLOIS
loiter .... LAG
Loki's daughter .... HEL, HELA
Loki's son .... NARE
Loki's wife .... SIGYN
London district .... SOHO
long .... YEN, PINE,
    CRAVE, YEARN, ASPIRE
long ago .... ELD, YORE
long journey .. TREK, ODYSSEY
d long line (fishing) with hooks
    TROT
long live! .... VIVA, VIVE
long-suffering .... MEEK
look .... LO, SEE
look after ...... MIND, TEND
look askance .... LEER
look at .... EYE, SCAN, VIEW
look here! .... HIST
look narrowly PEEK, PEEP, PEER
look slyly .... LEER, OGLE
loom, heddles of ...... CAAM
loom, lever in .... LAM
loon genus .... GAVIA
loon, kind of .... DIVER
loop, edging .... PICOT
loophole .... MUSE, MEUSE
looplike structure, anat. ANSA
loose .... LAX
loose coat PALETOT, MANTEVIL
loose robe .... SIMAR
loosen .... UNDO, UNTIE
lop ... SNED, PRUNE, SNATHE
lopsided .... ALOP, ALIST
loquat tree .... BIWA
Lord High Executioner in
    "Mikado" .... KOKO
Lord: Jacobite Church .. MAR
lord, Oriental .... KHAN
lord, Pers. .... KAAN,
    KAUN, KAWN, KHAN
lord, privileged .... PALATINE

Lord

a
lord, Scot. .... LAIRD
lore, Norse .... RUNE
lorica .... CUIRASS
"Lorna Doone" character RIDD
lose .... AMIT
"Lost Chord" finale .... AMEN
lot .... FATE
Lotan's father .... SEIR
Lot's birthplace .... UR
Lot's father .... HARAN
Lot's son .... MOAB
lottery prize .... TERN
lotus enzyme .... LOTASE
Lotus: poet .... LOTE
lotus tree .... SADR
loud: music .... FORTE
loud-voiced one .... STENTOR
loudness, measurement unit
PHON
loudspeaker for high sound
TWEETER
loudspeaker for low sound
WOOFER
Louis XVI's nickname .. VETO
Louisiana county ..... PARISH

b
Louisiana native ..... CREOLE
lounge .... LOAF, LOLL
love . JO, GRA, ADORE, AMOUR
love: Anglo-Irish ...... GRA
love apple .... TOMATO
love feast .... AGAPE
love god
LOVE GOD . see GOD OF LOVE
LOVE GODDESS . see GODDESS
OF LOVE
love, inflame with
ENAMOR, ENAMOUR
love knot .... AMORET
love to excess ... DOAT, DOTE
lover .... ROMEO
"Love's Labour's Lost" constable
DULL
loving
FOND, AMATIVE, AMATORY
low .... MOO, BASE
low caste Hindu .. PASI, TELI
low caste Indian .... DOM,
MAL, GADDI
Lowell, poetess .... AMY
lower ABASE, DEBASE, NETHER
lower: arch. .... VAIL
lower jaw, bird's .... MALA
lower world gods, Rom. MANES
lowest deck .... ORLOP
lowest part of base ... PLINTH

c
lowest point .... NADIR
loyal .... LEAL,
TRUE, STANCH, STAUNCH
loyalist .... TORY
lozenge ..... PASTIL, ROTULA
TROCHE, PASTILE, PASTILLE
loyalty fulfilling religious
obligations: Rom. . PIETAS
Lubeck, pert. to .... LUBS
lucerne .... MEDIC, ALFALFA
luck: Ir. .... CESS
luck, pert. to ..... ALEATORY
lucky stroke .... FLUKE
lugubrious .... SAD
lukewarm .... TEPID
lumber along ...... LOB, LOBB
Lumber State .... see page 208
lumberman .... SAWYER
lumberman's boot .... PAC
lumberman's boots
PACS, OVERS
lumberman's hook ..... PEVY,
PEAVY, PEEVY, PEAVEY,
PEEVEY
luminaire .... LAMP
luminary .... STAR

d
lump .... NUB, WAD,
CLOT, NODE, SWAD
lunar crater .... LINNE
lunar god, Phrygian ..... MEN
luncheon .... TIFFIN
lurch .... CAREEN
lure .... BAIT, DECOY
luster .... GLOSS, SHEEN
lusterless .. DIM, MAT, MATTE
lustrous .... NITID
lute, Oriental .... TAR
luxuriant .... LUSH, RANK
luxuriate .... BASK
Luzon native .... ATA, ITA,
AETA, ATTA, TAGAL,
TAGALA
Luzon negrito .... ATA,
AETA, ITA, ATTA
Luzon pagan .... ITALON
Lynette's knight .... GARETH
lynx, Afr. .... SYAGUSH
lynx, Pers. .... CARACAL
lyrebird genus ...... MENURA
lyric .... ODE, MELIC
lyric Muse .... ERATO
Lytton heroine .... IONE

M

macaque Indian **BRUH, RHESUS**
macaw .... **ARA, ARARA**
macaw, Braz.
    ARA, ARARA, MARACAN
mace-bearer .... **BEADLE**
macerate .... **RET, STEEP**
machine, finishing .... **EDGER**
machine, grain cleaner **AWNER**
machine gun .... **BREN, STEN**
machine, hummeling .. **AWNER**
machine, ore-dressing **VANNER**
machine part
    CAM, PAWL, TAPPET
machine, rubber .. **EXTRUDER**
mackerel net .... **SPILLER**
mackerel, young .... **SPIKE**
Madagascar mammal .. **LEMUR**
Madagascar native .... **HOVA**
madam .... **MUM, MAAM**
madder ..... **RUBIA, MUNJEET**
madder, common Eu. **GARANCE**
madder shrub genus ... **EVEA**
madness .... **MANIA**
mafura tree .... **ROKA**
maggot .... **LARVA**
Magi, one of .... **GASPAR**
magic .... **RUNE**
magic: Hindustan **JADU, JADOO**
magic, pert. to .... **GOETIC**
magic stone .... **AGATE**
magic: W. Ind. .... **OBEAH**
magician .... **MAGE,**
    MAGI, MAGUS, MERLIN
magistrate, Athens **ARCHON**
magistrate, It. .... **DOGE**
magistrate, Rom. ..... **EDILE,**
    AEDILE, CONSUL, PRETOR
magnate ... **MOGUL, TYCOON**
magnifying glass .... **LENS**
Magog, ruler of .... **GOG**
magpie .. **MAG, PIE, MAGG,**
    PIET, PIOT, PYAT, PYET,
    NINUT, PIANET
magpie genus .... **PICA**
mah-jongg piece .... **TILE**
mahatma
    ARAHT, ARHAT, ARAHAT
mahogany pine ...... **TOTARA**
mahogany, Sp. .... **CAOBA**
mahogany streak .... **ROE**
mahogany tree, Ind. ... **TOON**
MAHOMET .. see MOHAMMED
MAHOMETAN ... see MOSLEM
maid .... **LASS, BONNE**
maid, lady's .... **ABIGAIL**
maid-of-all-work ..... **SLAVEY**
maid, Oriental
    AMA, IYA, AMAH, EYAH
maiden .... **DAMSEL**

maiden name, signifying.. **NEE**
maiden of myth .... **IO**
mail .... **POST, SEND**
mail, coat of . **BRINIE, BYRNIE**
mail, India **DAK, DAUK, DAWK**
main point ... **NUB, GIST, PITH**
maintain. **AVER, HOLD, ASSERT**
maize .... **CORN**
maize bread .... **PIKI**
maize genus .... **ZEA**
major: music .... **DUR**
major third: Gr. mus. .. **DITONE**
make .... **RENDER**
make as one: obs. ...... **UNE**
make evident .... **EVINCE**
make fast: naut. ...... **BELAY**
make good by action . **REDEEM**
make happy .... **ELATE**
make public: Old Eng. **DELATE**
Makua .... **KUA**
malarial fever .... **AGUE**
malarial poison
    MIASM, MIASMA
Malay apple .... **KAWIKA**
Malay canoe
    PRAH, PRAO, PRAU, PROA
Malay chief or headman. **DATO,**
    DATU, DATTO
Malay dagger ... **CRIS, KRIS,**
    CREES, KREES, CREESE, KREESE
Malay lanseh tree ..... **DUKU**
Malay law .... **ADAT**
Malay lugger .... **TOUP**
malay negrito ..... **ATA, ITA**
Malay nerve ailment ... **LATA**
MALAY OUTRIGGER see MALAY
    CANOE
Malay title of respect .. **TUAN**
Malay ungulate ...... **TAPIR**
Malay verse form ... **PANTUN**
Malay vessel
    PRAH, PRAO, PRAU, PROA
Malay, word meaning dark **AETA**
Malayan ape .... **LAR**
male cat .... **GIB, TOM**
male figure, used as support
    ATLAS, TELAMON
male swan .... **COB**
malefic .... **EVIL**
malic acid, fruit with
    ATTA, APPLE, GRAPE
malign .... **REVILE**
malignant .... **EVIL**
malignant spirit ... **KER, KERES**
malleable ..... **SOFT, DUCTILE**
mallet .... **MALL, GAVEL**
malt drink, pert. to ..... **ALY**
malt infusion .... **WORT**
maltreat .... **ABUSE**

Mammal

MAMMAL .. see also ANIMAL
mammal, sea aquatic .. SEAL,
OTTER, WHALE, DUGONG,
MANATEE
mammoth .... GIANT
man-eating monster ... LAMIA
man, handsome ...... ADONIS
man, rich .... CROESUS
man's name .. ELI, GUY, IAN,
IRA, JOB, LEE, RAY, REX,
ADAM, ALAN, AMOS,
BRAM, CARL, DANA, DION,
EBEN, EMIL, ENOS, ERIC,
EVAN, EZRA, HANS, HUGH,
HUGO, IVAN, JOEL, JOHN,
JOSE, JUAN, JUDE, KARL,
KNUT, LEON, LUKE, MARC,
MARK, NEIL, NOEL, OTTO,
OWEN, PAUL, SEAN, SETH,
TEIG, BASIL, CALEB,
CLARE, ENOCH, HIRAM,
HOMER, SERGE, STEVE,
TERRY, DEXTER, GASPAR,
GEORGE, OLIVER, SAMSON,
STEVEN, WARREN
man's nickname. AL, ABE, ALF,
BEN, BOB, DON, GUS, JIM,
JOE, KIT, LEW, LON, LOU,
MAC, MAT, MAX, MOE,
NED, PAT, ROB, SAM, SID,
SIM, TED, TOM, ABIE,
ALGY, ANDY, BART, BERT,
BILL, BONY, DAVE, DAVY,
DICK, DODE, FRED, GENE,
JACK, JAKE, JOCK, JOEY,
MART, MIKE, MOSE, NOLL,
PETE, PHIL, RUBE, TOBY,
TONY, WALT, ZACH, ZEKE
manageable .... YARE
manager .... GERENT
Manasseh, city of ...... ANER
Manasseh, son of ..... AMON
mandarin's home
YAMEN, YAMUN
manducate .... EAT
maned .... JUBATE
manger ...... CRIB, CRECHE
mangle .... MAUL
mango, P. I. ...... CARABAO
mania .... CRAZE
manifest .... SHOW,
OVERT, ATTEST, EVINCE
manifestation .... AURA
manifestation of god of lower
world .... SERAPIS
maniple FANO, FANON, FANUM
manner
AIR, WAY, MIEN, MODE
manner of walking ..... GAIT
manners .... MORES
manor .... DEMENE, DEMESNE

mantis crab .... SQUILLA
mantle .... CAPE
manual training, Swed. . SLOID,
SLOYD
manuao .... IAO
Manxman .... GAEL
many .... MAINT
many-colored
PIED, PINTO, MOTLEY
many-colored stone ... AGATE
Maori tattooing .... MOKO
Maori village ... KAIK, KAIKA
Maori wages .... UTU
Maori war club MERE, MARREE
Maori war-club wood ... RATA
map .... PLAT
map in a map .... INSET
maple fruit, seed .... SAMARA
maple genus .... ACER
maple tree tap .... SPILE
mar .... DEFACE
marabou .... ARGALA
marble MIB, MIG, TAW, MIGG,
AGATE, AGGIE, MARMOR,
MEALIE, SHOOTER
marble, Belgian RANCE, RANSE
marble, choice ALAY, ALLEY
marble, It. .... CARRARA
marble, Rom. .... CIPOLIN
marble, white .... DOLOMITE
marbles, game at ...... TAW
March King .... SOUSA
mare: Gypsy .... GRASNI
margin .... RIM, EDGE, MARGE
marginal reading, Hebrew
Bible .... KRI
margosa tree .... NIM, NEEM
Marie Wilson, character played
by .... IRMA
MARINE .. see also SEA
marine annelid .... LURG
marine fish, E. Ind. ... DORAB
marine measure, Jap. ..... RI
marine snail
WELK, WILK, WHELK
marine snail genus .. NERITA
marine turtle genus..CARETTA
marine worm .... SYLLID
marionette maker ...... SARG
mark .... STIGMA, STIGMATA
mark, diacritic TILDE, MACRON
mark of omission ..... CARET
mark, reference
OBELI, OBELUS, OBELISK
mark, short vowel .... BREVE
marked with spots: bot. NOTATE
marker, Gr. & Rom. ... STELA,
STELE, STELAE, STELAI

96

a market .... MART, SELL,
                    VEND, RIALTO
market: India .... PASAR
market, Oriental
                SUQ, SOOK, SOUK
market place BAZAR, BAZAAR
market place, Gr. .... AGORA
marksman .... AIMER
marmalade tree
                MAMEY, SAPOTE
marmoset .... MICO
marmoset, S. Am. .. TAMARIN
"Marner, — " Eliot novel SILAS
marriage, absence of .. AGAMY
marriage notice BAN, BANNS
marriage portion, pert. to
                DOTAL
marriage portion: Scot.
                DOS, DOTE
marriage settlement
DOS, DOT, DOWRY, DOWERY
marriage vows .... TROTH
marriageable .... NUBILE
marrow .... PITH
marry .... WED, WIVE
Mars .... ARES
Mars' outer satellite .. DEIMOS
Mars, pert. to .... AREAN
"Marseillaise" author ... LISLE

b marsh .... BOG, FEN,
            SLUE, LIMAN, SWALE
marsh elder .... IVA
marsh fever .... HELODES
marsh gas .... METHANE
marsh hen .... RAIL
marsh mallow .... ALTEA
marsh marigold ...... CAPER
marsh plant
        REED, SEDGE, FESCUE
marshal, Waterloo .... NEY
marshy . PALUDAL, PALUDINE
marsupial, arboreal
        COALA, KOALA, POSSUM
marten .... SOBOL
martyr, 1st Christian . STEPHEN
marvel .... MIRACLE
Mascagni heroine .... LOLA
MASCULINE
            see also MALE, MAN'S
mashy .... IRON
masjid ...... MOSK, MOSQUE
mask, half .... DOMINO
mask topknot, Gr. ..... ONKOS
masons' pickax ...... GURLET
masquerade cloak ... DOMINO
mass ...... GOB, WAD, BULK
mass book .... MISSAL
mass meeting .... RALLY
mass, pert. to .... MISSATICAL
mass, rounded .... BOLUS
mast .... SPAR

c mast: obs. .... SPIR
mast, support .... BIBB
mast, wood for .... POON
master: archaic .... DAN
master, India
        MIAN, SAHEB, SAHIB
master, pert. to .... HERILE
master, S. Afr. .... BAAS
master-stroke .... COUP
mastic tree .... ACOMA
masticate ...... CHAW, CHEW
mat, ornamental ...... DOILY
match, friction . FUSEE, FUZEE
match, wax .... VESTA
matchmaker .... EROS
MATERIAL ... see also FABRIC
maternity goddess, Egypt . APET
matgrass .... NARD
math quantity .SINE, OPERAND
math ratio, quantity .. PI, SINE
math term, hyperbolic function
        COSH, SECH, SINH, TANH
matter: law .... RES
matter-of-fact ...... LITERAL
matter: philos. .... HYLE
mattress case .... TICK
mature ...... AGE, RIPE, RIPEN
mature reproductive cell
                GAMETE

d maul .... MALLET
Mau Mau territory .... KENYA
Mauna — .... LOA
mausoleum, at Agra ..... TAJ
maw: dialect .... MAA
maxilla .... JAW, MALA
maxim . SAW, ADAGE, AXIOM,
        GNOME, MOTTO, SAYING
maxwell per ampere turn . PERM
May 1, Celtic ...... BELTANE
May fly .... DUN
MAYAN . see MAYAN INDIAN,
                page 192
Mayan year .... HAAB
Mayan year-end days .. UAYEB
mayor, Sp. . ALCADE, ALCALDE
meadow .... LEA, MEAD
meadow barley .... RIE
meadow grass genus ..... POA
meadow mouse .... VOLE
meadow saxifrage ..... SESELI
meadowsweet SPIREA, SPIRAEA
meager .... SCANT,
            LENTEN, SCANTY
meal .... REPAST
meal, boiled .... MUSH
meal, fine .... FARINA
meal, grain . PINOLA, PINOLE
meal, Indian, Hindu ATA, ATTA
meal, light .... BEVER

Meaning

meaning .... **SENSE, PURPORT**
meantime .... **INTERIM**
MEASURE ... Area, Liquid, Dry
Length, Distance
      see SPECIAL SECTION
measure ...... **EM, EN, GAGE,
METE, PACE, GAUGE**
MEASURE, BIB. .. see HEBREW
MEASURE
measure, Chin. length .... **LI**
"Measure for Measure"
    character ...... **ANGELO**
MEASURE, DRY, BIB. .... see
HEBREW DRY MEASURE
measure, Jap. distance ... **RI**
measure of distance, Ang.-Ind.
COSS
measure of spirits .... **PEG**
measure, old Arab ...... **SAA**
measure, old length ...... **ELL**
measure, poetry .... **SCAN**
measure, square .... **AR, ARE**
meat, cut of ...... **HAM, RIB,
CHOP, LOIN, FILET,
STEAK, FILLET**
meat on skewer ...... **CABOB,
KABOB, KEBAB**
meat roll, fried ...... **RISSOLE**
Mecca pilgrim garb .... **IHRAM**
Mecca shrine .... **CAABA,
KAABA, KAABEH**
Mecca, trip to .... **HADJ**
mechanical man ...... **ROBOT**
mechanical part .... **CAM**
mechanics, branch of . **STATICS**
mechanics of motion
DYNAMICS
meddle .... **PRY, TAMPER**
Medea's father .... **AEETES**
median line of valve ... **RAPHE**
medical .... **IATRIC**
medical fluid .... **SERUM**
medicinal capsule .... **CACHET**
medicinal fruit shrub ... **ALEM**
medicinal gum .... **KINO**
medicinal herb .... **ALOE,
IPECAC, BONESET**
medicinal plant .... **ALOE**
medicinal plant, leaves **SENNA**
medicinal tablet ..... **TROCHE**
medicine man ...... **SHAMAN**
medicine man, S. Am.
PEAI, PIAY
medieval lyric .... **ALBA**
medieval society **GILD, GUILD**
medieval tale, poem . **LAI, LAY**
Medina Arab .... **AUS**
MEDITERRANEAN .... see also
GAZETTEER
Mediterranean, East of.**LEVANT**
Medit. grass .... **DISS**

Medit. herb genus ...... **AMMI**
Medit. island: It. .... **RODI**
Medit. resort .... **NICE**
medlar .... **MESPIL**
medley .... **OLIO**
Medusa's slayer ..... **PERSEUS**
meet .... **SIT**
meeting ..... **TRYST, SESSION**
meeting, political .... **CAUCUS**
megapode .... **MALEO**
melancholy . **SAD, BLUE, DREAR**
melancholy: poet. ..... **DOLOR**
mellow .... **AGE, RIPE**
melodic .... **ARIOSE**
melodious .... **ARIOSO**
melody .... **AIR, ARIA,
TUNE, MELOS**
melon .... **PEPO, CASABA**
melt together ..... **FUSE, FUZE**
melted .... **MOLTEN**
membership .... **SEAT**
membrane .... **WEB, TELA,
VELA, VELUM**
memento .... **RELIC**
memorabilia .... **ANA**
memorandum .... **CHIT, NOTE**
memorial post, Indian .. **TOTEM**
memory, pert. to
MNESIC, MNEMONIC
Memphis chief god .... **PTAH**
Memphis street, famous.**BEALE**
men .... **SONS**
mendacious person ...... **LIAR**
mender, chief .... **TINKER**
mendicant, Mos.
FAKIR, FAKEER
Menelaus' wife .... **HELEN**
menhaden fish .... **POGY**
menhaden, young ... **SARDINE**
Mennonite .... **AMISH**
Menotti heroine ...... **AMELIA**
men's party .... **STAG**
mental .... **PHRENIC**
mental deficiency ... **AMENTIA**
mental deficient **IDIOT, MORON**
mention .... **CITE**
Mercator .... **MAP, CHART**
mercenary . **VENAL, HIRELING**
merchandise .... **WARES**
merchant .... **TRADER**
merchant: India .... **SETH**
"Merchant of Venice" heiress
PORTIA
merchant ship .... **ARGOSY**
merchant vessel, Gr. . **HOLCAD**
Mercury, Gr. .... **HERMES**
Mercury's wand ... **CADUCEUS**
mercy, show .... **SPARE**
mere .... **SIMPLE**
merely .... **ONLY**

merganser duck **SMEW, GARBILL**
merge .... **MELD**
merit .... **EARN**
merriment .... **GLEE**
merry-go-round ... **CAROUSAL,
CAROUSEL, CARROUSAL**
"Merry Widow" composer **LEHAR**
"Merry Wives" character
.... **PISTOL**
mesh .... **NET, WEB**
Mesopotamia ..... **IRAK, IRAQ**
Mesopotamian boat **GUFA, KUFA**
Mesopotamian city ..... **URFA**
mesquite bean flour ... **PINOLE**
mess, to make a ...... **BOTCH**
mestizo .... **METIS**
metal .... **TIN, MONEL**

metal alloy .... **BRASS,
MONEL, BRONZE**
metal, bar of .... **INGOT**
metal bar on house door . **RISP**
metal casting .... **PIG, INGOT**
metal, coat with .**PLATE, TERNE**
metal-decorating art .. **NIELLO**
metal disk .... **MEDAL**
metal dross .... **SLAG**
metal filings .... **LEMEL**
metal fissure .... **LODE**
metal leaf .... **FOIL**
metal mixture .... **ALLOY**
metal refuse .... **SCORIA**
metal spacer: print. ..... **SLUG**
metal suit .... **MAIL**
metal sulfide, impure . **MATTE**
metal, white .... **TIN**
metallic rock .... **ORE**
metalware, lacquered .... **TOLE**
metalwork, god of .. **VULCAN**
metarabic acid ..... **CERASIN**
meteor .... **LEONID**
meteor, exploding
.... **BOLIS, BOLIDE**
meter, Dutch .... **EL**
meter, one-millionth .. **MICRON**
meters, 100 sq. ...... **AR, ARE**
metheglin .... **MEAD**
method .... **PLAN, ORDER**
Methuselah's grandson .. **NOAH**
methyl-phenol
.... **CRESOL, CRESSOL**
metric measure ..... **AR, ARE,
GRAM, KILO, LITER, METER,
STERE, DECARE, HECTARE**
metric "quart" .... **LITER**
metrical beat .... **ICTUS**
metrical unit .... **MORA**
metropolitan .... **URBAN**
mew .... **GULL**
mew, cat's .... **MIAU, MIAW,
MIAOU, MIAUL**

Mexican dollar .... **PESO**
Mex. mush .... **ATOLE**
Mex. painter .... **RIVERA**
Mex. persimmon .... **CHAPOTE**
Mex. plant .... **JALAP**
Mex. president ...... **ALEMAN,
CALLES, MADERO**
Mex. resin tree .... **DRAGO**
Mex. rodent .... **TUCAN**
Mex. slave .... **PEON**
Mex. spiny tree ...... **RETAMA**
Mex. timber tree ...... **ABETO**
Mex. wind instrument . **CLARIN**
mezzanine .... **ENTRESOL**
miasma .... **MALARIA**
mica, kind of .... **BIOTITE**
mica of muscovite ...... **TALC**
microbe .... **GERM**
microspores .... **POLLEN**
middle .... **MESAL,
MESNE, MEDIAN**
middle, in the ...... **ATWEEN**
middle, toward .... **MESAD**
middling .... **SOSO**
Midgard Serpent slayer .. **THOR**
midge .... **GNAT**
midship, off .... **ABEAM**
"Midsummer Night's Dream"
character .. **PUCK, SNUG**
midwife: India .... **DHAI**
MID-EAST land .. **IRAK, IRAQ**
mien .... **AIR**
might .... **POWER**
mignonette ... **GREEN, RESEDA**
migrate .... **TREK**
migratory worker
.... **OKIE, ARKIE**
Mikado's court . **DAIRI, DAIRO**
Milanion's wife ... **ATALANTA**
Milan's "Met" ... **LA SCALA**
mild ...... **SHY, MEEK, SOFT,
BLAND, GENTLE**
mildness .... **LENITY**
mile: naut. .... **KNOT**
mile, part of, Burma ... **DHA**
Miled, son of .... **IR, ITH, EBER**
milestone .... **STELE**
milfoil .... **YARROW**
military award .... **DSO**
military cap .... **KEPI**
military command ... **AT EASE**
military group . **CADRE, CORPS**
military maneuvers ... **TACTICS**
milk, coagulated ...... **CURD**
milk coagulator ..... **RENNIN**
milk, curdled .... **CLABBER**
milk, part of **SERUM, LACTOSE**
milk, pert. to .... **LACTIC**
milk: pharm. .... **LAC**
milk protein .... **CASEINE**

Milk

a

milk, watery part of .... **WHEY**
milkfish .... **AWA, SABALO**
Milky Way .... **GALAXY**
mill .... **QUERN**
MILLET
   see also GRAIN SORGHUM
millet, India **JOAR,JUAR,CHENA**
millimeter, 1000th part **MICRON**
millstone support ...... **RYND**
millwheel board .... **LADE**
millwheel bucket .... **AWE**
Milton, masque by .... **COMUS**
Milton rebel angel ..... **ARIEL**
mime .... **APER**
mimic ...... **APE, APER, MIME**
mimicking, practice of . **APISM**
mimosa .... **ACACIA**
minced oath .. **GAD, GED, GEE,**
   LUD, DRAT, EGAD, HECK,
   OONS, SWOW, MAFEY,
   MACKINS
mind .... **CARE, TEND**
mind, opposite of: Hindu
   ATTA, ATMAN
mind: philos. .... **NOUS**
Mindanao native, Indonesian
   ATA, AETA, MORO
mine ceiling .... **ASTEL**
mine entrance .... **ADIT**
mine narrow veins ..... **RESUE**

b

mine passage .... **STULM**
mine roof support .... **NOG**
mine shaft drain pit .... **SUMP**
mine step .... **LOB**
mineral, alkaline ..... **TRONA**
mineral, blue .... **IOLITE**
mineral group ...... **URANITE**
mineral group, pert. to . **SALIC**
mineral, hard **SPINEL, SPINELLE**
mineral, lustrous .... **SPAR**
mineral, raw, native ..... **ORE**
mineral salt .... **ALUM**
mineral, soft .... **TALC**
mineral spring .... **SPA**
mineral tar .... **BREA**
mineral, transparent ... **MICA**
mineral used gun-powder **NITER**
Minerva .... **ATHENA**
minim .... **DROP**
mining refuse .... **ATTLE**
mining road .... **BORD**
mining tool ..... **GAD, BEELE**
minister, Moslem **VIZIR, VIZIER**
minister (to) .... **CATER**
mink, Amer. .... **VISON**
minority, legal ...... **NONAGE**
Minos' daughter .... **ARIADNE**
Minotaur's slayer .... **THESEUS**
minstrel .... **RIMER**
minstrel, medieval ... **GOLIARD**
minstrel, Norse . **SCALD, SKALD**

c

mint .... **COIN**
mint, Europ. ... **CLARE, CLARY,**
   CLARRY, HYSSOP, DITTANY
mint genus .... **MENTHA**
mint herb .... **SAGE**
mints, the .... **NEPETA**
minus .... **LESS**
minute .... **WEE, TINY, SMALL**
mira .... **STAR**
miracle, scene of first .. **CANA**
mirage .... **SERAB**
miscellany .... **ANA**
mischief .... **HOB**
mischievous spirit ...... **PUCK**
misconceive .... **ERR**
Mishnah section . **ABOT, ABOTH**
Mishnah section festivals .**MOED**
misinterpret .... **ERR**
mislay .... **LOSE**
misplay .... **ERROR**
misrepresent .... **BELIE**
Miss Dombey's suitor .. **TOOTS**
missile .... **DART, SNARK**
missile, guided ... **JUNO, NIKE,**
   THOR, ATLAS, TITAN,
   BOMARC, JUPITER, PERSH-
   ING, REGULUS, REDSTONE,
   BOLD ORION,MINUTEMAN
mist .... **HAZE, SMUR, MISLE**
mist: Eng. .... **RAG**

d

mistake, stupid .... **BONER**
mistakes .... **ERRATA**
mistakes, make .... **ERR**
mite .... **ACARI, ATOMY,**
   ACARID, ACARUS
mite genus .. **ACARI, ACARUS**
mite, tick, order of
   ACARIDA, ACARINA
mitigate . **EASE, ABATE, ALLAY**
mix .... **STIR, ADDLE, KNEAD**
mixture .... **OLIO**
mixture, mineral .... **MAGMA**
Moab city, chief .... **UR**
Moab king .... **MESHA**
Moabites, Bibl. .... **EMIM**
moat .... **FOSS, FOSSE**
"Moby Dick" pursuer .. **AHAB**
moccasin .... **PAC**
mock ..... **GIBE, JIBE, FLEER,**
   TAUNT, DERIDE
mock blow .... **FEINT**
mock orange ...... **SYRINGA**
mockingbird genus .... **MIMUS**
model, perfect ..... **PARAGON**
moderate .... **BATE,**
   ABATE, LESSEN
modernist .... **NEO**
modest .... **SHY, DEMURE**
modify .... **VARY, ALTER,**
   EMEND, TEMPER
Mogul emperor ...... **AKBAR**

a MOHAMMEDAN .. see MOSLEM
Mohammedanism ...... ISLAM
Mohammed's adopted son . ALI
Mohammed's birthplace .MECCA
Mohammed's daughter .FATIMA
Mohammed's descendant
    SAID, SEID, SAYID
Mohammed's son-in-law .. ALI
Mohammed's supporters .ANSAR
Mohammed's title .... ALI
Mohammed's tomb city MEDINA
Mohammed's uncle .... ABBAS
Mohammed's wife ..... AISHA
Mohawk, city on .... UTICA
Mohicans, last of the .. UNCAS
moiety .... HALF
moist .... WET, DAMP, DANK,
    DEWY, UVID, HUMID
moist spot, rock-ledge .... SIPE
moisten ... DAMPEN, IMBRUE
moisture, having medium MESIC
mojarra fish .... PATAO
molasses .. TREACLE, TRIACLE
molasses, rum made from
    TAFIA
mold .... MUST
mold, hole in casting .GIT, GEAT
molded clay .... PUG
b molding .. CYMA, GULA, OGEE,
    TORUS, REGLET, REEDING
molding, concave
    CONGE, SCOTIA
molding, convex
    OVOLO, TORUS, ASTRAGAL
molding, curved . CYMA, OGEE
molding, edge of . ARIS, ARRIS
molding, flat .... FILLET
molding, rounded TORI, TORUS
molding, S-shaped ...... OGEE
molding, square ...... LISTEL
moldings, quarter-round .OVOLI
moldy .... MUSTY
mole .... NEVUS, NAEVUS
mole cricket, S. Am. .. CHANGA
mole genus .... TALPA
molecule part .... ION
molelike mammal ... DESMAN
MOLLUSK.see also GASTROPOD
mollusk ...... CLAM, CHITON,
    MUSSEL, ABALONE
mollusk, bivalve ..... SCALLOP
mollusk, chamber-shelled
    NAUTILUS
mollusk, gastropod
    SNAIL, ABALONE
mollusk genus ARCA, MUREX,
    OLIVA, ANOMIA
mollusk, largest ...... CHAMA
mollusk's rasp organ .. RADULA
molt .... MEW, SHED

c molten rock ... LAVA, MAGMA
moment ..... MO, JIFF, TRICE
Monaco, pert. to
    MONACAN, MONEGASQUE
monad .... ATOM, UNIT
monastery .... MANDRA
monastery church .. MINSTER
MONEY . see also SPECIAL
    SECTION COINS
money ... CASH, CUSH, GELT
money, Amer. Ind. .. WAMPUM
money, bronze .... AES
money certificate .BOND, SCRIP
money, copper .... AES
money: dialect .... SPENSE
money, early Eng. .... ORA
money drawer .... TILL
money exchange fee .... AGIO
money, fishhook . LARI, LARIN
money, medieval .... ORA
money of account .... ORA
money, piece of .... COIN
money premium .... AGIO
money, put in .... INVEST
money reserve .... FUND
money, shell . SEWAN, SEAWAN
money, trade unit .... UNITAS
moneylender .... USURER
moneylender, Ind. .. MAHAJAN
d Mongol ... HU, ELEUT, TATAR,
    ELEUTH, TARTAR
Mongol dynasty .... YUAN
Mongol warrior .... TATAR
Mongolian tent .... YURT
Mongoloid .... TURK, DURBAN
Mongoloid in Indo-China .SHAN
mongrel .... CUR, MUTT
monitor lizard .... URAN
monk .. FRA, FRIAR, CENOBITE
monk, Buddhist ...... ARAHT,
    ARHAT, ARAHAT
monk, Eng. ...... BEDA, BEDE
monk, Gr. Church ... CALOYER
monk, head .... ABBOT
monk settlement.SCETE, SKETE
monk's hood .... COWL
monk's title ..... FRA, ABBOT
monkey .... APE, LAR, SAI,
    SIME, SIMIAN, MARMOSET
monkey, Afr. .... MONA,
    WAAG, GRIVET
monkey, Asia .... LANGUR
monkey, capuchin .... SAI
monkey, Chin. .... DOUC
monkey genus .... CEBUS
monkey, guenon ... NISNAS
monkey, howling ...... ARABA
monkey, P. I. .... MACHIN
monkey puzzle .... PINON
monkey, red, Afr. ..... PATAS
monkey, small .... LEMUR

monkey, S. Am. .. **SAKI, TITI, ACARI, ARABA, SAJOU, TETEE, PINCHE, SAGUIN, SAMIRI, SAIMIRI, SAPAJOU**
monkey, spider, genus.**QUATA, ATELES, COAITA**
monkshood .... **ATIS, ATEES, ACONITE**
monolith .... **MENHIR**
monopoly ..... **TRUST, CARTEL**
monosaccharide .... **OSE**
Mons, language of ...... **PEGU**
monster .. **GOUL, GOWL, OGRE**
monster, Gr. myth .. **CHIMERA**
monster, half-man-bull **MINOTAUR**
monster: med. ...... **TERAS**
monster, 100 eyes ..... **ARGUS**
monster slain by Hercules **HYDRA**
month, Egypt. .... **AHET, APAP, TYBI**
month, first day, Rom. **CALENDS, KALENDS**
month, Hindu .... **ASIN, JETH, KUAR, MAGH**
month, in last .... **ULTIMO**
month, Jewish ancient ..... **AB** (11th), **BUL** (8th), **ZIF** (8th), **ABIB** (7th), **ADAR** (6th), **ELUL** (12th), **IYAR**, (8th), **NISAN** (7th), **SEBAT** (5th), **SIVAN** (9th), **TEBET** (4th), **TIZRI** (1st), **TEBETH** (4th), **TISHRI** (1st)
month, Moslem .... **RABIA, RAJAB, SAFAR, SHABAN, RAMADAN**
month, Nisan .... **ABIB**
monument, stone.**LECH, CAIRN, DOLMEN, CROMLECH**
moon . **LUNA, DIANA, PHOEBE**
moon, age at beginning of calendar year ..... **EPACT**
moon angel .... **MAH**
moon flower .... **ACHETE**
moon god, Babyl. .. **SIN, ENZU**
moon goddess ...... **ASTARTE**
moon goddess, Gr. .... **SELENA, SELENE, ARTEMIS**
moon goddess, Rom. ... **LUNA, DIAN, DIANA**
moon nearest earth, point **PERIGEE**
moon valley ..... **RILL, RILLE**
moor grass .... **NARD**
moorhen .... **GORHEN**
Moorish .... **MORISCAN**
moose genus .... **ALCES**
mop .... **SWAB, SWOB**

Moqui, one of .... **HOPI**
morals overseer ...... **CENSOR**
morass .... **QUAG, MARSH**
moray .... **EEL**
Mordecai, enemy of .. **HAMAN**
more .... **PLUS**
more! ...... **BIS, PIU, ENCORE**
more than enough ...... **TOO, EXTRA, EXCESS**
More's island .... **UTOPIA**
morepork, N. Z. .. **PEHO, RURU**
morindin dye .... **AL**
moringa seed .... **BEN**
morning glory .... **IPOMEA**
morning music ...... **AUBADE**
morning: P. I. .... **UMAGA**
morning prayer ...... **MATINS**
morning song .... **MATIN**
Moro .... **SULU, LANAO**
Moro chief **DATO, DATU, DATTO**
Moro mantle .... **JABUL**
Moroccan Berber ...... **RIFF**
Moroccan land, public .. **GISH**
Moroccan native .... **MOOR**
moron .... **AMENT, IDIOT**
morose ... **BLUE, GLUM, GRUM**
morsel .... **ORT**
mortar implement .... **PESTLE**
mortar ingredient ...... **LIME**
mortar mixer ... ... **RAB**
mortar tray .... **HOD**
mortise insert .... **TENON**
Mosaic law .... **TORA, TORAH**
mosaic piece .... **TESSERA**
Moselle, river to .... **SAAR**
Moses, law given to here **SINA, SINAI**
Moses' brother ...... **AARON**
Moses' death mountain .. **NEBO**
Moses' father-in-law .. **JETHRO**
Moses' spy in Canaan .. **CALEB**
MOSLEM ..... see also MECCA
Moslem .... **TURK**
Moslem ablution before prayer **WIDU, WUDU, WUZU**
Moslem, Afr. .... **MOOR**
Moslem beggar .**FAKIR, FAKEER**
Moslem bible .... **KORAN**
Moslem call to prayer **ADAN, AZAN**
Moslem chief .... **AGA, IMAM, DATTO**
Moslem chief gold coin.**DINAR**
Moslem converts ..... **ANSAR**
Moslem deity ... **JANN, ALLAH**
Moslem demon .. **JANN, EBLIS**
Moslem Easter .... **EED**
Moslem fast ...... **RAMADAN**
Moslem festival ...... **BAIRAM**

Moslem fiat .... **IRADE**
Moslem fourth Caliph .... **ALI**
Moslem grant of property
.... **WAKF, WAQF, WUKF**
Moslem guide .... **PIR**
Moslem holy city ..... **MECCA**
Moslem holy man
.... **IMAM, IMAUM**
Moslem, hostile to Crusaders
.... **SARACEN**
Moslem in Turkestan ... **SALAR**
Moslem judge .. **CADI, CAZI,**
CAZY, KADI, KAZI, KAZY
Moslem leader . **IMAM, IMAUM**
Moslem marriage.**MOTA, MUTA**
Moslem marriage settlement
.... **MAHR**
MOSLEM MORO ... see MORO
.... **CHIEF**
Moslem mystic .... **SUFI**
Moslem name .... **ALI**
Moslem Negroids .... **MABA**
Moslem noble .... **AMIR, EMIR,**
AMEER, EMEER
Moslem, N. W. India ... **SWAT**
Moslem official .... **AGA**
Moslem, orthodox ..... **HANIF**
Moslem, P.I. .... **MORO**
Moslem potentate .... **AGA**
Moslem prayer .... **SALAT**
Moslem prayer place ... **IDGAH**
Moslem priest . **IMAM, IMAUM**
Moslem prince ... **AMIR, EMIR,**
AMEER, EMEER
Moslem principle .... **IJMA**
Moslem pulpit ...... **MIMBAR**
Moslem reformer .... **WAHABI**
Moslem religion .... **ISLAM**
Moslem religious college
.... **ULEMA**
Moslem ruler .... **HAKIM**
Moslem saber ...... **SCIMITAR**
Moslem saint .... **PIR**
Moslem school ..... **MADRASA**
Moslem spirit ... **JINN, JINNI**
Moslem spiritual guide ... **PIR**
Moslem teacher .. **ALIM, COJA**
Moslem temple.**MOSK, MOSQUE**
Moslem theologians ... **ULEMA**
Moslem title .... **AGA, RAIS,**
REIS, SEID, SIDI, SYED,
SYUD, CALIF, SAYID,
SEYID, CALIPH
Moslem tunic .. **JAMA, JAMAH**
Moslem weight .... **ROTL**
Moslem woman's dress .. **IZAR**
Moslems, Sunnite .... **SART**
Moslemized Bulgarian . **POMAK**
mosque .... **MASJID**
mosque, central .... **JAMI**
mosque, Jerusalem .... **OMAR**
mosque student .... **SOFTA**

mosquito, genus, yellow-fever
.... **AEDES**
mossbunker fish .... **POGY**
moss of Ceylon .... **AGAR**
moth .... **IO, LUNA,**
EGGER, TINEA
moth, clearwing, genus . **SESIA**
moth, clothes .... **TINEA**
moth, green .... **LUNA**
mother goddess; Baby. . **ERUA**
mother goddesses. Hindu **MATRIS**
mother of Arthur .... **IGRAINE**
mother of gods .... **RHEA**
MOTHER OF IRISH GODS .. see
.... page 200
mother-of-pearl .... **NACRE**
mother-of-pearl shell.**ABALONE**
mother turned to stone . **NIOBE**
mother's side, related on
.... **ENATE, ENATIC**
mother's side, relation on
.... **ENATE, ENATION**
motherless calf .. **DOGY, DOGIE**
motion, producing .... **MOTILE**
motionless ..... **INERT, STILL**
motive ...... **CAUSE, REASON**
motmot, S. Am. ..... **HOUTOU**
motor part .... **ROTOR**
mottled .... **PIED, PINTO**
mottled, as wood .... **ROEY**
MOULDING .... see MOLDING
mound ...... **TUMP, BARROW**
mound, Polyn. .... **AHU**
Mount of Olives ...... **OLIVET**
mountain, Alps ...... **BLANC**
mountain ash .. **SORB, ROWAN**
mountain, Asia Minor ..... **IDA**
mountain, Bibl. .. **HOR, NEBO,**
SEIR, SINA, HOREB,
SINAI, ARARAT
(see others on page 197)
mountain chain .... **SIERRA**
mountain climbing staff .**PITON**
mountain crest .... **ARETE**
mountain, Crete .... **IDA**
mountain, Edom .... **HOR**
mountain, fabled Hindu . **MERU**
mountain, famous .... **IDA**
mountain, Gr. ...... **HELICON**
mountain in Thessaly ... **OSSA**
mountain lion .... **PUMA**
mountain mint .... **BASIL**
mountain, Moab .... **NEBO**
mountain pass .... **COL**
mountain pass, Alps **CENIS**
mountain pass, India
.... **GAUT, GHAT**
mountain peak .... **ALP**
mountain pool .... **TARN**
mountain recess .... **CWM**
mountain ridge .... **ARETE**

mountain ridge, Port. .. **SERRA**
mountain, 2nd highest N.A.
    LOGAN
mountain sickness **PUNA, VETA**
mountain spinach ..... **ORACH**
mountain spur .... **ARETE**
mountains, Asia ...... **ALTAI**
mountains, myth ... **KAF, QAF**
mourn .... **WEEP,**
    GRIEVE, LAMENT
mournful .... **SAD, DIRE**
mourning band .... **CRAPE**
mouse .... **VOLE**
mouse, field .... **VOLE**
mouse genus .... **MUS**
mousebird ..... **COLY, SHRIKE**
mouth .... **OS, ORA**
mouth, away from .... **ABORAL**
mouth open .... **AGAPE**
mouth, river .... **DELTA**
mouth, tidal river ...... **FRITH**
mouth, toward .... **ORAD**
mouthful .... **SIP, SUP**
mouthlike orifice ...... **STOMA**
mouthpiece ..... **REED, BOCAL**
move .... **STIR, AFFECT**
move a camera .... **PAN**
move back ..... **EBB, RECEDE**
move to and fro
    WAG, FLAP, SWAY
movement: biol. .... **TAXIS**
movement, capable of . **MOTILE**
movement: music ...... **MOTO**
movement,with:music **CONMOTO**
movie: Sp. .... **CINE**
moving part .... **ROTOR**
mow, barn's .... **LOFT**
mow of hay .... **GOAF**
mowed strip .... **SWATH**
Mowgli's bear friend ... **BALU,**
    BALOO
Mozambique native ...... **YAO**
muck .... **MIRE**
mud .... **MIRE, MURGEON**
mud deposit .... **SILT**
mud, slimy .... **OOZE**
mud, stick in .... **MIRE**
mud, viscous .... **SLIME**
mud, volcano .... **SALSE**
muddle .... **MESS, ADDLE**
muddy .... **ROIL**
muffin .... **GEM**
mug .... **STEIN, NOGGIN**
mug, small .... **TOBY**
mugger .... **GOA**
mulatto .... **METIS**
mulberry bark cloth .... **TAPA**
mulberry genus ...... **MORUS**
mulberry, India ...... **AL, AAL**
mulct .... **FINE, AMERCE**
mullet, red .... **SUR**

multiform .... **DIVERSE**
multiplicand: math. . **FACIEND**
multiplier: math. .... **FACIENT**
multitude ...... **HOST, HORDE**
mum .... **ALE**
munch .... **CHAMP**
mundane .... **TERRENE**
Munich's river .... **ISAR**
municipal officer, Sp. . **ALCADE,**
    ALCAID, ALCAIDE,
    ALCAYDE
muntjac deer . **KAKAR, RATWA**
murder by suffocation . **BURKE**
murder fine, Scot. .... **CRO**
murderer, first .... **CAIN**
murmuring sound
    CURR, PURL, PURR
Musci, plant of .... **MOSS**
muscle .... **THEW, SINEW**
muscle coordination, lack of
    ATAXIA
muscle, deep, pert. to
    SCALENE
muscle, kind of
    ERECTOR, LEVATOR
muscle, like .... **MYOID**
muscle, round, rolling .. **TERES**
muscle, stretching .... **TENSOR**
muscles .... **BRAWN**
muscular action, irregular
    ATAXIA
muscular spasm .... **TIC**
Muse, chief .... **CALLIOPE**
muse in reverie .... **REVE**
Muse of astronomy ... **URANIA**
Muse of comedy ..... **THALIA**
Muse of dancing .**TERPSICHORE**
Muse of history .... **CLIO**
Muse of lyric poetry
    CLIO, ERATO
Muse of music ...... **EUTERPE**
Muse of poetry .... **ERATO**
Muse of sacred lyric
    POLYMNIA
Muse of tragedy . **MELPOMENE**
Muses, 9 .... **PIERIDES**
Muses' region .... **AONIA**
Muses, The .... **NINE**
musette .... **OBOE**
museum head ...... **CURATOR**
mush .... **ATOLE, SEPON**
mushroom .... **MOREL, MORIL**
mushroom cap .... **PILEUS**
music: as written .... **STA**
music character .... **DOT,**
    CLEF, REST
music drama .... **OPERA**
music for nine .... **NONET**
music for three .... **TRIO**
music for two .... **DUET**
music from the sign: abbr. . **DS**

a music hall .... **ODEA,**
ODEON, ODEUM
music interval ...... **TRITONE**
music: it proceeds .... **VA**
music lines .... **STAFF**
music piece
SERENATA, SERENATE
music, sacred
CHORAL, CHORALE
music symbols, old ... **NEUME**
MUSICAL .... see also MUSIC
musical beat .... **TAKT**
musical composition, India
RAGA
musical direction . **STA, TACET**
musical instrument ..... **ASOR,**
DRUM, FIFE, GIGA, HARP,
HORN, LUTE, LYRE, OBOE,
PIPE, REED, TCHE, TUBA,
TURR, VINA, VIOL, CELLO,
RAPPEL, SPINET, CLAVIER,
HELICON, OCARINA
musical sign .. **DOT, CLEF, REST**
musical study .... **ETUDE**
musical work .... **OPUS**
musician, 11th century . **GUIDO**

c musket ball, India ...... **GOLI**
Musketeer .... **ATHOS,**
ARAMIS, PORTHOS
mussel, fresh-water ..... **UNIO**
must .... **STUM**
mustache monkey ... **MOUSTOC**
mustard family plant ... **CRESS**
musteline animal
OTTER, RATEL
mustiness .... **FUST**
mutilate .... **MAIM**
muttonbird .... **OII**
muttonfish .... **SAMA**
"My Name is —" ..... **ARAM**
mysteries .... **ARCANA**
mysterious .... **OCCULT**
mystery .... **RUNE**
mystic word, Hindu ...... **OM**
mystic writing .... **RUNE**
mythical land ...... **LEMURIA**
mythical stream .... **STYX**
mythical submerged island
ATLANTIS
mythical warrior ...... **ARES**
MYTHOLOGY .... see SPECIAL
SECTION, Page 198

N

b nab .... **GRAB, ARREST**
Nabal's wife: Bibl. ... **ABIGAIL**
NaCl .... **SALT**
nahoor sheep .... **SNA**
nail .... **CLAW, TALON,**
UNGUES, UNGUIS
nail, hooked .... **TENTER**
nail, mining, surveying .. **SPAD**
nail, thin .... **BRAD**
nail with aperture ...... **SPAD**
nails, 100 lbs. .... **KEG**
namaycush .... **TOGUE**
NAME .... see also MAN'S
NAME, WOMAN'S NAME
name .... **DUB, TERM, CLEPE,**
NOMEN, TITLE, ENTITLE
name: Dan. ..... **NAAM**
name plate, shop's .... **FACIA**
named ... **Y-CLEPT, Y-CLEPED**
namely .... **VIZ**
Naomi, name claimed by **MARA**
Naomi's daughter-in-law . **RUTH**
naos .... **CELLA**
nap, coarse, long .... **SHAG**
nap-raising device ... **TEASEL,**
TEASLE, TEAZEL, TEAZLE
nap-raising machine ...... **GIG**
nap, to raise .... **TEASE**
napoleon, game like ..... **PAM**

d Napoleon's brother-in-law
MURAT
Napoleon's isle .... **ELBA**
Napoleon's marshal general **NEY**
Napoleonic victory .**JENA, LODI**
Narcissus, nymph who loved
ECHO
narcotic .... **DOPE, DRUG,**
HEROIN, OPIATE
narcotic, India . **BANG, BHANG**
narcotic plant .... **DUTRA**
narcotic shrub
KAT, KAAT, KHAT
narcotic shrub, S. Am.
COCA, CUCA
narrate .... **TELL**
narrow ...... **LINEAL, STRAIT**
nasal .... **RHINAL**
Nata's wife: myth ..... **NANA**
nation: Ger. .... **VOLK**
nation, pert. to ...... **STATAL**
NATIVE .... see TRIBES in
SPECIAL SECTION, Page 191
native ... **ITE, RAW, NATAL,**
ENDEMIC, INDIGENE
natural luster, having ... **NAIF**
natural talent . **DOWER, FLAIR**
nature ...... **OUSIA, ESSENCE**
nature goddess ...... **CYBELE**

Nature

a
nature principal: Hindu . **GUNA**
nature spirit .... **NAT**
nature story writer ..... **SETON**
nautical .... **MARINE**
nautical cry
    AHOY, OHOY, AVAST
Navaho hut .... **HOGAN**
naval hero .... **PERRY**
navy jail .... **BRIG**
near . **AT, NIGH, ABOUT, CLOSE**
Near East native . **ARAB, TURK**
Near East river valley .. **WADI**
near the ear .... **PAROTIC**
near to .... **BY, ON**
nearest .... **NEXT**
nearsighted person .... **MYOPE**
nearsightedness ..... **MYOPIA**
neat ...... **TIDY, TOSH, TRIG,**
    TRIM, SPRUCE
neat cattle .... **NOWT**
neatly .... **FEATLY**
necessitate .... **ENTAIL**
neck, nape of .... **NUCHA**
necklace ..... **BEADS, RIVIERE**
neckline shape
    VEE, BOAT, CREW
neckpiece ...... **ASCOT, STOLE**
neckpiece, feather ...... **BOA**
neckpiece, woman's .... **FICHU**
NECKTIE .... see TIE

b
need .... **WANT, REQUIRE**
needle .... **PROD, BODKIN**
needle bug .... **NEPA**
needle case .... **ETUI**
needle-shaped ...... **ACUATE,**
    ACERATE
needlefish .... **GAR**
needlelike bristle .... **ACICULA**
negative .... **NE, NO, NAY,**
    NON, NOT
negative pole ...... **CATHODE**
neglect .... **OMIT**
neglected school subject:
    abbr. .... **LAT.**
negligent .... **LAX**
negotiate .... **TREAT**
negrito . **ATA, ATI, ITA, AETA,**
    ATTA
NEGRO .... see also TRIBES in
    SPECIAL SECTION
Negro dance .... **JUBA**
Negro: India .... **HUBSHI**
NEGRO TRIBE .... see SPECIAL
    SECTION
Nelson's victory site ..... **NILE**
nematocyst .... **CNIDA**
nemesis .... **BANE**
Nepal Mongoloid .... **RAIS**
Nepal native .... **KHA**
Nepal people .... **RAIS**
nephew .... **NEPOTE**

c
nephew, Fijian .... **VASU**
Neptune .... **LER**
Neptune's spear ...../. **TRIDENT**
nerve cell .... **NEURON**
nerve-cell process ...... **AXON**
nerve layers, brain ..... **ALVEI**
nervous .... **EDGY**
nervous disease ...... **CHOREA**
nest .... **NID, NIDE,**
    NIDI, NIDUS
nest, eagle's .... **AERY, AERIE,**
    EYRY, EYRIE
nested boxes .... **INRO**
nestling .... **EYAS**
net .... **CLEAR**
net, fishing .... **SEINE,**
    STENT, TRAWL
net of hair-lines ..... **RETICLE**
NETHERLANDS
    see SPECIAL SECTION
netlike .... **RETIARY**
nettle family .. **RAMIE, RAMEE**
network .... **WEB, MESH,**
    RETE, RETIA
neuroglia .... **GLIA**
neve .... **FIRN**
— Nevis, Gt. Brit. peak .. **BEN**
new .... **NOVEL, RECENT**
New Caledonia bird .... **KAGU**
New England state: abbr. .. **RI**

d
New Guinea area ..... **PAPUA**
New Guinea tribesman . **KARON**
New Guinea victory .... **GONA**
New Guinea wild hog .... **BENE**
New Jerusalem foundation
    JASPER
new, lover of .... **NEO**
new star .... **NOVA**
new wine .... **MUST**
New York harbor isle .... **ELLIS**
New Zealand aborigine ... **ATI**
N.Z. bird .... **HUIA, KAKI,**
    PEHO, RURU
N.Z. clan .... **ATI**
N.Z. evergreen .... **TAWA**
N.Z. fruit pigeon .... **KUKU**
N.Z. laburnum .... **GOAI**
N.Z. mollusk .... **PIPI**
N.Z. native .... **MAORI**
N.Z. native fort ..... **PA, PAH**
N.Z. parson bird .... **KOKO**
N.Z. plant .... **KARO**
N.Z. rail bird .... **WEKA**
N.Z. scabbard fish ...... **HIKU**
N.Z. shrub .... **KARO**
N.Z. shrub, poisonous .. **TUTU**
N.Z. subtribe .... **HAPU**
N.Z. timber tree . **GOAI, HINO,**
    MIRO, PELU, RATA, RIMU,
    HINAU, HINOU, KAURI,
    KAURY, TOTARA

a N.Z. tree ... AKE, KOPI, NAIO,
PUKA, TORO
N.Z. tree, lightwood ... WHAU
N.Z. tribe .... ATI
N.Z. wages .... UTU
N.Z. wood hen .... WEKA
news agency, Eng. ... REUTERS
news agency, Europ. ... ANETA
news agency, Jap. ..... DOMEI
news agency, Rus. Soviet . TASS
news paragraph .... ITEM
newspaper service ... AP, UP,
INS, UPI, REUTERS
newspapers .... PRESS
newt ..... EFT, EVET, TRITON
nibble ... GNAW, KNAB, KNAP
niche .... RECESS
Nichols' hero .... ABIE
Nick Charles' dog .... ASTA
Nick Charles' wife ...... NORA
nickel steel alloy ...... INVAR
nicotine acid .... NIACIN
nictitate .... WINK
Niger delta native .... IJO
NIGERIA
see SPECIAL SECTION
Nigerian Negro ..... ARO, IBO
Nigerian tribe .... EDO
NIGERIAN TRIBE OR PEOPLE
see also SPECIAL SECTION
page 191
b niggard .... MISER
nigh .... NEAR
night, Norse ..... NATT, NOTT
nightingale, Pers. .... BULBUL
nightjar .... POTOO
nightmare demon, Teut. .MARA
nightmare, the ...... INCUBUS
nightshade, black
MOREL, MORIL
Nile, as god .... HAPI
Nile island .... RODA
Nile native .... NILOT
Nile sailboat .... CANGIA
Nile valley depression ... KORE
Nile, waste matter on
SADD, SUDD
Nilotic Negro ...... JUR, LUO,
LWO, SUK
nimble .... SPRY, AGILE
nimbus .... HALO, NIMB
nimrod .... HUNTER
nine-angled polygon .NONAGON
nine, based on ..... NONARY
nine, group of ...... ENNEAD
nine inches .... SPAN
nine, music for .... NONET
Nineveh's founder ..... NINUS
ninth day, every ...... NONAN
ninth: mus. .... NONA
niton .... RADON

c nitrogen .... AZO, AZOTE
Noah, pert. to .... NOETIC
Noah's landing ..... ARARAT
Noah's 1st son .... SEM, SHEM
Noah's 2nd son .... HAM
Nobel prize, literature '04
MISTRAL
Nobel prize, science .... UREY
noble, nobleman .. DUKE, EARL,
LORD, PEER, BARON, COUNT
noble: Ger. ..... GRAF, RITTER
NOBLEMAN ...... see NOBLE
nobleman, Jap .... KAMI
nocturnal mammal BAT, LEMUR
nod .... BOW, BECK
Nod, west of .... EDEN
nodding .... NUTANT
noddy tern: Hawaii ..... NOIO
node .... KNOB, KNOT,
KNUR, NODUS
"— noire" .... BETE
nomad .... ARAB, SCENITE
Nome in Greece .... ELIS
nomenclature .... NAME
nominal value .... PAR
nominate .... NAME
non-gypsy: Romany ..... GAJO
non-Jew .... GOI, GOY
non-Moslem of Turkey or
d Ottoman Empire RAIA, RAYA
non-professional ... LAY, LAIC
non-union worker .... SCAB
nonchalant .... COOL
none: dialect .... NIN
nonsense . PISH, POOH, HOOEY
nonsense creature ...... GOOP
noodles: Yiddish FARFEL, FERFEL
nook, sheltered .... COVE
noose .... LOOP
Norn, one of URD,URTH,WYRD
Norse "Adam" .... ASKR
Norse bard .... SCALD, SKALD
Norse chieftain .. JARL, YARL
Norse epic .... EDDA
Norse explorer ..... ERIC, LEIF
NORSE GOD or GODDESSES
see also GODS and GODDESSES
and see also SPECIAL SEC-
TION Page 200
Norse gods .... VANS,
AESIR, VANIR
Norse letter .... RUNE
Norse myth. hero EGIL, EGILL
Norse myth. king .... ATLI
Norse myth. "Life" force LIF
Norse myth. woman .... IDUN
Norse neighbor .... FINN
Norse poetry .... RUNES
Norse prose .... EDDA
Norse sea goddess ...... RAN
Norseman ..... DANE, SWEDE

107

North African .... **BERBER**
N. Afr. outer garment .. **HAIK**
North Carolina college .. **ELON**
North Carolinian .... **TARHEEL**
North Caucasian language
   UDI, AVAR, UDIC, UDISH
North, Mrs. of fiction . **PAMELA**
North Sea fishing boat . **COBLE**
North Sea, river into **ELBE, TEES**
North Star .... **POLARIS**
North Syrian deity .... **EL**
northern .... **BOREAL**
northern Scandinavian ... **LAPP**
northern tribe, China ..... **HU**
northernmost land ..... **THULE**
Northumberland river ... **TYNE**
Norway coin .... **ORE**
Norway territorial division.**AMT**
Norwegian author ... **HAMSUN**
Norwegian composer .... **GRIEG**
Norwegian county **AMT, FYLKE**
Norwegian saint .... **OLAF**
nose .... **CONK, NASI,**
   NASUS, SNOOP
nose, having large ... **NASUTE**
nose, having snub .... **SIMOUS**
nose openings .. **NARES, NARIS**
nose, snub .... **PUG**
nostrils .... **NARES, NARIS**
nostrils, of .... **NARIC,**
   NARIAL, NARINE
"— Nostrum," Mediterranean
   MARE
not at home .... **OUT**
not ever: poet. .... **NEER**
not genuine .... **TIN**
not in style ...... **OUT, PASSE**
not long ago .... **LATELY**
not moving ... **INERT, STATIC**
not one .... **NARY, NONE**
not so great .... **LESS, FEWER,**
   SMALLER
notch ... **KERF, NICK, NOCK,**
   CRENA, CRENAE
notched .. **SERRATE, SERRATED**
note .... **CHIT, MEMO**
note, double, whole .... **BREVE**
note, Guido's .... **UT, ELA**
note, Guido's low ..... **GAMUT**
note, half .... **MINIM**
note, high, highest .... **ELA**
note, marginal
   POSTIL, APOSTIL
note: music .. **DI, DO, FA, FI,**
  LA, LE, LI, ME, MI, RA, RE,
  RI, SE, SI, SO, TE, TI, SOL
note, old Gr. musical .... **NETE**
note, old musical .... **ELA**
NOTE, SCALE ...... see NOTE:
   MUSIC
notes, furnish with . **ANNOTATE**

notes in Guido's scale .. **ELAMI**
nothing . **NIL, NIX, NUL, NULL,**
   ZERO, NIHIL
notion .... **BEE, IDEA**
notion, capricious ..... **WHIM**
notional .... **IDEAL**
notorious .... **ARRANT**
Nott's son .... **DAG**
notwithstanding .... **YET**
nought .... **ZERO, NULL**
NOUN ENDING
   see SUFFIX, noun
noun form .... **CASE**
noun suffix of condition .. **ATE**
noun with only 2 cases. **DIPTOTE**
nourish .... **FEED, FOSTER**
nourishment ...... **PABULUM**
Nova Scotia .... **ACADIA**
novel, advocate of .... **NEO**
novel by A. France ..... **THAIS**
novelty .... **FAD**
novice .... **TIRO, TYRO**
now: dial. .... **NOO**
noxious .... **MIASMIC**
Nubian .... **NUBA**
nucha .... **NAPE**
nuclear element ...... **PROTON**
nudge .... **POKE**
nuisance .... **PEST**
nullify .... **NEGATE**
nullify, legally .... **VOID**
number, describable by .**SCALAR**
number under 10 ...... **DIGIT**
number, whole ..... **INTEGER**
numbered: Bib. .... **MENE**
numerous .. **MANY, MULTIPLE**
nun, Franciscan .... **CLARE**
nun, head .... **ABBESS**
nun's dress .... **HABIT**
nunbird .... **MONASE**
nuque .... **NAPE**
nurse, Oriental, India .. **AMA,**
  IYA, AMAH, AYAH, EYAH
nurse, Slavic .... **BABA**
nursemaid: Fr. .... **BONNE**
nut ...... **COLA, KOLA, LICHI,**
  ALMOND, CASHEW,
  LICHEE, LITCHI
nut, beverage .... **COLA, KOLA**
nut, hickory .... **PECAN**
nut, pert. to .... **NUCAL**
nut, P. I. .... **PILI**
nut, pine .... **PINON**
nut, stimulating ...... **BETEL**
nut tree, Afr. .... **COLA, KOLA**
nuts for food .... **MAST**
nuthatch genus .... **SITTA**
nutlike drupe .... **TRYMA**
nutmeg husk .... **MACE**
nutria .... **COYPU**

a nutriment ... **FOOD, ALIMENT**
nutritive .... **ALIBLE**
nymph .... **MAIA, LARVA**
nymph, fountain ...... **EGERIA**
nymph, laurel .... **DAPHNE**
nymph, Moslem .... **HOURI**

c nymph, mountain ..... **OREAD**
nymph, ocean ...... **OCEANID**
nymph, water . **NAIAD, NEREID**
nymph, wood . **DRYAD, NAPEA,**
NAPAEA, HAMADRYAD
Nyx's daughter .... **ERIS**

O, plural .... **OES**
oaf .... **LOUT**
oak, Calif. .... **ENCINA**
oak, dried fruit of ... **CAMATA**
oak, evergreen .... **HOLM**
oak moss .... **EVERNIA**
oak, Turkey .... **CERRIS**
oakum, seal with ...... **CALK**
oar .... **ROW, BLADE, PROPEL**
oar at stern .... **SCULL**
oasis, N. Afr. ... **WADI, WADY**
oat genus .... **AVENA**
oats as rent .... **AVENAGE**
oath, knight's .... **EGAD**
oath, old-fashioned . **ODS, EGAD**
oath, say under ...... **DEPOSE**
obeisance, Oriental
BOW, SALAAM
b obey .... **HEED, MIND**
object ... **AIM, CAVIL, DEMUR**
object of art .... **CURIO**
objection, petty .... **CAVIL**
objective .... **AIM, GOAL**
obligation .... **TIE, DEBT**
DUTY, ONUS
oblique .... **CANT, BEVEL,**
SLANT, SLOPE
obliterate .... **ERASE, EFFACE**
obliteration .... **RASURE**
oblivion ..... **LETHE, LIMBO**
oblivion stream .... **LETHE**
obscure ..... **DIM, FOG, DARK**
BEDIM, CLOUD
obscure, render ...... **DARKLE**
observe .. **SEE, NOTE, BEHOLD,**
REMARK, CELEBRATE
obstinate .... **SET, HARD**
obstruction, petty .... **CAVIL,**
obtain .... **GET**
obvious ...... **OPEN, PATENT**
obvious, not . **SUBTLE, SUBTILE**
occasional .... **ODD**
Occident .... **WEST**
occipital protuberances ... **INIA**
occultism .... **CABALA**
occupant .... **TENANT**
occupation .... **TRADE**
occupy .... **USE, FILL**
occurrence .... **EVENT**

ocean's rise, fall ...... **TIDE**
oceanic .... **PELAGIC**
oceanic tunicate .... **SALP**
ocher, black ..... **WAD, WADD**
octave, designating high .. **ALT**
octave of church feast ... **UTAS**
octopus .... **POULPE**
octoroon **METIS,MESTEE,MUSTEE**
odd-job man .... **JOEY**
Odin. **WODAN, WODEN, WOTAN**
Odin's brother ...... **VE, VILI**
Odin's granddaughter . **NANNA**
Odin's son ... **TY, TYR, THOR,**
TYRR, VALE, VALI
Odin's wife .... **RIND**
odor .... **AROMA, SCENT**
ODYSSEUS ... see also ULYSSES
Odysseus' companion . **ELPENOR**
d Odysseus' friend ..... **MENTOR**
Odyssey beggar .... **IRUS**
Odyssey singer .... **SIREN**
Oedipus' father .... **LAIUS**
Oedipus' mother .... **JOCASTA**
of speed of sound ...... **SONIC**
of the age: abbr. .... **AET**
off .... **AWAY**
offend .... **CAG**
offense .... **CRIME**
offense: law .. **MALA, MALUM**
offer .... **BID, TENDER**
offered up .... **OBLATE**
offhand .... **CASUAL**
office, ecclesiastic .. **MATINS**
office, priest's ...... **MATINS**
office, R. C. curia
DATARY, DATARIA
officer, church ...... **BEADLE**
officer, court: Scot. .... **MACER**
officer, municipal: Scot. **BAILIE**
officer, Rom. .... **LICTOR**
officer, synagogue .... **PARNAS**
officer, university
DEAN, BEADLE, BURSAR
official, Moslem .... **HAJIB**
official, Rom.
EDILE, AEDILE, TRIBUNE
official, subordinate .. **SATRAP**
official, weights .... **SEALER**
offspring .... **SONS, HEIRS**

Ogygian

a

ogygian .... AGED
Ohio college town .... ADA
oil .... FAT, LARD, LUBE,
        ATTAR, OLEUM
oil beetle .... MELOE
oil bottle ..... CRUCE, CRUET,
      CRUSE, CRUIZE
oil, cruet .... AMPULLA
oil, edible .... ACEITE
oil, orange .... NEROLI
oil, pert. to .... OLEIC
oil, rub with .... ANOINT
oil-yielding Chinese tree . TUNG
oil-yielding tree ... EBO, EBOE
oilfish .... ESCOLAR
oilstone .... HONE
oily ketone .... IRONE
ointment ...... BALM, NARD,
    SALVE, CERATE, POMADE
Ojibway secret order
           MEDA, MIDE
O.K. .... ROGER
okra .... GOMBO, GUMBO
old .... AGED, ANILE, SENILE
"Old Curiosity Shop" girl . NELL
old English army .... FYRD
old Eng. gold piece ..... RYAL
old Eng. rune .... WEN, WYN
old Greek coin .... OBOL
old Irish coin .... RAP
old Persian money .... DARIC
OLD TESTAMENT see BIBLICAL
    and SPECIAL SECTION
Old Testament objects ... URIM

b

Old Test. people . PHUD, PHUT
old person .... DOTARD
old Sp. gold coin ...... DOBLA
old times .... ELD, YORE
old-womanish .... ANILE
oleaginous .... OILY
oleander genus ...... NERIUM
oleic acid salt ...... OLEATE
oleoresin .... ANIME,
    ELEMI, BALSAM
olive fly genus .... DACUS
olive genus .... OLEA
olive, inferior .... MORON
olive, stuffed .... PIMOLA
Oliver's nickname ...... NOLL
Olympian deity-god-goddess
    ARES, HERA, APOLLO,
    ATHENA, HERMES, AR-
    TEMIS, DEMETER
Olympus, mountain near . OSSA
Olympus queen .... HERA
Olympus, region by .... PIERIA
omen .... BODE, PRESAGE
omission, vowel ...... ELISION
omit .... DELE, PASS, SKIP
omit in pronunciation .. ELIDE

c

omitted, having part
    ELLIPTIC, ELLIPTICAL
onager .... ASS
once: dial. .... ANES
one .... AIN, UNIT
one-base hit .... SINGLE
one behind other .... TANDEM
one-eighth Troy ounce .. DRAM
one-eyed giant ..... CYCLOPS
one-horse carriage ..... SHAY
one hundred sq. meters AR, ARE
one hundred thousand rupees
           LAKH
one, music by .... SOLI, SOLO
one-spot .... ACE
one thousand .... MIL
one-year record ...... ANNAL
O'Neill heroine .... ANNA
onion .... CEPA
onion, Welsh .... CIBOL
onionlike plant .. CIVE, LEEK,
  CHIVE, SHALLOT, ESCHALOT
only ...... MERE, SAVE, SOLE
onward .... AHEAD, FORTH
onyx, Mex. .... TECALI
oorial .... SHA
ooze .... LEAK, SEEP, SEIP,
    SIPE, SYPE, EXUDE
open .... AJAR, OVERT,
  BROACH, PATENT, UNWRAP

d

open court .... AREA
open plain .... VEGA
opening .... GAP, HOLE,
  RIFT, SLOT, VENT, HIATUS
opening, long ...... RIMA, SLOT
opening, mouthlike
      STOMA, STOMATA
opening, slit-like .... RIMA
opening, small .... PORE
opera ... AIDA, BORIS, ORFEO
opera, Beethoven .... FIDELIO
opera, Bizet .... CARMEN
opera composer, modern
    BRITTEN, MENOTTI
opera, Gounod .... FAUST
opera hat .... GIBUS
opera heroine ... AIDA, ELSA,
  MIMI, SENTA, ISOLDE
opera house, Milan .... SCALA
opera, Massenet
      MANON, THAIS
opera, Puccini .... TOSCA
opera scene .... SCENA
opera singer .... MELBA
opera soprano, star.ALDA, PONS
 BORI, RISE, RAISA, STEBER
opera star .... DIVA
opera, Verdi ... AIDA, ERNANI
opera, Wagner .... RIENZI
operate .... RUN, MANAGE
operetta composer ..... FRIML

a opium poppy seed ...... **MAW**
opossum, S. Am. ...... **QUICA**
opponent .. **FOE, ANTI, RIVAL**
opportune .... **TIMELY**
opportunity .... **CHANCE**
oppose .... **IMPUGN**
opposed, one .... **ANTI**
opposed to solo .... **TUTTI**
opposite extremities ... **POLES**
opposite .... **REVERSE**
Ops' daughter .... **CERES**
Ops' husband .... **SATURN**
optical glass .... **LENS**
optical illusion ...... **MIRAGE**
optical instrument lines **RETICLE**
optimistic .... **ROSY, ROSEATE**
oracle, Apollo's .... **DELOS**
oracle, Gr. .. **DELPHI, DELPHOI**
oral .... **PAROL**
orange-red stone .... **SARD**
orange tincture, Her. .. **TENNE**
orangutan, Malay ...... **MIAS**
orarion .... **STOLE**
orator .... **OTIS, RHETOR**
orb of day .... **SUN**
orbit point .... **APSIS, APOGEE**
orchid genus .... **DISA**
orchid leaves for tea
FAAM, FAHAM
orchid tuber .... **SALEP**
b ordain .... **DECREE**
order .... **BID, FIAT,**
ARRAY, EDICT, DECREE
order, one of Catholic. **MARIST**
order, put in .... **TIDY, SETTLE**
orderliness .... **SYSTEM**
ordinance .... **LAW**
ordnance piece ...... **MORTAR**
ore deposit ...... **LODE, MINE**
ore of iron .... **OCHER, OCHRE**
ore receptacle ...... **MORTAR**
organ .... **EAR, EYE**
organ of algae .... **PROCARP**
organ part .... **STOP**
organ pipe .... **REED**
organ pipe, displayed **MONTRE**
organ prelude .... **VERSET**
organ, seed-bearing .... **PISTIL**
organ stop **REED,SEXT,DOLCAN,**
CELESTE, MELODIA
organism, 1-cell
AMEBA, AMOEBA
organism, simple
MONAD, MONAS
organization .... **SETUP**
orgy .... **REVEL**
Orient .... **EAST**
Oriental ...... **ASIAN, TATAR**
Oriental dwelling .... **DAR**

c Oriental lute .... **TAR**
Oriental nursemaid .... **AMA,**
IYA, AMAH, AYAH, EYAH
Oriental plane tree .. **CHINAR**
Oriental porgy .... **TAI**
Oriental potentate ...... **AGA**
Oriental sailing ship ... **DHOW**
Oriental servant ..... **HAMAL**
Oriental ship captain .... **RAS**
Oriental weight .... **ROTL**
orifice.**PORE, STOMA, OSTIOLE**
orifices, sponge ...... **OSCULA**
origin .... **SEED**
original .... **NEW**
original sin .... **ADAM**
originate **ARISE, START, CREATE**
Orinoco tributary .... **ARO**
oriole, golden .... **LORIOT**
ornament .... **FRET**
ornament, curly ..... **SCROLL**
ornament in relief ... **EMBOSS**
ornament, spire .... **EPI**
ornamental border .... **DADO**
ornamental grass .. **EULALIA**
ornamental nailhead .... **STUD**
Orpheus' destination ... **HADES**
Orpheus' instrument ..... **LYRE**
orris .... **IRIS**
orris-root ketone, oil ... **IRONE**
oscillate .... **WAVE**
osier .... **WITHE**
d Osiris' brother .... **SET**
Osiris' wife, sister .... **ISIS**
ostentation .... **POMP**
ostracism ..... **TABU, TABOO**
ostrich, Am. .... **RHEA**
ostrich-like bird
EMU, EMEU, RATITE
Otaheite apple .... **HEVI**
Othello was one .... **MOOR**
Othello's lieutenant, foe **IAGO**
otherwise .... **ELSE**
otic .... **AURAL**
otologist .... **AURIST**
otter brown, color ... **LOUTRE**
otter genus .... **LUTRA**
Ottoman .... **TURK**
Ottoman court .... **PORTE**
Ottoman official ...... **PASHA**
"Our Mutual Friend," ballad-
seller in .... **WEGG**
oust .... **EJECT, EVICT**
out .... **AWAY, FORTH**
out-and-out .... **ARRANT**
out: Dutch .... **UIT**
out of style .... **PASSE**
out of the way .... **ASIDE**
outbreak, unruly .... **RIOT**
outburst, sudden ...... **SPATE**
outcast
LEPER, PARIAH, ISHMAEL

a
outcome, final .... **UPSHOT**
outcry .... **CLAMOR**
outer .... **ECTAL**
outer portion of earth ... **SIAL**
outfit .. **KIT, RIG, GEAR, SUIT**
outfit, queer .... **GETUP**
outlet .... **VENT**
outline .... **PERIMETER**
outlook .... **VISTA**
outmoded .... **PASSE**
OUTRIGGER see MALAY CANOE
outward .... **ECTAD**
ova .... **EGGS**
oval ... **ELLIPTIC, ELLIPTICAL**
oven .... **KILN, OAST**
oven, annealing .. **LEER, LEHR**
oven, Polyn. native ...... **UMU**
over .... **ATOP, ABOVE,**
AGAIN, ENDED, ACROSS
over-nice .... **FINICAL**
overnice person .... **PRIG**
over: poet. .... **OER**
over there ..... **YON, YONDER**
overact .... **EMOTE**
overcoat ... **ULSTER, PALETOT**
overdue payment ..... **ARREAR**
overflow .... **DEBORD**
overfond, be ..... **DOAT, DOTE**
overjoy .... **ELATE**
overlay .... **CEIL**
overripe grain .... **BRITE**
overseer, ranch: Sp. Am.
CAPORAL
overshadow .... **DOMINATE**
overshoe
GOLOE, GALOSH, GALOSHE
overskirt .. **PANIER, PANNIER**
overspreading mass ..... **PALL**

c
overt .... **OPEN, FRANK**
overwhelm .... **DELUGE**
overwhelming amount .... **SEA**
Ovid's "— Amatoria" .... **ARS**
ovule .... **SEED**
ovum .... **EGG**
owala tree .... **BOBO**
owl, barn, Samoa ...... **LULU**
owl, eagle .. **BUBO, KATOGLE**
owl, horned .... **BUBO**
owl, S. Asia .... **UTUM**
owl's cry .... **HOOT**
own up to .... **AVOW**
ownership, of land, old law
ODAL, UDAL
ox, extinct wild .... **URUS**
ox, forest .... **ANOA**
ox, long-haired .... **YAK**
ox of Caesar's time .... **URUS**
ox, wild .... **ANOA**
ox, wild: India .... **GAUR**
GOUR, ZEBU, GAYAL
oxalis, S. Amer. .... **OCA**
oxen .... **KINE**
oxhide strap ..... **REIM, RIEM**
oxide .... **CALX**
oxidize .... **RUST**
oxygen compound **OXID, OXIDE**
oxygen, form of ..... **OZONE**
oxygen radical .... **OXYL**
oyster bed material
CULCH, CUTCH, CULTCH
oyster drill .... **BORER**
oyster farm: Fr. .... **PARC**
oyster, young .... **SPAT**
oysterfish .... **TAUTOG**
Ozarks, town west of in Okla.
ADA
Oz books author ...... **BAUM**

b
pace .... **RATE, STEP**
pachisi, kind of .... **LUDO**
pachyderm .... **ELEPHANT**
Pacific aroid food plant **TARO**
Pacific Island cloth ..... **TAPA**
Pacific pine .... **HALA**
Pacific shrub .... **SALAL**
pacify
CALM, SOOTHE, PLACATE
pack .... **WAD, STOW**
pack animal .... **ASS,**
BURRO, LLAMA, SUMPTER
pack horse .... **SUMPTER**
pack down .... **RAM, TAMP**
package, India .... **ROBBIN**
package of spun silk .. **MOCHE**
pad .... **TABLET**

d
padded jacket under armor
ACTON
padnag .... **TROT, AMBLE**
Padua, town near ...... **ESTE**
pagan god .... **IDOL**
page, "Love's Labor Lost" **MOTH**
page number .... **FOLIO**
pageantry .... **POMP**
"Pagliacci" character ... **CANIO**
"Pagliacci" heroine ... **NEDDA**
pagoda, Chinese ..... **TA, TAA**
pagoda ornament ... **EPI, TEE**
paid notice .... **AD**
pail .... **SKEEL**
pain, dull .... **ACHE**
pain reliever **OPIATE, ANODYNE**
paint, face .... **FARD, ROUGE**

pain-killer alkaloid source **COCA**
painted bunting: Creole .. **PAPE**
PAINTER .. see also ARTIST
and country of each artist
painter, modernist
KLEE, MIRO, ERNST
painting style .... **GENRE**
painting, wall .... **MURAL**
pair .... **DUO, DIAD,
DUAD, DYAD, MATE**
pair of horses ... **SPAN, TEAM**
pairing .... **MATING**
palanquin .... **JAUN**
palanquin bearer ..... **HAMAL**
palanquin, Jap. .... **KAGO**
palatable, very .... **SAPID**
pale .... **WAN, ASHY,
ASHEN, PASTY**
pale color .... **PASTEL**
pale-colored .... **MEALY**
Palestine in Jewish use **ERETS**
palisade: fort. .... **RIMER**
Pallas .... **ATHENA**
pallid .... **WAN, PALE**
palm ...... **TI, COCO, TALA,
TALIPAT, TALIPOT, TALI-
PUT**
palm, Afr. .... **DUM**
palm, Asia .... **ARENG, BETEL**
palm, betel .... **ARECA**
palm, book .... **TARA**
palm, Brazil .... **ASSAI**
palm, climbing ...... **RATTAN**
palm cockatoo .... **ARARA**
palm, dwarf genus ..... **SABAL**
palm fiber **DOH, TAL, RAFFIA**
palm fiber, S. Amer. **DATIL**
palm genus .... **ARECA**
palm genus, Asia ... **ARENGA**
palm juice, fermented .. **SURA**
palm leaf
OLA, OLE, OLAY, OLLA
palm-leaf mat .... **YAPA**
palm lily .... **TI**
palm, liquor ..... **BENO, BINO**
palm, N. Z. .... **NIKAU**
palm, nipa ..... **ATAP, ATTAP**
palm off .... **FOB, FOIST**
palm, palmyra leaf ..... **OLA,
OLE, OLLA, OLAY**
palm sago, Malay ... **GOMUTI**
palm sap .... **TODDY**
palm starch .... **SAGO**
palm, W. Ind. **GRIGRI, GRUGRU**
palmetto .... **SABAL**
palmyra leaf .... **OLA, OLE,
OLAY, OLLA**
palmyra palm .... **BRAB**
palp .... **FEELER**
palpitation .... **PALMUS**

pamper .... **COSHER, COSSET**
pamphlet .... **TRACT**
panacea .... **ELIXIR**
Panama gum tree **COPA, YAYA**
Panama, old name ... **DARIEN**
Panama tree, large .. **CATIVO**
Panay negrito .... **ATI**
panda .... **WAH, BEAR**
panel .... **PANE**
panel of jurors ...... **VENIRE**
pang .... **THROE**
pangolin .... **MANIS**
panic .... **FEAR, FUNK**
pannier .... **DOSSER**
Panopolis, chief god of .. **MIN,
KHEM**
pant .... **GASP**
pantry .... **AMBRY, LARDER,
SPENCE, BUTTERY**
— Paulo, Brazil .... **SAO**
papal cape ... **FANO, FANON,
FANUM, ORALE, PHANO,
FANNEL**
papal church .... **LATERAN**
papal collar .. **FANO, FANON,
FANUM, ORALE, PHANO,
FANNEL**
papal court ...... **SEE, CURIA**
papal fanon .... **ORALE**
papal letter ... **BULL, BULLA**
papal scarf .... **ORALE**
papal veil .... **FANO, FANON,
FANUM, ORALE, PHANO,
FANNEL**
papal vestment .... **FANO,
FANON, FANUM, ORALE,
PHANO, FANNEL**
paper folded once ..... **FOLIO**
paper, imperfect, poor
CASSE, CASSIE, RETREE
paper, lighting .... **SPILL**
paper measure .. **REAM, QUIRE**
paper mulberry .... **KOZO**
paper mulberry bark .... **TAPA**
paper size
DEMY, POTT, OCTAVO
paper, thin crisp ...... **PELURE**
par, 2 under .... **EAGLE**
Para, Brazil, capital .. **BELEM**
parade .... **MARCH, STRUT**
paradise .... **EDEN**
paradise, Buddhist ...... **JODO**
paradise, like .... **EDENIC**
"Paradise Lost" angel .. **ARIEL**
paragraph .... **ITEM**
parallelogram .... **RHOMB**
paralysis .... **PARESIS**
parapet, solid portion of **MERLON**
parasite .... **LEECH**

Parasite

parasite in blood .... TRYP
parasitic insect MITE, ACARID
parasitic plant MOSS, DODDER
paravane .... OTTER
Parcae .... FATES
Parcae, one of
NONA, MORTA, DECUMA
parcel of land .... LOT, PLAT
parchment, book
FOREL, FORREL
pardon .... REMIT, CONDONE
pardon, general .... AMNESTY
pare .... PEEL
Paris art exhibit ...... SALON
Paris, first bishop of
DENIS, DENYS
Paris section .... PASSY
Paris subway .... METRO
Paris thug .... APACHE
Paris' father .... PRIAM
Paris' wife .... OENONE
parish head .... RECTOR
parley .... PALAVER
Parliament report .. HANSARD
parol .... ORAL
paroxysm .... FIT, SPASM
parrot
KEA, LORY, VASA, VAZA
parrot, Brazil ... ARA, ARARA
parrot-fish
LORO, LAUIA, SCARID
parrot, hawk .... HIA
parrot, monk .... LORO
parrot, N. Z. large KEA, KAKA
parrot, P. I., green .... CAGIT
parrot, sheep-killing .... KEA
parrot's bill, part of .... CERE
parrotlike .... ARINE
parry .... FEND, EVADE
Parsi priest .... MOBED
Parsi scripture .... AVESTA
parsley camphor .... APIOL
parsley, plant kin to
ANISE, CELERY
parson bird
POE, TUE, TUI, KOKO
parsonage .... MANSE
part .... ROLE, SOME, PIECE,
BREAK, SEVER, SHARE,
CLEAVE, ELEMENT
part, Greek play
EXODE, EXODOS
part of church .... BEMA
NAVE, AISLE, ALTAR
part of horse's foot .. PASTERN
part of speech .. NOUN, VERB
parted .... PARTITE
participle ending .... ING
parti-colored .... PIED, PINTO

parti-colored horse
ROAN, CALICO
particle ...... ACE, BIT, ION,
JOT, ATOM, IOTA, DROP,
MITE, MOTE, GRAIN,
SHRED, TITTLE
particle, electrically charged
ION
particle in cosmic rays MESON
particle of chaff ...... PALEA
particle, small
JOT, ATOM, IOTA, MOTE
particular .... ITEM
Partlet .... HEN, BIDDY
partnership: Hawaii HUI, HOEY
partridge call ... JUCK, JUKE
partridge, sand ...... SEESEE
partridge, snow ...... LERWA
party .... SECT
parvenu .... UPSTART
pasha .... DEY
pass .... HAND, ELAPSE
pass a rope through ... REEVE
pass between peaks ..... COL
pass by .... BYGO
pass on .... RELAY
pass over ... OMIT, SKIP, ELIDE
pass through .... REEVE
pass through mountains .. COL,
DEFILE
passable .... SOSO
passage .... GUT, ITER,
CANAL, TRANSIT
passage, bastion .... POSTERN
passage, covered .... ARCADE
passage: hist. .... ALURE
passage: music TUTTI, STRETTA
passage out .... EXIT, EGRESS
passageway ADIT, HALL, AISLE
Passover ..... PASCH, PASCHA
Passover meal SEDAR, SEDER
passport endorsement VISA, VISE
past AGO, GONE, OVER, AGONE
paste .... STRASS
pasteboard .... CARD
pasted-up art work .. COLLAGE
pastel .... TINT
pastoral .... IDYLLIC
pastoral place ...... ARCADIA
pastoral poem ... IDYL, IDYLL
pastoral staff .. PEDA, PEDUM
pastry
PIE, FLAN, TART, ECLAIR
pasture .... LEA
pasture: N. Eng. .... ING
pasture, to .... AGIST
pasty .... DOUGHY
pat .... DAB, TAP
pat, very .... APT
Patagonian cavy ...... MARA
patchwork, literary .... CENTO

a patella .... ROTULA
paten .... ARCA, ARCAE
patent from monarch .. BERAT
path: Anglo-Ir. ..... CASAUN
path: math. .... LOCUS
path of planet .... ORBIT
pathos, false .... BATHOS
patriarch Jacob ...... ISRAEL
patriarch's title .... NASI
patron .... CLIENT
patron saint of France
DENIS, DENYS
patronage ...... EGIS, AEGIS
pattern .... NORM, TYPE,
IDEAL, MODEL, PARAGON
pattern, large square DAMIER
Paul, Apostle .... SAUL
Paul's birthplace ..... TARSUS
paulownia tree .... KIRI
pause .... REST
pause: poet. & music
SELAH, CESURA, CAESURA
paver .... TUP
paver's mallet .... TUP
pavilion .... TENT
paving stone .... FLAG, SETT
paw .... PUD, FOOT
pawl .... DETENT
b pawn .... HOCK
Pawnee Indian rite .... HAKO
Pawnee tribes .... CHAUI
pay .... ANTE, WAGE, REMIT
pay dirt .... ORE
pay, fixed .... STIPEND
pay for another ...... TREAT
pay homage: feudal law
ATTORN
pay one's part .... ANTE
pay out .... SPEND
payable .... DUE
paymaster, India ...... BUXY
payment back .... REBATE
payment for a bride, S. Afr.
LOBOLA
payment for death, feudal CRO
payment for homicide ... ERIC
payment, press for ...... DUN
payment to owner: Fr. law CENS
pea .... LEGUME
peace .... PAX
peace god, Anglo-Saxon .. ING
peace of mind .... REST
peaceful ... IRENE, IRENICAL
peach, clingstone ...... PAVY
peacock .... MAO, PAVO
peacock blue .... PAON
peacock butterfly .... IO
peacock fish .... WRASSE
peacock genus .... PAVO
peacock: Kipling .... MAO

c peak ...... ALP, TOR, ACME,
APEX, PITON, ZENITH
peak: Scot. .... BEN
peanut ...... MANI, GOOBER
pear, autumn .... BOSC
pear cider .... PERRY
pearl blue color ...... METAL
Pearl Buck heroine ..... OLAN
pearl, imitation ...... OLIVET
pearl millet ... BAJRA, BAJRI
pearlweeds .... SAGINA
peasant. CARL, CEORL, CHURL
peasant, India .... RYOT
peasant, Scot.
COTTAR, COTTER
peat .... TURF
peat spade .... SLADE
pecan tree .... NOGAL
peccary, collared .... JAVALI
peck .... DAB, NIP, KNIP
pedal .... TREADLE
peddle ... HAWK, SELL, VEND
peddle: Eng. .... TRANT
pedestal .... GAINE
pedestal part .. DADO, PLINTH
peduncle, plant .... SCAPE
peel . BARK, PARE, RIND, SKIN
peep-show .... RAREE
PEER .... see also NOBLE
peer .... PEEK, PEEP
d Peer Gynt's mother ...... ASE
peevish .... PETULANT
peg .... KNAG
peg, golf .... TEE
peg, wooden
NOG, TRENAIL, TREENAIL
Pegu ironwood .... ACLE
Peleg's son .... REU
pellucid ...... CLEAR, LIMPID
pelma .... SOLE
pelota court .... FRONTON
pelt ...... FELL, SKIN, STONE
pelvic bone, pert. to .... ILIAC
pelvic bones .... ILIA
pen name, Dickens .... BOZ
pen name, G. Russell ...... AE
pen name, Lamb .... ELIA
pen point .... NEB, NIB
pen-text .... RONDE
penman, Yutang .... LIN
penalty .... FINE
pendulum weight .... BOB
Penelope's father .... ICARIUS
penetrate
GORE, ENTER, PERMEATE
penitential season ..... LENT
penmanship .... HAND
pennies .... PENCE
Pennsylvania sect ..... AMISH
Pentateuch .... TORA, TORAH

People

PEOPLE .. see also TRIBES In SPECIAL SECTION
people .... MEN, FOLK, ONES, RACE, DEMOS
people, ancient Asian ... SERES
people: Ger. .... VOLK
people: Ir. .... DAOINE
people, Nigerian . BENI, BENIN
people: Sp. .... GENTE
people, spirit of ...... ETHOS
people, the .... DEMOS
pepper, climbing ...... BETEL
pepper, garden .... PIMIENTO
pepper plant, Borneo .... ARA
pepper shrub AVA, CAVA, KAVA, KAWA
pepper vine .... BETEL
Pequod's captain ...... AHAB
"per —" ..... DIEM, ANNUM
perceive .. SEE, SENSE, DESCRY
perception . EAR, TACT, SENSE
perch .... SIT, ROOST
perch genus .... PERCA
perchlike fish .... DARTER
percolate .. OOZE, SEEP, LEACH
peregrine .... ALIEN
perenially shifting sands region AREG
perfect .... IDEAL, MODEL
perforate ...... BORE, DRILL, PUNCH, RIDDLE
perform .... RENDER
performer DOER, ACTOR, ARTISTE
perfume ATAR, OTTO, AROMA, ATTAR
perfume base .... MUSK
perfume with incense .. CENSE
perfumed pad .... SACHET
Pericles' consort .... ASPASIA
periphery ... RIM, PERIMETER
period .... DOT
period, time AGE, EON, ERA, STAGE
periodic as Med. winds ETESIAN
permit .. LET, ALLOW, LICENSE
permission .... LEAVE
pernicious, something .... PEST
perplex BAFFLE, CONFUSE, BEWILDER
Persephone ..... CORA, KORE
Persephone's husband HADES, PLUTO
Persia .... IRAN
Persian .... IRANI
Persian coin, ancient .. DARIC
Pers. demigod .... YIMA
Pers. elf .... PERI
Pers. enameled tile ..... KASI
Pers. fairy .... PERI
Pers. governor, old ... SATRAP
Pers. headdress, ancient TIARA

Pers. lord ..... KAAN, KHAN
Pers. mystic .... SUFI
Pers. native .... LUR
Pers. poet .... OMAR
Pers. potentate .... SHAH
Pers. priestly caste ..... MAGI
Pers. province, ancient .. ELAM
Pers. race, tribesman LUR,KURD
Pers. rug .. SENNA, HAMADAN
Pers. ruler .... SHAH
Pers. ruler of dead ..... YIMA
Pers. sect .... BABI
Pers. sprite .... PERI
PERS. TITLE .... see TITLE, PERSIAN
Pers. tribe member ..... LUR
Pers. weight .... SER
persimmon, E. Ind. GAB, GAUB
person of mixed blood METIS, MESTIZO
person, overnice .... PRIG
personage .... NIBS
personification of folly ... ATE
personification of light: Polyn. AO
personnel .... STAFF
perspiration .. SUDOR, SWEAT
perspire .... EGEST, SWEAT
pert girl .... CHIT, MINX
pertaining to the chin MENTAL
pertinent .... APT, PAT
perturb .... DERANGE, DISTURB, AGITATE, TROUBLE
PERU INDIAN .. see page 193
peruse ..... CON, READ, SCAN
peruser .... CONNER
Peruvian fertility goddess MAMA
Peruvian plant .... OCA
pervade .... PERMEATE
pester .... ANNOY, TEASE
pestle .... PILUM
pestle vessel .... MORTAR
pet .... CADE
pet lamb ...... CADE, COSSET
"Peter Pan" dog ...... NANA
"Peter Pan" pirate ...... SMEE
petiole .... STIPE
Petrarch's love .... LAURA
petrol .... GAS
peyote .... MESCAL
phantoms .... EIDOLA
Pharaoh .... RAMESES
Pharaoh after Rameses I .. SETI
phase .... FACET, STAGE
pheasant brood NID, NYE, NIDE
pheasant, Himal. . CHIR, CHEER
pheasant, India ...... MONAL
Phidias statue .... ATHENA
philippic .... TIRADE
PHILIPPINE ISLANDS see also SPECIAL SECTION

a Philippine Islands attendant ...... **ALILA**
P.I. bast fiber ...... **CASTULI**
P.I. cedar .... **CALANTAS**
P.I. chief **DATO, DATU, DATTO**
P.I. DWARF see P. I. NEGRITO
P.I. dyewood tree
TUI, IPIL, TUWI
P.I. food .... **POI, SABA**
P.I. fort .... **COTA, KOTA**
P.I. grass ...... **BOHO, BOJO**
P.I. lighter .... **CASCO**
P.I. lizard .... **IBID, IBIT**
P.I. Moslem .... **MORO**
P.I. negrito, native, dwarf
**ATA, ATI, ITA,
AETA, ATTA**
P.I. palm wine ... **BENO, BINO**
P.I. peasant .... **TAO**
P.I. poisonous tree .... **LIGAS**
P.I. rice ...... **PAGA, MACAN**
P.I. sash .... **TAPIS**
P.I. servant .... **ALILA**
P.I. shrub, rope **NABO, ANABO**
P.I. skirt .... **SAYA**
P.I. tree .... **DAO, IBA, TUA,
TUI, BOGO, DITA, IFIL,
IPIL, YPIL**
P.I. warrior .... **MORO**
Philistine city .... **GATH,
GAZA, EKRON**
b Philistine deity, principal **DAGON**
philosopher's stone .... **ELIXIR**
philosophical element ... **RECT**
philosophical theory **MONISM**
philosophy, pert. to Gr. **ELEATIC**
phloem .... **BAST**
phoebe .... **PEWEE, PEWIT**
Phoebus .... **SOL, SUN**
Phoenician city .... **TYRE**
Phoenician goddess .. **ASTARTE**
Phoenician port .... **SIDON**
Phoenician princess .. **EUROPA**
phonetic notation system
ROMIC
phonetical sound .... **PALATAL**
phosphate of lime ... **APATITE**
photo-developing powder **METOL**
photography solution ... **HYPO**
Phrygian god .... **ATTIS**
Phrygian lunar god ..... **MEN**
physical ... **SOMAL, SOMATIC**
physician ..... **GALEN, MEDIC**
physician's group .... **AMA**
physician's symbol **CADUCEUS**
physicist, Am. .... **EINSTEIN**
physicist, Eng. .... **BOYLE**
physicist, Fr. .... **CURIE**
physicist, Nobel prize-winner
1944 .... **RABI**
physiological individual .. **BION**

c piano, upright ...... **CLAVIAL**
pick, miner's: Eng.
MANDREL, MANDRIL
pick out .... **CULL, GLEAN**
picket .... **PALE**
pickled bamboo shoots **ACHAR**
pickled meat .... **SOUSE**
pickling fluid .... **BRINE**
pickling herb .... **DILL**
pickpocket .... **DIP**
"Picnic" author .... **INGE**
picture ... **DRAW, PORTRAIT**
picture border .... **MAT**
picture, composite .. **MONTAGE**
picturesque .... **SCENIC**
pie, meat, small .... **PASTY**
piebald .... **PINTO**
piebald pony ... **PIED, PINTO**
piece of eight .... **REALS**
piece out .... **EKE**
piece, thin .... **SLAT**
pier .... **KEY, DOCK,
MOLE, QUAI, QUAY**
pier, architectural ..... **ANTA**
pier support .... **PILE, PILING**
pierce ... **GORE, STAB, SPEAR**
pig.**HOG, SOW, SHOAT, SHOTE**
pig, wild .... **BOAR**
pig, young .... **ELT, GRICE**
pigs .... **SUS**
d pigs' feet .... **PETTITOES**
pigs, litter of .... **FARROW**
pigs, red .... **DUROC**
pigeon ... **NUN, BARB, DOVE,
POUTER, ROLLER**
pigeon hawk .... **MERLIN**
pigeon pea.**DAL, TUR, GANDUL**
piglike animal ..... **PECCARY**
pigment, blue-green ..... **BICE**
pigment, brown .... **SEPIA**
pigment, brown, from soot
BISTER, BISTRE
pigment, deep blue .... **SMALT**
pigment, red .... **LAKE**
pigment test crystalline **DOPA**
pigment, without .... **ALBINO**
pigmentation, lack of
ACHROMA
pigtail .... **CUE, QUEUE**
pike, full grown . **LUCE, LUCET**
pike, walleyed .... **DORE**
pilaster .... **ANTA**
pilchard .. **FUMADO, SARDINE**
pilchard-like fish ...... **SPRAT**
pile ...... **NAP, HEAP, SPILE**
pile driver .... **OLIVER**
pile driver ram .... **TUP**
pile of hay .... **RICK, STACK**
pilfer .... **STEAL**
pilgrim .... **PALMER**

Pilgrimage

a
pilgrimage city .... MECCA
pilgrimage to Mecca .... HADJ
pill, large .... BOLUS
pillage .... LOOT, SACK, STEAL
pillage .... RAPINE
pillar, as of ore .... JAMB
pillar, Hindu .... LAT
pillar, resembling ..... STELAR
pillar, tapering ...... OBELISK
pillow .... BOLSTER
pilot .... GUIDE, STEER
pimento or —spice ..... ALL
pin .... BROOCH
pin, firing .... TIGE
pin, gunwale .... THOLE
pin, machine .... COTTER
pin, metal .... RIVET
pin, pivot .... PINTLE
pin, rifle firing .... TIGE
pin, Roman .... ACUS
pin, small, very LILL
pin, splicing .... FID
pin, wooden .. FID, NOG, PEG,
COAG, COAK, DOWEL
pin wrench .... SPANNER
pinafore .... TIER
pincer claw .... CHELA
pinch .... NIP
pinched with cold ..... URLED
Pindar work .... ODE
b
pine-cone, like a ...... PINEAL
pine, Mex. .... OCOTE, PINON
pine, Scot. .... RIGA
pine, textile screw
ARA, PANDAN
pineapple NANA, PINA, ANANA
pineapple genus .... PUYA
pinfeather .... PEN
pinion .... WING
pink .... DAMASK
pinnacle .... TOP, APEX
pinnacle, ice .... SERAC
pinniped .... SEAL
pinochle score, term
DIX, MELD
pint, half .... CUP
pintado fish .... SIER
pintail .... SMEE
pinworm .. ASCARID, ASCARIS
pious Biblical Jew ..... TOBIT
pipe .... TUBE, RISER
pipe, Irish .... DUDEEN
pipe joint, fitting .... TEE
pipe, pastoral .... REED
pipe, tobacco
BRIAR, BRIER, DUDEEN
pipe, water. HOOKAH, NARGILE
pipe with socket ends
HUB, HUBB
pipelike .... TUBATE
pique .... PEEVE

c
pirate ...... ROVER, CORSAIR
pirate in War of 1812 LAFITTE
pismire .... ANT, EMMET
pistil part .... CARPEL
pistol .... DAG, DAGG,
MAUSER, SIDEARM
pistol: slang .... HEATER
pit ..... HOLE, ABYSS, STONE
pit for roots, Maori ..... RUA
pit: medical .... FOSSA
pit, small .. FOVEA, LACUNA
pitch .... KEY, TAR, TONE
pitcher .... JUG, EWER
pitcher's false move .... BALK
pith .... NUB, GIST
pith helmet .... TOPI, TOPEE
pithy .... TERSE
pithy plant .... SOLA
pitiful quality ...... PATHOS
pittance .... DOLE
pitted .... FOVEATE
pity .... RUTH
placard .... POSTER
place .... SET, LIEU, LOCI,
SPOT, LOCUS, STEAD, LO-
CALE
place before .... APPOSE
place, camping .... ETAPE
place case is tried .... VENUE
place in office again .. RESEAT
d
place, in relation .... POSIT
place, market .... FORUM
place of shelter .. GITE, HAVEN
placid .... CALM, SERENE
plagiarize .... STEAL
plague .... PEST, TEASE
plain, arctic .... TUNDRA
plain, Argentine ...... PAMPA
plain, Asia .... CHOL
plain, Palestine .... ONO
plain, Russia .... STEPPE
plain, S. Am. .... LLANO
plain, treeless ..... SAVANNA
plain, treeless Arctic TUNDRA
plain, upland .. WOLD, WEALD
Plains Indian .... see page 193
plainly woven .... UNI
plait .... PLY, BRAID
plan .... PLOT, INTEND
plane, Fr. .... SPAD
plane, Ger. .... STUKA
plane, Jap. .... ZERO
plane part .... FLAP,
NOSE, TAIL, WING
plane, Russ. fighter ...... MIG
planets (in order of distance from
sun) MERCURY (1), VE-
NUS (2), EARTH (3),
MARS (4), JUPITER (5),
SATURN (6), URANUS (7),
NEPTUNE (8), PLUTO (9)

a planets in distance from Earth (closest first)

1—VENUS	5—SATURN
2—MARS	6—URANUS
3—MERCURY	7—NEPTUNE
4—JUPITER	8—PLUTO

planets in size (largest first)

1—JUPITER	6—VENUS
2—SATURN	7—PLUTO
3—NEPTUNE	8—MARS
4—URANUS	9—MERCURY
5—EARTH	

planetarium .... ORRERY
planetary aspect **CUSP, TRINE**
plank's curve on ship ..... SNY
plant .... SOW, SEED
plant, bayonet .... DATIL
plant broom .... SPART
plant, bulb **CAMAS, CAMASS, CAMMAS**
plant cutter bird ...... RARA
plant cutting .. SLIP, PHYTON
plant disease .... RUST, SMUT
plant joined to another GRAFT
plant life .... FLORA
PLANT, LILY ...... see LILY
plant, lily-like **CAMAS, CAMASS, CAMMAS**
plant louse .... APHID
plant, male .... MAS
b plant, medicinal, S. Am. **ALOE, SENNA, IPECAC**
plant modified by environment to abnormal development **ECAD**
plant, mustard family **KALE, CRESS**
plant organ .... LEAF
plant pod .... BOLL
plant, poisonous .... LOCO
plant, sea-bottom ... ENALID
plant stem: bot. ..... CAULIS
plant stem tissue ...... PITH
plant used as soap ... AMOLE
plants of area .... FLORA
plantain lily genus ..... HOSTA
plantation, osier .... HOLT
planter .... SEEDER
plaster .... SMEAR
plaster, artist's painting. GESSO
plaster of Paris .... GESSO
plastic .... LUCITE
plate, battery .... GRID
plate, Eucharist .... PATEN
plate, reptile's .... SCUTE
plate to hurl .... DISCUS
plateau .... MESA
plateau, Andes .... PUNA
platform ...... DAIS, STAGE
platform, ancient ...... BEMA

c platform, mine shaft **SOLLAR, SOLLER**
platinum, of .... OSMIC
platinum wire loop ..... OESE
Plato's "Idea" ... EIDE, EIDOS
play .... DRAMA
play on words .... PUN
play, part of ..... ACT, SCENE
play unskillfully ...... STRUM
player .... ACTOR
playing card, old It. ... TAROT
playwright .... INGE
plea, to end: law ... ABATER
plead .... SUE, ENTREAT
pleading: law .... OYER
please .... SUIT
pleasing .... NICE
pleasure god, Egypt. . BES, BESA
pledge .... VOW, **GAGE, OATH, PAWN, TROTH, ENGAGE**
pledge, Rom. law .... VAS
plexus .... RETE, RETIA
pliable .... WAXY
pliant .... LITHE
plinth .... ORLO, SOCLE
plot .... LOT, **PLAT, CABAL, CONSPIRE**
plow, cutter **COLTER, COULTER**
d plow part .... SHETH, SHEATH
plow, sole of .... SHARE
plowed field .... ERD, ARADA
plug .... BUNG, **CORK, SPILE, STOPPER**
plum .... GAGE, SLOE
plume ..EGRET, PREEN, AIGRET
plummet .... FATHOM
plump child .... FUB
plunder .... ROB, LOOT, PREY, **SACK, BOOTY, RAVEN, RAVIN, REAVE, PILFER, RAPINE, RAVAGE, RAVINE**
plunder ruthlessly ... MARAUD
plunge .... DIVE, DOUSE
plural ending .... EN, ES
plus .... AND
Pluto .... DIS, HADES, ORCUS
Pluto's mother-in-law DEMETER
pneumonia, kind of .... LOBAR
Po tributary .... ADDA
pochard .... SMEE
pocket billiards .... POOL
pocket gopher, Mex. ..... TUZA
pod, cotton .... BOLL
pods for tanning .... PIPI
Poe poem .... RAVEN
poem .... ODE, ELEGY, EPODE
poem division, or part . CANTO
poem, 8 line .... TRIOLET

Poem

a
poem, long heroic .. **EPIC, EPOS**
poem, love .... **SONNET**
poem, lyric ...... **ODE, EPODE**
poem, mournful .... **ELEGY**
poem, of a .... **ODIC**
poem, old Fr. .... **DIT**
poem, sacred .... **PSALM**
poet .... **BARD, ODIST**
poet, A.-S. .... **SCOP**
poet, Bengal .... **TAGORE**
poet, blind, epic ..... **HOMER**
poet, lyric .... **ODIST**
poet, Norse ... **SCALD, SKALD**
poet, poor .... **RIMER**
poetry .... **EPOS, POESY**
poetry, early .... **RUNE**
poetry, Finnish .... **RUNES**
poetry, mournful, pert. to
.... **ELEGIAC**
poetry, Norse god of
.... **BRAGE, BRAGI**
poi, source of .... **TARO**
point **END, TIP, BARB, PUNTO**
point in moon's orbit nearest
earth .... **PERIGEE**
point of curve .... **NODE**
point of land .... **SPIT**
point of moon .... **CUSP**
point of view .... **ANGLE**

b
point on mariner's compass
.... **RUMB**
point on tooth's crown .. **CUSP**
point, tennis or golf .... **ACE**
point won .... **GOAL**
pointed ..... **SHARP, ACUATE**
pointed arch .... **OGEE**
pointed end .... **CUSP**
pointed missile **DART, SPEAR**
pointed remark .... **BARB**
pointed staff .... **PIKE**
pointer .... **WAND**
pointless .... **INANE**
poison .... **BANE, TAINT**
poison, arrow ... **INEE, UPAS,
URALI, URARE, URARI,
CURARE, CURARI**
poison, hemlock ..... **CONINE**
poison, India **BISH, BISK, BIKH**
poisonous protein **RICIN, RICINE**
poisonous weed .... **LOCO**
poke ..... **JAB, PROD, NUDGE**
poker stake ...... **POT, ANTE**
pokeweed ..... **POCAN, SCOKE**
Polar explorer .... **BYRD**
pole .... **MAST**
pole, Gaelic games
.... **CABER, CABIR**
Pole .... **SLAV**
pole, naut. .... **MAST, SPRIT**
pole to handle fish ... **PEW**
pole to pole, from **AXAL, AXIAL**

c
polecat, Cape **ZORIL, ZORILLA**
police line .... **CORDON**
policeman ...... **COP, PEELER**
policeman, state .... **TROOPER**
policeman, S. Afr. ...... **ZARP**
polish .... **RUB, WAX,
SHINE, LEVIGATE**
POLISH ... see also POLAND
SPECIAL SECTION
Polish assembly ... **SEIM, SEJM**
Polish cake .... **BABA**
Polish general .. **BOR, ANDERS**
Polish title of address
.... **PAN, PANI**
polished ...... **SHINY, SLEEK,
URBANE, ELEGANT**
polisher .... **EMERY**
polishing material
.... **RABAT, ROUGE**
polite .... **CIVIL**
political booty .... **GRAFT**
pollack fish .... **SEY**
pollen brush .. **SCOPA, SCOPAE**
Pollux or Castor .... **ANAX**
Pollux' mother .... **LEDA**
Pollux' twin .... **CASTOR**
polo stick .... **MALLET**
Polynesian .... **MAORI**
Polyn. "Adam" .... **TIKI**
Polyn. chestnut .... **RATA**

d
Polyn. cloth .... **TAPA**
Polyn. dance .... **SIVA**
Polyn. deity, demon
.... **AKUA, ATUA**
Polyn. drink .... **AVA**
Polyn. for nature's power **MANA**
Polyn. god .... **ATEO**
Polyn. god of forest .... **TANE**
Polyn. herb .... **PIA**
Polyn. hero .... **MAUI**
Polyn. island group ... **SAMOA**
Polyn. languages
.... **MAORI, MAHORI**
Polyn. lily .... **TI**
Polyn. stone heap .... **AHU**
pome .... **APPLE**
"Pomp and Circumstance" Com-
poser .... **ELGAR**
pompous .... **TURGID**
pond .. **MERE, POOL, LOCHAN**
ponder .... **MUSE, PORE**
pontiff .... **POPE**
pony .... **CAVY**
pony, student's .... **CRIB**
pool .... **MERE, TARN,
LAGOON, PUDDLE**
pool: Scot. .... **DIB, CARR,
LINN, LLYN**
poon tree **DILO, DOMBA, KEENA**
poor .... **NEEDY**
poor joe .... **HERON**

a   poor player .... **DUB**
poorly .... **ILL**
POPE .. see also PAPAL
Pope ... **JOHN, PIUS, ADRIAN**
Pope, English .... **ADRIAN**
Pope John XXIII first name
                ANGELO
Pope John XXIII last name
               RONCALLI
Pope Pius XI .... **RATTI**
Pope Pius XII ...... **PACELLI**
POPE'S CAPE, COLLAR ... see
    PAPAL CAPE, COLLAR
Pope's triple crown **TIAR, TIARA**
poplar .... **ALAMO, ASPEN**
poplar, white ... **ABELE, ASPEN**
poppy red .... **GRANATE**
poppy seed .... **MAW**
populace, the .... **DEMOS**
popular girl .... **BELLE**
porcelain
    CHINA, SEVRES, LIMOGES
porcelain, ancient .... **MURRA**
porcelain, Chin. .... **JU, KO**
porcelain, Eng. .... **SPODE**
porch .... **ANTA, STOOP,**
    VERANDA, VERANDAH
porch, Gr. .... **STOA**
porch, Hawaiian ...... **LANAI**
b   porch swing .... **GLIDER**
porcupine anteater .. **ECHIDNA**
porcupine, Canada .... **URSON**
pore .... **PORUS, STOMA,**
    OSTIOLE, STOMATA
porgy .... **SCUP**
porgy, Europ. .... **PARGO**
porgy genus .... **PAGRUS**
porgy, Jap. (Oriental) .... **TAI**
porkfish .... **SISI**
porous rock ..... **TUFA, TUFF**
porpoise .... **DOLPHIN**
porridge .... **POB, BROSE**
porridge, corn meal ..... **SAMP**
porridge: Sp. Am. ...... **ATOLE**
Porsena of Clusium ..... **LARS**
PORT .. see also SPECIAL SEC-
    TION — GAZETTEER
port .... **HAVEN**
port, banana, Honduras .. **TELA**
port, Black Sea ...... **ODESSA**
Port Moresby land ... **PAPUA**
port of Rome .... **OSTIA**
port opp. Gibraltar .... **CEUTA**
port, South Seas .... **APIA**
port, Suez .... **SAID**
port wine city .... **OPORTO**
portable chair .... **SEDAN**
portal .... **DOOR, GATE**
portend **BODE, AUGUR, PRESAGE**

c   portent .... **OMEN, SIGN**
porter, Orient
    HAMAL, HAMMAL
Portia's waiting woman **NERISSA**
portico .... **STOA**
portion. **PART, SOME, SEGMENT**
portion out **DOLE, METE, ALLOT**
portray .... **DRAW,**
    LIMN, DEPICT, DELINEATE
Portuguese coin .... **REI**
Port. colony, India ...... **GOA**
Port. folk tune .... **FADO**
Port. lady .... **DONA**
Port. man .... **DOM**
Port. navigator .... **GAMA**
Port. title ..... **DOM, DONNA**
pose .... **SIT**
Poseidon .... **NEPTUNE**
Poseidon's son .... **TRITON**
posited .... **SET**
position ...... **SITUS, STATUS**
position without work **SINECURE**
positive .... **THETIC**
positive pole, terminal **ANODE**
possession, landed .... **ESTATE**
possum .... **COON**
possum, comic-strip ..... **POGO**
post .... **MAIL, SEND**
post-hole digger (slick) ...**LOY**
d   postpone .... **DEFER**
postulate .... **POSIT**
posture .... **STANCE**
pot .... **OLLA**
pot, chem. .... **ALUDEL**
pot, earthen .... **CRUSE**
pot herb .... **WORT**
pot, India **LOTA, LOTO, LOTAH**
pot liquor .... **BREWIS**
pot metal .... **POTIN**
potassium .... **KALITE**
potassium chloride .. **MURIATE**
potassium nitrate
    NITER, GROUGH
potation, small .... **DRAM**
potato .... **SPUD**
potato, sweet .. **YAM, BATATA**
pother .... **ADO**
potpourri .... **OLIO**
potter's blade .... **PALLET**
pottery fragment .... **SHARD**
pottery, pert. to .... **CERAMIC**
pouch .... **SAC**
pouch-shaped ...... **SACCATE**
poultry .... **HENS, BIRDS**
poultry disease .... **PIP, ROUP**
pounce .... **SWOOP**
pound .... **TUND**
pound down ...... **RAM, TAMP**
pour .... **RAIN, TEEM**
pour off gently ...... **DECANT**

121

Pour

pour out .... **LIBATE**
poverty .... **NEED, WANT**
powder, astringent .... **BORAL**
powder, mineral ingredient
.... **TALC**
powder of aloes .... **PICRA**
powdered pumice .... **TALC**
power .. **DINT, MANA, FORCE**
practical joke .... **HOAX**
practice .... **HABIT**
practice exercise, musical **ETUDE**
praise **LAUD, EXTOL, EXTOLL**
prance .... **CAPER**
prank .... **DIDO, CAPER**
prate .... **GAB, YAP**
prate: India ..... **BUKH, BUKK**
pray: Yiddish .... **DAVEN**
prayer **AVE, BEAD, BENE, PLEA,**
       CREDO, MATIN, ORISON
prayer form .... **LITANY**
prayer, 9-day ...... **NOVENA**
prayer-rug, Hindu ..... **ASANA**
prayer stick, Am. Ind.
       BAHO, PAHO, PAJO
prayers, deacon's
       ECTENE, EKTENE
prayerbook
       ORDO, PORTAS, PORTASS
praying figure .... **ORANT**
preacher, Gospel .... **EVANGEL**
precepts .... **DICTA**
precipice, Hawaii .... **PALI**
precipitous .... **STEEP**
preclude ...... **AVERT, DEBAR**
preconceive .... **IDEATE**
predicament .... **SCRAPE**
predicate
       BASE, FOUND, AFFIRM
predict
AUGUR, FORECAST, FORETELL
predisposed .... **PRONE**
preen .... **PLUME, PRINK**
preface .... **PROEM**
prefecture, Jap. .... **KEN**
PREFIX:
  about .... **PERI**
  above .... **HYPER**
  across .... **DIA, TRANS**
  again .... **RE**
  against .... **ANTI**
  ahead .... **PRE**
  an .... **AE**
  apart .... **DIS**
  away .... **DE, DI, APO**
  back .... **ANA**
  backward .... **RETRO**
  bad .... **MAL**
  badly .... **MIS**
  beauty .... **CALLI**
  before ..... **OB, PRE, ANTE**
  blood .... **HAEM, HEMO**

both .... **AMBI**
CHEMICALS .. see page 29
common .... **PRE**
distant .... **TEL, TELE**
double .... **DI**
down .... **DE, CATA**
eight ... **OCT, OCTA, OCTO**
equal .... **ISO**
far .... **TEL, TELE**
faulty .... **MIS**
fire .... **PYR**
former, formerly .... **EX**
four .... **TETRA**
from .... **EC**
half ..... **DEMI, HEMI, SEMI**
ill .... **MIS**
mountain .... **ORO**
negative .... **IR, NON**
new .... **NEO**
not ... **IL, IM, IR, UN, NON**
not fully .... **SEMI**
numerical .... **UNI**
of atmospheric pressure **BARO**
of the stars .... **ASTRO**
on this side .... **CIS**
one .... **UNI**
out of .... **EC, EX**
outer ..... **ECT, EXO, ECTO**
outer skin .... **EPI**
outside .... **ECT, EXO**
over .... **EPI, SUPER,**
       SUPRA, SUPERB
partly .... **SEMI**
people .... **DEMO**
pray .... **ORA**
recent .... **NEO**
same .... **ISO, EQUI, HOMO**
separation .... **DIS**
single .... **MONO**
ten .... **DEC, DECA**
thousand .... **KILO**
three .... **TER, TRI**
thrice .... **TER, TRIS**
threefold .... **TRI**
through .... **DIA, PER**
to .... **AP**
together .... **COM**
town .... **TRE**
turning .... **ROTO**
twice .... **BI**
two .... **DI, DUA**
twofold .... **DI**
under .... **SUB**
upon .... **EPI**
upward ..... **ANA, ANO**
with .... **SYN**
within .... **ENDO**
wrong .... **MIS**

a
prehistoric implement ... **CELT**
prehistoric mound ...... **TERP**
prejudice .... **BIAS**
prelate, high .... **PRIMATE**
prelude .... **PROEM**
premium, exchange ..... **AGIO**
prepare .... **FIT, GIRD,**
MAKE, ADAPT, EQUIP
prepare for publication .. **EDIT**
prepared opium
CHANDU, CHANDOO
preposition ...... **AT, IN, ON,**
UP, INTO
presage
OMEN, HERALD, PORTEND
prescribed .... **THETIC**
prescribed quantity .... **DOSE**
present .. **GIFT, GIVE, DONATE**
present, be .... **ATTEND**
present in brief .... **SUM**
presently. **ANON, ENOW, SOON**
preserve .... **CAN, JAM, KEEP,**
SAVE, PROTECT, MAINTAIN
preserve in brine .. **CORN, SALT**
Presidential nickname ... **ABE,**
CAL, IKE, TEDDY
press together .... **SERRY**
pressure .... **DURESS**
pressure unit .. **BARAD, BARIE**
pretend .. **FAKE, SHAM, FEIGN**
b
pretense .... **SHAM**
pretensions .... **AIRS**
pretentious .... **SIDY**
prevail .... **WIN**
prevail on .... **INDUCE**
prevalent .... **RIFE**
prevent ... **DETER, PRECLUDE**
prevent by law .... **ESTOP**
prey .... **RAVIN**
prey upon
RAVEN, RAVIN, RAVINE
Priam's son
PARIS, HECTOR, HEKTOR
price .... **RATE**
price of transportation .. **FARE**
prickle .... **SETA**
prickles .... **SETAE**
prickly pear
TUNA, NOPAL, CACTUS
prickly plant ... **BRIAR, BRIER,**
NETTLE
prickly seed coat .. **BUR, BURR**
pride .... **PLUME**
PRIEST .. see also CLERGYMAN
priest
FRA, ABBE, CURE, PADRE
priest, Celtic .... **DRUID**
priest, Gr. .... **MYST**

c
PRIEST, HIGH, see HIGH PRIEST
priest in "Iliad" .... **CALCHAS**
priest, Mongol ...... **SHAMAN**
priest, Moro **SARIP, PANDITA**
priestess, Gr. .... **AUGE**
priestess, Rom. ...... **VESTAL**
priesthood, Rom. ...... **SALII**
priestly caste ... **MAGI, MAGUS**
prima donna .... **DIVA**
PRIMA DONNA ...... see also
OPERA SOPRANO
prime minister: Brit. ... **EDEN,**
PEEL
primeval .... **OLD,**
EARLY, PRIMAL, PRISTINE
prince, Abyssin. .... **RAS**
prince, Arabian .. **EMIR, SAYID,**
SAYYID, SHERIF, SHEREEF
prince, India
RAJA, RANA, RAJAH
prince of Argos ...... **DANAE**
Prince of Darkness .... **SATAN**
prince, Oriental .... **KHAN**
prince, Persian .. **AMIR, AMEER**
prince, petty .... **SATRAP**
prince, Slavic .... **KNEZ**
Prince Val's father ... **AGUAR**
princeling .... **SATRAP**
princely .... **ROYAL**
princess, Gr. myth ...... **IOLE**
princess, India .. **RANI, RANEE**
d
principal .... **TOP, ARCH**
MAIN, CHIEF
principal commodity .. **STAPLE**
principle, accepted
AXIOM, PRANA, TENET
print .... **STAMP**
print measure .... **EM, EN**
printer, 1st colonial .... **DAYE**
printer's direction ...... **STET**
printer's mark .... **DELE**
printer's mistake
TYPO, ERRATUM
printer's mistakes .... **ERRATA**
printing plate .... **STEREO**
printing roller .... **PLATEN**
prison. **JUG, GAOL, JAIL, QUOD**
prison sentence .... **RAP**
prison spy .... **MOUTON**
privation .... **LOSS**
privilege, commercial .. **OCTROI**
prize .... **PRY, AWARD**
pro .... **FOR**
"— pro nobis" .... **ORA**
probe, medical .... **STYLET**
problem .... **POSER**
proboscis .... **SNOUT**
proboscis monkey ...... **KAHA**
proceed ... **WEND, ADVANCE**
proceedings .... **ACTA**

123

procession .... TRAIN, PARADE, MOTORCADE
proclaim .... CRY, VOICE, HERALD, DECLARE
prod .... URGE
produce .... BEGET, YIELD CREATE, INWORK, GENERATE
produce as an effect ... BEGET
produced, quantity ..... YIELD
producing cold ...... ALGIFIC
production, artistic .. FACTURE
profane .... VIOLATE
profane, Hawaiian ...... NOA
profession ART, CAREER, METIER
professional, not LAIC, LAICAL
profit ... GAIN, VAIL, AVAIL
profit, to yield .... NET
profits, taker of: law . PERNOR
profitable ...... FAT, USEFUL
profound .... DEEP
"— profundis" .... DE
progenitor ..... SIRE, PARENT
progeny .... ISSUE
prohibit .... BAN, BAR, VETO, DEBAR, ESTOP
prohibition BAN, VETO, EMBARGO
Prohibition, against ...... WET
project ...... JUT, IDEA, PLAN
projectile .... MISSILE
projecting edge RIM, FLANGE
projecting piece ARM, RIM, TENON, FLANGE
projecting rim .... FLANGE
projecting tooth .... SNAG
projection . EAR, BARB, PRONG
projection, fireplace. HOB, HOBB
projection, jagged SNAG, TOOTH
projection, studlike .... KNOP
promenade .... MALL
promise .... WORD
promise to pay .... IOU, NOTE
"Promised Land" fountain AIN
promontory ..... CAPE, NASE, NAZE, NESS
promontory, Orkneys .... NOUP
promontory, rocky ...... TOR
promote .... FOSTER
prompt .... CUE, YARE
prone .... APT, FLAT
prong .... TINE, TOOTH
pronghorn .... CABREE, CABRET, CABRIE, CABRIT
pronoun .. IT, ME, US, WE, YE, HER, HIM, ONE, SHE, THAT, THIS, THEE, THEM, THEY, THOU, THESE, THOSE

pronoun, possessive . MY, HER, HIS, ITS, OUR, HERS, MINE, OURS, YOUR
pronounce indistinctly ... SLUR
pronounce strongly .... STRESS
pronouncement DICTA, DICTUM
proof, corrected ...... REVISE
proof, printer's .... GALLEY
proofreader's mark DELE, STET, CARET
prop .... HOLD, STAY, BRACE, BOLSTER, SUSTAIN
propeller .... OAR
proper .... DUE, FIT
properly .... FEATLY
property, hold on .... LIEN
property, India .... DHAN
property, item of ASSET, CHATTEL
property, landed ...... ESTATE
property owned absolutely ALOD, ALLOD, ALODIUM, ALLODIUM
property, receiver of .. ALIENEE
prophesy .... FORETELL
prophet .... SEER, AUGUR, PREDICTOR, FORETELLER
PROPHETS, BIBLICAL ..... see SPECIAL SECTION
prophets .... VATES
prophetic ... VATIC, VATICAL
proportion .... RATIO
proportionally assess PRORATE
proposition THESES, THESIS, PREMISE
proposition, logic ..... LEMMA
proposition: math. .. THEOREM
prosecutor .... SUER
prosecutor: abbr. .... DA
proselyte to Judaism .... GER
"— prosequi," .... NOLLE
Proserpina ...... CORA, KORE
prospect .... VISTA
prosperity .... WEAL
prosperity god, Teut. .... FREY
Prospero's servant ..... ARIEL
prostrate .... PRONE, REPENT
protagonist .... HERO
protected .... HOUSED
protection .... EGIS, AEGIS
protection right, Old Eng. MUND
protective building .... REDAN
protective influence EGIS, AEGIS
Protestant denomination: abbr. ME, PE, BAP, PRESB
prototype .... IDEAL
protozoan order .... LOBOSA
protuberance ..... JAG, NUB, HUMP, KNOB, KNOT, NODE, WART, KNURL, TORUS

124

a protuberant .... **TOROSE**
prove: law .... **DERAIGN**
proverb ...... **SAW, ADAGE,**
AXIOM, MAXIM, SAYING
provide ...... **ENDOW, ENDUE**
provided .... **IF**
provided that .... **SO**
province, Rom. .... **DACIA**
provisional clause ... **PROVISO**
proviso .... **CLAUSE**
provoke............ **IRE, RILE,**
ANGER, ANNOY
prow .... **BOW, STEM**
prune: prov. Eng. ...... **SNED**
pruning knife .... **DHAW**
Prussian spa, town ...... **EMS**
pry .... **NOSE, LEVER, SNOOP**
Psalm, 51st .... **MISERERE**
Psalmist .... **DAVID**
Psalms, selection of .. **HALLEL**
Psalms, word in .... **SELAH**
pseudonym ...... **NOM, ALIAS**
pseudonym of Louise Del La
Ramee .... **OUIDA**
psyche .... **SOUL**
psychiatrist
JUNG, ADLER, FREUD
Ptah, embodiment of ... **APIS**
ptarmigan .... **RYPE**
b pteropod genus ...... **CLIONE**
pua hemp ....:......... **POOA**
public .... **OPEN, OVERT**
public: Chin. .... **KUNG**
public esteem .... **REPUTE**
public, make ... **AIR, DELATE**
public vehicle .... **BUS, TAXI**
publication, style of . **FORMAT**
publish .... **ISSUE, PRINT**
publish illegally ...... **PIRATE**
Puccini heroine .... **MIMI**
puck, hockey .... **RUBBER**
pudding......... **DUFF, SAGO**
pueblo dweller .... **HOPI**
Pueblo Indian ... **HOPI, ZUNI,**
KERES, MOQUI, TANOA
Pueblo sacred chamber .. **KIVA**
Pueblo, Tanoan .... **HANO**
Puerto Rican plant ...... **APIO**
puff up .... **ELATE**
puffbird, Brazil .... **DREAMER**
puffbird genus .... **MONASA**
puffer fish .... **TAMBOR**
Pulitzer poet .... **FROST**
pull .. **TOW, TUG, DRAG, HALE**
pull with nautical tackle **BOUSE**
pulley .... **SHEAVE**
pulp, fruit .... **POMACE**
pulpit .... **AMBO, BEMA**
pulpy mass left in cider **POMACE**
pulverize .... **MICRONIZE**

c pump handle .... **SWIPE**
pumpkin .... **PEPO**
punch .... **JAB**
"Punch and Judy" dog .. **TOBY**
punch, engraver's .. **MATTOIR**
punctuation mark **DASH, COLON**
pungent .. **TEZ, SPICY, TANGY**
punish by fine ...... **AMERCE**
punishment .... **FERULE**
punishment, of .... **PENAL**
punitive .... **PENAL**
Punjab native .... **JAT**
punk .... **AMADOU**
pupa .... **INSTAR**
pupil of eye .... **GLENE**
puppet .... **DOLL**
puppet, famous **JUDY, PUNCH**
puppeteer, famous ...... **SARG**
pure sirup .... **CLAIRCE**
pure thought .... **NOESIS**
purification, ancient Roman
LUSTRUM
purloin .... **STEAL**
purple
MAUVE, MODENA, TYRIAN
purple dye source .... **MUREX**
purple medic
LUCERN, ALFALFA, LUCERNE
purple ragwort ...... **JACOBY**
purple seaweed . **SION, LAVER**
d purport, general ...... **TENOR**
purpose .... **AIM, END,**
GOAL, SAKE, INTENT
purposive .... **TELIC**
purse net .... **SEINE**
pursy .... **STOUT**
push up .... **BOOST**
put aside .... **DAFF**
put away .... **STORE**
put back .... **REPLACE**
put forth .... **EXERT**
put in bank .... **DEPOSIT**
put off .... **DEFER**
put out .... **OUST, EJECT**
put up .... **ANTE**
puzzle .... **POSER,**
REBUS, BAFFLE, ACROSTIC
puzzles .... **CRUCES**
Pygmalion's statue .. **GALATEA**
pygmy .... **ATOMY**
pygmy people, Congo
AKKA, ACHUAS
pygmy people, Equatorial Africa
BATWA, ABONGO, OBONGO
Pylos, kin of .... **NESTOR**
Pyramus, lover of .... **THISBE**
pyromaniac .... **FIREBUG**
Pythias' friend .... **DAMON**
python .... **BOA**

Q

qua .... **AS**
"— qua non" .... **SINE**
quack **IMPOSTOR, CHARLATAN**
quack medicine .... **NOSTRUM**
quadrant .... **ARC**
quadrate .... **SQUARE**
"quae —" which see .... **VIDE**
quaff .... **DRINK**
quail .... **COLIN, COWER**
quake .... **SHAKE, SHIVER, TREMOR, TREMBLE**
Quaker .... **FRIEND**
Quaker Poet .... **WHITTIER**
quaking .... **TREPID**
qualify .... **FIT, ADAPT, EQUIP, PREPARE**
qualified .... **FIT, ABLE**
quality .... **CALIBER, CALIBRE**
quantity, indeterminate . **SOME**
quantity: math. **SCALER, VECTOR**

quarrel .... **ROW, FEUD, SPAT, TIFF**
quarter of a year: Scot. **RAITH**
quartz .... **JASPER**
quartz, green .... **PRASE**
quartz, translucent ... **PRASE**
quash: law .... **CASSARE**
quaternion .... **TETRAD**
quay .... **LEVEE**
Quebec, district, town ... **LEVIS**
Quebec's patron saint .. **ANNE**
Queen .... **CLEO**
queen: Moslem **BEGUM, BEEGUM**
queen of gods, Egypt. ... **SATI**
queen of gods, Rom. ... **HERA, JUNO**
Queen of Italy .... **ELENA**
Queen of Ithaca ... **PENELOPE**
Queen of Roumania ... **MARIE**
Queen of Scots .... **MARY**
Queen of Spain, last ..... **ENA**
queen, "Romeo and Juliet" **MAB**

queenly .... **REGAL, REGINAL**
Queensland hemp plant **SIDA**
Queensland tribe .... **GOA**
quell .... **CALM, CRUSH**
quench .... **SLAKE**
quench steel ..... **AUSTEMPER**
quern .... **MILL**
query .... **ASK**
queue .... **LINE**
question .... **ASK, GRILL**
question, hard .... **POSER**
quetzal .... **TROGON**
quibble .... **CAVIL, EVADE**
quick .... **FAST, AGILE, ALIVE, RAPID**
quick: music .... **TOSTO**
quicken ... **HASTEN, ENLIVEN**
quickly .... **CITO, APACE, PRESTO, PRONTO**
quickly, move **SCAT, SCUD, SKITE**
quicksilver ...... **HEAUTARIT**
quid .... **CUD**
"quid — quo," equivalent . **PRO**
quiescent **LATENT, DORMANT**
quiet .... **CALM, LULL, STILL, SMOOTH**
quiet! .... **SH, PST, TST**
quilkin .... **FROG, TOAD**
quill .... **PEN, SPINE**
quill feathers **REMEX, REMIGES**
quill for winding silk ..... **COP**
quilt .... **EIDER, COVER**
quince, Bengal .... **BEL, BHEL**
quinine .... **KINA**
quintessence ... **PITH, ELIXIR**
quirt, cowboy's ...... **ROMAL**
quit .... **CEASE, LEAVE**
quite .... **ALL**
quivering ... **ASPEN, TREMOR**
"quod — demonstrandum" **ERAT**
"Quo Vadis" tyrant character **NERO**
quoits, mark of .... **MOT**
quote .... **CITE**

126

R

Ra, consort of .... **MUT**
Ra, son of .... **SU, SHU**
rabbi, law-teaching ... **AMORA**
rabbit cage .... **HUTCH**
rabbit, Europ. . **CONY, CONEY**
rabbit, female .... **DOE**
rabbit fur .... **LAPIN**
rabbit home .... **WARREN**
rabbit, small swamp .. **TAPETI**
rabbit, So. Am. .... **TAPETI**
rabble .... **MOB**
rabies .... **LYSSA**
raccoon-like mammal .. **COATI**
RACE .. see also TRIBES in
SPECIAL SECTION
race, boat .... **REGATTA**
race, kind of .... **RELAY**
race, short .... **SPRINT**
race-track .... **OVAL**
race-track circuit ...... **LAP**
race-track tipster ..... **TOUT**
races, pert. to ...... **ETHNIC**
Rachel's father ...... **LABAN**
racing boat .... **GIG**
racket, game .... **PELOTA**
radar screen .... **SCOPE**
radiate .... **EMANATE**
radical .... **RED**
radicle .... **STEMLET**
radio advertiser .... **SPONSOR**
radio bulletin ..... **NEWSCAST**
radio-guided bomb ..... **AZON**
radio wave ..... **MICROWAVE**
radio wire .... **LITZ**
radio-TV awards ..... **EMMIES**
radioactive counter .... **GEIGER**
radioactive element ... **NITON**
radioactive ray ...... **GAMMA**
radium discoverer ...... **CURIE**
radium emanation .... **NITON**
radius, pert. to ...... **RADIAL**
radon .... **NITON**
raft, kind of ... **CATAMARAN**
raft, Maori .... **MOKI**
rag doll .... **MOPPET**
rage .... **RAMP, RANT,
RESE, STORM**
ragged person: Sp. ...... **ROTO**
raging monster, Bibl. .. **RAHAB**
ragout, game .... **SALMI**
ragweed genus .... **IVA**
raid .... **FORAY, INROAD**
raid, soldier's .... **COMMANDO**
rail at .... **REVILE**
rail bird **SORA, WEKA, CRAKE**
railing .... **PARAPET**

railroad bridge ...... **TRESSEL,
TRESTLE**
railroad light .... **FLARE**
railroad signal
TRIMMER, SEMAPHORE
railroad tie .... **SLEEPER**
railroad timber .... **TIE**
railway station: Fr. ..... **GARE**
rain after sunset ...... **SEREIN**
rain, fine .... **MISLE**
rain forest .... **SELVA**
rain gauge .... **UDOMETER**
rain serpent, Hindu .... **NAGA**
rain spout: Scot. ...... **RONE**
rain tree .... **SAMAN**
rainbow .... **ARC, IRIS**
rainbow goddess .... **IRIS**
rainbow, pert. to ..... **IRIDAL**
raincoat .... **PONCHO**
rainy .... **WET**
raise . **REAR, BREED, ELEVATE**
raised .... **BRED**
raisin: Sp. .... **PASA**
raising device .... **JACK**
Rajah's lady ... **RANI, RANEE**
rake ...... **ROUE, LOTHARIO**
rake with gunfire .. **ENFILADE**
ram . **TUP, BUTT, TAMP, ARIES**
ram, male .... **TUP**
ram-headed god, Egypt
AMEN, AMON, AMUN
Ramachandra, wife of .. **SITA**
ramble .... **GAD, ROVE**
Ramee, de la, penname . **OUIDA**
rammed earth building material
PISE
rampart ..... **AGGER, VALLUM**
range .... **AREA, GAMUT,
SCOPE, SIERRA**
Rangoon's state ...... **PEGU**
rank .... **ROW, RATE, DEGREE**
ranks, press in .... **SERRY**
rankle .... **FESTER**
ransom .... **REDEEM**
rapeseed ..... **COLSA, COLZA**
rapid, more: music .. **STRETTA,
STRETTE, STRETTI, STRETTO**
rapids, river .... **SOO**
rapidly .... **APACE**
rapier .... **BILBO**
rare earth element ... **ERBIUM**
rascal .... **IMP, ROGUE**
rase .... **INCISE**
rasorial .... **GNAWING**
rasp .... **FILE, GRATE**

127

Raspberry

a raspberry, variety . BLACKCAP
rasse .... CIVET
rat .... DESERTER
rat, Ceylon, India . BANDICOOT
rat hare .... PIKA
rate .... ESTIMATE
rate, relative .... AT
ratify .... SEAL
ratio .... RATE
RATIO: MATH see MATH, RATIO
rational .... SANE
rational integer .... NORM
rational principle ...... LOGOS
rationalize .... THOB
ratite bird ...... CASSOWARY
rattan .... CANE
rattlesnake
RATTLER, CROTALUS
rave .... RANT
"Raven" author .... POE
"Raven" character .... LENORE
ravine
GAP, DALE, VALE, GORGE
ravine, Afr. .... WADI, WADY
ravine, Arabia .. WADI, WADY
rawboned .... LEAN
rawboned animal ...... SCRAG
ray fish .... SKATE
rays, like .... RADIAL
rayon ... ACETATE, CELANESE
b raze .... DEVASTATE
razor-billed auk
ALCA, MURR, MURRE
reach across .... SPAN
react .... RESPOND
read, inability to ..... ALEXIA
read metrically .... SCAN
read publically ...... PRELECT
reader, first .... PRIMER
reading desk .... AMBO
reading substituted: Bibl.
KERE, KERI
ready: dialect .... YARE
ready-made tie .... TECK
real being, pert. to .... MCCOY
real thing .... MCCOY
reality .... FACT
realm .... DOMAIN
reamer .... BROACH
rear ... ERECT, RAISE, ARRIERE
rear, to the
AFT, ABAFT, ASTERN
rearhorse .... MANTIS
rearing of horse ...... PESADE
reason .... NOUS
reason, deprive of ... DEMENT
reasoning .... LOGIC
reasoning, deductive .. APRIORI
reata
LAZO, ROPE, LASSO, LARIAT

c rebec of India .... SAROD
Rebecca's hairy son ..... ESAU
rebound .. CAROM, RICOCHET
rebuff .... SLAP, SNUB
rebuke
CHIDE, SCOLD, REPROVE
recalcitrant .... RENITENT
recant .... RETRACT
recede .... EBB
recent
NEO, NEW, LATE, NEOTERIC
receptacle .... BIN, BOX,
TRAY, VESSEL
reception, a.m. .... LEVEE
reception: Fr. .... ACCUEIL
reception, India ..... DURBAR
recess .... APSE, ALCOVE
recess, wall .... NICHE
recipient .... DONEE
recite metrically .... SCAN
reckon .... ARET, COUNT
reckoning .... TALLY
reclaim .... REDEEM
recline .... LOLL
recluse .... ASCETIC, EREMITE,
ANCHORET, ANCHORITE
recoil .... SHY, RESILE
recommit .... REMAND
recompense .. PAY, FEES, MEED
reconnaissance RECCO, RECON
d reconnoiter .... SCOUT
reconstruct .... REMODEL
record .. TAB, NOTE, ENROL,
ENTER, ENTRY, REGISTER
record of investigation REPORT
record, ship's .... LOG
record, year's .... ANNAL
records .... ANNALS
recorded proceedings ... ACTA
recording device .... TAPE
records, one who ..... NOTER
recourse, have .... REFER
recover strength ...... RALLY
recovery, legal .... TROVER
recruit .... BOOT
rectifier, current ...... DIODE
rectify ...... AMEND, EMEND
recurring pattern ..... CYCLE
red .... CARMINE,
MAGENTA, NACARAT
red, Brazil .... ROSET
red cedar .... SAVIN, SAVINE
red circle: Her. .... GUZE
red currant .... RISSEL
red deer .... ELAPHINE
red dye root ... CHAY, CHOY
red garden flower .... CANNA
red: Her. .... GULES
red horse .... BAY, ROAN
red ocher .... KEEL, KIEL,
TIVER, RADDLE, RUDDLE

128

red pigment .... **ROSET,
ASTACIN, ASTACENE**
red pine .... **RIMU**
red planet .... **MARS**
red powder, India .... **ABIR**
red, painter's .... **ROSET**
Red River Rebellion leader
RIEL
red: Sp. .... **ROJO**
red squirrel ...... **CHICKAREE**
red swine .... **DUROC**
red, Venetian .... **SIENA**
red-yellow color ...... **ALOMA**
redact .... **EDIT**
redbreast .... **ROBIN**
redcap .... **PORTER**
reddish yellow .... **SUDAN**
redeem .... **RANSOM**
redshank .... **CLEE**
reduce .... **PARE, DEMOTE**
reduce sail .... **REEF**
reduce taxes .... **DERATE**
reebok .... **PEELE**
reedbuck .... **NAGOR**
reek .... **FUG, FUME**
reef .... **SHOAL**
reel, fishing-rod .... **PIRN**
refer .... **PERTAIN**
refer to repeatedly ..... **HARP**
refined grace ...... **ELEGANCE**
reflection .... **GLARE**
refracting device .... **LENS**
refractor, light .... **PRISM**
refrain .... **FORBEAR**
refrain in songs .. **FALA, LALA,
DERRY, LUDDEN**
refrigerant .... **FREON**
refuge ...... **HAVEN, SHELTER**
refugee .... **EMIGREE**
refuse .... **DENY**
refuse .... **ORT, DROSS,
SCUM, OFFAL, TRASH**
refuse, bit of .... **SCRAP**
refuse, flax .... **POB**
refuse: law .... **RECUSE**
refuse, metal . **DROSS, SCORIA**
refuse, wool ·.......... **COT**
refute .... **REBUT, DISPROVE**
regale .... **FETE**
regard ...... **ESTEEM, RESPECT**
regarding ...... **RE, ANENT**
regenerate .... **RENEW**
regiment's framework .. **CADRE**
REGION .... see also DISTRICT
region .... **CLIME, SECTOR**
region, Afr. .. **CONGO, NUBIA**
region, Boeotia ...... **AONIA**
region, Cent. Afr.
SUDAN, SOUDAN
region, Fr. .... **ALSACE**

region, Gr. .... **DORIC**
region, Indo-China ..... **LAOS**
region, pert. to .... **AREAL**
register .... **ENROL,
ENROLL, RECORD**
reiterate .... **REPEAT**
regret .... **RUE, DEPLORE**
reign: India .... **RAJ**
reign, pert. to .... **REGNAL**
reigning .... **REGNANT**
reigning beauty .... **BELLE**
reimbursed .... **PAID**
reindeer .... **CARIBOU**
reindeer, Santa's .... **DASHER,
DONDER, BLITZEN,
PRANCER**
reinstate .... **REVEST**
reject .... **SPURN, REPULSE**
relate .... **TELL,
RECITE, NARRATE**
related .... **AKIN, TOLD,
COGNATE, GERMANE**
related by blood .... **SIB**
related on mother's side **ENATE**
relation .... **SIB**
relative. **SIB, SIS, AUNT, NIECE**
relative amount ...... **RATION**
relative pronoun .... **WHO,
THAT, WHAT**
relative speed .... **TEMPO**
relatives .... **KIN**
relatives, favoring .. **NEPOTAL**
relax .... **EASE**
relaxing of state tensions
DETENTE
relay of horses ..... **REMUDA**
release .... **LOOSE**
release: law .... **REMISE**
release, phonetic .... **DETENTE**
relevant .... **GERMANE**
reliable .... **HONEST**
relief, — .... **BAS**
relief .... **DOLE**
relieve .... **EASE, ALLAY**
relieve: Scot. .... **LISS**
religieuse .... **NUN**
religion .... **FAITH**
religion, Jap. .... **SHINTO**
religious art, work of .. **PIETA**
religious brother .... **FRA,
MONK, FRIAR**
religious festival ..... **EASTER**
religious festival, India .. **MELA**
religious law, Rom. ...... **FAS**
religious laywoman .. **BEGUINE**
religious opinion .... **DOXY**
religious order, one in . **OBLATE**
religious sayings ...... **LOGIA**
relinquish .... **CEDE,
WAIVE, YIELD**

a reliquary .... APSE, ARCA,
ARCAE, CHEST
relish .... GUSTO
reluctant ..... LOATH, AVERSE
rely .... TRUST
remain .... BIDE, STAY
remainder .... REST
remaining .... OVER
remark, witty .... MOT, SALLY
remiss .... LAX
remit .... SEND
remnant .... END, SHRED
remora fish . PEGA, LOOTSMAN
remove .. DELE, DOFF, DELETE
remove interior .... GUT
remove: law .... ELOIN,
ELOIGN, ELOIGNE
remunerate .... PAY
rend ...... RIP, TEAR, WREST
render fat .... TRY
rendezvous .... TRYST
renegade .... APOSTATE
renounce .... ABNEGATE
renovated hat ..... MOLOKER
renown .... FAME, NOTE,
EMINENCE, PRESTIGE
rent .... LET, HIRE, TEAR,
TORN, LEASE
rent, old Eng. law .... TAC
renter .... LESSEE
b repair .... DARN, MEND
repartee .... RIPOST, RIPOSTE
repast .... MEAL
repay .... REQUITE
repay in kind .... RETALIATE
repeat .... ECHO, ITERATE
repeat: music .... BIS
repeat performance .. ENCORE
repeat sign: music .... SEGNO
repeat tiresomely .. DIN, DING
repeated phrase ..... REPRISE
repeatedly hit ...... POMMEL
repetition .... ROTE
replete .... FULL
report, small .... POP
repose .... EASE, REST
representation .... IDOL
representative .... AGENT
reproach ..... BLAME, TAUNT
reproach, old term ..... RACA
reproductive body .. GAMETE
reproductive cell ..... SPORE
reptile, pert. to ..... SAURIAN
repulse .... REPEL
reputation .... NAME, REPUTE
repute .... CHARACTER
request .... PLEA
rescind .... REPEAL
resentment .... IRE
reserve supply .... STORE

c residence ..... HOME, ABODE
residence, ecclesiastical. MANSE
resident of .... ITE
resign .... QUIT, DEMIT
resin ..... GUM, LAC, ANIME,
COPAL, ELEMI, JALAP,
MYRRH, BALSAM, MASTIC
resin, fossil . AMBER, GLESSITE
resin, fragrant .... ELEMI
resist .... OPPOSE
resist authority .... REBEL
resisting pressure ... RENITENT
resistor, current ... RHEOSTAT
resort .... SPA
resort, Fr. .... PAU,
NICE, CANNES
resources .... FUND,
MEANS, ASSETS
respect .... ESTEEM
respond .... REACT
rest .... SIT, EASE, REPOSE
rest, lay at .... REPOSE
restaurant, small ..... BISTRO
resthouse ...... CHAN, KHAN
resting .... ABED
restive .... BALKY
restore .... RENEW
restrain .. CURB, REIN, DETER,
d STINT, TETHER
restrict .... LIMIT
retaliate .... REPAY
retain .... HOLD, KEEP
retaliation .... TALION
retinue .... SUITE, TRAIN
retort, quick . RIPOST, RIPOSTE
retract .... RECANT
retreat .... RECEDE
retreat, cosy . DEN, NEST, NOOK
retribution .... NEMESIS
retribution, get .... VENGE
retrograde .... RECEDE
return ...... RECUR, RESTORE
return a profit .... PAY
return blow .... TIT
return on investment .. YIELD
returning .... REDIENT
reunion, hold a .... REUNE
reveille, call to .... DIAN
revelry, cry of .... EVOE
revelry, drunken .... ORGY
revenue, church: Scot. ANNAT
reverberate .... ECHO
reverberating ...... REBOANT
revere ...... HONOR, HONOUR
reverence .... AWE
reversed in order .. CONVERSE
reversion to type .... ATAVISM

a **revert to state (land)**
　　　　　　　ESCHEAT
revise .... **EDIT, AMEND**
revive wine .... **STUM**
revoke legacy, grant .. **ADEEM**
Revolution hero . **HALE, ALLEN**
revolutions per minute .. **REVS**
revolve . **SPIN, TURN, ROTATE**
revolve: logging .... **BIRL**
revolver.**GAT, GUN, ROD, COLT**
reward .... **MEED**
rhebok .... **PEELE**
Rhine city .... **MAINZ**
Rhine tributary .... **AAR**
rhinoceros beetle ...... **UANG**
rhinoceros, black
　　　　BORELE, NASICORN
rhinoceros: obs.
　　　　　　ABADA, ABATH
Rhone tributary ...... **SAONE**
rhythm .... **TIME, METER,**
　　　　　METRE, CADENCE
rhythmical accent ...... **BEAT**
rhythmical swing .... **LILT**
rib .... **COSTA**
rib. pert. to .... **COSTAL**
rib, woman from .... **EVE**
ribs, with .... **COSTATE**
ribbed fabric ..... **REP, CORD,**
　　　　　　REPP, PIQUE
b **ribbon, badge ...... CORDON**
ribbon: comb. form ..... **TENE**
ribbonfish .... **GUAPENA**
rice .... **PADI, PADDY**
rice dish ...... **PILAU, PILAW**
rice field, Java .... **PADI**
rice grass, P.I. .... **BARIT**
rice in husk .... **PALAY**
rice paste, Jap. .... **AME**
rice polishings .... **DARAC**
rich man .... **MIDAS,**
　　　　　NABOB, NAWAB
rich silk cloth .... **CAFFA**
riches .... **PELF**
rid .... **FREE**
riddle .... **ENIGMA**
ridge .... **ARETE,**
　　　　SPINE, MOUNTAIN
ridge, camp's .... **RIDEAU**
ridge, glacial, sandy ...... **OS,**
　　OSAR, ESKER, OESAR
ridge on cloth .... **WALE**
ridge on skin .... **WELT**
ridge, stony .... **RAND**
ridges, rounded .... **GYRI**
ridged area, Balkan .... **BILO**
ridicule .... **GUY, MOCK,**
　　　　RAZZ, DERIDE
ridicule personified, Gr.
　　　　　　　　MOMUS

c **riding academy** ..... **MANEGE**
riding dress .... **HABIT**
rifle .... **KRAG, MINIE,**
　　　GARAND, CARBINE
rifle ball .... **MINIE**
rifleman, Ger. .... **JAGER**
right conduct, Buddhist ... **TAO**
right conduct: Taoism ..... **TE**
right hand: music .... **DM**
right-hand page .. **RO, RECTO**
right: law .... **DROIT**
right, pert. to .... **DEXTER**
right to speak .... **SAY**
right, turn .... **GEE**
rights, of ...... **JURAL, UDAL**
Rigoletto's daughter .. **GILDA**
rigorous ...... **HARSH, STERN,**
　　STRICT, SEVERE, AUSTERE
rim ...... **LIP, EDGE, FLANGE**
rim of wheel .. **FELLY, FELLOE**
"Rime cold giant" .**YMER, YMIR**
ring ...... **PEAL, TOLL, KNELL**
ring, boxing .... **ARENA**
ring for reins . **TERRET, TERRIT**
ring, gun carriage ..... **LUNET**
ring, harness pad
　　　　　TERRET, TERRIT
ring, lamp condensing ... **CRIC**
ring, little .... **ANNULET**
ring, naut. .... **GROMMET**
d **ring of light** .... **HALO, NIMB,**
　　NIMBUS, AUREOLA,
　　　　　　　AUREOLE
"Ring of the Nibelung" goddess
　　　　　　　　ERDA
"Ring of the Nibelung" smith
　　　　　　　　MIME
ring out .... **PEAL**
ring, part of .... **CHATON**
ring, rubber jar .... **LUTE**
ring, seal .... **SIGNET**
ring-shaped ...... **CIRCINATE**
ring-shaped piece .... **QUOIT**
ring, stone of .... **CHATON**
ringlet .... **CURL, TRESS**
ringworm ..... **TINEA, TETTER**
ripening agent .... **AGER**
ripple ...... **LAP, RIFF, WAVE**
rise above .... **TOWER**
rise aloft .... **TOWER**
rise: old Eng. .... **RIS**
risible .... **GELASTIC**
rites, religious .... **SACRA**
ritual .... **RITE**
RIVER . see also GAZETTEER in
　　SPECIAL SECTION
river .... **RIO**
river, Balmoral Castle's ... **DEE**
river bank .... **RIPA**
river bank, growing by
　　　　　　RIPARIAN

131

River

a river-bank stair, Ind.
    GAUT, GHAT
river bed, dry, Afr.
    WADI, WADY
river between Europe and Asia
    KARA
river, Bremen's .... **WESER**
river Caesar crossed . **RUBICON**
river, Dutch Meuse ..... **MAAS**
river in Baltic .... **ODER**
river in Essex .... **CAM**
river in Orleans .... **LOIRE**
river in Petrograd ...... **NEVA**
river into Moselle ...... **SAAR**
river into Rhone ...... **SAONE**
river islet .... **AIT**
river, "Kubla Khan" .... **ALPH**
river, Munich's .... **ISAR**
river mouth ..... **LADE, DELTA**
river nymph .... **NAIS**
river to the Humber
    OUSE, TRENT
River of Woe ..... **ACHERON**
river, Southwest .... **PECOS**
river: Sp. .... **RIO**
river: Tagalog .... **ILOG**
river to Medit. .... **EBRO**
river valley .... **STRATH**
rivulet .... **RILL**
road .... **VIA, PATH,**
    ITER, AGGER
b road: Roman .... **ITER**
road: Gypsy .... **DRUN**
roadhouse .... **INN**
roam .... **GAD, ROVE**
roast .... **CALCINE**
roasted meat strip .... **CABOB**
roasting rod .... **SPIT**
rob .... **REAVE, DESPOIL**
Rob Roy .... **CANOE**
robber .... **THIEF**
ROBE ..... see also GARMENT
robe .... **MANTLE**
robe to ankles .... **TALAR**
"Roberta" composer .... **KERN**
robot drama .... **RUR**
rock aggregate .... **AUGE**
rock, basic igneous ..... **SIMA**
rock cavity ..... **VOOG, VUGG,**
    VUGH, GEODE
rock, dangerous ...... **SCYLLA**
rock, dark .... **BASALT**
rock, fine grained ...... **TRAP**
rock, flintlike .... **CHERT**
rock, granitoid **DUNITE, GNEISS**
rock, hard .... **WHIN**
rock, jutting .... **TOR**
rock, laminated ...... **SHALE**
    SLATE, GNEISS
rock, melted .... **LAVA**
rock, mica-bearing ... **DOMITE**

c rock, projecting ... **TOR, CRAG**
rock, rugged .... **CRAG**
rock snake .... **PYTHON**
rock whiting genus ..... **ODAX**
rock-wren .... **TURCO**
ROCKET .. see under MISSILE,
    GUIDED
rocket's goal .... **MOON**
rockfish ... **RASHER, TAMBOR**
rockfish, Calif. .. **RENA, REINA**
rockweed .... **FUCI, FUCUS**
Rocky Mt. peak .... **ESTES**
Rocky Mt. range
    TETON, UINTA
rocky peak, eminence,
    pinnacle .... **TOR**
rod ... **POLE, WAND, BATON,**
    PERCH, STAFF
rod, barbecue .... **SPIT**
rod, basketry .... **OSIER**
rod, billiard .... **CUE**
rod, chastening ...... **FERULE**
rodent .... **RAT, HARE**
rodent genus .... **MUS**
rodent, rabbit-like ..... **PIKA**
rodent, S. Am. .. **CAVY, DEGU,**
    PACA, COYPU, AGOUTI
rodent, W. Ind. .... **HUTIA**
Rhoderick Dhu .... **SCOT**
rogue .... **PICARO**
roguish .... **SLY, ARCH**
d roister .... **REVEL**
Roland's destroyer ...... **GAN,**
    GANO, GANELON
roll and heave .... **TOSS**
roll of bread: dialect. .... **BAP**
roll of cloth .... **BOLT**
roll of paper .... **SCROLL**
roll up .... **FURL**
romaine .... **COS**
ROMAN GODS
    see SPECIAL SECTION
Rom. assembly ...... **COMITIA**
Rom. authors .... **CATO, LIVY,**
    OVID, LUCAN, NEPOS,
    PLINY, CICERO, HOR-
    ACE, SENECA, SILIUS,
    VERGIL, SALLUST
Rom. barracks
    CANABA, CANNABA
Rom. box .... **CAPSA**
Rom. boxing glove ... **CESTUS**
Rom. bronze .... **AES**
Rom. brooch .... **FIBULA**
Rom. building .... **INSULA**
Rom. cap .... **PILEUS**
Rom. cavalry body
    TURM, TURMA
Rom. circus post .... **META**
Rom. clan ..... **GENS, GENTES**
Rom. cloak ... **TOGA, ABOLLA**

Rom. coin, ancient ..... **SEMIS, DINDER**
Rom. coins .... **AS, AES, ASSES, SOLIDUS**
Rom. Curia court ...... **ROTA**
Rom. date ...... **IDES, NONES**
Rom. dictator .... **SULLA**
Rom. dish .... **LANX**
Rom. emperor .... **NERO, OTHO, TITUS**
Rom. farce .... **EXODE**
Rom. galley **TRIREME, UNIREME**
Rom. gaming cube ..... **TALUS**
Rom. garment .. **TOGA, STOLA, TUNIC, PLANETA**
Rom. goal post in racing . **META**
Rom. highway ..... **VIA, ITER**
Rom. historian ... **LIVY, NEPOS**
Rom. judge .... **EDILE, AEDILE**
Rom. law control ..... **MANUS**
Rom. legendary king ... **NUMA**
Rom. liquid measure .... **URNA**
Rom. list ...... **ALBE, ALBUM**
Rom. magistrate or official **EDILE, AEDILE, ARCHON, CONSUL, PRETOR, TRIBUNE**
Rom. market ... **FORA, FORUM**
Rom. meal .... **CENA**
Rom. money, copper ..... **AES**
Rom. numerals 1-**I**, 5-**V**, 10-**X**, 50-**L**, 100-**C**, 500-**D**, 1000-**M**
ROMAN OFFICIAL see ROMAN MAGISTRATE
Rom. patriot .... **CATO**
Rom. philosopher **CATO, SENECA**
Rom. platter .... **LANX**
Rom. pledge .... **VAS**
Rom. poet ..... **OVID, LUCAN, HORACE, VERGIL, VIRGIL**
Rom. pound .... **AS**
Rom. province .... **DACIA**
Rom. public games ...... **LUDI**
Rom. public lands ...... **AGER**
Rom. religious festivals . **VOTA**
Rom. road .... **VIA, ITER**
Rom. robe .... **TOGA**
Rom. room, principal **ATRIA, ATRIUM**
Rom. scroll .... **STEMMA**
Rom. statesman .... **CATO**
Rom. sword .... **FALX**
Rom. vessel .... **PATERA**
Rom. war garb .... **SAGUM**
Rom. weight .... **AS**

Rom. well-curb ...... **PUTEAL**
Rom. writer .... **MACER**
romance, tale of . **GEST, GESTE**
ROMANIA .... see RUMANIA
Rome, a founder of ... **REMUS**
Rome's cathedral church **LATERAN**
Rome's conqueror ..... **ALARIC**
Rome's river .... **TIBER**
Romulus' twin .... **REMUS**
rood .... **CROSS**
roof .... **MANSARD**
roof edge .... **EAVE**
roof of mouth .... **PALATE**
roof of mouth, pert. to **PALATAL**
roof ornament .... **EPI**
roof, rounded . **DOME, CUPOLA**
roof, rounded like a ... **DOMAL**
roof, truncated .... **HIP**
roofing piece ...... **RAG, TILE**
roofing slate .... **TILE**
roofing timber .... **PURLIN**
rook's cry .... **CAWK**
room, Eng. college supply **BUTTERY**
room, snug .... **DEN**
room, rooms .... **SPACE, SUITE**
room, architecture ..... **OECUS**
room for household goods, linen, etc. . **EWRY, EWERY**
room, main, Rom. **ATRIA, ATRIUM**
room, mineshaft . **PLAT, PLATT**
room, Rom. .... **ALA**
roomy .... **WIDE**
roost .... **PERCH**
rooster .... **COCK**
root .... **RADIX, RADICES**
root, drug-yielding ..... **JALAP**
root, edible ..... **OCA, TARO, CASSAVA**
root, tree used for sewing **WATAP**
root, word .... **ETYM**
rootlet .... **RADICEL, RADICLE**
rootstock, edible ...... **TARO**
rootstock, fern (Maori) ... **ROI**
rootstock, fragrant .... **ORRIS**
rope ...... **JEFF, LAZO, LASSO, LONGE, REATA, RIATA, LARIAT, MARLINE**
rope, cringle **LEEFANG, LEEFANGE**
rope fiber .. **DA, COIR, FERU, HEMP, IMBE, JUTE, RHEA, ABACA, SISAL**
rope for animals ..... **TETHER**
rope guide: naut. ...... **WAPP**
rope loop .... **BIGHT**

133

Rope

rope, naut. ... **FOX, TYE, STAY, VANG, HAWSER, RATLIN, LANIARD, LANYARD, RATLINE, SNOTTER**
rope to tie boat ..... **PAINTER**
rope, weave .... **REEVE**
rope, yardarm ..... **SNOTTER**
ropes, unite .... **SPLICE**
rosary bead .... **AVE**
rose: Byron .... **GUL**
rose fruit .... **HIP**
rose genus .... **ROSA, ACAENA**
rose-like plant .... **AVENS**
rose of Sharon .... **ALTHEA, ALTHAEA**
rose oil derivative ..... **ATAR, OTTO, ATTAR, OTTAR**
rose ornament .... **ROSETTE**
rose, Pers. .... **GUL**
rosewood .... **MOLOMPI**
rosolic acid ... **AURIN, AURINE**
rostellum .... **ROSTEL**
roster .... **LIST, ROTA**
rotate .... **ROLL, GYRATE**
rotating muscle ..... **EVERTOR**
rotating part .... **CAM, ROTOR**
rotation producer .... **TORQUE**
rotten .... **PUTRID**
rouge ...... **RADDLE, RUDDLE**
rough .... **RUDE, UNEVEN**
rough, as country ...... **HILLY**
rough copy .... **DRAFT**
rough in voice .... **GRUFF**
rough rock .... **KNAR**
roughness, sea .... **LIPPER**
roulette bet ...... **BAS, NOIR, MILIEU**
round, a ...... **ROTA, ROTULA**
round hand .... **RONDE**
round room .... **ROTUNDA**
Round Table Knight .... **KAY, BORS, BORT, BALAN, BALIN, BOHORT, GARETH, GAWAIN, GALAHAD, PELLEAS**
round-up .... **RODEO**
rounded projection ...... **LOBE**
rounder .... **RAKE, ROUE**
roundworm .... **NEMA, ASCARID, ASCARIS**
rouse . **WAKE, AWAKE, WAKEN**
Rousseau novel, hero ... **EMILE**
route .... **WAY, PATH**
route, plane's fixed ..... **LANE**
routine, fixed .... **ROTE**
row .... **LINE, SPAT, TIER**
rowan tree .... **ASH, SORB**
rowdy: slang .... **B'HOY**
rower .... **OAR**
rower's bench .... **ZYGA, ZYGON, THWART**

royal authority ...... **SCEPTRE**
royal court, relating to . **AULIC**
royal edict: Fr. .... **ARRET**
royal family, Fr. ..... **VALOIS**
royal rights, having . **PALATINE**
royal rod .. **SCEPTER, SCEPTRE**
royal treasury ...... **FISC, FISK**
royalty, Hawaii .... **ALII**
rub harshly .... **GRATE**
rub off .... **ABRADE**
rub out .... **ERASE**
rub roughly .... **SCRAPE**
rub to polish .... **BUFF, SHINE**
rub to soreness .... **CHAFE**
rubber .... **PARA, LATEX, CAUCHO, ELASTIC**
rubber, black .... **EBONITE**
rubber source .... **KOKSAGYZ**
rubber, S. Am. . **PARA, CEARA**
rubber tree ...... **ULE, HULE, SERINGA**
rubber, wild .... **CEARA**
rubbery substance **GUTTA, NOREPOL**
rubbish .... **ROT, JUNK, CULCH, RUBBLE**
rubble masonry ..... **MOELLON**
rubella .... **MEASLES**
ruby .... **RED**
ruby red quartz ..... **RUBASSE**
ruby spinel ... **BALAS, BALASS**
rudder bushing .... **PINTLE**
rudder fish .... **CHOPA**
ruddle .... **KEEL, KIEL**
rudiment .... **GERM**
rudiments .... **ABC**
rue .... **REGRET**
rue herb genus .... **RUTA**
ruff, female ..... **REE, REEVE**
ruffed lemur .... **VARI**
ruffer .... **NAPPER**
ruffle .... **CRIMP**
ruffle, neck ... **JABOT, RUCHE**
RUG .... see also CARPET
rug, long narrow **KANARA, RUNNER**
ruin .... **DOOM**
rule ...... **LAW, DOMINEER**
"Rule Britannia" composer **ARNE**
rules, dueling .... **DUELLO**
ruler .... **REGENT**
ruler, Afghanistan ...... **EMIR, AMEER, CALIF, EMEER, CALIPH, SULTAN**
ruler, Arabian .. **EMIR, AMEER, CALIF, EMEER, CALIPH, SULTAN**
RULER, BIBLICAL .... see SPECIAL SECTION

a **RULER IN EAST**
         see RULER, ARABIAN
ruler, India .... **NAWAB**
ruler, Morocco
         SHERIF, SHEREEF
ruler, Moslem .. **EMIR, AMEER,
    CALIF, EMEER, CALIPH,
    SULTAN**
ruler of gods .... **ZEUS**
ruler, Oriental .... **CALIF**
ruler, Tunis .... **DEY**
RUMANIA
    see also SPECIAL SECTION
Rumanian composer ... **ENESCO**
Rumanian folk song ... **DOINA**
Rumanian king's title .. **DOMN**
rumen .... **CUD**
ruminant ...... **DEER, GOAT,
    CAMEL, LLAMA, ANTELOPE**
ruminant genus .... **CAPRA**
ruminant, horned **DEER, GOAT**
ruminate ..... **MULL, PONDER**
Rumor personified ...... **FAMA**
rumor, to .... **BRUIT,
        NORATE, REPORT**
b rumple .... **MUSS**
run at top speed ...... **SPRINT**
run before wind .... **SCUD**
run of the mill .... **PAR**
run out .... **PETER**
runner .... **SCARF,
        STOLO, STOLON**
runner, distance ...... **MILER**
runner, plant .. **STOLO, STOLON**
rupees, 100,000 .... **LAC**
rural .... **RUSTIC, PASTORAL**
rural deity ..:.. **PAN, FAUNUS**
rural poem .... **GEORGIC**
rush .... **HASTE, SPEED**
rush, marsh .... **SPART**
Russell's viper
        DABOIA, DABOYA
RUSSIA ...... see also SOVIET
        and SPECIAL SECTION
Russia, most northern town
        KOLA
Russian .... **RED, RUSS, SLAV,
        KULAK, TATAR**
Russ. basso........... **KIPNIS**
Russ. author .... **BUNIN**

c Russ. beer.**KVAS, QUAS, KVASS**
Russ. community .... **MIR**
Russ. convention ...... **RADA**
Russ. cooperative society.**ARTEL**
Russ. council .... **DUMA**
Russ. dress .... **SARAFAN**
Russ. edict .. **UKASE, DECREE**
Russ. emperor .... **CZAR,
        TSAR, TZAR**
Russ. fiddle .... **GUDOK**
Russ. folk dance .... **KOLO**
Russ. girl's name .... **OLGA**
Russ. hemp .... **RINE**
Russ. labor union ...... **ARTEL**
Russ. lagoon .... **LIMAN**
Russ. Lapland capital ... **KOLA**
Russ. leather .... **YUFT**
Russ. liquid measure ... **STOF,
        STOFF, STOOF**
Russ. log hut .... **ISBA**
Russ. marsh .... **LIMAN**
Russ. mile .... **VERST**
Russ. mountain range
        ALAI, URAL
d Russian mts., pert. to..**ALTAIC**
Russ. name, given . **AKIM, IGOR**
Russ. news agency ...... **TASS**
Russ. official .... **BERIYA**
Russ. opera .... **BORIS**
Russ. peninsula .... **KOLA**
Russ. sea, inland .... **ARAL,
        AZOF, AZOV**
Russ. secret police.**NKVD, OGPU**
Russ. tavern .... **CABACK**
Russ. tax, old .... **OBROK**
Russ. tea urn ...... **SAMOVAR**
Russ. trade guild .... **ARTEL**
Russ. vehicle .. **ARBA, ARABA**
Russ. village .... **MIR**
Russ. whip .... **PLET**
Russ. writer ... **GORKI, GORKY**
Russ. "yes" .... **DA**
rust .... **EAT, ERODE**
Rustam's father .... **ZAL**
rustic .... **BOOR, RUBE, CARL,
    CARLE, YOKEL, BUCOLIC,
    PEASANT**
Ruth's husband .... **BOAZ**
Ruth's son .... **OBED**
rye, disease of .... **ERGOT**

S

a sable .... **SOBOL, MARTEN**
sac .... **BURSA**
saccharine source .... **TAR**
sack fiber .... **JUTE**
sack, to .... **LOOT**
saclike cavity .... **BURSA**
sacred asp, symbol ... **URAEUS**
sacred bull, Egypt . **APIS, HAPI**
sacred chalice .... **GRAIL**
sacred city, India ... **BENARES**
sacred enclosure, Gr. .... **SEKOS**
sacred fig .... **PIPAL**
sacred Hindu word .... **OM**
sacred image .... **ICON, IKON**
sacred lily .... **LOTUS**
sacred object: Oceania .. **ZOGO**
sacred picture .... **ICON, IKON**
sacred place .... **SHRINE**
sacred place, Gr.
          ABATON, HIERON
sacred tree, Hindu .. **BO, PIPAL**
sacrifice, place of ..... **ALTAR**
b sacrificial drink, Zoroaster's
                    SOMA
sacrificial offerings .... **HIERA**
sad: comb. form .... **TRAGI**
sad cry .... **ALAS, ALACK**
sad: music .... **MESTO**
saddle horses, fresh . **REMUDA**
saddle knob .... **POMMEL**
saddle, rear of .... **CANTLE**
safe .... **SECURE**
safe place ...... **PORT, HAVEN**
safe: thief's slang ...... **PETE**
safety lamp .... **DAVY**
safflower .... **KUSUM**
saga .... **EDDA**
sage .... **WISE**
sagacious .... **WISE,**
          ASTUTE, SAPIENT
sage genus .... **SALVIA**
sail fastener .... **CLEW**
sail-line .... **EARING**
sail nearer wind .... **LUFF**
sail, square .... **LUG**
sail, square, edge of ... **LEECH**
sail, triangular .... **JIB**
sail yard: Scot. .... **RAE**
sail's corner .... **CLEW**
"Sails" of constellation Argo
                    VELA
sailboat .... **YAWL, KETCH**
sailing race .... **REGATTA**
SAILING VESSEL .... see
          VESSEL, SAILING
sailmaker's awl ..... **STABBER**

c sailor . **GOB, TAR, SALT, SEADOG**
sailor, India .... **LASCAR**
St. Anthony's cross ...... **TAU**
saint, British .... **ALBAN**
saint, Buddhist
      ARAHT, ARHAT, ARAHAT
St. Catherine's home ... **SIENA**
saint, female: abbr. ...... **STE**
saint, 14th century ..... **ROCH**
St. Francis' birthplace .. **ASSISI**
St. John's-bread ..... **CAROB**
"St. Louis Blues" composer
                    HANDY
saint, Moslem .... **PIR**
St. Paul, deserter from . **DEMAS**
St. Vitus dance ...... **CHOREA**
sainte: abbr. .... **STE**
saint's relic box ...... **CHASSE**
salad green ...... **UDO, CRESS,**
          KERSE, CRESSE, ENDIVE
salamander .. **EFT, EVET, NEWT**
salient angle .... **CANT**
Salientia, the .... **ANURA**
sally .... **START, SORTIE**
"Sally in Our Alley" composer
                    CAREY
salmon, female .... **HEN**
d salmon, male .... **COCK**
salmon net .... **MAUD**
salmon, silver .... **COHO**
salmon, third year ..... **MORT**
salmon, 2 yr. .. **SMOLT, SPROD**
salmon, young .. **PARR, GRILSE**
salt .... **SAL, HALITE, SALINE**
salt factory .... **SALTERN**
salt lake, Turkestan ..... **SHOR**
salt of tartaric acid .. **TARTAR**
salt pond or spring ... **SALINA**
salt, resembling ...... **HALOID**
salt, rock .... **HALITE**
salt, solution .. **BRINE, SALINE**
salt tax .... **GABELLE**
salt tree, Tamarisk ..... **ATLE**
salted .... **ALAT**
saltpeter ...... **NITER, NITRE**
saltwort .... **KALI**
saltworks , ... **SALINA**
salty water .... **BRINE**
salutation .... **AVE**
salutation: Ir. .... **ACHARA**
Salvation Army leader . **BOOTH**
salver .... **TRAY**
salvia .... **CHIA**
Sambal language .... **TINO**
sambar deer .... **MAHA, RUSA**
same .... **ILK, DITTO**

a
same place: abbr. .... **IBID**
samlet .... **PARR**
Samoan maiden ...... **TAUPO**
Samoan mollusk .... **ASI**
Samoan political council. **FONO**
Samuel, king killed by .. **AGAG**
Samuel, teacher of .... **ELI**
Samuel's son .... **ABIA**
samurai, straying ..... **RONIN**
sanction .... **AMEN, FIAT**
sanctuary ...... **BEMA, FANE,**
NAOS, CELLA
sand .... **GRIT**
sand bar .... **REEF, SHOAL**
sand expanses .... **AREG**
sand hill .... **DENE, DUNE**
sand island .... **BAR**
sand, sea bottom .... **PAAR**
sand snake genus ...... **ERYX**
sandal, Egypt .... **TATBEB**
sandal, Mex.
HUARACHE, HUARACHO
sandalwood tree .... **MAIRE**
sandarac powder .... **POUNCE**
sandarac tree .... **ARAR**
sandbox tree genus ..... **HURA**
sandpiper .... **REE, RUFF, STIB,**
REEVE, STINT
sandpiper, Europ. ...... **TEREK**

b
sandpiper, red .... **KNOT**
sandpiper, small .... **KNOT,**
PUME, STINT
sandstone .... **GRIT**
sandstorm .... **HABOOB**
sandwich .... **HERO**
Sandwich Island discoverer
COOK
sandy .... **ARENOSE**
Sankhya philos. term ... **GUNA**
Sanskrit dialect .... **PALI**
Sanskrit precept
SUTRA, SUTTA
Sanskrit school .... **TOL**
Sao —, Brazil .... **PAULO**
Sao Salvador .... **BAHIA**
sap spout .... **SPILE**
sapodilla ... **SAPOTA, SAPOTE**
sapota tree .... **ACANA**
Saracen ..... **MOOR, MOSLEM**
Sarah's slave .... **HAGAR**
sarcasm .... **IRONY**
Sardinia gold coin ... **CARLINE**
sargeant fish .... **SNOOK**
Sargon's capital ...... **ACCAD**
Sarmatia cave-dwellers . **TAURI**
sartor .... **TAILOR**
sash, C. Amer. .... **TOBE**
sash, Jap. kimono .... **OBI**
sassafras tree .... **AGUE**
Satan .... **DEVIL**
Satan: Arab .... **EBLIS**

c
satellite .... **MOON, PLANET**
satellite .... **LUNIK, SPUTNIK,**
PIONEER, EXPLORER,
VANGUARD, ATLAS-
SCORE, DISCOVERER
satellite, navigation . **TRANSIT**
satellite, television .... **TIROS**
satellite's path .... **ORBIT**
satiate .. **CLOY, GLUT, SATE**
satirical .... **DRY**
satisfaction Maori ...... **UTU**
satisfy ... **SATE, SUIT, PLEASE**
saturate . **SOAK, IMBUE, STEEP**
Saturn, satellite of ..... **DIONE**
Saturn's rings projection. **ANSA**
Saturn's wife .... **OPS**
Saturnalia .... **ORGY**
satyr .... **FAUN**
sauce .... **GRAVY**
sauce, Chinese, Oriental .. **SOY**
sauce, fish .... **ALEC**
sauce, peppery ..... **TABASCO**
sauce, tomato ...... **CATSUP,**
CATCHUP, KETCHUP
saucy .... **PERT**
Saul's army leader .... **ABNER**
Saul's chief herdsman .. **DOEG**
Saul's father .... **KISH**
Saul's grandfather . **NER, ABIEL**
Saul's successor .... **DAVID**
Saul's uncle .... **NER**
Sault Ste. Marie .... **SOO**
saurel fish .... **SCAD**

d
sausage, spiced ..... **SALAME,**
SALAMI
savage .... **FERAL**
Savage Island language . **NIUE**
save .... **HOARD, STINT,**
REDEEM, CONSERVE
saviour .... **REDEEMER**
savory .... **SAPID, TASTY**
saw .... **ADAGE, AXIOM,**
MAXIM, SAYING
saw-leaved centaury
BEHN, BEHEN
saw, notched like .... **SERRATE**
saw notching .... **REDAN**
saw, surgical **TREPAN,TREPHINE**
sawbill duck .... **SMEW**
sawlike organ, or part .. **SERRA**
sawlike parts . **SERRAS, SERRAE**
sawtooth ridge .... **SIERRA**
saxhorn .... **TUBA**
Saxon god .... **ER, EAR**
Saxon king ...... **INE, ALFRED**
Saxony natives .... **SORBS**
say .... **UTTER**
say again .... **ITERATE**
saying ... **MOT, SAW, ADAGE,**
AXIOM, MAXIM
sayings .... **LOGIA**

a scabbard fish .... HIKU
scabbard, put into .. SHEATHE
scaffolding .... STAGING
scale .... GAMUT
scale, syllable of .. DO, FA, LA,
MI, RE, SO, TI, SOL
scale under blossom
PALEA, PALET
scales, having large . SCUTATE
scallop ..... CRENA, CRENAE
scallops, cut in small .... PINK
scalloped .... CRENATE
scalp disease .... FAVI, FAVUS
scamp ...... ROGUE, RASCAL
SCANDINAVIAN
see also NORSE
SCANDINAVIAN . see also
SWEDEN, NORWAY, in
SPECIAL SECTION
Scandinavian ... DANE, SWEDE
Scand., ancient .... NORSE
Scand. countryman ..... GEAT
Scand. explorer .... ERIC
Scand. fertility god .... NJORD
Scand. legend .... SAGA
Scand. measure .... ALEN
Scand. nation .... GEATAS
Scandinavians in Russia
ROS, RUS
b scanty .... SPARSE
scar, resembling a .... ULOID
scarce .... RARE
scarcely: Lat. VIX
scare away .... SHOO
scarf .... BOA, TIE,
ASCOT, ORALE
scarf, long .... STOLE
scarf, Sp. Am. .... TAPALO
scarlet flower .... SALVIA
Scarlett O'Hara's home .. TARA
scatter ... SOW, TED, STREW
scatter: dial. .... SCOAD
scatter on .... LITTER
scattered: Her. .... SEME
scenario .... SCRIPT
scene .... VIEW, TABLEAU
scene of action. ARENA, SPHERE
scenic view .... SCAPE
scent .... ODOR, AROMA
scented .... OLENT
schedule .... LIST
scheme .... PLAN, PLOT
schism .... RENT
scholar .... PEDANT
scholars, Moslem .... ULEMA
scholarship .... BURSE
school, boy's .... PREP
school, Fr. ...... ECOLE, LYCEE
school grounds ...... CAMPUS

c SCHOONER ... see also BOAT,
SHIP, VESSEL
schooner, 3-masted ..... TERN
sciences .... ARTS
scientific farmer . AGRONOMIST
scientific study: abbr. . ANAT.
scientist, Am. . UREY, HOOTON,
PARRAN, COMPTON,
WAKSMAN, MILLIKAN
scientist, Austr. .... MEITNER
scientist, Czech .... CORI
scientist, Dan. .... BOHR
scientist, Eng. ...... HOGBEN,
FLEMING, HALDANE
scientist, Ger. .. BAADE, HABER
scientist, Ital. .... FERMI
scissors .... SHEARS
scoff .... GIBE, JEER, JIBE,
RAIL, SNEER
scold .... JAW, NAG, RATE
scold: dialect .... FRAB
scone: Scot. ..... FARL, FARLE
scoop .... DIP
scoot: Scot. ..... SKYT, SKITE
scope .. AREA, AMBIT, RANGE
scorch .... CHAR, SEAR,
SERE, SINGE
score .... TALLY
scoria .... SLAG, DROSS
d scorpion fish .... LAPON
Scotch cake .... SCONE
scoter .... COOT
Scotland .... SCOTIA
Scott character .... ELLEN
Scott heroine .... ELLEN
Scott, poem by .... MARMION
SCOTTISH
see Pages of SCOTTISH WORDS
Scot. alderman .... BAILIE
Scot. author .... BARRIE
Scot. chemist .... URE, DEWAR
Scot. chief landholder
THANE, THEGN
Scot. cultural congress ... MOD
Scot. explorer .... RAE
Scot. highlander ...... GAEL
Scot. king .... BRUCE
Scot. lord ..... THANE, THEGN
Scot. pillory .... JOUG
Scot. playwright ...... BARRIE
Scot. poet .... BURNS
Scot. pottage .... BROSE
Scot. proprietor ...... LAIRD
Scot. scholar .... NICOLL
Scot. singer .... LAUDER
SCOTTISH WORDS:
accept .... TAE
advise .... REDE
afraid .... RAD, RADE
age .... EILD

a

against .... **GIN**
alder tree ..... **ARN, ELLER**
an .... **AE**
animal, lean .... **RIBE**
any .... **ONY**
article .... **TA**
ashes .... **ASE**
ask .... **AX**
at all .... **AVA**
away .... **AWA**
awry .... **AJEE**
babbler .... **HAVEREL**
ball .... **BA**
bank .... **BRAE**
barter .... **TROKE**
beg .... **SORN**
bind .... **OOP**
biscuit .... **BAKE**
blockhead .... **CUIF, NOWT**
bloodhound .... **LYAM**
bone .... **BANE**
bound .... **STEND**
breeches .... **TREWS**
broth .... **BREE, BROO**
brow of hill .... **SNAB**
built .... **BAG**
burden .... **BIRN**
bushel .... **FOU**
calves ...... **CAUR, CAURE**

b

came .... **CAM**
catch .... **KEP**
chalk .... **CAUK**
check .... **WERE**
chest .... **KIST**
child .... **BAIRN**
church .... **KIRK, KURK**
comb .... **KAME**
contend .... **KEMP**
court, bring to .... **SIST**
cut .... **KNAP, SNEG**
dairymaid .... **DEY**
damage .... **TEEN**
damaged .... **LESED**
dare .... **DAUR**
devil .... **DEIL**
did not know ...... **KENNA**
die .... **DEE**
dig .... **HOWK**
dining room .... **SPENCE**
do .... **DAE, DIV**
do not know .... **KENNA**
dread .... **DREE**
drip .... **SIE, SYE**
dusty .... **MOTTY**
earth .... **EARD**
elder .... **ELLER**
else .... **ENSE**
empty .... **TOOM**
endeavor .... **ETTLE**
endure .... **DREE**

c

extra .... **ORRA**
eye .... **EE**
eyes .... **EEN, EES**
family .... **ILK**
fidget .... **FIKE**
firth .... **KYLE**
fishing expedition ... **DRAVE**
fit of sulks .... **GEE**
flax refuse ...... **PAB, POB**
fog ..... **DAG, HAR, HAAR**
foretell .... **SPAE**
give .... **GIE**
glimpse .... **STIME**
grandchild .... **OY, OYE**
grant as property . **DISPONE**
great-grandchild .... **IEROE**
grief .... **TEEN**
have .... **HAE**
hawk .... **ALLAN**
heavy .... **THARF**
hill . **BEN, DOD, BRAE, DODD**
hillside .... **BRAE**
howl .... **YOWT**
hurt .... **LESED**
injure .... **TEEN**
injured .... **LESED**
intent .... **ETTLE**
keg .... **KNAG**

d

kinsman .... **SIB**
kiss .... **PREE**
knead .... **ELT**
knock .... **KNOIT**
lake .... **LOCH**
leap .. **LOUP, LOWP, STEND**
learning .... **LEAR**
list of candidates ..... **LEET**
loaf .... **SORN**
lop .... **SNATHE**
lout .... **CUIF**
love .... **LOE**
loyal .... **LEAL**
marriage portion ..... **DOTE**
millrace .... **LADE**
mire .... **GLAUR**
mist .... **URE**
mountain .... **BEN**
mouth, river .... **BEAL**
mouth .... **BEAL**
mud .... **GLAIR**
must .... **MAUN**
name .... **IAN**
near, nearest .... **NAR**
no .... **NAE**
none .... **NANE**
not matched .... **ORRA**
now .... **NOO**
nowhere .... **NAEGATE**
oak .... **AIK**

(Scottish words continued 140)

Scottish

oatmeal dish .... **BROSE**
odd .... **ORRA**
old age .... **EILD**
once .... **ANES**
one .... **AIN, ANE, YIN**
otherwise .... **ELS**
out .... **OOT**
own ...... **AIN, ANE, AWN**
pantry .... **SPENCE**
parlor .... **BEN**
payment .... **MENSE**
paw ground .... **PAUT**
peat cutter .... **PINER**
pig .... **GRICE**
pike .... **GED, GEDD**
pillory .... **TRONE**
pipe .... **CUTTY**
pluck wool .... **ROO**
pool .... **DIB, CARR,**
LINN, LLYN
present .... **GIE**
pretty .... **GEY**
prop .... **RANCE**
propriety .... **MENSE**
prune .... **SNED**
puddle .... **DUB**
pull .... **PU**
quagmire .... **HAG**
quarter of a year ... **RAITH**
relieve .... **LISS**
revenue, church .... **ANNAT**
ridge of a hill .... **SHIN**
river .... **DOON**
rowboat .... **COBLE**
sailyard .... **RAE**
same .... **ILK**
scone .... **FARL, FARLE**
scoot .... **SKYT, SKITE**
scratch .... **RIT**
seep .... **SIPE**
seize .... **VANG**
self .... **SEL**
serve .... **KAE**
severe blow .... **DEVEL**
sheepfold .... **REE**
sheepstick .... **KED**
sheep walk .... **SLAIT**
shelter ...... **BIELD, SHEAL**
sift .... **SIE**
since .... **SIN, SYNE**
slope .... **BRAE**
slouch .... **LOUCH**
sly .... **SLEE**
small .... **SMA**
snow .... **SNA**
so .... **SAE**
son of .... **MAC**
song .... **STROUD**
sore .... **SAIR**
sorrow .... **TEEN**
sow .... **SOO**

steward .... **MORMAOR**
stipend .... **ANNAT**
stone.**STANE, STEAN, STEEN**
stretch .... **STENT**
stupid one .... **CUIF**
suffer .... **DREE**
summit .... **DOD, DODD**
sweetheart .... **JO**
than .... **NA**
to .... **TAE**
toe .... **TAE**
tone .... **TEAN**
trench .... **GAW**
truant, play .... **TRONE**
try .... **ETTLE**
tune .... **PORT**
turnip .... **NEEP**
uncanny .... **UNCO**
uncle .... **EME**
urge .... **ERT**
very .... **VERA**
vex .... **FASH**
village .... **REW**
void, to render ...... **CASS**
waterfall ... **LIN, LYN, LINN**
wealthy .... **BIEN**
weep .... **ORP**
week .... **OUK**
well .... **AWEEL**
weighing machine ... **TRON,**
TRONE
wet .... **WAT**
whirlpool ..... **WEEL, WIEL**
whiskey drink ..... **ATHOL,**
ATHOLE
widow's third .... **TERCE**
workhouse .... **AVER**
year, 1/4 of .... **RAITH**
yell .... **GOWL**
scoundrel .... **ROGUE, VARLET**
scout unit . **DEN, PACK, TROOP**
scow .... **BARGE, LIGHTER**
scow: Fr. .... **ACON**
scrap, table .... **ORT**
scraps of literature ...... **ANA**
scrape ... **RAKE, RASP, GRAZE**
scrape bottom .... **DREDGE**
scratch .... **MAR, RAKE**
scrawny animal .... **SCRAG**
screamer bird .... **CHAJA**
screed .... **TIRADE**
screen .... **SIFT, SHADE**
screen, altar .... **REREDOS**
screen, wind ...... **PARAVENT**
script, modern Syriac ... **SERTA**
script, upright .... **RONDE**
scripture, early .... **ITALA**
scripture passage .... **TEXT**
scriptures, occult interpretation
CABALA
scrutinize .... **EYE, SCAN**

a
scuffle .... MELEE
sculptor of "Thinker" . RODIN
scum, metal .... DROSS
scup .... BREAM, PORGY
scuppernong ..... MUSCADINE
scuttle .... HOD
scuttle, coal .... HOD
scythe .... SY, SYE
scythe handle . SNATH, SNEAD,
SNEED, SNATHE
sea anemone .. POLYP, OPELET
sea bird ... ERN, ERNE, GULL,
SKUA, SCAUP, TERN, FUL-
MAR, GANNET, PETREL,
SCOTER
sea bird, north .... PUFFIN
sea cow . DUGONG, MANATEE
sea cucumber ...... TREPANG
sea demon, Teut. ...... WATE
sea duck ...... COOT, EIDER,
SCAUP, SCOTER
sea eagle .... ERN, ERNE
sea-ear .... ABALONE
sea: Fr. .... MER
sea girdles .... CUVY
sea god .... LER, TRITON,
NEPTUNE
sea god, Gr. . NEREUS, TRITON,
POSEIDON
sea god, Rom. ...... NEPTUNE
sea god, Teut. .. HLER, AEGIR
sea goddess, Norse ...... RAN
b
sea green .... CELADON
sea gull, Eur. .... MEW
sea, kept bow on . ATRY, ATRIE
sea lettuce ..... ALGA, LAVER
sea lettuce genus ULVA, ULUA
sea marker .... DAN
sea pheasant .... SMEE
sea robber .... PIRATE
sea mile, Austral. ...... NAUT
sea nymph .... NEREID
sea shell .... TRITON
(see also SHELL)
sea skeleton .... CORAL
sea slug genus . DOTO, ELYSIA
sea snail . WELK, WILK, WHELK
sea snake, Asia ...... KERRIL
sea soldier .... MARINE
sea worm . SAO, LURG, NEREIS
seal .... SIGIL
seal, eared .... OTARY
seal, fur .... URSAL
seal, letter .... CACHET
seal, official .... SIGNET
seal, papal .... BULLA
seal, young .... PUP
seals, group of .... POD
seamark .... BEACON
seamen: Brit. .... RATINGS
seamlike ridge .... RAPHE

c
seams of boat, fill ..... CALK
SEAPORT .... see PORT
search .... GROPE
search for .... HUNT, SEEK
search for food ...... FORAGE
season ...... AGE, FALL, SALT,
TIDE, SPRING
season, church . LENT, ADVENT
season, Fr. .... ETE
seasons, goddesses of .. HORAE
seasonal phenomenon .. EPACT
seasoning .... SAGE, SALT
seasoning herb .... SAGE,
BASIL, THYME
seat, chancel .... SEDILE
seat, long ...... PEW, SETTEE
seat of oracle of Zeus. DODONA
seat, Rom. .... SELLA
seaweed ..... ORE, AGAR, ALGA,
KELP, ALGAE, LAVER,
VAREC
seaweed ashes .... KELP
seaweed, brown .... KELP
seaweed, edible .... AGAR
seaweed, edible Hawaiian . LIMU
seaweed, purple .... LAVER
seaweed, purple, Jap. ... NORI
seaweed, red .... DULSE
Seb, consort of .... NUT
d
secluded .... REMOTE
second . ABET, TRICE, MOMENT
second brightest star ... BETA
second-growth crop ... ROWEN
Second Punic War's end,
site of .... ZAMA
second team .... SCRUB
secondary .... BYE, LESS
secret .... RUNE, ARCANE,
COVERT, MYSTERY,
ESOTERIC
secret agent .... SPY
secret society, Afr. . EGBO, PORO
secret society in Sierra Leone
PORO
secrets .... ARCANA
secrets, one learning ... EPOPT
secretion, sweet
LAAP, LERP, LAARP
sect .... CULT
sect, Nepal . ACHAR, ACHARA
section of journey .... LEG
secular ... LAY, LAIC, LAICAL
secure .. FIX, GET, PIN, FAST,
NAIL, SAFE, FASTEN
secure firmly . MOOR, ANCHOR
secure with rope .... BELAY
security .... BOND
Sec'y of State, 1933-44 .. HULL
sedate .... STAID
sedative .... NEMBUTAL

141

Sediment

sediment .... LEES, SILT, DREGS, SILTAGE
see .... ESPY, LOOK
see: Lat. .... VIDE
seed .... PIP, PIT, GRAIN, SPORE, PYRENE
seed coat or covering .. ARIL, HULL, HUSK, TESTA, TEGMEN, TESTAE, TEGUMEN, TEGIMINA
seed, edible ...... PEA, BEAN, LENTIL, PINOLE
seed, edible, Asia .... SESAME
seed, immature .... OVULE
seed, lens-shaped ..... LENTIL
seed, nutlike .... PINON
seed, opium poppy ..... MAW
seed plant .... ENDOGEN
seeds, remove .... GIN
seedless plant .... FERN
seek to attain .... ASPIRE
seem .... LOOK
seesaw .... TEETER
segment, last .... TELSON
segment of body ..... SOMITE
segment of circle .... ARC
segment, pert. to ...... TORIC
seine .... NET
seize .... NAB, GRAB, GRASP, USURP, ARREST, COLLAR
seize: archaic .... REAVE
selections, literary ANA, ANALECTA
self .... EGO
self-assurance .... APLOMB
self-defense, art of ..... JUDO
self-denying .... ASCETIC
self-education doctrine BIOSOPHY
self-locking nut ..... PALNUT
self-reproach .... REMORSE
sell .... VEND
seller .... COSTER, VENDER, VENDOR
semblance .... GUISE
semester .... TERM
semi-precious stone ONYX, SARD
semicircular room ...... APSE
semidiameter .... RADIUS
semidiameters .... RADII
Seminole chief ..... OSCEOLA
Semitic deity .... BAAL
sen, tenth of .... RIN
senate house .... CURIA
senate houses .... CURIAE
Senator, former .... BORAH
send back ... REMIT, REMAND
send money .... REMIT

send out .... EMIT, ISSUE
sending forth .... EMISSIVE
Senegambia gazelle ... KORIN
senility .... DOTAGE
senior .... ELDER
senior: Fr. .... AINE
senna, source of ...... CASSIA
sennet .... SPET
sense .... FEEL
senseless .... INANE
sensitive .... SORE
sentence, analyze ...... PARSE
sentence part .... CLAUSE
"Sentimental Journey" author STERNE
sentinel, mounted ... VEDETTE
separate . SIFT, APART, SECERN
separated .... APART
separation .... SCHISM
sequence, 3-card ..... TIERCE
sequester .... ISOLATE
Sequoia national park ... MUIR
seraglio .... HAREM, SERAI
serene .... SERENO
serf .... ESNE
serf, Rom. .... COLONA
serf, Spartan, ancient .. HELOT
sergeant fish .... COBIA
series .... SET, GAMUT
series, in a .... SERIATIM
series of tones .... SCALE
serious ..... GRAVE, EARNEST
sermon .... HOMILY
serow .... JAGLA
SERPENT ..... see also SNAKE
serpent, Egypt. myth .... APEPI
serpent goddess, Egypt. . BUTO
serpent, Gr. .... SEPS
serpent, large .. BOA, PYTHON
serpent monster ...... ELLOPS
serpent, myth. .... BASILISK
serpent worship ...... OPHISM
serpentine .... OPHITE
servant.......... BOY, MAN, MAID, MENIAL
servant, India .... HAMAL, FERASH, HAMMAL
servant, man's .... VALET
servant, P. I. .... BATA
servants, for .... MENIAL
serve soup .... LADLE
server .... TRAY
service, religious .... MASS
service tree .... SORB
servile .... MENIAL
serving boy .... PAGE
sesame .... TIL, TEEL
sesame oil ...... BENI, BENNE
sesame seed .... GINGILI
session, hold .... SIT, MEET

142

set aside .... DEFER
set in type .... PRINT
set limits to .... STINT
set price .... RATE
set system .... ROTE
set thickly .... STUD
setback .... REVERSE
Seth's brother .... CAIN
Seth's mother .... EVE
Seth's son .... ENOS
setting .... SCENE, MILIEU
setting sun, Egyp. god of.TEM,
　　TUM, ATMU, ATUM
settled .... ALIT
settler .... BOOMER
seven .... SEPT
Seven Dwarfs ... DOC, DOPEY,
　HAPPY, GRUMPY, SLEEPY,
　SNEEZY, BASHFUL
seven, group of .... HEPTAD,
　PLEIAD, SEPTET, SEPTETTE
"Seventh Heaven" heroine
　　　　　　　　DIANE
seventh order, of ...... SEPTIC
seventh, pert. to ..... SEPTAN
sever .... CUT, LOP, REND
severe .... STERN
severely criticize ...... PAN,
　　　　SLATE, ROAST
sew hawk's eyelids ..... SEEL
"Seward's —," Alaska . FOLLY
sexes, common to both.EPICENE
shabby .... WORN
shabby woman .... DOWD
shackle .... BOND, GYVE,
　　　　IRON, FETTER
shad .... ALLIS, ALOSA,
　　　　ALOSE, ALLICE
shaddock .. POMELO, PUMELO
shade .... HUE, SCREEN
shade of difference .. NUANCE
shade of meaning ... NUANCE
shaded walk .... MALL
shadow .... TAIL
shadow, eclipse .... UMBRA
shaft .... POLE, SPINDLE
shaft column, feather .. SCAPE
shaft horse .... THILLER
shaft of column .... FUST
shaft, wooden .... ARROW
shafter .... HORSE
shake ..... JAR, JOLT, NIDGE
Shakespeare's elf ...... PUCK
Shakespeare's river .... AVON
Shakespeare's theatre .. GLOBE
Shakespeare's wife .... ANNE
Shakesperian clown .. BOTTOM
Shakesperian forest ... ARDEN
Shakesperian king ...... LEAR

Shakesperian shrew ..... KATE
Shakesperian villain ..... IAGO
shallow receptacle ...... TRAY
sham .... FAKE
Shamash, wife of .... AI, AYA
"Shane," star of .... LADD
Shang dynasty .... YIN
shank .... CRUS, SHIN
shanks .... CRURA
shanty .... HUT
shape .... FORM, MOLD
shaped like a club .. CLAVATE
shaped like a needle
　　ACUATE, ACERATE
shaping tool ... LATHE, SWAGE
share .... LOT, RATION
share .... PARTAKE
shark .... TOPE
shark, Eur. small .... TOPE
shark, long-nosed ..... MAKO
shark, nurse .... GATA
shark parasite fish ... REMORA
sharp .... ACERB,
　　ACUTE, ACUATE
sharp .... CHEAT
sharp ridge .... ARETE
sharpen ... EDGE, HONE, WHET
sharpshooter .. JAGER, SNIPER
shavetail: abbr. .... LT
shawl ..... MAUD, PAISLEY
shea tree .... KARITE
sheaf of grain: Her. .... GERB
shear .... CLIP
sheath, petiole .... OCREA
Sheba: Lat. .... SABA
shed, as feathers MOLT, MOULT
shed for sheep .... COTE
sheen .... GLOSS
sheep .... EWE, RAM, MERINO
sheep, Afr. domestic ... ZENU
sheep, Afr. wild
　ARUI, UDAD, AOUDAD
sheep, Asia wild .... ARGALI
sheep, Asia, wild, mountain
　SHA, SNA, RASSE, URIAL,
　BHARAL, NAHOOR, OORIAL
sheep cry .... BAA, MAA
sheep disease .. COE, GID, ROT
sheep dog .... COLLIE
sheep, Eng. black-faced LONK
sheep, female .... EWE
sheep genus .... OVIS
sheep in 2nd year
　　TEG, TEGG, BIDENT
sheep, India, wild .. SHA, SNA,
　URIAL, NAHOOR, OORIAL
sheep, large-horned
　　AOUDAD, ARGALI
sheep, Leicester ...... DISHLEY
sheep, male .... RAM, TUP

Sheep

a sheep, N. Afr. wild
   ARUI, UDAD, AOUDAD
sheep, of .... **OVINE**
sheep owner, Bibl. .... **NABAL**
sheep pasture, old Eng. .. **HEAF**
sheep, pert. to .... **OVINE**
sheep, Tibet .... **SHA, SNA,**
  URIAL, BHARAL, NAHOOR,
  OORIAL
sheep tick .... **KED, KADE**
sheep, unshorn .. **HOGG, HEDER**
sheep walk: Scot. .... **SLAIT**
sheep, wild .. **SHA, SNA, ARUI,**
  UDAD, RASSE, BHARAL,
  NAHOOR, AOUDAD, AR-
  GALI, OORIAL
sheep, young ...... **TAG, TEG**
sheepfold .... **REE, COTE**
sheeplike .... **OVINE**
sheepskin leather ..... **BOCK,**
   ROAN, SKIVER
sheerly .... **SOLELY**
shekel, ¼, Hebrew ...... **REBA**
shelf .... **LEDGE**
shelf above altar ... **RETABLE**
shell .... **BOMB**
shell .. **TEST, LORICA, TUNICA**
shell beads .... **PEAG**
shell, large .... **CONCH**
shell, marine .... **TRITON**
shell money .... **ULLO,**
b   **COWRY, UHLLO, COWRIE**
shellfish, edible
 CRAB, ABALONE, SCALLOP
shelter .... **LEE, COTE,**
  SHED, HAVEN, SCREEN
shelter, hillside .... **ABRI**
shelter: Scot. .. **BIELD, SHEAL**
shelter, to .... **ALEE**
sheltered .... **ALEE**
Shem descendant ..... **SEMITE**
Shem's brother .... **HAM**
Shem's son
 LUD, ARAM, ELAM, ASSHUR
Sheol .... **HADES**
shepherd prophet ...... **AMOS**
shepherd's crook **PEDA, PEDUM**
shepherd's pipe .... **OAT, REED**
shepherd's song .. **MADRIGAL**
shepherdess, "Winter's Tale"
   MOPSA
sheriff substitute ..... **ELISOR**
sheriff's men .... **POSSE**
Sherwood .... **FOREST**
Shetland court president **FOUD**
Shetland hill pasture ... **HOGA**
shield .... **ECU, EGIS, AEGIS,**
  PAVIS, DEFEND, PROTECT
shield, Athena's .... **AEGIS**
shield, Austral. .... **MULGA**
shield-bearing or border. **ORLE**

c shield, medieval .... **ECU**
shield, Rom.
 SCUTA, SCUTUM, CLIPEUS
shield-shaped **PELTATE, SCUTATE**
shield, small .... **ECU**
shield strap .... **ENARME**
shield's corner: Her. **CANTON**
shift .... **VEER**
shift position. **GIBE, GYBE, JIBE**
shin .... **CNEMIS**
shine **GLOW, GLISTEN, ERADIATE**
shingle, wedge-shaped .. **SHIM**
shingles .... **ZONA**
shining .... **NITID**
Shinto deity .... **KAMI**
Shinto temple .... **SHA**
Shinto temple gate .... **TORII**
ship ..... **KEEL, SEND, LINER,**
 TANKER, TENDER, VESSEL,
 CARAVEL
ship, back part .... **STERN**
ship boat .... **GIG, DORY**
ship body or frame ..... **HULL**
ship bow, curve of ...... **LOOF**
ship canvas .... **SAIL**
ship clock .... **NEF**
d ship drainage hole .. **SCUPPER**
ship employee ...... **STEWARD**
ship, 1st Northwest Passage
   GJOA
ship, forward part **BOW, PROW**
ship, fur-hunting ..... **SEALER**
ship, ironclad ...... **MONITOR**
ship: Jap. ...... **MARO, MARU**
ship keel, rear part ..... **SKEG**
ship, large .... **TONNER**
ship, lowest part ...... **BILGE**
ship, Medit. ... **SETEE, SETTEE**
ship, middle part ...... **WAIST**
ship mooring place
  DOCK, BERTH
ship, oar-propelled ... **GALLEY**
ship, part of
 RIB, DECK, HULL, KEEL
ship plank .... **STRAKE**
ship platform .... **DECK**
ship pole .... **MAST, SPAR**
ship shaped clock .... **NEF**
ship side, opp. middle **ABEAM**
ship timber, bevel ..... **SNAPE**
ship timber curve .... **SNY**
ship timber, extra ..... **RIDER**
ship wheel .... **HELM**
ship, wrecked .... **HULK**
ship, 1-masted .... **SLOOP**
ship, 2-masted ... **BRIG, SNOW**
ship's kitchen .... **GALLEY**
shipboard covering .... **CAPOT**

shipbuilding curve ..... SNY
shipbuilding piece
SPALE, THWART
shipworm .... BORER, TEREDO
shipwreck, causing
NAUFRAGEOUS
shirk .... GOLDBRICK
SHIRT .... see also GARMENT
shirt .... KAMIS, CAMISE
shirt, Oriental .... CAMISE
shoal .... REEF
shoal water deposit .... CULM
shock .... STUN,
APPAL, APPALL, TRAUMA
shock absorber ..... SNUBBER
shod, as monks ..... CALCED
shoe .... GAITER, SANDAL
shoe form .... LAST
shoe front .... VAMP
shoe gripper .... CLEAT
shoe, heavy. BROGAN, BROGUE
shoe latchet .... TAB
shoe, mule .... PLANCH
shoe part
LAST, RAND, WELT, INSOLE
shoe strip ...... RAND, WELT
shoe, wooden ... GETA, SABOT
shoe, wooden-soled ..... CLOG
shoes .... SHOON
shoes, Mercury's winged
TALARIA
shoelace .... LACET
shoemakers' saint ... CRISPIN
shoemaker's tool .... AWL
shoot .... BAG, POT
shoot at from ambush SNIPE
shoot at, marble to ...... MIG
shoot, cotton .... RATOON
shoot, plant .... BINE, CION,
GEMMA, SPRIT,
STOLO, STOLON
shoot, small .... SPRIG
shoot, sugar cane ... RATOON
shooter, hidden .... SNIPER
shooter marble .... TAW,
AGATE, AGGIE
shooting match .... TIR
shooting match: Fr. ...... TIR
shooting star .... LEONID
shop .... STORE
shop, Rom. wine ... TABERNA
shops, Rom. wine .. TABERNAE
shop's name plate ..... FACIA
shore .... COAST, STRAND
SHORE BIRD . see BIRD, SHORE
short .... CURT,
BRIEF, TERSE, STUBBY

short-breathed .... PURSY
short comedy sketch .... SKIT
short-spoken ... CURT, TERSE
short tail .... SCUT
shorten .... CUT, DELE, ELIDE
shortly
ANON, SOON, PRESENTLY
Shoshonean .... UTE
shoulder blade ..... SCAPULA
shoulder, of the
ALAR, SCAPULAR
shoulder ornament
EPAULET, EPAULETTE
shoulder, road .... BERM
shoulder wrap .... SHAWL
shout.CRY, CALL, ROAR, YELL
shove .... PUSH
shovel .... SPADE
show as false .... BELIE
show off .... FLAUNT
show place, Rom. .... CIRCUS
show, street .... RAREE
"Showboat" author .... FERBER
showy .... LOUD
shrew .... ERD, TARTAR
shrewd.SAGE, CANNY, ASTUTE
shrike genus .... LANIUS
shrill .... PIPY
shrill, to .... STRIDULATE
shrimplike crustacean PRAWN
shrine .... ALTAR
shrink .... CONTRACT
shroud-stopper: naut. ... WAPP
SHRUB .... see also TREE
shrub and tree .... ALDER
shrub, Asia .... CHE
shrub, berry-bearing ... ELDER
shrub, berry, Pacific ... SALAL
shrub, Chin. .... TEA
shrub, Congo medical .. BOCCA
shrub, desert
RETEM, OCOTILLO
shrub, Eng. .... HEATH
shrub, evergreen .. BOX, YEW,
TITI, ERICA, HEATH, SAL-
AL, OLEANDER
shrub, flowering ITEA, AZALEA,
PRIVET, SPIREA, SPIRAEA,
SYRINGA
shrub genus BIXA, INGA, ITEA,
ROSA, ALDER, IXORA,
AZALEA
shrub, Hawaiian ..... OLONA
shrub, low spiny .... GORSE
shrub, Medit. .... CAPER
shrub, poisonous
SUMAC, SUMACH
shrub, prickly .... CAPER

Shrub

a
shrub, Rhus genus **SUMAC, SUMACH**
shrub, strong-scented .. **BATIS**
shrub with grapelike fruit **SALAL**
shrub, yellow flowers **OLEASTER**
shun .... **AVOID, DODGE**
shut up .... **IMMURE**
shy .... **JIB, BALK**
SIAM .. see also SPECIAL SECTION
Siamese .... **THAI**
Siam. coin .... **ATT**
Siam. garment ...... **PANUNG**
Siam. group .... **KUI, LAO**
Siam. monetary unit .... **BAHT**
Siamese twin ... **ENG, CHANG**
SIBERIAN .. see also RUSSIAN
Siberian .... **TATAR**
Siberian wild cat ..... **MANUL**
Siberian squirrel ..... **MINIVER**
sibilant sound .... **HISS**
Sicilian resort .... **ENNA**
sickle, curved like ... **FALCATE**
sickle: variant .... **SIVE**
side, jewel's .... **FACET**
side arm .... **GUN, SWORD, PISTOL, REVOLVER**

b
side: Lat. .... **LATUS**
side of head ... **LORA, LORUM**
side, pert. to **COSTAL, LATERAL**
side-post, door's ...... **JAMB**
sidetrack .... **SHUNT**
side street, Chin. ... **HUTUNG**
side timber: naut. ..... **BIBB**
side, toward the .... **LATERAD**
sidereal .... **ASTRAL**
sidewalk .... **PAVEMENT**
sidewalk edge ... **CURB, KERB**
sidewinder .... **CROTALUS**
sidle .... **EDGE**
Siegfried's murderer ... **HAGEN**
siesta .... **NAP**
sieve .... **SIFT, PUREE, BOLTER**
sieve for clay .... **LAUN**
Sif, son of .... **ULL, ULLR**
sift .... **SCREEN**
sift: dialect .... **REE**
sift: old Eng. .... **LUE**
sift: Scot. .... **SIE**
sifter .... **SIEVE**
sigh .... **SOUF, SOUGH**
sight, come into .... **LOOM**
sight, dimness of ..... **CALIGO**
sight on gun .... **BEAD**
sight, pert. to .... **OCULAR**
sign ... **MARK, OMEN, TOKEN**

c
sign, music .... **PRESA, SEGNO**
sign: old Eng. .... **SEIN**
sign, pert. to .... **SEMIC**
sign up ..... **ENROL, ENROLL**
signal for attention ...... **PST**
signal for parley ... **CHAMADE**
signal to act .... **CUE**
signal to begin .... **CUE**
signature, affix **SIGN, ENDORSE**
signet .... **SIGIL**
signify ...... **MEAN, DENOTE**
"Silas Marner" author .. **ELIOT**
silence .... **GAG, HUSH**
silence: music .... **TACET**
silent ... **MUM, MUTE, TACIT**
silica .... **SAND, SILEX**
silica, rich in .... **ACIOLIC**
silicate .... **MICA**
silk-cotton tree **CEIBA, KAPOK**
silk-cotton tree fiber **KAPOK, KUMBI**
silk fabric ..... **GROS, MOFF, PEKIN, SATIN, TULLE**
silk filament .... **BRIN**
silk, fine .... **CRIN, TULLE**
silk, heavy .... **GROS**
silk in cocoon .... **BAVE**
silk, India ... **ROMAL, RUMAL**
silk, old heavy ..... **CAMACA**

d
silk, raw .... **GREGE**
silk substitute .... **NYLON, RAYON, ORLON, DACRON**
silk thread .... **FLOSS**
silk, twilled .... **ALMA**
silk, unravel .... **SLEAVE**
silken .... **SERIC**
silkworm, Assam ... **ERI, ERIA**
silkworm, China ...... **TASAR**
silkworm disease .... **UJI**
silly .... **INANE**
silver: Her. .... **ARGENT**
silver lactate .... **ACTOL**
silver ore .... **PACO**
silver, uncoined, in ingots **SYCEE**
silverfish .. **TARPON, TARPUN**
silverize .... **PLATE**
silvery .... **ARGENT**
silvery-white metal .. **COBALT**
simian .... **APE**
similar .... **LIKE, SUCH**
Simon .... **PETER**
simper .... **SMIRK**
simple .... **EASY, MERE**
simple sugar .... **OSE**
simpleton .... **ASS, DAW, OAF, BOOB, COOT, FOOL, GABY, GAWK, GOWK, SIMP, GOOSE**
simulate **APE, SHAM, FEIGN, PRETEND**

a   sin .... ERR, EVIL
sin, grief for ..... ATTRITION
Sinai .... HOREB
Sinbad's bird .... ROC
since .... AGO
since: Scot. .... SIN, SYNE
Sinclair Lewis character   CASS
sine — non .... QUA
sine qua — .... NON
sinew .... TENDON
sinewy .... WIRY
sing .... LILT, CAROL
sing, as a round ...... TROLL
sing softly .... CROON
sing, Swiss style
        JODEL, YODEL, YODLE
singer, synagogue ... CANTOR
singing bird .... OSCINE
singing girl, Egyptian .. ALMA,
    ALME, ALMAH, ALMAI,
    ALMEH
singing, suitable for .... MELIC
single .... ONE, BILL, MONO,
        ONLY, UNAL
single out .... CHOOSE
single: prefix .... MONO
single thing ...... ONE, UNIT
singleton .... ACE
sink, as putt .... HOLE
sink: geol. .... DOLINA
b   sinuous .. WAVY, SERPENTINE
sinus cavities .... ANTRA
Sioux, Siouan .... OTO, OTOE
sir: India .... MIAN
sir: Malay .... TUAN
siren, Rhine .... LORELEI
Sisera's killer .... JAEL
sister .... NUN, SIB
"Sistine Madonna" painter
            RAPHAEL
sitatunga, Afr. ...... NAKONG
sitting
        POSING, SEANCE, SESSION
sitting on .... ASTRIDE
situation, difficult .... STRAIT
siva snake .... COBRA
Siva, wife of DEVI, KALI, SATI
six, group of
        SENARY, SESTET, SEXTET
six-line verse SESTET, SESTINA
six on a die .. CISE, SICE, SISE
six, series of .... HEXAD
six: Sp. .... SEIS
sixpence: slang .... SICE
sixteen annas .... RUPEE
sixth: music .... SEXT
sixth sense: abbr. .... ESP
size of shot ...... BB, FF, TT
sizing .... SEALER
skate .... RAY
skate genus .... RAIA

c   skating area .... RINK
skegger .... PARR
skein of yarn .... RAP, HANK
skeletal .... BONY
skeleton, sea animal
        CORAL, SPONGE
skeptic .... AGNOSTIC
sketch ...... DRAW, OUTLINE
ski, heel spring .... AMSTUTZ
ski race .... SLALOM
ski run ..... SCHUSS, SLALOM
ski wax .... KLISTER
skier, mark of ..... SITZMARK
skiing position .... VORLAGE
skiing, zigzag .... SLALOM
skilled person .... ADEPT
skillful ..
    ABLE, DEFT, ADEPT, HABILE
skillfully .... ABLY
skim over .... SKIP
skin .... FLAY, DERMA
skin, deeper layer ..... CUTIS
skin, design on
        TATOO, TATTOO
skin disease ... ACNE, MANGE,
        PSORA, TETTER
skin disease, horse's .. CALORIS
skin disease, Peru ...... UTA
skin infection .... LEPRA
skin layer .... DERM, CUTIS,
d   DERMA, CORIUM, ENDERON
skin of a beast .... FELL
skin, pert. to .. DERIC, DERMIC
skinflint .... MISER
skink, Egypt. .... ADDA
skip .... OMIT
skip a stone .... DAP
skip happily .... CAPER
skipjack .... ELATER
skirmish .... MELEE
skirt, ballet .... TUTU
skirt section .... PANEL
skittle .... PIN
skulk .... LURK
skull, pert. to .. INIAL, INION
skull protuberance .... INION
skullcap, Arab. ..... CHECHIA
skunk .. CHINCHA, CHINCHE
sky .... FIRMAMENT
sky god, Assyrian ...... ANAT
sky: Chin. .... TIEN
sky god, Babyl. .... ABU, ANU
sky god, Norse .... TIU,
        TIW, TYR, ZIO, ZIU
sky, highest part .... ZENITH
sky: Polyn. .... LANGI
sky serpent, Vedic ...... AHI
slab, engraved .... TABLET
slab, flooring, decorative DALLE
slag .... DROSS, SCORIA

Slam

a
slam .... BANG
slam in cards .... VOLE
slander ...... LIBEL, ASPERSE
slang .... ARGOT
slant .... BEVEL, SLOPE
slanted edge .... BEVEL
slanted: naut. .... ARAKE
slanting .... SKEW, ASKEW
slanting type .... ITALIC
slantingly, drive .... TOE
slap .... CUFF, SPANK
slash .... JAG, SLISH
slater's tool, same as slate-
   trimming tool
slate-trimming tool
          SAX, ZAT, ZAX
Slav .... SERB
Slav, ancient
     VEND, WEND, VENED
Slav, E. Ger. .... WEND
Slav in Saxony .... SORB
slave .... ESNE, SERF, THRALL
slave, fugitive ..... MAROON
slave, Spartan .... HELOT
sled, Swiss .... LUGE
sled to haul logs ...... TODE
sleep .... NAP, NOD, DOZE
sleep, deep .... SOPOR
sleep lightly .... DOZE

b
sleeping .... DORMANT
sleeping place BED, COT, BERTH
sleeping sickness fly .. TSETSE
sleeve, large .... DOLMAN
sleigh .... PUNG
sleight-of-hand .... MAGIC
slender .... LANK, LEAN,
       SLIM, THIN, REEDY
slender woman .... SYLPH
slice, bacon .... RASHER
slice of meat .... COLP
slice, thick .... SLAB
slick .... LOY
slide .... SKID, SLUE
sliding door, Jap. ... FUSUMA
sliding piece .... CAM
sliding valve .... PISTON
slight .... MERE, SLIM, FAINT
slight intentionally SLUR, SNUB
slimy .... OOZY
sling around .... SLUE
slip.ERR, BONER, GLIDE, LAPSE
slip by .... ELAPSE
slip out of course ...... SLUE
slip, plant .... CION, CUTTING
slipknot .... NOOSE
slipper ...... MULE, MOYLE
slipper, P. I. .... CHINELA
slope ...... RAMP, GRADIENT
slope: fort. .... GLACIS

c
slope of vein or lode ... HADE
slope: Scot .... BRAE
slope of land ...... VERSANT
slope, steep ... SCARP, ESCARP
sloping edge
       BASIL, BEZEL, BEZIL
sloth, three-toed .... AI
sloth, two-toed .... UNAU
slouch: Scot. .... LOUCH
slow .... POKY
slow loris .... KOKAM
slow: music .. TARDO, LARGO
     LENTO, ADAGIO, ANDANTE
slower: music .... RIT
sluggish .... DOPEY
sluice .... CLOW
slump .... RECESSION
slur over .... ELIDE
slushy mass .... POSH
sly look .... LEER, OGLE
sly: old Eng. .... SLEE, SLOAN
sly: Scot: .... SLEE
smack ...... BUSS, KISS, SLAP
small .... WEE, TINY,
      PETIT, PETTY, PETITE
small amount .. DRAM, MINIM
small arachnid .... MITE
small bottle .... VIAL
small bunch .... WISP

d
small case .... ETUI
small cluster .... SPRIG
small coin .... MITE
small creature MITE, MINIMUS
small dog .... POM, PUG,
         PUP, PEKE, FEIST
small goby, Atlantic ... MAPO
small: law .... PETIT
small marine animal .... SALP
small monkey .... LEMUR
small pearl .... PEARLET
small poem .... ODELET
small: Scot. .... SMA
small stream RUN, RILL, RILLET
small: suffix .... ING
small weight ... GRAM, MITE
smallest .... LEAST
smallest integer .... ONE
smallpox .... VARIOLA
smaragd .... EMERALD
smart .... STING
smart CHIC, ASTUTE, CLEVER
smartly dressed ... CHIC, TRIG
smear on .... DAUB
smell, disagreeable
      OLID, REEK, FETOR
smelting mixture ..... MATTE
smelting waste .. SLAG, DROSS
smirch .... SULLY
smith, aided Siegfried .. MIME

a smock .... **CAMISE**
smoke .... **FUME, REEK**
smoke-colored .... **FUMOUS**
smoke, wisp of .... **FLOC**
smoked beef ...... **PASTRAMI**
smokeless powder ..... **FILITE**
smoking .... **AREEK**
smoking pipe ... **BRIAR, BRIER**
smoking pipe, Oriental
    HOOKAH, NARGILE
smoky .... **FUMID**
smooth
    EVEN, IRON, LEVEL, PREEN
smooth-breathing ...... **LENE**
smooth, make ..... **LEVIGATE**
smooth: phonetics ...... **LENE**
smooth-spoken .... **GLIB**
smoothing tool .... **PLANE**
snail, large. **WHELK, ABALONE**
snail, marine .... **TRITON**
snake ..... **ASP, BOA, ADDER,**
    VIPER, PYTHON, REPTILE
snake, Amer. .. **ADDER, RACER**
snake-bite antidote
    GUACO, CEDRON
snake, black .... **RACER**
snake charmer's clarinet **BEEN**
snake-haired woman **GORGON,**
    MEDUSA, STHENO, EURYALE
b snake, India .... **COBRA,**
    KRAIT, DABOIA, DABOYA
snake-like .... **SINUOUS**
snake, S. Amer. .... **ABOMA**
snake, tree .... **LORA**
snake, venomous, Ind.. **BONGAR**
snakes, pert. to ..... **OPHIOID**
snakebird .... **DARTER**
snakeroot, white ...... **STEVIA**
snap up bargains ...... **SNUP**
snapper .... **SESI, PARGO**
snapper fish: Maori .. **TAMURE**
snapper: N. Z. ...... **TAMURE**
snare .. **GIN, NET, WEB, TRAP**
snarl .... **GNAR, GNARR**
snatch .... **GRAB, SEIZE**
sneer. **GIBE, JIBE, FLEER, SCOFF**
sniff .... **NOSE**
snipe, Europ. .... **BLEATER**
snipe's cry .... **SCAPE**
snoring .... **STERTOR**
snow field, Alpine. **FIRN, NEVE**
snow goose genus ...... **CHEN**
snow, ground down .... **LOLLY**
snow house
    IGLU, IGLOE, IGLOO, IGLOU
snow leopard .... **OUNCE**
snow lily .... **VIOLET**
snow, living in .... **NIVAL**
snow mouse .... **VOLE**

c snow panther .... **OUNCE**
snow runner .... **SKI, SKEE**
snow: Scot. .... **SNA**
SNOW WHITE
    see **SEVEN DWARFS**
snuff .... **RAPPEE**
snuffbox bean
    CACOON, MACKAYBEAN
snug .... **COSY, COZY**
snuggery .... **NEST**
so .... **THUS, TRUE, VERY**
so be it! .... **AMEN**
so much: music ...... **TANTO**
so: Scot. .... **SAE**
soak .... **RET, SOG, SOP, WET**
soak flax .... **RET**
soap, fine .... **CASTILE**
soap-frame bar .... **SESS**
soap: pharm. .... **SAPO**
soap plant .... **AMOLE**
soap substitute ...... **AMOLE**
soap vine .... **GOGO**
soapstone .... **TALC**
soapy mineral .... **TALC**
sober .... **GRAVE, STAID**
social affair .... **TEA**
social division .... **CASTE**
social unit or group .... **SEPT**
society, entrance into .. **DEBUT**
d society swell .... **NOB**
sock, Jap. .... **TABI**
sock, Rom. .... **UDO**
sod .... **TURF**
sodium alum .... **MENDOZITE**
sodium carbonate .... **TRONA**
sodium chloride .... **SALT**
sodium chloride: pharm. .. **SAL**
sodium compound ..... **SODA**
sodium nitrate .. **NITER, NITRE**
sofa .... **DIVAN**
soft
    LOW, EASY, WAXY, TENDER
soft area on bill .... **CERE**
soft drink
    ADE, POP, COLA, SODA
soft feathers ... **DOWN, EIDER**
soft ice from floes ..... **LOLLY**
soft job ..... **SNAP, SINECURE**
soft mass .... **WAD**
soft palate .... **VELUM**
soft palate lobe ...... **UVULA**
soft palate, pert. to
    VELAR, UVULAR
soft palates .... **VELA**
soft-spoken .... **MEALY**
soften in temper ..... **RELENT**
softly: music .... **SOAVE**
soil: comb. form .... **AGRO**
soil, organic part ..... **HUMUS**

a
soil, rich .... **LOAM**
soil, sticky .. **GOMBO, GUMBO**
soil, type of .... **PEDOCAL**
solar disc ...... **ATEN, ATON**
solar over lunar year,
    excess of .... **EPACT**
soldier: Am. Rev. .. **BUCKSKIN**
soldier, Austral., N. Z. **ANZAC**
soldier, Brit. .... **ATKINS**
soldier, former .... **LANCER**
soldier, Gr. .... **HOPLITE**
soldier, Indo-Brit. ...... **SEPOY**
soldier, native India ... **SEPOY**
soldier's shelter ..... **FOXHOLE**
sole .... **PELMA**
sole of foot .... **VOLA**
sole of plow .... **SLADE**
solemn declaration. **VOW, OATH**
solicit .... **BEG, URGE,**
    COURT, CANVASS
solicitor's chamber ...... **INN**
solicitude .... **CARE**
solid .... **CONE, CUBE, PRISM**
solid, become **GEL, SET, HARDEN**
solid: comb. form .... **STEREO**
solidify ... **GEL, SET, HARDEN**
solitary .... **LONE, ONLY, SOLE**
solo .... **ARIA**
Solomon's aid giver ... **HIRAM**

b
Solomon's temple rebuilder
    HIRAM
solution .... **KEY**
solution, strength of
    TITER, TITRE
solvent .... **ACETONE**
solvent, treat with .. **SOLUTIZE**
some .... **ANY**
somite .... **MEROSOME**
son: Fr. .... **FILS**
son-in-law .... **GENER**
son: Ir. .... **MAC**
son of .... **MAC**
son of Agrippina .... **NERO**
son of Joktan .... **OPHIR**
son of Reuben .... **PALLU**
son of: Scot. .... **MAC**
song .... **LAY, ODE, DITE,**
    DITTY, MELOS, TROLL
song, Christmas
    NOEL, CAROL, WASSAIL
song for solo voices ..... **GLEE**
song: Ger. .... **LIED**
song, Hawaiian .... **MELE**
song, Jap. .... **UTA**
song, morning: poet. .. **MATIN**
song, of a .... **MELIC**
song of praise, joy
    PEAN, PAEAN, ANTHEM
"Song of the South" Uncle
    REMUS

c
song, operatic .... **ARIA**
song, religious
    HYMN, CHANT, ANTHEM
song, sacred
    HYMN, CHANT, ANTHEM
song, sad .... **DIRGE**
song: Scot. .... **STROUD**
song, simple .... **DITTY**
song, Sp. .... **CANCION**
song thrush ... **MAVIE, MAVIS**
sonship .... **FILIETY**
soon .... **ANON**
sooner .... **ERE, ERER**
soot .... **COOM, SMUT**
soot: old Eng. .... **SOTE**
soothe .... **EASE, LULL**
soothing **ANODYNE, LENITIVE**
soothsayer .... **SEER**
Sophocles, play by ... **OEDIPUS**
soprano, prima donna .. **ALDA,**
    BORI, PONS, RISE,
    RAISA, CALLAS, STEBER
sora bird .... **RAIL**
sorceress .... **CIRCE**
sorceress, Hindu .... **USHA**
sorceress, myth. .... **LAMIA**
sorceress, "Odyssey," Greek
    CIRCE

d
sorcery, W. Ind.
    OBE, OBI, OBEAH
sore, make .... **RANKLE**
sore: Scot. .... **SAIR**
sorghum variety .... **MILO**
sorrow .... **DOLOR, REMORSE**
sorrow, feel
    RUE, LAMENT, REPENT
sorrowful . **SAD, BLUE, DOLENT**
sort .... **KIND,**
    CLASS, GROUP, SPECIES
sortie .... **SALLY**
sortilege .... **LOT**
sorting machine ..... **GRADER**
soul .... **ANIMA**
soul, Egyp. .... **BA, KA**
soul, Hindu .. **ATMA, ATMAN**
sound .. **TONE, NOISE, VALID**
sound, kind of ..... **PALATAL**
sound loudly .. **BLARE, LARUM**
sound, monotonous
    HUM, DRONE
sound perception .... **EAR**
sound, pert. to ...... **SONANT**
sound reasoning .... **LOGIC**
sound, resemblance of
    ASSONANT
sound, solid .... **KLOP**
sound the ocean
    PLUMB, FATHOM

a sound waves, of ...... **AUDIO**
sound, without ..... **ASONANT**
sounding .... **SONANT**
soundless .... **ASONANT**
soup, heavy .. **PUREE, POTAGE**
soup spoon .... **LADLE**
soup, thick .... **BISK, HOOSH, PUREE, BISQUE**
soup vessel .... **TUREEN**
soupfin shark .... **TOPE**
sour .... **ACID, ACERB, ACIDIC, ACETOSE**
sour curdled milk: Nor. .. **SKYR**
sour-leaved plant ..... **SORREL**
sour milk drink.**LEBAN, LEBEN**
source, mineral .... **ORE**
source, obsidian's ...... **LAVA**
soursop .... **ANNONA**
south: Sp. .... **SUR**
South African .... **BOER**
SOUTH AFRICA ..... see also SPECIAL SECTION
S. Afr. assembly .... **RAAD**
S. Afr. dialect .... **TAAL**
S. Afr. Dutch .... **BOER, TAAL**
S. Afr. garter snake .... **ELAPS**
S. Afr. grass country .... **VELD**
S. Afr. greenhorn ..... **IKONA**
S. Afr. gully .... **DONGA**
S. Afr. "out" .... **UIT**
b S. Afr. town .... **STAD**
S. Afr. village .... **KRAAL**
SOUTH AMERICA .... see also SPECIAL SECTION
South American animal . **TAPIR**
S. Amer. bird ... **GUAN, JACU, SYLPH, TURCO, SERIEMA**
S. Amer. game bird **TINAMOU**
S. Amer. Indian group .... **GES**
S. Amer. lizard .... **TEJU**
S.Amer.tree **VERA,CEBIL,FOTUI**
S. Amer. ungulate .... **TAPIR**
"South Pacific" hero .... **EMILE**
Southern Cross constellation **CRUX**
Southern France .... **MIDI**
Southern river .... **PEEDEE**
Southern state: abbr. .... **ALA**
Southwest river .... **RED**
sovereign (coin) .... **SKIV**
sovereignty .... **EMPERY**
SOVIET .... see also RUSSIAN
Soviet news agency ..... **TASS**
Soviet newspaper .... **PRAVDA**
sow .... **PIG, GILT**
sow .... **SEED, PLANT**
sow: Prov. Eng. .... **YELT**
sow: Scot. .... **SOO**
sower .... **SEEDER**
sown: her. .... **SEME**
soybean .... **SOJA, SOYA**

c spa, Bohemian .... **BILIN**
spa, Eng. .... **BATH**
spa, Ger. .... **EMS, BADEN**
space between bird's eye and bill ..... **LORA, LORE, LORUM**
space between triglyphs **METOPE**
space, small **AREOLA, AREOLE**
spaces on bird's face **LORAE, LORES**
spade .... **LOY, SHOVEL**
spade, narrow .... **LOY, SPUD**
spade-shaped .... **PALACEOUS**
spade, turf .... **SLANE**
Spain, ancient .... **IBERIA**
SPANISH see also SPAIN, SPECIAL SECTION
SP. ARTIST see SP. PAINTER
Sp. belle .... **MAJA**
Sp. cellist .... **CASALS**
Sp. coin, old .... **PISTOLE**
Sp. dance .... **JOTA, BOLERO**
Sp. epic .... **CID**
Sp. explorer **CORTEZ, BALBOA, CORTES**
d Sp. fabric .... **CREA**
Sp. fortress commander .. **CAID**
Sp. game of ball .... **PELOTA**
Sp. general, duke.**ALBA, ALVA**
Sp. hero .... **CID**
Sp. kettle .... **OLLA**
Sp. lady .... **DONA, SENORA**
Sp. length unit .... **VARA**
Sp. man .... **DON, SENOR**
Sp. nun .... **AVILA**
Sp. painter **GOYA, MIRO, SERT, PICASSO**
Sp. poet .... **ENCINA**
Sp. pot .... **OLLA**
Sp. title.**DON, SENOR, SENORA**

SPANISH WORDS:
(tilde omitted throughout)
abbey .... **ABADIA**
afternoon .... **TARDE**
annatto seeds ... **ACHIOTE**
another .... **OTRO**
article .... **EL, LA, LAS, LOS, UNO**
ass .... **ASNO**
aunt .... **TIA**
bay .... **BAHIA**
bean .... **HABA**
before .... **ANTES**
being .... **ENTE**
black .... **NEGRA**
blue .... **AZUL**
box canyon .... **CAJON**

151

Spanish

a

boy	NINO
bravo!	OLE
bull	TORO
but	PERO
canal	CANO
chaperon	DUENA, DUENNA
chest	CAJETA
chief	JEFE, ADALID
child	NINO
church	IGLESIA
city	CIUDAD
clay building	ADOBE, TAPIA
cloak	CAPA
clothes	ROPA
corral	ATAJO
cut	TAJO
day	DIA
dining hall	SALA
dove	PALOMA
drawing room	SALA
estuary	RIA
evening	TARDE
evil	MALO
first	PRIMUS
for	POR
friend	AMIGO
funds	CAJA
girl	NINA
God	DIOS
gold	ORO

b

good-bye	ADIOS
grass fiber rope	SOGA
grille	REJA
gulch	ARROYO
gypsy	GITANO
hall	SALA
hamlet	ALDA
harbor entrance	BOCA
health	SANO
hello	HOLLA
hill	ALTO, CERRO, MORRO
hillside	FALDA
hotel	POSADA
house	CASA
Indian	INDIO
inlet	RIA, ESTERO
jail keeper	CAID
judge	JUEZ
king	REY
lady	DAMA
lake	LAGO
landmark	SENAL
latter	ESTE
lawsuit	ACTO
letter	CARTA
lime	LIMA
love	AMOR
man	HOMBRE
manservent	MOZO
mayor	ALCADE, ALCALDE

c

mouth	BOCA
movie house	CINE
meadow	VEGA
my	MIO
of	DE
open space	COSO
other	OTRA
parish priest	CURA
peak	PICO
people	GENTE
pine	PINO
pole	PALO
pole, wooden	PALO
porridge	ATOLE
post office	CORREO
pot	OLLA
priest	CURA, PADRE
queen	REINA
ragged person	ROTO
raisin	PASA
red	ROJO
river	RIO
road	CAMINO
room	SALA
rum	RON
saint, feminine	SANTA
she	ELLA
silver	PLATA
six	SEIS

d

snake	CULEBRA
song	CANCION
south	SUR
street	CALLE, CALLI
sweet potato	CAMOTE
tall	ALTA
this	ESTA, ESTE
three	TRES
to be	SER, ESTE
tomorrow	MANANA
trench	TAJO
uncle	TIO
very	MUY
water	AGUA
wax	CERA
wit	SAL
with	DE
work	OBRA
yes	SI
you	TE

spar	BOX, BOOM, GAFF, MAST, YARD, SPRIT
spar for colors	GAFF
spar, heavy	BARITE
spar, loading	STEEVE
spar, small	SPRIT
spare	LEAN, EXTRA, GAUNT, LENTEN
sparkle	GLITTER
sparkling, as wine	MOUSSEUX
sparrow, hedge	DONEY

a Sparta queen .... **LEDA**
Spartan army division .. **MORA**
Spartan magistrate ... **EPHOR**
spasm .... **FIT, TIC, JERK**
spawning place .... **REDD**
speak
 UTTER, ORATE, DECLAIM
speak: comb. form ..... **LALO**
speak, inability to ... **ALALIA**
speak theatrically ..... **EMOTE**
speaker ... **ORATOR, LOCUTOR**
speaking tube, pilot's.**GOSPORT**
spear .... **DART, LANCE**
spear, Afr. **ASSAGAI, ASSEGAI**
spear, fish .... **GIG, GAFF**
spear-like weapon **PIKE, LANCE**
spear-shaped .... **HASTATE**
spear, 3-prong ...... **TRIDENT**
spear thrower, Austral.
 WOMERA
special: Moslem law
 KHAS, KHASS
species .... **KIND, SORT**
specific date .... **DAY**
specified time .... **DATE**
specimen .... **SAMPLE**
speck .... **DOT, MOTE, FLECK**
speckle .... **DOT, STIPPLE**
spectacle .... **PAGEANT**
specter .... **BOGY, BOGEY,**
b **GHOST, SHADE**
speech ... **LECTURE, ORATION**
speech, art of ..... **RHETORIC**
speech defect
 LISP, ALOGIA, STAMMER
speech goddess, Hindu
 VAC, DEVI, VACH
speech, local .... **PATOIS**
speech, long .... **SPIEL**
speech, loss of ...... **APHASIA**
speech peculiarity ..... **IDIOM**
speech, violent ...... **TIRADE**
speechless ...... **DUMB, MUTE**
speed ..... **HIE, RUN, PACE,**
 RACE, HASTE, HASTEN,
 RAPIDITY
speed, at full .... **AMAIN**
spelt .... **ADOR, EMMER**
Spenser heroine .... **UNA**
Spenser's name for Ireland
 IRENA
sphere .... **ORB**
sphere of action ..... **ARENA**
spice .... **MACE**
spice ball .... **FAGOT, FAGGOT**
spicknel .... **MEU, MEW**
spicy .... **RACY**
spider crab genus **MAIA, MAJA**
spider fluid: Pharm. **ARANEIN**

c spider monkey
 QUATA, ATELES, COAITA
spider nest .... **NIDUS**
spigot .... **TAP**
spike .... **EAR, GAD, BROB**
spikenard .... **NARD**
spin
 BIRL, REEL, TWIRL, ROTATE
spinal column ... **AXIS, AXON**
spinal cord .... **MYELON**
spinal membrane ...... **DURA**
spindle .... **COP, AXLE**
spindle, yarn .... **HASP**
spine .... **AXIS, AXON**
spine bones .... **SACRA**
spine, slender .... **SETA**
spineless cactus ...... **CHAUTE**
spiniform .... **SPINATE**
spinning jenny .... **MULE**
spiny shrub genus ...... **ULEX**
spiral formation ..... **VOLUTE**
spire ornament .... **EPI**
spirit .... **ELAN, SOUL, METAL**
spirit: Egyp. myth ..... **BA, KA**
spirit: Ger. .... **GEIST**
spirit, Ir. . **BANSHEE, BANSHIE**
spirit lamp .... **ETNA**
spirit, Moslem .... **JIN, JINN,**
 GENIE, GENII, JINNI, JINNEE
spirit of air .... **ARIEL**
spirit of evil .. **DEMON, DEVIL**
d spirit of man: Egypt ..... **AKH**
spirit raiser .. **ELATER, ELATOR**
spirits and water ...... **GROG**
spirits of the dead .... **MANES**
spirited .... **EAGER, CONMOTO**
spirited horse .... **STEED**
spiritual body: Egypt. ... **SAHU**
spiritual struggle ..... **PENIEL**
spiritualist meeting ... **SEANCE**
splash .... **LAP**
spleen .... **MILT**
splendid .... **GRAND**
splendor .... **ECLAT**
splendor, goddess of: Hindu
 UMA
split .... **RIT, RENT, RIVE,**
 CLEFT, RIVEN, CLEAVE
split pulse .... **DAL**
spoil .... **ROT, BOTCH**
spoil, as eggs .... **ADDLE**
spoils of war .... **LOOT**
spoken .... **ORAL**
spoken word .... **AGRAPH**
spokes, having .... **RADIAL**
sponge, calcareous ... **LEUCON**
sponge gourd ... **LOOF, LOOFA**
sponge on ..... **MUMP, LEACH**
sponge spicule, bow-shaped
 OXEA, TOXA, PINULUS
sponge, young .... **ASCON**

a
spongewood .... SOLA
sponsor .... PATRON
sponsorship .... EGIS, AEGIS
spool .... REEL
spore .... SEED
spore cluster .... SORUS
spore fruit of rust fungi
    AECIA, TELIA, AECIUM,
         TELIUM
spore sac, fungus ASCI, ASCUS
sport .... RUX, GAME,
     GOLF, PLAY, POLO
sports arena STADIA, STADIUM
sports center ... RINK, ARENA
sports hall .... GYM
spot in mineral ..... MACLE
spot on card .... PIP
spotted .... PIED, PINTO,
    DAPPLED, MACULOSE
spotted cavy .... PACA
spotted deer KAKAR, CHITAL
spotted moth ...... FORESTER
spotted sting-ray ..... OBISPO
spotted, to make
    DAPPLE, STIPPLE
spouse .... MATE, WIFE
spray .... ATOMIZE
spray, sea .... LIPPER

b
spread .... TED
spread by peening .... RIVET
spread by report
    BRUIT, NORATE
spread out .... FAN
spread rumor .... GOSSIP
spread the word .... TELL
spread to dry, as hay ... TED
sprightly .... PERT, PEART
spring .... SPA
spring back .... RESILE
spring: Bible .... AIN
spring-like .... VERNAL
spring: old Eng. .... KELD
spring, mineral .... SPA
spring rice, India ...... BORO
spring, small .... SEEP
springs, warm ...... THERMAE
springboard .... BATULE
sprinkle DEG, WATER, SPARGE
sprinkling: her. .... SEME
sprint .... RUN, RACE
sprite .. ELF, FAY, PIXY, PIXIE
sprite, tricksy .... ARIEL
sprout ... CION, GROW, SCION
spruce ... TRIG, TRIM, NATTY
spruce, Jap. .... YEDDO
spruce, white ...... EPINETTE
spume .... FOAM
spun wool .... YARN
spur .... GAD, GOAD, CALCAR
spur of mountain ..... ARETE

c
spur part .... ROWEL
spur wheel .... ROWEL
spurs, having .... CALCARATE
spurt .... JET, GUSH
spy, garment-trade slang KEEK
spy, British, Revolution ANDRE
squama .... ALULA
squander .... SPEND
square dance .... REEL
square-meshed net ..... LACIS
squash .... PEPO,
    CRUSH, GOURD, FLATTEN
squash bug .... ANASA
squaw .... MAHALA
squawfish .... CHUB
squid genus .... LOLIGO
squirrel fur, Siberian
    CALABAR, CALABER
squirrel, ground Europ. .. SISEL
squirrel-like animal DORMOUSE
squirrel skin .... VAIR
squirrel's nest ... DRAY, DREY
ST. .... see SAINT
stab .... GORE
stabilize .... STEADY
stable .... FIRM, SOLID
stable compartment ... STALL
stable-keeper, royal .. AVENER
stables, royal .... MEWS
stableman .... OSTLER

d
stack of hay .... RICK
staff .... ROD, MACE
staff-bearer .... MACER
staff, bishop's ...... CROSIER
staff of office .... MACE
staff, royal SCEPTER, SCEPTRE
stag ..... DEER, HART, MALE
stage direction
    MANET, SENET, EXEUNT
stage equipment ...... PROPS
stage extra ..... SUPE, SUPER
stage horn signal .... SENNET
stage setting .... SCENE
stage whisper .... ASIDE
stagger .... REEL
stagger: Prov. Eng. ...... STOT
stagnation .... STASIS
stagnation, blood ..... STASIS
stain, DYE, SOIL, SPOT, TASH
stair part ...... RISER, TREAD
stair post .... NEWEL
staircase spindle .... SPEEL
stake .... ANTE, WAGER
stake, like a .... PALAR
stake, pointed ..... PALISADE
stake, poker .... ANTE
stakes .... POT
stakes, —, Epsom Downs Race
        OAKS
stale .... TRITE
stalk .... STEM

a
stalk, flower .. **SCAPE, PEDICEL**
stalk, frond .... **STIPE**
stalk, plant .... **CAULIS**
stalk, short .... **STIPE**
stalk, sugarcane ..... **RATOON**
stall in mud .... **STOG**
stammer .... **HAW, HEM**
stammering sound .... **ER**
stamp .... **MARK, SIGIL**
stamp battery block ..... **VOL**
stamp of approval .... **OK**
stamp-sheet part .... **PANE**
stamping device .... **DIE**
stamping machine ..... **DATER**
stanch .... **STEM**
stand .... **RISE**
stand .. **BEAR, ABIDE, ENDURE**
stand, cuplike .... **ZARF**
stand in awe of .... **FEAR**
stand, small
    TABORET, TAROURET
stand, 3-legged **TRIPOD, TRIVET**
standard . **PAR, FLAG, ENSIGN**
standard.**NORM, TYPE, NORMA**
standard of chemical strength
    TITER
standard, Turk .... **ALEM**
standing .... **STATUS**
stannum .... **TIN**
stanza, last .... **ENVOY**
b
stanza, Nor. .... **STEV**
stanza, part of .... **STAVE**
star .... **ASTRO**
star, blue .... **VEGA**
star, brightest .... **COR**
star cluster, distant
    NEBULA, NEBULAE
star, day .... **SUN**
star, evening ...... **VENUS,**
  HESPER, VESPER, HESPERUS
star facet .... **PANE**
star, fixed .... **SUN, ALYA**
star: Fr. .... **ETOILE**
star in Aquarius .... **SKAT**
star in Aquilla .... **ALTAIR**
star in Argo .... **NAOS**
star in Big Dipper ..... **PHAD**
star in Bootes .... **IZAR**
star in Cetus .... **MIRA**
star in Cygenus **SADR, DENEB**
star in Draco .... **ADIB, JUZA**
star in Eridanus ... **AZHA, BEID**
star in Leo .. **DUHR, REGULUS**
star in Lyra ... **VEGA, WEGA**
star in Orion .... **RIGEL**
star in Pegasus **ENIF, MATAR**
star in Pleiades .... **MAIA**
star in Perseus .... **ATIK**
star in Scorpio ..... **ANTARES**

c
star in Serpens .... **ALYA**
star in Taurus ..**NATH, PLEIAD**
star in Virgo .... **SPICA**
star near Mizar .... **ALCOR**
star, new .... **NOVA**
star-shaped .... **STELLATE**
star-shaped spicule
    ACTER, ACTINE
star, temporary .... **NOVA**
stars, dotted with ...... **SEME**
stars, pert. to .... **ASTRAL**
starch .... **AMYL, ARUM,**
  SAGO, FARINA, CASSAVA
starchy rootstock .... **TARO**
starfish .... **ASTEROID**
stark mad .... **RAVING**
starnose .... **MOLE**
— Starr, comic strip character
    BRENDA
starred lizard **AGAMA, HARDIM**
start ... **BEGIN, SALLY, ROUSE**
starvation .... **INEDIA**
starwort .... **ASTER**
state .... **AVER**
STATE .. see also GAZETTEER
STATE FLOWERS . see page 208
state, New England: abbr. .. **RI**
state of affairs .... **PASS**
state, pert. to .... **CIVIL**
d
state of: suffix .... **ERY**
state of being: suffix .... **URE**
state precisely ...... **SPECIFY**
stately home .. **DOME, ESTATE**
statements, confused
    RIGMAROLE
statesman, Brit. .... **PITT**
station .. **POST, DEPOT, PLACE**
stationary .... **FIXED, STATIC**
stationary motor part **STATOR**
statistician .... **STATIST**
statute .... **ACT, LAW**
stave, barrel .... **LAG**
stay .... **WAIT, TARRY**
stay rope .... **GUY**
stays .... **CORSET**
stead .... **LIEU, PLACE**
steal **COP, ROB, GLOM, SNITCH**
steal cattle .... **RUSTLE**
steal: Eng. .... **GLOM**
steal, Eng. dialect .... **NIM**
steel beam .... **GIRDER**
steel: Ger. .... **STAHL**
steel splint, armor skirt
    TACE, TASSE, TASSET
steep .... **RET, SOP**
steep .... **SHEER**
steep in lime .... **BOWK**
steer wildly .... **YAW**
steer, young: Prov. Eng. .. **STOT**

Steering

steering, direct ship's **COND, CONN**
steersman .... **COX**
stellar ...... **ASTRAL, STARRY**
stem **CION, CORM, SCAPE, STALK**
stem, fungus .... **STIPE**
stem, hollow .... **CANE**
stem, jointed .... **CULM**
stem of hop .... **BINE**
stem, rudimentary .. **CAULICLE**
stem, ship's .... **PROW**
stench .... **ODOR, FETOR**
stentorian .... **LOUD**
step .... **GRADE, PHASE**
step ... **PACE, STAIR, TREAD**
step, dance ..... **ΓAS, CHASSE**
step up to mark .... **TOE**
step, upright part of .. **RISER**
steps, outdoor .... **PERRON**
steps over fence ...... **STILE**
steppes, storm on ..... **BURAN**
stern **GRIM, HARSH, AUSTERE**
steward: Scot. ..... **MORMAOR**
stick .. **BAR, BAT, ROD, CANE, WAND, BATON, MUNDLE**
stick .... **GLUE, PASTE, ADHERE, CLEAVE**
stick, conductor's ..... **BATON**
stick together ...... **COHERE**
stick used in hurling .. **CAMAN**
sticks, bundle of ...... **FAGOT**
stickler for formality .. **TAPIST**
sticky substance ... **GOO, GUM**
stiffly nice .... **PRIM**
stigma .... **BRAND**
stigmatic point of mango **NAK**
still .... **BUT, YET**
stimulant, coffee **CAFFEIN, CAFFEINE**
stimulant, tea **THEIN, THEINE**
stimulate .. **FAN, WHET, ELATE**
sting .... **BITE, SMART**
stinging ant .... **KELEP**
stinging herb .... **NETTLE**
stingy .... **MEAN**
stint .... **TASK**
stipend, church ..... **PREBEND**
stipend: Scot. .... **ANNAT**
stipulation .... **CLAUSE**
stir .. **ADO, MIX, TODO, ROUSE**
stir up .... **RILE, ROIL**
stitch .... **PUNTO**
stitchbird .... **IHI**
stitched fold .... **TUCK**
stithy .... **ANVIL**
stock .... **BREED**
stock .... **STORE**
stock exchange, membership in **SEAT**
stock exchange, Paris **BOURSE**

stock market crash .... **PANIC**
stockade: Russ. .... **ETAPE**
stocking run .... **LADDER**
stockings .... **HOSE**
stocky .... **STUB**
stolen goods .... **SWAG**
stomach .... **MAW, CRAW**
stomach division, ruminant's **OMASUM**
stomach, first .... **RUMEN**
stomach, ruminant's ... **TRIPE**
stone .. **AGATE, LAPIS, SLATE**
Stone Age tool .... **CELT, EOLITH, NEOLITH**
stone, aquamarine .... **BERYL**
stone, breastplate .... **JASPER**
stone chest .... **CIST**
stone chip .... **SPALL**
stone: comb. form ..... **LITH**
stone-cutter's chisel .... **DROVE**
stone fruit .... **DRUPE**
stone, green .. **BERYL, OLIVINE**
stone hammer .... **MASH**
stone, hard .... **ADAMANT**
stone heap .... **CARN, KARN, CAIRN, CARNE, CAIRNE**
stone, hollow .... **GEODE**
stone implement ..... **CELT, EOLITH, NEOLITH**
stone, like a .... **LITHOID**
stone, monument .... **MENHIR**
stone paving block ..... **SETT**
stone pillar .... **STELE**
stone, red ..... **SARD, SPINEL**
stone roller fish ...... **TOTER**
stone, rough .... **RUBBLE**
stone: Scot. .... **STEAN, STEEN**
stone set .... **PAVER**
stone, squared ...... **ASHLAR**
stone to death ..... **LAPIDATE**
stone, woman turned to **NIOBE**
stone worker .... **MASON**
stone, yellow **TOPAZ, CITRINE**
stonecrop **ORPIN, SEDUM, ORPINE**
stonecutter **MASON, LAPICIDE**
stonecutter's chisel ... **DROVE**
stoneware: Fr. .... **GRES**
stool pigeon .... **NARK**
stop .... **DAM, BALK, HALT, STEM, WHOA, DESIST**
stop, as engine .. **CONK, STALL**
stop by accident ...... **STALL**
stop: naut. ... **AVAST, BELAY**
stop short .... **BALK**
stoppage .... **JAM**
stopper .... **BUNG, PLUG**
storage battery plate ... **GRID**
storage place **BIN, BARN, SILO**
store, army .... **CANTEEN**
store fodder .... **ENSILE**

156

a storehouse .... ETAPE
storehouse, army ..... DEPOT
storehouse, India .... GOLA
storehouse, public ..... ETAPE
stork .... MARABOU
storm FUME, FURY, RAGE, RAVE
storm, away from ...... ALEE
storm, dust .... SIMOON
storm: Fr. .... ORAGE
storm god, Babyl. ZU, ADAD,
ADDA, ADDU
story, Norse .... SAGA
story, short .... CONTE
stoss, opposite of .... LEE
stout .... BURLY
stout, kind of .... PORTER
stove .... ETNA, RANGE
"Stowe" character
EVA, TOM, TOPSY
straight .... DIRECT
straight-edge .... RULER
strain .... EXERT
strained .... TENSE
strainer .... SIEVE
strainer, wool cloth ... TAMIS
Straits Settlement region
PENANG
strange .... ODD
strap on falcon's leg .... JESS
strap-shaped .... LORATE
b strass .... PASTE
stratagem .... RUSE, WILE
stratagem, sudden ...... COUP
stratum .... LAYER
straw hat ...... BAKU, MILAN
stray .... ERR
stray .... WAIF
stray animal .... CAVY
streak .... ROE, LINE, VEIN,
STRIA, STRAKE, STRIAE
streaky .... LINY, ROWY
stream
FLOW, RILL, BOURN, RIVER
streamlet ...... RILL, RUNNEL
street Arab .... GAMIN
street: It., Sp. .. CALLE, CALLI
street, narrow .... LANE
street roisterer .... MUN
street urchin .... ARAB
street, Venice water .. RIO, RII
strength .... POWER
strengthening .... ROBORANT
stress .... ICTUS
stressed beat, syllable .. ARSIS
stretch: Scot. .... STENT
stretched out ...... PROLATE
stretcher .... LITTER
stretching frame .... TENTER,
STENTER
strewn with flowers: Her. SEME

c strife .... WAR
strife, civil .... STASIS
strike .. BAT, HIT, RAP, CONK,
SLOG, SLUG, SOCK, SWAT,
WHAM, SMITE
strikebreaker ..... FINK, SCAB
striking effect .... ECLAT
string of mules .... ATAJO
stringy .... ROPY
strip .. BARE, DIVEST, STRAKE
strip of land ... DOAB, DUAB
strip of wood .... LATH
strip off skin .... FLAY
strip, oxhide, S. Afr. ... RIEM
strip, wood, metal ... SPLINE
stripe .... BAR, BAND, WALE,
WEAL, STREAK
stripe of color: zool. .. PLAGA
stripling .... BOY, LAD
strive .... AIM, VIE
strobile .... CONE
stroke .... FIT, ICTUS
stroke, brilliant .... COUP
stroll .... AMBLE
strong-arm man .... GOON
strong, as cigars ... MADURO
strong desire .... HUNGER
strong man .... SAMSON
strong man, Gr. .... ATLAS
strong point .... FORTE
d strong-scented ... OLID, RANK
strongbox .... SAFE
stronghold .. FORT, SION, ZION
struck with horror ... AGHAST
structure, tall .... TOWER
struggle .... COPE
struggle helplessly. FLOUNDER
struggled .... HOVE
stud .... BOSS
student in charge ... MONITOR
studio, art .... ATELIER
study ...... CON, PORE, READ
study group .... SEMINAR
stuff .... PAD, RAM, CRAM
stuffing .... KAPOK
stum .... MUST
stumble: prov. Eng. ..... STOT
stump of branch ...... SKEG
stunted trees .... SCRUB
stupefied .... MAZED
stupefy .... DAZE, MAZE,
STUN, BESOT
stupid .... CRASS, DENSE
stupid person ..... ASS, OAF
CLOD, COOT, DOLT, LOON,
LOUT, LOWN, MOKE
stupor .... COMA, SOPOR
sturgeon, small .... STERLET
style .... MODE, NAME
style of art .... DADA, GENRE

Stylet

a
stylet, surgical ...... TROCAR
stymie .... IMPEDE
Styx ferryman ...... CHARON
subbase .... PLINTH
subdued shade .... PASTEL
subject ...... TOPIC, VASSAL
subject in grammar .... NOUN
subjoin .... ADD
sublime .... NOBLE
submarine PIGBOAT, SNORKEL
submit .... BOW, YIELD
subordinate
　　　MINOR, DEPENDENT
subside
EBB, SINK, ABATE, RELAPSE
substance, lustrous .... METAL
substances, class of .... LIPIN
substantiate .... VERIFY
substantive word .... NOUN
substitute
　　　VICE, PROXY, ERSATZ
substitute for: suffix .... ETTE
subtle emanation ...... AURA
subtle variation ..... NUANCE
subtract .... DEDUCT
subway, Eng. .... TUBE
subway entrance ...... KIOSK
subway, Fr. .... METRO
success .... HIT, WOW
b
succession .... LINE
successively .... AROW
succinct .... TERSE
succor .... AID
succulent plant .. ALOE, HERB
such .... SO
sucking fish ... PEGA, REMORA
Sudan lake .... CHAD
Sudan native .... FUL
Sudan Negroid .... SERE
Sudan people .... HAUSA
sudden attack: Med. .. ICTUS
suet .... TALLOW
suffer .... LET, BIDE
suffer from hunger
　　　　CLEM, STARVE
suffer: Scot. .... DREE
sufficient: poet. .... ENOW

SUFFIXES:
act of .... TION
action .... ANCE
adjective .... ENT, IAL, INE,
　　　ISH, IST, ITE, OUS
agent .... URE
alcohol .... OL
carbohydrate .... OSE
chemical or chemistry . ANE,
ENE, IDE, INE, OLE, ONE,
ENOL, ITOL, OLIC

c
common ending ENT, INE,
　　　　ING, ION
common suffix ..... ES, ESE,
ESS, INE, IVE, ETTE,
YNONE
condition .... ATE, ILE, ISE,
ANCE, SION, STER
comparative ...... IER, IOR
compound .... ICAL, ILITY
diminutive .... ET, IE, ULA,
ULE, ETTE
feminine ... INA, INE, ELLA
feminine noun .... ESS
follower .... IST, ITE
forming nouns from verbs. ER
full of .... OSE
inflammation .... ITIS
inhabitant of .... ITE
into .... EN
like .... OID
little .... ET
made of .... EN
make .... ISE
medical .... IA, OMA
mineral .... ITE, LITE
native of .... ITE
noun ... IA, OR, ATE, ENT,
ERY, ESS, IER, ISE, IST,
ITE, ANCY, ENCE, ENSE,
STER
d
noun ending .... STER
noun forming diminutive. CLE
number .... TEEN
or ordinal number .... ETH
oil .... OL, OLE
one who .... IST, STER
one who does .... IST
order of animals .... INI
ordinal .... ETH
origin, denoting ...... OTE
participle .... ING
person .... ER
plural .... (old EN), ES
quality .... ANCE, ILITY
rocks, of .... ITE, LITE
science of .... ICS
skin .... DERM
small .... ING
state of .... ERY, ANCE
state of being .... URE
substitute for .... ETTE
superlative .... EST
sympathizer .... ITE
town .... TON
tumor .... OMA
verb .... ISE, ESCE
with mineral names ... LITE
zoological .... ATA
Sufi disciple .... MURID
sugar .... OSE, SUCROSE
sugar cane disease ..... ILIAU

a

sugar cane residue .. **BAGASSE**
sugar, crude .... **GUR**
sugar, fruit .... **KETOSE**
sugar, raw ...... **CASSONADE**
sugar, simple .... **OSE**
sugar source .... **CANE**
suggestion .... **CUE, HINT**
suit of mail .... **ARMOR**
suitable. **APT, FIT, PAT, PROPER**
suitcase ... **BAG, GRIP, VALISE**
suitor .... **SWAIN**
sullen .. **DOUR, GLUM, MOROSE**
sullen, act .... **MOPE**
sullen, be ...... **POUT, SULK**
sully .... **SOIL, DIRTY**
sultan, Turkish .... **SELIM**
sultan's order .... **IRADE**
sultan's residence ...... **SERAI**
sultanate .... **OMAN**
sultry .... **HUMID**
Sulu Moslem .... **MORO**
"sum," infinitive following **ESSE**
sum paid as punishment .. **FINE**
sumac genus .... **RHUS**
sumac, P. I. .... **ANAM, ANAN**
Sumatra squirrel shrew .. **TANA**
Sumatra wildcat ...... **BALU**
Sumatran silk .... **IKAT**

b

"summa — laude" ...... **CUM**
summary
DIGEST, PRECIS, EPITOME
summer: Fr. .... **ETE**
summer-house
ARBOR, PERGOLA
summer, pert. to ..... **ESTIVAL**
summit
APEX, KNAP, PEAK, SPIRE
summits .... **APICES**
summon .... **CALL, CITE,**
PAGE, CLEPE, EVOKE
sun .... **SOL, HELIOS**
sun apartments ..... **SOLARIA**
sun bittern .... **CAURALE**
sun: comb. form .... **HELIO**
sun disk .... **ATEN, ATON**
sun-dried brick
DOBE, DOBY, ADOBE, DOBIE
sun god, Babyl. .. **UTU, UTUG,**
BABBAR, SHAMASH
sun god, Egypt. ..... **RA, TEM,**
TUM, AMON, AMEN,
AMUN, ATMU, ATUM
sun god, Gr., Rom. ...... **SOL,**
APOLLO, HELIOS
sun god, Inca .... **INTI**
sun, halo around .... **CORONA**
sun, pert. to .... **SOLAR**
sun porches .... **SOLARIA**
sun tree, Jap. .... **HINOKI**

c

sunbaked building
DOBE, DOBY, ADOBE, DOBIE
Sunday of Lent, 4th .. **LAETARE**
sunder
PART, REND, SPLIT, DIVIDE
sundial, style of ..... **GNOMON**
sunfish .... **BREAM**
sunfish genus .... **MOLA**
sunken fence .... **AHA, HAHA**
sunset, occurring at **ACRONICAL**
sunspot center
UMBRA, UMBRAE
supercilious person ..... **SNOB**
superfluous: Fr. ...... **DE TROP**
superintendent, office
MANAGER
superior, most .... **BEST, TOPS**
superior quality: Fr. .... **LUXE**
superiority, belief in .. **RACISM**
superlative, absolute .. **ELATIVE**
superlative ending ...... **EST**
supernatural .... **OCCULT**
supernatural being, Melanesia
ADARO
supernatural power, E. Afr. **NGAI**
supernatural power, Polyn.
MANA
superscribe .... **DIRECT**
superstition, object of
FETICH, FETISH

d

supper .... **TEA**
supplication, make ..... **PRAY**
supply .... **STOCK, ENDUE**
supply, fresh .... **RELAY**
supply of horses ...... **REMUDA**
support ...... **LEG, RIB, ABET,**
BACK, PROP, BRACE
support, one-legged .. **UNIPOD**
suppose ... **ASSUME, IMAGINE**
suppose: archaic .... **TROW**
suppress ...... **ELIDE, QUASH**
Supreme Being, Hebrew . **IHVH,**
JHVH, JHWH, YHVH, YHWH
surety agreement ...... **BOND**
surf, roar of .... **ROTE**
surface, attractive ... **VENEER**
surface of gem .... **FACET**
surface of a tool .... **FACE**
surfeit .... **CLOY, GLUT, SATE**
surfeited .... **BLASE**
surge .... **TIDE, BILLOW**
surgeon's instrument .. **TREPAN,**
TROCAR, ABLATOR, LE-
VATOR, SCALPEL
surgical thread .... **SETON**
Surinam toad .... **PIPA**
surly .... **GRUFF, SULLEN**
surmise .. **INFER, GUESS, OPINE**
surnamed: Fr. .... **DIT**

Surpass

a
surpass ...... **CAP, TOP, BEST**
surplice, chorister's .... **COTTA**
surplus .... **EXTRA, EXCESS**
surrender
    CEDE, YIELD, DEDITION
surrender: law .... **REMISE**
surround **GIRD, BESET, INARM**
surrounding area ...... **ZONE**
surtout .... **COAT**
survey .... **MAP, POLL**
surveyor's assistant .. **RODMAN**
surveyor's instrument
    ROD, ALIDADE
surveyor's rod, sight on **TARGET**
Susa inhabitant ..... **ELAMITE**
suspend .... **HANG**
suspenders .... **BRACES**
suture .... **SEAM**
svelte .... **SLIM, TRIM**
swab .... **MOP**
swain .... **LOVER**
swallow **BOLT, GULP, MARTIN**
swallow, sea .... **TERN**
swamp ..... **BOG, FEN, MARSH,**
  MORASS, SLEW, SLOO, SLUE
swamp gas .. **MIASM, MIASMA**
swamp, S. Afr. ... **VLEI, VLEY**
swampy belt, India ..... **TERAI**
swan, female .... **PEN**
swan genus .... **OLOR**

b
swan, male .... **COB**
swan, whistling .... **OLOR**
swap .... **TRADE**
sward .... **SOD, TURF**
swarm .... **NEST, HORDE**
swarthy .... **DUN, DARK**
swastika .... **FYLFOT**
sway .... **ROCK, ROLL**
swear .... **AVER, CURSE**
sweat ...... **SUDOR, PERSPIRE**
SWEDISH .... see also SPECIAL
  SECTION—SWEDEN
Swedish:
  beer .... **OL**
  tea .... **TE**
  toe .... **TA**
  you .... **ER**
Swedish coin .... **ORE**
Swedish county, district .. **LAN**
Swedish explorer ...... **HEDIN**
Swedish order of merit .. **VASA**
Swedish royal guard **DRABANT**
Swedish sculptor ..... **MILLES**
sweep, scythe's ...... **SWATH**
sweet flag .. **SEDGE, CALAMUS**
sweet gale .... **GAGL**
sweet liquid .... **NECTAR**
sweet potato
  YAM, BATATA, OCARINA
sweet potato: Sp. .... **CAMOTE**

c
sweet red wine .... **ALICANTE**
sweet-smelling
  OLENT, REDOLENT
sweet spire .... **ITEA**
sweetfish .... **AYU**
sweetheart: Ir. .... **GRA**
sweetheart: Scot. .... **JO**
sweetmeat: Fr. .... **DRAGEE**
sweetsop .... **ATA,**
  ATES, ATTA, ANNONA
swell .... **DILATE**
swell of water .... **WAVE**
swelling **LUMP, NODE, EDEMA**
swelling on plants ..... **GALL**
swerve .... **SHY, SKEW**
swift .... **FAST, FLEET**
swift, common ....**CRAN**
swift horse .. **ARAB, PACOLET**
swiftly, run ...... **DART, SCUD**
swimming .... **NATANT**
swimming bell .. **NECTOPHORE**
swindle **GIP, GYP, DUPE, SWIZ**
swindler .... **COZENER**
swine .. **HOG, PIG, SOW, BOAR**
swine, feeding of ... **PANNAGE**
swine fever .... **ROUGET**
swine genus .... **SUS**
swing music .... **JIVE**
swing musician ...... **HEPCAT**

d
swinish .... **PORCINE**
swipe .... **GLOM**
swirl .... **EDDY, GURGE**
SWISS .. see also SPECIAL SEC-
  TION—SWITZERLAND
Swiss capital ... **BERN, BERNE**
Swiss card game .... **JASS**
Swiss critic .... **AMIEL**
Swiss patriot .... **TELL**
Swiss state .... **CANTON**
switch .... **TOGGLE**
swollen .... **TURGID**
swoon .... **FAINT**
swoon: old Eng. .... **SWEB**
sword ... **PATA, EPEE, BLADE,**
  SABER, SABRE, RAPIER
sword, Arthur's
  EXCALIBAR, EXCALIBUR
sword, curved .. **SABER, SABRE**
sword, fencing .... **EPEE**
sword, matador's ... **ESTOQUE**
sword, medieval ...... **ESTOC**
sword, Norse myth. ... **GRAM**
sword, put away .... **SHEATHE**
sword, St. George's
  ASCALON, ASKELON
sword-shaped ...... **ENSATE**
sword, Siegfried's ..... **GRAM**
sword, slender .... **RAPIER**
swordsman's dummy stake **PEL**
syllable, last .... **ULTIMA**

160

a syllable, scale .... **DO, FA, LA, MI, RE, SO, TI, SOL**
syllable, short .. **MORA, MORAE**
sylvan deity **PAN, FAUN, SATYR**
SYMBOL, CHEMICAL .... see SPECIAL SECTION
symbol .... **TOKEN**
symbol of authority ... **MACE**
symbol of Crusaders ... **CROSS**
symbol of protection .... **EGIS**
sympathizer: suffix ...... **ITE**
synagogue .... **SHUL, TEMPLE**
syncopated music ...... **RAG**
syncope ...... **FAINT, SWOON**
synod, Russian .... **SOBOR**
syntax, give the .... **PARSE**

c synthetic fabric or fiber **NYLON, ORLON, RAYON, DACRON**
synthetic rubber **BUNA, ELASTOMER**
Syria, ancient .... **ARAM**
Syrian, ancient port ... **SIDON**
Syrian bear .... **DUBB**
Syrian bishop's title .... **ABBA**
Syrian city, old ...... **ALEPPO**
system .... **ISM**
system of rule ...... **REGIME**
system of rules .... **CODE**
system of weights ..... **TROY**
system of worship ...... **CULT**
systematic regulation ... **CODE**

T

b T-shaped .... **TAU**
tab .... **FLAP, LABEL**
tabard .... **CAPE**
table mountain, Abyssin. **AMBA**
tableland .... **MESA**
tablet .... **PAD, SLATE**
taboo, opposite of .... **NOA**
tabor, Moorish **ATABAL, ATTABAL**
Tacoma's Sound ...... **PUGET**
tack: naut. .... **BUSK**
tact .... **FINESSE**
tackle, anchor .... **CAT**
tael, part of .... **LI**
tag .... **LABEL**
tag, metal .... **AGLET, AIGLET**
Tagalog for river .... **ILOG**
Tahitian national god ... **ORO**
Tai race branch .... **LAO**
tail, of ... **CAUDAL, CAUDATE**
tail of coin .... **VERSO**
tail, rabbit's .... **SCUT**
tail: zool. .... **CAUDA**
tailor .... **SARTOR**
Taino fetish ..... **ZEME, ZEMI**
Taj Mahal site .... **AGRA**
take away by force ... **REAVE**
take away: law .... **ADEEM**
take back .... **RECANT**
take effect again ..... **REVEST**
take off .... **DOFF**
take one's ease .... **REST**
take on cargo ... **LADE, LOAD**
take out **DELE, ELIDE, EXPUNGE**
take part .... **SIDE**
take up again ...... **RESUME**
take up weapons .... **ARM**
tale .... **SAGA, YARN, STORY**
tale, medieval Fr. .... **LAI**

tale, Norse .... **SAGA**
"Tale of Two Cities" girl **LUCIE**
"Tales of a Wayside —" .. **INN**
talent .... **FLAIR**
talented .... **SMART**
talisman .... **CHARM**
talisman, Afr. .... **GRIGRI**
talk .... **GAB, GAS, CHAT, PRATE, PALAVER**
d talk: slang .... **YAK**
talk freely .... **DESCANT**
talk pompously **ORATE, HARANGUE**
talk, rambling ... **RIGMAROLE**
talk wildly ..... **RANT, RAVE**
Tallinn .... **REVAL**
tallow tree .... **CERA**
tally .... **SCORE**
Talmud commentary .. **GEMARA**
talon .... **CLAW, NAIL**
tamarack .... **LARCH**
tamarisk .... **ATLE**
tame, as hawks .... **MAN**
tan .... **BUFF, BEIGE**
tan skins .... **TAW**
tanager ..... **YENI, REDBIRD**
tanager, S. Am. **HABIA, LINDO**
tanbark .... **ROSS**
tangle ...... **SNARL, SLEAVE**
tangled mass ..... **MAT, SHAG**
tanning gum .... **KINO**
tanning, plant for ..... **ALDER**
tanning shrub **SUMAC, SUMACH**
tanning tree, India **AMLA, AMLI**
tantalize .... **TEASE**
Tantalus' daughter .... **NIOBE**
tantra .... **AGAMA**
tantrum .... **RAGE**
tap **PAT, COCK, SPIGOT, FAUCET**

Tapering

tapering dagger ..... ANLACE
tapering piece .... SHIM
tapestry ARRAS, TAPIS, DOSSER
tapestry center .... ARRAS
tapeworm .... TAENIA
tapeworm larva ..... MEASLE
tapioca-like food ..... SALEP
tapioca source
    CASAVA, CASSAVA
tapir, S. Amer. ...... DANTA
Tapuyan .... GE
tarboosh .... FEZ
target .... BUTT
Tariff Act writer ..... SMOOT
Tarkington character .... SAM
tarnish .... SPOT, SULLY
taro ... GABE, GABI, DASHEEN
taro paste .... POI
taro root ... EDO, EDDO, KALO
tarpaulin .... PAULIN
tarpon .... SABALO
tarradiddle .... FIB, LIE
tarry .... BIDE, WAIT,
    STAY, LINGER
tarsus .... ANKLE
tarsus, insect .... MANUS
tart .... ACID
tartar, crude .. ARGAL, ARGOL
Tartini's B-flat .... ZA
task .... DUTY, CHORE,
    STENT, STINT
task, punishing ...... PENSUM
taste ...... SIP, SUP, SAPOR,
    SNACK, PALATE
tasteful .... ELEGANT
tasty .... SAPID
Tatar .... HU
Tatar dynasty, China .... WEI
Tatar tribe, W. Siberia .. SHOR
tattle .... BLAB
tattler, idle .... GOSSIP
Tattler publisher ...... STEELE
tau cross .... ANKH
taunt ..... JEER, MOCK, TWIT
taut .... TENSE
taut, pull .... STRETCH
tavern .... INN
tax .. CESS, GELD, LEVY, SCOT,
    SESS, STENT, ASSESS, EX-
    CISE, IMPOST
tax, church .... TITHE
tea .... CHA, CHAA
tea, black
    PECO, BOHEA, PEKOE
tea bowl .... CHAWAN
tea box
    CADDY, CALIN, CANISTER
tea, China .... BOHEA
tea, Chin. green ...... HYSON

tea genus .... THEA
tea-growing region ... ASSAM
tea, kind of
    OOPAK, OOLONG, OOPACK
tea, Labrador .... LEDUM
tea, marsh .... LEDUM
tea, medicinal PTISAN, TISANE
tea, oriental .... CHA
tea, Paraguay .. MATE, YERBA
tea, rolled .. CHA, TCHA, TSIA
tea tree .... TI
teacake .... SCON, SCONE
teacher .... DOCENT, MENTOR
teacher, Hebrew ...... RABBI
teacher, Islam religious
    ALIM, MOLLA, MULLA
teacher, Jewish .... RAB, REB
teacher, Moslem
    ALIM, MOLLA, MULLA
teacher, Xenophon's .ISOCRATES
teacher's association: abbr. NEA
team of horses .... SPAN
team, 3-horse ..... RANDEM
teamster's command GEE, HAW
tear ...... RIP, REND, RENT
tear apart
    REND, TATTER, DIVULSE
tease .... TWIT, BOTHER
technical name: biol. ... ONYM
technique .... ART
tedious writer .... PROSER
teem .... RAIN, POUR
teeth, false ...... DENTURES
teeth, incrustation .. TARTAR
Telamon's son .... AJAX
telegraph inventor .... MORSE
telegraph key ...... TAPPER
telegraph signal ... DOT, DASH
telegraph, underwater .. CABLE
telegraphic speed unit .. BAUD
telephone exchange CENTRAL
telephone inventor ..... BELL
telephone wire .... LINE
telescope part .... LENS
television .... VIDEO
television broadcast TELECAST
television cable .... COAXIAL
television recording KINESCOPE
television tube
    MONOSCOPE, ICONSCOPE
tell IMPART, RELATE, NARRATE
tell in detail .... RECOUNT
Tell, site of legend ..... URI
telling blow ...... COUP, ONER
temper .... ANNEAL
temper, fit of .... PET
temperament: Ger. .... GEMUT
"Tempest" sprite ..... ARIEL
"Tempest" slave ... CALIBAN
temple .. FANE, RATH, RATHA
temple, Asian .... PAGODA

a
temple chamber, Gr. ... **NAOS**
temple, inner part ..... **CELLA**
temple: Siam. .... **VAT, WAT**
temple tower, India .. **SHIKARA**
tempo: music .... **TAKT**
temporary decline ..... **SLUMP**
temporary fashion .... **FAD**
temporary relief ... **REPRIEVE**
tempt .... **LURE, TOLE**
temptation .... **ALLURE**
ten .... **DECAD**
ten ares .... **DECARE**
Ten Commandments
    DECALOG, DECALOGUE
"Ten Days that Shook the
    World" author ..... **REED**
ten million ergs .... **JOULE**
tenant .... **LESSEE**
tenant, early Ir. .... **SAER**
tend .... **SERVE**
tender .... **SOFT, OFFER**
tending toward .... **FOR**
tendril: bot. .... **CAPREOL**
tennis score .... **LOVE, DEUCE**
tennis shoe .... **SNEAKER**
tennis stroke **ACE, LOB, LOBB**
tennis term .... **LET**
Tennyson character .... **ENID,**
b   **ARDEN**
Tennyson heroine
    ELAIN, ELAINE
Tennyson sailor ...... **ENOCH**
tenon .... **COG**
tenonlike piece .. **COAG, COAK**
tenor, famous ..... **MELCHIOR**
tense .... **TAUT**
tent dweller
    KEDAR, SCENITE
tent dwelling Arabs ... **KEDAR**
tent flap .... **FLY**
tentmaker, the .... **OMAR**
tents .... **CAMP**
tentacle .... **FEELER**
tenth part .... **DECI, TITHE**
tepid .... **WARM**
Tereus' son .... **ITYS**
term .... **NAME**
term .... **SESSION**
term: algebra .... **NOME**
TERM, GEOMETRY .... see
    GEOMETRY, GEOMETRIC
term in office .... **TENURE**
term, math. .... **SINE, COSINE**
term of address .... **SIR, SIRE,**
                MADAM
termagant .... **SHREW**
terminable .... **ENDABLE**
termite, P. I. ..... **ANAI, ANAY**
tern .... **SKIRK**

c
tern, black .... **DARR**
tern genus .... **STERNA**
tern, Hawaii .... **NOIO**
terpene alcohol ...... **NEROL**
terpene compound . **TEREBENE**
terrapin .... **EMYD,**
    POTTER, SLIDER
terrapin, red-bellied
    POTTER, SLIDER
terrestrial .... **GEAL**
terrible .... **DIRE**
terrier, kind of .. **SKYE, CAIRN**
terrier, Scottish breed of . **SKYE**
terrified .... **AFRAID**
territorial division .... **AMT**
territory .... **LAND, SOIL**
territory, additional
    LEBENSRAUM
territory, enclosed .. **ENCLAVE**
terror .... **PANIC**
terrorist .... **GOON**
tessellated .... **MOSAIC**
tessera .... **TILE**
test .... **ASSAY, TEMPT,**
    TRIAL, EXAMINE
test ground .... **BOSE**
testament .... **WILL**
testifier .... **DEPONENT**
testify ...... **DEPONE, DEPOSE**
d tetrachord, upper tone of . **NETE**
Teutonic, ancient ...... **GOTH**
Teutonic barbarian ..... **GOTH**
Teutonic deity .... **ER**
Teut. Fate ..... **NORN, URTH**
TEUTONIC GODS, GODDESSES,
  DEITY see **NORSE SPECIAL**
  SECTION
Teut. legendary hero ... **OFFA**
Teut. letter of alphabet . **RUNE**
Teut. people .... **GEPIDAE**
Teut. sea goddess .... **RAN**
Teut. sky god .. **TY, TIU, TIW,**
    TYR, ZIO, ZIU, TYRR
Texas shrine .... **ALAMO**
textile screw pine
    ARA, PANDAN
texture .... **WALE,**
    WOOF, GRAIN
Thailand .... **SIAM**
Thames estuary .... **NORE**
than: Ger. .... **ALS**
than: Scot. .... **NA**
thankless person .... **INGRATE**
that is: abbr. .... **E.G., I.E.**
that not .... **LEST**
that one: Lat. .... **ILLE**

That

a
that which follows .... **SEQUEL**
thatch, grass to .... **NETI**
thatching palm .... **NIPA**
the: Ger. .... **DAS, DER**
"The Ballad of Reading —"
                                 GAOL
"The Jairite" .... **IRA**
"The Lion of God" .... **ALI**
"The Red" .... **ERIC**
the same: Lat. .... **IDEM**
the squint .... **SKEN**
theatre .... **ODEA, ODEON,**
                    ODEUM, STAGE
theatre box seat .... **LOGE**
theatre district ...... **RIALTO**
theatre floor .... **PIT**
theatre, Grecian ...... **ODEA,**
                 ODEON, ODEUM
theatre group .... **ANTA**
theatre, part of Greek . **SKENE,**
     SCENA, SCENAE, SKENAI
theatre sign .... **SRO**
"Theban Bard" .... **PINDAR**
Thebes deity ... **AMEN, AMON,**
  AMUN, MENT, AMENT, MENTU
Thebes, king of
            CREON, OEDIPUS
theme .... **MOTIF**
theme: music .... **TEMA**
then .... **ANON**

b
then: music .... **POI**
theoretical .... **PLATONIC**
there: Fr. .... **VOILA**
therefore .... **ERGO**
theseli veil .... **TEMPE**
Theseus' father ..... **AEGEUS**
thesis, opp. of .... **ARSIS**
thespian .... **ACTOR**
Thessaly, king of .... **AEOLUS**
Thessaly mountain ...... **OSSA**
Thessaly valley .... **TEMPE**
they: Fr. .... **ILS**
thick-lipped .... **LABROSE**
thicket .. **BOSK, SHAW, COPSE,**
        COPPICE, SPINNEY
thicket: dialect .... **RONE**
thicket, game .... **COVERT**
thickness .... **PLY**
thief, gypsy .... **CHOR**
thief: Yiddish .... **GANEF,**
         GANOF, GONOF
thigh bone .... **FEMUR**
thigh, of the .... **FEMORAL**
thin ...... **LANK, LEAN, RARE,**
    SHEER, DILUTE, PAPERY,
        SPARSE, TENUOUS
thin cake .... **WAFER**
thin: comb. form .... **SERO**
thin disk .... **WAFER**
thin layer .... **FILM**

c
"Thin Man" dog ...... **ASTA**
"Thin Man" wife .... **NORA**
thin-toned .... **REEDY**
thin out .... **ATTENUATE**
thing: law (Latin) .... **RES**
things added ...... **ADDENDA**
things done .... **ACTA**
things to be done
        AGENDA, AGENDUM
think ... **DEEM, TROW, OPINE**
think: archaic .... **WIS**
think (over) .... **MULL, MUSE**
third: comb. form .... **TRIT**
third day, every .... **TERTIAN**
third king of Judah ...... **ASA**
third: music .... **TIERCE**
Third Reich special police: abbr.
                       SS
thirst-tortured king: Gr. myth
             TANTALUS
thirsty .... **DRY, ADRY**
thirty: Fr. .... **TRENTE**
thirty, series of .... **TRENTAL**
this: Fr. .... **CE**
this: Sp. .... **ESTA, ESTE**
this one: Lat. ..... **HIC, HAEC**
thither .... **THERE**
Thomas Hardy heroine ... **TESS**
thong .... **STRAP**
thong, braided .... **ROMAL**
thong-shaped .... **LORATE**

d
thong, S. Afr. .... **RIEM**
Thor's stepson ..... **ULL, ULLR**
Thor's wife .... **SIF**
thorax, crustacean's . **PEREION**
thorn ... **BRIAR, BRIER, SPINE**
thorn apple .... **METEL**
thorn, bearing a ..... **SPINATE**
thornback ray .. **DORN, ROKER**
Thorne Smith character. **TOPPER**
thorny plant ... **BRIAR, BRIER**
thorny shrub .... **NABK, NUBK**
thoroughfare .... **WAY, ROAD,**
        AVENUE, STREET
thoroughgoing ...... **ARRANT**
those .... **YON, YOND**
those in power or office ... **INS**
thou: Fr. .... **TU**
thought .... **IDEA**
thought: comb. form .... **IDEO**
thoughts, form .... **IDEATE**
thousand .... **MIL**
thousand: comb. form . **MILLE**
Thrace, ancient people of **EDONI**
thrall .... **ESNE, SLAVE**
thrash .... **LAM, BEAT**
thread: comb. form .... **NEMA**
thread, cotton .... **LISLE**
thread, guiding ball of .. **CLEW**
thread-like .... **NEMALINE**
thread-like process ..... **HAIR**

a thread-like structure ... **FILUM**
thread, of a .... **FILAR**
threads, cross .... **RETICLE**
threads crossed by woof . **WARP**
threads crossing warp
              WEFT, WOOF
threads, lengthwise .... **WARP**
threaded fastener .... **NUT**
threaten ... **IMPEND, MENACE**
three ...... **TER, TRIO, TRIAD**
three: Ger. .... **DREI**
three: Ital. .... **TRE**
three-legged stand
           TRIPOD, TRIVET
three-masted ship
           XEBEC, FRIGATE
3 parts, divided into: Her.
             TIERCE
3.1416 .... **PI**
three: Sp. .... **TRES**
three-spot .... **TREY**
threefold .... **TRINE, TREBLE,**
         TERNARY, TERNATE
threefold: comb. form .... **TER**
threshold .... **SILL**
threshold, psychology ... **LIMEN**
thrice: music .... **TER**
thrifty ..... **FRUGAL, SAVING**
thrive ..... **BATTEN, PROSPER**
b throat .... **GORGE, GULLET**
throat: Lat. .... **GULA**
throat, pert. to .... **GULAR**
throb .. **BEAT, PULSE, PULSATE**
throe .... **PANG**
throng .. **MOB, HORDE, SWARM**
through .... **PER**
through: prefix .... **DIA**
throw .... **CAST, PITCH**
throw aside .... **FLING**
throw back .... **REPEL**
thrush ...... **VEERY, MISSEL**
thrush, Hawaiian ..... **OMAO**
thrush, India .... **SHAMA**
thrush, missel . **MAVIE, MAVIS**
thrust .... **LUNGE**
thrust back .... **REPEL**
thrust down .... **DETRUDE**
thunderfish .... **RAAD**
thurible .... **CENSER**
Thuringian city .... **JENA**
Thursday, source of name. **THOR**
thus .... **SO, SIC**
thus far .... **YET**
thwart .... **FOIL**
Tiber tributary .... **NERA**
Tibetan chief .... **POMBO**
Tibetan ox .... **YAK**
Tibetan priest .... **LAMA**
Tibetan tribe .... **CHAMPA**

c tibia .... **CNEMIS**
Tichborne Claimant ... **ORTON**
tick .... **ACARID**
tick genus .... **ARGAS**
tick, S. Amer. ..... **CARAPATO**
tickets, sell illegally ... **SCALP**
tickle .... **TITILLATE**
Ticonderoga's commander **GATES**
tidal flood ...... **BORE, EAGRE**
tidal wave, flow or bore.**EAGRE**
tidbit .... **CATE**
tide, lowest high .... **NEAP**
tidings .... **NEWS, WORD**
tidings, glad .... **GOSPEL,**
     EVANGEL, EVANGILE
tidy ...... **NEAT, REDO, TRIM**
tie ...... **BIND, BOND, LASH,**
       TRUSS, CRAVAT
tie, kind of .... **ASCOT**
tie-breaking game ... **RUBBER**
tie off .... **LIGATE**
tie, railroad .... **SLEEPER**
tier .... **ROW**
tiger cat, S. Amer. .... **CHATI**
tiger, Persian ..... **SHER, SHIR**
tight ... **SNUG, TAUT, TENSE**
tight place .. **FIX, JAM, MESS**
tighten: naut. .... **FRAP**
tightly stretched .... **TENSE**
til .... **SESAME**
d tile, hexagonal .... **FAVI**
tile, roofing .... **PANTILE**
tilelike .... **TEGULAR**
till the earth .... **FARM, PLOW**
tilled land ... **ARADA, ARADO**
tiller .... **HELM**
tilt .... **TIP, CANT, LIST**
tilt .... **JOUST**
tilting: naut. .... **ALIST**
timber bend .... **SNY**
timber, flooring ...... **BATTEN**
timber, nautical .... **KEVEL**
timber, pine: Asia .... **MATSU**
timber rot .... **DOAT, DOTE**
timber truck .... **WYNN**
timber wolf .... **LOBO**
timbrel ..... **TABOR, TABOUR**
time ..... **ERA, TEMPI, TEMPO**
time before .... **EVE**
time being .... **NONCE**
time gone by .... **PAST**
time out .... **RECESS**
time, space of .... **WHILE**
time value, equalling in
            DIMORIC
times, old .... **ELD, YORE**
timetable .... **SCHEDULE**
timid .... **SHY, PAVID**
timorous .... **TREPID**
timothy .... **HAY**
Timothy's mother: Bib. ... **LOIS**

a
tin .... CAN, STANNUM
tin, containing .... STANNOUS
tin foil .... TAIN
tin plate .... TAIN
tin roofing .... TERNE
tinamou .... YUTU
tincture: Her. .... OR, GULES,
   VERT, AZURE, SABLE,
   ARGENT, PURPURE
tinder .... PUNK, AMADOU
tine .... PRONG
tine of antler .... SNAG
tinge .... TAINT
tinge deeply .... IMBUE
tingle of feeling ...... THRILL
tinkle .... TING
tiny bird, W. Ind. ...... TODY
tip .... END, FEE, APEX, KNAP
tip .... CANT, LEAN,
   TILT, CAREEN
tipping .... ALIST, ATILT
tiptoe, on .... ATIP
tire .... FAG, JADE
tire casing .... SHOE
tire, face of .... TREAD
tire support .... RIM
tissue .... TELA
tissue, of a .... TELAR
tissue, pert. to .... TELAR

b
TITAN . see SPECIAL SECTION,
   GREEK MYTH page 200
Titania's husband .... OBERON
titanic iron-ore sand . ISERENE
titlark .... PIPIT
title ..... EARL, NAME, TERM
title, baronet's .... SIR
title, Benedictine .... DOM
title, church .... PRIMATE
title, East .... COJA, HOJA
title, Ethiopian .... RAS
title Hindu gives Moslem
          MIAN
title, India .... AYA, NAWAB,
   SAHEB, SAHIB
title, Jewish . RAB, REB, RABBI
title, knight's .... SIR
title, king's .... SIRE
title, lady's ... DAME, MADAM
title, Moslem ...... AGA, ALI,
   MOLLA, MULLA,
   SHERIF, SHEREFF
title of address .. MME., MRS.,
   SIR, MAAM, MADAM
title of honor, Moslem . SAYID,
   SAIYID, SAYYID
title of kings of Edessa . ABGAR
title of respect ..... SIR, SIRE,
   MADAME
title of respect, Afr. ..... SIDI

c
title of respect, India .... SRI,
   SHRI, SAHIB, SHREE,
   HUZOOR
title of respect, Malay .. TUAN
title, Oriental .... BABA
title, Persian MIR, AZAM, KHAN
title, Spanish DOM, DON, SENOR
title to property or land . DEED
title, Turkish .. PACHA, PASHA
titleholder .... TITLIST
titmice, genus of ...... PARUS
titmouse .... MAG, PARUS
tittle .... JOT, IOTA, WHIT
Titus Andronicus' daughter
          LAVINIA
Tiwaz .... ER, TIU
to .... FOR, UNTO
to: prefix .... AP
to: Scot. .... TAE
to be: Fr. .... ETRE
to be: Lat. .... ESSE
"to be," part of ...... AM, IS,
   ARE, WAS
to go: Fr. .... ALLER
to love: Fr. .... AIMER
to the point that ...... UNTIL
to use: Lat. .... UTOR
toad genus .... BUFO
toad, huge .... AGUA
toad, order of .... ANURA

d
toad, tree genus .... HYLA
toadfish .... SAPO
toast, bit of .... SIPPET
toasting word .... SALUD,
   SKOAL, PROSIT
tobacco ash . DOTTEL, DOTTLE
tobacco, chewing .... QUID
tobacco, coarse
      SHAG, CAPORAL
tobacco, Cuban .... CAPA
tobacco, low grade ...... SHAG
tobacco, Peru .... SANA
tobacco, roll .... CIGAR
toddy palm juice ...... SURA
toe .... DIGIT
toe, fifth .... MINIMUS
toe: Scot. .... TAE
togs .... DUDS
toilet case .... ETUI
Tokyo Bay city .... CHIBI
Tokyo, old name ... EDO, YEDO
tolerable .... SOSO
toll .... FEE, KNELL
Tolstoi heroine .... ANNA
tomb, Moslem TABUT, TABOOT
tomboy .... HOIDEN, HOYDEN
tomcat .... GIB
tone down .... SOFTEN
tone, lack of .... ATONY
tone, of .... TONAL
tone quality .... TIMBRE

a tone: Scot. .... TEAN
tones, series of ...... OCTAVE
tongue, gypsy .... CHIB
tongue of Agni .... KALI
tongue, pert. to ..... GLOSSAL
tongue, using the ..... APICAL
tongue, wagon .... NEAP
tonic .... ROBORANT
tonic, dried India
      CHIRATA, CHIRETTA
tonic herb ...... ALOE, TANSY
Tonkin native .... THO
too early .... PREMATURE
too much: Fr. .... TROP
tool, boring .... AWL, BIT,
          AUGER, GIMLET
tool, cutting .. AX, ADZ, AXE,
    HOB, SAW, SAX, SYE, ADZE
tool, engraver's
        BURIN, MATTOIR
tool, enlarging ...... REAMER
tool, grass-cutting .... SITHE,
          SCYTHE, SICKLE
tool, machine .... LATHE
tool, molding .... DIE
tool, pointed .... BROACH
tool, post hole digging .... LOY
tool shaper .... SWAGER
tool, splitting .... FROE, FROW
b tool, stone, prehistoric
        CELT, EOLITH
tool, threading ...... CHASER
tool's biting edge .... BIT
tooth ..... COG, TINE, MOLAR,
      CANINE, CUSPID, FANG
tooth-billed pigeon ... DODLET
tooth, canine .... CUSPID
tooth: comb. form .... ODONT
tooth, gear .... COG
tooth: Lat. .... DENS
tooth-like ornament .. DENTIL
tooth, long FANG, TUSH, TUSK
tooth pulp .... NERVE
toothed formation ..... SERRA
toothed margin, having
        DENTATE
toothed wheel .... GEAR
toothless .... EDENTATE
toothless mammals . EDENTATA
top .... APEX, CAP, LID
top-notch .... AONE
top ornament ..... EPI, FINIAL
topaz humming bird ..... AVA
topee material .... SOLA
toper .... SOT, SOUSE
topic .... THEME
topmast crossbar support .. FID
topsail .... RAFFE
torment ...... BAIT, ANNOY,
      DEVIL, HARRY, TEASE
torn: archaic .... REFT

c torn place .... RENT
torrid region or zone .. TROPIC
tortoise .... GALAPAGO
tortoise, fresh water .... EMYD
tortoise, marsh genus ... EMYS
tortoise, order of ... CHELONIA
torturer .... RACKER
"Tosca" villain ...... SCARPIA
toss ...... CAST, FLIP, HURL,
          FLING, PITCH
tosspot ... . SOT
total ...... ADD, SUM, UTTER
total abstinence .. NEPHALISM
totalitarian ruler ... DICTATOR
totem pole .... XAT
toucan .... TOCO
toucan, S. Am. .... ARACARI
touch .... ABUT
touch lightly .... PAT
touch, organ of .... PALP
touch, pert. to HAPTIC, TACTIC,
      TACTILE, TACTUAL
touch sense, pert. to .. HAPTIC
touchwood .... PUNK
tough .... WIRY, HARDY,
          ROWDY, CHEWY
tour: It. .... GIRO
tourmaline, colorless
        ACHROITE
d tow .... PULL, DRAW
towai .... KAMAHI
toward: Lat. .... AD
toward stern ..... AFT, ABAFF,
      ABAFT, ASTERN
towel .... WIPER
towel fabric .... HUCK, TERRY
tower, Bibl. .... BABEL
tower, India .... MINAR
tower, little .... TURRET
tower, mosque, slender
        MINARET
towering .... STEEP
towhead .... BLOND, BLONDE
town, Arcadia ancient ... ALEA
town: Cornish prefix ..... TRE
town: Dutch .... STAD
town: Ger. .... STADT
town, India pilgrimage . SORON
town: It. .... CASAL, CASALE
town: Jap. .... MACHI
town: suffix .... TON
township, ancient Attica . DEME
townsman .... CIT
toxic protein .... ABRIN
toy with .... TRIFLE
trace .... TINGE, VESTIGE
track .... TRACE
track, animal ... RUN, SLOT,
          SPUR, SPOOR
track circuit .... LAP

Track

a
track of ship .... **WAKE**
track, deer's .... **SLOT**
track, otter's .... **SPUR, SPOOR**
track, put off .... **DERAIL**
track, put on another
SHUNT, SWITCH
tracker, India .... **PUGGI**
tract .... **LOT, AREA**
tract of farm land ...... **FIELD**
trade .... **SWAP, SWOP**
BARTER, TRAFFIC
trade .... **METIER**
trade agreement ..... **CARTEL**
trader ..... **DEALER, MONGER**
trader selling to soldiers
SUTLER
trading exchange .... **PIT**
trading vessel of Ceylon
DONI, DHONI
traditional story .... **SAGA**
traduce .... **SLUR, DEFAME**
traffic .... **TRADE**
trail .... **SLOT, SPOOR, TRACK**
train of attendants
SUITE, RETINUE
train, overhead .... **EL**
train, slow, many-stops . **LOCAL**
tramp .... **BO, HOBO**
trample .... **TREAD**
tranquil or tranquilize
SERENE, SOOTHE

b
transaction ...... **DEAL, SALE**
transfer .... **CEDE**
transfer, property
DEED, GRANT
transfer, sovereignty .. **DEMISE**
transferer, property .. **ALIENOR**
transform .... **CONVERT**
transgress .... **ERR, SIN**
transit coach .... **BUS**
"— transit gloria mundi" . **SIC**
translator of Freud, Amer.
BRILL
transmit .... **SEND**
transom .... **TRAVE**
transpire .... **OCCUR, HAPPEN,**
DEVELOP
transverse pin .... **TOGGLE**
trap .... **SNARE, ENSNARE**
trap door .... **DROP**
trap, mouse: dial. .... **TIPE**
trap, rabbit: dial. ...... **TIPE**
trappings .... **REGALIA**
travel .... **TREK**
traveler .... **PASSENGER**
tray .... **SALVER, SERVER**
tread softly ..... **PAD, SNEAK**
treasure .... **ROON, TROVE**
treasurer, college ..... **BURSAR**
treasury agents .... **TMEN**
treat .... **USE**

c
treat with acid ..... **ACIDIZE**
treat with malice .... **SPITE**
treatment .... **USE**
tree   (3 letters) **ASH, ELM,**
FIR,   LIN,   OAK,   YEW;
(4 letters) **AKEE, AMLA,**
AMLI,   ANAM,   ANDA,
ARAR, ASAK, AULU, AUSU,
AUZU, BARU, BIJA, BITO,
BIWA, BOBO, BOGO, DALI,
DILO, DOON, DOUM, DUKU,
EBOE, EJOO, GOAI, GUAO,
HINO, IFIL, IPIL, KINO,
KIRI, KOPI, KOZO, LIME,
LINN,   MAKO,   MYXA,
NAIO, NEEM, NIOG, NIPA,
ODUM, OHIA, PALM, PELU,
PINE, PUKA, RATA, RIMU,
ROKA, SAUL, SHEA, SUPA,
TALA, TARA, TAWA, TEAK,
TEIL, TEYL, TOON, TORO,
TUNG, TUNO, TUWI, UPAS,
WHAU, YATE, YAYA, YPIL;
(5 letters) **ASPEN**; (6 let-
ters) **LINDEN**

tree, African .... **AKEE, BAKU,**
COLA, KOLA, ROKA,
SHEA, AEGLE, ARTAR

d
tree, Afr. & Asia .... **SIRIS**
tree, Afr. gum .... **BUMBO**
tree, Afr. tallow .... **ROKA**
TREE, AMER. TROPICAL...see
TREE, TROPICAL AMER.
tree, Argentine timber ... **TALA**
TREE, ASIATIC .. see ASIATIC
TREE
tree, arrow poison ...... **UPAS**
TREE, AUSTRAL. .... see
AUSTRAL. TREE
tree, Bengal quince ...... **BEL**
tree, black gum ...... **TUPELO**
tree, body of .... **TRUNK**
tree, boxwood yielding . **SERON**
tree, buckwheat .... **TITI**
tree, butter .... **SHEA**
tree, caucho-yielding ..... **ULE**
tree, chicle .... **SAPOTA**
tree, Chin. ... **GINKO, GINKGO**
tree clump, prairie .... **MOTTE**
tree cobra .... **MAMBA**
tree, coniferous (cone) .. **FIR,**
YEW, PINE, LARCH
TREE. E. IND. ... see E. IND.
TREE and TREE, IND.
TREE, EVERGREEN .... see
EVERGREEN
tree, flowering ..... **CATALPA**
tree genus .... **MABA**
tree genus, Afr. .... **OCHNA**

168

a tree genus, elms
　　　　ULMUS, CELTIS
tree genus, small ... CATALPA
tree, gum .... ICICA
tree, hardwood ASH, OAK, IPIL
tree, India .... DAR, MEE, SAJ,
　　SAL, AMLA, AMLI, DHAK,
　　MYXA, NEEM, SHOQ, MA-
　　HUA, BANYAN
tree knot .... BURL
tree, locust .... ACACIA
tree, maidenhair ..... GINKGO
tree, Malay .... TERAP
tree, Medit. .... CAROB
tree, mimosaceous ...... SIRIS
tree moss .... USNEA
tree, N. Am.
　　TAMARAC, TAMARACK
TREE, N. Z.
　　see NEW ZEALAND TREE
tree, oak .... ENCINA
tree of olive family ..... ASH
tree, Pacific .... KOU
tree, palm .. GRIGRI, GRUGRU
tree, palm, Asiatic .... ARENG
TREE, P.I. ..... see P. I. TREE
tree, pod .... CAROB
tree, resinous ...... FIR, PINE,
　　　　BALSAM
b tree, showy Asia .... ASAK
tree-snake .... LORA
tree, sun, Jap. .... HINOKI
tree, swamp .... ALDER
tree, tamarisk salt ...... ATLE
tree, tea .... TI
tree, thorny .... ACACIA
tree tiger .... LEOPARD
tree toad genus .... HYLA
tree, tropical .... EBOE, PALM,
　　BALSA, MANGO, COLIMA,
　　SAPOTA, LEBBEK
tree, tropical Amer. CEBA, DALI,
　　GUAO, CEIBA, COLIMA,
　　GUAMA, CEDRON
tree trunk .... BOLE
tree, W. Ind. .... GENIP,
　　　　SAPOTE, LIBIDIBI
trees of a region .... SILVA
treeless plain .... PAMPAS,
　　　　TUNDRA, STEPPES
tremble ...... QUAKE, DIDDER
trembling .... ASPEN, TREPID
trench .... SAP
trench extension .... SAP
trench, rear wall of .. PARADOS
trend .... TENOR
trespass .. INFRINGE, INTRUDE

c trespass for game .... POACH
trespass to recover goods
　　　　TROVER
triad .... TRIO
trial .... TEST
triangle .... TRIGON, SCALENE
triangle, side of .... LEG
triangular insert .... GORE
tribal symbol .... TOTEM
TRIBE
　　see also SPECIAL SECTION
tribe ...... CLAN, FOLK, RACE
TRIBE, BIBLICAL .... see
　　　　SPECIAL SECTION
tribe: Bib. tent-dwellers. KEDAR
tribe division, Rom.
　　　　CURIA, CURIAE
TRIBE, ISRAELITE .... see
　　　　ISRAELITE TRIBE
TRIBESMAN .. see TRIBES in
　　SPECIAL SECTION
tribulation .... TRIAL
tribunal .... BAR, FORUM
tribute .... SCAT, SCATT
tribute: Gaelic .... CAIN
trick FLAM, GAWD, JEST, RUSE,
　　WILE, DODGE, FICELLE,
　　STRATAGEM
tricks, game for no .... NULLO
tricks, win all .... CAPOT
d Trieste measure .. ORNA, ORNE
trifle ...... TOY, DOIT, FICO,
　　STRAW, NIGGLE, PALTER
trifling ...... SMALL, SLIGHT
trig .... NEAT, TRIM
trigonometry function
　　　　SINE, COSINE
trigonometry line ..... SECANT
trill, bird's .... TIRALEE
trim .... NEAT, TRIG,
　　　　ADORN, DECORATE
trimmed .... SNOD
trimming, dress . GIMP, RUCHE
trimmings, overlapping . FLOTS
Trinidad tree .... CYP
trinket .... GAUD
triple .... TRI, TREBLE
triplet .... TRIN
tripletail, P. R. .... SAMA
tripod, 6-footed .... CAT
Tripoli: measure . see page 188
"Tristram Shandy" author
　　　　STERNE
Tristram's beloved .... ISOLT,
　　YSEUT, ISAUDE, ISAULT,
　　ISEULT, ISOLDE, ISOLTA,
　　ISOUDE, ISULTE
trite .. BANAL, CORNY, STALE
triton ...... EFT, EVET, NEWT

Troche

a troche ...... **PASTIL, ROTULA,**
       PASTILE, PASTILLE
TROJAN .... see also **TROY**
Trojan hero .. **PARIS, ENEAS,**
    AENEAS, AGENOR, DARDAN,
    HECTOR, HEKTOR, ACHILLES
trolley .... **TRAM**
troop-carrying group: abbr.
          ATS
troop, division, Gr. .... **TAXIS**
troops .... **MEN**
troops, spread .... **DEPLOY**
trophy .... **CUP**
tropic .... **SOLAR**
tropical Am. bird genus
       CACICUS
tropical disease . **BUBA, BUBAS**
tropical fever .... **DENGUE**
TROPICAL FRUIT .... see
     FRUIT, TROPICAL
tropical plant .... **TARO**
tropical shrub genus **INGA, SIDA**
trot .... **JOG, AMBLE**
trouble ... **ADO, AIL, WORRY,**
    EFFORT, MOLEST
troubles .... **ILLS**
troublesome person
    PEST, AGITATOR
trough, inclined ...... **CHUTE**
trough, mining .... **SLUICE**
b trout, British .. **SEWEN, SEWIN**
trout, brook .... **CHAR**
trowel, plasterers' .... **DARBY**
Troy .... **ILION, ILIUM**
Troy, founder of .... **ILUS**
Troy, land of .... **TROAS**
Troy, last king of ..... **PARIS,**
    PRIAM, PRIAMOS
Troy, of ancient **ILIAC, ILIAN**
Troy: poetic .... **ILIUM**
truant, play: Scot. .... **TRONE**
truck .... **LORRY, CAMION**
trudge .... **PACE, PLOD, SLOG**
true copy: law .... **ESTREAT**
true olives .... **OLEA**
trumpet ..... **HORN, CLARION**
trumpet call, reveille .... **DIAN**
trumpet, mouth of .... **CODON**
trumpet shell .... **TRITON**
trumpeter perch .... **MADO**
trumpeter, pigeon-like . **AGAMI**
trundle, as ore .... **RULL**
trunk of body .... **TORSO**
trunkfish .... **CHAPIN**
truss up .... **TIE**
trust .... **RELY, TROW,**
    RELIANCE
trustee of a wakf.**MUTAWALLI**
trusting .... **RELIANT**
truth: Chin. .... **TAO**

c truth drug ...... **PENTOTHAL**
Truth personified .... **UNA**
try .... **TEST, ESSAY, ATTEMPT**
try to equal ... **VIE, EMULATE**
tsetse fly .... **MAU, KIVU**
tsetse fly genus .... **GLOSSINA**
tub ...... **VAT, KNAP, KNOP**
tub, brewer's .... **KEEVE**
tub, broad .... **KEELER**
tub, wooden: dialect ...... **SOE**
tube .... **DUCT**
tube, glass ... **PIPET, PIPETTE**
tube, plane's .... **PITOT**
tuber delicacy ...... **TRUFFLE**
tuber, edible **OCA, OKA, YAM,**
    TARO, POTATO
tuber, orchid .... **SALEP**
tuber, S. Amer. .... **OCA, OKA**
Tuesday, god who gave name to
    TIU, TYR
tuft .... **CREST**
tuft: bot. .... **COMA**
tufted plant .... **MOSS**
tulip tree .... **POPLAR**
TUMERIC ..... see **TURMERIC**
tumor .... **OMA, WEN**
tumor, skin .... **WEN**
tumult .... **RIOT**
tune .... **AIR, ARIA,**
    SONG, MELODY
tune, bagpipe .... **PORT**
d tune: Scot. .... **PORT**
tungstite ..... **OCHER, OCHRE**
tuning fork ...... **DIAPASON**
Tunis, ruler of ...... **BEY, DEY**
tunnel, train, Alps .... **CENIS**
tunny .... **AMIA, TUNA**
turban, Oriental .... **MANDIL**
turbid, make .... **ROIL**
turf .... **SOD**
turf, bit of: golf ...... **DIVOT**
Turkestan town dwellers . **SART**
turkey buzzard .... **AURA**
turkey, red .... **MADDER**
turkeys, collection of .. **RAFTER**
Turkic person **TATAR, TARTAR**
Turkic person, 8th century
    OGOR
Turkish army corps ..... **ORDU**
Turkish army officer ..... **AGA**
Turkish caliph .... **ALI**
Turkish chamber .. **ODA, ODAH**
Turkish chieftain ...... **AMIR,**
    ZAIM, AMEER
Turkish commander . **AGA, ALI**
Turkish copper coin .... **PARA**
Turkish decree .... **IRADE**
Turkish flag .... **ALEM**
Turkish general .... **AGA**
Turkish gold coin ...... **LIRA,**
    ALTUN, MAHBUB

a Turkish government .... **PORTE**
Turkish govt. summer residence
YALI
Turkish governor .. **VALI, WALI**
Turkish hostelry ..... **IMARET**
Turkish judge .... **CADI, KADI**
Turkish leader .... **AGA**
Turkish liquor .... **MASTIC**
Turkish magistrate.**CADI, KADI**
Turkish military district . **ORDO**
Turkish money of account
ASPER
Turkish officer .. **AGA, AGHA**
Turkish oxcart . **ARBA, ARABA**
Turkish palace .... **SERAI**
Turkish pavilion .... **KIOSK**
Turkish president, former
INONU
Turkish regiment .... **ALAI**
Turkish standard . **ALEM, TOUG**
Turkish sultan .... **SELIM**
Turkish title .... **AGA, AGHA,
BABA, EMIR, EMEER,
PASHA, BASHAW**
Turkish tribesman ..... **TATAR**
Turkish tribesman, Persia
GHUZ
Turkoman tribesman **SEID, SHIK**
turmeric .... **REA, ANGO**
b turmoil .... **WELTER**
turn ..... **BEND, GYRE, VEER,
ROTATE, SWERVE**
turn aside.**SKEW, VEER, SHUNT**
turn back to .... **REVERT**
turn direction .... **VERT**
turn inside out .... **EVERT**
turn over: mus. .... **VERTE**
turning point ... **CRISES, CRISIS**
turning: prefix .... **ROTO**
turnover .... **PIE**
turnip ... **BAGA, NEEP, SWEDE**
turnip: Scot. .... **NEEP**
turpentine derivative
ROSIN, PINENE
turpentine distillate .... **ROSIN**
turpentine resin
ALK, GALLIPOT, GALIPOT
turtle, Amazon .... **ARRAU**
turtle, edible
TERAPIN, TERRAPIN
turtle, edible part of . **CALIPEE**
turtle enclosure ...... **CRAWL**
turtle genus .... **EMYS**
turtle, hawkbill .... **CARET**
turtle, order of .... **CHELONIA**
Tuscany art city .... **SIENA**
tusk, elephant .... **IVORY**
tutelary god ..... **LAR, LARES**
tutor .... **TUTE**

c TV advertiser ...... **SPONSOR**
"Twelfth Night" clown .. **FESTE**
"Twelfth Night" heroine
VIOLA
twelve and one-half cents . **BIT**
twenty-fourth part
CARAT, KARAT
twenty quires .... **REAM**
twice .... **BIS**
twice: prefix .... **BI**
twig, willow .. **WITHE, WITHY**
twilight .... **EVE, DUSK,
GLOAM, EVENTIDE**
twilled coth .... **REP**
twilled wool fabric ..... **SERGE**
twin .... **GEMEL**
twin crystal .... **MACLE**
twin gods, Teut. .... **ALCIS**
twine .... **COIL, WIND, TWIST**
twining stem .... **BINE**
twist ..... **PLY, COIL, FEAK,
KINK, SKEW, GNARL,
WREATHE, CONTORT**
twist inwards .... **INTORT**
twist out of shape ..... **WARP**
twisted .... **AWRY, SKEW,
TORTILE**
twisted roll of fibers .... **SLUB**
twisted spirally .... **TORSE**
twitch .... **TIC**
d twitching .... **TIC**
two .... **DUO, DUAD, PAIR**
two ears, affecting the **DIOTIC**
two elements, having . **BINARY**
two feet, verse of .... **DIPODY**
two-footed ... **BIPED, BIPEDAL**
two-horse chariot ..... **BIGA**
two-hulled boat . **CATAMARAN**
two-masted ship . **YAWL, ZULU**
two-month period .. **BIMESTER**
two, music for .... **DUET**
two notes, group of .... **DUOLE**
two-pronged, as sponges
DICELLATE
two-pronged weapon .. **BIDENT**
two-spot .... **DEUCE**
two tenacles, having.**DICEROUS**
two-toed sloth .... **UNAU**
two-wheeled vehicle **GIG, CART**
two-year-old sheep
TEG, TEGG, BIDENT
"Two Years Before the Mast"
author .... **DANA**
twofold .. **DUAL, TWIN, BINAL**
twofold: prefix .... **DI**
tycoon .... **NABOB**
tymp arch of furnace ... **FAULD**
Tyndareus, wife of ..... **LEDA**
type collection .... **FONT**

Type

type, conforming to . **TYPICAL**
type face .... **RUNIC, CASLON**
type, 5½ point .... **AGATE**
type, jumbled .... **PI, PIE**
type, kind of .... **ELITE**
type measure .... **EM, EN**
type metal piece ...... **QUAD**
type, mixed .... **PI, PIE**
type of script .... **RONDE**
type part .... **KERN**
type set .... **FONT**

type size ..... **PICA, AGATE,**
BREVIER
type, slanting .... **ITALIC**
type square .... **EM**
type tray .... **GALLEY**
typewriter roller ..... **PLATEN**
Tyr, Norse war god .... **ER**
tyrant .... **DESPOT**
tyrant of Rome .... **NERO**
Tyre, king of .... **HIRAM**
Tyre, princess of .... **DIDO**
tyro .... **NOVICE**

U

Uganda native .... **KOPI**
ukase .... **EDICT**
Ukraine legislature ..... **RADA**
"Ulalume" author .... **POE**
ulexite .... **TIZA**
ultra-conservative ...... **TORY**
ULYSSES ... see also ODYSSEUS
Ulysses' swineherd ... **EUMAEUS**
Ulysses' voyages .... **ODYSSEY**
umbrella .... **GAMP**
umbrella finial, Burma .... **TEE**
umbrella, India ...... **CHATTA**
umbrella part .... **RIB**
umpire .... **REFEREE**
unaccented vowel sound **SCHWA**
unadulterated .... **PURE**
unaffected .. **SIMPLE, ARTLESS**
Unalaskan .... **ALEUT**
unaspirate .... **LENE**
unassuming
MODEST, NATURAL
unbeliever .... **HERETIC**
unbleached ..... **ECRU, BEIGE**
unburnt brick .. **DOBE, ADOBE**
Uncas' beloved .... **CORA**
uncanny ...... **EERY, EERIE,**
WEIRD
unceasing **ETERNAL, PERPETUAL**
uncinate .... **HAMATE**
uncivil .... **RUDE**
uncle, dial. .... **EME**
uncle: Scot. .... **EME**
"Uncle Remus" author
HARRIS
"Uncle Remus" rabbit ... **BRER**
unclean: Jewish law .... **TREF**
unclose .... **OPE, OPEN**
uncommon .... **RARE, SPECIAL**
unconcerned .... **CALM, OPEN,**
SERENE
unconscious state ...... **COMA**
unconstrained .... **EASY**

uncouth person ... **CAD, BOOR,**
YAHOO, GALOOT
unction .... **BALM**
unctuous .... **OILY, SUAVE**
under .... **INFRA, NEATH,**
SOTTO, NETHER
under: Fr. .... **SOUS**
under: naut. .... **ALOW**
under: prefix .... **SUB**
under side, pert. to .. **VENTRAL**
undergo: obs. .... **DREE**
underground bud .... **BULB**
underground reservoir, natural
water .... **CENOTE**
underground stream, S. Afr.
AAR
underhand, throw .... **LOB**
undersong .... **TIERCE**
undershirts .... **SKIVVIES**
undersized animal ...... **RUNT**
understand .... **GRASP**
understanding ... **KEN, SENSE,**
ENTENTE
underwater box .... **CAISSON**
underworld .... **HADES, SHEOL**
underworld, Egypt.
DUAT, AMENTI
underworld god ... **DIS, PLUTO**
underworld god, Egypt. **OSIRIS,**
SERAPIS
underworld goddess ...... **HEL**
underwrite ... **ENSURE, INSURE**
undeveloped .... **LATENT**
undraped .... **NUDE**
undulant fever .. **BRUCELLOSIS**
undulating .... **WAVY**
undulation .... **WAVE**
unequal .... **UNIQUE**
unequal angled ..... **SCALENE**
unequal conditions ...... **ODDS**
uneven ...... **ODD, EROSE**
unevenly shaped .... **EROSE**

_a_ unfadable .... FAST
unfair move .... FOUL
unfair shove in marbles . FULK
unfasten ..... UNTIE, LOOSEN
unfavorable .... BAD, ILL
unfeeling ... HARSH, CALLOUS
unfermented grape juice
                     STUM
unfit to eat, make . DENATURE
unfledged bird .... EYAS
unfold .... EVOLVE
unguent, Roman wrestlers'
                 CEROMA
ungula .. CLAW, HOOF, NAIL
ungulate, S. Am. ...... TAPIR
unhappy .... SAD, BLUE,
       MOROSE, RUEFUL
unicorn fish ...... LIJA, UNIE
uniform .... EVEN
uniform in hue .. FLAT, FLOT
uninteresting .... DULL
union .... MERGER
union, labor ... AFL, CIO, ILA,
          ITA, ILGWU
union, political .... BLOC
union, Russ. workers' ... ARTEL
unique person .... ONER
unique thing: slang ..... ONER
unit .... ACE, ONE

_b_ unit of capacity ...... FARAD
unit of conductance ..... MHO
unit of electrical intensity:
    abbr. .... AMP
unit of electrical resistance or
    reluctance .... REL
unit of electricity . OHM, WATT,
       FARAD, WEBER
unit of electromotive force
                 VOLT
unit of energy .... ERG,
       RAD, ERGON
unit of fluidity .... RHE
unit of force .... DYNE
unit of heat .... CALORIE
unit of illumination ..... PHOT
unit of jet propulsion .... JATO
unit of light .... PYR, LUMEN,
       HEFNER
unit of power .... DYNE
unit of power, electric ... OHM,
    WATT, FARAD, WEBER
unit of pressure BARAD, BARIE
unit of reluctance .... REL
unit of resistance .... OHM
unit of weight .... WEY
unit of work ..... ERG, ERGON
unit, pert. to ...... MONADIC
unit, power ratio .... BEL

_c_ unite .... WED, ALLY, JOIN,
    KNIT, WELD, YOKE,
    MERGE, INTEGRATE
unite edges .... RABBET
UNITED STATES
         see AMERICAN
unity .... ONE
univalent element .... MONAD
universal .. WORLD, GENERAL
universal language ... RO, IDO
universe ... WORLD, COSMOS
universe: Hindu .... LOKA
universe, pert. to ..... COSMIC
university degree-holder
         LICENTIATE
University in Conn. ..... YALE
unkeeled .... RATITE
unkind ILL
unknown Hindu god ...... KA
unless .... BUT, SAVE
unless: Lat. .... NISI
unlock .... OPE, OPEN
unmarried .... CELIBATE
unmatched .... ODD
unmixed .... PURE, SHEER
unmusical clang ..... TONK
unnecessary .... NEEDLESS
unplowed strip .... HADE
unpredictable .... ERRATIC

_d_ unprincipled person .... CAD,
    SCAMP, BOUNDER,
    REPROBATE
unprofitable, as rents .... SECK
unrefined .... EARTHY
unrelenting . IRON, ADAMANT
unruffled ..... CALM, SERENE
unruly outbreak .... RIOT
unruly person .... RANTIPOLE
unsophisticated .... NAIVE
unsorted flour .... ATA, ATTA
unspoken .... TACIT
unstable ... ASTATIC, ERRATIC
unsuitable ..... INAPT, INEPT
untamed .... WILD, FERAL
untidy person .... SLOB
untidiness .... MESS, MUSS
until .... TILL
untrained .... RAW
unusual .... RARE, EXO[1]IC
unusual person or thing . ONER
unwavering .... SURE, STEADY
unwholesome ILL
unwieldly thing .... HULK
unwilling ..... LOTH, LOATH,
       AVERSE
unwilling, be: archaic ... NILL
unyielding .. FIRM, ADAMANT
unyielding: naut. .... FAST

Up

a

up: comb. form .... **ANO**
Upanishad .... **ISHA**
upland plain .... **WOLD**
upbraid ...... **CHIDE, SCOLD,
REPROACH**
upon ...... **EPI, ATOP, ONTO**
upon: law .... **SUR**
Upper Nile Negro ...... **MADI**
Upper Nile tribesman ... **MADI**
Upper Silurian .... **ONTARIAN**
uppermost part .... **TOP**
upright ...... **ERECT, HONEST**
upright column .... **STELE**
upright piece .... **JAMB, STUD**
uprising .... **REVOLT**
uproar .... **DIN**
upward, heave: naut. ... **SCEND**
uraeus .... **ASP**
Uranus' satellite .... **ARIEL**
urban office-holder ... **MAYOR**
urchin ..... **IMP, TAD, GAMIN**
Urfa, modern .... **EDESSA**
urge .... **EGG, PLY, YEN,
IMPEL, PRESS**
urge: Scot. .... **ERT**

c

urial .... **SHA**
urticaria .... **HIVES**
urus .... **TUR**
us: Ger. .... **UNS**
usage .... **WONT**
use a divining rod ..... **DOWSE**
use, be of .... **AVAIL**
use exertions .... **STRIVE**
use one's efforts .... **EXERT**
used up ...... **ATE, DEPLETED**
useful ..... **UTILE, PRACTICAL**
useless .... **IDLE, FUTILE,
OTIOSE, INUTILE**
usual .... **NORMAL**
Utah State flower ...... **SEGO**
utmost .... **LAST, FINAL,
GREATEST**
utmost hyperbole .... **ELA**
utter .... **SAY, SHEER,
SPEAK, STARK**
utter, as greeting .... **BID**
utter loudly ..... **VOCIFERATE**
uttered ... **ORAL, SAID, SPOKE**
utterly .... **STARK**
Uz, brother of .... **ARAN**

b

V-shaped piece ...... **WEDGE**
vacant .... **IDLE, EMPTY**
vacuum .... **VOID**
vacuum, opposite of .. **PLENUM**
vacuum tube .... **DIODE**
vagabond . **VAG, HOBO, TRAMP**
vague .... **HAZY, LOOSE**
vainglory .... **PRIDE**
valance, short .... **PELMET**
vale ..... **DALE, DELL, VALLEY**
Vali, mother of .... **RIND**
valiant ... **BRAVE, STALWART**
Valkyrie .... **DIS, NORN**
valley ..... **DALE, DELL, VAIL,
VALE, GLADE**
valley, deep .... **COULEE**
valley, Jordan .... **GHOR**
value .... **RATE, PRIZE,
WORTH, APPRAISE**
value, thing of little ... **TRIFLE**
valve .... **COCK**
vampire .... **LAMIA**
van .... **FORE**
vandal .... **HUN**
vanish .... **EVANESCE**
vanity .... **PRIDE**
vanity case .... **ETUI**
vantage, place of ...... **COIGN**
vapid .... **INANE, STALE**

d

vapor .... **STEAM**
vapor: comb. form ..... **ATMO**
vapor: dialect.......... **ROKE**
vapor in air ...... **HAZE, MIST**
Varangians .... **ROS**
variable .... **PROTEAN**
variable, most ...... **PROTEAN**
variable star .... **MIRA, NOVA**
variation, small
SHADE, NUANCE
variegated .... **SHOT**
variegated in color
PIED, CALICO
variety .... **KIND**
variety of bean
SOY, LIMA, PINTO
various: comb. form
VARI, VARIO
varnish ingredient
LAC, COPAL, RESIN
varnish, kind of
SHELLAC, SHELLACK
varnish material .... **ELEMI**
vase .... **URN**
vat ...... **BAC, TUB, CISTERN**
vat, beer ... **GAAL, GAIL, GYLE**
vat, brewer's ... **KIVE, KEEVE**
vat, large .... **KEIR, KIER**
vault .... **SAFE**

a vault, church .... **CRYPT**
vaulted alcove .... **APSE**
vaunt .... **BRAG, BOAST**
vector, that which turns a
.... **VERSOR**
Vedic dialect .... **PALI**
VEDIC GODS
see SPECIAL SECTION
veer ..... **SHY, TURN, SHIFT**
veer off .... **SHEER**
vegetable ... **PEA, BEAN, BEET,**
KALE, OCRA, OKRA, OKRO,
CHARD, ENDIVE, TOMATO,
WOBBIE, CELTUCE
vegetable fuel .... **PEAT**
vegetables, pod .... **PEASE**
vehicle .... **CAR, CART,**
CYCLE, HANSOM
vehicle, Am. Ind.
TRAVOIS, TRAVOISE
vehicle 4-wheeled .... **LANDAU**
vehicle, light, India ... **TONGA**
vehicle, Near East ..... **ARABA**
vehicle, Russ. .... **TROIKA**
vehicle, war .... **TANK**
veil, chalice .... **AER**
vein: Lat. .... **VENA**
b vein of body .... **CAVA**
vein, ore .... **LODE, SCRIN**
vein, ore: prov. Eng. .... **ROKE**
vein, ore beside .... **RIDER**
vein, throat .... **JUGULAR**
vellum .... **PARCHMENT**
velocity per second ..... **VELO**
velum .... **PALATE**
velvet .... **PANNE**
velvet grass .... **HOLCUS**
vend .... **SELL**
vendetta .... **FEUD**
venerable .... **OLD, HOARY**
"Venerable" monk ...... **BEDE**
venerate ..... **ESTEEM, REVERE**
veneration .... **AWE**
Venetian nobleman ..... **DOGE**
Venetian painter ..... **TITIAN**
Venetian red .... **SIENA**
Venetian resort .... **LIDO**
Venetian rose .... **SIENA**
Venetian traveler ...... **POLO**
Venezuela copper center **AROA**
Venezuela Ind. language **PUME**
vengeance goddess ...... **ARA**
Venice marble bridge ..**RIALTO**
Venice canals .... **RII**
Venice district .... **RIALTO**
ventral .... **HEMAD, HAEMAD**
venture .... **DARE**

c Venus, island of ..... **MELOS**
Venus' son .... **CUPID**
Venus, youth loved by **ADONIS**
veranda, Dutch, S. Afr. **STOEP**
veranda, Hawaii ...... **LANAI**
veranda, India .... **PYAL**
verb form .... **IS, AM, ARE,**
WAS, TENSE
verbal .... **ORAL**
verbal ending .. **ED, ER, ES, ING**
verbal noun .... **GERUND**
verbal rhythm .... **METRE**
verbally .... **ALOUD**
Verdi heroine .... **AIDA**
verily .... **YEA, AMEN**
verity .... **TRUTH**
versatile .... **MOBILE**
verse .... **LINE, STICH**
verse, Fr. .... **RONDEL**
verse, Ir. .... **RANN**
verse, pert. to kind of **IAMBIC**
version, Bible .... **ITALA**
vertebral bones **SACRA, SACRUM**
verticle line, in a ..... **APEAK**
verticle timber: naut. ... **BITT**
vertigo .... **DINUS**
very .... **SO**
very abundant ... **LUXURIANT**
very: Fr. .... **TRES**
very: Scot. .... **VERA**
d very: Span. .... **MUY**
Ve's brother .... **ODIN**
vesicle, skin .... **BLISTER**
VESSEL .. see also BOAT, SHIP,
GALLEY
vessel .... **ARK**
vessel, anat. ...... **VAS, VASA**
vessel, Arab .... **DOW, DHOW**
vessel, chemical .... **ETNA**
vessel, coasting, E. Ind.
PATAMAR
vessel, cooking .... **PAN, POT**
vessel, drinking ...... **GOURD**
vessel for liquors .. **DECANTER**
vessel, glass .... **BOCAL**
vessel, Gr. **CADUS, AMPHORA**
vessel, heating .... **ETNA**
vessel, large .... **TANK**
vessel, liquor .... **FLAGON**
vessel, Medit. .. **SETEE, MISTIC**
vessel, Rom. .... **PATERA**
vessel, sacred ...... **PIX, PYX**
vessel, sailing .... **SAIC,**
SETEE, XEBEC
vessel, shallow .... **BASIN**
vessel, supply .... **COALER**
vessel, 3-masted
XEBEC, FRIGATE
vessel, 2-masted **YAWL, ZULU**

Vessel

a vessel with two handles, Gr. **DIOTA**
vessel's curved planking .. **SNY**
vestal .... **CHASTE**
vestige .. **IOTA, RELIC, TRACE**
vestment .. **ALB, COPE, AMICE, EPHOD, STOLE**
vestment, white .. **ALB, AMICE**
vesuvianite, brown ... **EGERAN**
vetch .... **TARE**
vetch, bitter .... **ERS**
vetch, India .... **AKRA**
vetiver, grass .... **BENA**
vex **GALL, RILE, ROIL, HARRY**
vex persistently ...... **NETTLE**
vex: Scot. .... **FASH**
vexed .... **RILY**
via .... **PER**
viands .... **DIET**
viands, dainty .... **CATES**
Viaud's pseudonym ..... **LOTI**
vibrate .... **THRILL**
vibration: music .... **TREMOLO**
vice .... **SIN**
viceroy .... **VALI**
Vichy Premier .... **LAVAL**
vicious man .... **YAHOO**
victim .... **PREY**
victorfish .... **AKU**
victor's crown .... **LAUREL**
victory, Eng. .. **CRECY, CRESSY**
victory trophy .... **SCALP**
b victuals .... **FOOD**
"— victus," woe to the con-
    quered .... **VAE**
"—vide," "which see" .. **QUAE**
vie with .... **EMULATE**
Viennese park .... **PRATER**
view .... **SCENE, VISTA**
vigilant .... **WARY, ALERT**
vigor .... **PEP, VIM, VIS, ZIP, FORCE**
Viking ... **ERIC, OLAF, ROLLO**
Viking explorer .... **ERIC**
vilify .... **REVILE**
village .. **DORP, VILL, HAMLET**
village, Afr. .... **KRAAL**
village, Java .... **DESSA**
village, Russ. .... **MIR**
village, Scot. .... **REW**
village, S. Afr. native ... **STAD**
villain .... **KNAVE**
villein .... **CEORL**
vindicate .... **AVENGE**
vindication .... **REVENGE**
vine .... **IVY, BINE**
vine: comb. form .... **VITI**
vine, N. Z. .... **AKA**
vine, P. I. .... **IYO**

c vine, woody .. **ABUTA, LIANA**
"vin du —," wine of the
    country .... **CRU**
vinegar of ale .... **ALEGAR**
vinegar, pert. to ...... **ACETIC**
vinegar worm .... **EEL, NEMA**
vinous .... **WINY**
viol, ancient type ...... **REBEC**
viol, bass .... **GAMBA**
viol, Shetlands .... **GUE**
viola .... **ALTO**
violent .... **HOT**
violet-odored ketone .. **IRONE**
violin, bass .... **CELLO**
violin, early .. **REBAB, REBEC**
violin, famous .... **STRAD**
violin, It. .. **AMATI, CREMONA**
violin, small .... **KIT**
violin, tenor ..... **ALTO, VIOLA**
violinist ...... **ELMAN, YSAYE**
viper .... **ASP, ADDER**
viper genus .... **ECHIS**
viper, horned ...... **CERASTES**
Virgil's hero .. **ENEAS, AENEAS**
Virgin Mary pictured mourning **PIETA**
virus-fighting substance **ANTIVIRAL**
visage .... **FACE**
viscous
d   **LIMY, ROPY, SIZY, SLIMY**
viscous substance .. **TAR, SLIME**
Vishnu, incarnation, 7th **RAMA**
Vishnu, soul of universe **VASU**
Vishnu's bow .... **SARAN**
Vishnu's serpent ...... **NAGA**
visible juncture .... **SEAM**
Visigoth king **ALARIC, ALARIK**
vision, defective ..... **ANOPIA**
vision, pert. to .... **OPTIC**
visionary ...... **AIRY, IDEAL, DREAMY, UNREAL, IDEALIST**
visit ...... **SEE, CALL, HAUNT**
visit at sea .... **GAM**
visit between whalers ... **GAM**
vison .... **MINK**
vital energy .... **HORME**
vital fluid .... **SAP**
vital principle .... **SOUL**
vitalize .... **ANIMATE**
vitamin ... **CITRIN, ADERMIN, ANEURIN, TORULIN**
vitamin B **NIACIN, THIAMINE**
vitamin B2 .... **FLAVIN**
vitamin H .... **BIOTIN**
vitiate .... **SPOIL, TAINT, POLLUTE, INVALIDATE**
vitriol-infused earth .... **SORY**
vituperate .... **SCOLD**

a vivacious ..... AIRY, BRIGHT
vivacity .... ELAN, LIFE
vocal flourish ...... ROULADE
vocation .... CAREER
"— voce" .... SOTTO
voice .... SAY
voice
    ALTO, BASS, VOCE, TENOR
voice: It. .... VOCE
voice: Lat. .... VOX
voice, loss of ...... APHONIA
voiced .... SONANT
voiced, not .... ASONANT
voiceless .... SPIRATE
voiceless consonant ..... SURD
void .... NUL, NULL,
    ABYSS, SPACE, INVALID
void, to make.ANNUL, CANCEL
void, to render: Scot. ... CASS
voided escutcheon ...... ORLE
volcanic cinder .... SCORIA
volcanic islands, Atlantic
                    FAROE
volcanic rock
    TUFA, TUFF, LATITE
volcanic scoria-matter
                LAVA, SLAG
volcano .. ETNA, AETNA, PELEE
volcano crater .... MAAR
volcano hole .... CRATER

c volcano, Martinique Is. .. PELEE
volcano mouth ...... CRATER
volcano, P. I. .... APO
volcano pit .... CRATER
volcano, Sicily   ETNA, AETNA
volcano, W. Indies .... PELEE
volition .... WILL
volt-ampere .... WATT
Voltaire .... AROUET
Voltaire play: Fr. ..... ZAIRE
voluble .... GLIB
volume .... MO, TOME
vomiting .... EMESIS
voodoo charm .... MOJO
voodoo snake deity .... ZOMBI
vote .... BALLOT
vote into office .... ELECT
vote, right to .... FRANCHISE
vote, take a .... POLL
votes ...... AYES, NOES, YEAS
vouch for .... SPONSOR
voucher .... CHIT, NOTE
"vous —": Fr., you are .. ETES
vowel, line over ..... MACRON
vowel suppression .... ELISION
voyaging .... ASEA
vulcanite .... EBONITE
Vulcan's wife .... MAIA
vulgar .... COARSE
vulture AURA, URUBU, CONDOR

W

b "W", old English .... WEN
wade across .... FORD
wading bird IBIS, RAIL, CRANE,
    EGRET, HERON, STILT,
    AVOCET, AVOSET, JAC-
    ANA, FLAMINGO
wag .... WIT
wages .... PAY
Wagner heroine . ELSA, SENTA,
                    ISOLDE
Wagnerian role .... ERDA
wagon .. CART, DRAY, WAIN
wagon pin .... CLEVIS
wagon, Russ. .... TELEGA
wagon shaft .... THILL
wagon tongue .... NEAP, POLE
wagtail .... LARK
wahoo, fish .... PETO
wail .... KEEN, LAMENT
waist ...... CAMISA, TAILLE
waistcoat VEST, GILET, JERKIN
wait .... BIDE
waken ...... ROUSE, AROUSE

d wale .... WELT
Wales emblem .... LEEK
walk ..... PACE, STEP, TREAD
walk affectedly .... MINCE
walk heavily .... PLOD, SLOG
walk, inability to .... ABASIA
walk lamely .... LIMP
walk stiffly .... STALK
walk, tree-lined .... ALAMEDA
walking stick ... CANE, STILT
wall, arena .... SPINA
wall around fortified place
                RAMPART
wall, divided by .... SEPTATE
wall: Fr. .... MUR
wall material .... COB
wall, of a .... MURAL
wall paneling .... WAINSCOT
wall piece TEMPLET, TEMPLATE
wall section .... DADO, PANEL
wall, squeeze against .. MURE
walls .... SEPTA
wallaba tree, Brazil ..... APA
walled city, Nigeria ..... KANO

177

a

wallflower	KEIRI
wallop	LAM
wallow	WELTER
walrus	MORSE
wampum	PEAG, SEWAN, SEAWAN
wan	ASHY, PALE, ASHEN
wand	BATON
wander	ERR, HAAK, ROAM, ROVE, RAMBLE, DIGRESS
wander idly	GAD
wanderer	VAG, NOMAD
"Wandering Jew" author	SUE
wane	EBB
want	LACK, NEED, DESIRE
wapiti	ELK
war-club, medieval	MACE
war correspondent	PYLE, BALDWIN
war cry, ancient Gr.	ALALA
war god	ARES, MARS
war god, Babyl.	IRA, IRRA
war god, Norse	TY, TYR, TYRR
war god, Teut.	ER
war goddess, Gr.	ENYO
war horse	CHARGER
war, religious	CRUSADE
war, Russ.-Eng.	CRIMEA
war vessel	CRUISER
warble	SING, TRILL, YODEL

b

ward off	FEND, AVERT, PARRY, REPEL, STAVE
ward politician	HEELER
warden, fire	RANGER
warehouse	DEPOT
warehouse room	LOFT
warm	CALID, TEPID
warning of danger: biol.	SEMATIC
warning signal	SIREN
warning system, attack	DEW, BMEWS
warp yarn	ABB
warrant, from monarch	BERAT
warrior, Samoa	TOA
warship, sailing	FRIGATE
wary	CAGY
was not: dialect	NAS
wash	LAVE
wash leather	LOSH
wash out	ELUTE
washings: chem.	ELUATE
Washington Irving character	RIP
wasp	HORNET
wasps, the	VESPA
waste	LOSS
waste allowance	TRET
waste away	GNAW, ATROPHY
waste fiber	NOIL
waste land	MOOR
waste matter	DROSS
waste silk	KNUB, FRISON

c

waste time	IDLE
wastes, growing in	RUDERAL
watch	SEE, GLOM
watch chain	FOB
watchdog, Hel's	GARM
watchful	ALERT
watchful guardian	ARGUS
watchful, name meaning	IRA
watchman, alert	ARGUS
watchman, night	SERENO
watchtower	MIRADOR
water	SPRINKLE, IRRIGATE
water arum	CALLA
water chestnut, Chin.	LING
water cock	KORA
water, covered by	AWASH
water: Fr.	EAU, EAUX
water: Lat.	AQUA
water lily	LOTUS
water passage	SLUICE, STRAIT
water pipe	HOOKA, HOOKAH, NARGILE
water raising device	TABUT, TABOOT
water reservoir, natural	CENOTE
water scorpion genus	NEPA
water, seek	DOUSE
water, sound of	PLASH
water: Sp.	AGUA

d

water spirit	ARIEL, SPRITE, UNDINE
water sprite	NIX, NIXIE
water sprite: Gaelic	KELPIE
water surface	RYME
water vessel, India	LOTA, LOTO, LOTAH
water wheel	NORIA, DANAIDE, TURBINE
water wheel, Persian	NORIA
water's surface: naut.	RYME
watercourse	LADE, BROOK, CANAL, RIVER, STREAM
watered apearance	MOIRE
watered silk	MOIRE
waterfall, Scot.	LIN, LYN, LINN
watering place	SPA, BADEN
waterproof canvas	TARP
waterskin	MATARA
watertight, make	CALK, CAULK
waterway	BAYOU, CANAL
waterway, narrow	STRAIT
watery	SEROUS
watery: comb. form	SERO
wattle tree	BOREE
wattled honeyeater	IAO, MANUAO
wave	FLY, SEA
wave-crest comb.	COOM
wave: Fr.	ONDE
wave, huge	SEA

waver ...... **FALTER, TEETER**
wavy: Her.
     UNDE, UNDY, NEBULE
wax .... **CERE**
wax ointment .... **CERATE**
wax, pert. to .... **CERAL**
wax: Sp. .... **CERA**
wax, yellow or white **CERESIN**
waxy chemical .... **CERIN**
waxy substance .... **CERIN**
way ...... **VIA, MODE, ROUTE**
way of walking .... **GAIT**
way out .... **EGRESS**
wayside — .... **INN**
wayside stop, India .. **PARAO**
we: Lat. .... **NOS**
weak .... **PUNY, FRAIL,**
    DEBILE, EFFETE, FEEBLE
weak cider .... **PERKIN**
weaken .... **SAP, LABEFY,**
    VITIATE, ENERVATE, EN-
    FEEBLE
weakfish, S. Am. .... **ACOUPA**
weakness .... **ATONY**
weal .... **WALE**
wealth, man of .... **NABOB**
wealthy: Scot. .... **BIEN**
weapon .... **LANCE,**
  SPEAR, SWORD, MUSKET
weapon, ancient .... **CELT**
weapon, dagger-like .. **BALAS**
weapon: Fr. .... **ARME**
weapon, gaucho's **BOLA, BOLAS**
weapon, Maori .... **PATU**
weapon, medieval ..... **ONCIN**
weapon, N. Z. .... **PATU**
weapon, P. I. .... **BOLO**
weapon, S. Am. .. **BOLA, BOLAS**
wear away **EAT, ERODE, ABRADE**
wear away slowly ... **CORRODE**
wear by friction .... **RUB**
wear off .... **ABRADE**
wearing down .... **ATTRITION**
weary .... **BORE, TIRE**
weasel **VARE, ERMINE, FERRET**
weasel: Eng.
   STOT, STOAT, STOTE
weather indicator **BAROMETER**
weathercock .... **VANE**
weaverbird ..... **BAYA, MAYA**
weaverbird, S. Afr. .... **TAHA**
weaver's bobbin on shuttle **PIRN**
weaver's reed .... **SLEY**
weaving frame .... **LOOM**
weaving term .... **LISSE**
weaving tool .... **EVENER**

web .... **TELA**
web-footed bird . **DUCK, LOON,**
               GOOSE
web-like membrane ..... **TELA**
web-spinning
    RETIARY, TELARIAN
wed .... **MARRY**
wedding anniversaries 1st,
  PAPER; 2nd, COTTON;
  3rd, CANDY OR LEATHER;
  4th, SILK, FRUIT, FLOW-
  ERS, or LEATHER; 5th,
  WOODEN; 6th, IRON OR
  CANDY; 7th, WOOL, COP-
  PER, OR FLORAL; 8th,
  WOOL, BRONZE, OR POT-
  TERY; 9th, WILLOW OR
  POTTERY; 10th, TIN; 11th,
  STEEL; 12th, SILK OR LIN-
  EN; 13th, LACE; 14th,
  IVORY; 15th, CRYSTAL;
  20th, CHINA; 25th, SIL-
  VER; 30th, PEARL; 35th,
  CORAL; 40th, RUBY OR
  EMERALD; 45th, RUBY OR
  SAPPHIRE; 50th, GOLDEN;
  55th, EMERALD; 75th,
  DIAMOND
wedge, entering . **COIN, COIGN,**
    QUOIN, COIGNE
wedge-like piece ..... **QUOIN**
wedge-shaped ...... **CUNEATE**
wedge-shaped piece **GIB, SHIM**
wedge, steel .... **FROE**
Wednesday, source of name
    WODEN
weed .... **TARE, DARNEL**
weed, coarse .... **DOCK**
week ..... **SENNET, SENNIGHT**
week day .... **FERIA**
weep
  CRY, SOB, BOHO, LAMENT
weep, Scot. .... **ORP**
weeping statue .... **NIOBE**
weeping woman, Gr. myth **NIOBE**
weft .... **WOOF**
WEIGHT .. see also SPECIAL
  SECTION
weight .... **TON, HEFT**
weight allowance **TARE, TRET**
weight, ancient
    MINA, TALENT
weight, ancient: var. ... **MNA**
weight, Asiatic .... **TAEL**
weight, balance .... **RIDER**

Weight

weight, Danish .... **ORT**
weight, India .... **SER, TOLA**
weight machine: Scot.
.... **TRON, TRONE**
weight, metric unit of .. **GRAM**
weight of England ..... **STONE**
weight of silk before
  degumming .... **PARI**
weight, pert. to .... **BARIC**
weight system .... **TROY**
weir .... **DAM**
weird .... **EERY, EERIE**
welcome .... **GREET**
well, Bib. .... **AIN**
well-bred people .... **GENTRY**
"well done" .. **EUGE, BRAVO**
well done: Eng. .... **EUGE**
well: Fr. .... **BIEN**
well: It. & Lat. .... **BENE**
well: Scot. .... **AWEEL**
Welsh dog .... **CORGI**
Welsh god of sea .... **DYLAN**
Welshman .... **CELT**
welt .... **WALE**
wen .... **TALPA**
Wend of Saxony .... **SORB**
wergeld .... **CRO**
W. Australia capital ... **PERTH**
W. Afr. timber tree ... **ODUM**
W. Afr. tribe **IBO, BUBE, BUBI**
W. Ind. bayberry **AUSU, AUZU**
W. Ind. fish
.... **BOGA, CERO, TESTAR**
W. Ind. idol. ..... **ZEME, ZEMI**
W. Ind. isle ... **CUBA, HAITI**
W. Ind. key .... **CAY**
W. Ind. scrapper .... **CAJI**
W. Ind. shrub plant .... **ANIL**
West Point mascot ..... **MULE**
West Pointer
.... **PLEB, CADET, PLEBE**
West Saxon king .... **INE**
Western division of Osset **DIGOR**
Western European **CELT, KELT**
Western Indian .... **UTE**
Western shrub .... **SAGE**
"Western Star" author **BENET**
Western state .... **UTAH**
Westphalian city ..... **HERNE**
wet: Scot. .... **WAT**
wet .... **ASOP, MOIST**
whale .... **CET, ORC, ORK,**
CETE, BELUGA, GRAMPUS
whale carcass **KRANG, KRENG**
whale hunter .... **AHAB**
whale oil cask .... **RIER**
whale-shark .... **MHOR**
whale tail part .... **FLUKE**
whale, white .... **BELUGA**

whale, white Caspian
.... **HUSE, HUSO**
whales .... **CETE**
whales, herd of ... **GAM, POD**
whales, pert. to .... **CETIC**
whales, school of .. **GAM, POD**
whalebone .... **BALEEN**
wharf..**KEY, PIER, QUAI, QUAY**
what is it? obs. .... **ANAN**
whatnot .... **ETAGERE**
wheal .... **WALE, WEAL**
wheat disease .... **BUNT**
wheat, German **EMMER, SPELT**
wheat, India ..... **SUJI, SUJEE**
wheat, kind of **EMMER, SPELT**
wheat middlings .. **SEMOLINA**
wheedle .... **COG, COAX**
wheedling .... **BUTTERY**
wheel .... **ROTA**
wheel band .... **STRAKE**
wheel center **HOB, HUB, NAVE**
wheel, furniture ..... **CASTER**
wheel, grooved ...... **SHEAVE**
wheel horse .... **POLER**
wheel part .... **HUB, RIM,**
FELLY, SPOKE
wheel projection .... **CAM**
wheel shaft .... **AXLE**
wheel-shaped .... **ROTATE**
wheel spindle .. **AXLE, ARBOR**
wheel tread .... **TIRE**
wheels, pert. to .... **ROTAL**
where: Lat. .... **UBI**
whetstone, fine . **BUHR, HONE**
whey of milk .. **SERA, SERUM**
which see: abbr. .... **QV**
whiff .... **PUFF**
while .... **AS, WHEN**
whimper .... **MEWL, PULE**
whin .... **GORSE**
whine .... **PULE**
whinny .... **NEIGH**
whip **CAT, BEAT, FLOG, LASH**
whip, cowboy .... **CHICOTE**
whip mark ..... **WALE, WEAL**
whip, Russ. .... **KNOUT**
whipsocket .... **SNEAD**
whirl .... **REEL, SPIN**
whirlpool ...... **EDDY, GURGE,**
VORTEX
whirlpool: Scot. ... **WEEL, WIEL**
whirlwind in Atlantic ...... **OE**
whirring sound .... **BIRR**
whiskers .... **BEARD, GOATEE**
whiskey: Ir. .... **POTEEN**
whiskey drink: Scot.
.... **ATHOL, ATHOLE**
whist win .... **SLAM**
whistle .... **PIPE, SIREN**
whit .... **BIT, JOT,**
ATOM, DOIT, IOTA

a
white acid, pert. to .. **TROPIC**
white alkaline .... **SODA**
white ant, P. I. ... **ANAI, ANAY**
white, bitter compound **LININ**
white: comb. form ..... **ALBO**
"White Elephant" land .. **SIAM**
white ermine **LASSET, MINIVER**
white-flecked .... **ROAN**
White Friar ...... **CARMELITE**
white: Ir. .... **BAWN**
white man: P. I. ... **CACHILA**
white matter, brain .... **ALBA**
white oak .... **ROBLE**
white poplar .... **ABELE**
white spruce ...... **EPINETTE**
white with age .... **HOAR**
whitefish .... **CISCO**
whiten .... **ETIOLATE**
whitish .... **HOARY**
whitlow grass .... **DRABA**
Whittier heroine .... **MAUD**
whiz ..... **PIRR, WHIR, ZIZZ**
whoa .... **HOLLA**
whole amount .... **GROSS**
whole: comb. form ...... **TOTO**
wholesome .... **SALUTARY**
wholly .... **ALL**
wicked .... **EVIL**
wicker basket .... **CESTA, KIPSY, PANNIER**

b
wicker basket, Guiana **PEGALL**
wickerwork .... **RATAN**
wickerwork hut .... **JACAL**
wicket, croquet .... **HOOP**
wide-mouthed vessel **EWER, OLLA**
widgeon .... **SMEE**
widgeon genus ...... **MARECA**
widow .... **RELICT**
widow in cards .... **SKAT**
widow monkey .... **TITI**
widow's bit or coin ..... **MITE**
widow's third: Scot. .... **TERCE**
wield .... **PLY, USE**
wife, Moroccan ruler's **SHERIFA**
wife ... **FEME, FRAU, FEMME**
wife's property .... **DOS**
wig .... **PERUKE**
wigwam .. **TIPI, TEPEE, TEEPEE**
wild .... **FERAL, SAVAGE**
wild animals, collection of **ZOO, MENAGERIE**
wild animal's trail **SLOT, SPUR, SPOOR**
wild apple .... **CRAB, DOUCIN**
wild ass, Afr. ...... **QUAGGA**
wild ass, Asia .... **ONAGER**
wild boar genus .... **SUS**
wild buffalo, India **ARNA, ARNI, ARNEE**

c
wild buffalo, Malay ... **GAUR, SLADANG, SALADANG, SELADANG**
wild cat, Siberia, Tibet, steppes **MANUL**
wild cattle, India **GAUR, GOUR**
wild cry .... **EVOE**
wild dog .... **DHOLE**
wild dog genus .... **THOS**
wild dog, Japan ..... **TANATE**
"Wild Duck" author .... **IBSEN**
wild garlic .... **MOLY**
wild ginger .... **ASARUM**
wild hog .... **BOAR**
wild honeybee, E. Ind. **DINGAR**
wild horse of Tartary **TARPAN**
wild lime .... **COLIMA**
wild olive tree ..... **OLEASTER**
wild ox .... **ANOA**
wild ox, Malay. .... **BANTENG**
wild plum .... **SLOE**
wild plum, Calif. .... **ISLAY**
wild sheep, Asia **RASSE, ARGALI**
wild sheep, horned . **MOUFLON**
wild sheep, India ... **SHA, SNA, URIAL, NAHOOR, OORIAL**
wild sheep, N. Afr. **ARUI, UDAD, AOUDAD**
wild sheep, Tibet .... **SHA**

d
SNA, BHARAL, NAHOOR
wild turnip .... **NAVEW**
wild vanilla .... **LIATRIS**
wildcat .... **BALU, LYNX**
wildcat, Afr. & India .. **CHAUS**
wildcat, S. Am. .... **EYRA**
wildcat, Sumatra ...... **BALU**
wildebeest .... **GNU**
wile .... **ART**
will addition .... **CODICIL**
will, one inheriting from **DEVISEE**
will, one making .... **DEVISOR**
will power, loss of .... **ABULIA**
William: Ir. .... **LIAM**
William I, half brother of **ODO**
William the Conqueror's daughter .... **ADELA**
willingly .... **LIEF**
willow .... **ITEA, OSIER**
willow, Europ. .... **SALLOW**
willow genus, Virginia ... **ITEA**
Wilson's thrush .... **VEERY**
wilt .... **FADE, DROOP**
wily .... **FOXY**
wimple .... **GORGET**
win .... **GAIN**
winch .... **WHIN**
wind .... **GALE**
wind, Adriatic .... **BORA**

Wind

a wind, Andes ... **PUNA, PUNO**
wind, Austral. ...... **BUSTER**
wind, away from .... **ALEE**
wind, cold Malta .... **GREGALE**
wind, cold Medit. .... **MISTRAL**
wind, cold Swiss Alps **BISE, BIZE**
wind: comb. form .... **ANEMO**
wind-deposited loam ... **LOESS**
wind, dry, from Sahara .. **LESTE**
wind, east .... **EURUS**
wind god, Babyl.
      ADAD, ADDA, ADDU
wind god, Hindu ...... **VAYU**
wind god, pert. to
      EOLIAN, AEOLIAN
wind, hot, dry ...... **KAMSIN,**
  SIMOOM, SIMOON, SIROCCO
wind, hot, Medit. .... **SOLANO**
wind indicator .. **SOCK, VANE**
wind instrument
  HORN, OBOE, PIPE, BUGLE
wind, Levant .... **ETESIAN**
wind, Madeira .... **LESTE**
wind, Medit. .... **ETESIAN**
wind, Medit., poet. ..... **SIROC**
wind, Mesop. .... **SHAMAL**
wind, north .... **BOREAS**
wind off Faroe Islands .... **OE**
wind, Peru Andes **PUNA, PUNO**
wind, sand-laden
  SAMIEL, SIMOOM, SIMOON
b wind, Sahara .... **LESTE**
wind, South .. **NOTUS, AUSTER**
wind, southeast .... **EURUS**
wind, southwest .... **AFER**
wind, Trieste, cold ..... **BORA**
wind, warm dry **FOHN, FOEHN**
wind, west .... **AFER**
winds, south, Peru ..... **SURES**
windborne .... **AEOLIAN**
windflower .... **ANEMONE**
windlass .... **CAPSTAN**
windmill sail .... **AWE**
window lead .... **CAME**
window ledge .... **SILL**
window part .... **SASH**
window, semipolygonal .. **ORIEL**
window setter .... **GLAZIER**
windrow .... **SWATH**
windstorm
  OE, BURAN, TORNADO
windstorm, Asia **BURA, BURAN**
wine ...... **VIN, HOCK, PORT,**
  SACK, VINO, MEDOC, TO-
  KAY, CLARET, MALAGA,
  MUSCAT, SHERRY, MO-
  SELLE
wine, Am. .... **CATAWBA**
wine, ancient .... **MASSIC**
wine cask .... **TUN, BUTT**
wine city, It. .... **ASTI**

c wine cup .... **AMA**
wine, delicacy of: Fr. ... **SEVE**
wine disorder .... **CASSE**
wine district, Calif. .... **NAPA**
wine drink .... **NEGUS**
wine, dry .... **SEC, BRUT**
wine, golden .... **BUAL**
wine, heavy .... **TOKAY**
wine, honey and ...... **MULSE**
wine, Madeira .... **BUAL**
wine measure, Trieste
      ORNA, ORNE
wine merchant .... **VINTNER**
wine, new .... **MUST**
wine pitcher, Gr. .... **OLPE**
wine, red **PORT, TINTA, CLARET**
wine, sweet .... **MUSCAT**
wine, sweet: Fr. ..... **MASDEU**
wine, to make .... **VINT**
wine vessel ...... **AMA, OLPE,**
    AMULA, CHALICE
wine, white .... **HOCK,**
  SHERRY, SAUTERNE
wineberry, N. Z. ...... **MAKO**
wing .... **ALA, PENNA,**
  PINNA, PINION
wing, bastard .... **ALULA**
wing, beetle .... **TEGMAN,**
  TEGMINA, TEGUMEN
wing: Fr. .... **AILE**
d wing-footed animal .. **ALIPED**
winglike .... **ALAR**
wing-like part ..... **ALA, ALAE**
wing movement .... **FLAP**
wing tip, pert. to ... **ALULAR**
wings .... **ALAE**
wings, divested of
  DEALATA, DEALATED
wings, having .. **ALAR, ALATE**
wings: her. .... **VOL, AILE**
winged figure, Gr.
  IDOLON, IDOLUM, EIDOLON
winged fruit, indehiscent
    SAMARA
winged god ..... **EROS, CUPID**
winged seed .... **SAMARA**
winged victory .... **NIKE**
wingless .... **APTERAL**
wingless invertebrates **APTERA**
wink rapidly .... **BAT**
winning at bridge ...... **SLAM**
winnow .... **FAN**
winter, pert. to .... **BRUMAL,**
  HIEMAL, HYEMAL, HIBERNAL
winter squash ...... **CUSHAW**
wipe out .... **ERASE**
wire measure .... **MIL**
wire service .... **AP, UP,**
  INS, UPI, REUTERS

a wires, cross .... **RETICLE**
Wisconsin college ...... **RIPON**
wisdom ...... **LORE, GNOSIS**
wisdom god of: Babyl.
NABU, NEBO
wisdom goddess of: Gr.
ATHENA, PALLAS
wisdom, goddess of: Rom.
MINERVA
wise .... **SAGE, SENSIBLE**
wise adviser .... **MENTOR**
wise man
SAGE, SOLON, NESTOR
Wise Men .... **MAGI, GASPAR, MELCHIOR, BALTHASAR**
wise men, A-S .... **WITAN**
wisecrack .. **GAG, JOKE, QUIP**
wish for ..... **YEARN, DESIRE**
wish undone .... **RUE**
wisp of hair .... **TATE**
wit .... **WAG, HUMOR**
wit: Sp. .... **SAL**
witless chatter .... **GAB**
witch ... **HAG, HECAT, LAMIA, HECATE, HECCAT, HEKATE**
witch city .... **SALEM**
witch doctor .... **GOOFER**
witch in "Faerie Queene"
DUESSA
witchcraft .... **OBEAH**
b with: Fr. .... **AVEC**
with: Ger. .... **MIT**
with joy .... **FAIN**
with: prefix .... **SYN**
withdraw .. **RECEDE, REMOVE, RETIRE, SECEDE, RETRACT**
wither .... **FADE**
withered .... **SERE**
within ...... **INTO, INTERIOR**
within: comb. form
ESO, ENDO, ENSO, ENTO
within: prefix .... **ENDO**
without: comb. form ..... **ECT**
without energy .... **ATONY**
without: Fr. .... **SANS**
without: Ger. .... **OHNE**
without: Lat. .... **SINE**
without: poetic .... **SANS**
without teeth, claws, lion
MORNE
without veins ...... **AVENOUS**
witness .... **SEE**
witness, law . **TESTE, DEPONENT**
witness, to bear ...... **ATTEST**
witty remark ..... **MOT, QUIP**
witty reply .... **REPARTEE**
wobble .... **TEETER**
Woden .... **ODIN**
woe .... **MISERY**
woe is me .... **ALAS**

c wolf, gray .... **LOBO**
wolf, Odin's ...... **GERE, GERI**
wolf, timber .... **LOBO**
wolfhound .... **ALAN**
wolfish .... **LUPINE**
wolframite .... **CAL**
wolverine genus .... **GULO**
woman diplomat, first U.S.
OWEN
woman: Gr. .... **GYNE**
woman, ill-tempered
SHREW, VIRAGO
woman personified, Ir.
EMER, EIMER
woman's name (3 letters) **ADA, AMY, ANN, EVA, EVE, FAY, IDA, INA, MAE, MAY, NAN, RAE, UNA, ZOE,** (4 letters) **AFRA, ALIX, ALMA, ALYS, ANNA, ANNE, AVIS, BONA, CARA, CLOE, CORA, DORA, EDNA, ELLA, ELSA, EMMA, ENID, ERMA, ETTA, INEZ, JANE, JEAN, JOAN, JUNE, LEAH, LIDA, LILA, LOIS, LORA, LUCY, MARY, MAUD, MYRA, NONA, NORA, OLGA, RITA, ROSA, ROSE, RUTH, SARA, VERA, VIDA,** (5 letters) **ALICE,**
d **ANITA, CLARE, DELIA, DIANA, ELAIN, ELSIE, ERICA, FAITH, FLORA, GRACE, IRENE, SARAH, SELMA,** (6 letters) **ALTHEA, BERTHA, DAPHNE, EDWINA, ELAINE, EMILIA, PHOEBE,** (7 letters) **ABIGAIL, CELESTE, LAVINIA**
woman's nickname **CAT, DEB, HAT, KIT, LOU, MAB, MAG, MEG, SAL, SUE, ABBY, ADDY, BESS, BETH, CARO, DORA, GAIL, JILL, JOSY, JUDY, JULE, KATE, KATY, LINA, LISA, LULU, MART, MIMI, MINA, MOLL, NELL, NINA, ROXY, SUSY, TAVE, TAVY, TESS, TINA, XINA, SALLY, SALLIE**
Wonderland girl ...... **ALICE**
wont .... **HABIT**
wood .... **ALOE**
wood apple, Ind. .... **BEL**
wood, black .... **EBONY**
wood, flexible .... **EDDER**
wood, fragrant . **ALOES, CEDAR**
wood: comb, form ...... **XYLO**
wood: Fr. .... **BOIS**
wood gum .... **XYLAN**

183

Wood

wood, light .... **BALSA**
wood, long piece .... **POLE**
wood: obsolete .... **WOLD**
wood, piece of .... **SLAT,
SPRAG, BILLET**
wood pussy .... **SKUNK**
wood robin, N. Z. ...... **MIRO**
wood sorrel .... **OCA, OKA**
wood, timber: P. I. ... **CAHUY**
woodchuck .... **MARMOT**
woodchuck: dialect **MOONACK**
wooden .... **TREEN**
wooden brick .... **DOOK**
wooden collar, convict's **CANG**
wooden pail .... **SOE**
wooden peg .... **SKEG**
wooden shoe **SABOT, PATTEN**
woodland deity **FAUN, SATYR**
woodland god .... **PAN**
woodpecker genus **JYNX, YUNX**
woodpecker, green **HICKWALL**
woodpecker group ...... **PICI**
woodpecker, red-bellied . **CHAB**
woodpecker, small ... **PICULE**
woodpeckers, of ...... **PICINE**
woodwind
OBOE, BASSOON, CLARINET
woodworking tool ..... **SAPPER**
woodworm .... **TERMITE**
woody fiber .... **BAST**
woody hill .... **HOLT**
woody plant .... **TREE**
woof .... **WEFT**
wool ...... **ANGORA, MERINO**
wool cluster .... **NEP**
wool, coarse .... **GARE**
wool fat . **LANOLIN, LANOLINE**
wool: Lat. .... **LANA**
wool measure .... **HEER**
wool package .... **FADGE**
wool, reclaimed ...... **MUNGO**
woolen cloth .... **ETAMINE**
woolen cloth, coarse, twilled
KERSEY
woolen fabric .... **FRISCA**
woolen thread .... **YARN**
woolly ...... **LANATE, LANOSE**
woolly pyrol .... **URD**
word by word .... **LITERAL**
word expressing action .. **VERB**
word meanings, pert. to
SEMANTIC
word of affirmation .... **AMEN**
word of choice .... **OR**
word of God .... **LOGOS**
word of honor, promise
PAROL, PAROLE
word of mouth, by
PAROL, PAROLE
word of ratification .... **AMEN**
word, scrambled ... **ANAGRAM**

work

**MOIL, TOIL, CHARE, LABOR
WORK** ..see also COMPOSITION
work aimlessly .... **POTTER**
work at steadily .... **PLY**
work hard
PEG, MOIL, TOIL, SLAVE
work, in terms of heat **ERGON**
work, musical
OPUS, OPERA, ORATORIO
work persistently .... **PEG**
work, piece of .... **JOB, STINT**
work: Sp. .... **OBRA**
work unit .... **ERG, ERGON**
workbasket .... **CABA, CABAS**
worker .... **HAND,
OPERANT, OPERATOR**
worker ant .... **ERGATE**
worker: comb. form .. **ERGATE**
worker's group, worldwide .. **ILO**
worker's union, Soviet .. **ARTEL**
workhorse: Scot .... **AVER**
working boat, Chesapeake Bay
FLATTIE
workman, mine .... **CAGER**
workman, S. Afr. .... **VOLK**
workshop .... **ATELIER**
world: Hindu myth ...... **LOKA**
world, holder of .... **ATLAS**
World War I battle site
MONS, MARNE
World War I group . **AEF, AMEX**
World War II area ...... **ETO**
worm .. **ESS, TINEA, ANNELID**
worm, African .... **LOA**
worm, bait .... **LURG**
worm, eye-infesting ...... **LOA**
worm, S-shaped .... **ESS**
worm track, fossil .. **NEREITE**
worn, as rope .... **MAGGED**
worn by friction .... **ATTRITE**
worn out .... **EFFETE**
worn-out horse
NAG, HACK, PLUG
worry .... **RUX, CARE, CARK,
FRET, STEW**
worship .... **ADORE**
worship, form of ..... **RITUAL**
worship, house of ..... **BETHEL**
worship, object of ...... **IDOL**
worship of saints ...... **DULIA**
worship, place of
ALTAR, TEMPLE
worthless **BAD, RACA, TRASHY**
worthless bit from table .. **ORT**
worthless rock ...... **GANGUE**
wound: Her. .... **VULN**
wound mark .... **SCAR**
wrangle .... **HAGGLE**
wrap .... **SWATHE, SWADDLE**

a wrapping .... PLIOFILM
wrath .... IRE
wrathful .... IRATE
wreath .... CHAPLET
wreath: Her. .... TORSE
wreathe .... COIL, WIND
wrest .... REND
wrestle .... TUSSLE
wrestling throw ... HIPE, HYPE
wriggling .... EELY
wrinkle .... RUCK, RUGA,
    SEAM, RUGAE, RIMPLE
wrinkled ... RUGATE, RUGOSE
wrist .... CARPUS
wrists .... CARPI
wrist bone .... CARPAL
wrist guard .... BRACER
writ of execution ..... ELEGIT
writ, sheriff's .... VENIRE
writ to arrest .... CAPIAS

c write .... PEN, SCRIVE
write comments ...... POSTIL
write music .... NOTATE
writer .... DITER, SCRIBE
writer, Ger. .... MANN
writing instrument ...... PEN
writing on the wall
    MENE, TEKEL
writing paper size ...... CAP
writing table .... ESCRITOIRE
writing well, art of .. RHETORIC
wrong ...... OUT, EVIL, AMISS
wrong: Lat. ... MALA, MALUM
wrong, legal .... TORT
wrong: prefix .... MIS
wrongdoing .... EVIL
wrongdoing, serious .... CRIME
wryneck .... LOXIA
Wyoming peak, highest
               GANNETT

Y

Y, in Middle Eng. .. YOK, YOGH
Y's .... WIES
yacht .... SAIL
yacht pennant .... BURGEE
Yale .... ELI
b yam, Hawaii .... HOI
yam, white
    UBE, UBI, UVE, UVI
Yang, opposite of ...... YIN
Yangtze tributary .... HAN
Yap Island stone money ... FEI
yarn ... GARN, TALE, CREWEL
yarn count .... TYPP
yarn for warp .... ABB
yarn measure ..... LEA, HEER
yarn projection KNAP, KNOP
yarn, quantity of ...... SKEIN
Yarura language .... PUME
yataghan .... BALAS
yaupon holly ...... CASSENA
yawn .... GAPE
yawn: obs. .... GANE
yearly .... ETESIAN
yearly church payment ANNAT
yearn .... ACHE, LONG
year's crops .... ANNONA
yeast .... BEES
yeast, brewer's .... BARM
yeast, Jap. .... KOJI
yeast, wild .... ANAMITE
yell: Scot. .... GOWL
yellow ...... AMBER, OCHER,
  OCHRE, MELINE, CITRINE
yellow-brown .... TOPAZ
yellow bugle .... IVA

yellow dye plant .... AMIL
yellow fish .... ORF, ORFE
yellow ide ...... ORF, ORFE
yellow iris .... SEDGE
yellow ocher .... SIL
d yellow pigment .... SIL
yellow wood .... AVODIRE
yellowhammer, Eur. .. AMMER
yellowish .... SALLOW
yelp .... KIYI, YOUP
Yemenite .... ARAB
Yemen's capital .... SANA
yes: Sp. .... SI
yesterday: Fr. .... HIER
yesterday, pert. to HESTERNAL
yet .... E'EN, STILL
yew, pert. to .... TAXINE
yield CEDE, ACCEDE, CONCEDE
Yogi .... SWAMI
yoke bar, S. Afr. .... SKEY
yokel ...... OAF, HICK, RUBE
yolk of egg .... VITELLUS
yolky .... EGGY
yon .... THERE
yorker: cricket .... TICE
Yorkshire city .... LEEDS
Yorkshire river .... URE, OUSE
you: It. .... TU
you: Sp. .... TE
young animal
    CUB, PUP, COLT, WHELP
young female hog ...... GILT
young girl of Burma ... MIMA
young hog .... SHOAT, SHOTE
young kangaroo .... JOEY

Young

young man, handsome **ADONIS**
young ox: Eng. .... **STOT**
young plant .... **SET**
young rowdy ...... **HOODLUM**
youngest son .... **CADET**
youngster
KID, TAD, TOT, SHAVER
youth .... **LAD**
youth .... **GOSSOON**
youth shelter .... **HOSTEL**

youthful: zool. .... **NEANIC**
Yucatan Indian .... **MAYA**
yucca-like plant .... **SOTOL**
Yugoslav .... **SERB, CROAT**
Yugoslav leader .... **TITO**
Yum-Yum's friend
KOKO, NANKIPOO
Yutang .... **LIN**

Z

zeal .... **ELAN, ARDOR**
zealot .... **BIGOT**
zealous .... **AVID**
Zebedee, son of **JOHN, JAMES**
zebra, young .... **COLT**
zebrawood .... **ARAROBA**
zebu-yak hybrid **ZO, ZOH, ZOBO**
zenith .... **TOP, ACME, PEAK**
zenith, opposite of .... **NADIR**
Zeno's follower .... **STOIC**
zeppelin .... **BLIMP**
Zeppelin .... **GRAF**
zero .... **CIPHER**
zest .... **TANG**
zetetic .... **SEEKER**
Zeus, epithet of ..... **AMMON**
Zeus, maiden loved by
IO, LEDA, EUROPA
Zeus, mother of .... **RHEA**
Zeus, old Doric name for **ZAN**
Zeus' daughter
ATE, HEBE, IRENE
Zeus' sister .... **HERA**

Zeus' son ..... **ARES, ARCAS,
MINOS, APOLLO**
Zeus' wife ..... **HERA, METIS**
Zilpah's son ..... **GAD, ASHER**
zinc in slabs .... **SPELTER**
zinc ingot .... **SPELTER**
Zionist group .... **ITO**
zipper .... **TALON**
zodiac sign ...... **LEO, ARIES,
LIBRA, VIRGO, CANCER,
PISCES, TAURUS, SCORPIO**
Zola novel .... **NANA**
zone .... **AREA**
zone: Lat. .... **ZONA**
zoophyte, marine ...... **CORAL**
Zophah, son of ...... **BEERA**
Zoroastrian .. **PARSI, PARSEE**
Zoroastrian bible .... **AVESTA**
zounds .... **OONS**
Zulu headman ..... **INDUNA**
Zulu language .... **BANTU**

SPECIAL SECTION

READY REFERENCE WORD LISTS

In one compact section, here are lists of the most useful and widely-used word categories. Some of these words, having certain customary definitions, are also listed in the definitions' section of this book, but these complete word lists will be of greatest help when you are confronted with GENERALIZED definitions such as "Roman goddess," "South American Indian," "Heraldic term," or "African tribe."

All words in each separate listing are placed according to the number of their letters. This is a tremendous advantage to puzzle solvers, who are more concerned with the length of a word than with its alphabetical placement.

MEASURES

AREA MEASURES

AR, ARE, ACRE, DECARE (10 ARES), CENTIAR, CENTIARE
Annam .... MAU, QUO, SAO
Bengal .... BEGA
Czechoslovakia ... LAN, MIRA
Dutch E. Ind. .... BOUW
England, Old .... HYDE
Japan .... BU, SE, TAN
Norway .... MAL, MAAL
Paraguay .... LINO
Poland .... MORG
Rome, Ancient ...... CLIMA, CLIMATA
Serbia .... RIF, RALO
Shetlands, Orkney .... URE
Siam .... RAI, NGAN
Sweden .... MORGEN

DRY MEASURES

PECK, PINT, STERE
Algeria .... TARRI
Austria .... MUTH
Borneo .... GANTANG
Brazil .... MOIO
Burma .... TENG
Calcutta .... KUNK, RAIK
Channel Is. .... CABOT
China .... HO, HU
Dutch .... KOP, ZAK
Egypt .... KADA, KILAH
Hebrew .... CAB, KAB, KOR, EPHA, OMER, SEAH, EPHAH
Italy .... SALM, SALMA
Japan .... SHO
Morocco .... SAHH
Netherlands .... KOP, ZAK
Portugal .... MEIO, PIPA
Russia .... LOF
Tangier .... MUDD
Tunis ..... SAA, SAAH, UEBA

LENGTH, DISTANCE MEASURES

ELL, ROD, FOOT, HAND, INCH, MILE, YARD, METER, METRE, PERCH, MICRON, FURLONG
Annam .... LY, GON, NGU
Brazil .... PE
Calcutta .... DHAN, JAOB
China .... HU, LI, PU, TU, CH'IH, TCHI, TSUN
Czechoslovakia .. SAH, LATRO
Denmark FOD, MIL, MUL, ALEN
Domin. Repub. .... ONA
Dutch .... DUIM, VOET
D. E. Indies .... DEPA
Egypt .. PIC, PIK, KHET, THEB
Eritrea .... CUBI
Estonia .... LIIN, SULD
France .... AUNE
Greece .. PIC, PIK, BEMA, PIKI POUS, ACAENA
Hebrew .... EZBA
Iceland .... FET, ALIN, LINA
India .. GAZ, GEZ, GUZ, JOW, KOS, JAOB, KOSS
Italy .... CANNA
Japan .. BU, JO, RI (marine), CHO, DJO, KEN, RIN, HIRO

Java .... PAAL
Libya .... DRA, PIK, DRAH
Malabar .... ADY
Malacca .... ASTA
Netherlands .... DUIM, VOET
Norway .... FOT, ALEN
Persia ...... GAZ, GEZ, GUZ, ZAR, ZER
Poland .... MILA, PRET
Prussia .... RUTE
Rangoon . LAN, DAIN, TAUN
Rome, ancient ...... ACTUS, .. GRADUS, STADIA, STADIUM
Russia .... FUT, VERST
Siam .... WA, KUP, NIU, SEN, SOK, WAH, NIOU, SAWK
Spain .... BARA, CODO, DEDO, VARA
Sweden ...... FOT, REF, FAMN
Switzerland .... TOISE
Tripoli .... DRA, DRAA
Turkey .... PIC, PIK, KHAT, ZIRA

(liquid measures on page 189)

WEIGHTS

KIP, TON, GRAM, KILO, CARAT, GRAIN, OUNCE, CENTRAL

Abyssinia .... KASM, NATR, OKET, ALADA, NETER
Annam .... BINH
Arabia .... KELA
Austria .... UNZE
Bavaria .... GRAN
Brazil .... ONCA
Bulgaria .... OKA, OKE
Burma ...... VIS, KYAT, VISS
Calcutta .. PANK, PAWA, RAIK
China .... LI, FEN, HAO, KIN, SSU, TAN, YIN, TAEL
Columbia .... SACO
Denmark ES, ORT, VOG, ESER, PUND
Dutch .... ONS, LOOD
Dutch E. Ind ...... TJI, HOEN, TALI, WANG
Egypt ... KAT, KET, OKA, OKE, HEML, KHAR, OHIA, OKIEH
England .... STONE
Estonia .... NAEL, PUUD
Ethiopia .... See Abyssinia
France .... GROS
Germany .... LOT, LOTE, LOTH, STEIN
Greece .... MNA, MINA, OBOLE, OBOLUS
Guinea .... AKEY, PISO, UZAN, SERON

Hebrew .... BEKA, REBA
India .... SER, BHAR, PALA, RATI, TOLA, VISS, RATTI
Italian .... SALM, SALMA
Japan ...... KIN, SHI, MORIN
Malay .... CHEE
Malta .... SALM, SALMA
Mexico .... LIBRA, ONZA
Mongolia .... LAN
Morocco .... ARTEL
Moslem .... ROTL
Netherlands ...... ONS, LOOD
Norway .... PUND
ORIENT ...... MANN, ROTL, TAEL, ARTAL
Palestine ...... ROTLA, ZUZA
Persia .... SER
Poland .... LUT
Portugal GRAO, ONCA, LIBRA
Rangoon .... RUAY
Rome, Ancient ...... AS, BES, LIBRA, SOLIDUS
Russia .... LAN, PUD, DOLA, POOD, POUD
Siam .... PAI, KLAM, KLOM, TICAL
Shetland Island .. URE (ounce)
Spain .... ONZA
Sweden ASS, ORT, STEN, UNTZ
Turkey ..... OCK, OKA, OKE, KILE, OCHA, KERAT

LIQUID MEASURES

TUN, DRAM, GILL, PINT, MINIM

Abyssinia ...... CUBA, KUBA
Annam .... TAO
Arabia .... SAA
Austria .... FASS
Brazil .... PIPA
Burma .... BYEE, SEIT
China .... KO, QUEI, SHIH
Cyprus .... CASS
Dutch .. (old) AAM, AUM, KAN
Egypt .... HIN
England .... PIN, CRAN
Ethiopia .... see ABYSSINIA
Germany .... AAM, EIMER
Hebrew .... HIN

Hungary .... AKO
Japan .... KOKU, SHO
Malaya .... PAU
Netherlands . AAM, AUM, KAN
Portugal .... BOTA, PIPA
Rangoon .... BYEE, SEIT
Rome, Ancient .... URNA
Russia ... STOF, STOFF, STOOF
Somaliland .... CABA
Spain .... COPA
Sweden .... AM, AMAR, KAPP
Switzerland ..... IMMI, SAUM
Tangier .... KULA
Trieste .... ORNA, ORNE
Yugoslavia .... AKOV

COINS, MONEY

Abyssinia ..... BESA, GIRSH, TALARÍ
Afghanistan .... AMANIA
Albania .... LEK
Anglo-Saxon .... ORA, SCEAT
Annam .... QUAN
Austria .... DUCAT
Biblical .. BEKA, MITE (small), SHEKEL, TALENT
Brazil .... REI
Bulgaria ... LEV, LEW, DINAR
Chile .... COLON
China .. LI, CASH, TAEL, TIAO, YUAN, PU (early)
Colombia .... REAL
Costa Rica .... COLON
Czechslovakia ...... DUCAT, KRONE (plural, KRONEN)
Denmark ... ORA, ORE, ORAS, KRONE (plural, KRONER)
Dutch OORD, DALER, GULDEN, STIVER
D. E. Indies ..... BONK, DUIT
Egypt .... GIRSH
England ... ORA, RIAL (gold), RYAL, RYEL, GROAT, PENCE, FLORIN, GUINEA
Equador .... SUCRE
Ethiopia ..... see ABYSSINIA
Europe .... (old) GROS, DUCAT
France .. ECU (old), SOL, SOU, AGNEL (old), FRANC, LIARD (old), LOUIS, OBOLE, BESANT or BEZANT (old).
Genoa .... JANE (old)
Germany ..... MARK, KRONE (former), TALER, THALER
Ger. E. Africa .... PESA
Greece .. OBOL or OBOLI (old), STATER (old)
Hungary ...... GARA, PENGO
Iceland .... AURAR, EYRIR, KRONA
India. LAC, PIE, ANNA, DAWM, FELS, HOON, LAKH, PICE (small bronze), TARA, MOHUR (old), RUPEE
Iran .... see PERSIA
Iraq .... DINAR
Ireland .... RAP (old)

Italy .... LIRA, LIRE, SOLDO, TESTER, TESTON, TESTONE, TESTOON
Japan .... BU, RIN, SEN, YEN, OBAN
Latvia .... LAT, LATU
Lithuania .. LIT, LITAI, LITAS
Macao .... AVO
Malaya TRA (tin, pewter), TRAH
Mexico ...... PESO, CENTAVO
Montenegro .... PARA
Morocco .... OKIA, RIAL
Nepal .... MOHAR
Netherlands .... DAALDER
Norway .... ORE, KRONE (KRONER)
Oman .... GAJ, GAZ, GOZ, GHAZI
Persia. PUL, KRAN, POUL, RIAL DARIC, DINAR, MOHUR (old), TOMAN, STATER
Peru .... SOL, DINERO
Poland .... DUCAT
Portugal ..... JOE, REI, PECA, DOBRA (former)
Rome, ancient . SEMIS, DINDER
Roman ...... AS, AES, ASSES, SOLIDUS
Rumania ..... LEU, LEY, BANI
Russia . COPEC, KOPEK, RUBLE
Siam .... AT, ATT, BAHT, TICAL or TIKAL
Sicily .... TARI
Somaliland .... BESA
South Africa ...... DAALDER
Spain ..... COB, DURO, PESO, REAL, DOBLA (old), PESETA, PISTOLE (old)
Sweden ORE, KRONA (KRONOR), KRONE (KRONER)
Switzerland .... BATZ
Thailand .... see SIAM
Timor .... AVO
Turkey .... LIRA (gold), PARA, ALTUN (gold), ASPER, MAHBUB (gold), PIASTER
United States .. CENT, DIME, EAGLE
Venice .... BETSO (old silver)
Yugoslavia .... DINAR

TRIBES (Including Peoples, Natives)

EUROPE:
Albania .... GEG, CHAM, GHEG, TOSK
Balto-Slav .... LETT
Celtic on Danube .... BOII
Finnish near Volga ..... VEPS, VEPSA
Finnish, Ingria .... VOT, VOTE, VOTH, WOTE
Lithuania .... BALT
Syryenian .... KOMI
Teuton, ancient .... UBII

MIDDLE EAST:
Arab .... AUS, IBAD
Bedouin .... ABSI, HARB
Turkey .... KURD
East Turkey .... KURD
Persia .... see under ASIA

ASIA:
Afghanistan .... SAFI
Assam ..... AO, AKA; AHOM, GARO, NAGA
Borneo .. DYAK, IBAN; DAYAK
Burma .... WA, LAI, KAW, MON, WAS; AKHA, CHIN, KADU, KUKI, TSIN; KAREN
Caucasus ... IMER, KURI, LASI, LAZE, LAZI, SVAN; OSSET, SVANE
Celebes, Malayan .... BUGI
China, Miao .... HEH
China, Nord .... USUN, UZUN; USSUN
China, Tatar .... TOBA
India .... AWAN, BHIL, BHEEL, TURI
Kolarian (India) .... BHAR
Japan, aborigine .. AINO, AINU
Madagascar .... HOVA
Manchu .... DAUR
Mongol .... CHUD
Nepal .... AOUL, KHAS
Persia .... LUR, KURD, FARSI, IRANIAN
Tibet .... CHAMPA

AFRICA:
Abyssinian .... SHOA
Bantu .... KUA; BANE, BAYA, BIHE, BULE, FANG, FUNG, GOGO, GOLO, GOMA, GUHA, HAKU, HEHE, JAGA, LUBA, MAKA, NAMA, SOGA, SUKU, VIRA, YAKA, ZULU (largest); KAFIR; KAFFIR
Bedouin .... ABSI
Berber DAZA, RIFF, TEDA, TIBU
Bushman ... SAN, SAAN, QUNG
Congo .... FIOT, SUSU
Central Africa ... ABO; BULO, DOMA, KALI, KURI, LURI, YAKO; LUREM
Dahomey .... FON, FONG
East Africa ... JUR, LUR, YAO; AKKA, ALUR, ASHA, BARI, BONI, GOLO, MADI, NUER, VITI
Gold Coast .... AKAN, AKIM, AKRA
Hamitic ... AFAR, BEJA, BENI, BOGO, GALA, HIMA
Kaffir .... XOSA, ZULU
Kenya .... BONI
Lake Albert ..... ALUR, LURI
Liberia .... GI, KRA, KRU, TOMA, VAI, VEI, KROO
Libya ..... FUL, FULA, MZAB
Mozambique .... YAO
Nigeria .. ARO, EDO, IBO, IJO; BENI, BINI, EBOE, EKOI, IDJO, IDYO, IDZO, NUPE; BENIN
Nilotic .... SUK, BARI
Pygmy .... AKKA, DOKO
Slave Coast .... EGBA
Sudan ... FUL, FUR, VEI; FULA, GOLO, MABA, MEGE, NUBA, SUSU, TAMA
West Africa ... GA; AJA, EWE, IBO, KRU, KWA; AGNI, AKIM, APPA, BAGA, BINI, EFIK, EGBA, EKOI, GENG, GOLA, HABE, IKWE, JEBU, JOAT, JOLA, KETU, NALU, ONDO, REMO, SAPE, TCHI, TSHI, VACA, WARI

ALASKA:
Aleutians .... ATKA

GREENLAND .... ITA

AUSTRALIA .... KOKO
NEW GUINEA .... KARON

SOUTH AMERICA:
Fr. Guiana .... BONI

INDIANS, INDIAN TRIBES

Alaska .... ALEUT, SITKA

Algonquin or Algonkian
Indians ... FOX, SAC, WEA;
CREE, SAUK; MIAMI; LEN-
APE, OTTAWA, PIEGAN;
SHAWNEE

Amazon .... (lower) MURA,
(upper) ANDOA

Apache .... LIPAN

Araucanian .... AUCA

Arawak ..... ARAUA, CAMPA,
INERI

Arikara .... REE

Arizona .. HANO, HOPI, MOKI,
PIMA, TEWA, YUMA;
MOQUI; APACHE

Athapascan Indians ..... DENE,
HUPA, TAKU; LIPAN,
TINNE; APACHE, NAV-
AHO

Aymara .... COLLA

Bolivia ...... ITE, URO, URU;
ITEN, LECA, MOJO, MOXO,
URAN; CHOLO

Brazil ...... GE; YAO; CAME,
DIAU, MAKU, MURA, PURI,
PURU, TUPI; ACROA,
ANDOA, ARAUA, CARIB,
GUANA, SIUSI; ZAPARO

Caddoan Indians .. REE; ADAI;
IONI, CADDO, BIDAI;
PAWNEE

California ...... HUPA, KOSO,
MONO, NOZI, POMO, SERI,
TATU, YANA; MAIDU,
YANAN; SALINA

Canada .... AHT, CREE, DENE,
TAKU; NISKA, TINNE;
SARCEE

Carib .... YAO, TRIO

Carolina .... CATAWBA

Chaco .... TOBA

Chile .... AUCA

Colorado .... UTE

Colombia .... BORO, DUIT,
MUSO, MUZO, TAMA,
TAPA; CHOCO; COLIMA

Costa Rica ...... BOTO VOTO

Cowichan Indians .. NANAIMO

Dakotas .. REE, SIOUX, TETON;
MANDAN, SANTEE;
ARIKARA

Delaware .... LENAPE

Ecuador: ..... CARA (extinct);
ANDOA, ARDAN

Eskimo .... ATKA; ALEUT

Florida: .... CALUSA

Fuegan .... ONA

Great Lakes .... ERIE; HURON

Guatemala ...... MAM; CHOL,
ITZA, IXIL, IXLI, MAYA,
ULVA, VOTO; KICHE, PIPIL

Honduras .... PAYA

Iowa .... FOX, SAC; SAUK

Indiana .... WEA; MIAMI

Iroquoian Indians,
Iroquois: .... ERIE, HURON,
CAYUGA, MOHAWK,
ONEIDA, SENECA

Jalisco: .... CORA

Keresan Indians: . SIA; ACOMA

Kusan .... COOS

Lesser Antilles .... INERI

Mayan Indians: ... MAM, CHOL

Mexico ... MAM, CHOL, CORA,
MAYA, MIXE, PIMA, PIME,
SERI, TECA, TECO, WABI;
AZTEC, OTOMI, SERIA;
TOLTEC

Miami .... WEA

Mississippi ..... TIOU, BILOXI

Montana ...... CROW, HOHE

Muskohegan Indians: . CREEK,
YAMASI, CHOCTAW,
SEMINOLE

Nebraska .... KIOWA

Nevada .... PAIUTE

New Mexico . SIA, PIRO, TANO,
TAOS, TEWA, ZUNI;
ACOMA, KERES, PECOS

New York .... SENECA

Nicaragua . MIXE, RAMA, ULVA

Oklahoma .. KAW, OTO; LOUP,
OTOE; CADDO, CREEK,
KANSA, KIOWA, OSAGE,
PONCA; PAWNEE

Oregon ...... COOS, KUSAN,
MODOC, CHINOOK

Panamint .... KOSO
Panama .... CUNA, CUEVA
Pawnee Indians .... LOUP
Payaguas .... AGAZ
Peru: .... ANDE, ANTI, BORO,
    CANA, INCA, INKA, LAMA,
    PEBA, PIBA, PIRO, YNCA;
    CAMPA, CHIMU, CHOLO,
    COLAN, YUNCA; CHANCA;
    QUICHU
Peru South .... CANA, COLLA,
                        CHANCA
Piman Indians .. CORA, JOVA,
    MAYO, PIMA, XOVA, YAKI,
    YAQUI
Plains Indians ... CREE, CROW;
    KIOWA, OSAGE; PONCA,
    TETON, PAWNEE
Pueblo Indians .. HOPI, MOKI,
    TANO, TAOS, ZUNI;
    KERES, MOQUI
Rio Grande .... TANO
Sacramento Valley ..... YANA
Salishan Indians ..... ATNAH,
                        LUMMI
Shoshonean Indians .... UTE;
    HOPI,   KOSO,   MOKI,
    MONO; MOQUI,   PIUTE;
    UINTA, PAIUTE
Siouan Indians ... KAW, OTO;
    CROW,   IOWA,   OTOE;

KANSA, OMAHA, OSAGE,
PONCA; BILOXI, DAKOTA,
MANDAN; CATAWBA
Sonora .... JOVA, PIMI, SERI
South America (widely
    distributed) .... GES, ONA,
    YAO; LULE, MOXO, PANO,
    PIRO, TOBA;   CARIB,
    INERI; ARAWAK
South Carolina ..... CATAWBA
Tacanan Indians ..... CAVINA
Tanoan .... TEWA
Tapuyan Indians .... GE, GES,
                GHES, ACROA
Texas .... LIPAN
Tierra del Fuego: .... ONA
Tlingit: .... AUK, SITKA
Tupian .... ANTA
Utah: .... UTE
Washington .... HOH, LUMMI,
                        MAKAH
Yucatan .... MAYA
Yukian .... TATU
Yukon .... TAKU
Yuncan .... CHIMU

ARMOR

Head .... **COIF, HELM; ARMET, VISOR; BEAVER, CAMAIL; BASINET, HAUBERK**
Neck .... **GORGET**
Shoulder .... **AILETTE, PAULDRON, EPAULIERE, PASSEGARDE**
Body .... **TACE; CULET, TASSE; CORIUM, GORGET, LORICA, TASSET; CUIRASS, HAUBERK, SURCOAT; BRAGUETTE**
Arm .... **BRASSARD, PALLETTE, VAMBRACE; CUBITIERE, REREBRACE**
Hand .... **GAUNTLET**
Thigh .... **CUISH, TASSE, TUILE; CUISSE, TASSET, TUILLE**
Leg, foot .... **JAMB, JAMBE; GREAVE; CHAUSSE, PEDIEUX; SOLLERET**
Complete suit .... **BARD, MAIL; BARDE**

HERALDRY—HERALDIC TERMS

Heraldic bearings: **BEND, ENTE, FESS, ORLE, FESSE, GIRON, GYRON, LAVER, PHEON; SALTIRE**
Heraldic tinctures:
  gold, **OR**; fur, **PEAN, VAIR, VAIRE**; green, **VERT**; blue, **AZURE**; red, **GULES**; black, **SABLE**; orange, **TENNE**; silver, **ARGENT**; blood-red, **MURREY**; purple, **PURPURE**
attitude of animal
  SEJANT, GARDANT, PASSANT, RAMPANT
ball .... **ROUNDEL**
band ..... **FESS, ORLE, FESSE**
barnacle .... **BREY**
bend .... **COTISE**
bird .... **MARTLET**
circle .... **BEZANT, ANNULET**
colter .... **LAVER**
creature .. **LION, PARD; BISSE, WYVER; CANNET, WYVERN; GRIFFON, MARTLET**
cross .. **CRUX, NOWY, PATY; FLORY, FORMY, PATEE, PATTE; CLECHE; SALTIRE**
curved in middle ...... **NOWY**
curves, made of ..... **NEBULE**
division .... **PALE, PALY**
dog, short-eared ...... **ALANT**
drops, seme of .... **GUTTE**
duck ..... **CANNET, CANETTE**
fillet .... **ORLE**
fish trap .... **WEEL**
flower strewn .... **SEME**

flying in air .... **FLOTANT**
fountain .... **SYKE**
grafted .... **ENTE**
headless .... **ETETE**
horizontal band ......see band
leaves, having .... **POINTE**
lines .... **UNDE, UNDY, URDY, NEBULY**
lozenge ..... **FUSIL, MASCLE**
manacle .... **TIRRET**
pointed .... **URDE**
powdered .... **SEME**
scattered .... **SEME**
sheaf of grain .. **GERB, GERBE**
shield .... **PAVIS**
shield division .... **ENTE**
shield's corner ...... **CANTON**
silver .... **ARGENT**
sitting .... **ASSIS**
snake .... **BISSE**
sown .... **SEME**
spangled .... **SEME**
star-strewn .... **SEME**
strewn .... **SEME**
three parts, divided into
TIERCE
triangle ..... **GIRON, GYRON**
two-winged .... **VOL**
voided escutcheon ...... **ORLE**
walking .... **PASSANT**
wavy .... **ONDE, UNDE, UNDY, UNDEE, NEBULE**
winged .... **VOL, AILE**
wound .... **VULN**
wreath .... **ORLE, TORSE**

194

CHEMICAL ELEMENTS

METALLIC ELEMENTS	NON-METALLIC ELEMENTS	GASEOUS ELEMENTS
TIN	ARGON	ARGON
GOLD	BORON (inert)	CHLORINE
IRON	CARBON	FLUORINE
LEAD	HELIUM	HELIUM
ZINC	IODINE	HYDROGEN
CERIUM	NEON (inert)	KRYPTON
CESIUM	RADON-NITON	NEON (inert)
COBALT	SILICON	NITROGEN
COPPER	XENON	OXYGEN
ERBIUM		XENON
NICKEL		
RADIUM		
SILVER		
SODIUM		
YTTRIUM		

CHEMICAL SYMBOLS

Solver: Important Note—it is not necessary to list for you the chemical symbol of every element. The Chemical Symbol of any element not given below is found simply by writing down the first 2 letters of the name of the element. For example: Ruthenium's chemical symbol is simply RU.

Alabamine, **AB**
antimony, **SB;**
arsenic, **AS;**
boron, **B;**
cadmium, **CD;**
cesium, **CS;**
chlorine, **CL;**
chromium, **CR;**
columbium, **CB;**
copper, **CU;**
curium, **CM;**
gadolinium, **GD;**
gold, **AU;**

hafnium, **HF;**
iron, **FE**
lead, **PB;**
magnesium, **MG;**
manganese, **MN;**
mercury, **HG;**
neodymium, **ND;**
palladium, **PD;**
protoactinium, **PA;**
platinum, **PT;**
radon, **RN;**
rhenium, **RE;**
rubidium, **RB;**

samarium, **SM;**
silver, **AG;**
sodium, **NA;**
strontium, **SR;**
terbium, **TB;**
thallium, **TL;**
thulium, **TM;**
tin, **SN;**
ytterbium, **YB;**
zinc, **ZN;**
zirconium, **ZR;**

BIBLICAL REFERENCES

BOOKS OF THE BIBLE

Names and order of books of the:

OLD TESTAMENT

1 GENESIS	11 KINGS 1	21 ECCLESIASTES	30 AMOS
2 EXODUS	12 KINGS 2	22 SONG OF	31 OBADIAH
3 LEVITICUS	13 CHRONICLES 1	SOLOMON	32 JONAH
4 NUMBERS	14 CHRONICLES 2	23 ISAIAH	33 MICAH
5 DEUTERONOMY	15 EZRA	24 JEREMIAH	34 NAHUM
6 JOSHUA	16 NEHEMIAH	25 LAMENTATIONS	35 HABAKKUK
7 JUDGES	17 ESTHER	26 EZEKIEL	36 ZEPHANIAH
8 RUTH	18 JOB	27 DANIEL	37 HAGGAI
9 SAMUEL 1	19 PSALMS	28 HOSEA	38 ZECHARIAH
10 SAMUEL 2	20 PROVERBS	29 JOEL	39 MALACHI

Names and order of books of the:

NEW TESTAMENT

1 MATTHEW	9 GALATIANS	15 TIMOTHY 1	23 JOHN 1
2 MARK	10 EPHESIANS	16 TIMOTHY 2	24 JOHN 2
3 LUKE	11 PHILIPPIANS	17 TITUS	25 JOHN 3
4 JOHN	12 COLOSSIANS	18 PHILEMON	26 JUDE
5 THE ACTS	13 THESSALON-	19 HEBREWS	27 REVELATION
6 ROMANS	IANS 1	20 JAMES	
7 CORINTHIANS 1	14 THESSALON-	21 PETER 1	
8 CORINTHIANS 2	IANS 2	22 PETER 2	

BIBLICAL PROPHETS

AMOS (minor), ESAY, EZRA, JOEL (minor), HOSEA (minor), JONAH (minor), MICAH (minor), MOSES, DANIEL (major), NAHUM (minor), ELISHA, HAGGAI (minor), ISAIAH (major), EZEKIEL (major), JEREMIAH (major)

BIBLICAL PATRIARCHS

REU; ADAM, EBER, ENOS, NOAH, SETH, SHEM; ISAAC, JACOB, JARED, NAHOR, PELEG, SERUG, TERAH; LAMECH

BIBLICAL RULERS

OG; ASA (Judah), GOG, IRA; AGAG, AHAB, AHAZ, AMON, ELAH, JEHU, OMRI, SAUL; CYRUS, DAVID, DEBIR, HEROD, HIRAM, JORAM, NADAB, PEKAH, PIRAM, REZIN, SIHON, ZIMRI; ABIJAH, BAASHA. CAESAR, DARIUS, HEZION, HOSHEA, JAPHIA, JOSHUA, JOSIAH, JOTHAM, UZZIAH

BIBLICAL PEOPLES—TRIBES

DAN, GOG; ANAK, ARAD, CUSH, EMIM, MOAB, PHUD, PHUT (o.t.); ARKITE, HAMITE, HIVITE, KENITE, SEMITE, SHELAH, SINITE; EDOMITE, HITTITE, LEHABIM, MOABITE, REPHAIM

BIBLICAL PLACES

City . DAN, GATH, GAZA, ZOAR; BABEL, EKRON, SODOM; HEBRON

Country .... EDOM, ENON, SEBA; SHEBA

Hill, Jerusalem's .... ZION

Kingdom .... ELAM, MOAB; SAMARIA

Land .... NOD

Land of plenty .... GOSHEN

Mt. HOR, EBAL, NAIN, NEBO, PEOR; HOREB, SEIR, SINA, SINAI, TABOR; ARARAT, GIL-EAD, HERMON

Place .... ENON, AENON; JORDAN, SHILOH

Pool .... SILOAM

Region .. ARAM, EDAR; BASHAN

Town ...... CANA (1st miracle), NAIN (miracle site); BETHEL

River .... ARNON, JORDAN

BIBLICAL MEN

OG, UZ; ARA, DAN, ELI, GOG, HAM, IRA, LOT, NUN, URI; ABEL, AMOS, BOAZ, CAIN, CUSH, DOEG, EBAL, ENON, ENOS, ESAU, HETH, IRAD, JADA, JEHU, JOAB, KISH, LEVI, MASH, MOAB, OBAL, OBED, OMAR, OREB, OZEM, SETH, SODI, ULAM, UNNI, URIA; AARON (high priest), ABIAH, ABIEL, AHIRA, AMASA, ANNAS, CALEB, CHUZA, ENOCH, HAMAN, HARAN, HIRAM, HOHAM, IBZAN, ISAAC, JACOB, JAMES, JARED, MASSA, MOREH, NABAL, NAHBI, NAHOR, OPHIR, REZON, SACAR, TERAH, URIAH, ZAHAM; SAMSON; ANANIAS, ISHMAEL

BIBLICAL WOMEN

EVE; ADAH, JAEL, LEAH, MARY, RUTH; DINAH, EGLAH, HAGAR, JULIA, JUNIA, LYDIA, MERAB, NAOMI, PHEBE, RAHAB, SARAH, SARAI, SHUAH, TAMAR; ABITAL, BILHAH, DORCAS, ESTHER, HAN-NAH, HOGLAH, MAACAH, MAHLAH, MICHAL, MILCAH, MIRIAM, PERSIS, RACHEL, RIZPAH, SALOME, VASHTI, ZILLAH, ZILPAH; ABIGAIL, HAMUTAL

BIBLICAL NAMES

ED, ER; IRI, NER, ONO, REI, TOI; ABIA, ADER, ANER, ANIM, ASOM, DARA, ELON, ENOS, IRAD, IVAH, REBA; ABIAM, AHIRA, AMASA, ASEAS

GODS (DEITIES), GODDESSES AND MYTHOLOGY

ASSYRIAN GODS
ANAT (sky), ASUR or ASSUR (war)

BABYLONIAN GODS
Chief gods: EA, ABU or ANU, BEL
EA (chief), ZU (wind), ABU or ANU (chief, sky, sun), BEL (chief), HEA (see EA), IRA (war), SIN (moon), UTU (sun), ADAD or ADDA or ADDU (wind, storm), APSU (chaos), ENKI (see EA), ENZU (see SIN), IRRA (war), NABU or NEBO (wisdom), UTUG (sun), DAGAN (earth), ETANA (eagle rider), SIRIS (alcoholic drinks), BABBAR (sun), SHAMASH (sun)

BABYLONIAN GODDESSES
AI or AYA (consort of Shamash), ERUA (mother), NINA (watery deep), NANAI (daughter of Anu), ISTAR or ISHTAR (chief, love)

BRYTHONIC GODDESS
DON (ancestress of gods)

CELTIC GODS—GODDESS
ANA, ANU, DANA, DANU (mother, queen), LER (sea), LUG, LUGH (light, sun), DAGDA (chief)

CYMRIC GODS
GWYN, LLEU, LLEW (solar)

EGYPTIAN GODS
RA (sun), SU (solar deity), BES (evil, pleasure), GEB (earth), KEB (earth), MIN (procreation), SEB (earth), SET (evil), SHU (see SU), TEM or TUM (sun), AANI (dog-headed ape, sacred to Thoth), AMEN (king), AMON (sun and king), AMUN (king), ATMU or ATUM (sun), BESA (see BES), HAPI (the Nile as a god), KHEM (see MIN), MENT (falcon-headed), PTAH (Memphis god), SETH (evil), SOBK (crocodile-headed), AMMON (see AMEN), HORUS (hawk-headed), MENTU (see MENT), SEBEK (see SOBK), THOTH (wisdom, magic), OSIRIS (underworld), SERAPIS (see OSIRIS)

EGYPTIAN GODDESSES
MA (same as MAAT), MUT (Amen's wife), NUT (heavens), ANTA, APET (maternity), BAST (cat- or lion-headed), BUTO (serpent), ISIS (cow-headed, Horus' mother), MAAT (truth, justice), SATI (queen), ATHOR (see HATHOR), HATHOR (love, mirth, cow-headed)

EGYPTIAN MYTH

BA (soul of man), KA (body of man), NU (chaos), AKH (spirit of man), NUN (see NU), APIS (sacred bull), ATEN (solar disk), DUAT (see AMENTI), HAPI (Nile or Amenti's jinnee), AMENTI (underworld region)

GREEK GODS

DIS (underworld), PAN (field, flocks, forest), ZAN (old name for Zeus), ARES (war, Eris' brother), EROS (love), ZEUS (chief of Olympian gods), COMUS (mirth and revelry), EURUS (southeast wind), HADES (underworld), KOMOS (see COMUS), MOMUS (ridicule), PLUTO (underworld), AEOLUS (wind), APOLLO (sun, youth), AUSTER (south wind), BOREAS (north wind), CRONUS (a Titan, Rhea's spouse; harvest), HELIOS (sun), HERMES (herald), KRONOS (see CRONUS), NEREUS (sea), PLUTUS (wealth), TRITON (sea), BACCHUS (wine), POSEIDON (sea)

GREEK GODDESSES

GE (earth, mother of Titans), ARA (destruction, retribution, vengeance), ATE (discord, mischief, infatuation), EIR (healing), EOS (dawn), ALEA (ATHENA), CORA (see KORE), DICE or DIKE (one of Horae), ENYO (Ares' mother, war), ERIS (discord, sister of Ares), GAEA or GAIA (see GE), HEBE (youth), HERA (queen), HORA (one of Horae), KORE (vegetation), LEDA (Tyndareus' wife), NIKE (victory), RHEA (mother of gods, wife of Kronos), UPIS, ARTEMIS, HORAE (three goddesses of seasons), IRENE (peace), METIS (Zeus' first wife), MOIRA (fate or Fates), ATHENA (wisdom), CLOTHO (a Fate, thread spinner), CYBELE (nature), EIRENE (see IRENE), HECATE (moon, magic), MOERAE (see MOIRA), PALLAS (wisdom), SELENA and SELENE (moon), ARTEMIS (moon, woods, nature), ATROPOS (one of the Fates, thread cutter), DEMETER (grain, agriculture), CHLORIS (flowers), NEMESIS (revenge), LACHESIS (one of the Fates, thread length), APHRODITE (love)

GREEK MYTH

IO (Zeus' beloved changed to a heifer), INO (Cadmus' daughter), PAN (field, flocks, forest), ANAX (one of Dioscuri), AUGE (Arcadian princess), CEYX (Halcyone's husband turned into kingfisher), CLIO (Muse of History), FAUN (see PAN), IDAS (hero, killed Castor), IOLE (Hercules' captive), LETO (Apollo's mother), MAIA (Hermes' mother), OTUS (giant killed by Apollo), ALTIS (sacred grove, Olympic games), ATLAS (held up heavens), CREON (Oedipus' brother-in-law), DIONE (Aphrodite's mother), ENEAS (Troy's defender), ERATO (Clio's sister), HADES (underworld), HELLE (fell into Hellespont with golden fleece), HYDRA (9-headed monster), MINOS (king), NIOBE (weeping stone), SATYR (part-horse demigod), THEIA (Hyperion's sister, wife), ADONIS (beautiful youth), AENEAS (see ENEAS), AGENOR (Trojan warrior), ALECTO (a Fury), DAPHNE (Apollo's nymph turned into tree), EUROPA (carried off by Zeus in form of white bull), HECTOR (Trojan warrior), NEREID (sea nymph to Poseidon), NESTOR (wise king, fought Troy), THETIS (Achilles' mother), TITHON (see TITHONUS), TRITON (sea demigod,

Poseidon's son), **URANIA** (astronomy), **ARIADNE** (Theseus' love), **ATHAMAS** (Ino's husband), **CENTAUR** (half man, half horse), **CYCLOPS** (1-eyed giant), **ERINYES**, (avenging spirits), **EUTERPE** (Muse of Music), **SILENUS** (woodland deity, horse-goat-human), **ATALANTA** (picked up golden apples—lost the race), **TARTARUS** (infernal regions), **TITHONUS** (immortal king of Troy, Eos' favorite), **TISIPHONE** (one of Erinyes)
The Gorgons: **MEDUSA, STHENO, EURYALE**
The Graces: **AGLAIA, THALIA**
The Titans or Titanesses: primeval deities: **GAEA** or **GE** (mother of Titans). **URANUS** (father of Titans). Titans: **RHEA, COEUS, CREUS, THEIA, CRONUS** or **KRONOS, PHOEBE, THEMIS**

HINDU GODS
KA (unknown), **AGNI** (fire), **AKAL** (immortal), **CIVA** (see SIVA), **DEVA** or **DEWA** (divine being), **KAMA** (love), **RAMA** (incarnation of Vishnu), **SIVA** (supreme), **VAYU** (wind), **YAMA** (judge of dead), **BHAGA** (love), **DYAUS** (heaven, sky), **VISHNU** (supreme), **KRISHNA** (avatar of Vishnu)

HINDU GODDESSES
SRI (beauty, wealth, luck, Vishnu's wife), **UMA** (splendor), **VAC** (speech), **DEVI** (any divinity, Siva's consort), **KALI** (evil), **SHRI** (see SRI), **USAS** (dawn), **VACH** (see VAC), **SHREE** (see SRI), **MATRIS** (mothers), **LAKSHMI** (see SRI)

HINDU MYTH
BANA (1,000-arm giant), **KALI** (tongue of Agni), **KETU** (Rahu's tail), **NAGA** (Vishnu's serpent), **RAHU** (dragon, swallows sun), **USHA** (Bana's daughter)

INCA GOD
INTI (sun)

IRISH—see **CELTIC**

NORSE GODS
ER (war), **TY** (see TIU), **VE** (Odin's brother, slayed Ymir), **EAR** (see ER), **LOK** (see LOKI), **TIU** (sky, war, Tiwaz), **TIW** (see TIU), **TYR** (sky, war), **ULL** (bow skill), **VAN** (sea), **ZIO** (sky), **ZIU** (see ZIO), **FREY** (fertility), **HLER** (sea), **HOTH** (blind god), **LOKE** or **LOKI** (discord, mischief), **ODIN** chief god, war, wisdom, slayed Ymir), **THOR** (thunder), **TYRR** (war), **ULLR** (see ULL), **VALE** (see VALI), **VALI** (Odin's son), **VANS** (see VANIR), **VILI** (Odin's brother), **AEGIR** (sea), **AESIR** (chief), **ALCIS** (twin gods), **BALDR** (see BALDER), **BRAGE** or **BRAGI** (poetry), **DONAR** (see THOR), **HODER** or **HOTHR** (see HOTH), **VANIR** (early race of gods), **WODAN** or **WODEN** or **WOTAN** (see ODIN), **BALDER** or **BALDUR** (light)
The Aesir or chief gods: **TIU, TYR, ULL, FREY, LOKI, ODIN, THOR, VALI, BRAGI, DONAR, WODEN, BALDER**

NORSE GODDESSES

EIR (healing), HEL (Loki's daughter, underworld, dead), RAN (sea, death, wife of Aegir), SIF (Thor's wife), URD (destiny), VOR (betrothal), ERDA (earth), FREA or FRIA (see FRIGG), GERD (Frey's wife), HELA (see HEL), NORN (fate), RIND (Odin's wife, Vali's mother), SAGA (golden beaker), URTH (see URD), FREYA (love, beauty), FRIGG (Odin's wife), NANNA (flowers), NORNA or NORNS (see NORN), FREYJA (see FREYA)

NORSE MYTH

ASK (see ASKR), DIS (female spirit), ASKR (first man), ATLI (king), EGIL (story hero), GARM (Hel's watchdog, slays Tyr), GERI (Odin's wolf), IDUN (Bragi's wife), MARA (nightmare demon), NATT or NOTT (night), WATE (giant), YMIR or YMER ("rime-cold giant"), EGILL (see EGIL), MIMIR (giant), ASGARD (abode of gods)

PHOENICIAN GODDESS

ASTARTE (fertility, love)

ROMAN GODS

DIS (underworld), SOL (sun), AMOR (love), FAUN (field, herds, half goat), JOVE (chief god), MARS (war), MORS (death), COMUS (mirth, joy), CUPID (love), EURUS (southeast wind), KOMOS (see COMUS), MANES (spirits of dead, gods of underworld), ORCUS (dead), APOLLO (sun, music), AUSTER (south wind), BOREAS (north wind), FAUNUS (rural deity), VULCAN (fire), NEPTUNE (sea)

ROMAN GODDESSES

NOX or NYX (night), OPS (harvest, plenty), DIAN (moon, chase, woods), IRIS (rainbow, Zeus' messenger), JUNO (queen), LUNA (moon), MAIA (Vulcan's consort), NONA (Fate), SPES (hope), CERES (earth, grain, agriculture, vegetation), DIANA (see DIAN), EPONA (horses), FIDES (faith), FAUNA (field), FLORA (flowers), MORTA (a Fate), PARCA (a Fate), SALUS (prosperity), TERRA (earth), VENUS (love), VESTA (hearth), ANNONA (crops), AURORA (dawn), DECUMA (a Fate), PARCAE (the Fates), VACUNA (Sabine huntress)
The Fates or Parcae: NONA, MORTA, DECUMA

TEUTONIC GODS—see NORSE GODS

TEUTONIC GODDESSES—see NORSE GODDESSES

VEDIC GODS—see HINDU GODS

VEDIC GODDESSES—see HINDU GODDESSES

WELSH GOD

DYLAN

FIRST AND LAST NAMES

(common to crossword puzzles)

You often find in crossword puzzles definitions like "Writer Aldous ———" or "——— Pavlova." The following list contains the most commonly used names, first names and last names. The part of the name which is usually given in the definition is here in light-face type, arranged alphabetically. The rest of the person's name follows in bold-face type.

Aaron .... **BURR**	Anita .... **LOOS**	Billy . **ROSE, SUNDAY**
Abbott .... **BUD**	Anna .. **CASE, HELD,**	Blanche ..... **RING,**
Adams .... **MAUDE**	**STEN, NEAGLE**	**SWEET**
Addams ...... **JANE**	Anthony .... **EDEN,**	Blandish ... **SERENA**
Adelina ..... **PATTI**	**SUSAN, TUDOR**	Blas ...... **GIL, RUY**
Adolph ...... **OCHS**	Anton ...... **DOLIN**	Bloch .... **RAY**
Adolphe .... **ADAM**	Anya .... **SETON**	Blum .... **LEON**
Adoree ..... **RENEE**	Arden ... **EVE, TONI**	Blyth .... **ANN**
Aherne ..... **BRIAN**	Arnaz .... **DESI**	Bohr .... **NIELS**
Alan .. **HALE, LADD,**	Arnold .... **HAP**	Boleyn ...... **ANNE**
PATON, REED	Arsene ..... **LUPIN**	Bolger .... **RAY**
Albani ...... **EMMA**	Artemus ..... **WARD**	Bolivar ..... **SIMON**
Alban .... **BERG**	Arthur Conan.**DOYLE**	Bonar .... **LAW**
Albert ..... **ANKER,**	Ataturk ... **KEMAL**	Bonheur ..... **ROSA**
CAMUS	Attlee ... **CLEMENT**	Bowman .... **LEE**
Aldo .... **RAY**	Auguste .... **RODIN**	Boyd .... **ORR**
Aldous .... **HUXLEY**	Autry .... **GENE**	Bradley ..... **OMAR**
Alexis ...... **KIVI**	Axel .... **GADE**	Brendel .... **EL**
Alexander	Bagnold ...... **ENID**	Bret ...... **HARTE**
FLEMING, POPE,	Bailey ...... **PEARL**	Brigham ... **YOUNG**
SEROV	Bainter .... **FAY**	Brodie ...... **STEVE**
Alexandre .. **DUMAS**	Bambi ...... **LINN**	Brown ... **JOE EVAN**
Alfred ..... **DRAKE,**	Bampton ..... **ROSE**	Broz .... **TITO**
LUNT	Barkley .... **ALBEN**	Bruce ..... **CABOT**
Alfred B. ... **NOBEL**	Bartok .... **BELA**	Brynner .... **YUL**
Alighieri .... **DANTE**	Barton ..... **CLARA**	"Buffalo Bill" . **CODY**
Allegra ...... **KENT**	Basie .... **COUNT**	Bull .... **OLE**
Allen ...... **ETHAN,**	Baxter ...... **ANNE**	Burl .... **IVES**
IDA, MEL	Bayes .... **NORA**	Burns .... **BOB**
Allison ...... **FRAN**	Beerbohm .... **MAX**	Burr .... **AARON**
Allyson ...... **JUNE**	Beery .... **NOAH**	Burrows .... **ABE**
Alois .... **LANG**	Begley .... **ED**	Byington ... **SPRING**
Alonzo ...... **CANO**	Ben .... **HOGAN**	Cabeza de ... **VACA**
Ambler .... **ERIC**	Bennett ...... **CERF**	Calloway ..... **CAB**
Ambrose ... **BIERCE,**	Benzell ...... **MIMI**	Cameron ...... **ROD**
FLEMING	Berg ...... **ALBAN**	Camillo Benso
Amon ..... **CARTER**	Berger ...... **ERNA**	**CAVOUR**
Amundsen .. **ROALD**	Bernard .... **SHAW**	Canada .... **LEE**
Anatole ... **FRANCE**	Bernhardt .. **SARAH**	Cantor .... **IDA**
Andersen ... **HANS**	Bernie .... **BEN**	Capek ...... **KAREL**
Andre .... **GIDE**	Bert .... **LAHR**	Carl .... **CORI**
Andrews .... **DANA**	Best .... **EDNA**	Carl Marie von
Andy ...... **DEVINE**	Bette ...... **DAVIS**	**WEBER**
Aneurin Bevan . **NYE**	Betty .... **FIELD**	Carney .... **ART**
Angelo ... **GIOTTO,**	Bevin ..... **ERNEST**	Carnera .... **PRIMO**
MOSSO, PATRI	Billings ...... **JOSH**	Carrel ..... **ALEXIS**

Carrie Chapman ...... CATT
Carrie Jacobs . BOND
Carrillo .... LEO
Carroll . BAKER, LEO
Carter ...... AMON
Case .... ANNA
Cassals ..... PABLO
Castle ...... IRENE,
      VERNON
Cather ..... WILLA
Catherine .... PARR
Cavalieri .... LINA
Celeste ..... HOLM
Champion .. GOWER
Chaney .... LON
Channing ... CAROL
Chaplin ..... LETA,
      OONA
Chapman ..... CEIL
Charisse ...... CYD
Charles .... BEARD,
   BUSH, DANA,
   ELIOT, GREY,
   LAMB, LEVER,
   READE
Charlie ..... CHASE
Charlotte . BRONTE,
      CORDAY
Chase .... ILKA
Chekhov ... ANTON
Chic .... SALE
Christie ... AGATHA
Claire .... INA
Clare . BOOTH LUCE
Clarence ..... DAY
Clark .... MARK
Claude .... MONET,
      RAINS
Clemens .... MARK
      TWAIN
Cleveland .. AMORY
Clifton ...... WEBB
Cobb ...... LEE, TY
Cole .. NAT "KING"
Columbo .... RUSS
Conde .... NAST
Connelly .... MARC
Conquest ..... IDA
Conway ..... SHIRL
Cordell ...... HULL
Cornel .... WILDE
Correll, C. J. . ANDY
Coty .... RENE
Count ...... BASIE
Coward ...... NOEL
Cox .... WALLY
Crane .... HART
Cregar ..... LAIRD
Cronyn ..... HUME
Curie .. EVE, MARIE

D.D.E. .... IKE
Dailey .... DAN
Dale .... EVANS
Daniel ...... DEFOE
Davis .... JEFF
Day ...... LARAINE
de l'Enclos . NINON
de Leon .... PONCE
de Maupassant . GUY
Deborah ..... KERR
Deems .... TAYLOR
Delmar ...... VINA
Dennis .. DAY, KING
Descartes .... RENE
De Valera .. EAMON
Devine ...... ANDY
Dewey .... TOM
Dionne .. ANNETTE,
   CECILE, EMELIE,
   MARIA, OLIVA,
   YVONNE
Dolin ...... ANTON
Donald ...... COOK,
   CRISP, MEEK,
   NOVIS
Donlevy .... BRIAN
Donna ...... REED
Dorfmann ... ANIA
Doris . DAY, DOLON,
      DUKE
Dorothy . DIX, GISH,
      STONE
Dors .... DIANA
Doubleday .. ABNER
Doyle ..... ARTHUR
      CONAN
Drew .... ELLEN
Duke .... DORIS
Dumas .... AINE
Duncan ..... SARA,
      TODD
Dunn .... EMMA
Dunne ...... IRENE
Durocher . LEO, LIP,
      LIPPY
Duryea .... DAN
Dvorak .... ANTON
Dwight .... MOODY
Eakers .... IRA
Eames ...... EMMA
Eamon de .. VALERA
Early ...... STEVE
Eartha .... KITT
Eckener ..... HUGO
Eddie .... FOY
Edgar .... POE
Edith . ADAMS, DAY,
      PIAF
Edna . BEST, FERBER,
      MILLAY
Edouard .... MANET

Eduard ...... BENES
Eduard ...... LALO
Edvard ...... GRIEG
Edward ..... ELGAR,
      GAY, SILL
Edward Everett. HALE
Edwards ...... GUS
Edwin ..... BOOTH,
      WEEKS
Eggerth ... MARTA
Egon .... PETRI
Ekberg ..... ANITA
Eleanor ... STEBER
Eleanora ..... DUSE
Elias .... HOWE
Elihu .... ROOT
Ellen .... TERRY
Ellington .... DUKE
Ellsworth .... VINES
Emerson .... FAYE,
      RALPH WALDO
Emile .... ZOLA
Emily ..... BRONTE,
      POST
Emma ...... EAMES
En-lai .... CHOU
Enoch ...... ARDEN
Enrico ...... FERMI
Erik .... SATIE
Erikson .... LIEF
Ernest ...... BEVIN,
      SETON
Ernie ... FORD, PYLE
Errol .... LEON
Ethan ..... ALLEN,
      FROME
Ethel ..... WATERS
Ethelbert ... NEVIN
Eugene . DEBS, FIELD
Eva .... GABOR
Eva Marie ... SAINT
Evans .... DALE
Ewell .... TOM
Eydie ...... GORME
Eyre .... JANE
Ezra ...... POUND,
      STONE
F.P.A. ..... ADAMS
Fabrizi ...... ALDO
Ferber ...... EDNA
Ferdinand ... FOCH
Fernando ... LAMAS
Ferrer .. JOSE, MEL
Filippino ... LIPPI
Fitzgerald .... ELLA
Fitzhugh ...... LEE
Florence ... BATES,
      REED
Foch .... NINA
Ford .... EDSEL,
   ERNIE, HENRY

203

Foscolo ...... **UGO**
Fournier ... **ALAIN**
Fra Filippo ... **LIPPI**
Frances ...... **ALDA**
Francis .... **BACON, DRAKE**
Francis Scott ... **KEY**
Francesco ... **NITTI**
Franchot .... **TONE**
Franck ..... **CESAR**
Francoise ... **SAGAN**
Frank ..... **BACON, BUCK, CAPRA, CRAVEN, FAY**
Frankie .... **CARLE, LAINE**
Frans .... **HALS**
Franz ...... **LEHAR**
Frome ..... **ETHAN**
Gabor . **EVA, MAGDA, ZSA ZSA**
Gale . **STORM, ZONA**
Gam .... **RITA**
Gardner . **AVA, ERLE**
Gavin .... **MUIR**
George .... **ADE, BROWN, CLARK, CUSTER, DEWEY, ELIOT, GOBEL, OHM , PATTON, SAND**
George Bernard **SHAW**
Geraldine .... **PAGE**
Gershwin ...... **IRA**
Gertrude .... **BERG, STEIN**
Gil .... **BLAS**
Giuseppe .... **BELLI**
Glasgow ..... **ELLEN**
Glenn ...... **FORD**
Gluck ...... **ALMA**
Gorin .... **IGOR**
Gosden, F. F. . **AMOS**
Gould .... **JAY**
Graham ..... **BILLY**
Grant ...... **WOOD**
Gray ... **ASA, ZANE**
Greco .... **JOSE**
Gregor .... **MENDEL**
Griffith ..... **ANDY**
Gueden .... **HILDE**
Guido .... **RENI**
Guiseppe .... **VERDI**
Guitry ...... **SACHA**
Gustavus ... **SWIFT**
Guy ...... **MOLLET**
Gypsy Rose .... **LEE**
H.S.T. .... **TRUMAN**
Hagen .... **UTA**
Hal .... **MARCH**

Hale .... **ALAN**
Hallstrom .... **IVAR**
Hals .... **FRANS**
Halsey .... **BULL**
Hansson ...... **OLA**
Harold . **TEEN, UREY**
Harriet Beecher **STOWE**
Harris .. **JOEL, PHIL**
Hart ...... **CRANE**
Harte .... **BRET**
Havoc .... **JUNE**
Hayward .... **SUSAN**
Hayworth .... **RITA**
Hazel ...... **SCOTT**
Heifetz .... **JASCHA**
Heinrich .... **HEINE**
Held .... **ANNA**
Henri ..... **PETAIN**
Henrik ..... **IBSEN**
Henry .... **HUDSON**
Herbert ..... **ALAN**
Herbert George **WELLS**
Hernando de .. **SOTO**
Hess .... **MYRA**
Heywood .. **BROUN**
Hobson .... **LAURA**
Hogan ...... **BEN**
Holt .... **TIM**
Holtz .... **LOU**
Horace ..... **MANN**
Horne .... **LENA**
Houston ...... **SAM**
Howard ..... **PYLE**
Howe .... **ELIAS**
Hubbel .... **CARL**
Hugh ..... **LAING**
Hunter .. **IAN, KIM, TAB, EVAN**
Hus .... **JAN**
Hyerdahl .... **THOR**
Ian ...... **HUNTER**
Ida Bailey ... **ALLEN**
Igor .... **GORIN**
Ilka .... **CHASE**
Immanuel ... **KANT**
Ina .... **CLAIRE**
Inonu ...... **ISMET**
Irene ...... **CASTLE, DUNNE, RICH**
Iris .... **MANN**
Irving ..... **BERLIN**
Irvin S. ..... **COBB**
Isaac .... **STERN**
Ismet ...... **INONU**
Italo .... **TAJO**
Ives .... **BURL**
J. Carrol .... **NAISH**
Jack ..... **LONDON, OAKIE, PARR,**

WEBB
Jacob .... **RIIS**
Jagger ..... **DEAN**
James .... **BARRIE, BARTON, BEARD, FARLEY, HILL, AGEE, WATT**
James Montgomery **FLAGG**
Jan .. **HUS, PEERCE, SMUTS, STEEN**
Jane **AUSTEN, COWL, EYRE**
Janet ...... **BLAIR, GAYNOR, LEIGH**
Janis .... **PAIGE**
Jannings ...... **EMIL**
Jay .... **GOULD**
Jean-Paul .. **MARAT**
Jeanmaire ... **RENEE**
Jeanne ..... **CRAIN, EAGELS**
Jeffreys ..... **ANNE**
Jenkins .... **ALLEN**
Jenny .... **LIND**
Jerome .... **KERN**
Jessica ..... **TANDY**
Jimmy ..... **SAVO**
Joel Chandler **HARRIS**
Johan .... **SARS**
Johann Sebastian **BACH**
John.**AGAR, ALDEN, BROWN, DALY, DEWEY, DREW, GAY, GOLDEN, HAY, KEATS, LITEL, LODER, LUND, RAITT**
John Godfrey . **SAXE**
John Philip . **SOUSA**
John Wilkes . **BOOTH**
Johnnie ...... **RAY**
Johnny ... **MERCER**
Johnson . **OSA, VAN**
Jolson .... **AL**
Jonas .... **SALK**
Jonathan .... **SWIFT**
Jonson .... **BEN**
Johnston .... **ALVA**
Jose .... **GRECO**
Juanita ...... **HALL**
Jobal .... **EARLY**
Juhani .... **AHO**
Jules ...... **VERNE**
Julia Ward .. **HOWE**
Julie ...... **ADAMS**
June ...... **HAVER, HAVOC, LANG**
Kaltenborn .. **HANS**

Karel ..... CAPEK
Karl .... MARX
Kay .... STARR
Kaye .... NORA
Kazan .... ELIA
Keith .... IAN
Kelly . GENE, EMMET
Kenton ...... STAN
Khachaturian .ARAM
Khan .. AGA, ALI,
ALY
Kibbee .... GUY
Kiepura ...... JAN
Kim .... HUNTER
Kitchell .... IVA
Knight .... ERIC
Koussevitzky . SERGE
Kovacs ...... ERNIE
Kurt .... ADLER
Kyser .... KAY
Lafcadio ... HEARN
Lagerkvist .... PAR
Lagerlof .... SELMA
Lahr .... BERT
Laing ...... HUGH
Lanchester ... ELSA
Lange ...... HOPE
Lanny .... ROSS
Lardner ..... RING
Lauck, Chester . LUM
Laura Hope . CREWS
Laurel .... STAN
Laurence .. STERNE,
OLIVIER
Laurie ...... PIPER
Law .... BONAR
Lazarus ..... EMMA
Learned ..... HAND
Lee . OMA, CANADA
Le Gallienne ... EVA
Lehmann ... LOTTE
Lehr .... LEW
Lena .... HORNE
Leslie ...... BANKS
Levant ..... OSCAR
Levene ...... SAM
Levenson ..... SAM
Lew .. AYRES, CODY
Lewin, Liliane . LILO
Lewis . ADA, JOHN,
LAWES, STONE,
TED
"Light-horse Harry"
LEE
Lillian . GISH, ROTH
Lillie ... BEA, PEEL
Lily .... PONS
Linkletter .... ART
Linn .... BAMBI
Liszt ...... FRANZ
Lollobrigida .. GINA

Lombardo ..... GUY
Long .... HUEY
Loos .... ANITA
Loren ..... SOPHIA
Lorre .... PETER
Louise ..... ANITA
Lowell .... AMY
Lucas .. FOSS, SCOTT
Lucrezia ..... BORI
Ludwig ...... EMIL
Lugosi .... BELA
Luise ...... RAINER
Lupescu ... MAGDA
Lupino .... IDA
Lynn .... BARI
Lyons .... GENE
Mack .... TED
MacMahon .. ALINE
Madame de .. STAEL
Madge ..... EVANS
Magnani ..... ANNA
Major ..... BOWES
Malbin ... ELAINE
Mann IRIS, HORACE
Marco ...... POLO
Maria ..... CALLAS
Marie ...... CURIE
Mario ...... LANZA
Mark ...... CLARK
Markey ...... ENID
Marner ..... SILAS
Marquette .... PERE
Marquis ...... DON
Marshall ..... ALAN
Martha HYER, RAYE
Martini ..... NINO
Mary .... ASTOR,
GARDEN, URE
Mary Baker .. EDDY
Marx ..... CHICO,
HARPO, KARL
Masaryk JAN, TOMAS
Mason ..... JAMES,
PAMELA
Massey CURT, ILONA
Mata .... HARI
Maude .... ADAMS
Maurice .... RAVEL
Maxwell ..... ELSA
Maynard ..... KEN
McCarey ..... LEO
McCoy .... TIM
Meg .... MUNDY
Mel .. ALLEN, OTT,
TORME
Menken.ADA, HELEN
Merimee PROSPER
Meriwether .. LEWIS
Merkel .... UNA
Merman ..... ETHEL
Meyerson .... BESS

Milton ...... CROSS
Miranda .... ISA
Mischa ..... AUER,
ELMAN
Mitzi ...... GREEN
Mollet .... GUY
Montagu ..... LOVE
Montez ..... LOLA,
MARIA
Moorhead .. AGNES
Morgana FATA, NINA
Morini ...... ERICA
Mostel ...... ZERO
Mowbray .... ALAN
Mundt ...... KARL
Munson .... ONA
Murray .. DON, JAN,
KEN, MAE
Musial .... STAN
Myra .... HESS
Nahum .... TATE
Nazimova ... ALLA
Ned ...... SPARKS
Neilson .... ADA
Nelson ...... GENE,
MILES
Nethersole ... OLGA
Nicholas .... AMATI
Nicholas Murray
BUTLER
Nikolaidi ... ELENA
Niels .... BOHR
Noel ..... COWARD
Nora . BAYES, KAYE
Novello ..... IVOR
O. Henry . PORTER
O'Casey ..... SEAN
O'Connor ..... UNA
Ogden . NASH, REID
Oley ...... SPEAKS
Oliver ..... HARDY
Olsen .... OLE
Oma .... LEE
Onegin .... EUGEN
O'Neill ..... OONA
Opie .... READ
Oren .... ROOT
Orlando .... LASSO
Oscar .... LEVANT,
WILDE
Ott .... MEL
Page .... PATTI
Paine .... TOM
Palmer LILLI
Parker ...... FESS
Pastor ...... TONY
Pasternak ... BORIS
Paton ...... ALAN
Paul ..... DRAPER,
MUNI, POTTER
Pauline ...... LORD

Pauling ..... LINUS
Pavlova .... ANNA
Peerce .... JAN
"Peewee" .... REESE
Peggy .... WOOD
Pendleton .... NAT
Peron . EVA, EVITA,
JUAN
Peter ...... ARNO,
LORRE, MUNCH
Petina .... IRRA
Petri .... EGON
Philip .. HALE, NERI
Picon ...... MOLLY
Pierre ...... CURIE,
LOTI
Pieter ..... HOOCH
Pinky .... LEE
Polo .... MARCO
Ponce de .... LEON
Pons .... LILY
Ponselle ..... ROSA
Porter ...... COLE
Pound ...... EZRA
Preminger .... OTTO
Priscilla ... ALDEN,
MULLEN
Proust .... MARCEL
Pyle .... ERNIE
Rainer ...... LUISE
Raines .... ELLA
Rains ..... CLAUDE
Ralph Adams . CRAM
Rathbone .... BASIL
Ray .... ALDO,
BLOCH, NOBLE
Read .... OPIE
Rebecca ..... WEST
Red, the ..... ERIC
Reed ALAN, DONNA
Reese .. "PEEWEE"
Regan ...... PHIL
Rehan .... ADA
Reinhardt .... MAX
Rene .... COTY
Rex .... BEACH,
BELL, STOUT
Rhodes ...... CECIL
Richard .... BYRD,
CONTE, DIX,
HOWE, LONG
Rip .... TORN
Rita .... GAM
Robb .... INEZ
Robert .... ALDA,
BURNS, DONAT,
FULTON, PEEL,
TAFT
Rodzinski .. ARTUR
Roger ..... BACON,
PRYOR, RICO

Romain .. ROLLAND
Romero .... CESAR
Rooney .... PAT
Root . ELIHU, OREN
Rosa .... RAISA
Rubinstein . ANTON
Rudolf ...... BING
Ruth .... DRAPER
Rutherford .... ANN
S.F.B. ..... MORSE
Saint, — Marie EVA
St. John .... ADELA
St. Vincent Millay
EDNA
Salmon P. .. CHASE
Sam .... HOUSTON,
SNEAD
Samuel .... LOVER,
MORSE
Sand ..... GEORGE
Sande .... EARL
Sandra .... DEE
Sayao .... BIDU
Scheffer ...... ARY
Schipa ...... TITO
Scholem ..... ASCH
Seegar ...... ALAN
Segovia ... ANDRES
Seton ...... ANYA
Sevareid ..... ERIC
Shaw ...... ARTIE
Shawn .... TED
Sheldon ..... HERB
Shelley .... PERCY
BYSSHE, WINTERS
Short .... ADAM
Shriner ...... HERB
Shubert ...... LEE
Siddons .... SARAH
Sidney .... LANIER
Signe ...... HASSO
Silvers .. PHIL, SID
Sinclair .... LEWIS
Skinner ...... OTIS
Slagle ...... SUSIE
Slavenska .... MIA
Smith . AL, ALFRED
Snead .... SAM
Sonny ...... TUFTS
Sophia .... LOREN
Sothern ...... ANN
Sparks .... NED
Speaker ..... TRIS
Speaks ...... OLEY
Spewack ..... BELLA
Spitalny .... PHIL
Stanford ... WHITE
Steen .... JAN
Stephen .. CRANE,
LONG
Stephen V. .. BENET

Sterling .... JAN
Steve ...... BRODY
Stevens MARK, RISE
Stoker ...... BRAM
Storm .... GALE
Stravinsky .... IGOR
Struthers .... BURT
Sullivan .... ED
Sunday .... BILLY
Susan B. . ANTHONY
Syngman .... RHEE
Tab ...... HUNTER
Tajo ...... ITALO
Tamiroff .... AKIM
Tanguay ..... EVA
Tarbell .... IDA
Tarkington .. BOOTH
Taylor ..... DEEMS
Teasdale .... SARA
Tegner .... ESAIAS
Templar ... SIMON
Templeton .. ALEC
Tennessee .. ERNIE
Teresa ..... AVILA
Terry ...... ELLEN
Tex .... RITTER
Theda ...... BARA
Thelma .... RITTER
Thomas ARNE, BATA,
DYLAN, GRAY,
HARDY, HICKS,
HOOD, MANN,
NAST, WOLFE
Thornton .. WILDER
Tilden .... BILL
Tillstrom ... BURR
Tim .... HOLT
"Tinker to —"
EVERS, CHANCE
Tiselius ...... ARNE
Tito .... BROZ
Tolstoy .... LEO
Tom ...... EWELL,
MIX, PAINE
Torme .... MEL
Torn .... RIP
Truex ...... ERNIE
Truman ... CAPOTE
Trygve .... LIE
Tse-tung .... MAO
Turpin .... BEN
Twain ...... MARK
Uriah .... HEEP
Ulric ..... LENORE
Vallee ...... RUDY
Van .... GUS
Vance ...... ETHEL
Velez ...... LUPE
Venerable, the BEDE
Verdon .... GWEN
Verdugo .... ELENA

Verne ...... JULES
Vernon .... CASTLE
Victor BORGE, HUGO
Vincent ..... PRICE
Vitus ..... BERING
Vivien ..... LEIGH
Vivienne .... SEGAL
Vladimir ... LENIN
W.C. ...... FIELDS
W. Mackenzie . KING
Wallace .. HENRY,
          AGARD, LEW
Wallach .... ELI
Wally .... PIP
Walter ..... ABEL,
    BRUNO, REED
Warburg .... OTTO
Washington
          BOOKER
Waugh ...... ALEC
Webb .... ALAN

Weber and —
          FIELDS
Weill .... KURT
Wheeler ..... BERT
White .... PEARL,
    WILLIAM ALLEN
Whitelaw .... REID
Whitfield .... MAL
Whitman .... WALT
Whitney ..... ELI
Wilbur ..... CROSS
Wilhelm von . OPEL
Willa .... CATHER
William .. BOOTH,
    HANDY, HART,
    HOLDEN, HULL,
    INGE, PENN,
    PITT
William Butler YEATS
William Cullen
          BRYANT

William Randolph
          HEARST
William Rose BENET
William Sidney
          PORTER
Williams ... ROGER,
          TED
Wills CHILL, HELEN
Winslow .... HOMER
Winterhalter . HUGO
Wolfert ...... IRA
Wynn .... ED
Xavier ..... CUGAT
Young ... CY, GIG,
          ALAN
Youskevitch .. IGOR
ZaSu .... PITTS
Zebulon ..... PIKE
Zernial ...... GUS
Zetterling .... MAI
Zola ...... EMILE
Zorina ...... VERA

PRESIDENTS OF THE UNITED STATES

(In order)

1. GEORGE WASHINGTON
2. JOHN ADAMS
3. THOMAS JEFFERSON
4. JAMES MADISON
5. JAMES MONROE
6. JOHN QUINCY ADAMS
7. ANDREW JACKSON
8. MARTIN VAN BUREN
9. WILLIAM HENRY HARRISON
10. JOHN TYLER
11. JAMES KNOX POLK
12. ZACHARY TAYLOR
13. MILLARD FILLMORE
14. FRANKLIN PIERCE
15. JAMES BUCHANAN
16. ABRAHAM LINCOLN
17. ANDREW JOHNSON
18. ULYSSES SIMPSON GRANT
19. RUTHERFORD BIRCHARD
    HAYES
20. JAMES ABRAM GARFIELD

21. CHESTER ALAN ARTHUR
22. GROVER CLEVELAND
23. BENJAMIN HARRISON
24. GROVER CLEVELAND
25. WILLIAM McKINLEY
26. THEODORE ROOSEVELT
27. WILLIAM HOWARD TAFT
28. WOODROW WILSON
29. WARREN GAMALIEL HARDING
30. CALVIN COOLIDGE
31. HERBERT CLARK HOOVER
32. FRANKLIN DELANO
    ROOSEVELT
33. HARRY S. TRUMAN
34. DWIGHT DAVID EISENHOWER
35. JOHN FITZGERALD KENNEDY
36. LYNDON BAINES JOHNSON
37. RICHARD MILHOUS NIXON
38. GERALD RUDOLPH FORD
39. JAMES EARL CARTER
40. RONALD WILSON REAGAN

U.S. STATE GENERAL INFORMATION TABLE

STATE	Abbreviation	Rank by Area	Rank by Population
ALABAMA	Ala.	29	19
ALASKA	Alas., Alsk.	1	50
ARIZONA	Ariz.	6	35
ARKANSAS	Ark.	27	32
CALIFORNIA	Calif., Cal.	3	2
COLORADO	Colo.	8	33
*CONNECTICUT	Conn.	48	26
*DELAWARE	Del., Dela.	49	46
†DISTRICT OF COLUMBIA	D.C.		
FLORIDA	Fla.	22	12
*GEORGIA	Ga.	21	16
HAWAII	H., Haw.	47	44
IDAHO	Id., Ida.	13	42
ILLINOIS	Ill.	24	4
INDIANA	Ind.	38	10
IOWA	Ia.	25	23
KANSAS	Kan., Kans.	14	29
KENTUCKY	Ky.	37	21
LOUISIANA	La.	31	20
MAINE	Me.	39	36
*MARYLAND	Md.	42	22
*MASSACHUSETTS	Mass.	45	9
MICHIGAN	Mich.	23	7
MINNESOTA	Minn.	12	18
MISSISSIPPI	Miss.	32	28
MISSOURI	Mo.	19	13
MONTANA	Mont.	4	41
NEBRASKA	Nebr.	15	34
NEVADA	Nev.	7	49
*NEW HAMPSHIRE	N.H.	44	45
*NEW JERSEY	N.J.	46	8
NEW MEXICO	N.M.	5	39
*NEW YORK	N.Y.	30	1
*NORTH CAROLINA	N.C.	28	11
NORTH DAKOTA	N.D.	17	43
OHIO	O.	35	6
OKLAHOMA	Okla.	18	27
OREGON	Ore.	10	31
*PENNSYLVANIA	Penna., Pa., Penn.	33	3
*RHODE ISLAND	R.I.	50	37
*SOUTH CAROLINA	S.C.	40	25
SOUTH DAKOTA	S.D.	16	40
TENNESSEE	Tenn.	34	17
TEXAS	Tex.	2	5
UTAH	Ut.	11	38
VERMONT	Vt.	43	47
*VIRGINIA	Va.	36	15
WASHINGTON	Wash.	20	24
WEST VIRGINIA	W. Va.	41	30
WISCONSIN	Wisc., Wis.	26	14
WYOMING	Wyo.	9	48

†District   *One of The Thirteen Original States

State Capital	State Nickname	State Flower
Montgomery	Yellow Hammer, Cotton, Heart of Dixie	Goldenrod
Juneau	The Last Frontier	Forget-Me-Not
Phoenix	Grand Canyon, Sunset Land, Apache	Saguaro Cactus
Little Rock	Wonder, Land of Opportunity, Bear	Apple Blossom
Sacramento	Golden, Grizzly Bear	Golden Poppy
Denver	Centennial, Rover	Columbine
Hartford	Constitution, Nutmeg	Mountain Laurel
Dover	First, Diamond, Blue Hen	Peach Blossom
		American Beauty Rose
Tallahassee	Sunshine, Everglade, Live Oak, Peninsula	Orange Blossom
Atlanta	Empire State of the South, Peach, Cracker	Cherokee Rose
Honolulu	Paradise of the Pacific	Hibiscus
Boise	Gem, Potato	Lewis Mockorange
Springfield	Prairie, Sucker	Violet
Indianapolis	Hoosier	Peony
Des Moines	Hawkeye, Corn	Wild Rose
Topeka	Sunflower, Corn Cracker, Garden, Jayhawk	Sunflower
Frankfort	Blue Grass	Goldenrod
Baton Rouge	Pelican, Creole, Sugar	Magnolia
Augusta	Pine Tree, Lumber, Potato	Pine Cone and Tassel
Annapolis	Old Line, Free, Cockade	Black-Eyed Susan
Boston	Bay, Old Colony	Arbutus
Lansing	Wolverine	Apple Blossom
St. Paul	North Star, Gopher, Land of 10,000 Lakes	Moccasin Flower
Jackson	Magnolia, Bayou	Magnolia
Jefferson City	Show Me, Bullion	Hawthorn
Helena	Treasure, Bonanza	Bitterroot
Lincoln	Beef, Cornhusker, Antelope	Goldenrod
Carson City	Sagebrush, Silver, Battle-Born	Sagebrush
Concord	Granite	Lilac
Trenton	Garden	Violet
Santa Fe	Sunshine	Yucca
Albany	Empire, Excelsior	Rose
Raleigh	Tar Heel, Old North, Turpentine	Dogwood
Bismarck	Sioux, Flickertail	Wild Prairie Rose
Columbus	Buckeye	Scarlet Carnation
Oklahoma City	Sooner	Mistletoe
Salem	Beaver, Webfooter	Oregon Grape
Harrisburg	Keystone, Quaker	Mountain Laurel
Providence	Little Rhody, Gunflint	Violet
Columbia	Palmetto	Yellow Jessamine
Pierre	Coyote, Sunshine	Pasque Flower
Nashville	Volunteer, Big Bend	Iris
Austin	Lone Star	Bluebonnet
Salt Lake City	Beehive, Mormon	Sego Lily
Montpelier	Green Mountain	Red Clover
Richmond	Old Dominion, Cavalier, "Mother of Presidents"	Dogwood
Olympia	Evergreen, Chinook	Rhododendron
Charleston	Mountain, Panhandle	Great Rhododendron
Madison	Badger, Cheese	Violet
Cheyenne	Equality	Indian Paintbrush

GAZETTEER

OR

GEOGRAPHICAL DICTIONARY

Cities, States, Countries, Counties, Provinces, Towns, Rivers, Communes, Ports and Harbors, Regions, Lakes, Mountains, Islands, Volcanoes, Settlements, Kingdoms, Districts, Divisions, Peninsulas, Mountain Ranges, Nomes, etc.; n = North; s = South

A

ABYSSINIA ..... city, **HARAR, GONDAR, HARRAR**; town, **ADOWA,** (s) **MEGA,** province, **TIGRE**; river, **OMO, ABBA**; lake, **TANA, TSANA**

ADRIATIC ... port and harbor, **FIUME**; peninsula, **ISTRIA**; resort, **LIDO**

AEGEAN .... river, **STRUMA**; island, **MELOS, SAMOS, TENOS**; gulf, **SAROS**

AFGHANISTAN .. city, **HERAT**

AFRICA .... (see also SOUTH AFRICA page 216)

AFRICA .. (n) country, **TUNIS, UGANDA, ALGERIA, TUNISIA, TUNISIE**; lake, **NYASA**; province, **LAGOS, NATAL**; river, **UMO, NILE, TANA, CONGO, NIGER**; city (n) **ORAN, DAKAR, TUNIS**; mountains, **ATLAS**; region, **CONGO, NUBIA, SUDAN, SOUDAN**; port (w) **DAKAR**

ALABAMA ...... city, **SELMA ANNISTON**

ALASKA .. city, **NOME, SITKA**; island, **ADAK, ATKA, ATTU**; peninsula, **UNGA**; mountain, **ADA**; inlet, **COOK**; river, **YUKON**; highest peak in North Amer., **McKINLEY**; glacier, **MUIR**

ALBANIA ... capital, **TIRANA**; river, **DRIN**

ALEUTIANS ... islands, **ADAK, ATKA, ATTU**

ALGERIA .... city, port, **ORAN**

ALPS ...... mountain, **BLANC, MATTERHORN**

ANNAM .. .... capital, **HUE**

ANTARCTIC .... sea, **ROSS**

ARABIA .. city, **ADEN, BEDA, BERA, SANA**; state, **ASIR, OMAN, YEMEN**; port, **ADEN**; district, **TEMA**; kingdom, **NEJD**; gulf, **ADEN, OMAN**

ARCTIC .. gulf, **OB**; sea, **KARA**

ARIZONA . city, **MESA, YUMA**; river, **GILA**

ARMENIA .... river, **ARAS**

ASIA . mountains, **ALTAI**; lake, **ARAL**; sea, **ARAL**; river, **OB, ILI, AMUR, LENA, ONON, TIGRIS**; kingdom, **NEPAL, SIAM**; country, **ANAM, IRAK, IRAN, BURMA, CHINA, KOREA, SYRIA, TIBET, SITSANG**; kingdom E. Asia, **KOREA**; desert, **GOBI**

ASIA MINOR .. district, **IONIA**; mountains, **IDA**

ASIATIC .... (see ASIA)

AUSTRIA .. city, **GRAZ, WEIN, VIENNA**; river, **MUR, ENNS, RAAB, RABA**

AUSTRALIA .. peninsula, **EYRE**; river, **SWAN**; city **PERTH**

AZORES ..... port and harbor, **HORTA**; island, **PICO, FAYAL, FLORES**; volcano, **PICO, (ALTO)**

B

BALEARIC ISLANDS .... port, **PALMA**; island, **MAJORCA**

BALTIC island, **OSEL** (opposite **RIGA**); gulf, **RIGA**; capital, **RIGA**; river, **ODER**

BAVARIA .. river, **NAB, ISAR, NAAB**
BELGIAN CONGO .. river, **UELE**

BELGIUM .. city, **HUY, MONS, GHENT, LIEGE, MALINES**; commune (town), **ANS, ATH, SPA, LEDE, MONS, NIEL, ROUX, NAMUR**; river, **LYS, YSER, MEUSE, SENNE**; port and harbor, **OSTEND**; province, **LIEGE**

BOHEMIA .. river, **ELBE, ISER**; mountains, **ORE**

BOMBAY .. city, **POONA**; district, **SURAT**; seaport and harbor, **SURAT**

BOTHNIA .... islands, **ALAND**

BRAZIL .... city, **RIO, BELEM**; port and harbor, **PARA, BELEM, NATAL, SANTOS, PELOTAS**; state, **PARA, BAHIA**; river, **APA, ICA, PARA**; capital, **RIO**

BRITISH WEST INDIES . island, **NEVIS**

BULGARIA ..... capital, **SOFIA**

BURMA (see also INDIA) . capital (former) **AVA**, (present) **RANGOON**; district, **PROME**

C

CALIFORNIA .... city, **LODI,**

NAPA, POMONA, ALAMEDA, SALINAS; town, **OJAI**; county, **NAPA, YOLO, MODOC, MADERA**; lake, **TAHOE**; mountain peak, **LASSEN, SHASTA**; valley, **NAPA**

CANADA .. mountains, **LOGAN, ROBSON**; peninsula, **GASPE**; province, **ALBERTA (ALTA.), BRITISH COLUMBIA (B.C.), MANITOBA (MAN.) NEW BRUNSWICK (N.B.), NEWFOUNDLAND (NEWF.), NOVA SCOTIA (N.S.), ONTARIO (ONT.), PRINCE EDWARD ISLAND (P.E.I.), QUEBEC (QUE.), SASKATCHEWAN (SASK.)**; national park, **JASPER**

CANAL ZONE .. city, **ANCON, COLON**; lake, **GATUN**

CARIBBEAN .... island, **CUBA**

CAROLINES .. island, **PALAU (PELEW), PONAPE, TRUK, YAP**

CAPE VERDE . island, **SAL, FOGO**

CASPIAN .. seaport and harbor, **BAKU**

CENTRAL AFRICA ..... region, **SUDAN, SOUDAN**

CENTRAL AMERICA .... river, **LEMPA**

CEYLON .... province, **UVA**

CHANNEL ISLANDS island, **SARK**

CHILE ..... river, **LOA**; port, harbor, town, **ARICA**

CHINA .. city, **AMOY, IPIN, CANTON**; port and harbor, **AMOY**; kingdom old, **WU, SHU, WEI**; river, **SI, HAN, KAN, PEI, AMUR, HWAI, CANTON**; province, **AMOY, AMUR, HONAN**; mountains, **OMEI**; division, **MIAO**

COLORADO .... city, **LAMAR, PUEBLO, DURANGO**; park, **ESTES**; town, **OURAY**; range, **RATON**; mountain, **OSO, EOLUS**; peak, **OSO**; county, **OTERO**; resort, **ASPEN**

COLOMBIA .... river,
MAGDALENA; city, CALI

CONGO .... river, UELE

CONNECTICUT town, DARIEN,
ANSONIA, MERIDEN

CORSICA ... port and harbor,
BASTIA

CRETE .... port and harbor,
CANDIA; capital, CANEA;
mountain, IDA

CRIMEA .... port and harbor,
KERCH; river, ALMA

CUBA .... town, GUINES

CYCLADES .. island, IOS, NIOO,
MILO, SYRA, DELOS, MELOS,
TENOS, THERA

CZECHOSLAVAKIA ..... city,
BRNO; BRUNN; river, EGER,
GRAN, HRON, IPEL, ISER,
ODER, OHRE, MOLDAU; region,
SUDETEN; capital, PRAGUE
(PRAHA); mountains, ORE

D

DENMARK .... island off, ALS,
AERO; islands, FAROE

DOMINICAN REPUBLIC .. city,
MOCA

DUTCH ...... see Netherlands

DUTCH EAST INDIES .. island,
BALI, JAVA NIAS; island group,
ARU, ALOR, LETI; gulf, BONI;
capital, BATAVIA

E

EAST ASIA .. kingdom, KOREA

EAST EUROPEAN . river, DRAU,
TISA, DRAVA, DRAVE, TISZA,
THEISS

EAST INDIES . see also (Dutch)
East Indies) island, BORNEO

ECUADOR ..... province, ORO

EGYPT .. city, SAIS, CAIRO;
ancient city, THEBES; town,

KISH; province, GIZA; river,
NILE

ENGLAND .. city, ELY, BATH,
YORK, LEEDS, COVENTRY; port
and harbor, HULL, DOVER,
POOLE; town, ETON; river, ALN,
CAM, DEE, EXE, NEN, URE,
AVON, NENE, OUSE, TEES,
TYNE, TRENT; county, KENT,
YORK, BERKS, BUCKS, DERBY,
DEVON, ESSEX, HANTS, WILTS,
DORSET, SURREY, SUSSEX

ESTONIA ..... island, SAARE;
province, SAARE; capital, REVAL

ETHIOPIA ...... see Abyssinia

EUROPE .... river, ISAR,
OISE, URAL, DANUBE; lake,
BALATON (largest); peninsula,
IBERIA; resort, LIDO

F

FIJI .... capital, SUVA

FINLAND .. port and harbor,
ABO, KEM, PORI; town, northern, ENARE; lake, ENARE;
islands, ALAND

FLORIDA ...... county, DADE;
resort, DELAND; city, OCALA;
cape, SABLE

FRANCE .... city, AIX, DAX,
PAU, AGEN, ALBI, CAEN,
LAON, LYON, METZ, NICE,
OPPY, VAUX, ARLES, ARRAS,
BLOIS, DINAN, LILLE, (n)
NESLE, PARIS, SEDAN, TULLE,
CANNES, NANTES, SEVRES;
colony, ALGERIA; commune, EU,
AUX, AUBY, BRON, ISSY, LOOS,
MERU, ORLY, SENS, VIMY,
VIRE, CENON; port and har-
bor, CAEN, MEZE, (s) SETE,
BREST; resort, PAU, NICE,
CANNES; department, VAR,
GARD, JURA, NORD, ORNE,
MEUSE, VENDEE; river, AIN,
LOT, LYS, AIRE, AUDE, CHER,
EURE, LOIR, OISE, ORNE, RHIN,
SAAR, YSER, AISNE, ISERE,
LOIRE (largest), MARNE, MEUSE,
SAONE, SARRE, SEINE, SELLE
(small), (n) VESLE, MOSELLE;
Mount, BLANC; mountains,
JURA; region, ANJOU, ALSACE

FRENCH EQUATORIAL AFRICA
river, **SHARI**

FRENCH INDO-CHINA
see Indo China

FRENCH MOROCCO .. capital,
RABAT; city, **RABAT**

FRENCH WEST AFRICA
city, **DAKAR**

FRIENDLY ISLANDS .. **TONGA**

G

GEORGIA ..... city, **MACON,
SPARTA, AUGUSTA**

GERMANY ... city, **EMS, ULM,
BONN** (capital W. Germany),
**GERA, JENA, LAHR, LINZ,
EMDEN, ESSEN, NEUSS**; com-
mune town, **AUE, WALD**; spa,
AIX, BADEN; canal, **KIEL**;
river, **EMS, ALLE, EDER, EGER,
ELBE, ISAR, MAIN, ODER, PRUT,
REMS, RUHR, SAAR, LIPPE,
MOSEL, REGEN, RHINE, SAONE,
WESER**; mountain, **ORE, HARZ**;
state, **HESSE**; district, **ALSACE**;
region, **SUDETEN**

GOLD COAST . port and harbor,
KETA

GREAT BARRIER ISLAND **OTEA**

GREECE .... city, **ELIS,
SPARTA, SPARTE**; colony, an-
cient, **IONIA**; island, **COS, IOS,
KOS, NIO, MILO, SCIO, SERO,
CRETE, DELOS, MELOS, PAROS,
SAMOS, IONIAN**; mountain,
OETA, OSSA, HELICON; nome,
ELIS; river, **ARTA**; peninsula,
MOREA; region, **DORIS**; dis-
trict, ancient, **ATTICA**

GREENLAND .... town, settlement, base, **ETAH**

GUAM .. city, capital, **AGANA**;
port and harbor, **APRA**

GUATEMALA .. volcano, **AGUA**

H

HAWAII .. chief city, **HILO**;
island, **MAUI, OAHU**; district,

HANA; islet, **KURE**

HEBRIDES, INNER ..... island,
IONA, SKYE, UIST

HOLLAND .. see NETHELANDS

HONDURAS ...... port. **TELA**

HONSHU .... bay, **ISE**; port
and harbor, **KOBE**

HUNGARY ...... city, **BUDA,
PECS**; commune, town, **ERLAU**;
river, **RAAB**

HYOGO .... capital, **KOBE**

I

IDAHO ...... capital, **BOISE**;
town, **ARCO**

ILLINOIS . city, **PANA, ALEDO,
ELGIN, PEKIN, CANTON, MO-
LINE, PEORIA, SPARTA**

INDIA .. capital, **MADRAS**;
city, **AGRA, DELHI, POONA,
SIMLA, MADRAS, BENARES**;
commune, town, **ARCOT, SOR-
ON**; kingdom (n) **NEPAL**; state,
**DHAR, JATH, JIND, ASSAM,
MYSORE, GWALIOR**; province,
**SIND, SWAT, ASSAM, BERAR,
DELHI, MADRAS**; Portuguese
possession, **GOA**; river, **SIND,
SWAT, GANGA, INDUS, KABUL,
GANGES**; district, **SIMLA, SA-
TARA**

INDIA, NORTH
see NORTH INDIA

INDIANA .... city **GARY,
PERU, MARION**

INDOCHINA . country, **ANAM,
ANNAM**; kingdom, **ANAM,
ANNAM**: city, **HUE, HANOI,
SAIGON**; region, **LAOS**; state,
ANAM, LAOS; port and harbor,
ANNAM

INDONESIA .... island. **AROE,
BALI, JAVA, TERNATE,
CELEBES**; island group, **KAI,
OBI**

IOWA .. city **AMES** (college);
county, **IDA**

IRAQ ..... capital, **BAGDAD,
BAGHDAD;** port and harbor,
BASRA

IRAN .... see PERSIA

IRELAND .. old capital, **TARA;**
port and harbor, **COBH, TRALEE;**
county, **MAYO, CLARE;** island,
ARAN; river, **LEE, BANN, ERNE;**
NORE; lake, **REE, ERNE;** town,
TARA

ISLE OF WIGHT .... port and
harbor, **COWES**

ISRAEL ..... port and harbor,
ACRE, HAIFA; plain, **SHARON;**
desert, **NEGEB**

ITALY .. capital, **ROMA, ROME;**
city, **BARI, COMO, PISA, ROMA,
ROME, MILAN, PARMA, SIENA,
TRENT, NAPLES, SIENNA,
VENICE,** (s) **CASERTA;** commune
or town, **BRA, ARCO, ASTI,
ATRI, DEGO, ESTE, LARI, NOLA,
SAVA, TODI, ADRIA, ASOLA,
PADUA, TURIN, EMPOLI;** re-
sort, **LIDO;** port and harbor,
OSTIA, TRANI; province, **ALBA,
CONI, POLA, ROMA, ZARA,
UDINE;** river, **PO, ADDA, ARNO,
NERA, RENO, PIAVE, TIBER;**
lake, **COMO, ISEO, NEMI;** strait,
OTRANTO; gulf, **SALERNO**

J

JALAUN ...... capital, **ORAI**

JAPAN ..... capital, **TOKIO,
TOKYO** (old name **EDO**); resort
city, **HONSHU;** capital, **NARA;**
city, **KOBE, KOFU, CHIBA,
OSAKA, OTARU, TOKIO,
TOKYO;** harbor or port or seaport, **OSAKA, OTARU;** island,
HONDO (largest), **SADO;** volcano, **ASO, FUJI;** bay, **ISE;**
province, old, **ISE, IYO, YA-
MATO;** mountain, **FUJI**

K

KANSAS .. city, **ARMA, IOLA,
SALINA;** county, **OSAGE;** river,
OSAGE

KOREA ... city, **KEIJO, SEOUL**

KASHMIR .... river, **INDUS**

KENTUCKY .. county, **ADAIR
LA RUE**

KENYA .. (Africa) river, **TANA**

L

LATVIA .. capital, port, **RIGA;**
river, **AA**

LEBANON ...... port, **SIDON**

LIBYA ..... port and harbor,
DERNA; capital, **TRIPOLI**

LITHUANIA .. seaport, **VILNA**

LITTLE AMERICA .. sea, **ROSS**

LUZON ...... province, **ABRA**
river, **ABRA, AGNO**

M

MAINE ... bay, **CASCO;** town,
BATH, (University) **ORONO;** city,
SACO

MALAYA ...... state, **PERAK,
JOHORE;** region, **PENANG;**
island, **BALI, JAVA, TIMOR;**
port, **PEKAN**

MALAY ARCHIPELAGO
island, **CELEBES**

MALTA .... island, **GOZO**

MARTINIQUE . volcano, **PELEE**

MASSACHUSETTS ...... city,
SALEM, NEWTON; cape, **ANN,
COD;** mountain, **TOM**

MEDITERRANEAN . island, **IOS,
GOZO, RODI, CAPRI, CRETE,
MALTA;** gulf, **TUNIS;** resort,
LIDO, NICE

MESOPOTAMIA .. river, **TIGRIS**

MEXICO .... town, **TULA;**
state, **COLIMA;** lake, **CHAPALA**

MICHIGAN ..... city, **ALMA,
CLARE, FLINT, SPARTA;** county,
EATON

MINDANAO ... volcano, **APO**; gulf, **DAVAO**

MISSISSIPPI .... city, **BILOXI**; river, **YAZOO**

MISSOURI .... city, **SEDALIA**; resort, **AVA**; river, **SAC**

MOLUCCA ...... island, **OBI**, **TERNATE**

MONGOLIA ..... desert, **GOBI**

MONTANA ..... city, **BUTTE**; river, **TETON**

MOROCCO .. region, **RIF, RIFF**; mountains, **ANTI ATLAS**; province, **SUS**; port and harbor, **RABAT**; town, **IFNI**

MOZAMBIQUE ... town, **IBA**; port and harbor, **BEIRA**

N

NEBRASKA .. city, **ORD**; river, **LOUP, PLATTE**; county, **OTOE**; capital, **LINCOLN**

NEPAL .... mountain, **API**

NETHERLANDS ... city, **EDAM, UTRECHT**; commune or town, **EDE, EPE, BEEK, ECHT, ELST, OLST, UDEN, GEMERT**; port and harbor, **EDAM**; river, **EEM, MAAS** (Dutch Meuse), **MAES, RIJN, WAAL**; island, **SUMATRA**

NEVADA ... city, **ELY, ELKO, RENO**; lake, **TAHOE**

NEW GUINEA .. city, port and harbor, **LAE**; island, **PAPUA**

NEW HAMPSHIRE .... lake, **OSSIPEE**; city, **KEENE, NASHUA, LACONIA**; county, **COOS**

NEW HEBRIDES .... port and harbor, **VILA**; island, **EPI, TANA, EFATE, TANNA**

NEW JERSEY .. city, **TRENTON**; river, **RARITAN**

NEW MEXICO .. town, **TAOS**; river, **GILA**; resort, **TAOS**

NEW YORK ...... city, town, **ROME, TROY, OLEAN, UTICA, ELMIRA, MALONE, OSWEGO**; island, **STATEN**; county, **TIOGA**; village, **ILION**

NEWFOUNDLAND peninsula, **AVALON**

NEW ZEALAND ...... lake, **TAUPO**; island, reef, **OTEA**

NIGERIA .. town, **ABA, IWO, LERE**; region, **BENIN**

NICARAGUA ..... city, **LEON**

NORMANDY ..... town, **ST. LO**

NORTH CAROLINA .... river, **HAW, TAR, PEE DEE** (Yadkin); cape, **FEAR**; county, **ASHE**

NORTH DAKOTA . city, **MINOT**

NORTHUMBERLAND river, **TYNE**

NORTH INDIA kingdom, **NEPAL**

NORTH VIETNAM capital, **HANOI**

NORWAY .... capital, **OSLO**; river, **TANA**; city, **HAMAR**

O

OHIO .... county, **ROSS**; city, **ADA** (college town Ohio Northern), **KENT, LIMA, BEREA, ELIDA, NILES, XENIA, CANTON, FOSTORIA**

OKINAWA .. port and harbor, **NAWA, NAHA**

OKLAHOMA ...... city, **ADA, ENID, SHAWNEE**

OREGON .... city, **SALEM, ASTORIA**; peak, **HOOD**

ORKNEYS .... island, **HOY**

P

PACIFIC ISLANDS ... island, **LAU, YAP, FIJI, GUAM, SULU, TRUK, WAKE, LEYTE, SAMOA, TAHITI**; island group, **PELEW**

PAKISTAN .... city, **LAHORE;** river, **INDUS**

PALESTINE .. (see also separate Biblical lists on page 197); mountain, **EBAL, SION, ZION, TABOR, HERMON** (highest); valley, **GHOR;** plain, **ONO;** area, **BEISAN;** port, **ACRE, GAZA;** town, **GAZA**

PANAMA .... port, **COLON**

PARAGUAY ...... city, **ITA;** river, **APA**

PENNSYLVANIA .. city, **ERIE, EASTON, CHESTER, TYRONE;** port, **ERIE**

PERSIA ... city, **NIRIZ, SUSA, RESHT**

PERU ...... department, **ICA;** capital, **LIMA;** city, **ICA;** cold district, **PUNO;** port and harbor, (s) **ILO, CALLAO;** river, **ICA**

PHILIPPINE ISLANDS (see also Luzon and Mindanao); city, **IBA, CEBU, NAGA, ILOILO;** mountain or peak, **IBA, APO;** volcano, **APO;** port and harbor, **ILOILO, BATANGAS;** province, **DAPA;** island, **CEBU, SULU, BATAN SAMAR, PANAY**

POLAND ... city, **LIDA, LODZ, LWOW, POSEN, SRODA;** river, **SAN, STYR, BIALA, VISLA, STRYPA, VISTULA**

PORTUGAL ...... cape, **ROCA**

PUNJAB .... river, **INDUS**

Q

QUEBEC .... peninsula, **GASPE;** district and town, **LEVIS**

R

RAJPUTANA ... district, **ABU**

ROUMANIA ..... city, **ARAD, IASI;** department, **ALBA;** river, **OLT**

RUSSIA .... city, **KIEF, OMSK, OREL;** port and harbor, **OREL,** ODESSA; commune, town, **KOLA;** river, **OB, OM, DON, ILI, OKA, ROS, UFA, DUNA, LENA, NEVA, ONON, SEIM, URAL, TEREK;** lake, **ONEGA;** sea, **ARAL, AZOF, AZOV;** mountains, **ALAI, URAL, ALTAI;** peninsula, **KOLA, KRIM, CRIMEA;** lake in European Russia, **SEG;** state in Dagestan, **AVAR;** region, **OMSK**

S

SAMOA
    port, capital and harbor, **APIA**

SAVAGE ISLAND . island, **NIUE**

SAXONY . commune, town, **AUE**

SCOTLAND .. port and harbor, **OBAN;** seaport, **AYR;** county, **AYR, BUTE;** river, **DEE, TAY** (largest), **DOON, SPEY, TYNE, AFTON;** city, **AYR;** mountains, **IME;** lake, **AWE, LOCH;** district, **ATHOLE, ATHOLL;** island off. **ARRAN**

SERBIA ...... department or capital, **NIS, NISH**

SIBERIA .... (see also Russia) river, **OB, ENISEI, YENISEI**

SICILY ...... volcano, **ETNA, AETNA;** commune, town, **RAGUSA;** city, **ENNA;** province, **ENNA;** resort, **ENNA**

SOCIETY ISLANDS
    island, **TAHITI**

SOUTH AFRICA district, **RAND;** river, **VAAL**

SOUTHEAST AFRICA
    district, **NIASSA, NYASSA**

SOUTHWEST AFRICA
    port and harbor, **DAKAR**

SOUTH AMERICA . river, **BENI, PLATA, YAPURA;** district, **CHACO;** mountains, **ANDES**

SOUTH CAROLINA
    river, **SANTEE**

SOUTH DAKOTA capital, **PIERRE**

SOUTH PACIFIC .... isle, **FIJI,
BALI, COOK, SAMOA**

SOUTHWEST .... river, **PECOS**

SPAIN .... city, **JACA, JAEN,
LEON, AVILA;** province, **ADRA,
JAEN, LEON, LUGO, AVILA,
MALAGA;** port and harbor,
**ADRA, NOYA, VIGO, PALOS,
MALAGA;** river, **EBRO, MINHO,
TAGUS;** kingdom, **LEON, CAS-
TILE;** commune, town, **ORIA**

SPANISH MOROCCO (see also
Morocco) port and harbor,
CEUTA; district, **IFNI**

SUMATRA .... district, **DELI**

SWEDEN .. river, **UME, LULE;**
island off **ALAND;** port and harbor, **MALMO, OREBRO;** strait,
ORESUND

SWITZERLAND .... city, **BEX,
BALE, BERN, GENF, SION,
BASLE, BERNE, LOCARNO;**
commune, town, **AY, BAAR,
BIEL, CHUR, RUTI, WALD,
AARAU, MORAT;** canton, **URI
ZUG, BERN, VAUD, ZOUG,
BASLE, BERNE;** river, **AAR,
AARE;** lake, **ZUG, JOUY,
LUCERNE;** mountain, **TODI,
VISO, MATTERHORN;** resort,
DAVOS; capital, **BERN, BERNE;**
town, see commune

SYRIA .... city, **ALEP, HOMS,
ALEPPO;** port and harbor,
SIDON

T

TAHITI .... capital, **PAPEETE**

TEXAS .... county, **CLAY,
CARSON;** city, **WACO, LAREDO,
ABILENE**

TIBET . capital, **LASSA, LHASA;**
river, **INDUS**

TRANS-JORDON .. mountain,
HOR; mountain range, **SEIR**

TUNISIA ..... capital, **TUNIS**

TURKEY .... city, **ADANA,
ANGORA;** river, **ARAS;** vilayet,
ORDU, URFA; island, **TENEDOS**
TUSCANY ...... river, **ARNO**

U

UTAH .... city,
HEBER, LOGAN;
mountains, **UINTA**

V

VENEZUELA .... state, **LARA;**
island, **ARUBA;** river, **PAO**

VERMONT ...... city, **BARRE**

VIRGINIA .... river, **DAN,
RAPIDAN**

VIRGIN ISLANDS
capital, **CHARLOTTE AMALIE**

W

WALES .... river, **DEE, USK;**
lake, **BALA**

WASHINGTON .. city, **TACOMA**

WEST AUSTRALIA capital,
PERTH

WEST INDIES .... isle, island,
CUBA, HAITI, NEVIS

WISCONSIN .... city, **RIPON,
RACINE**

WYOMING .... city, **CASPER,
LARAMIE;** highest mountain
peak, **GANNETT;** range, **TETON**

Y

YEMEN .... capital, **SANA**

YORKSHIRE .... river, **OUSE;**
city, **LEEDS**

YUGOSLAVIA ... island, **RAB,
ARBE, SOLTA;** city, **NIS;** river,
SAVA, DRINA, NARENTA; dis-
trict and province, **BANAT**

YUKON .... city,
DAWSON; river, **HESS, PEEL,
ROSS**

THE WORD-FINDER
with cross-references

FOR THE SOLVER

You can complete any unfinished 2-, 3-, or 4-letter word in the crossword you are working by using this WORD-FINDER. Even though you are at first unable to locate it in the Definition section for some reason, if you have just two letters of your wanted word (just one if it's a 2-letter word) you can find it here.

The WORD-FINDER words are listed according to the following Letter-Combination system:

XX - -	(for cases when the first two letters are known)
- XX -	(when the second and third letters are known)
- - XX	(when the last two letters are known)
X - - X	(when the first and last letters are known)

Let us say that you need to complete a word that is four letters long.

STEP ONE: Find the Letter-Combination that is the same as the letters which you have written into the crossword puzzle. Have you, for example, found "ON" as the end of a 4-letter word? Then turn to the "- - ON" Letter-Combination. Of course, since the WORD-FINDER is thorough-going, a number of words, all containing the same letter combination, are listed under this Letter-Combination.

- - ON   Acon, agon, Amon, anon, Avon, axon, azon, bion, boon, cion, coon, Dion, doon, ebon, Enon, Eton, faon, Gaon, hoon, icon, iron, Leon, lion, loon, moon, neon, **etc.**

STEP TWO: You may know, after looking through the words listed under your Letter-Combination, the word which is the only correct possibility. If not, you now begin to eliminate words in the list by working with the words in the crossword puzzle which CROSS your unfinished word. You do this by experimentally inserting words from the Letter-Combination list. When the experimental insert produces such impossible-looking combinations with the crossing word as "bv," "pv" etc. it can be discarded.

STEP THREE: After eliminating the words which make highly unlikely or "impossible" combinations with the crossing words, you still may not be sure how to complete your unfinished puzzle. Here you make use of the invaluable CROSS-REFERENCE listings following the words in the WORD-FINDER. Each number following a word is the number of the page of the Definitions Section on which the word and one of its definitions will be found. The alphabetical letters a, b, c, d indicate in exactly which section of the definition page you will be able to locate the word with its meaning.

Example: **adat** (90b,95d)

On page 90 of this Dictionary, in section b of the page, you will find the word ADAT in bold face type. The definition is "law, D. E. Ind". On page 95, section d, you will find another cross-reference to ADAT. The definition reads "Malay law."

STEP FOUR: Now re-examine the definition in your puzzle. Eliminate words in the WORD-FINDER by comparing definitions until you arrive at the "logical candidate" word for which you have been looking. Definitions in this dictionary and those in your puzzle will not always agree in exact wording. In that case, let the general meaning of the definitions be your guide. Everyday words are not always cross-referenced in this WORD-FINDER, nor are some words of exceptional terminology. Only some of the words listed in the Special Section are cross-referenced. If your definition calls for a word likely to be found in the Special Section, it is recommended that you look there first.

TWO-LETTER WORDS

A -   **Aa** (47a), **aa** (90b), **Ab** (48d,75b,102a), **ab** (63d), **AC** (39d), **ad** (90a,112d,167d), **ae** (42b,43c,d,122b,139a), **Ae** (82c,115d), **ah** (52c), **ai** (143c,148c), **al** (8c,80c,102c,104b), **am** (166c,175c), **an** (11b, 13b), **Ao** (13d,88b,c,116c), **AP** (107a,182d), **ap** (122d,166c), **ar** (88b,91c,98a,99b,110c), **as** (51b,67b,92b,126a,133a,b,180d), **at** (25c,32c,106a,123a,128a), **au** (63a,69c), **aw** (44a), **ax** (40c,139a, 167a), **ay** (7c,8b,9b,28d,55a,60a)

- A   **Aa** (47a), **aa** (90b), **BA** (42a), **Ba** (150d,153c), **ba** (139a), **da** (9b,37a, 56a,133d,135d), **DA** (124d), **ea** (43c), **EA** (15b,68a), **fa** (108b,138a, 161a), **Ga** (69c), **ha** (52c), **ia** (43d,158c), **ja** (66d), **ka** (45c), **Ka** (68c, 77b,150d,153c,173c), **la** (13b,61a,83a,108b,138a,151d,161a), **ma, MA** (42a), **Ma** (69a,b,85d), **na** (140c,163d), **NA** (36c), **oa** (43c,d), **pa** (60b,106d), **ra** (108b), **Ra** (159b), **SA** (36c), **ta** (112d,139a,160b), **VA** (83a), **va** (105a), **wa** (188), **Wa** (24c,d,88c), **ya, za** (162a)

B -   **BA** (42a), **ba** (139a,150d,153c), **bb** (147b), **be, bi** (122d,171c), **bo** (23d,24c,136a,168a), **bu** (190), **by** (18b,32c,106a)

- B   **ab** (63d,) **Ab** (48d,75b,102a), **bb** (147b), **FB** (59c), **HB** (59c), **ob** (122b), **QB** (59c)

C -   **ce** (62d,164c), **CE** (42a)

- C   **DC** (39d), **ec** (122c)

D -   **da** (9b,37a,56a,133d,135d), **DA** (124d), **DC** (39d), **DD** (42a), **de** (63d,89b,122b,122c,124a,152c,d), **di** (68c,89b,108b,122b,122c, 122d,171d), **dm** (131c), **do** (108b,138a,161a)

- D   **ad,** (90a,112d,167d), **DD** (42a), **ed** (175c), **Ed** (18d), **id** (26d, 40c,51c,57a,b,d), **od** (8d,59d,79c), **td** (32a)

E -   **ea** (43c), **EA** (15b,68a), **ec** (122c), **ed** (175c), **Ed** (18d), **ee** (139c), **EE** (42a), **ef** (91c), **eg** (59d,163d), **eh** (52c), **el** (13b,42a,47a,99b, 151d,168a), **El** (68a,108a), **em** (91c,98a,123d,172a,c), **en** (15b, 29c,50a,91c,98a,119d,123d,158c,d,172a), **eo** (34a), **er** (35b,76c, 137d,155a,158c,d,160b,175c), **Er** (18d,68c,85c,163d,166c,172c, 178a), **es** (49b,50a,66c,119d,158c,d,175c), **et** (10b,61a,b,89a,158c), **ex** (60b,91c,122c)

- E   **ae** (42b,43c,d,122b,139a), **Ae** (82c,115d), **be, CE** (42a), **Ce** (62d), **ce** (164c), **de** (63d,89b,122b,c,124a,152c,d), **ee** (139c), **EE** (42a), **Ge** (47d,69a), **he** (91c), **ie** (74c,158c,163d), **LE** (59c), **le** (13b,61a, 108b), **me** (108b,124b), **Me.** (124d), **ne** (35b,106b), **oe** (43c,54d, 82d,180d,182a,b), **pe** (91c), **Pe.** (124d), **re** (6b,10b,35d,108b,122b, 129b,138a,161a), **RE** (59c), **se** (35b,108b), **te** (43a,62d,108b,131c, 152d,160b,185d), **Ve** (63c,109c), **we** (48c,124b), **We** (92b), **ye** (124b)

F -   **fa** (108b,138a,161a), **FB** (59c), **ff** (147b), **Fi** (108b), **Fo** (23d), **fu** (42c,84c), **Fu** (30b)

- F   **ef** (91c), **ff** (147b), **if** (35d,125a), **LF** (16d), **of** (6b), **RF** 16d)

G - Ga (69c), Ge (47d,69a), Gi (91d), go (64c,90d)

- G eg (59d,163d), Og (16d,18c)

H - ha (52c), HB (59c), he (91c), hi (52c), ho (39b,79a), Ho (87c), Hu (101c,108a,162b)

- H ah (52c), eh (52c), oh (52c), Rh (20c), sh (17b,43c,79c,126d), th (43c)

I - ia (43d,158c), id (26d,40c,51c,57a,b,d), ie (74c,158c,163d), if (35d, 125a), il (122c), im (122c), in (9d,123a), io (74b,74c,103c,115b), Io (25a,85d,95c,186b), ir (9d,122c), Ir (10a,28a,82b), is (51a,166c, 175c), Is (15b,23c,86c), it (124b)

- I ai (143c,148c), bi (122d,171c), di (68c,89b,108b,122b,c,d,171d), fi (108b), Gi (91d), hi (52c), ji (30a,b,37b,98a,108b,161b), mi (43b, 108b,138a,161a), pi (71b,85d,91c,165a,172a), ri (84c,96d,98a, 108b), RI (106c), si (108b,152d,185d), ti (92b,108b,113a,b,120d, 138a,161a,162c,169b), xi (91c)

J - ja (66d), jo (140c,160c), Jo (8c,94b), ju (121a)

K - ka (45c), Ka (68c,77b,150d,153c,173c), ko (22c,87c,121a)

- K OK (155a)

L - la (13b,61a,83a,108b,138a,151d,161a), le (13b,61a,108b), LE (59c), Lf (16d), li (30a,b,37b,98a,108b,161b), Lt (143c), LT (59c), lu (65a), lo (17d,93d)

- L al (8c,80c,102c,104b), Al (96b), el (13b,42a,47a,99b,151d,168a), El (68a,108a), il (122c), ol (29c,158b,d,160b)

M - ma, Ma (69a,b,85d), MA (42a), me (108b,124b), Me. (124d), mi (43b,108b,138a,161a), mo (21d,81c,101c), Mo (88c,177c), mu (10a, 30a,60c,71a,91c), my (52c,124c)

- M am (166c,175c), em (91c,98a,123d,172a,c), dm (131c), im (122c), om (49a,77a,77b,105c,136a), um (52c,76c)

N - na (140c,163d), NA (36c), ne (35b,106b), no (42b,106b), No (84b), nu (71b,91c), Nu (29a,49a)

- N an (11b,13b), en (15b,29c,50a,91c,98a,119d,123d,158c,d,172a), in (9d,123a), on (8b,9a,60c106a,123a), un (34c,122c)

O - oa (43c,d), ob (122b), od (8d,59d,79c), oe (43c,54d,82d,180d, 182a,b), of (6b), Og (16d,18c), oh (52c), OK (155a), ol (29c, 158b, d,160b), om (49a,77a,b,105c,136a), on (8b,9a,60c,106a,123a), oo (34a,74b), or (9b,36a,37b,69c,158c,166a,184b), os (21d,67b,104a, 131b), ow (52c), ox (10c,22c), oy (139c)

- O Ao (13d,88b,c,116c), bo (23d,24c,136a,168a), do (108b,138a 161a), eo (34a), Fo (23d), go (64c,90d), ho (39b,79a), Ho (87c), io (74b,c,103c,115b), Io (25a,85d,95c,186b), jo (140c,160c), Jo (8c, 94b), ko (22c,87c,121a), lo (17d,93d), mo (21d,81c,101c), Mo (88c, 177c), no (42b,106b), No (84b), oo (34a,74b), Ro (13c,81d,88c,131c, 173c), so (76a,108b,125a,138a,158b,161a,165b,175c), to (10b, 13c), uo (43d), vo (91a), yo, zo (13d,186b)

P - pa (60b,106d), pe (91c), Pe. (124d), pi (71b,85d,91c,165a,172a), pu (30b,140a)

- P ap (122d,166c), AP (107a,182d), up (123a), UP (107a,182d)

Q - QB (59c), q.v. (180d)

R - ra (108b), Ra (159b), re (6b,10b,35d,108b,122b,129b,138a,161a), RE (59c), RF (16d), Rh (20c), ri (84c,96d,98a,108b), RI (106c), Ro (13c,81d,88c,131c,173c), RT (59c)

- R ar (88b,91c,98a,99b,110c), er (35b,76c,137d,155a,158c,d,160b, 175c), Er (18d,68c,85c,163d,166c,172c,178a), ir (99d,122c), Ir (10a, 28a,82b), or (9b,36a,37b,69c158c,166a,184b), Ur (6b,28d,94a, 100d)

S - SA (36c), se (35b,108b), Se, sh (17b,43c,79c,126d), si (108b,152d, 185d), so (76a,108b,125a,138a,158b,161a,165b,175c), SS (16d, 164c), Su (127a), Sw (35b), Sy (141a)

- S as (51b,67b,92b,126a,133a,b,180d), es (49b,50a,66c,119d,158c, d,175c), is (51a,166c,175c), Is (15b,23c,86c), os (21d,67b,104a, 131b), S.S. (16d,164c), us (124b)

T - ta (112d,139a,160b), td (32a), te (43a,62d,108b,131c,152d,160b, 185d), th (43c), ti (92b,108b,113a,b,120d,138a,161a,162c,169b), to (10b,13c), tt (147b), tu (83c,164d,185d), Ty (68c,109c,163d, 178a)

- T at (25c,32c,106a,123a,128a), et (10b,61a,b,89a,158c), It (124b), Lt (143c), LT (59c), RT (59c), tt (147b), ut (72b,108b), Ut (67a)

U - um (52c,76c), un (34c,122c), Uo (43d), up (123a), Ur (6b,28d, 94a,100d), UP (107a,182d), us (124b), ut (72b,108b), Ut (67a), Uz (48c)

- U au (63a,69c), bu (190), fu (42c,84c), Fu (30b), Hu (101c,108a, 162b), ju (121a), lu (65a), mu (10a,30a,60c,71a,91c), nu (71b, 91c), Nu (29a,49a), pu (30b,140a), Su (127a), tu (83c, 164d, 185d), Wu (30b), Zu (68c,157a)

V - va (105a), Va (83a), Ve (63c,109c), vo (91a)

- V q.v. (180d)

W - wa (188), Wa (24c,d,88c), we (48c,124b), We (92b), Wu (30b), wy (91c)

- W aw (44a), ow (52c), sw (35b)

X - xi (91c)

- X ax (40c,139a,167a), ex (60b,91c,122c), ox (10c,22c)

Y - ya, ye (124b), yo

- Y ay (7c,8b,9b,28d,55a,60a), by (18b,32c,106a), my (52c,124c), sy (141a), oy (139c), Ty (68c,109c,163d,178a), wy (91c)

Z - za (162a), zo (13d,186b), Zu (68c,157a)

- Z Uz (48c)

THREE-LETTER WORDS

AA - aal (47c,80c,104b), aam (47a,49d,93a), aar (172d), Aar (131a)

A - A aba (12a,25d,32b,33a,65b), Ada (110a,112c,183c), aea (26a,36d), aga (35a,39a,48b,102d,103a,b,111c,166b,170d,171a), aha (52c,55c, 159c), aka (88b,c,176b), Aka (13d), ala (6d,13a,15c,61a,133d,

182c,d), **Ala** (151b), **ama** (26a,28d,31a,35b,39c,95b,108d,111c, 117b,182c), **ana** (10b,33c,60d,93a,98c,122b,d,140d,142b), **Ana** (28a,68d,100c), **apa** (23a,177d), **ara** (33a,114a,116a,118b,163d), **Ara** (9b,18c,36b,c,68d,69b,c,85a,95a,175b), **Asa** (6a,18c,71a,84d, 86d,164c), **ata** (58d,97d,158d,160c,173d), **Ata** (79c,80d,94d, 95d,100a,106b,117a,), **ava** (78d,86a,116a,120d,139a,167b), **Ava** (24c), **awa** (100a,139a), **aya** (77b,166b)

- AA   **baa** (143d), **maa** (97d,143d), **saa** (98a), **taa** (112d)

AB -   **aba** (12a,25d,32b,33a,65b), **abb** (58b,178b,185b), **ABC** (134d), **Abe** (71a,96a,123a), **Abi** (76c), **Abo** (25d), **Abt** (34c), **abu** (17a), **Abu** (15b,42a,55a,68a,c,147d)

A - B   **abb** (58b,178b,185b), **alb** (65b,176a)

- AB   **Bab** (15a), **cab** (75c), **dab** (46a,57b,58b,d,114d,115c), **gab** (29b, 78a,116c,122a,161c,183a), **jab** (120b,125c), **kab** (75c), **lab, Mab** (54b,126b,183d), **nab** (13b,26c,27b,142a), **pab** (139c), **rab** (17c,75c, 85b,102d,162c,166b), **Rab** (45a), **tab** (29b,39c,58b,86a,128d,145a)

AC -   **ace** (7a,26c,52d,57a,77d,110c,114c,120b,147a,163a,173a), **ach** (8b, 48a,52c,66b,80c), **aci** (29c), **act** (41d,55b,119c,155d), **acu** (34c), **acy** (34c)

A - C   **ABC** (134d), **arc** (31b,39d,92a,126a,127c,142a)

- AC   **bac** (31b,55c,174d), **fac** (41c), **lac** (53c,99d,130c,135b,174d), **Mac** (96a,140b,150b), **pac** (73b,94c,100d), **sac** (15d,121d), **Sac** (80c), **tac** (34d,130a), **Vac** (153b), **zac** (27c)

AD -   **Ada** (110a,112c,183c), **add** (10d,11d,14c,158a,167c), **ade** (18c, 149d), **Ade** (9c,53b), **ado** (22b,24d,35b,64c,78d,121d,156b,170a), **ady** (188), **adz** (40c,167a)

A - D   **aid** (14a,15b,64c,75d,158b), **add** (10d,11d,14c,158a,167c), **and** (36a,119d)

- AD   **bad** (55a,173a,184d), **cad** (22b,23b,75c,172c,173d), **dad, fad** (38b, 108c,163a), **gad** (58c,100a,b,127d,132b,153c,154b,178a), **Gad** (84a, 186d), **had, lad** (22c,25b,55b,157c,186a), **mad** (10c,82b), **pad** (39d, 59c,76c,157d,161a,168b), **rad** (50b,138d,173b), **sad** (29c,42c,94c, 98c,104a,150d,173a), **tad** (22c,174a,186a), **wad** (94d,97b,109c, 112b,149d)

AE -   **aea** (26a,36d), **AEF** (184d), **aer** (8b,28d,34a,b,175a), **aes** (23c, 89a,101c,132d,133a,b), **aet** (89a,109d), **Aex** (46d)

A - E   **Abe** (71a,96a,123a), **ace** (7a,26c,52d,57a,77d,110c,114c,120b, 147a,163a,173a), **ade** (18c,149d), **Ade** (9c,53b), **age** (51d,66a,92a, 97c,98c,116b,141c), **ake** (60a,107a), **ale** (17c,18c,50c,55d,92d, 104c), **ame** (37a,62d,131b), **ane** (61c,140a,158b), **ape** (36d,79d, 100a,101d,146d), **are** (51a,88b,98a,99b,110c,166c,175c), **ase** (51a, 139a), **Ase** (79b,115d), **ate** (81a,108c,158c,174c), **Ate** (20c,68b,d, 69a,b,116c,186b), **ave** (54c,71d,73a,122a,134a,136d), **awe** (81d, 100a,130d,175b,182b), **axe** (30c,40c,167a), **aye** (7c,9b,55a,60a)

- AE   **dae** (139b), **eae** (34b), **hae** (139c), **kae** (84a,140b), **Mae** (183c), **nae** (139d), **rae** (136b,138d,140b), **Rae** (183c), **sae** (140b,149c), **tae** (138d,140c,166c,d), **vae** (176b)

AF -   **AFL** (173a), **Afr.** (36c), **aft** (14a,15b,17d,128b,167d)

A - F   **AEF** (184d), **Alf** (96a)

223

- AF   **gaf** (12b), **kaf** (12b), **Kaf** (104a), **oaf** (22a,45b,146d,157d,185d), **Qaf** (104a)

AG -   **aga** (35a,39a,48b,102d,103a,b,111c,166b,170d,171a), **age** (51d, 66a,92a,97c,98c,116b,141c), **ago** (25a,69d,114d,147a)

- AG   **bag** (26c,139a,145b,159a), **cag** (81d,109d), **dag** (11b,118c,139c), **Dag** (108c), **fag** (55a,166a), **gag** (146c,183a), **hag** (140a,183a), **jag** (124d,148a), **lag** (93c,155d), **mag** (73b,95b,166c), **Mag** (183d), **nag** (73d,78b,138c,184d), **rag** (59b,77c,100c,133c,161a), **sag** (46b), **tag** (45a,54c,65a,87b,144a), **vag** (174b,178a), **wag** (85b,104a,183a), **zag** (84a)

AH -   **aha** (52c,55c,159c), **Ahi** (32c,147d), **ahu** (24c,41d,65d,103d,120d)

A - H   **ach** (8b,48a,52c,66b,80c), **akh** (153d), **ash** (24d,33c,49c,73d,134b, 168c,169a), **auh** (52c)

- AH   **bah** (52c), **dah** (24c,87a), **hah** (52c), **Jah** (84d), **Mah** (10b,57c, 102b), **pah** (52c,60b,106d), **rah** (29b), **sah** (188), **wah** (113c), **yah** (52c)

AI -   **aid** (14a,15b,64c,75d,158b), **aik** (139d), **ail** (170a), **aim** (42d,43d, 67d,109b,125d,157c), **ain** (18d,91c,110c,124b,140a,154b,180a), **air** (11c,12c,42b,44c,53a,96b,98c,99d,125c,170c), **ait** (82d,132a), **Aix** (46d)

A - I   **Abi** (76c), **aci** (29c), **Ahi** (32c,147d), **Ali** (7b,12a,25c,48b,55a,60c, 92d,101a,103a,164a,166b,170d), **ami** (61d), **ani** (19b,d,20b,39b), **api** (34a,76d), **Ari** (18d), **asi** (137a), **ati** (106d,107a), **Ati** (45d,106b, 113c,117a)

- AI   **hai** (55c), **kai** (59c), **Kai** (14d,84c), **lai** (98b,161b), **Lai** (24c,d,88c), **mai** (62a), **rai** (188), **sai** (101d), **tai** (84b,111c,121b), **Tai** (80d), **Vai** (91d)

- AJ   **gaj** (190), **raj** (129c), **saj** (48a,169a), **taj** (75a,97d)

AK -   **aka** (176b), **Aka** (13d,88b,c), **ake** (60a,170a), **akh** (153d), **ako** (189), **aku** (57c,176a)

A - K   **aik** (139d), **alk** (171b), **ark** (21a,29d,38a,58b,60d,175d), **ask** (38b, 82a,126c), **auk** (19b)

- AK   **dak** (95c), **hak** (46d), **lak** (38a), **nak** (156b), **oak** (73d,168c,169a), **sak** (37c), **Sak** (88c), **yak** (112c,161d,165b), **zak** (188)

AL -   **ala** (6d,13a,15c,61a,133d,182c,d), **Ala.** (151b), **alb** (65b,176a), **ale** (17c,18c,50c,55d,92d,104c), **Alf** (96a), **Ali** (7b,12a,25c,48b,55a,60c, 92d,101a,103a,164a,166b,170d), **alk** (171b), **all** (35c,118a,126d, 181a), **alp** (24b,103d,115c), **als** (66d,163d), **alt** (66c,76c,109c), **aly** (95d)

A - L   **aal** (47c,80c,104b), **AFL** (173a), **ail** (170a), **all** (35c,118a,126d,181a), **awl** (145b,167a)

- AL   **aal** (47c,80c,104b), **bal** (9d,37b,61a,61b), **cal** (183c), **Cal** (123a), **dal** (117d,153d), **gal, Hal** (69d), **ial** (158b), **mal** (34a,b,44a,52b,62c, 122b), **Mal** (94b), **pal** (35b,38d), **sal** (29c,48a,136d,149d,152d, 169a,183a), **Sal** (183d), **tal** (40c,77a,113b), **Zal** (135d)

AM -   **ama** (26a,28d,31a,35b,39c,95b,108d,111c,117b,182c), **ame** (37a, 62d,131b), **ami** (61d), **amo** (79a,89c), **amp** (49b,173b), **amt** (37d, 40d,108a,163c), **amy** (63c), **Amy** (8c,94b,183c)

A - M　aam (47a,49d,93a), aim (42d,43d,67d,109b,125d,157c), arm (22d, 60c,81b,92b,124b,161b), aum (189)

- AM　aam (47a,49d,93a), bam (29b), cam (48b,65d,95a,98b,134a,139b, 148b,180c), dam (30c,49c,55b,156d,180a), gam (76b,176d,180c), ham (98a,144b), Ham (18d,107c), jam (123a,156d,165c), lam (51b, 58b,93d,164d,178a), Mam (192), pam (26c,65a,87a,105b), Ram (36b), ram (17a,45b,50b,79c,112b,121d,143d,157d), Sam (96a, 162a), tam (74d), yam (48c,121d,160b,170c)

AN -　ana (10b,33c,60d,93a,98c,122b,d,140d,142b), Ana (28a,68d,100c), and (36a,119d), ane (61c,140a,158b), ani (19b,d,20b,39b), Ann (183c), ano (19d,20b,34d,122d,174a), Ans (92a), ant (49d,60b,81b, 118c), Anu (15b,28a,68a,d,75b,88c,147d), any (14b,150b)

A - N　ain (18d,91c,110c,124b,140a,154b,180a), Ann (183c), arn (8c, 139a), awn (12c,17b,140a)

- AN　ban (81d,97a,124a), can (24c,36c,123a,166a), dan (24c,97c), Dan (18c,39c,77d,83a,84a,141b), ean (17d,23b,88a), fan (43a,154b), 156b,182d), Gan (132d), Han (16c,30b,185b), Ian (85b,96a,139d), kan (93a), lan (37b,37d,160b), man (29c,60c,64c,65a,142d,161d), Nan (183c), pan (34a,61a,104a,175d), Pan (56a,68a,68b,76b,120c, 135b,161a,184a), ran (73d), Ran (7c,107d,141a,163d), san (91c, San (24d), tan (23d,33c,46a,72d,90d), van (7b,59d,60a,63d,90c), wan (113a), Zan (186b)

A - O　Abo (25d), ado (22b,24d,35b,64c,78d,121d,156b,170a), ago (25a, 69d,114d,147a), ako (189), amo (79a,89c), ano (19d,20b,34d, 122d,174a), Apo (122b,177c), Aro (107a,111c), Aso (84c), azo (107c)

- AO　dao (117a), hao (189), iao (78a,96c,178d), Lao (80d,88c,146a, 161b), mao (115b), Mao (30b), sao (141b), Sao (113c), tao (10d, 131c,170b), Tao (117a), Yao (30a,c,104b)

AP -　apa (23a,177d), ape (36d,79d,100a,101d,146d), api (34a,76d), apo (122b), Apo (177c), apt (11d,23b,32b,58a,80b,92b,114d,116d, 124b,159a)

A - P　alp (24b,103d,115c), amp (49b,173b), asp (7b,32b,149a,174a, 176c)

- AP　bap (93b,132d), Bap (124d), cap (19d,39a,43a,53a,74d,160a,167b, 185c), dap (43b,c,46b,91b,147d), gap (11b,23a,29b,76c,110d,128a), hap (17d,28d), Jap, lap (31b,37d,59b,127a,131d,153d,167d), map (27a,29b,54a,98d,160a), nap (65a,117d,146b,148a), pap (59c), rap (90d,110a,147c,157c), sap (45d,52d,85c,169b,176d,179a), tap (55a,114d,153c), yap (16c,29b,122a)

AR -　ara (33a,114a,116a,118b,163d), Ara (8c,9b,36b,c,68d,69b,c, 85a,95a,175b), arc (31b,39d,92a,126a,127c,142a), are (51a,88b, 98a,99b,110c,166c,175c), Ari (18d), ark (21a,29d,38a,58b,60d, 175d), arm (22d,60c,81b,92b,124b,161b), arn (8c,139a), Aro (107a, 111c), ars (13b,89a), Ars (112c), art (22d,38b,39c,43b,56c,124a, 162c,181d), aru (80c,82b), Aru (82d)

A - R　aar (172d), Aar (131a), aer (8b,28d,34a,b,175a), Afr. (36c), air (11c,12c,42b,44c,53a,96b,98c,99d,125d,170c)

- AR　aar (172d), Aar (131a), bar (37c,39a,46a,52c,76d,78b,91a,124a,

137a,156a,157c,169c), **car** (16a,61d,93b,175a) **dar,** (65c,111b, 169a), **ear** (14c,d,28c,63d,64a,73c,111b,116a,124b,137d,150d, 153c), **far** (44c), **gar** (57b,c,d,106b), **har** (139c), **jar** (31d,70d,143b), **lar** (24c,51d,67a,78d,95d,101d,171b), **mar** (40b,44a,79a,d,81a, 140d), **Mar** (93d), **nar** (139d), **oar** (20b,124c,134b), **par** (15a,51a, 51b,c,69d,107c,135b,155a) **sar** (57d), **tar** (8c,68a,94d,111c,118c, 136a,c,176d), **war** (157c), **yar** (72a), **zar** (188)

AS - **Asa** (6a,18c,71a,84d,86d,164c), **ase** (51a,139a), **Ase** (79b,115d), **ash** (24d,33c,49c,73d,134b,168c,169a), **asi** (137a), **ask** (38b,82a, 126c) **Aso,** (84c), **asp** (7b,32b,149a,174a,176c), **ass** (17b,20c,45b, c,59c,110c,112b,146d,157d)

A - S **aes** (23c,89a,101c,132d,133a,b), **als** (66d,163d), **Ans** (92a), **ars** (13b,89a), **Ars** (112c), **ass** (17b,20c,45b,c,59c,110c,112b,146d, 157d), **aus** (66c), **Aus** (98b)

- AS **bas** (62a,d,129d,134b), **das** (13b,15d,36d,66b,d,164a), **fas** (44d,89d, 129d), **gas** (10b,29b,59a,116d,161c), **has, kas** (32c,47a), **las** (13b, (151d), **mas** (34b,55b,119a) **nas** (74a,89c,178b), **pas** (40d, 156a), **ras** (6c,26b,48b,51d,53d,61c,75a,111c,123c,166b), **vas** (46d, 89d,119c,133b,175d), **was** (166c,175c), **Was** (24d)

AT - **ata** (58d,97d,158d,160c,173d), **Ata** (79c,80d,94d,95d,100a, 106b,117a), **ate** (81a,108c,158c,174c), **Ate** (20c,68b,d,69a,b, 116c,186b), **ati** (106d,107a), **Ati** (45d,106b,113c,117a), **att** (146a)

A - T **Abt** (35c), **act** (41d,55b,119c,155d), **aet** (89a,109d), **aft** (14a,15b, 17d,128b,167d), **ait** (82d,132a), **alt** (66c,76c,109c), **amt** (37d,40d, 108a,163c), **ant** (49d,60b,81b,118c), **apt** (11d,23b,32b,58a,80b,92b, 114d,116d,124b,159a), **art** (22d,38b,39c,43b,56c,124a,162c,181d), **att** (146a), **aut** (34d,89d)

- AT **bat** (39c,107c,156a,157c,182d), **cat** (10a,45b,55b,71d,161b,169d, 180d,183d), **eat** (37b,96b,135d,179b), **fat** (110a,124a), **gat** (28d, 72c,131a), **hat** (74d), **Hat** (183d), **Jat** (80d,125c), **kat** (105d), **lat** (24a,33d,106b,118a), **mat** (46d,50d,94d,117c,161d), **Mat** (96a), **nat** (7a,24c,24d,106a), **oat** (15a,28b,70b,144b), **pat** (11d,116d, 159a,161d,167c), **Pat** (96a), **rat** 16a,42d,73b,132c), **sat** (13d), **tat** (48c,72d,87c), **Tat** (82a), **vat** (31b,36c,163a,170c), **wat** (73d,140d, 163a,180b), **xat** (167c), **zat** (148a)

AU - **auh** (52c), **auk** (19b), **aum** (189), **aus** (66c), **Aus** (98b), **aut** (34d, 89d), **aux** (6d,61a)

A - U **abu** (17a), **Abu** (15b,42a,55a,68a,c,147d), **acu** (34c), **ahu** (24c,41d, 65d,103d,120d), **aku** (57c,176a), **Anu** (15b,28a,68a,d,75b,88c, 147d), **aru** (80c,82d), **Aru** (82d), **ayu** (160c)

- AU **eau** (63a,178c), **gau** (66d,67a), **mau** (170c,188), **pau** (130c), **Pau** (48c,76a), **tau** (71b,91c,136c,161a), **vau** (91c), **Yau** (30c)

AV - **ava** (78d,86a,116a,120d,139a,167b), **Ava** (24c), **ave** (54c,71d,73a, 122a,134a,136d)

- AV **gav** (72d), **lav** (72d), **tav** (91c)

AW - **awa** (100a,139a), **awe** (81d,100a,130d,175b,182b), **awl** (145b,167a), **awn** (12c,17b,140a)

- AW **baw** (52c), **caw** (19b,d), **daw** (39a,70b,84a,146d), **gaw** (140c), **haw** (35a,52c,74d,91a,155a,162c), **jaw** (97d,138c), **law** (26b,33a,40a,

48c,60b,85d,91a,111b,134d,155d), **maw** (38b,d,72c,111a,121a, 142a,156c), **paw** (32d,59c,73c), **raw** (20c,39a,105d,173d), **saw** (7a, 11b,40c,54c,97d,125a,137d,167a), **taw** (90d,91c,96c,d,145b,161d), **waw** (12b,91c), **yaw** (43a,155d)

AX -   axe (30c,40c,167a)

A - X   **Aex** (46d), **Aix** (46d), **aux** (6d,61a)

- AX   **lax** (93d,130a), **Max** (96a), **pax** (89d,115b), **sax** (40c,148a,167a), **tax** (13a,14a,80a,91d), **wax** (28b,72a,80b,120c), **zax** (148a)

AY -   **aya** (77b,143c,166b), **aye** (7c,9b,55a,60a), **ayu** (160c)

A - Y   **acy** (34c), **ady** (188), **aly** (95d), **amy** (63c), **Amy** (8c,94b,183c), **any** (14b,150b)

- AY   **bay** (12d,16c,33c,73d,78b,81b,90a,128d), **cay** (82d,180b), **day** (153a), **fay** (32c,54b,154b), **Fay** (183c), **gay, Gay** (17d), **hay** (52c, 55c,165d), **jay** (19b,91c), **kay** (82d), **Kay** (13b,134b), **lay** (16a,25c,80a,98b,107d,141d,150b), **may** (74d), **May** (183c), **nay** (42b,106b), **pay** (35b,128c,130a,d,177b), **ray** (38a,49a,57b, 58b,147b), **Ray** (96a), **say** (131c,174c,177a), **way** (37d,96b,134b, 164d)

AZ -   **azo** (107c)

A - Z   **adz** (40c,167a)

- AZ   **gaz** (188,190), **Laz** (27d)

BA -   **baa** (143d), **Bab** (15a), **bac** (31b,55c,174d), **bad** (55a,173a,184d), **bag** (26c,139a,145b,159a), **bah** (52c), **bal** (9d,37b,61a,b), **bam** (29b), **ban** (81d,97a,124a), **bap** (93b,132d), **Bap.** (124d), **bar** (37c, 39a,46a,52c,76d,78b,91a,124a,137a,156a,157c,169c), **bas** (62a,d, 129d,134b), **bat** (39c,107c,156a,157c,182d), **baw** (52c), **bay** (12d, 16c,33c,73d,78b,81b,90a,128d)

B - A   **baa** (143d) **boa** (36c,55b,106a,125d,138b,142d,149a)

- BA   **aba** (12a,25d,32b,33a,65b), **iba** (117a)

B - B   **Bab** (15a), **bib, bob** (57c,115d), **Bob** (96a), **bub** (22c)

- BB   **abb** (58b,178b,185b), **ebb** (6a,15b,41c,43c,104a,128c,158a,178a)

B - C   **bac** (31b,55c,174d), **BSC** (42a)

- BC   **ABC** (134d)

B - D   **bad** (55a,173a,184d), **bed** (60c,148b), **bid** (35a,82a,109d,111b, 174c), **bud** (22c)

BE -   **bed** (60c, 148b), **bee** (46b,81b,91c,108c), **beg** (38b,150a), **bel** (64a, 93c,168d,173b,183d), **Bel** (15b,68a,126d), **ben** (78c,81b,102c,115c), **Ben** (12d,77c,96a,106c,139d,140a), **ber** (85c), **Bes** (68b,119c), **bet, bey** (70b,170d)

B - E   **bee** (46b,81b,91c), **bye** (38c,141d)

- BE   **Abe** 71a,96a,123a), **obe** (31d,87d,150d), **ube** (185b)

B - G   **bag** (26c,139a,145b,159a), **beg** (38b,150a), **big, bog** (97a,160a), **bug** (24b,66b,81b)

B - H   **bah** (52c), **boh** (24c)

BI -   **bib, bid** (35a,82a,109d,111b,174c), **big, Bim** (16c), **bin** (22c,59a, 78a,128c,156d), **bis** (50a,90a,102c,130b,171c), **bit** (46a,86b,114c, 167a,b,171c,180d), **biz**

- BI   Abi (76c), **obi** (55d,67b,84c,137b,150d), **ubi** (90a,180d,185b)

B - K   Bok (9c)

B - L   bal (9d,37b,61a,61b), bel (64a,93c,168d,173b,183d), Bel (15b,68a, 126d), Bul (25d,102a)

B - M   bam (29b), Bim (16c), bum (21b)

B - N   ban (81d,97a,124a), ben (78c,81b,102c,115c,139d,140a), Ben (12d, 77c,96a,106c), bin (22a,59a,78a,128c,156d), bon (30a,61d,86b,88c), Bon (84b), bun (25b,73b)

BO -   boa (36c,55b,106a,125d,138b,142d,149a), bob (57c,115d), Bob (96a), bog (97a,160a), boh (24c), Bok (9c), bon (30a,61d,86b,88c), Bon (84b), boo, Bor (120c), Bos (27c), bot (59a,88d), bow (11c,21b, 39d,60a,107c,109a,125a,144d,158a), box (36a,128c,145d,152d), boy (142d,157c), Box (43b,115d)

B - O   boo

- BO   Abo (25d), ebo (28b,110a), Ibo (107a,180a)

B - P   Bap. (124d), bap (93b,132d)

B - R   bar (37c,39a,46a,52c,76d,78b,91a,124a,137a,156a,157c,169c), ber (85c), Bor (120c), bur (123b)

BS -   BSC (42a)

B - S   bas (62a,d,129d,134b), Bes (68b,119c), bis (50a,90a,102c,130b, 171c), Bos (27c), bus (125b,168b)

B - T   bat (39c,107c,156a,157c,182d), bet, bit (46a,86b,114c,167a,b, 171c,180d), bot (59a,88d), but (36a,52b,156b,173c)

- BT   Abt (35c)

BU -   bub (22c), bud (22c), bug (24b,66b,81b), Bul (25d,102a), bum (21b), bun (25b,73b), bur (123b), bus (125b,168b), but (36a,52b, 156b,173c), buy

- BU   abu (17a), Abu (15b,42a,55a,68a,c,147d)

B - W   baw (52c), bow (11c,21b,39d,60a,107c,109a,125a,144d,158a)

B - X   box (36a,c,128c,145d,152d)

BY -   bye (38c,141d)

B - Y   bay (12d,16c,33c,73d,78b,81b,90a,128d), bey (70b,170d), boy (142d,157c), buy

B - Z   biz, Box (43b,115d)

CA -   cab (75c), cad (22b,23b,75c,172c,173d), cag (81d,109d), cal (183c), Cal (123a), cam (48b,65d,95a,98b,134a,139b,148b,180c), can (24c, 36c,123a,166a), cap (19d,39a,43a,53a,74d,160a,167b,185c), car (16a,61d,93b,175a), cat (10a,45b,55b,71d,161b,169d,180d), Cat (183d), caw (19b,d) cay (82d, 180b)

C - A   cha (162b,c)

- CA   ECA (8a), oca (48c,112c,116d,133d,170c,184a), Uca (56a)

C - B   cab (75c), cob (28c,78b,95d,160b,177d), cub (92d,185d)

C - D   cad (22b,23b,75c,172c,173d), Cid (151c,d), cod (57b,c), cud (126c, 135a)

CE -   cee (91c), cep (63a), ces (62b), cet (62d,180b)

C - E   cee (91c), che (145d), cie (61b,63b), cle (158d), coe (143d),

228

Coe (33c), **cue** (7a,27b,92c,117d,124b,132c,146c,159a)

- CE ace (7a,26c,52d,57a,77d,110c,114c,120b,147a,163a,173a), **ice** (30a, 36d,42d,63d)

C - G cag (81d,109d), **cig, cog** (33a,65d,163b,167b,180c)

CH - cha (162b,c), **che** (145d), **chi** (91c), **Chi** (69c), **cho** (188)

- CH ach (8b,48a,52c,66b,80c), **ich** (66c), **och** (8b), **tch** (52c)

CI - Cid (151c,d), **cie** (61b,63b), **cig, CIO** (173a), **cis** (34c,122c), **cit** (81a,167d)

C - I chi (91c), **Chi** (69c)

- CI aci (29c), **ici** (61d), **Ici** (9b), **LCI** (21b)

- CK ock (189), **tck** (52c)

CL - cle (158d)

C - L cal (183c), **Cal** (123a), **col** (103d,114c)

C - M cam (48b,65d,95a,98b,134a,139b,148b,180c), **com** (122d), **cum** (159b), **cwm** (31b,37b,103d)

C - N can (24c,36c,123a,166a), **con** (7d,29b,83c,116d,157d)

CO - cob (28c,78b,95d,160b,177d), **cod** (57b,c), **coe** (143d), **Coe** (33c), **cog** (33a,65d,163b,167b,180c), **col** (103d,114c), **com** (122d), **con** (7d,29b,83c,116d,157d), **coo** (19b), **Coo** (82d), **cop** (36a,120c, 126d,153c,155d), **cor** (36c,75b,155b), **cos** (91d,132d), **cot** (129b, 148b), **cow** (22c,45b,81d), **cox** (156a), **coy** (16d), **coz**

C - O cho (188), **CIO** (173a), **coo** (19b), **Coo** (82d), **cro** (104c,115b,180a)

C - P cap (19d,39a,43a,53a,74d,160a,167b,185c), **cep** (63a), **cop** (36a, 120c,126d,153c,155d), **cup** (46b,69d,118b,170a), **cyp** (169d)

CR - cro (104c,115b,180a), **cru** (63a,176c), **cry** (25c,124a,145c,179d)

C - R car (16a,61d,93b,175a), **cor** (36c,75b,155b), **cur** (101d)

C - S ces (62b), **cis** (34c,122c), **cos** (91d,132d)

- CS ics (158d)

C - T cat (10a,45b,55b,71d,161b,169d,180d,183d), **cet** (62d,180b), **cit** (81a,167d), **cot** (148b), **cut** (30c,32b,145c)

- CT act (41d,55b,119c,155d), **ect** (35a,122d,183b), **oct** (34a,122c)

CU - cub (92d,185d), **cud** (126c,135a), **cue** (7a,27b,92c,117d,124b,132c, 146c,159a), **cum** (159b), **cup** (46b,69d,118b,170a), **cur** (101d), **cut** (30c,32b,145c)

C - U cru (63a,176c)

- CU acu (34c), **ecu** (58a,144b,c)

CW - cwm (31b,37b,103d)

C - W caw (19b,d), **cow** (22c,45b,81d)

C - X cox (156a)

CY - cyp (169d)

C - Y cay (82d,180b), **coy** (16d), **cry** (25c,124a,145c,179d)

- CY acy (34c), **icy** (65d)

C - Z coz

DA - dab (46a,57b,58b,d,114d,115c), **dad, dae** (139b), **dag** (11b,118c, 139c), **Dag** (108c), **dah** (24c,87a), **dak** (95c), **dal** (117d,153d), **dam**

(30c,49c,55b,156d,180a), **dan** (24c,97c), **Dan** (18c,39c,77d,83a, 84a,141b), **dao** (117a), **dap** (43b,c,46b,91b,147d), **dar** (65c,111b, 169a), **das** (13b,15d,36d,66b,d,164a), **daw** (39a,70b,84a,146d), **day** (153a)

D - A   **dea** (68d,89b), **dha** (99d), **dia** (122b,d,152a,165b), **dra** (188), **dua** (122d)

- DA   **Ada** (110a,112c,183c), **Ida** (103d,183c), **oda** (74a,170d)

D - B   **dab** (46a,57b,58b,114d,115c), **deb, Deb** (183d), **dib** (21b,43b,c, 120d,140a), **dub** (25c,46a,c,87a,105b,121a,140a)

D - C   **dec** (122d), **doc** (143a), **duc** (61c)

DD -   **DDS** (42a)

D - D   **dad, did, dod** (11a,32a,43b,140c), **dud** (21c,54a)

- DD   **add** (10d,11d,14c,158a,167c), **odd** (46b,53a,109b,157a,172d,173c)

DE -   **dea** (68d,89b), **deb, Deb** (183d), **dec** (122d), **dee** (91c), **Dee** (131d, 139b), **deg** (154b), **dei** (68d), **den** (38b,44d,74b,130d,133c,140d), **der** (13b,66b,d,164a), **des** (13b,61a,62b,d), **dev** (42a,b), **dew** (41a), **dey** (8d,84a,114c,135a,139b,170d)

D - E   **dae** (139b), **dee** (91c), **Dee** (131d,139b), **die** (27b,54a,65a,155a, 167a), **doe** (41d,55b,127a), **due** (7b,115b,124c), **dye** (33c,154d)

- DE   **ade** (18c,149d), **Ade** (9c,53b), **Ede** (35b,65d), **ide** (40c,57a,b,d, 158b), **ode** (26b,79c,94d,118a,119d,120a,150b)

D - G   **dag** (11b,118c), **Dag** (108c,139c), **deg** (154b), **dig** (52b), **dog** (10b, 45b,59b), **dug**

DH -   **dha** (99d), **dhu** (40b), **Dhu** (28a,87d)

D - H   **dah** (24c,87a), **doh** (113b)

- DH   **edh** (91c)

DI -   **dia** (122b,d,152a,165b), **dib** (21b,43b,c,120d,140a), **did, die** (27b, 54a,65a,155a,167a), **dig** (52b), **dii** (68d), **dim** (47a,48b,54a,74d, 94d,109b), **din** (31c,130b,174a), **dip** (26a,79d,117c,138c), **dis** (122b,d), **Dis** (68b,73a,119d,172d,174b), **dit** (62b,d,120a,159d), **div** (42b,139b), **dix** (118b), **Dix** (60b)

D - I   **dei** (68d) **dii** (68d), **dui** (46d)

- DI   **Udi** (108a)

DJ -   **djo** (188)

D - K   **dak** (95c)

D - L   **dal** (117d,153d)

D - M   **dam** (30c,49c,55b,156d,180a), **dim** (47a,48b,54a,74d,94d,109b), **dom** (121c,166b,c), **Dom** (94b), **dum** (45c,67b,113a)

D - N   **dan** (24c,97c), **Dan** (18c,39c,77d,83a,84a,141b), **den** (38b,44d,74b, 130d,133c,140d), **din** (130b,174a), **don** (151d,166c), **Don** (96a), **dun** (19a,39d,46d,71a,97d,115b,160b)

DO -   **Doc** (143a), **dod** (11a,32a,43b,140c), **doe** (41d,55b,127a), **dog** (10b, 45b,59b), **doh** (113b), **dom** (121c,166b,c), **Dom** (94b), **don** (151d, 166c), **Don** (96a), **dop** (39c,43b), **dor** (17d,24b,32b,46b,47a,81b, 85d), **dos** (45d,61a,97a,181b), **dot** (45d,97a,104d,105a,116b,153a, 162d), **dow** (17d,87a,88d,175d)

230

D - O   **dao** (117a) **djo** (188), **DSO** (99d), **duo** (46d,113a,171d)

- DO   **ado** (22b,24d,35b,64c,121d,156b,170a), **edo** (162a), **Edo** (107a, 166d), **Ido** (13c,81d,88c,173c), **Odo** (181d), **udo** (28a,30c,48c,84b, c,d,136c,149d)

D - P   **dap** (43b,c,46b,91b,147d), **dip** (26a,79d,117c,138c), **dop** (39c,43b)

DR -   **dra** (188), **dry** (46d,85a,137c,164c)

D - R   **dar** (111b,169a), **der** (13b,66b,d,164a), **dor** (17d,24b,32b,46b,47a, 81b,85d), **dur** (95c)

DS -   **DSO** (99d)

D - S   **das** (13b,15d,36d,66b,d,164a), **DDS** (42a), **des** (13b,61a,62b,d), **dis** (122b,d), **Dis** (68b,73a,119d,172d,174b), **dos** (45d,61a,97a,181b)

- DS   **DDS** (42a), **ods** (109a)

D - T   **dit** (62b,d,120a,159d), **dot** (45d,97a,104d,105a,116b,153a,162d)

DU -   **dua** (122d), **dub** (25c,46a,c,87a,105b,121a,140a), **duc** (61c), **dud** (21c,54a), **due** (7b,115b,124c), **dug, dui** (46d), **dum** (45c,67b,113a), **dun** (19a,39d,46d,71a,97d,115b,160b), **duo** (46d,113a,171d), **dur** (95c), **dux** (31d,64a,90c)

D - U   **dhu** (40b), **Dhu** (28a,87d)

D - V   **dev** (42a,b), **div** (42b,139b)

D - W   **daw** (39a,70b,84a), **dew** (41a), **dow** (17d,87a,88d,175d)

D - X   **dix** (118b), **Dix** (60b), **dux** (31d,64a,90c)

DY -   **dye** (33c,154d)

D - Y   **day** (153a), **dey** (8d,84a,114c,135a,139b,170d), **dry** (46d,85a,137c, 164c)

- DY   **ady** (188)

- DZ   **adz** (40c,167a)

EA -   **eae** (34b), **ean** (17d,23b,88a), **ear** (14c,d,28c,63d,64a,73c,111b, 116a,124b,137d,150d,153c), **eat** (37b,96b,135d,179b), **eau** (63a, 178c)

E - A   **ECA** (8a), **ela** (21c,53c,72b,76c,108b,174c), **Ena** (8c,126b), **era** (8a, 51a,116b,165d), **ESA** (8a), **eta** (71a,84c,91c), **Eva** (157a,183c)

- EA   **aea** (26a,36d), **dea** (68d,89b), **Hea** (15b), **kea** (114a,b), **lea** (56a, 97d,114d,185b), **Lea** (22d), **N.E.A.** (162c), **pea** (32d,91b,142a,175a), **rea** (9c,171a), **sea** (19a,52d,58c,112c,178d), **tea** (13d,18c,79c,81a, 145d,149c,159d), **Wea** (192), **yea** (7c,175c), **zea** (95c)

EB -   **ebb** (6a,15b,41c,43c,104a,128c,158a,178a), **ebo** (28b,110a)

E - B   **ebb** (6a,15b,41c,43c,104a,128c,158a,178a), **elb** (85c)

- EB   **deb, Deb** (183d), **Geb** (47d), **Keb** (47d), **neb** (17b,19a,d,115d), **reb** (35d,75c,85b,162c,166b), **Seb** (47d), **web** (50d,70a,98c,99a,106c, 149b)

EC -   **ECA** (8a), **ect** (35a,122d,183b), **ecu** (58a,144b,c)

E - C   **etc** (10b)

- EC   **dec** (122d), **sec** (46c,182c), **tec** (43a)

ED -   **Ede** (35b,65d), **edh** (91c), **edo** (162a), **Edo** (107a,166d)

E - D   **Eed** (102d), **eld** (10b,93c,110b,165d), **end** (8b,67d,120a,125d,130a, 166a), **erd** (47d,119d,145c)

- ED   **bed** (60c,148b), **Eed** (102d), **fed**, **ged** (100a,140a), **ked** (140b,144a), **led**, **Ned** (96a), **ped** (16d,34b), **red** (33c,38d,59a,127b,134c,135b), **Red** (151b), **sed** (89a), **ted** (74d,138b,154b), **Ted** (96b), **wed** (97a, 173c), **zed** (91c)

EE -   **Eed** (102d), **eel** (36a,49c,57a,b,88a,102c,176c), **een** (52a,139c, 185d), **eer** (9b,52a), **ees** (139c)

E - E   **eae** (34b), **Ede** (35b,65d), **eke** (14c,117c), **ele** (48c), **eme** (38d,70a, 140c,172b), **ene** (35b,158b,c), **ere** (17d,150c), **ese** (35b,158c), **ete** (36c,62d,141c,159b), **eve** (47a,131a,143a,165d,171c), **Eve** (183c), **ewe** (88a,143d), **Exe** (43a), **eye** (93d,111b,140d)

- EE   **bee** (46b,81b,91c,108c), **cee** (91c), **dee** (91c), **Dee** (131d,139b), **fee** (29a,58a,70d,166a,d), **gee** (35a,91c,100a,131c,139c,162c), **lee** (74b, 144b), **Lee** (9c,31c,96a), **mee** (169a), **nee** (19d,22b,25c,60b,95c), **pee** (91c), **ree** (12c,50a,80c,134d,137a,140b,144a,146b), **Ree** (25a), **see** (20a,43c,44a,51c,53c,93d,109b,113c,116a,176d,178c,183b), **tee** (39d,52b,69d,91c,112d,115d,118b,172a), **vee** (58a,91c,106a), **wee** (52c,100c,148c), **zee** (81b,91c)

EF -   **eft** (93b,107a,136c,169d)

E - F   **elf** (54b,154b)

- EF   **AEF** (184d), **kef** (12a,46c,75d,88c), **nef** (32b,144c,d), **ref**

EG -   **egg** (32d,80b,81c,112c,174a), **ego** (51a,79a,142b)

E - G   **egg** (32d,80b,81c,112c,174a), **eng** (48a,146a), **erg** (50b,173b, 184c)

- EG   **beg** (38b,150a), **deg** (154b), **Geg** (8c), **keg** (27a,105b), **leg** (37d, 92b,141d,159d,169c), **Meg** (8c,183d), **peg** (38c,46b,54d,98a,118a, 184c), **teg** (45a,54b,171d)

E - H   **edh** (91c), **eth** (91c,158d)

- EH   **Heh** (191), **reh** (8d)

EI -   **ein** (66b,c), **Eir** (69a,75a), **eis** (66c)

E - I   **Eli** (18c,d,76c,96a,137a,185a), **epi** (56c,61c,d,111c,112d,122d, 133c,153c,167b,174a), **eri** (13d,21c,146d), **Eri** (18c)

- EI   **dei** (68d), **fei** (16a,185b), **hei** (65a), **lei** (65b,74c), **rei** (89b,121c), **Rei** (18d), **Vei** (91d), **Wei** (30b,162b)

EK -   **eke** (14c,117c)

E - K   **elk** (22c,90d,178a)

- EK   **lek** (65c)

EL -   **ela** (21c,53c,72b,76c,108b,174c), **elb** (85c), **eld** (10b,93c,110b, 165d), **ele** (48c), **elf** (54b,154b), **Eli** (18c,d,76c,96a,137a,185a), **elk** (22c,90d,178a), **ell** (10d,24b,32c,98a), **elm** (168c), **els** (140a), **elt** (87a,117c,139d), **Ely** (27c,50b)

E - L   **eel** (36a,49c,57a,b,88a,102c,176c), **ell** (10d,24b,32c,98a)

- EL   **bel** (64a,93c,168d,173b,183d), **Bel** (15b,68a,126d), **eel** (36a,49c, 57a,b,88a,102c,176c), **gel** (32d,73d,150a), **Hel** (68d,93c,172d), **mel** (77d), **pel** (55c,160d), **rel** (49b,173b), **sel** (62c,140b), **tel** (34a, b,122c), **zel** (40c)

EM -   **eme** (38d,70a,140c,172b), **Ems** (125a,151c), **emu** (19b,58c,111d)

E - M   **elm** (168c)

- EM   **gem** (104b), **hem** (22a,36a,48b,52c,155a), **mem** (91c), **Sem** (107c), **Tem** (143a,159b)

EN -   **Ena** (8c,126b), **end** (8b,67d,120a,125d,130a,166a), **ene** (35b,158b, c), **eng** (48a,146a) **ens** (17d,18a,51a,52d), **ent** (34d,158b,c)

E - N   **ean** (17d,23b,88a), **een** (52a,139c,185d), **ein** (66b,c), **eon** (8a,37b, 51d,116b), **ern** (19c,d,47b,54b,141a)

- EN   **ben** (78c,81b,102c,115c), **Ben** (12d,77c,96a,106c,139d,140a), **den** (38b,44d,74b,130d,133c,140d), **een** (52a,139c,185d), **fen** (21c,97a, 160a), **gen** (31d,76b), **hen** (19a,60c,114c,136c), **ken** (60b,87c,122b, 172d), **men** (38c,116a,117b,170a), **Men** (94d), **pen** (36a,50a,80d, 118b,126d,160a,185c), **sen** (190), **ten** (19a,26c,41c,42b), **wen** (40c, 72a,110a,170c,177b), **yen** (33b,42d,93c,174a), **Zen** (24a)

EO -   **eon** (8a,37b,51d,116b), **Eos** (14d,41a,68d)

E - O   **ebo** (28b,110a), **edo** (162a), **Edo** (107a,166d), **ego** (51a,79a,142b), **eso** (34d,183b), **ETO** (184d), **exo** (122d)

- EO   **geo** (34a,47d), **Leo** (36b,c,92d,186d), **Meo** (27b,80c), **neo** (34a,b, c,100d,106d,108c,122c,d,128c), **Reo** (26c)

EP -   **epi** (56c,61c,d,111c,112d,122d,133c,153c,167b,174a)

E - P   **e.s.p.** (147b)

- EP   **cep** (63a), **hep** (52c), **kep** (139b), **nep** (27c,32d,56a,87c,184b), **pep** (50b,176b), **rep** (53b,d,131a,171c), **yep**, **Zep**

ER -   **era** (8a,51a,116b,165d), **erd** (47d,119d,145c), **ere** (17d,150c), **erg** (50b,173b,184c), **eri** (13d,21c,146d), **Eri** (18c), **ern** (19c,d,47b,54b, 141a), **err** (21a,43a,67d,100c,d,147a,148b,157b,168b,178a), **ers** (20a,176a), **ert** (140c,174a), **ery** (155d,158c,d)

E - R   **ear** (14c,d,28c,63d,64a,73c,111b,116a,124b,137d,150d,153c), **eer** (9b,52a), **Eir** (69a,75a), **err** (21a,43a,67d,100c,d,147a,148b,157b, 168b,178a), **Eur.** (36c)

- ER   **aer** (8b,28d,34a,b,175a), **ber** (85c), **der** (13b,66b,d,164a), **eer** (9b, 52a), **ger** (8d,36d,75c,124d), **her** (124b,c), **ier** (50a,158c), **Ker** (71b, 95d), **Ler** (23d,28a,b,64b,106c,141a), **mer** (62c,141a), **ner** (137c), **o'er** (6b,112a), **per** (25c,122d,165b,176a), **ser** (80d,83b,d,116c, 152d,180a), **ter** (34d,122d,165a), **xer** (34a), **zer** (188)

ES -   **ESA** (8a), **ese** (35b,158c), **eso** (34d,183b), **esp** (147b), **ess** (39d,78a, 91c,158c,184d), **est** (50a,61c,62a,79b,89c,158d,159c)

E - S   **ees** (139c), **eis** (66c), **els** (140a), **Ems** (125a,151c), **ens** (17d,18a, 51a,52d), **Eos** (14d,41a,68d), **ers** (20a,176a), **ess** (39d,78a,91c,158c, 184d)

- ES   **aes** (23c,89a,101c,132d,133a,b), **Bes** (68b,119c), **ces** (62b), **des** (13b,61a,62b,d), **ees** (139c), **Ges** (151b), **les** (13b,61a), **mes** (62b), **nes** (26b), **oes** (109a), **pes** (59d), **res** (80a,89d,91a,97c,164c), **ses** (61d), **yes** (7c,55a)

ET -   **eta** (71a,84c,91c), **etc** (10b), **ete** (36c,62d,141c,159b), **eth** (91c, 158d), **ETO** (184d)

E - T   **eat** (37b,96b,135d,179b), **ect** (35a,122d,183b), **eft** (93b,107a,136c, 169d), **elt** (87a,117c,139d), **ent** (34d,158b,c), **ert** (140c,174a), **est** (50a,62a,79b,89c,158d,159c)

- ET aet (89a,109d), **bet, cet** (62d,180b), **get** (44d,64b,109b,141d), **jet** (20b,35a,154c), **ket** (189), **let** (9a,76d,77c,116b,130a,158b,163a), **met** (28d), **net** (26c,32a,50d,53b,60d,99a,124a,142a,149b), **pet** (26d,37c,55a,59b,162d), **ret** (58b,95a,149c,155d), **set** (7b,11d,13a, 23c,32b,33c,37c,58a,73d,109b,118c,121c,142c,150a,186a), **Set** (52b, 68a,b,111d), **vet, wet** (40d,46a,101a,124a,127c,149c), **yet** (18b, 24d,64c,77c,80a,108c,156b,165b)

EU - **Eur.** (136c)

E - U **eau** (63a,178c), **ecu** (58a,144b,c), **emu** (19b,58c,111d)

- EU **feu** (55d,61c,88b), **heu** (8b,30c,52c), **jeu** (61d), **leu** (190), **meu** (153b), **peu** (62a), **Reu** (115d)

EV - **Eva** (157a,183c), **eve** (47a,131a,143a,165d,171c), **Eve** (183c)

- EV **dev** (42a,b), **lev** (33b) **rev**

EW - **ewe** (88a,143d)

- EW **dew** (41a), **few, hew** (40a), **Jew, lew** (190), **Lew** (96a), **mew** (25b, 27b,50a,55b,72c,74d,101b,141b,153b), **new** (11a,63c,88d,111c, 128c), **pew** (30d,52c,57d,120b,141c), **rew** (75c,140c,176b), **sew, yew** (36a,52a,b,145d,168c,d)

EX - **Exe** (43a), **exo** (122d)

- EX **Aex** (46d), **hex** (18c), **lex** (90b), **rex** (86c,96a), **sex, vex** (7c,10d, 44c,82c)

EY - **eye** (93d,111b,140d)⁻

E - Y **Ely** (27c,50b), **ery** (155d,158c,d)

- EY **bey** (70b,170d), **dey** (8d,84a,114c,135a,139b,170d), **fey** (49c), **gey** (140a), **hey** (25c,52c), **key** (14c,82d,88b,117c,118c,150b,180c), **ley** (190), **Ney** (63b,97b,105d), **rey** (86c,152b), **sey** (120c), **wey** (173b)

- EZ **fez** (75a,162a), **gez** (188), **nez** (62b), **tez** (125c), **yez**

FA - **fac** (41c), **fad** (38b,108c,163a), **fag** (55a,166a), **fan** (43a,154b, 156b,182d), **far** (44c), **fas** (44d,89d,129d), **fat** (110a,124a), **fay** (32c,54b,154b), **Fay** (183c)

F - A **Fha** (8a), **fra** (23c,63c,101d,123b,129d)

- FA **MFA** (42a)

F - B **fib** (162a), **fob** (29b,59b,113b,178c), **fub** (29b,119d)

F - C **fac** (41c)

F - D **fad** (38b,108c,163a), **fed, fid** (16b,54d,118a,167b), **fod** (188)

FE - **fed, fee** (29a,58a,70d,166a,d), **fei** (16a,185b), **fen** (21c,97a,160a), **feu** (55d,61c,88b), **few, fey** (49c), **fez** (75a,162a)

F - E **fee** (29a,58a,70d,166a,d), **fie** (52c,59d), **foe** (111a)

- FE **ife** (22c,75d)

- FF **off** (6b,15c,44c,76a)

F - G **fag** (55a,166a), **fig, fog** (109b), **fug** (129a)

FH - **FHA** (8a)

F - H **foh** (52c)

FI - **fib** (162a), **fid** (16b,54d,118a,167b), **fie** (52c,59d), **fig, fin** (86a), **fir** (16a,36a,52a,168c,d,169a), **fit** (7a,11d,51b,75a,114a,123a, 124c,126a,153a,157c,159a), **fix** (7b,10a,13a,14c,43a,c,141d,165c)

F - I   **fei** (16a,185b)

FL -   **flo, flu, fly** (58c,81b,163b,178d)

F - L   **Ful** (158b)

- FL   **AFL** (173a)

F - N   **fan** (43a,154b,156b,182d), **fen** (21c,97a,160a), **fin** (86a), **Fon** (40b), **fun**

FO -   **fob** (29b,59b,113b,178c), **fod** (188), **foe** (111a), **fog** (109b), **foh** (52c), **Fon** (40b), **foo** (42c), **fop** (38a,40d,46d), **for** (123d,163a, 166c), **fot** (188), **fou** (139a), **fox** (134a)

F - O   **Flo, foo** (42c), **fro** (15b)

- FO   **Ufo** (59a)

F - P   **fop** (38a,40d,46d)

FR -   **fra** (23c,63c,101d,123b,129d), **fro** (15b), **fry** (57d)

F - R   **far** (44c), **fir** (16a,36a,52a,168c,d,169a), **for** (123d,163a,166c), **fur**

- FR   **Afr.** (36c)

F - S   **fas** (44d,89d,129d)

F - T   **fat** (110a,124a), **fit** (7a,11d,51b,75a,114a,123a,124c,126a,153a, 157c,159a), **fot** (188), **fut** (188)

- FT   **aft** (14a,15b,17d,128b,167d), **eft** (93b,107a,136c,169d), **oft** (63c)

FU -   **fub** (29b,119d), **fug** (129a), **Ful** (158b), **fun, fur, fut** (188)

F - U   **feu** (55d,61c,88b), **flu, fou** (139a)

F - W   **few**

F - X   **fix** (7b,10a,13a,14c,43a,c,141d,165c), **fox** (134a)

F - Y   **fay** (32c,54b,154b), **Fay** (183c), **fey** (49c), **fly** (58c,81b,163b,178d), **fry** (57d)

F - Z   **fez** (75a,162a)

GA -   **gab** (29b,78a,116c,122a,161c,183a), **gad** (58c,100a,127d,132b, 153c,154b,178a), **Gad** (84a,186d), **gaf** (12b), **gag** (146c,183a), **gaj** (190), **gal, gam** (76b,176d,180c), **Gan** (132d), **gap** (11b,23a,29b, 76c,110d,128a), **gar** (57b,c,d,106b), **gas** (10b,29b,59a,116d,161c), **gat** (28d,72c,131a), **gau** (66d,67a), **gav** (72d), **gaw** (140c), **gay, Gay** (17d), **gaz** (188,190)

G - A   **goa** (65d,104b,126c), **Goa** (121c), **gra** (59b,94b,160c)

- GA   **aga** (35a,39a,48b,102d,103a,b,111c,166b,170d,171a)

G - B   **gab** (29b,78a,116c,122a,161c,183a), **Geb** (47d), **gib** (17b,38b,95d, 166d,179d), **gob** (97b,136c)

G - D   **gad** (58c,100a,b,127d,132b,153c,154b,178a), **Gad** (84a,186d), **ged** (140a), **Ged** (100a), **gid** (143d), **god** (42a), **God** (84d)

GE -   **Geb** (47d), **Ged** (100a,140a), **gee** (35a,91c,100a,131c,139c,162c), **Geg** (8c), **gel** (32d,73d,150a), **gem** (104b), **gen** (31d,76b), **geo** (34a, 47d), **ger** (8d,36d,75c,124d), **Ges** (151b), **get** (44d,64b,109b,141d), **gey** (140a), **gez** (188)

G - E   **gee** (35a,91c,100a,131c,139c,162c), **gie** (139c,140a), **gue** (176c)

- GE   **age** (51d,66a,92a,97c,98c,116b,141c)

G - F   **gaf** (12b)

G - G gag (146c,183a), **Geg** (8c), **gig** (26d,28d,57c,105b,127a,144c,153a, 171d), **gog** (95b)

- GG egg (32d,80b,81c,112c,174a)

GH - ghi (24d)

- GH ugh (52c)

GI - gib (17b,38b,95d,166d,179d), **gid** (143d), **gie** (139c,140a), **gig** (26d,28d,57c,105b,127a,144c,153a,171d), **gin** (37c,92d,139a,142a, 149b), **gip** (29b,160c), **git** (101a)

G - I ghi (24d), **goi** (107c), **gri** (75c,78b)

G - J gaj (190)

G - L gal, gel (32d,73d,150a), **gul** (134a)

G - M gam (76b,176d,180c), **gem** (104b), **gum** (7b,53c,80b,130c,156b), **gym** (154a)

GN - gnu (11a,181d)

G - N gan (132d), **gen** (31d,76b), **gin** (37c,92d,139a,142a,149b), **gon** (188), **gun** (56d,131a,146a)

GO - goa (65d,104b,126c), **Goa** (121c), **gob** (97b,136c), **god** (42a), **God** (84d), **gog** (95b), **goi** (107c), **gon** (188), **goo** (156b), **Gor** (81a), **got, goy** (107c), **goz** (190)

G - O geo (34a,47d), **goo** (156b)

- GO ago (25a,69d,114d,147a), **ego** (51a,79a,142b)

G - P gap (11b,23a,29b,76c,110d,128a), **gip** (29b,160c), **gup** (70a), **gyp** (29b,42a,160c)

GR - gra (59b,94b,160c), **gri** (75c,78b), **grr** (52c), **gry** (78b)

G - R gar (57b,c,d,106b), **ger** (8d,36d,75c,124d), **Gor** (81a), **grr** (52c), **gur** (159a)

G - S gas (10b,29b,59a,116d,161c), **Ges** (151b), **Gus** (96a)

G - T gat (28d,72c,131a), **get** (44d,64b,109b,141d), **git** (101a), **got, gut** (114d,130a)

GU - gue (176c), **gul** (134a), **gum** (7b,53c,80b,130c,156b), **gun** (56d, 131a,146a), **gup** (70a), **gur** (159a), **Gus** (96a), **gut** (114d,130a), **guy** (55b,131b,155d), **Guy** (96a), **guz** (188)

G - U gau (66d,67a), **gnu** (11a,181d)

- GU ngu (188

G - V gav (72d)

G - W gaw (140c)

GY - gym (154a), **gyp** (29b,42a,160c)

G - Y gay, **Gay** (17d), **gey** (140a), **goy** (107c), **gry** (78b), **guy** (55b,131b, 155d), **Guy** (96a)

G - Z gaz (188,190), **gez** (188), **goz** (190), **guz** (188)

HA - had, **hae** (139c), **hag** (140a,183a), **hah** (52c), **hai** (55c), **hak** (46d), **Hal** (69d), **ham** (98a,144b), **Ham** (18d,107c), **Han** (16c,30b,185b), **hao** (189) **hap** (17d,28d), **har** (139c), **has, hat** (74d), **Hat** (183d), **haw** (35a,52c,74d,91a,155a,162c), **hay** (52c,55c,165d)

H - A Hea (15b), **hia** (114b), **hoa** (39b)

236

- HA	aha (52c,55c,159c), cha (162b,c), dha (99c), FHA (8a), Kha (88d, 106b), sha (110c,143d,144a,c,174c,181c)
H - B	hob (40c,56d,100c,124b,167a,180c), hub (28b,118b,180c)
H - C	hic (52c,90a,164c)
H - D	had, hid, hod (23b,32d,102d,141a)
HE -	Hea (15b), Heh (191), hei (65a), Hel (68d,93c,172d), hem (22a,36a, 48b,52c,155a), hen (19a,60c,114c,136c), hep (52c), her (124b,c), heu (8b,30c,52c), hew (40a), hex (18c), hey (25c,52c)
H - E	hae (139c), hie (79a,153b), hoe (39c), hue (33c,143b)
- HE	che (145d), rhe (59a), she (124b), She (73a), the (13b)
H - G	hag (140a,183a), hog (45b,117c,160c), hug (32c,49d)
H - H	hah (52c), Heh (191), Hoh (80d), hsh (79c), huh (52c)
HI -	hia (114b), hic (52c,90a,164c), hid, hie (79a,153b), him (124b), hin (189), hip (52c,54b,85b,133c,134a), hir (76a), his (124c), hit (32d,157c,158a)
H - I	hai (55c), hei (65a), hoi (52c,74b,185b), hui (14a,30b,56d,114c)
- HI	Ahi (32c,147d), chi (91c), Chi (69c), ghi (24d), ihi (57c,156b), phi (91c)
H - K	hak (46d)
H - L	Hal (69d), Hel (68d,93c,172d)
H - M	ham (98a,144b), Ham (18d,107c), hem (22a,36a,48b,52c,155a), him (124b), hum (24d,46b,150d)
- HM	ohm (49b,67a,173b)
H - N	Han (16c,30b,185b), hen (19a,60c,114c,136c), hin (189), Hun (16c,21d,174b)
HO -	hoa (39b), hob (40c,56d,100c,124b,167a,180c), hod (23b,32d,102d, 141a), hoe (39c), hog (45b,117c,160c), Hoh (80d), hoi (52c,74b, 185b), hop (40b), Hor (103d), hot (10c,176c), how, hoy (16c,52c)
H - O	hao (189)
- HO	cho (188), mho (49b,173b), oho (52c), Rho (71b,91c), sho (188), tho (52a), Tho (167a), who (129c)
H - P	hap (17d,28d), hep (52c), hip (52c,54b,85b,133c,134a), hop (40b), hup (35a), hyp
H - R	har (139c), her (124b,c), hir (76a), Hor (103d), Hur (91d)
- HR	ihr (66d)
HS -	hsh (79c)
H - S	has, his (124c)
H - T	hat (74d), Hat (183d), hit (32d,157c,158a), hot (10c,176c), hut (143c)
HU -	hub (28b,118b,180c), hue (33c,143b,) hug (32c,49d), huh (52c), hui (14a,30b,56d,114c), hum (24d,46b,150d), Hun (16c,21d,174b), hup (35a), Hur (91d), hut (143c)
H - U	heu (8b,30c,52c)
- HU	ahu (24c,41d,65d,103d,120d), dhu (40b), Dhu (28a,87d), phu (38c), Shu (30b,127a)

H - W   haw (35a,52c,74d,91a,155a,162c), hew (40a), how

H - X   hex (18c)

HY -   hyp

H - Y   hay (52c,55c,165d), hey (25c,52c), hoy (16c,52c)

- HY   shy (16d,99d,128c,160c,165d,175a), thy, why (52c)

IA -   ial (158b), Ian (85b,96a,139d), iao (78a,96c,178d)

I - A   iba (117a), Ida (103d,183c), Ila (16b), ILA (173a), ina (158c), Ina (183c), Ira (18c,d,41a,68c,82c,96a,164a,178a,c), Ita (51b,71d, 94d,95d,106b,117a), ITA (173a), iva (76a,97b,127b,185b) iwa (63c), iya (95b,108d,111c)

- IA   dia (122b,d,152a,165b), hia (114b), Lia (82b), mia (83c), pia (13b, 22d,48a,120d), ria (38c,51d,81b,152a,b), Sia (80c), tia (151d), via (132a,133a,b,179a)

IB -   iba (117a), Ibo (107a,180b)

- IB   bib, dib (21b,43b,c,120d,140a), fib (162a), gib (17b,38b,95d,166d, 179d), jib (38b,136b,146a), mib (8d,96c), nib (17b,19d,115d), rib (37c,85b,90c,98a,144d,159d,172a), sib (86b,129c,139d,147b)

IC -   ice (30a,36d,42d,63d), ich (66c), ici (61d), Ici (9b), ics (158d), icy (65d)

- IC   hic (52c,90a,164c), pic (188), sic (90a,165b,168b), tic (104d,153a, 171c,d)

ID -   Ida (103d,183c), ide (40c,57a,b,d,158b), Ido (13c,81d,88c,173c)

I - D   Ind (80c)

- ID   aid (14a,15b,64c,75d,158b), bid (35a,82a,109d,111b,174c), Cid (151c,d), did, fid (16b,54d,118a,167b), gid (143d), hid, kid (67d, 85b,90d,186a), lid (167b), mid (9d,28b,73b), nid (72a,106b,c,116d), oid (158c), rid (32a,44a,60d), Sid (96a)

IE -   ier (50a,158c)

I - E   ice (30a,36d,42d,63d), Ide (40c,57a,b,d,158b), ife (22c,75d), Ike (123a), ile (62a,63b,158c), ine (29c,158b,c), Ine (10c,137d,180b), ire (10c,30c,52b,64c,125a,130b,185a), ise (40d,158c,d), Ise (78a, 84c), ite (59b,81a,105d,130c,158b,c,d,161a), ive (158c)

- IE   cie (61b,63b), die (27b,54a,65a,155a,167a), fie (52c,59d), gie (139c,140a), hie (79a,153b), lie (53a,69d,162a), nie (53c), pie (42d,85d,95b,114d,171b,172a), rie (28c,70d,97d), sie (46c,66d, 139b,140b,146b), tie (10a,14c,38b,45d,51a,88d,109b,127c,138b, 170b), vie (36c,157c,170c)

IF -   ife (22c,75d)

- IF   Lif (107d), rif (188), Sif (164d), vif (62a), Zif (102a)

I - G   ing (114b,d,148d,158c,d,175c), Ing (10c,115b)

- IG   big, cig, dig (52b), fig, gig (26d,28d,57c,105b,127a,144c, 153a,171d), jig (40b,d), mig (8d,96c,145b), Mig (118d), nig (33b, 40a,46a), pig (27a,45b,99a,151b,160c), rig (51b,112a), tig (46b), wig (73b), zig (84a)

IH -   ihi (57c,156b), ihr (66d)

I - H   ich (66c), ish (158b), Ith (10a,28a,82b,99d)

I - I ici (61d), ici (9b), ihi (57c,156b), ini (158d), iri (18a,d,75a)

- II dii (68d), oii (105c), rii (157b,175b)

IJ - ijo (107a)

IK - ike (123a)

I - K ilk (31d,54c,86b,136d,139c,140b), ink (20b,40c), irk (10d)

- IK aik (139d), pik (188)

IL - ila (16b), ILA (173a), ile (62a,63b,158c), ilk (31d,54c,86b,136d, 139c,140b), ill (43d,121a,173a,c,d), ILO (184c), ils (62b,d,164b)

I - L ial (158b), ill (43d,121a,173a,c,d)

- IL ail (170a), kil (82b), lil (72d), mil (80b,110c,164d,182d), Mil (10a), nil (108c), oil (11a,71a), pil (34b), sil (30c,185c,d), til (142d)

IM - imp (42b,127d,174a), imu (15d)

I - M ism (45a,79b,161c)

- IM aim (42d,43d,67d,109b,125d,157c), Bim (16c), dim (47a,48b,54a, 74d,94d,109b), him (124b), Jim (96a), Kim (86d), lim (21a), mim (12b), nim (96d,155d), rim (22a,48b,96d,116b,124b,166a,180c), Sim (96b), Tim (43b), vim (50b,176b)

IN - ina (158c), Ina (183c), Ind (80c), ine (29c,158b,c), Ine (10c, 137d,180b), ing (114b,d,158c,d,175c) Ing (10c,115b), ini (158d), ink (20b,40c), inn (72b,73b,78c,132b,150a,161c,162b,179a), Inn (41a), Ino (14b,25b), ins (164d), INS (107a,182d)

I - N Ian (85b,96a,139d), inn (72b,73b,78c,132b,150a,161c,162b,179a), Inn (41a), ion (11c,29a,49b,101b,114c,158c)

- IN ain (18d,91c,110c,124b,140a,154b,180a), bin (22c,59a,78a,128c, 156d), din (31c,130b,174a), ein (66b,c), fin (86a), gin (37c,92d, 139a,142a,149b), hin (189), jin (42b,153c), kin (30b,81c,129d) Kin (30b), lin (140c,168c,178d), Lin (115d,186c), Min (29d,68b, 113c), nin (107d), pin (45d,54d,141d,147d), rin (33b,142b), sin (91c,140b,147a,168b,176a), Sin (102b), tin (36c,99a,b,108b,155a, 179c), vin (63a,182b), win (7a,17b,64b,123b), yin (140a), Yin (30b, 143c,185b)

IO - ion (11c,29a,101b,114c,158c), ior (50a,158c), ios (74d), IOU (124b)

I - O iao (78a,96c,178d), Ibo (107a,180b), Ido (13c,81d,88c,173c), Ijo (107a), ILO (184c), Ino (14b,25b), iso (34a,122c,d), Ito (84a,c, 186d), iyo (7d,176b)

- IO CIO (173a), mio (152c), rio (33a,131d,132a,152c,157b), Rio (23a), tio (152d), Zio (147d,163d)

I - P imp (42b,127d,174a)

- IP dip (26a,79d,117c,138d), gip (29b,160c), hip (52c,54b,85b,133c, 134a), kip (17c,72d,76c,189), lip (48b,58b,80a,131c), nip (20c, 29b,45d,46a,b,115c,118a), pip (11d,44a,121d,142a,154a), Pip (43b), rip (87b,130a,162c), Rip (178b), sip (46b,79d,104a,162b), tip (26b,d,50a,70d,77b,78a,120a,165d), yip (16c), zip (24b,50b, 176b)

IR - ira (18c,d,41a,68c,82c,96a,164a,178a,c), ire (10c,30c,52b,64c,

125a,130b,185a), **Iri** (18a,d,75a), **irk** (10d)

I - R **ier** (50a,158c), **ihr** (66d), **ior** (50a,158c)

- IR **air** (11c,12c,42b,44c,53a,96b,98c,99d,125b,170c), **Eir** (69a,75a), **fir** (16a,36a,52a,168c,d,169a), **hir** (76a), **mir** (29d,135c,d,166c,176b), **pir** (103a,b,136c), **sir** (163b,166b), **tir** (61d,62c,87a,145b), **vir** (89c)

IS - **ise** (40d,158c,d), **Ise** (78a,84c), **-ish** (158b), **ism** (45a,79b,161c), **iso** (34a,122c,d), **ist** (7b,34b,43a,59b,66c,158c,d)

I - S **ics** (158d), **ils** (62b,d,164b), **ins** (164d), **INS** (107a,182d), **ios** (74d), **its** (124c)

- IS **bis** (50a,90a,102c,130b,171c), **cis** (34c,122c), **dis** (122b,d), **Dis** (68b,73a,119d,172d,174b), **eis** (66c), **his** (124c), **lis** (54b, 58b,60c,62a,92b), **Lis** (47a), **mis** (122b,c,d,185c), **nis** (23d,67d, 68a,87c), **Nis** (19d), **ris** (131d), **sis** (67b,129c), **tis**, **vis** (59d,89b,d, 90b,176b), **wis** (79d,164c)

IT - **Ita** (51b,71d,94d,95d,106b,117a), **ITA** (173a), **ite** (59b,81a,105d, 130c,158b,c,d,161a), **Ite** (130c), **Ith** (10a,28a,82b,99d), **Ito** (84a, c,186d), **its** (124c)

I - T **ist** (7b,34b,43a,59b,66c,158b,c,d)

- IT **ait** (82d,132a), **bit** (46a,86b,114c,167a,b,171c,180d), **cit** (81a, 167d), **dit** (62b,d,120a,159d), **fit** (7a,11d,51b,75a,114a,123a,124c, 126a,153a,157c,159a), **git** (101a), **hit** (32d,157c,158a), **kit** (112a, 176c), **Kit** (96a,183d), **lit, mit** (56c,66d,183b), **nit** (48d), **pit** (52b, 142a,164a,168a), **rit** (148c,140b,153d), **sit** (98c,116a,121c,130c, 142d), **tit** (19c,130d), **uit** (47a,111d,151a), **wit** (78d,85b,177b)

I - U **imu** (15d), **I.O.U.** (124b)

- IU **piu** (102c), **Tiu** (7c,68c,147d,163d,166c,170c), **Ziu** (147d,163d)

IV - **iva** (76a,97b,127b,185b), **ive** (158c), **ivy** (32b,38c,176b)

- IV **div** (42b,139b), **Liv** (93b)

IW - **iwa** (63c)

- IW **Tiw** (68c,147d,163d)

- IX **Aix** (46b), **dix** (118b), **Dix** (60b), **fix** (7b,10a,13a,14c,43a,c,141d, 165c), **mix** (156b), **nix** (23d,108c,178d), **pix** (31a,51d,175d), **six** (26c), **vix** (89d,138b)

IY - **iya** (95b,108d,111c), **iyo** (7d,176b)

I - Y **icy** (65d), **ivy** (32b,38c,176b)

- IZ **biz, viz** (105b)

JA - **jab** (120b,125c) **jag** (124d,148a) **Jah** (84d), **jam** (123a,156d,165c), **Jap, jar** (31d,70d,143b), **Jat** (80d,125c), **jaw** (97d,138c), **jay** (19b, 91c)

J - B **jab** (120b,125c), **jib** (38b,136b,146a), **job** (30d,184c), **Job** (96a)

JE - **jet** (20b,35a,154c), **jeu** (61d), **Jew**

J - E **Joe** (96a)

J - G **jag** (124d,148a), **jig** (40b,d), **jog** (82c,85c,170a), **jug** (118c,123d)

J - H **Jah** (84d)

JI - **jib** (38b,136b,146a), **jig** (40b,d), **Jim** (96a), **jin** (42b,153c)

- JI **tji** (189), **uji** (146d)

J - M jam (123a,156d,165c), Jim (96a), jum (39c)

J - N jin (42b,153c)

JO - job (30d,184c), Job (96a), Joe (96a), jog (82c,85c,170a), jot (82a, 114c,166c,180d), jow (188), joy

- JO djo (188), Ijo (107a)

J - P Jap

J - R jar (31d,70d,143b), Jur (107b)

J - S jus (61d,90b)

J - T Jat (80d,125c), jet (20b,35a,154c), jot (82a,114c,166c,180d), jut 53a,124a)

JU - jug (118c,123d), jum (39c), Jur (107b), jus (61d,90b), jut (53a, 124a)

J - U jeu (61d)

J - W jaw (97d,138c), Jew, jow (188)

J - Y jay (19b,91c), joy

KA - kab (75c), kae (84a,140b), kaf (12b), Kaf (104a), kai (59c), Kai (14d,84c), kan (93a), kas (32c,47a), kat (105d), kay (82d), Kay (13b,134b)

K - A kea (114a,b), Kha (88d,106b), koa (74c), Kra (11b,91d), Kua (95c)

- KA aka (176b), Aka (13d,88b,c), oka (170c,184a,189)

K - B kab (75c), Keb (47d), kob (11a)

K - D ked (140b,144a), kid (67d,85b,90d,186a)

KE - kea (114a,b), Keb (47d), ked (140b,144a), kef (12a,46c,75d,88c), keg (27a,105b), ken (60b,87c,122b,172d), kep (139b), Ker (71b, 95d), ket (189) key (14c,82d,88b,117c,118c,150b,180c)

K - E kae (84a,140b)

- KE ake (60a,107a), eke (14c,117c), Ike (123a), oke (189)

K - F kaf (12b), Kaf (104a), kef (12a,46c,75d,88c)

K - G keg (27a, 105b)

KH - Kha (88d,106b)

- KH akh (153d)

KI - kid (67d,85b,90d,186a), kil (82b), Kim (86d), kin (30b,81c, 129d), Kin (30b), kip (17c,72d,76c,189), kit (112a,176c), Kit (96a, 183d)

K - I kai (59c), Kai (14d,84c), koi (26d), kri (75c,96d), Kri (75c), Kui (86a,88c,146a)

- KI ski (149c)

K - L kil (82b), Kol (18b), kyl (76d,79b)

K - M Kim (86d)

K - N kan (93a), ken (60b,87c,122b), kin (30b,81c), Kin (30b)

KO - koa (74c), kob (11a), koi (26d), Kol (18b), kop (76d), kor (75c), Kos (77c,82d), kou (169a)

- KO ako (189), TKO (22c)

K - P kep (139b), kip (17c,72d,76c,189), kop (76d), kup (188)

KR - Kra (11b,91d), kri (75c,96d), Kru (91d)
K - R Ker (71b,95d), kor (75c)
K - S kas (32c,47a), Kos (77c,82d)
K - T kat (105d), ket (189), kit (112a,176c), Kit (96a,183d)
KU - Kua (95c), Kui (86a,88c,146a), kup (188)
K - U kou (169a), Kru (91d)
- KU aku (57c,176a)
KY - kyi (76d,79b)
K - Y kay (82d), Kay (13b,134b), key (14c,82d,88b,117c,118c,150b, 180c)
- KY sky (56d)

LA - lab, lac (53c,99d,130c,135b,174d), lad (22c,25b,55b,157c,186a), lag (93c,155d), Lai (24c,d,88c), lai (98b,161b), lak (38a), lam (51b, 58b,93d,164d,178a), lan (37b,d,160b), Lao (80d,88c,146a,161b), lap (31b,37d,59b,127a,131d,153d,167d), lar (24c,51d,67a,78d,95d, 101d,171b), las (13b,151d) lat (24a,33d,106b,118a), lav (72d), law (26b,33a,40a,48c,60b,85d,91a,111b,134d,155d), lax (93d,130a), lay (16a,25c,80a,98b,107d,141d,150b), Laz (27d)
L - A lea (56a,97d,114d,185b), Lea (22d), Lia (82b), loa (7d,53c,97d,184d)
- LA ala (6d,13a,15c,61a,133d,182c,d), Ala. (151b), ela (21c,53c,72b, 76c,108b,174c), lla (16b), ILA (173a), ola (113b), ula (72c,158c)
L - B lab, LLB (42a), lob (15d,23b,94c,100b,163a,172d)
- LB alb (65b,176a), elb (85c), LLB (42a)
LC - LCI (21b)
L - C lac (53c,99d,130c,135b,174d)
L - D lad (22c,25b,55b,157c,186a), led, lid (167b), LLD (42a), lud (100a), Lud (23c,144b)
- LD eld (10b,93c,110b,165d), LLD (42a), old (8a,71a,77c,123c,175b)
LE - lea (56a,97d,114d,185b), Lea (22d), led, lee (74b,144b), Lee (9c, 31c,96a), leg (37d,92b,141d,159d,169c), lei (65b,74c), lek (65c), Leo (36b,c,92d,186d), Ler (23d,28a,b,64b,106c,141a), les (13b, 61a), let (9a,76d,77c,116b,130a,158b,163a), leu (190), lev (33b), lew (190), Lew (96a), lex (90b), ley (190)
L - E lee (74b,144b), Lee (9c,31c,96a), lie (53a,69d,162a), loe (139d), lue (146b), lye (8d,27d,93b)
- LE ale (17c,18c,50c,55d,92d,104c), cle (158d), ele (48c), ile (62a,63b, 158c), ole (24b,29b,113b,152a,158b,d), ule (23a,27d,134c,158c, 168d)
L - F Lif (107d), lof (188)
- LF Alf (96a), elf (54b,154b)
L - G lag (93c,155d), leg (37d,92b,141d,159d,169c), log (64a,128d), lug (27a,45d,47b,73c,136b), Lug (28b)
LI - Lia (82b), lid (167b), lie (53a,69d,162a), Lif (107d), lil (72d), lim (21a), lin (92c,140c,168c,178d), Lin (115d,186c), lip (48b,58b,80a, 131c), lis (54b,58b,60c,62a,92b), Lis (47a), lit, Liv (93b)

L - I   lai (98b,161b), Lai (24c,d,88c), LCI (21b), lei (65b,74c), loi (62a)

- LI   Ali (7b,12a,25c,48b,55a,60c,92d,101a,103a,164a,166b,170d), Eli (18c,d,76c,96a,137a,185a)

L - K   lak (38a), lek (65c), Lok (15d,68b)

- LK   alk (171b), elk (22c,90d,178a), ilk (31d,54c,86b,136d,139c,140b)

LL -   LLB (42a), LLD (42a)

L - L   lil (72d)

- LL   all (35c,118a,126d,181a), ell (10d,24b,32c,98a), ill (43d,121a,173a, c,d), Ull (7c,68c,146b,164d)

L - M   lam (51b,58b,93d,164d,178a), lim (21a), lum (30a)

- LM   elm (168c), olm (48c), ulm (49c), Ulm (40d)

L - N   lan (37b,d,160b), lin (140c,168c,178d), Lin (115d,186c), Lon (86c, 96a), lyn (140c,178d)

LO -   loa (7d,53c,97d,184d), lob (15d,23b,94c,100b,163a,172d), loe (139d), lof (188), log (64a,128d), loi (62a), Lok (15d,68b), Lon (86c, 96a), loo (65a), lop (30c,40a,46b,143a), los (13b,151d), lot (24b, 28d,55a,65d,114a,119c,143c,150d,168a), Lot (6b,73d), Lou (96a, 183d), low (16c,149d), loy (121c,148b,151c,167a)

L - O   Lao (80d,88c,146a,161b), Leo (36b,c,92d,186d), loo (65a), Luo (107b), Lwo (107b)

- LO   Flo, ILO (184c), ulo (34b,80d)

L - P   lap (31b,37d,59b,127a,131d,153d,167d), lip (48b,58b,80a,131c), lop (30c,40a,46b,143a)

- LP   alp (24b,103d,115c)

L - R   lar (24c,51d,67a,78d,95d,101d,171b), Ler (23d,28a,28b,64b,106c, 141a), Lur (116c)

LS -   Lst (21a,b,88b)

L - S   las (13b,151d), les (13b,61a), lis (54b,58b,60c,62a,92b), Lis (47a), los (13b,151d), lys (58b,92b)

- LS   als (66d,163d), els (140a), ils (62b,d,164b)

L - T   lat (24a,33d,106b,118a), let (9a,76d,77c,116b,130a,158b,163a), lit, lot (24b,28d,55a,65d,114a,119c,143c,150d,168a), Lot (6b,73d), Lst (21a,b,88b), lut (189)

- LT   alt (66c76c,109c), elt (87a,117c,139d), Olt (41a)

LU -   lud (100a), Lud (23c,144b), lue (146b), lug (27a,45d,47b,73c,136b), Lug (28b), lum (30a), Luo (107b), Lur (116c), lut (189), lux (79d)

L - U   leu (190), Lou (96a,183d)

- LU   flu, ulu (87a)

L - V   lav (72d), lev (33b), Liv (93b)

LW -   Lwo (107b)

L - W   law (26b,33a,40a,48c,60b,85d,91a,111b,134d,155d), lew (190), Lew (96a), low (16c,149d)

L - X   lax (93d, 130a), lex (90b), lux (79d)

LY -   lye (8d,27d,93b), lyn (140c,178d), lys (58b,92b)

L - Y   lay (98b,107d,141d,150b), ley (190), loy (121c,148b,151c,167a)

- LY aly (95d), **Ely** (27c,50b), **fly** (58c,81b,163b,178d), **ply** (59b,90b, 118d,164b,171c,174a,181b,184c), **sly** (13b,38b,64c,81b,132c)

L - Z **Laz** (27d)

MA - maa (97d,143d), **Mab** (54b,126b,183d), **Mac** (96a,140b,150b), **mad** (10c,82b), **Mae** (183c), **mag** (73b,95b,166c), **Mag** (183d), **Mah** (10b, 57c,102b), **mai** (62a), **mal** (34a,b,44a,52b,62c,122b), **Mal** (94b), **Mam** (192), **man** (29c,60c,64c,65a,142d,161d), **mao** (115b), **Mao** (30b), **map** (27a,29b,54a,98d,160a), **mar** (40b,44a,79a,d,81a,140d), **Mar** (93d), **mas** (34b,55b,119a), **mat** (46d,50d,94d,117c,161d), **Mat** (96a), **mau** (170c,188), **maw** (38b,d,72c,111a,121a,142a,156c), **Max** (96a), **may** (74d), **May** (183c)

M - A maa (97d,143d), **MFA** (42a), **mia** (83c), **mna** (71d,179d), **moa** (19b), **Mya** (31c)

- MA ama (26a,28d,31a,35b,39c,95b,108d,111c,117b,182c), **oma** (158c,d, 170c), **sma** (140b,148d), **Uma** (43a,69b,153d)

M - B **Mab** (54b,126b,183d), **mib** (8d,96c), **mob** (39a,127a,165b)

M - C **Mac** (96a,140b,150b)

M - D mad (10c,82b), **mid** (9d,28b,73b), **Mod** (138d), **mud** (6c)

ME - mee (169a), **Meg** (8c,183d), **mel** (77d), **mem** (91c), **men** (38c,116a, 117b,170a), **Men** (94d), **Meo** (27b,80c), **mer** (62c,141a), **mes** (62b), **met** (28d), **meu** (153b), **mew** (25b,27b,50a,55b,72c,74d,101b,141b, 153b)

M - E **Mae** (183c), **mee** (169a), **Mme.** (166b), **Moe** (96a)

- ME ame (37a,62d,131b), **eme** (38d,70a,140c,172b), **Mme.** (166b), **ume** (11d)

MF - **MFA** (42a)

M - G mag (73b,95b,166c), **Mag** (183d), **Meg** (8c,183d), **mig** (8d,96c, 145b), **Mig** (118d), **mug** (46b,54a,65a)

MH - mho (49b,173b)

M - H **Mah** (10b,57c,102b)

MI - mia (83c), **mib** (8d,96c), **mid** (9d,28b,73b), **mig** (8d,96c,145b), **Mig** (118d), **mil** (80b,110c,164d,182d), **Mil** (10a,82b), **mim** (12b), **Min** (29d,68b,113c), **mio** (152c), **mir** (29d,135c,d,166c,176b), **mis** (122b,c,d,185c), **mit** (56c,66d,183b), **mix** (156b)

M - I mai (62a), **Moi** (80d)

- MI ami (61d)

M - L mal (34a,b,44a,52b,62c,122b), **Mal** (94b), **mel** (77d), **mil** (80b,110c, 164d,182d), **Mil** (10a,82b), **mol** (58b,70c), **mul** (188)

MM - **Mme.** (166b)

M - M **Mam** (192), **mem** (91c), **mim** (12b), **mom**, **mum** (30d,95a,146c)

MN - mna (71d,179d)

M - N man (29c,60c,64c,65a,142d,161d), **men** (38c,116a,117b,170a), **Men** (94d), **Min** (29d,68b,113c), **mon** (15d,84b) **Mon** (24c), **mun** (157b)

MO - moa (19b), **mob** (39a,127a,165b), **Mod** (138d), **Moe** (96a), **Moi** (80d), **mol** (58b,70c), **mom**, **mon** (15d,84b), **Mon** (24c), **moo** (94b), **mop** (160a), **mos** (59b), **mot** (126d,130a,137d,183b), **mow** (32b,40a)

M - O   mao (115b), Mao (30b), Meo (27b,80c), mho (49b,173b), mio (152c), moo (94b), Mro (88c)

- MO   amo (79a,89c), omo (34d)

M - P   map (27a,29b,54a,98d,160a), mop (160a)

- MP   amp (49b,173b), imp (42b,127d,174a)

MR -   Mro (88c), Mrs. (166b), Mru (80d,88c)

M - R   mar (40b,44a,79a,d,81a,140d), Mar (93d), mer (62c,141a), mir (29d, 135c,d,166c,176b), mur (63a,177d)

M - S   mas (34b,55b,119a), mes (62b), mis (122b,c,d,185c), mos (59b), Mrs. (166b), Mus (104a,132c)

- MS   Ems (125a,151c)

M - T   mat (46d,50d,94d,117c,161d), Mat (96a), met (28d), mit (56c,66d, 183b), mot (126d,130a,137d,183b), mut (39c), Mut (9b,127a)

- MT   amt (37d,40d,108a,163c)

MU -   mud (6c), mug (46b,54a,65a), mul (188), mum (30d,95a,146c), mun (157b), mur (63a,177d), Mus (104a,132c), mut (39c), Mut (9b,127a), muy (152d,175d)

M - U   mau (170c,188), meu (153b), Mru (80d,88c)

- MU   emu (19b,58c,111d), imu (15d), SMU (40b), umu (112a)

M - W   maw (38b,d,72c,111a,121a,142a,156c), mew (25b,27b,50a,55b,72c, 74d,101b,141b,153b), mow (32b,40a)

M - X   Max (96a), mix (156b)

MY -   Mya (31c)

M - Y   may (74d), May (183c), muy (152d,175d)

- MY   amy (63c), Amy (8c,94b,183c)

NA -   nab (13b,26c,27b,142a), nae (139d), nag (73d,78b,138c,184d), nak (156b), Nan (183c), nap (65a,117d,146b,148a), nar (139d), nas (74a, 89c,178b), nat (7a,24c,d,106a), nay (42b,106b)

N - A   NEA (162c), noa (35b,124a,161a), NRA (8a,20d)

- NA   ana (10b,33c,60d,93a,98c,122b,d,140d,142b), Ana (28a,68d,100c), Ena (8c,126b), ina (158c), Ina (183c), mna (71d,179d), Ona (26b, 64a), sna (105b,140b,143d,144a,149c,181c,d), Una (54a,153b, 170c,183c)

N - B   nab (13b,26c,27b,142a), neb (17b,19a,d,115d), nib (17b,19d,115d), nob (38c,74d,84a,149d) nub (67b,94d,95c,118c,124d)

N - D   Ned (96a), nid (72a,106c,116d), nod (17c,46c), Nod (18d,25b)

- ND   and (36a), end (8b,67d,120a,125d,130a,166a), Ind (80c), und (66b)

NE -   N.E.A. (162c), neb (17b,19a,d,115d), Ned (96a), nee (19d,22b,25c, 60b,95c), nef (32b,144c,d), neo (34a,b,c,100d,106d,108c,122c,d, 128c), nep (27c,32d,56a,87c,184b), ner (137c), nes (26b), net (26c, 32a,50d,53b,60d,99a,124a,142a,149b), new (11a,63c,88d,111c, 128c, Ney (63b,97b,105d), nez (62b)

N - E   nae (139d), nee (19d,22b,25c,60b,95c), nie (53c,66c), NNE (35b), nye (72a,116d), Nye (9c,18b)

- NE   ane (61c,140a,158b), ene (35b,158b,c), ine (29c,158b,c), Ine (10c, 137d,180b), NNE (35b), one (79a,b,80b,d,124b,147a,148d,173a,c), une (13b,61a,62b,95c)

N - F nef (32b,144c,d)

NG - ngu (188)

N- G nag (73d,78b,138c,184d), nig (33b,40a,46a), nog (20c,46a,48d,54d, 100b,115d,118a)

- NG eng (48a,146a), ing (114b,d,148d,158c,d,175c), Ing (10c,115b)

N - H nth (42a)

NI - nib (17b,19d,115d), nid (72a,106c,116d), nie (53c,66c), nig (33b, 40a,46a), nil (108c), nim (96d,155d), nin (107d), nip (20c,29b,45d,46a,b,115c,118a), nis (23d,67d,68a,87c), Nis (19d), nit (48d), nix (23d,108c,178d)

- NI ani (19b,d,20b,39b), ini (158d), oni (11b), uni · (34c,118d,122c), Uni (51d)

N - K nak (156b)

- NK ink (20b,40c)

N - L nil (108c), nul (108c,177a)

N - M nim (96d,155d), nom (62b,125a), Nym (54c,76a)

NN - NNE (35b), NNW (35b)

N - N Nan (183c), nin (107d), non (34c,62b,89c,106b,122c,147a), nun (24c,91c,117d,147b), Nun (29a,85c)

- NN Ann (183c), inn (72b,73b,78c,150a,161c,162b,179a), Inn (41a)

NO - noa (35b,124a,161a), nob (38c,74d,84a,149d), nod (17c,46c,148a), Nod (18d,25b), nog (20c,46a,48d,54d,100b,115d,118a), nom (62b, 125a), non (34c,62b,89c,106b,122c,147a), noo (108c,139d), nor (10b,36a,37b,92b), nos (62b,90a,179a), not (78b,106b), now (60b, 79d), Nox (69b)

N - O neo (34a,b,c,100d,106d,108c,122c,d,128c), noo (108c,139d)

- NO ano (19d,20b,34d,122d,174a), Ino (14b,25b), ono (34a), Ono (18d,118d), uno (83c,151d)

N - P nap (65a,117d,146b,148a), nep (27c,32d,56a,87c,184b), nip (20c, 29b,45d,46a,b,115c,118a)

NR - NRA (8a,20d)

N - R nar (139d), ner (137c), nor (10b,36a,37b,92b), nur (67d)

N - S nas (74a,89c,178b), nes (26b), nis (23d,67d,87c), Nis (19d), nos (62b,90a,179a)

- NS Ans (92a), ens (17d,18a,51a,52d), ins (164d), INS (107a,182d), ons (38c), uns (66d,174c)

NT - nth (42a)

N - T nat (7a,24c,d,106a), net (26c,32a,50b,53d,60d,99a,124a,142a, 149b), nit (48d), not (78b,106b), nut (24c,32d,38b,54d,64a,65d, 86b,141c,165a), Nut (69a)

- NT ant (49d,60b,81b,118c), ent (34d,158b,c), TNT (53a)

NU - nub (67b,94d,95c,118c,124d), nul (108c,177a), nun (24c,91c,117d, 147b), Nun (29a,85c,129d), nur (67d), nut (24c,32d,38b,54d,64a, 65d,86b,141c,165a), Nut (69a)

N - U ngu (188)

- NU   **Anu** (15b,28a,68a,d,75b,88c,147d), **gnu** (11a,181d), **Unu** (24d)

N - W   **new** (11a,63c,88d,111c,128c), **NNW** (35b), **now** (60b,79d)

- NW   **NNW** (35b), **WNW** (35b)

N - X   **nix** (23d,108c,178d), **Nox** (69b), **Nyx** (69b)

NY -   **nye** (72a,116d), **Nye** (9c,18b), **Nym** (54c,76a), **Nyx** (69b)

N - Y   **nay** (42b,106b), **Ney** (63b,97b,105d)

- NY   **any** (14b,150b), **ony** (139a), **sny** (18a,39d,43d,87a,119a,144d,145a, 165d,176a)

N - Z   **nez** (62b)

OA -   **oaf** (22a,45b,146d,157d,185d), **oak** (73d,168c,169a), **oar** (20b,124c, 134b), **oat** (15a,28b,70b,144b)

O - A   **oca** (48c,112c,116d,133d,170c,184a), **oda** (74a,170d), **oka** (170c, 184a,189), **ola** (113b) **oma** (158c,d,170c), **Ona** (26b,64a), **OPA** (8a), **ora** (10c,40d,41b,45b,83a,c,101c,104a,122d,123d), **ova** (48d), **oxa** (29c)

- OA   **boa** (36c,55b,106a,125d,138b,142d,149a), **goa** (65d,104b,126c), **Goa** (121c), **hoa** (39b), **koa** (74c), **loa** (7d,53c,184d), **Loa** (97d), **moa** (19b), **noa** (35b,124a,161a), **poa** (20d,70d,97d), **roa** (23d,87a), **toa** (17c,178b), **Zoa** (20b)

OB -   **obe** (31d,87d,150d), **obi** (55d,67b,84c,137b,150d)

O - B   **orb** (50a,53c,67d,153b)

- OB   **bob** (57c,115d), **Bob** (96a), **cob** (28c,78b,95d,160b,177d), **fob** (29b, 59b,113b,178c), **gob** (97b,136c), **hob** (40c,56d,100c,124b,167a, 180c), **job** (30d,184c), **Job** (96a), **kob** (11a), **lob** (15d,23b,94c,100b, 163a,172d), **mob** (39a,127a,165b), **nob** (38c,74d,84a,149d), **pob** (121b,129b,139c), **rob** (119d,155d), **Rob** (96a), **sob** (39b,179d)

OC -   **oca** (48c,112c,116d,133d,170c,184a), **och** (8b), **ock** (189), **oct** (34a, 122c)

O - C   **orc** (28c,70c,180b)

- OC   **Doc** (143a), **roc** (19c,53b,54a,147a), **soc** (44c,85d)

OD -   **oda** (74a,170d), **odd** (46b,53a,109b,157a,172d,173c), **ode** (26b,79c, 94d,118a,119d,120a,150b), **Odo** (181d), **ods** (109a)

O - D   **odd** (46b,53a,109b,157a,172d,173c), **oid** (158c), **old** (8a,71a,77c, 123c,175b), **Ord** (25b,60b)

- OD   **cod** (57b,c), **dod** (11a,32a,43b,140c), **fod** (188), **god** (42a), **God** (84b), **hod** (23b,32d,102d,141a), **Mod** (138d), **nod** (17c,46c), **Nod** (18d,25b), **pod** (76b,78d,91b,141b,180c), **rod** (6a,72d,88b,131a, 154d,156a,160a), **sod** (160b,170d), **tod** (24d,60c,83d), **Vod** (16a)

OE -   **o'er** (6b,112a), **oes** (109a)

O - E   **obe** (31d,87d,150d), **ode** (26b,79c,94d,118a,119d,120a,150b), **oke** (189), **ole** (24b,29b,113b,152a,158b,d), **one** (79a,b,80d,124b,147a, 148d,173a,c), **ope** (172b,173c), **ore** (39a,99b,108a,115b,141c,151a, 160b), **ose** (102a,146d,158b,c,d,159a), **owe, ote** (158c), **oye** (139c)

- OE   **coe** (143d), **Coe** (33c), **doe** (41d,55b,127a), **foe** (111a), **hoe** (39c), **Joe** (96a), **loe** (139d), **Moe** (96a), **poe** (114b), **Poe** (9c,d,128a, 172a), **roe** (27d,41d,48d,57b,76d,95d,157b), **soe** (170c,184a), **toe** (43c,69d,148a,156a), **voe** (17a,81b), **woe** (25b), **Zoe** (36b,183c)

OF - off (6b,15c,44c,76a), oft (63c)

O - F oaf (22a,45b,146d,157d,185d), off (6b,15c,44c,76a), orf (57b,185c), ouf (52c)

- OF lof (188)

- OG bog (97a,160a), cog (33a,65d,163b,167b,180c), dog (10b,45b,59b), fog (109b), gog (95b), hog (45b,117c,160c), jog (82c,85c,170a), log (64a,128d), nog (20c,46a,48d,54d,100b,115d,118a), sog (149c), tog (46a), vog (189)

OH - ohm (49b,67a,173b), oho (52c)

O - H och (8b)

- OH boh (24c), doh (113b), foh (52c), Hoh (80d), poh (52c), soh (52c, 72d,) zoh (13d,186b)

OI - oid (158c), oii (105c), oil (11a,71a)

O - I obi (55d,67b,84c,137b,150d), oii (105c), oni (11b), ori (34a), ovi (34a)

- OI goi (107c), hoi (52c,74b,185b), koi (26d), loi (62a), Moi (80d), poi (44a,59c,74c,117a,162a,164b), roi (55c,62a,133d), toi (62b,d,63a), Toi (18d), yoi (52c,79a)

OK - oka (170c,184a,189), oke (189)

O - K oak (73d,168c,169a), ock (189), ork (180b), ouk (140c)

- OK Bok (9c), Lok (15d,68b), Rok (87c), sok (188), yok (10c,185a)

OL - ola (113b), old (8a,71a,77c,123c,175b), ole (24b,29b,113b,152a, 158b,d), olm (48c), Olt (41a)

O - L oil (11a,71a), owl

- OL col (103d,114c), Kol (18b), mol (58b,70c), sol (108b), Sol (117b, 159b), tol (137b), vol (155a,182d)

OM - oma (158c,d,170c), omo (34d)

O - M ohm (49b,67a,173b), olm (48c)

- OM com (122d), dom (121c,166b,c), Dom (94b), mom, nom (62b,125a), pom (45a,148d), rom (72d), tom (95d), Tom (96b,157a), yom (41a)

ON - Ona (26b,64a), one (79a,b,80b,d,124b,147a,148d,173a,c), oni (11b), ono (34a), Ono (18d,118d), ons (38c) ony (139a)

O - N own (6d)

- ON bon (30a,61d,86b,88c), Bon (84b), con (7d,29b,83c,116d,157d), don (151d,166c), Don (96a), eon (8a,37b,51d,116b), Fon (40b), gon (188), ion (11c,29a,49b,101b,114c,158c), Lon (86c,96a), mon (15d,84b), Mon (24c), non (34c,62b,89c,106b,122c,147a), ron (152c), Ron (86c,88a), son (42d,75d), ton (158d,167d,179d), von (66d,67a), won, yon (44c,112a,164d)

OO - oop (139a), oot (140a)

O - O Odo (181d), oho (52c), omo (34d), ono (34a), Ono (18d,118d), oro (34c,122c,152a), Oro (161b), oto (34a) Oto (147b)

- OO boo, coo (19b), Coo (82d), foo (42c), goo (156b), loo (65a), moo (94b), noo (108c,139d), roo (140a), soo (127d,140b,151b), Soo (137c), too (18b,102c), woo, zoo (181b)

OP - OPA (8a), ope (172b,173c), Ops (28c,69a,b,74a,137c), opt (30c)

248

O - P   oop (139a), orp (140c,179d)

- OP   cop (36a,120c,126d,153c,155d), dop (39c,43b), fop (38a,40d,46d), hop (40b), kop (76d), lop (30c,40a,46b,143a), mop (160a), oop (139a), pop (52d,53a,130b,149d), sop (23b,35d,149c,155d), top (38c,52b,118b,123d,160a,174a,186b), wop

OR -   ora (10c,40d,41b,45b,83a,c,101c,104a,122d,123d), orb (50a,53c, 67d,153b), orc (28c,70c,180b), Ord (25b,60b), ore (39a,99b,108a, 115b,141c,151a,160b), orf (57b,185c), ori (34a), ork (180b), oro (34c,122c,152a), Oro (161b), orp (140c,179d), orr (77c), ort (59b, 90d,91a,102c,129b,140d,180a,184d), ory (36c)

O - R   oar (20b,124c,134b), oer (6b,112a), orr (77c), our (124c)

- OR   Bor (120c), cor (36c,75b,155c), dor (17d,24b,32b,46b,47a,81b,85d), for (123d,163a,166c), Gor (81a), Hor (103d), ior (50a,158c), kor (75c), nor (10b,36a,37b,92b), por (152a), tor (38b,76d,85d,115c, 124b,132b,c), Vor (69a)

OS -   ose (102a,146d,158b,c,d,159a), ost (15d,86b)

O - S   ods (109a), oes (109a), ons (38c), Ops (28c,69a,b,74a,137c), ous (158b)

- OS   Bos (27c), cos (91d,132d), dos (45d,61a,97a,181b), Eos (14d,41a, 68d), ios (74d), Kos (77c,82d), los (13b,151d), mos (59b), nos (62b, 90a,179a), ros (37b), Ros (138a,174d), SOS

OT -   ote (158d), oto (34a), Oto (147b)

O - T   oat (15a,28b,70b,144b), oct (34a,122c), oft (63c), Olt (41a), oot (140a), opt (30c), ort (59b,90d,91a,102c,129b,140d,180a,184d), ost (15d,86b), out (6b,14b,60b,69d,80a,108b,185c)

- OT   bot (59a,88d), cot (129b,148b), dot (45d,97a,104d,105a,116b,153a, 162d), fot (188), got, hot (10c,176c), jot (82a,114c,166c,180d), lot (24b,28d,55a,65d,114a,119c,143c,150d,168a), Lot (6b,73d), mot (126d,130a,137d,183b), not (78b,106b), oot (140a), pot (120b, 145b,154d,175d), rot (22b,134c,143d,153d), sot (46c,167b,c), tot (186a), Vot (56d)

OU -   ouf (52c), ouk (140c), our (124c), ous (158b), out (6b,14b,60b,69d, 80a,108b,185c)

- OU   fou (139a), IOU (124b), kou (169a), Lou (96a,183d), sou (63b), you

OV -   ova (48d), ovi (34a)

OW -   owe, owl, own (6d)

- OW   bow (11c,21b,39d,60a,107c,109a,125a,144d,158a), cow (22c,45b, 81d), dow (17d,87a,88d,175d), how, jow (188), low (16c,149d), mow (32b,40a), now (60b,79d), pow, row (44c,56b,92c,109a,126b, 127d,165c), sow (45b,117c,119a,138b,160c), tow (45d,58b,75d, 125b), vow (119c,150a), wow (52c,158a), yow (52c)

OX -   oxa (29c)

- OX   box (36a,c,128c,145d,152d), cox (156a), fox (134a), Nox (69b), pox (44a), vox (90a,177a)

OY -   oye (139c)

O - Y   ony (139a), ory (36c)

- OY   boy (142d,157c), coy (16d), goy (107c), hoy (16c,52c), joy, loy (121c,148b,151c,167a), Roy, soy (17b,137c,74d), toy (169d)

- OZ   Boz (43b,115d), coz, goz (190)

PA -   pab (139c), pac (73b,94c,100d), pad (39d,59c,76c,157d,161a,168b), pah (52c,60b,106d), pal (35b,38d), pam (26c,65a,87a,105b), pan (34a,61a,104a,175d), Pan (56a,68a,b,76b,120c,135b,161a,184a), pap (59c), par (15a,51a,b,c,69d,107c,135b,155a), pas (40d,156a), pat (11d,116d,159a,161d,167c), Pat (96a), Pau (48c,76a,130c), paw (32d,59c,73c), pax (89d,115b), pay (35b,128c,130a,d,177b)

P - A   pea (32d,91b,142a,175a), pia (13b,22d,48a,120d), poa (20d, 70d,97d), pta (6a), pua (74c,76a)

- PA   apa (23a,177d), OPA (8a), spa (75b,100b,130c,154b,178d)

P - B   pab (139c), pob (121b,129b,139c)

P - C   pac (73b,94c,100d), pic (188)

P - D   pad (39d,59c,76c,157d,161a,168b), ped (16d,34b), pod (76b,78d, 91b,141b,180c), pud (59d,73c,115a)

PE -   pea (32d,91b,142a,175a), ped (16d,34b), pee (91c), peg (38c,46b, 54d,98a,118a,184c), pel (55c,160d), pen (36a,50a,80d,118b,126d, 160a,185c), pep (50b,176b), per (25c,122d,165b,176a), pes (59d), pet (26d,37c,55a,59b,162d), peu (62a), pew (30d,52c,57d,120b, 141c)

P - E   pee (91c), pie (42d,85d,95b,114d,171b,172a), poe (114b), Poe (9c, d,128a,172a), pre (17d,122b,c), pue (52c), Pye (50d,55a)

- PE   ape (36d,79d,100a,101d,146d), ope (172b,173c)

P - G   peg (38c,46b,54d,98a,118a,184c), pig (27a,45b,99a,151b,160c), pug (45a,101a,108a,148d)

PH -   phi (91c), phu (38c)

P - H   pah (52c,60b,106d), poh (52c)

PI -   pia (13b,22d,48a,120d), pic (188), pie (42d,85d,95b,114d, 171b,172a), pig (27a,45b,99a,151b,160c), pik (188), pil (34b), pin (45d,54d,141d,147d), pip (11d,44a,121d,142a,154a), Pip (43b), pir (103a,b,136c), pit (52b,142a,164a,168a) piu (102c), pix (31a,51d, 175d)

P - I   phi (91c), poi (44a,59c,74c,117a,162a,164b), psi (91c)

- PI   api (34a,76d), epi (56c,61c,d,111c,112d,122d,133c,153c,167b, 174a), UPI (107a,182d)

P - K   pik (188)

PL -   ply (59b,90b,118d,164b,171c,174a,181b,184c)

P - L   pal (35b,38d), pel (55c,160d), pil (34b), pul (190), Pul (14a)

P - M   pam (26b,65a,87a,105b), pom (45a,148d)

P - N   pan (34a,61a,104a,175d), Pan (56a,68a,b,76b,120c,135b,161a, 184a), pen (36a,50a,80d,118b,126d,160a,185c), pin (45d,54d,141d, 147d), pun (119c)

PO -   poa (20d,70d,97d), pob (121b,129b,139c), pod (76b,78d,91b,141b, 180c), poe (114b), Poe (9c,d,128a,172a), poh (52c), poi (44a,59c, 74c,117a,162a,164b), pom (45a,148d), pop (52d,53a,130b,149d), por (152a), pot (120b,145b,154d,175d), pow, pox (44a)

P - O   pro (59d,126d), Pwo (88c)

- PO apo (122b), **Apo** (177c)

P - P pap (59c), pep (50b,176b), pip (11d,44a,121d,154a), **Pip** (43b), pop (52d,53a,130b,149d), pup (141b,148d,185d)

PR - pre (17d,122b,c), pro (59d,126d), pry (52b,91d,98b,123d)

P - R par (15a,51a,b,c,69d,107c,135b,155a), per (25c,122d,165b,176a), pir (103a,b,136c), por (152a), pur, pyr (92a,b,122c,173b)

PS - psi (91c), pst (25c,126d,146c)

P - S pas (40d,156a), pes (59d), pus

- PS Ops (28c,69a,b,74a,137c)

PT - Pta (6a)

P - T pat (11d,116d,159a,161d,167c), **Pat** (96a), pet (26d,37c,55a,59b,162d), pit (52b,142a,164a,168a), pot (120b,145b,154d,175d), pst (25c,126d,146c), put (65a,69d,90b)

- PT apt (11d,23b,32b,58a,80b,92b,114d,116d,124b,159a), opt (30c)

PU - pua (74c,76a), pud (59d,73c,115a), pue (52c), pug (45a,101a,108a,148d), pul (190), **Pul** (14a), pun (119c), pup (141b,148d,185d), pur, pus, put (65a,69d,90b), puy (61d)

P - U Pau (48c,76a,130c), peu (62a), phu (38c), piu (102c)

PW - Pwo (88c)

P - W paw (32d,59c,73c), pew (30d,52c,57d,120b,141c), pow

P - X pax (89d,115b), pix (31a,51d,175d), pox (44a), pyx (31a,51d,175d)

PY - Pye (50d,55a), pyr (92a,b,122c,173b), pyx (31a,51d,175d)

P - Y pay (35b,128c,130a,d,177b), ply (59b,90b,118d,164b,171c,174a,181b,184c), pry (52b,91d,98b,123d), puy (61d)

- PY spy (44a,51c,52b,141d)

QA - Qaf (104a)

Q - A qua (13c,80a,89c,147a)

Q - E que (62d)

Q - F Qaf (104a)

Q - I qui (62d)

Q - O quo (188)

QU - qua (13c,80a,89c,147a), que (62d), qui (62d), quo (188)

RA - rab (17c,75c,85b,102d,162c,166b), **Rab** (45a), rad (50b,138d,173b), rae (136b,138d,140b), **Rae** (183c), rag (59b,77c,100c,133c,161a), rah (29b), rai (188), raj (129c), ram (17a,45b,50b,79c,112b,121d,143d,157d), **Ram** (36b), ran (73d), **Ran** (7c,107d,141a,163d), rap (90d,110a,147c,157c), ras (6c,26b,48b,51d,53d,61c,75a,111c,123c,166b), rat (16a,42d,73b,132c), raw (20c,39a,105d,173d), ray (38a,49a,57b,58b,147b), **Ray** (96a)

R - A rea (9c,171a), ria (38c,51d,81b,152a,b), roa (23d,87a), rua (118c), **Rua** (16b)

- RA ara (33a,114a,116a,118b,163d), **Ara** (9b,18c,36b,c,68d,69b,c,85a,95a,175b), dra (188), era (8a,51a,116b,165d), fra (23c,63c,101d,123b,129d), gra (59b,94b,160c), Ira (18c,d,41a,68c,82c,96a,164a,178a,c), **Kra** (11b,91d), **NRA** (8a,20d), ora (10c,40d,41b,45b,83a,c,

101c,104a,122d,123d), **tra** (33b)

R - B   **rab** (17c,75c,85b,102d,162c,166b), **Rab** (45a), **reb** (35d,75c,85b, 162c,166b), **rib** (37c,85b,90c,98a,144d,159d,172a), **rob** (119d, 155d), **Rob** (96a), **rub** (6b,24d,28c,43c,120c,179b)

- RB   **orb** (50a,53c,67d,153b)

R - C   **roc** (19c,53b,54a,147a)

- RC   **arc** (31b,39d,92a,126a,127c,142a), **orc** (28c,70c,180b)

R - D   **rad** (50b,138d,173b), **red** (33c,38d,59a,127b,134c,135b), **Red** (151b), **rid** (32a,44a,60d), **rod** (6a,72d,88b,131a,154d,156a,160a), **rud** (26d,57b)

- RD   **erd** (47d,119d,145c), **Ord** (25b,60b), **urd** (17b,184b), **Urd** (68d,107d)

RE -   **rea** (9c,171a), **reb** (35d,75c,85b,162c,166b), **red** (33c,38d,59a,127b, 134c,135b), **Red** (151b), **ree** (12c,50a,80c,134d,137a,140b,144a, 146b), **Ree** (25a), **ref, reh** (8d), **rei** (89b,121c), **Rei** (18d), **rel** (49b, 173b), **Reo** (26c), **rep** (53b,d,131a,171c), **res** (80a,89d,91a,97c), **ret** (58b,95a,149c,155d), **Reu** (115d), **rev, rew** (75c,140c,176b), **rex** (86c,96a), **rey** (86c,152b)

R - E   **rae** (136b,138d,140b), **Rae** (183c), **ree** (12c,50a,80c,134d,137a, 140b,144a,146b), **Ree** (25a), **rhe** (59a,173b), **rie** (28c,70d,97d), **roe** (27d,41d,48d,57b,76d,95b,157b), **rue** (76a,b,129c,150d,183a), **rye** (28b,70b,72d,92d)

- RE   **are** (51a,88b,98a,99b,110c,166c,175c), **ere** (17d,150c), **ire** (10c, 52b,30c,64c,125a,130b,185a), **ore** (39a,99b,108a,115b,141c,151a, 160b), **pre** (17d,122b,c), **tre** (37b,83c,122d,165a,167d), **ure** (40a, 139d,155d,158b,d), **Ure** (138d,185d)

R - F   **ref, rif** (188)

- RF   **orf** (57b,185c)

R - G   **rag** (59b,77c,100c,133c,161a), **rig** (51b,112a), **rug**

- RG   **erg** (50b,173b,184c)

RH -   **rhe** (59a,173b), **rho** (71b,91c)

R - H   **rah** (29b), **reh** (8d)

RI -   **ria** (38c, 51d, 81b, 152a, b), **rib** (37c, 85b, 90c, 98a, 144d, 159d,172a), **rid** (32a,44a,60d), **rie** (28c,70d,97d), **rif** (188), **rig** (51b, 112a), **rii** (157b,175b), **rim** (22a,48b,96d),116b,124b,166a,180c), **rin** (33b,142b), **rio** (33a,131d,132a,152c,157b), **Rio** (23a), **rip** (87b, 130a,162c), **Rip** (178b), **ris** (131d), **rit** (140b,148c,153d)

R - I   **rai** (188), **rei** (89b,121c), **Rei** (18d), **rii** (157b,175b), **roi** (55c,62a, 133d)

- RI   **Ari** (18d), **eri** (13d,21c,146d), **Eri** (18c), **gri** (75c,78b), **Iri** (18a,d, 75a), **kri** (75c,96d), **ori** (34a), **sri** (60c,77b,166c), **Sri** (17c), **tri** (122d,169d), **Uri** (162d)

R - J   **raj** (129c)

R - K   **Rok** (87c)

- RK   **ark** (21a,29d,38a,58b,60d,175d), **irk** (10d), **ork** (180b)

R - L   **rel** (49b,173b)

R - M   **ram** (17a,45b,50b,79c,112b,121d,143d,157d), **Ram** (36b), **rim** (22a,

48b,96d,116b,124b,166a,180c), **rom** (72d), **rum** (8c,92d)

- **RM**   **arm** (22d,60c,81b,92b,124b,161b)

R - N   **ran** (73d), **Ran** (7c,107d,141a,163d), **rin** (33b),142b), **ron** (152c), **Ron** (86c,88a), **run** (10d,23c,58d,110d,148d,153b,154b,167d)

- **RN**   **arn** (8c,139a), **ern** (19c,d,47b,54b,141a), **urn** (36c,174d)

RO -   **roa** (23d,87a), **rob** (119d,155d), **Rob** (96a), **roc** (19c,53b,54a,147a), **rod** (6a,72d,88b,131a,154d,156a,160a), **roe** (27d,41d,48d,57b,76d, 95b,157b), **roi** (55c,62a,133d), **Rok** (87c), **rom** (72d), **ron** (152c), **Ron** (86c,88a), **roo** (140a) **ros** (37b), **Ros** (138a,174d), **rot** (22b, 134c,143d,153d), **row** (44ᵇ,56b,92c,109a,126b,127d,165c), **Roy**

R - O   **Reo** (26c), **rho** (71b,91c), **rio** (33a,131d,132a,152c,157b), **Rio** (23a), **roo** (140a)

- **RO**   **Aro** (107a,111c), **cro** (104c,115b,180a), **fro** (15b), **Mro** (88c), **oro** (34c,122c,152a), **Oro** (161b), **pro** (59d,126d), **S.R.O.** (6a,164a), **Uro** (192)

R - P   **rap** (90d,110a,147c,157c), **rep** (53b,d,131a,171c), **rip** (87b, 130a,162c), **Rip** (178b)

- **RP**   **orp** (140c,179d)

R - R   **rur** (132b)

- **RR**   **err** (21a,43a,67d,100c,d,147a,148b,157b,168b,178a), **grr** (52c), **orr** (77c)

R - S   **ras** (6c,26b,48b,51d,53d,61c,75a,111c,123c,166b), **res** (80a,89d, 91a,97c,164c), **ris** (131d), **ros** (37b), **Ros** (138a,174d), **rus** (89b), **Rus** (138a)

- **RS**   **ars** (13b,89a), **Ars** (112c), **ers** (20a,176a), **Mrs.** (166b)

R - T   **rat** (16a,42d,73b,132c), **ret** (58b,95a,149c,155d), **rit** (140b,148c, 153d), **rot** (22b,134c,143d,153d), **rut** (73a)

- **RT**   **art** (22d,38b,39c,43b,56c,124a,162c,181d), **ert** (140c,174a), **ort** (59b,90d,91a,102c,129b,140d,180a,184d)

RU -   **rua** (118c), **Rua** (16b), **rub** (6b,24d,28c,43c,120c,179b), **rud** (26d, 57b), **rue** (76a,b,129c,150d,183a), **rug, rum** (8c,92d), **run** (10d,23c, 58d,110d,148d,153b,154b,167d), **rur** (132b), **rus** (89b), **Rus** (138a), **rut** (73a), **rux** (154a,184d)

R - U   **Reu** (115d)

- **RU**   **aru** (80c,82b), **Aru** (82d), **cru** (63a,176c), **Kru** (91d), **Mru** (80d,88c), **Uru** (192)

R - V   **rev**

R - W   **raw** (20c,39a,105d,173d), **rew** (75c,140c,176b), **row** (44c,56b,92c, 109a,126b,127d,165c)

R - X   **rex** (86c,96a), **rux** (154a,184d)

RY -   **rye** (28b,70b,72d,92d)

R - Y   **ray** (38a,49a,57b,58b,147b), **Ray** (96a), **rey** (86c,152b), **Roy**

- **RY**   **cry** (25c,124a,145c,179d), **dry** (46d,85a,137c,164c), **ery** (155d,158c, d), **fry** (57d), **gry** (78b), **ory** (36c), **pry** (52b,91d,98b,123d), **try** (7c, 10d,14c,50a,51c,130a), **wry** (13d)

SA -   **saa** (98a), **sac** (15d,121d), **Sac** (80c), **sad** (29c,42c,94c,98c,104a,

150d,173a), **sae** (140b,149c), **sag** (46b), **sah** (188), **sai** (101d), **saj** (48a,169a), **sak** (37c), **Sak** (88c), **sal** (29c,48a,136d,149d,152d, 169a,183a), **Sal** (183d), **Sam** (96a,162a), **san** (91c), **San** (24d), **sao** (141b) , **Sao** (113c), **sap** (45d,52d,85c,169b,176d,179a), **sar** (57d), **sat** (13d), **saw** (7a,11b,40c,54c,97d,125a,137d,167a), **sax** (40c,148a,167a), **say** (131c,174c,177a)

S - A   **saa** (98a), **sea** (19a,52d,58c,112c,178d), **sha** (110c,143d,144a,c, 174c,181c), **sia** (80c), **sma** (140b,148d), **sna** (105b,140b,143d,144a, 149c,181c,d), **spa** (75b,100b,130c,154b,178d), **sta** (13c,91b,104d, 105a), **sua** (89d),

- SA   **Asa** (6a,18c,71a,84d,86d,164c), **ESA** (8a)

S - B   **Seb** (47d), **sib** (86b,129c,139d,147b), **sob** (39b,179d), **sub** (90a, 122d,172c)

S - C   **sac** (15d,121d), **Sac** (80c), **sec** (46c,182c), **sic** (90a,165b,168b), **soc** (44c,85d)

- SC   **BSC** (42a)

S - D   **sad** (29c,42c,94c,98c,104a,150d,173a), **sed** (89a), **Sid** (96a), **sod** (160b,170d), **sud** (59a)

SE -   **sea** (19a,52d,58c,112c,178d), **Seb** (47d), **sec** (46c,182c), **sed** (89a), **see**   (20a,43c,44a,51c,53c,93d,109b,113c,116a,176d,178c,183b), **sel** (62c,140b), **Sem** (107c), **sen** (190) **ser** (80d,83b,d,116c, 152d,180a), **ses** (61d), **set** (7b,11d,13a,23c,32b,33c,37c,58a,73d, 109b,118c,121c,142c,150a,186a), **Set** (52b,68a,b,111d), **sew, sex, sey** (120c)

S - E   **sae** (140b,149c), **see** (20a,43c,44a,51c,53c,109b,113c,116a,176d, 178c,183b), **she** (124b), **She** (73a), **sie** (46c,66d,139b,140b,146b), **soe** (170c,184a), **SSE** (35b), **ste** (62c,136c), **sue** (119c), **Sue** (63a, 178a,183d), **sye** (40c,46c,139b,141a,167a)

- SE   **ase** (51a,139a), **Ase** (79b,115d), **ese** (35b,158c), **ise** (40d,158c,d), **Ise** (78a,84c), **ose** (102a,146d,158b,c,d,159a), **SSE** (35b), **use** (7b, 47a,49d,64c,109b,168b,c,181b)

S - F   **Sif** (164d)

S - G   **sag** (46b), **sog** (149c)

SH -   **sha** (110c,143d,144a,c,174c,181c), **she** (124b), **She** (73a), **sho** (188), **Shu** (30b,127a), **shy** (16d,99d,128c,160c,165d,175a)

S - H   **sah** (188), **soh** (52c,72d)

- SH   **ash** (24d,33c,49c,73d,134b,168c,169a), **hsh** (79c), **ish** (158b), **ush**

SI -   **Sia** (80c), **sib** (86b,129c,139d,147b), **sic** (90a,165b,168b), **Sid** (96a), **sie** (46c,66d,139b,140b,146b), **Sif** (164d), **sil** (30c,185c,d), **Sim** (96b), **sin** (91c,140b,147a,168b,176a), **Sin** (102b), **sip** (46b,79d, 104a,162b), **sir** (87a,163b,166b), **sis** (67b,129c), **sit** (98c,116a,121c, 130c,142d), **six** (26c)

S - I   **sai** (101d), **Sia** (80c), **ski** (149c), **sri** (60c,77b,166c), **Sri** (17c), **sui** (30b)

- SI   **asi** (137a), **psi** (91c)

S - J   **saj** (48a,169a)

SK -   **ski** (149c), **sky** (56d)

254

S - K   sak (37c), Sak (88c), sok (188), Suk (107b)

- SK   ask (38b,82a,126c)

SL -   sly (13b,38b,64c,81b,132c)

S - L   sal (29c,48a,136d,149d,152d,169a,183a), Sal (183d), sel (62c, 140b), sil (30c,185c,d), sol (108b), Sol (117b,159b)

SM -   sma (140b,148d), SMU (40b)

S - M   Sam (96a,162a), Sem (107c), Sim (96b), sum (8a,123a,167c)

- SM   ism (45a,79b,161c)

SN -   sna (105b,140b,143d,144a,149c,181c), sny (18a,39d,43d,87a,119a, 144d,145a,165d,176a)

S - N   san (91c), San (24d), sen (190), sin (91c,140b,147a,168b,176a), Sin (102b), son (42d,75d), sun (75d,111a,117b,155b), syn (122d,183b)

SO -   sob (39b,179d), soc (44c,85d), sod (160b,170d), soe (170c,184a), sog (149c), soh (52c,72d), sok (188), sol (108b) Sol (117b,159b), son (42d,75d), soo (127d,140b,151b), Soo (137c), sop (23b,35d, 149c,155d), SOS, sot (46c,167b,c), sou (63b), sow (45b,117c,119a, 138b,160c), soy (17b,137c,174d)

S - O   sao (141b), Sao (113c), sho (188), soo (127d,140b,151b), Soo (137c), S.R.O. (6a,164a)

- SO   Aso (84c), DSO (99d), eso (34d,183b), iso (34a,122c,d)

SP -   spa (75b,100b,130c,154b,178d), spy (44a,51c,52b,141d)

S - P   sap (45d,52d,85c,169b,176d,179a), sip (46b,79d,104a,162b), sop (23b,35d,149c,155d), sup (46b,104a,162b)

- SP   asp (7b,32b,149a,174a,176c), e.s.p. (147b)

S - Q   suq (22a,97a)

SR -   sri (60c,77b,166c), Sri (17c), S.R.O. (6a,164a)

S - R   sar (57d), ser (80d,83b,d,116c,152d,180a), sir (87a,163b,166b), sur (34a,62b,d,104b,151a,152d,174a)

SS -   SSE (35b), ssu (189), SSW (35b)

S - S   ses (61d), sis (67b,129c), SOS, sus (117c), Sus (160c,181b)

- SS   ass (17b,20c,45b,c,59c,110c,112b,146d,157d), ess (39d,78a,91c, 158c,184d)

ST -   sta (13c,91b,104d,105a), ste (62c,136c), sty (50a,53c)

S - T   sat (13d), set (7b,11d,13a,23c,32b,33c,37c,58a,73d,109b,118c, 121c,142c,150a,186a), Set (52b,68a,b,111d), sit (98c,116a,121c, 130c,142d), sot (46c,167b,c)

- ST   est (50a,61c,62a,79b,89c,158d,159c), ist (7b,34b,43a,59b,66c,158b, c,d), LST (21a,88b), ost (15d,86b), pst (25c,126d,146c), tst (81d, 126d)

SU -   sua (89d), sub (90a,122d,172c), sud (59a), sue (119c), Sue (63a, 178a,183d), Sui (30b), Suk (107b), sum (8a,123a,167c), sun (75d, 111a,117b,155b), sup (46b,104a,162b), suq (22a,97a), sur (34a,62b, d,104b,151a,152d,174a), sus (117c), Sus (160c,181b)

S - U   Shu (30b,127a), SMU (40b), sou (63b), ssu (189)

- SU   ssu (189)

S - W   saw (7a,14b,40c,54c,97d,125a,137d,167a), **sew, sow** (45b,117c, 119a,138b,160c), **SSW** (35b)

- SW   **SSW** (35b), **WSW** (35b)

S - X   sax (40c,148a,167a), **sex, six** (26c)

SY -   sye (40c,46c,139b,141a,167a), **syn** (122d,183b)

S - Y   say (131c,174c,177a), **sey** (120c), **shy** (16d,99d,128c,160c,165d, 175a), **sky** (56d), **sly** (13b,38b,64c,81b,132c), **sny** (18a,39d,43d,87a, 119a,144d,145a,165d,176a), **soy** (17b,137c,174d), **spy** (44a,51c, 52b,141d), **sty** (50a,53c)

TA -   taa (112d), **tab** (29b,39c,58b,86a,128d,145a), **tac** (34d,130a), **tad** (22c,174a,186a), **tae** (138d,140c,166c,d), **tag** (45a,54c,65a,87b, 144a), **tai** (84b,111c,121b), **Tai** (80d), **taj** (75a,97d), **tal** (40c,77a, 113b), **tam** (74d), **tan** (23d,33c,46a,72d,90d), **tao** (10d,131c, 170b), **Tao** (117a), **tap** (55a,114d,153c), **tar** (8c,68a,94d,111c,118c, 136a,c,176d), **tat** (43b,48c,72d,87c), **Tat** (82a), **tau** (71b,91c,136c, 161a), **tav** (91c), **taw** (90d,91c,96c,d,145b,161d), **tax** (13a,14a,80a, 91d)

T - A   taa (112d), **tea** (13d,18c,79c,81a,145d,149c,159d), **tia** (151d), **toa** (17c,178b), **tra** (33b), **tua** (117a)

- TA   ata (58d,97d,158d,160c,173d), **Ata** (79c,80d,94d,95d,100a,106b, 117a), **eta** (71a,84c,91c), **Ita** (51b,71d,94d,95d,106b,117a), **ITA** (173a), **Pta** (6a), **sta** (13c,91b,104d,105a), **uta** (53c,84d,93b,147c, 150b)

T - B   tab (29b,39c,58b,86a,128d,145a), **tub** (21a,27a,36c,174d)

TC -   tch (52c), **tck** (52c)

T - C   tac (34d,130a), **tec** (43a), **tic** (104d,153a,171c,d)

- TC   etc (10b)

T - D   tad (174a,186a), **ted** (74d,138b,154b), **Ted** (96b), **tod** (24d,60c,83d)

TE -   tea (13d,18c,79c,81a,145d,149c,159d), **tec** (43a), **ted** (74d,138b, 154b), **Ted** (96b), **tee** (39d,52b,69d,91c,112d,115d,118b,172a), **teg** (45a,54b,143d,144a,171d), **tel** (34a,b,122c), **Tem** (143a,159b), **ten** (19a,26c,41c,42b), **ter** (34d,122c,165a), **tez** (125c)

T - E   tae (138d,140c,166c,d), **tee** (39d,52b,69d,91c,112d,115d,118b, 172a), **the** (13b), **tie** (10a,14c,38b,45d,51a,88d,109b,127c,138b, 170b), **toe** (43c,69d,148a,156a), **tre** (37b,83c,122d,165a,167d), **tue** (114b), **tye** (28c,134a)

- TE   ate (81a,108c,158c,174c), **Ate** (20c,68b,d,69a,b,116c,186b), **ete** (36c,62d,141c,159b), **ite** (59b,81a,105d,130c,158b,c,d,161a), **ote** (158d), **ste** (62c,136c), **Ute** (145c,180b)

T - G   tag (45a,54c,65a,87b,144a), **teg** (45a,54b,143d,144a,171d), **tig** (46b), **tog** (46a), **tug** (45d,125b), **tyg** (46b)

TH -   the (13b), **tho** (52a), **Tho** (167a), **thy**

T - H   tch (52c)

- TH   eth (91c,158d), **Ith** (10a,28a,82b,99d), **nth** (42a)

TI -   tia (151d), **tic** (104d,153a,171c,d), **tie** (10a,14c,38b,45d, 51a,88d,109b,127c,138b,170b), **tig** (46b), **til** (142d), **Tim** (43b), **tin** (36c,99a,b,108b,155a,179c), **tio** (152d), **tip** (26b,d,50a,70d,77b,78a,

120a,165d), **tir** (61d,62c,145b), **tis, tit** (19c,130d), **Tiu** (7c,68c, 147d,163d,166c,170c), **Tiw** (68c,147d,163d)

T - I   **tai** (84b,111c,121b), **Tai** (80d), **tji** (189), **toi** (62b,d,63a), **Toi** (18d), **tri** (122d,169d), **tui** (47c,114b,117a), **Twi** (69c)

- TI   **ati** (106d,107a), **Ati** (45d,106b,113c,117a)

TJ -   **tji** (189)

T - J   **taj** (75a,97d)

TK -   **TKO** (22c)

T - K   **tck** (52c)

T - L   **tal** (40c,77a,113b), **tel** (34a,b,122c), **til** (142d), **tol** (137b)

T - M   **tam** (74d), **Tem** (143a,159b), **Tim** (43b), **tom** (95d), **Tom** (96b, 157a), **tum** (26d), **Tum** (143a,159b)

TN -   **TNT** (53a)

T - N   **tan** (23d,33c,46a,72d,90d), **ten** (19a,26c,41c,42b), **tin** (36c,99a,b, 108b,155a,179c), **ton** (158d,167d,179d), **tun** (23b,27a,182b)

TO -   **toa** (17c,178b), **tod** (24d,60c,83d), **toe** (43c,69d,148a,156a), **tog** (46a), **toi** (62b,d,63a), **Toi** (18d), **tol** (137b), **tom** (95d), **Tom** (96b, 157a), **ton** (158d,167d,179d), **too** (18b,102c), **top** (38c,52b,118b, 123d,160a,174a,186b), **tor** (38b,76d,85d,115c,124b,132b,c), **tot** (186a), **tow** (45d,58b,75d,125b), **toy** (169d)

T - O   **tao** (10d,131c,170b), **Tao** (117a), **tho** (52a), **Tho** (167a), **tio** (152d), **TKO** (22c), **too** (18b,102c), **two** (26c,37d,80a,93a)

- TO   **ETO** (184d), **Ito** (84a,c,186d), **oto** (34a), **Oto** (147b)

T - P   **tap** (55a,114d,153c), **tip** (26b,d,50a,70d,77b,78a,120a,165d), **top** (38c,52b,118b,123d,160a,174a,186b), **tup** (115a,117d,127d,143d)

TR -   **tra** (33b), **tre** (37b,83c,122d,165a,167d), **tri** (122d,169d), **try** (7c, 10d,14c,50a,51c,130a)

T - R   **tar** (8c,68a,94d,111c,118c,136a,c,176d), **ter** (34d,122d,165a), **tir** (61d,62c,145b), **tor** (38b,76d,85d,115c,124b,132b,c), **tur** (14d,27c, 68a,79b,117d,174c), **tyr** (7c,68c,147d,163d,170c,178a)

TS -   **tst** (81d,126d)

T - S   **tis**

- TS   **its** (124c)

T - T   **tat** (43b,48c,72d,87c), **Tat** (82a), **tit** (19c,130d), **TNT** (53a), **tot** (186a), **tst** (81d,126d), **tut** (52c)

- TT   **att** (146a)

TU -   **tua** (117a), **tub** (21a,27a,36c,174d), **tue** (114b), **tug** (45d,125b), **tui** (47c,114b,117a), **tum** (26d), **Tum** (143a,159b), **tun** (23b,27a, 182b), **tup** (115a,117d,127d,143d), **tur** (14d,27c,68a,79b,117d, 174c), **tut** (52c)

T - U   **tau** (71b,91c,136c,161a), **Tiu** (7c,68c,147d,163d,166c,170c)

- TU   **utu** (35b,137c), **Utu** (96c,107a,159b)

T - V   **tav** (91c)

TW -   **Twi** (69c), **two** (26c,37d,80a,93a)

T - W   **taw** (90d,91c,96c,d,145b,161d), **Tiw** (68c,147d,163d), **tow** (45d, 58b,75d,125b)

T - X   tax (13a,14a,80a,91d)

TY -   tye (28c,134a), tyg (46b), **Tyr** (7c,68c,109c,147d,163d,170c,178a)

T - Y   thy, toy (169d), try (7c,10d,14c,50a,51c,130a)

- TY   sty (50a,53c)

T - Z   tez (125c)

U - A   Uca (56a), ula (72c,158c), **Uma** (43a,69b,153d), **Una** (54a,153b, 170c,183c), **uta** (53c,84d,93b,147c,150b), uva (64a,70c)

- UA   dua (122d), **Kua** (95c), pua (74c,76a), qua (13c,80a,89c,147a), rua (118c), **Rua** (16b), sua (89d), tua (117a)

UB -   ube (185b), ubi (90a,180d,185b)

- UB   bub (22c), cub (92d,185d), dub (25c,46a,c,87a,105b,121a,140a), fub (29b,119d), hub (28b,118b,180c), nub (67b,94d,95c,118c 124d), rub (6b,24d,28c,43c,120c,179b), sub (90a,122d,172c), tub (21a,27a,36c,174d)

UC -   Uca (56a)

- UC   duc (61c)

UD -   Udi (108a), udo (28a,30c,48c,84b,c,d,136c,149d)

U - D   und (66b), urd (17b,184b), **Urd** (68d,107d)

- UD   bud (22c), cud (126c,135a), dud (21c,54a), lud (100a), **Lud** (23c, 144b), mud (6c), pud (59d,73c,115a), rud (26d,57b), sud (59a)

U - E   ube (185b), ule (23a,27d,134c,158c,168d), ume (11d), une (13b, 61a,62b,95c), ure (40a,139d,155d,158b,d), **Ure** (138d,185d), use (7b,47a,49d,64c,109b,168b,c,181b), **Ute** (145c,180b), uve (185b)

- UE   cue (7a,27b,92c,117d,124b,132c,146c,159a), due (7b,115b,124c), gue (176c), hue (33c,143b), lue (146b), pue (52c), que (62d), rue (76a,b,129c,150d,183a), sue (119c), **Sue** (63a,178a,183d), tue (114b)

UF -   ufo (59a)

- UF   ouf (52c)

UG -   ugh (52c)

- UG   bug (24b,66b,81b), dug, fug (129a), hug (32c,49d), jug (118c, 123d), lug (27a,45d,47b,73c,136b), **Lug** (28b), mug (46b,54a,65a), pug (45a,101a,108a,148d), rug, tug (45d,125b), vug (28a,66a)

U - H   ugh (52c), ush

- UH   auh (52c), huh (52c)

UI -   uit (47a,111d,151a)

U - I   ubi (90a,180d,185b), Udi (108a), uji (146d), uni (34c,118d,122c), **Uni** (51d), **UPI** (107a,182d), **Uri** (162d), uvi (185b)

- UI   dui (46d), hui (14a,30b,56d,114c), **Kui** (86a,88c,146a), qui (62d), **Sui** (30b), tui (47c,114b,117a)

UJ -   uji (146d)

- UK   auk (19b), ouk (140c), **Suk** (107b)

UL -   ula (72c,158c), ule (23a,27d,134c,158c,168d), **Ull** (7c,68c,146b, 164d), ulm (49c), **Ulm** (40d), ulo (34b,80d), ulu (87a)

U - L   **Ull** (7c,68c,146b,164d)

- **UL**   **Bul** (25d,102a), **Ful** (158b), **gul** (134a), **mul** (188), **nul** (108c,177a), **pul** (190), **Pul** (14a)

UM -   **Uma** (43a,69b,153d), **ume** (11d), **umu** (112a)

U - M   **ulm** (49c), **Ulm** (40d)

- **UM**   **aum** (189), **bum** (21b), **cum** (159b), **dum** (45c,67b,113a), **gum** (7b, 53c,80b,130c,156b), **hum** (24d,46b,150d), **Jum** (39c), **lum** (30a), **mum** (30d,95a,146c), **rum** (8c,92d), **sum** (8a,123a,167c), **tum** (26d), **Tum** (143a,159b)

UN -   **Una** (54a,153b,170c,183c), **und** (66b), **une** (13b,61a,62b,95c), **uni** (34c,118d,122c), **Uni** (51d), **uno** (83c,151d), **uns** (66d,174c), **Unu** (24d)

U - N   **urn** (36c,174d)

- **UN**   **bun** (25b,73b), **dun** (19a,39d,46d,71a,97d,115b,160b), **fun, gun** (56d,131a,146a), **Hun** (16c,21d,174b), **mun** (157b), **nun** (24c,91c, 117d,129d,147b), **Nun** (29a,85c), **pun** (119c), **run** (10d,23c,58d, 110d,148d,153b,154b,167d), **sun** (75d,111a,117b,155b), **tun** (23b, 27a,182b), **wun** (24c), **Yun** (88d)

U - O   **udo** (28a,30c,48c,84b,c,d,136c,149d), **ufo** (59a), **ulo** (34b,80d), **uno** (83c,151d), **Uro** (192)

- **UO**   **duo** (46d,113a,171d), **Luo** (107b), **quo** (188)

UP -   **UPI** (107a,182d)

- **UP**   **cup** (46b,69d,118b,170a), **gup** (70a), **hup** (35a), **kup** (188), **pup** (141b,148d,185d), **sup** (46b,104a,162b), **tup** (115a,117d,127d, 143d)

- **UQ**   **suq** (22a,97a)

UR -   **urd** (17b,184b), **Urd** (68d,107d), **ure** (40a,139d,155d,158b,d), **Ure** (138d,185d), **Uri** (162d), **urn** (36c,174d), **Uro** (192), **Uru** (192)

- **UR**   **bur** (123b), **cur** (101d), **dur** (95c), **Eur.** (36c), **fur, gur** (159a), **Hur** (91d), **Jur** (107b), **Lur** (116c), **mur** (63a,177d), **nur** (67d), **our** (124c), **pur, rur** (132b), **sur** (34a,62b,d,104b,151a,152d,174a), **tur** (14d,27c,68a,79b,117d,174c)

US -   **use** (7b,47a,49d,64c,109b,168b,c,181b), **ush**

U - S   **uns** (66d,174c)

-**US**   **aus** (66c), **Aus** (98b), **bus** (125b,168b), **Gus** (96a), **jus** (61d,90b), **Mus** (104a,132c), **ous** (158b), **pus, rus** (89b,138a), **sus** (117c), **Sus** (160c,181b)

UT -   **uta** (53a,84d,93b,147c,150b), **Ute** (145c,180b), **utu** (35b, 137c), **Utu** (96c,107a,159b)

U - T   **uit** (47a,111d,151a)

- **UT**   **aut** (34d,89d), **but** (36a,52b,156b,173c), **cut** (30c,32b,145c), **fut** (188), **gut** (114d,130a), **hut** (143c), **jut** (53a,124a), **lut** (189), **mut** (39c), **Mut** (9b,127a), **nut** (24c,32d,38b,54d,64a,65d,86b,141c, 165a), **Nut** (69a), **out** (6b,14b,60b,69d,80a,108b,185c), **put** (65a, 69d,90b), **rut** (73a), **tut** (52c)

U - U   **ulu** (87a), **umu** (112a), **Unu** (24d), **Uru** (192), **utu** (35b,137c), **Utu** (96c,107a,159b)

UV -   **uva** (64a,70c), **uve** (185b), **uvi** (185b)

- UX   aux (6d,61a), **dux** (31d,64a,90c), **lux** (79d), **rux** (154a,184d)

- UY   buy, **guy** (55b,131b,155d), **Guy** (96a), **muy** (152d,175d), **puy** (61d)

- UZ   guz (188)

VA -   Vac (153b), **vae** (176b), **vag** (174b,178a), **Vai** (91d), **van** (7b,59d, 60a,63d,90c), **vas** (46d,89d,119c,133b,175d), **vat** (31b,36c,163a, 170c), **vau** (91c)

V - A   via (132a,133a,b,179a)

- VA   ava (78d,86a,116a,120d,139a,167b), **Ava** (24c), **Eva** (157a,183c), **iva** (76a,97b,127b,185b), **ova** (48d), **uva** (64a,70c)

V - C   Vac (153b)

V - D   Vod (16a)

VE -   vee (58a,91c,106a), **Vei** (91d), **vet**, **vex** (7c,10d,44c,82c)

V - E   vae (176b), **vee** (58a,91c,106a), **vie** (36c,157c,170c), **voe** (17a,81b)

- VE   ave (54c,71d,73a,122a,134a,136d), **eve** (47a,131a,143a,165d,171c), **Eve** (183c), **ive** (158c), **uve** (185b)

V - F   vif (62a)

V - G   vag (174b,178a), **vog** (189), **vug** (28a,66a)

VI -   via (132a,133a,b,179a), **vie** (36c,157c,170c), **vif** (62a), **vim** (50b, 176b), **vin** (63a,182b), **vir** (89c), **vis** (59d,89b,d,90b,176b), **vix**, (89d,138b), **viz** (105b)

V - I   Vai (91d), **Vei** (91d)

- VI   ovi (34a), **uvi** (185b)

V - L   vol (155a,182d)

V - M   vim (50b,176b)

V - N   van (7b,59d,60a,63d,90c), **vin** (63a,182b), **von** (66d,67a)

VO -   Vod (16a), **voe** (17a,81b), **vog** (189), **vol** (155a,182d), **von** (66d, 67a), **Vor** (68d), **Vot** (56d), **vow** (119c,150a), **vox** (90a,177a)

V - R   vir (89c), **Vor** (68d)

V - S   vas (46d,89d,119c,133b,175d), **vis** (59d,89b,d,90b,176b)

V - T   vat (31b,36c,163a,170c), **vet**, **Vot** (56d)

VU -   vug (28a,66a)

V - U   Vau (91c)

V - W   vow (119c,150a)

V - X   vex (7c,10d,44c,82c), **vix** (89d,138b), **vox** (90a,177a)

V - Z   viz (105b)

- VY   ivy (32b,38c,176b)

WA -   wad (94d,97b,109c,112b,149d), **wag** (85b,104a,183a), **wah** (113c), **wan** (113a), **war** (157c), **was** (166c,175c), **Was** (24d), **wat** (73d, 140d,163a,180b), **waw** (12b,91c), **wax** (28b,72a,80b,120c), **way** (37d,96b,134b,164d)

W - A   Wea (192)

- WA   awa (100a,139a), **iwa** (63c)

W - B   web (50d,70a,98c,99a,106c,149b)

W - D   wad (94d,97b,109c,112b,149d), **wed** (97a,173c)

WE -   **Wea** (192), **web** (50d,70a,98c,99a,106c,149b), **wed** (97a,173c), **wee** (52c,100c,148c), **Wei** (30b,162b), **wen** (40c,72a,110a,170c,177b), **wet** (40d,46a,101a,124a,127c,149c), **wey** (173b)

W - E   **wee** (52c,100c,148c), **woe** (25b), **wye** (91c)

- WE   **awe** (81d,100a,130d,175b,182b), **ewe** (88a,143d), **owe**

W - G   **wag** (85b,104a,183a), **wig** (73b)

WH -   **who** (129c), **why** (52c)

W - H   **wah** (113c)

WI -   **wig** (73b), **win** (7a,17b,64b,123b), **wis** (79d,164c), **wit** (78d,85b, 177b)

W - I   **Wei** (30b,162b)

- WI   **Twi** (69c)

- WL   **awl** (145b,167a), **owl**

- WM   **cwm** (31b,37b,103d)

WN -   **WNW** (35b)

W - N   **wan** (113a), **wen** (40c,72a,110a,170c,177b), **win** (7a,17b,64b,123b), **won, wun** (24c) **wyn** (110a)

- WN   **awn** (12c,17b,140a), **own** (6d)

WO -   **woe** (25b), **won, woo, wop, wow** (52c,158a)

W - O   **who** (129c), **woo**

- WO   **Lwo** (107b), **Pwo** (88c), **two** (26c,37d,80a,93a)

W - P   **wop**

WR -   **wry** (13d)

W - R   **war** (157c)

WS -   **WSW** (35b)

W - S   **was** (166c,175c), **Was** (24d), **wis** (79d,164c)

W - T   **wat** (73d,140d,163a,180b), **wet** (40d,46a,101a,124a,127c), **wit** (78d,85b,177b)

WU -   **wun** (24c)

W - W   **waw** (12b,91c), **WNW** (35b), **wow** (52c,158a), **WSW** (35b)

W - X   **wax** (28b,72a,80b,120c)

WY -   **wye** (91c), **wyn** (110a)

W - Y   **way** (37d,96b,134b,164d), **wey** (173b), **why** (52c), **wry** (13d)

XA -   **xat** (167c)

- XA   **oxa** (29c)

XE -   **xer** (34a)

- XE   **axe** (30c,40c,167a), **Exe** (43a)

- XO   **exo** (122d)

X - R   **xer** (34a)

X - T   **xat** (167c)

YA -   **yah** (52c), **yak** (112c,161d,165b), **yam** (48c,121d,160b,170c), **Yao** (30a,c,104b), **yap** (16c,29b,122a), **yar** (72a), **Yau** (30c), **yaw** (43a, 155d)

Y - A yea (7c,175c)

- YA aya (77b,166b), **Aya** (143c), **iya** (95b,108d,111c), **Mya** (31c)

YE - yea (7c,175c), yen (33b,42d,93c,174a), yep, yes (7c,55a), yet (18b, 24d,64c,77c,80a,108c,156b,165b), yew (36a,52a,b,145d,168c,d) yez

- YE aye (7c,9b,55a,60a), bye (38c,141d), dye (33c,154d), eye (93d, 111b,140d), lye (8d,27d,93b), nye (72a,116d), **Nye** (9c,18b), oye (139c), **Pye** (50d,55a), rye (28b,70b,72d), sye (40c,46c,139b,141a, 167a), tye (28c,134a), wye (91c)

- YG tyg (46b)

Y - H yah (52c)

YI - yin (140a), **Yin** (30b,143c,185b), yip (16c)

Y - I yoi (52c,79a)

Y - K yak (112c,161d,165b), yok (10c,185a)

- YL kyl (76d,79b)

Y - M yam (48c,121d,160d,170c), yom (41a)

- YM gym (154a), **Nym** (54c,76a)

Y - N yen (33b,42d,93c,174a), yin (140a), **Yin** (30b,143c,185b), yon (44c,112a,164d), **Yun** (88d)

- YN lyn (140c,178d), syn (122d,183b), wyn (110a)

YO - yoi (52c,79a), yok (10c,185a), yom (41a), yon (44c,112a,164d), you, yow (52c)

Y - O **Yao** (30a,c,104b)

- YO iyo (7d,176b)

Y - P yap (16c,29b,122a), yep, yip (16c)

- YP cyp (169d), gyp (29b,42a,160c), hyp

Y - R yar (72a)

- YR pyr (92a,b,122c,173b), **Tyr** (7c,68c,109c,147d,163d,170c,178a)

Y - S yes (7c,55a)

- YS lys (58b,92b)

Y - T yet (18b,24d,64c,77c,80a,108c,156b,165b)

YU - **Yun** (88d)

Y - U **Yau** (30c), you

- YU ayu (160c)

Y - W yaw (43a,155d), yew (36a,52a,b,145d,168c,d), yow (52c)

- YX **Nyx** (69b), pyx (31a,51d,75d)

Y - Z yez

ZA - zac (27c), zag (84a), zak (188), **Zal** (135d), **Zan** (186b), zar (188), zat (148a), zax (148a)

Z - A zea (95c), **Zoa** (20b)

Z - C zac (27c)

Z - D zed (91c)

ZE - zea (95c), zed (91c), zee (81b,91c), zel (40c), **Zen** (24a), **Zep**, zer (188)

Z - E zee (81b,91c), **Zoe** (36b,183c)

262

Z - F   **Zif** (102a)

Z - G   **zag** (84a), **zig** (84a)

Z - H   **zoh** (13d,186b)

ZI -   **Zif** (102a), **zig** (84a), **Zio** (147d,163d), **zip** (24b,50b,176b), **Ziu** (147d,163d)

Z - K   **zak** (188)

Z - L   **Zal** (135d), **zel** (40c)

Z - N   **Zan** (186b), **Zen** (24a)

ZO -   **zoa** (20b), **Zoe** (36b,183c), **zoh** (13d,186b), **zoo** (181b)

Z - O   **Zio** (147d,163d), **zoo** (181b)

- ZO   **azo** (107c)

Z - P   **Zep**, **zip** (24b,50b,176b)

Z - R   **zar** (188), **zer** (188)

Z - T   **zat** (148a)

Z - U   **Ziu** (147d,163d)

Z - X   **zax** (148a)

FOUR-LETTER WORDS

AA - -   **Aalu** (6b,48d), **Aani** (45a,48d), **Aare, Aaru** (6b,48d)

- AA -   **baal** (142b), **baas** (97c), **caam** (93d), **Faam** (111a), **gaal** (23b,174d), **Haab** (97d), **haaf** (57d), **haak** (57b,178a), **haar** (139c), **kaan** (93d, 116c), **kaat** (105d), **laap** (51d,91b,141d), **maal** (188), **ma'am** (95a, 166b), **maar** (177a), **Maas** (132a), **Maat** (69a,b,85d), **Naab, naam** (44c), **Naam** (105b), **paal** (188), **paar** (28c,137a), **raab** (32d), **raad** (14a,49b,151a,165b), **Raad** (151a), **raas** (91b), **Saad** (12b), **saah** (188), **saal** (66c,73b), **Saan** (24d), **Saar** (63b,102d,132a), **Taal** (7d, 88c,151a), **taar** (12b), **Waac, waag** (71d,101d)

- - AA   **blaa, chaa** (162b), **draa** (188)

A - - A   **Abba** (20a,55a,161c), **Abfa** (76b), **Abia** (18d,137a), **abra** (26b), **Abra, acca** (53b,d), **acta** (41d,123d,128d,164c), **adda** (147d), **Adda** (68c,119d,157a,182a), **aera** (8a), **Aeta** (94d,100a,106b,117a), **Afra** (183c), **agha** (35a,171a), **agla** (7a), **agra** (26d,34d), **Agra** (161b), **agua** (152d,166c,178c), **Aida** (110d,175c), **Aira** (70d), **Akha** (86a,c), **akia** (74c), **Akka** (125d), **akra** (176a), **Akra** (191), **akua** (120d), **alba** (98b,181a), **Alba** (151d), **Alca** (14c,128b), **alda** (152b), **Alda** (110d,150c), **Alea** (14b,31c,167d), **alfa** (70d), **alga** (141b,c), **alia** (89d), **alla** (6d), **alma** (40d,53d,146d,147a), **Alma** 38d, 183c), **alta** (89c,152d), **Alva** (151d), **Alya** (155b,c), **amba** (161a), **amia** (22c,170d), **amla** (48a,161d,168c,169a), **amma** (6a), **amra** (77c), **anba** (36d), **anda** (23a,168c), **anna** (190), **Anna** (110c,166d, 183c), **anoa** (28a,60a,112c,181c), **ansa** (73c,93d,137c), **anta** (83d, 117c,d,121a), **Anta** (164a), **apia** (121b), **aqua** (90a,178c), **arba** (135d,171a), **arca** (9a,22c,29d,115a,130a), **Arca** (101b), **area** (37d, 38a,44c,53a,93b,110d,127d,138c,168a,186d), **aria** (8b,98c,150a,c, 170c), **arna** (24a,181b), **Aroa** (175b), **arpa** (83b), **arra** (47d,52c,82b),

Arta (72b), **Arya** (80d), **asea** (39b,177c), **Asha** (191), **Asia** (48a), **asta** (188), **Asta** (107a,164c), **Atka** (11a), **atma** (150d), **atta** (58d, 90c,97d,160c,173d), **Atta** (94d,95d,100a,106b,117a), **atua** (120d), **Auca** (192), **aula** (66c,73b), **aura** (44c,49c,66a,96b,158a,170d, 177c), **Ausa, Azha** (155b)

AB - - **abas** (61c), **Abba** (20a,55a,161c), **abbe** (32b,63b,123b), **Abby** (183d), **ABC's** (57a), **abed** (130c), **Abel** (7a,25b), **abet** (8b,15b,50a, 59b,75d,81c,141d,159d), **Abfa** (76b), **Abia** (18d,137a), **Abib** (102 a,b), **Abie** (96b,107a), **abir** (129a), **able** (26b,35b,126a,147c), **ably** (147c), **aboo** (17a), **Abot** (100c), **Abou** (48b,55a), **abox** (22d), **abra** (26b), **Abra, abri** (61c,62c,144b), **Absi** (191), **abut** (22a, 167c)

- AB - **baba** (108d,120c,166c,171a), **babe, Babi** (116c), **babu** (77a), **baby, caba** (184c), **Faba, gabe** (162a), **gabi** (162a), **gaby** (59c,146d), **haba** (151d), **habe** (191), **Maba** (103a,168d), **mabi** (58d), **nabk** (30d, 164d), **nabo** (117a), **Nabu** (68c,183d), **Raba, rabi** (38d,74a), **Rabi** (14b,117b), **saba** (56a,117a), **Saba** (143d), **sabe, tabi** (84c, 149d), **tabu** (59d,111d), **Wabi** (192)

- - AB **Ahab** (18c,26c,85b,86d,100d,116a,180b), **Arab** (30a,78b,c,106a, 107c,157b,160c,185d), **blab** (162b), **brab** (113b), **chab** (184a), **crab** (39b,144b,181b), **doab** (157c), **drab** (23d,29c,33d,46d,53b,d), **duab** (157c), **frab** (138c), **grab** (105b,142a,149b), **Haab** (97d), **Joab** (41a), **knab** (107a), **Moab** (18d,85a,86d,94a), **Naab, raab** (32d), **scab** (80b, 107d,157c), **slab** (148b), **snab** (23c,139a), **stab** (14c,87a,117c), **swab** (102b)

A - - B **Abib** (102a,b), **Adib** (155b), **Agib** (12a,42d), **Ahab** (18c,26c,85b, 86d,100d,116a,180b), **Arab** (30a,78b,c,106a,107c,157b,160c,185d)

AC - - **acca** (53b,d), **Acer** (96c), **ache** (79a,112d,185b), **acht** (66c), **achy, acid** (151a,162a), **Acis** (64b), **acle** (13d,82c,115d), **acme** (39c,115c, 186b), **acne** (147c), **acon** (62c,140d), **acor** (6d), **acre** (39b,56a,88b), **Acre, acta** (41d,123d,128d,164c), **acth** (13b), **acto** (152b), **Acts, actu** (7a,89a), **acus** (89d,118a), **acyl** (6d)

- A C - **Bach** (35c), **back** (75d,76d,159d), **Caca** (67a), **caco** (73b), **dace** (57a,b), **each, face** (159d,176c), **fact** (7a,128b), **hack** (40a,77c, 184d), **jaca** (84a), **jack** (26c,58a,127c), **Jack** (96b), **jacu** (19a,151b), **lace** (58b,179c), **lack** (178a), **lact** (34c), **lacy, mace** (49d,108d,153b, 154d,161a,178a), **mack, nach, paca** (132c,154a), **pace** (64b,98a, 153b,156a,170b,177d), **pack** (24b,140d), **paco** (9b,146d), **pacs** (94c), **pact** (8a), **raca** (19a,59c,130b,184d), **race** (116a,153b,154b, 169c), **rack** (32c,64b), **racy** (153b), **sack** (43d,118a,119d,182b), **saco** (189), **tace** (13a,155d), **tack** (28d,37d,54d), **tact** (43c,d,116a), **Vach** (153b), **Waco, Zach** (96b)

- - AC **utac** (22d), **Waac**

A - - C **aesc** (12d,64d), **alec** (10a,57c,d,76c,137c), **amic** (9d), **avec** (63a, 183a)

AD - - **adad** (52c,56a), **Adad** (68c,157a,182a), **Adah** (25b,51b), **Adam** (26b,96a,111c) **adan** (102d), **Adar** (85c,102a), **adat** (90b,95d), **adda** (147d), **Adda** (68c,119d,157a,182a), **Addu** (68c,157a,182a), **Addy** (183d), **aden** (34b), **Aden, Ader** (18d), **Ades** (73a), **Adib** (155b), **adit** (51a,100a,114d), **admi** (65d), **ador** (153b), **adry** (164c), **adze** (40c,167a)

264

- AD - Badb (82b), bade, cade (25c,27a,76c,85d,116d), Cade (50c), cadi (12a,103a,171a), cady (69d), Dada (13b,63a,157d), dado (41c,111c, 115c,177d), Eads (23b,24b,50b,82a), fade (181d,183b), fado (121c), fady, gade, hade (66a,148c,173c), hadj (98b,118a), jade (33c,65d,71d,166a), jadu (95a), jady, kada (188), kade (144a), kadi (103a,171a), Kadu (191), lade (24c,26d,43c,93b,100a,132a,139d, 161b,178d), Ladd (143c), lady, made, Madi (174a), mado (14d,57a, 170b), padi (131b), rada (135c,172a), rade (138d), sadd (33a,40b, 58c,107b), sade (91d), sadh (77a), sado (26d,84d), sadr (94a), Sadr (155b), vade (42c,67d,89b), wadd (109c), wade, wadi (46c,106a, 109a,128a,132a), wady (109a,128a,132a)

- - AD adad (52c,56a), Adad (68c,157a,182a), arad (13a,c,84a), bead (17a, 122a,146b), brad (54d,67c,105b), Chad (158b), clad (46a,82a), dead, diad (113a), duad (113a,171d), dyad (113a), ecad (73a, 119b), egad (100a,109a), Fuad (54d), glad (85c), goad (80b,154b), grad (28b), head (29d), Ibad (191), Irad (18d), Joad (50c), lead (35d,43d,72b,74d,81a), load (24c,26d,161b), mead (46a,78a,97d, 99b), Mead (78a), orad (104a), Phad (155b), quad (33c,172a), raad (14a,49b,151a,165b), read (116d,157d), road (37d,164d), Saad (12b), scad (31a,57a,78b,88d,137c), shad (27d,57a,b,c), spad (105b), Spad (118d), stad (151b,167d,176b), swad (94d), toad (10a, 17a,63d,126d), udad (143d,144a,181c), woad (20d,47c)

A - - D abed (130c), acid (151a,162a), adad (52c,56a), Adad (68c,157a, 182a), aged (110a), alod (51c,55d,88a,124c), amid (9d,50a), apod (59d), arad (13a,c,84a), arid (46c,85a), Arnd (67a), Arod (86c), avid (47b,71a,186b)

AE - - aera (8a), aeri (34a), aero (8b,34a,b,58c,59a), aery (47b,51d,106c), aesc (12d,64d), Aeta (94d,95d,100a,106b,117a)

- AE - Caen, daer (22b), daez, faex (46a), Gaea (47d,69a), Gael (28a,96c, 138d), haec (90a,164c), haem (122b), Jael (147b), laet (60d), nael (189), saer (163a), tael (91d,179d), waeg (19b,72c,87a), waer (40b)

- - AE alae (182d), blae (93b), brae (76d,139a,c,140b,148c), Irae (43c), koae (74b), quae (176b), spae (139c)

A - - E Aare, abbe (32b,63b,123b), Abie (96b,107a), able (26b,35b,126a, 147c), ache (79a,112d,185b), acle (13d,82c,115d), acme (39c,115c, 186b), acne (147c), acre (39b,56a,88b), Acre, adze (40c,167a), agee (13d,15c,38d), ague (30a,55d,95c,137b), aide (7b,14a,75d), aile (62b,63a,182c,d), aine (49b,62c,142c), aire (82c), Aire, ajee (15c,139a), akee (168c), alae (182d), albe (133a) alee (15c,75d,144b,157a,182a), Alle (14c), alme (40d,147a), aloe (7d,20a,76a,b,92b,98b,119b,158b,167a,183d), amie (61d), ance (158b,c,d), Ande (193), ange (61a), Anne (50c,84a,143b,183c), ante (87a,89a,115b,120b,122b,125d,154d), a-one (52b,167b), apse (9b, 20a,31a,128c,130a,142b,175a), arme (63a,179b), Arne (35c,50c, 134d), asse (25a,60d,74a), atle (136d,161d,169b), Aude, auge (123c,132b), aune (188), axle (153c,180c)

AF - - afar (44c), Afar (6c), afer (48a,182b), affy (18b), Afra (183c)

- AF - baff (69d), baft (14a,53b), cafe, daff (125d), daft (59c), gaff (57c, d,152d,153a), haft (76d), Kafa (6c), raff (75b), raft (27b,33c,58c, 75b), safe (141d,157d,174d), Safi (191), Taft (29d), Wafd (49a), waft (20d,58c)

- - AF   deaf, goaf (104b), Graf (37c,66b,67a,107c,186b), haaf (57d), heaf (144a), leaf (55c,73c,119b), loaf (79b,94b), neaf (58a,73c), Olaf (108a,176b), Piaf (63c), Wraf

A - - F   alef (91c), alif (12b), arif (127d), atef (39a,48d), Azof (20b,135d)

AG - -   Agag (18c,86c,137a), agal (17c,36d), Agao (6c,73c), agar (7d,28c, 39c,103c,141c), Agau (73c), Agaz (193), aged (110a), agee (13d, 15c,38d), ager (47c,56a,89b,c,131d,133b), agha (35a,171a), Agib (12a,42d), agio (52c,60a,101c,123a), Agis (86d), agla (7a), agni (88a,89c), Agni (56d,68b), agog (47b,52c,86b), agon (12c,36c,41b, 55d,71b), agra (26d,34d), Agra (161b), agri (89b), agro (149d), agua (152d,166c,178c), ague (30a,55d,95c,137b)

- AG -   baga (171b), bago (13d), cage (36a), cagy (178b), dagg (118c), dagh (76d), Dago, gage (28d,98a,119c,d), gagl (160b), hagg, hagi (84b), Iago (54b,111d,143c), Jaga (191), jagg, kago (113a), kagu (106c), Iago (83b,152b), mage (95b), magg (95b), Magh (102a), magi (123c), Magi (95b,116c,183a), naga (13d,33a,55b,127c), Naga (24c,77a,88c,176d), Nagy (78d), Paga (117a), page (51b,59b, 142d,159b), raga (56d,105a), rage (10c,30c,157a,161d), ragi (28b), saga (79b,91a,138a,157a,161b,c,168a), Saga, sage (13a,90d,100c, 141c,145c,180b,183a), sago (54c,59b,113b,125b,155c), sagy, vagi (38b), wage (27a,115b), yage (23a)

- - AG   Agag (18c,86c,137a), brag (21a,175a), coag (45d,118a,163b), crag (132c), drag (74a,125b), flag (16b,50d,82b,88c,115a,155a), knag (115d,139c), krag (131c), peag (144a,178a), quag (21c,102c), shag (73b,105b,161d,166d), skag (7d,46d), slag (46c,99a,138c,148d, 177a), snag (11b,27b,35c,87c,124b,166a), stag (65a,98d), swag (22a,156c), waag (71d,101d)

A - - G   Agag (18c,86c,137a), agog (47b,52c,86b), ajog, areg (116a,137a)

AH - -   Ahab (18c,26c,85b,86d,100d,116a,180b), Ahaz (86d), ahem, Ahet (49a,102a), ahey (52c), Ahir (27b), Ahom (88c), ahoy (106a), ahum

- AH -   bahi (60c), baho (122a), baht (146a), haha (55c,159c), kaha (123d), kahu (14d), maha (28c,88c,136d), mahr (103a), Oahu, paha (67b), pahi (21b,26a), paho (122a), Rahu (42b,48b), saha, sahh (188), Saho (6c), sahu (153d), taha (179b), tahr (68a,76d)

- - AH   Adah (25b,51b), Amah (95b,108d,111c), arah (52c), ayah (108d), blah, drah (188), Elah (18c,86d), Etah (51c,71d), eyah (95b,108d, 111c), Ivah (18d), kyah (19a), Leah (19a,84a,87b,183c), Noah (88a, 99b), odah (170d), opah (23b,57a,b,86d), prah (21b,26a,95c,d), Ptah (48d,98c), saah (188), seah (188), shah (116c), Utah (180b), yeah

A - - H   acth (13b), Adah (25b,51b), aich (9a), Alph (132a), amah (95b, 108d,111c), ankh (38d,162b), arah (52c), arch (29d,38b,39d,123d, 132c), ayah (108d)

AI - -   aich (9a), Aida (110d, 175c), aide (7b,14a,75d), aile (62b,63a,182c, d), aine (49b,62c,142c), Aino (84a,c), aint, Ainu (84a,c), aipi (27a), Aira (70d), aire (82c), Aire, airs (123b), airy (177a,176d)

- AI -   bail (43c), bain (61a), bait (15d,51a,94d,167b), caid (35a,151d, 152b), cain (169c), Cain (6a,7a,50d,88a,104c,143a), Dail (49a, 82b, c), dain (188), dais (119b), fail, fain (42d,67c,183b), fair (17a,55d),

266

fait (6d,61b), **Gaia** (47d,69a), **gail** (23b,174d), **Gail** (183d), **gain** (7a, b,124a,181d), **gait** (96b,179a), **haik** (57b,65b,108a), **hail** (6d,15a, 71d), **hair** (56b,164d), **jail** (123d), **Jain** (77b), **kaid** (29d,66a), **kaif** (88c), **kaik** (96c), **kail** (18c,22a.25a,79b), **Kain, kair, laic** (32b,90b, 107d,124a,141d), **laid, lain, lair** (37c,42b), **Lais** (17c), **lait** (62a), **Maia** (76b,109a,153b,155b,177c), **maid** (45b.142d), **mail** (12d,99b, 121c), **maim** (43d,81a,105c), **main** (29d,35d,123d), **mais** (61b), **Naia** (33a), **naid** (63c), **naif** (74b,105d). **naik, nail** (31d,54d,141d,161d, 173a), **naio** (107a,168c), **Nair** (45d), **nais** (63c,132a), **paid** (129c), **pail, pain** (7c), **pair** (22d,37d,85b,171d), **pais** (37d), **qaid** (35a), **raia** (107d), **Raia** (147b), **raid** (59d,80c), **raik** (188,189), **rail** (16b,19b,c, 37a,97b,138c,150c,177b), **rain** (121d,162d), **raip** (36d), **rais** (26c, 29d,75a,103b), **Rais** (106b), **saic** (86b,91d,175d), **said** (174c), **Said** (42d,101a,121b), **sail** (144c,185a), **sain** (20c,38d,48a), **sair** (140b, 150d), **sais** (48d,71d), **tail** (11d,27d,59b,143b), **tain** (166a), **tair** (68a,76d), **tait** (14d), **vail** (94b,124a,174b), **vain** (81a), **vair** (64c, 154c), **waif** (157b), **wail** (39b,88a), **wain** (177b), **Wain, wait** (26d, 42b,92c,155d,162a), **zaim** (170d), **zain** (41a)

--AI alai (171a), **Alai** (135c), anai (163b,181a), chai (72d), goal (106d, 168c), ngai (48a,159c), peai (98b), quai (88b,117c,180c), **Thai** (146a)

A--I **Aani** (45a,48d), **abri** (61c,62c,144b), **Absi** (191), **admi** (65d), **aeri** (34a), **agni** (88a,89c), **Agni** (56d,68b), **agri** (89b), aipi (27a), alai (171a), **Alai** (135c), **Albi** (58a), alii (74c,134c), ambi (34a,122c), amli (48a,161d,168c,169a), ammi (98c), amoi (62a), anai (163b, 181a), **Andi** (27d), anti (7d,111a,122b), **Anti** (193), apii (74c), arni (24a,181b), arui (11b,143d,144a,181c), asci (154a), assi (77d), **Asti** 83d,182b), **Atli** (14c,72b,79a,107d), **Atri, auri** (34a)

AJ-- ajar (110c), **Ajax** (71b,162d), ajee (15c,139a), ajog

-AJ- baju (84a), caja (152a), caji (180b), gajo (107c), haje (33a,48d), maja (151c), **Maja** (153b), majo, **Naja** (33a), pajo (122a), raja (77a, 123c), **Raja, tajo** (152a,d), yaje (23a)

AK-- **Akal** (56d), **Akan** (191), akee (168c), akey (189), **Akha** (86a,c), akia (74c), **Akim** (135d,191), akin (8b,92b,129c), **Akka** (125d), akov (189), akra (176a), **Akra** (191), akua (120d)

-AK- baka (52b), bake (139a), baku (26d,157b,168c), cake, caky, fake (123a,143c), faky, hake (57a,b), hakh (46d), hako (115b), haku (86d), jake (40d), **Jake** (96b), jako (71a), kaka (114b), kaki (84c, 106d), lake (117d), lakh (110c), laky, make (35b,36d,54a,123a) maki (91b), mako (18a,19a,20d,143c,168c,182c), **Maku** (192), oaks (154d), oaky, rake (41b,44c,134b,140d), **Saka** (10a), sake (84b,125d), saki (39c,84b,102a), take, takt (105a,163a), **Taku** (80c), taky, waka (26a), wake (134b,168a), wakf (103a), waky, **Yaka** (191), **Yaki** (193)

--AK **Anak** (67a), asak (13d,168c,169a), beak (19a), coak (45d,118a, 163b), dhak (48a,169a), **Dyak** (22b), feak (39d,171c), flak (11a), haak (57b,178a), **Irak** (99a,d), kiak (51c), kyak (51c), leak (110c), peak (9a,38c,159b,186b), siak (72d), soak (46c,137c), teak (41a, 48a,168c), weak (55b)

A--K amok (18b,63c), **Anak** (67a), asak (13d,168c,169a), asok (13d), **Atik** (155b)

267

AL · · alae (182d), alal (171a), Alai (135c), alan (45a,79a,183), Alan, alar (15c,145c,182d), alas (52c,136b,183b), alat (136d), alay (96c), alba (98b,181a), Alba (151d), albe (133a), Albi (58a), albo (34d,181a), Alca (14c,128b), alco (45b), alda (152b), Alda (110d, 150c), Alea (14b,31c,167d), alec (10a,57c,d,76c,137c), alee (15c, 75d,144b,157a,182a), alef (91c), alem (98b,155a,170d,171a), alen (40d,138a), alfa (70d), alga (141b,c), Algy (96b), alia (89d), alif (12b), alii (74c,134c), alim (103b,162c), alin (188), alit (44b,143a), Alix (183c), alky, alla (6d), Alle (14c), allo (34c), ally (14a,35c,d, 173c), alma (40d,53d,146d,147a), Alma (38d,183c), alme (40d, 147a), alms (29a), alod (51c,55d,88a,124c), aloe (7d,20a,76a,b,92b, 98b,119b,158b,167a,183d) alop (13d,46b,93d), alow (18a,172c), Alph (132a), Alps (85d), also (10b,18b,80a), alta (89c,152d), alto (152b,176c,177a), alum (14a,45c), Alur (191), Alva (151d), Alya (155b,c), Alys (183c)

· AL · Aalu (6b,48d), Bala (26c,66a), bald (16c), bale (24b,74a), bali, Bali, balk (118c,146a,156d), ball, balm (110a,172c), Balt (93a), balu (104b,159a,181d), cale (72d), calf, calk (78c,109a,141c,178d), call (145c,159b,176d), calm (8d,11d,112b,118d,126c,d,172b,173d), calo (72d), calp (92b), calx (23c,75c,112c), dale (43c,128a,174b), dali (168c,169b), fala (129b), fall (46b,141c), falx (133b), gala (55d), Gala (191), gale (181d), gali (6c), gall (19a,28c,29b,82c,160c, 176a), galt, hala (112b), hale (125b), Hale (9d,131a), half (101a), hall (37b,114d), halm, halo (14d,31b,92a,107b,131d), Hals (47a), halt (13b,28a,38d,156d), lalu (48d), kala (19a), kale (22a,25a, 119b,175a), kali (26d,67c,136d,167a), Kali (147b), kalo (162a), lala (129b), lalo (16b,34d,153a), Lalo (35c), mala (89b,c,90a,94b, 97d,109d,185c), male (154d), Male (45d), mali (27b), mall (95d,124b,143b), malm (32a,92b), malo (23a,74c,152a), malt (17c), Nala (77a), pala (189), Pala (88b), pale (113a,117c,178a), pali (122b), Pali (23d,24a,137b,175a), pall (32d,81b,112a), palm (59b, 168c,169b), palo (152c), palp (11a,55b,58b,167c), paly (194), rale (7c,23a,29d,41b), ralo (188), sala (152a,b,c), Sala (50c), sale (14c,61c,62b,c,168b), salp (109c,148d), salt (35d,105b,123a,136c, 141c,149d), tala (16d,113a,168c,d), talc (28d,63b,99c,100b,122a, 149c), tale (91a,185b), tali (189), talk, tall (118d), vale (54c,128a, 174b), Vale (7c,109c), vali (171a,176a), Vali (7c,109c), wale (70b, 131b,157c,163d,179a,180a,c,d), wali (171a), walk, wall, Walt (96b), Yale (173c), yali (171a)

· · AL agal (17c,36d), Akal (56d), Aral (135d), aval (70c), axal (120b), Baal (142b), beal (139d), bual (182c), coal (49c,64a), cral, deal (11d,16c,36c,44c,81a,168b), dhal (12b), dial (25c), dual (45c,171d), eral (51a), etal (89a), foal (78c), gaal (23b,174d), geal (47d,163c), goal (8b,109b,120b,125d), heal, ical (158c), keal (25a), kral, leal (54b,94c,139d), maal (188), meal (72a,130b), Neal, odal (48a,88b, 112c), opal (20a,65d,67b,82b) oral (114a,153d,174c,175c), oval (48d,49c,127a), paal (188), peal (131c,d), pyal (175c), real (7a), rial (190), ryal (110a,190), saal (66c,73b), seal (10c,d,54d,64c,96a, 118b,128a), sial (112a), Taal (7d,88c,151a), teal (19b,20d,46c,d), udal (76b,88b,131c), unal (147a), ural, Ural (135c), uval (70c), veal, vial (148c), weal (124d,157c,180c,d), zeal (12c,55d)

A · · L Abel (7a,25b), acyl (6d), agal (17c,36d), Akal (56d), amil (45a,48a,

268

185c), **amyl** (155c), **anil** (47c,80d,180b), **Aoul** (191), **Aral** (135d), **aril** (142a), **aval** (70c), **axal** (120b), **axil** (10c), **azul** (151d)

AM - - **amah** (95b,108d,111c), **amar** (189), **amba** (161a), **ambi** (34a,122c), **ambo** (125b,128b), **amen** (14a,80b,94a,137a,149c,175c,184b), **Amen** (86d,127d,159b,164a), **amer** (61b), **Ames** (9c,82a), **Amex** (184d), **amia** (22c,170d), **amic** (9d), **amid** (9d,50a), **amie** (61d), **amil** (45a,48a,185c), **amin** (9d), **amir** (7c,12a,103a,b,123c,170d), **amit** (94a), **amla** (48a,161d,168c,169a), **amli** (48a,161d,168c,169a), **amma** (6a), **ammi** (98c), **ammo** (9d), **ammu** (9d), **amoi** (62a), **amok** (18b,63c), **Amon** (86d,96d,127d,159b,164a), **amor** (152b), **Amor** (39c,68b), **Amos** (96a,144b), **Amoy** (88c), **amra** (77c), **Amun** (86d,127d,159b,164a), **amyl** (155c)

- AM - **came** (182b), **Came** (192), **camp** (163b), **dama** (65d,152b), **dame** (67b,87c,166b), **damn, damp** (101a), **Fama** (135a), **fame** (130a), **famn** (188), **Gama** (121c), **game** (64d,154a), **gamp** (172a), **hami** (78a), **iamb** (59c), **jama** (103b), **jamb** (12d,45c,118a,146b,174a), **jami** (103b), **Kama** (56d), **kame** (67b,139b), **kami** (68a,84b), **Kami** (88c,107c,144c), **lama** (23d,24a,91d,165b), **Lamb** (49c), **lame** (38d, 43d,73b), **lamp** (92a,94c), **mama, Mama** (116d), **mamo** (19a,d,74b), **Nama** (78c), **name** (8a,11b,d,25c,46c,107c,130b,157d,163b,166b), **Rama** (77a,80b,176d), **rame** (22d), **rami** (22d), **ramp** (65a,80b, 127b,148b), **sama** (105c,169d), **same** (44d,79b), **samh** (56b), **samp** (70b,77d,121b), **Tama** (192), **tame** (45a,b,66a), **Tame, tamp** (46b, 112b,121d,127d), **vamp** (80a,145a), **Yama** (57a,68a), **Zama** (73d, 141d)

- - AM **Adam** (26b,96a,111c), **anam** (159a,168c), **Anam, Aram** (18d,50c, 105c,144b,161c), **Azam** (166c), **beam, Bram** (96a), **caam** (93d), **cham** (20a,29d), **Cham** (8c), **clam** (20b,101b), **cram** (157d), **dram** (46b,110c,121d,148c), **edam** (29c), **Elam** (18d,37d,82a,116c,144b), **enam** (70c,77a), **Enam** (85c), **exam, Faam** (111a), **flam** (169c), **foam** (63d,154b), **gram** (29d,99b,148d,160d,180a), **Gram, Guam, imam** (25c,102d,103a), **klam** (189), **Liam** (181d), **loam** (47d,150a), **lyam** (139a), **ma'am** (95a,166b), **miam** (14d), **naam** (44c,105b), **ogam** (82b,c), **olam** (51a,d,75c,81a), **pram** (15a), **ream** (18c,37d, 50d,113d,171c), **roam** (178a), **seam** (85b,d,160a,176d,185a), **sham** (41c,55b,60d,80a,123a,b,146d), **Siam** (163d,181a), **slam** (180d, 182d), **swam, team** (38c,72a,113a), **Tiam, tram** (170a), **Ulam** (67b), **wham** (157c)

A - - M **Adam** (26b,96a,111c), **ahem, Ahom** (88c), **ahum, Akim** (135d,191), **alem** (98b,155a,170d,171a), **alim** (103b,162c), **alum** (14a,45c), **anam** (159a,168c), **Anam, Anim** (18d), **Aram** (18d,50c,105c,144b, 161c), **arum** (13a,39b,58d,92b,155c), **Arum** (66a), **asem** (9a,49a, 69c), **Asom** (18d), **atom** (101c,114c,180d), **Atum** (143a,159b), **Azam** (166c)

AN - - **anai** (163b,181a), **Anak** (67a), **anam** (159a,168c), **anan** (49a,159a, 180c), **Anas** (46c,d), **Anat** (138c,147d), **Anax** (43c,120c), **anay** (72b,163b,181a), **anba** (36d), **ance** (158b,c,d), **ancy** (158c), **anda** (23a,168c), **Ande** (193), **Andi** (27d), **Andy** (96b), **Aner** (18d,96b), **anes** (110c,140a), **anet** (43c), **anew** (7c), **ange** (61a), **ango** (171a), **anil** (47c,80d,180b), **Anim** (18d), **anis** (55c), **ankh** (38d,162b), **anna** (190), **Anna** (110c,166d,183c), **Anne** (50c,84a,143b,183c), anoa (28a,60a,112c,181c), anon (7d,14d,79d,80b,123a,145c,150c, 164a), ansa (73c,93d,137c), anse (61d), ansu (11d), anta (83d, 117c,d,121a), Anta (164a), ante (87a,89a,115b,120b,122b,125d, 154d), anti (7d,111a,122b), Anti (193), anzu (11d)

- AN -   Aani (45a,48d), Bana (67a), banc (61a,85c), band (72a,157c), bane (74a,106b,120b,139a), bang (75d,105d,148a), bani (190), bank (18a,58c), bans, bant (43c), Cana (57a,64b,100c), cane (17b, 128a,156a,159a,177d), Cane, cang (184a), cano (152a), cant (28d, 81b,84d,90c,109b,136c,165d,166a), Dana (28a,96a,171d), Dane (85d,107d,138a), dang, dank (40b,101a), dans (62a), Danu (28a), fana, fane (30d,137a,162d), fang (167b), Fano (51d,96b,113c,d), gane (185b), gang (38c), Gano (132d), hand (60c,114c,115d,184c), hang (160a), hank (147c), Hano (125b), Hans (66d,96a), hant (67a), jane (190), Jane (183c), Jann (102d), kana (84d), Kane (74c), k'ang (30a), Kano (84c,177d), kant (28d), Kant (67a), lana (58a,66a,90a,184b), land (44a,163c), lane (134b,157b), lank (148b,164b), lanx (133a,b), mana (30a,120d,122a,159c), mand (28b), mane, mani (115c), mann (189), Mann (9c,48c,185c), mano (71d,73d,74b,83b), Mans (30a), Manu (10a,76d,77a,b), Manx (27b, 28a,82d), many (108d), nana (118b), Nana (15c,105d,116d,186d), nane (139d), Pana, pane (113c,155a,b), pang (165b), Pani (120c), pank (189), pant, rana (77a,123c), Rana (63d), rand (16d,22a, 131b,145a,b), Rand (69c), rang, rani (72d,77b,123c,127c), rank (31d,55d,70b,92c,94d,157d), rann (175c), rant (41c,127b,128a, 161d), sana (56a,166d), Sana (185d), sand (71d,146c), sane (128a), sang, sank, sano (152b), sans (63a,183b), tana (159a), Tana (87d), Tane (120d), tang (30b,58b,186b), tanh (97c), tank (175a,d), Tano (192), uang (131a), vane (179b,182a), vang (72d,134a,140b), Vans (107d), wand (120b,132c,156a), wane (41c,43c), wang (189), want (41b,42d,87b,106b,122a), wany, Yana (192,193), yang (30b,70a), yank, Yank, zany (24a,32d,59c)

- - AN   adan (102d), Akan (191), alan (45a,79a,183c), Alan (96a), anan (49a,159a,180c), Aran (18c,48c,64d,82d,174c), Awan (191), azan (102d), bean (91b,142a,175a), bran (23c,39a,72a,79c,70b), Bran (23c,50c), chan (26c,130c), clan (169c), Coan (37b), cran (160c), cyan, dean (33c,109d), dhan (124c), dian (46c,130d,170b), Dian (68d,69a,c,102b), duan (64b), elan (12c,41a,50d,62a,153c,177a, 186b), Eoan (41a,85b), Evan (96a), Ewan, flan (39d,40a,114d), gean (29c), Goan, gran, guan (151b), Iban (47c), Iran (6a,48c, 116b), Ivan (40c,85b,96a), jean (37c), Jean (183c), Joan (183c), juan (113a), Juan (96a), kaan (93d,116c), khan (7c,26c,81b,93d, 116c,123c,130c,166c), kran (190), kuan (30b,c), Kuan, kwan (30b), lean (128a,148b,152d,164b,166a), loan, mean (15a,42b, 146c,156b), mian (97c,147b,166b), moan, ngan, oban (190), Olan (115c), Oman (159a), Onan (18c,85c), Oran, oxan, pean (65c), plan (99b,124a,138b), quan (190), roan (78b,c,114c,128d,144a, 181a), Saan (24d), Sean (85b,96a), Shan (13c,80d,88c,101d), scan (52b,93d,98a,116d,128b,c,140d), span (23b,107b,113a,128b,162c), Svan (27d), swan (19b,33a) tean (140c167a), than (35b), tran (7a), tuan (95d,147b,166c), ulan (27d,88a), uran (101d), Uran, uzan (189), wean (8d,42d), yean (88a), yuan (190), Yuan (30b,101d)

A - - N acon (62c,140d), adan (102d), aden (34b), **Aden, agon** (12c,36c, 41b,55d,71b), **Akan** (191), akin (8b,92b,129c), alan (45a,79a, 183c), **Alan** (96a), alen (40d,138a), alin (188), amen (14a, 80b,94a,137a,149c,175c,184b), \ **Amen** (86d,127d,159b,164a), amin (9d), **Amon** (86d,96b,127d,159b,164a), **Amun** (86d,127d, 159b,164a), anan (49a,159a,180c), anon (7d,14d,79d,80b,123a, 145c,150c,164a), **Aran** (18c,48c,64d,82d,174c), **Asin** (102a), aten (150a,159b), aton (150a,159b), **Avon** (143b), **Awan** (191) axon (106c,153c), ayin (91c), azan (102d), azon (127b)

AO - - aone (52b,167b), **Aoul** (191)

- AO - faon (33c,55a), gaol (123d), **Gaol** (164a), **Gaon** (85b), **jaob, Laos** (80d,129c), naos (28a,71c,137a,163a), **Naos** (155b), paon (115b), **Taos** (192), **Yaou** (30c)

- - AO **Agao** (6c,73c), dhao (24c), grao (189), guao (168c,169b), **Miao** (30a,b), omao (165b), prao (21b,26a,95c,d), tiao

A - - O aboo (17c), acto (152b), aero (8b,34a,b,58c,59a), **Agao** (6c,73c), agio (52c,60a,101c,123a), agro (149d), **Aino** (84a,c), albo (34d, 181a), alco (45b), allo (34c), also (10b,18b,80a), alto (152b,176c, 177a), ambo (125b,128b), ammo (9d), ango (171a), apio (125b), areo (34c), **Argo** (12c,36b,c), **Arno** (27a), aroo (80c,82b), arro (52c), arto (34a), asno (151d), **Ateo** (120d), atmo (34d,174d), auto (34d)

AP - - Apap (102a), apar (12d), aper (32d), **Apet** (97c), apex (39c,76c, 115c,118b,159b,166a,167b), apia (121b), apii (74c), apio (125b), **Apis** (17c,24b,49a,125a,136a), apod (59d), apse (9b,20a,31a,128c, 130a,142b,175a), **Apsu** (29a), **Apus** (36b,c)

- AP - capa (152a,166d), cape (75a,96c,124b,161a), caph (91c), capp (27a), gape (185b), gapo (60a), gapy, **Hapi** (66a,107b,136a), hapu (106d), jape (85a,b), kapa (74b), kaph (91d), kapp, **Lapp** (108a), mapo (68a,148d), napa (25c,67d,90d), **Napa** (182c), nape (15b, 108c,d), napu (29d,80d), papa, pape (19b,113a), rapt (6c,27a,50d), sapa (70c), sapo (149c,166d), tapa (16c,32c,53b,56a,74b,104b,112b, 113d,120d), tape (16a,19a,128d), tapu, wapp (54b,133d,145d), yapa (113b), **Yapp** (22a)

- - AP Apap (102a), atap (113b), chap (55b), clap (58b), drap (61b,c, 62a), flap (17b,59a,104a,118d,161a,182d), frap (45d,165c), heap (117d), knap (76d,107a,139b,159b,166a,170c,185b), laap (51d,91b, 141d), leap (26c), neap (165c,167a,177b), plap (54b), reap (7a,40a, 74a), shap, slap (24a,128c,148c), snap (23a,36d,38b,48b,54d,56c, 58c,149d), soap, swap (168a), trap (27b,67b,132b,149b), wrap (32b,51a)

A - - P alop (13d,46b,93d), Apap (102a), asop (180b), atap (113b), atip (14b,166a), atop (112a,174a)

AQ - - aqua (90a,178c)

- AQ - waqf (103a)

- - AQ Iraq (99a,d)

AR - - **Arab** (30a,78b,c,106a,107c,157b,160c,185d), arad (13a,c,84a), arah (52c), **Aral** (135d), **Aram** (18d,50c,105c,144b,161c), **Aran** (18c, 48c,64d,82d,174c), arar (137a,168c), **Aras, arba** (135d,171a), arca

271

(9a,22c,29d,115a,130a), **Arca** (101b), **arch** (29d,38b,39d,123d, 132c), **area** (37d,38a,44c,53a,93b,110d,127d,138c,168a,186d), **areg** (116a,137a), **areo** (34c), **Ares** (49b,51b,68c,76a,97a,105c,110b, 178a,186d), **aret** (128c), **Argo** (12c,36b,c), **aria** (8b,98c,150a,c, 170c), **arid** (46c,85a), **arif** (127d), **aril** (142a), **aris** (101b), **arme** (63a,179b), **arms, army** (78c), **arna** (24a,181b), **Arnd** (67a), **Arne** (35c,50c,134d), **arni** (24a,181b), **Arno** (27a), **arn't**, **Aroa** (175b), **Arod** (86c), **aroo** (80c,82b), **arow** (92c,158b), **arpa** (83b), **arra** (47d,52c,82b), **arro** (52c), **Arta** (72b), **arto** (34a), **arts** (138c), **arty, arui** (11b,143d,144a,181c), **arum** (13a,39b,58d,92b,155c), **Arum** (66a), **Arya** (80d)

- AR -   **Aare, Aaru** (6b,48d), **bara** (188), **barb** (20b,57d,78b,117d,120a,b, 124b), **bard** (12d,120a), **bare** (43d,157c), **bari** (79c), **Bari** (37c,83d), **bark** (115c), **barm** (185b), **barn** (156d), **baro** (71a,122c), **barr** (49b), **Bart** (96b), **baru** (168c), **cara** (83a), **Cara** (48b,183c), **card** (33d, 114d), **care** (11b,14c,35d,150a,184d), **cark** (26d,184d), **carl** (115c, 135d), **Carl** (96a), **carn** (156c), **caro** (83a,183d), **carp** (27d,38d, 40c,55a,56c,57a), **carr** (120d,140a), **cart** (171d,175a,177b), **Dara** (18d), **Dard, dare** (28d,41b,42a,74d,175b), **Dare** (57a), **dari** (38a, 70b), **dark** (47a,67d,109b,160b), **darn** (130b), **darr** (163c), **dart** (13b,88a,100c,120b,153a,160c), **Dart** (100c), **earl** (107c), **earn** (42d,64b,99a), **fard** (112d), **fare** (43c,59b,67d,123b), **farl** (138c, 140b), **farm** (165d), **faro** (65a), **gara** (190), **garb** (32c,46a), **gare** (61b,c,62c,127c,184b), **Garm** (178c), **garn** (67d,185b), **Garo** (88c), **Harb** (191), **hard** (109b), **hare** (91b,132c), **hark** (92d), **harl** (16b,56b, 59a), **harm** (40b,81a), **harp** (105a,129a), **hart** (41d,154d), **jarl** (40d, 107d), **kara** (132a), **Kari** (14d), **Karl** (96a), **karn** (156c), **karo** (106d), **Lara** (25c), **lard** (54d,61a,71a,110a), **lari** (78a,101c), **Lari** (72c), **lark** (19a,63d,177b), **larp** (51d), **Lars** (51d,121b), **mara** (114d), **Mara** (24a,d,105b,107b), **marc** (70c), **Marc** (96a), **mare** (78b,108b), **mari** (16a,61d), **mark, Mark** (52a,96a,146b,155a), **marl** (32a,42c, 55d), **maro** (144d), **Mars** (68c,118d,119a,178a), **mart** (49d,97a), **Mart** (96b,183d), **maru** (84c,144d), **Mary** (50c,126b,183c), **nard** (13a, 97c,102b,110a,153c), **Nare** (93c), **nark** (81a,156d), **nary** (108b), **oary, para** (134c,170d), **Para** (18a,51d), **parc** (62b,112c), **pard** (27b, 91b), **pare** (115c,129a), **pari** (34a,180a), **park, parr** (136d,147c), **pars** (89d), **part** (44d,60d,121c,159c), **paru** (57a), **rara** (119a), **rare** (138b,164b,172b,173d), **Sara** (24d,183c), **sard** (26d,28d,65d,111a, 142b,156d), **Sarg** (96d,125c), **sari** (48b,65b,77b), **Sark** (28d), **Sart** (82b, 103b, 170d), **tara** (22a, 55c, 113a, 168c), **Tara** (82b,c,138b), **tare** (9a,18d,41a,176a,179d), **tari** (47d,69a), **tarn** (87d,103d,120d), **taro** (13c,48c,49b,64b,112b,120a,133d,155c,170a, c), **tarp** (26b,178d), **tart** (114d), **vara** (151d), **vare** (179b), **vari** (34d,91b,134d,174d), **vary** (28d,43c), **ward** (31c,55c,86b), **ware** (27d,35a), **warf, warm** (7c,75b,163b), **warn** (7b), **warp** (36c,165a, 171c), **wart** (124d), **wary** (27d,176b), **yard** (152d), **yare** (96b,124b, 128b), **yark** (22c), **yarl** (40d,107d), **yarn** (154b,161b,184b), **yarr** (72a), **Yaru** (48d), **zarf** (39c,155a), **zarp** (120c)

- - AR   **Adar** (85c,102a), **afar** (44c), **Afar** (6c), **agar** (7d,28c,39c,103c,141c), **ajar** (110c), **alar** (15c,145c,182d), **amar** (189), **apar** (12d), **arar** (137a,168c), **asar** (67b), **atar** (58d,116c,134a), **Avar** (27d,108a), **bear** (27a,50b,113c,155a), **Bhar** (191), **boar** (77c,117c,160c,181c),

272

char (24d,138c,170b), **czar** (42d,49d,60b,135c), **dear, Dhar, duar, Edar** (18d), **fear** (113c,155a), **gear** (32c,112a,167b), **gnar** (72a), **guar** (46c,59d), **haar** (139c), **hear** (75b,c,92d), **hoar** (63d,71a, 181a), **inar** (65b), **Isar** (41a,104c,132a), **Iyar** (102b), **izar** (65b, 103b,155b), **joar** (100a), **juar** (100a), **khar** (189), **knar** (87c,134b), **kuar** (102a), **kyar** (33a), **lear** (139d), **Lear** (37a,143b), **liar** (98d), **maar** (177a), **near** (11d,32c,107b), **omar** (103b), **Omar** (48c,51b, 163b), **osar** (51b,67b,131b), **paar** (28c), **pear** (64a), **rear** (15b,23a, b,24a,51b,76d,127c), **roar** (145c) **Saar** (63b,102d,132a), **scar** (31a, 184d), **sear** (23d,27d,72d,138c), **soar** (59a), **spar** (22c,24c,64b, 97b,100b,144d), **star** (14a,21c,94c,100c), **taar** (12b), **tear** (67c, 87b,130a), **thar** (68a,76d), **tiar** (39a,75a,121a), **tsar** (42d,49d, 60b,135c), **tzar** (42d,49d,60b,135c), **usar** (8d,16c), **wear** (50b), **year, Zoar**

A - - R   **Abir** (129a), **Acer** (96c), **acor** (6d), **Adar** (85c,102a), **Ader** (18d), **ador** (153b), **afar** (44c), **Afar** (6c), **afer** (48a,182b), **agar** (7d,28c, 39c,103c,141c), **ager** (47c,56a,89b,c,131d,133b), **Ahir** (27b), **ajar** (110c), **alar** (15c,145c,182d), **Alur** (191), **amar** (189), **amer** (61b), **amir** (7c,12a,103a,b,123c,170d), **amor** (152b), **Amor** (39c,68b), **Aner** (18d,96b), **apar** (12d), **aper** (32d), **arar** (137a,168c), **asar** (67b), **Aser** (84a), **Askr** (107d), **asor** (75c,105a), **Asur** (68c), **atar** (58d,116b,134a), **Ater** (18c), **Auer** (79a), **Avar** (27d,108a), **aver** (7c,14a,15c,41c,95c,140d,155c,160b,184c)

AS - -   **asak** (13d,168c,169a), **asar** (67b), **asci** (154a), **asea** (39b,177c), **asem** (9a,49a,69c), **Aser** (84a), **Asha** (191), **ashy** (113a,178a), **Asia** (48a), **Asin** (102a), **Askr** (107d), **asno** (151d), **asok** (13d), **Asom** (18d), **asop** (180b), **asor** (75c,105a), **asse** (25a,60d,74a), **assi** (77d), **asta** (188), **Asta** (107a,164c), **Asti** (83d,182b), **Asur** (68c)

- AS -   **base** (6a,43b,44b,51c,60c,79b,94b,122b), **bash, bask** (94d), **bass** (57b,c,177a), **bast** (16c,56a,117b,184a), **Bast** (27b), **casa** (152b), **case** (22c,36c,81c,91a,108c), **cash** (101c), **cask, Caso** (82d), **cass** (140c,177a), **Cass** (147a), **cast** (165b,167c), **dash** (125c,162d), **dasi** (77a), **ease** (7c,8d,35a,100d,129d,130b,c,150c), **East** (111b), **easy** (54a,146d,149d,172b), **fash** (140c,176a), **fass** (189), **fast** (56d, 126c,141d,160c,173a,d), **gash** (40a), **gasp** (113c), **hase** (74d), **hash, hasp** (31d,54d,153c), **hast, jass** (160d), **kasa** (48a), **kasi** (116b), **kasm** (189), **lash** (58c,87b,165c,180d), **Lasi** (191), **lass** (95b, **last** (36c,50b,145a,174c), **masa** (37a), **mash** (39b,156c), **mask** (44a,45c), **mass** (8a,24b,35b,142d), **mast** (17c,108d,120b,144d,152d), **masu** (57a,84c), **nase** (26b,75a,124b), **Nash** (9c), **nasi** (34c,108a,115a), **Nast** (9c,27a), **oast** (15d,86b,112a), **pasa** (46a,127c,152c), **pasi** (94b), **pass** (110b,155c), **past** (25c,69d,165d), **rasa** (51c), **rase** (42b, d,91d), **rash** (75a), **rasp** (56b,70d,140d), **sasa** (55c), **sash** (18a,45c, 67b,182b), **sass, tash** (154c), **task** (156b), **Tass** (107a,135d,151b), **vasa** (46d,114a,160b,175d), **Vasa, vase, vast** (78d,79d), **vasu** (106c), **Vasu** (176d), **wash, wasp, wast**

- - AS   **abas** (61c), **alas** (52c,136b,183b), **Anas** (46c,d), **Aras, baas** (97c), **bias** (43b,123a), **blas** (6c,49c), **Blas** (67b), **bras** (61a), **Dyas** (66a), **ELAS** (71c), **eyas** (106c,173a), **gras** (78b), **Idas** (27b,71c), **Iras** (11b,32a), **khas** (153a), **kras** (76d), **kvas** (135c), **Lias** (66a), **Lyas** (66a), **Maas** (132a), **mias** (111a), **Nias** (82d), **oras** (40d), **quas**

273

(135c), upas (84d,120b,168c,d), **Usas** (68d), **utas** (49a,109c), **Xmas, yeas** (177c), **Zoas** (20b)

A - - S   abas (61c), **ABC's** (57a), **Acis** (64b), **Acts, acus** (89d, 118a), **Ades** (73a), **Agis** (86d), **Aias, Airs** (123b), alas (52c,136b,183b), **alms** (29a), **Alps** (85d), **Alys** (183c), **Ames** (9c,82a), **Amos** (96a,144b), **Anas** (46c,d), **Anes** (110c,140a), anis (55c), **Apis** (17c,24b,49a, 125a,136a), **Apus** (36b,c), **Aras, Ares** (49b,51b,68c,76a,97a,105c, 110b,178a,186d), aris (101b), **arms, arts** (138c), ates (160c), atis (76d,102a), **Aves** (19d), **Avis** (89a,183c), **avus** (89b), **axis** (28b, 41d,77c,153c), **ayes** (177c)

AT - -   atap (113b), atar (58d,116b,134a), atef (39a,48d), aten (150a, 159b), **Ateo** (120d), **Ater** (18c), ates (160c), **Atik** (155b), atip (14b,166a), atis (76d,102a), **Atka** (11a), atle (136d,161d,169b), **Atli** (14c,72b,79a,107d), atma (150d), atmo (34d,174d), **Atmu** (143a,159b), atom (101c,114c,180d), aton (150a,159b), atop (112a, 174a), **Atri, atry** (141b), atta (58d,90c,97d,160c,173d), **Atta** (94d, 95d,100a,106b,117a), **Attu, atua** (120d), **Atum** (143a,159b)

- AT -   bata (30a,142d), **bate** (43c,91b,100d), **bath, Bath** (50d,151c), **batt** (37c), **batz** (190), cata (122c), **cate** (165c), **Cato** (132d,133b), data (54a), **date** (64a,153a), dato (95c,102c,117a), datu (95c,102c, 117a), eats, **fate** (42d,52a,87a,94a), gata (143c), **gate** (51a,121b), **Gath** (117a), **hate** (6a,43a), **hath, Hati** (48d), jati (27b), jato (173b), **Kate** (143c,183d), kath (14a), **Katy** (183d), lata (85d,95d), **late** (128c), **lath** (157c), latu (190), **mate** (18c,35b,41d,113a,154a,162c), math (77a), **Matt, maty** (80c), **Nata** (15c,47c), **Nate** (22b), **Nath** (155c), **Nato** (6a,8d), natr (189), **Natt** (107b), **oath** (119c,150a), pata (32c,160d), **pate** (39a,74d), **path** (132a,134b), pato (46d), patu (179b), **rata** (29d,56b,89d,96c,106d,120c,168c), **rate** (11d,14a,31d, 36b,51d,52a,70b,85c,112b,123b,127d,128a,138c,143a,174b), **rath** (29a,76d,162d), rati (189), **rats, sate** (32d,52c,67d,70d,137c,159d), **sati, Sati** (49a,126b,147b), **tate** (183a), **tatt** (87c), **tatu** (12d), **Tatu, Wate** (141a), **watt, Watt** (82a,173b,177c), **yate** (51d,168c), **yati** (76d), **zati** (21d)

- - AT   adat (90b,95d), **alat** (136d), **Anat** (138c,147d), **beat** (58c,87b,131a, 164d,165b,180d), **bhat** (80c), **blat** (25b), **boat** (27b,106a), **brat, chat** (9b,19c,161c), **coat** (160a), **doat** (17a,94b,112a,165d), **drat** (100a), **Duat** (172d), **erat** (89c), etat (62d), **feat** (7a,52d), **fiat** (35a, 41d,48c,111b,137a), **Fiat** (83c), **flat** (41b,124b,173a), **frat, geat** (77d,101a), **Geat** (138a), **ghat** (32d,88b,103d,132a), **gnat** (59a, 81b,99c), **goat** (135a), **heat, ikat** (53b,159a), **kaat** (105d), **khat** (105d), **kyat** (189), **Maat** (69a,b,85d), **meat** (59b), **moat** (44d), **neat** (165c,169d), **peat** (64a,175a), **piat** (11a), **plat** (22d,96c,114a,119c, 133d), **pyat** (95b), **scat** (26b,67a,d,126c,169c), **seat** (98c,156b), **shat** (87d), **skat** (181b), **Skat** (155b), **slat** (58b,89a,117c,184a), **spat** (112c,126b,134b), **stat** (72d), **swat** (15d,20d,32d,157c), **Swat** (103a), **that** (42b,124b,129c), **what** (129c)

A - - T   abet (8b,15b,50a,59b,75d,81c,141d,159d), **Abot** (100c), **abut** (22a, 167c), **acht** (66c), **adat** (90b,95d), **adit** (51a,100a,114d), **Ahet** (49a,102a), **aint, alat** (136d), **alit** (44b,143a), **amit** (94a), **Anat** (138c,147d), **anet** (43c), **Apet** (97c), **aret** (128c), **arn't, aunt** (129c)

AU - -   **Auca** (192), **Aude, Auer** (79a), **auge** (123c,132b), **aula** (66c,73b),

274

aulu (74c,168c), **aune** (188), **aunt** (129c), **aura** (44c,49c,66a,96b, 158a,170d,177c), **auri** (34a), **Ausa, ausu** (168c,180b), **auto** (34d), **auza** (168c,180b)

- AU - **baud** (162d), **baul** (18b), **Baum** (9c,112c), **cauk** (139b), **caul** (16d, 74d), **caur** (139a), **daub** (148d), **dauk** (95c), **Daur** (139b), **dauw** (24c), **eaux** (178c), **faun** (56a,68b,137c,161a,184a), **gaub** (116c), **gaud** (169d), **gaue** (67a), **Gaul** (10a,60d,63c), **gaup, gaur** (112c, 181c), **gaus** (67d), **gaut** (88b,103d,132a), **haul** (27b,45d), **jaun** (113a), **kaun** (93d), **laud** (122a), **laun** (146b), **maud** (53d,136d, 143c), **Maud** (181a,183c), **Maui** (120d), **maul** (73c), **maun** (139d), **naut** (141b), **Paul** (96a), **paun** (18b), **paut** (140a), **Sauk** (192), **saul** (48a,168c), **Saul** (18c,86d,115a), **saum** (189), **taun** (188), **taut** (163b,165c), **Vaux** (63b), **yaup**

- - AU **Agau** (73c), **beau, Diau** (192), **Drau, Esau** (82c,84a,128c), **frau** (181b), **miau** (27b,99b), **prau** (21b,26a,95c,d), **sgau** (88c), **unau** (148c,171d), **whau** (107a,168c)

A - - U **Aalu** (6b,48d), **Aaru** (6b,48d), **Abou** (48b,55a), **actu** (7a,89a), **Addu** (68c,157a,182a), **Agau** (73c), **Ainu** (84a,84c), **ammu** (9d), **ansu** (11d), **anzu** (11d), **Apsu** (29a), **Atmu** (143a,159b), **Attu, aulu** (74c,168c), **ausu** (168c,180b), **auzu** (168c,180b)

AV - - **aval** (70c), **Avar** (27d,108a), **avec** (63a,183a), **aver** (7c,14a,15c,41c, 95c,140d,155c,160b,184c), **Aves** (19d), **avid** (47b,71a,186b), **avis** (89a), **Avis** (183c), **Avon** (143b), **avow** (6d,36a,41c,112c), **avus** (89b)

- AV - **bave** (61d,146c), **cava** (116a,175b), **cave** (27d), **cavy** (72b,120d, 132c,157b), **Dave** (96b), **Davy** (96b,136b), **eave** (133c), **favi** (138a, 165d), **gave, have, Java** (33a), **Jave** (84d), **kava** (18c,116a), **Kavi** (84d), **lava** (101c,132b,151a,177a), **lave** (16d,178b), **nave** (30d,31a, 78d,114b,180c), **navy** (33c,58b), **pave** (85a), **pavo** (115b), **Pavo** (36b,c), **pavy** (115b), **rave** (41c,157a,161d), **ravi, Ravi** (16b), **save** (52b,110c,123a,173c), **Tave** (183d), **Tavy** (183d), **wave** (19a, 59a,111c,131d,160c,172d), **wavy** (147b,172d), **yava**

- - AV **Muav** (66a), **Slav** (13c,40c,48b,52a,120b,135b)

A - - V **akov** (189), **Azov** (20b,135d)

AW - - **Awan** (191), **away** (6b,69d,76a,109d,111d), **awry** (13d,38d,171c)

- AW - **bawl, bawn** (181a), **cawk** (133c), **dawk** (95c), **dawm** (190), **dawn** (14d,41b), **fawn** (33c), **gawd** (169c), **gawk** (146d), **gawp, hawk** (19c, 115c), **jawy, kawa** (18c,116a), **Kawi** (84d), **kawn** (93d), **lawn** (20a, 37c,53b,92c), **pawa** (189), **pawl** (43a,95a), **pawn** (29c,119c), **sawk** (188), **sawn, tawa** (106d,168c), **yawl** (136b,171d,175d), **yawn, yawp**

- - AW **chaw** (97c), **claw** (29c,105b,161d,173a), **craw** (38d,72c,156c), **dhaw** (125a), **draw** (42c,53a,92b,117c,121c,167d), **flaw, gnaw** (20a,107a, 178b), **miaw** (27b,99b), **shaw** (164b), **Shaw** (50c,53b), **slaw, thaw**

A - - W **alow** (18a,172c), **anew** (7c), **arow** (92c,158b), **avow** (6d,36a,41c, 112c)

AX - - **axal** (120b), **axil** (10c), **axis** (28b,41d,77c,153c), **axle** (153c,180c), **axon** (106c,153c)

- AX - **saxe** (20d,33c), **taxi** (13a,125b), **taxo** (13a), **waxy** (119c,149d)

- - AX Ajax (71b,162d), **Anax** (43c,120c), **coax** (180c), **Crax** (19b,39d), **flax, hoax** (41c,122a), **Odax** (132c), **Olax** (52b)

A - - X abox (22d), **Ajax** (71b,162d), **Alix** (183c), **Amex** (184d), **Anax** (43d,120c), **apex** (39c,76c,115c,118b,159b,166a,167b),

AY - - ayah (108d), **ayes** (177c), **ayin** (91c)

- AY - baya (179b), **Baya** (191), **cayo, Daye** (123d), **days, hayz, kayo** (87c), **maya** (179b), **Maya** (23d,186c), **Mayo** (193), **raya** (19b,23c,76d, 107d), **saya** (117a), **Vayu** (68c,182a), **ways, yaya** (113c,168c)

- - AY alay (96c), **anay** (72b), **away** (6b,69d,76a,109d,111d), **blay** (57d), **bray, chay** (48a,128d), **Clay** (9d), **dray** (27a,154c,177b), **esay, flay** (147c,157c), **fray** (56b,60d), **gray** (33c,77c), **Gray** (50c), **okay** (8d), **olay** (113b), **piay** (98b), **play** (63d,154a), **pray** (18b,51a,159d), **quay** (88b,117c,180c), **ruay** (189), **shay** (110c), **slay, stay** (72d, 124c,130a,134a,162a), **sway** (104a)

A - - Y Abby (183d), **ably** (147c), **achy, Addy** (183d), **adry,** (164c), **aery** (47b,51d,106c), **affy** (18b), **ahey** (52c), **ahoy** (106a), **airy** (176d, 177a), **akey** (189), **alay** (96c), **Algy** (96b), **alky, ally** (14a,35c,d, 173c), **Amoy** (88c), **anay** (72b,163b,181a), **ancy** (158c), **Andy** (96b), **army, arty, ashy** (113a,178a), **atry** (141b), **away** (6b,69d,76a,109d, 111d), **awry** (13d,38d,171c)

AZ - - Azam (166c), **azan** (102d), **Azha** (155b), **Azof** (20b,135d), **azon** (127b), **Azov** (20b,135d), **azul** (151d)

- AZ - caza, cazi (103a), **cazy** (103a), **Daza** (191), **daze** (157d), **dazy, faze** (43d), **Gaza** (117a), **gaze, gazi, gazy, haze** (100c,174d), **hazy** (174b), **jazz, Kazi** (103a), **kazy** (103a), **laze** (79b), **Laze** (191), **Lazi** (191), **lazo** (88d,128b,133d), **lazy, maze** (87b,157d), **naze** (26b, 124b), **Nazi, raze** (42b,d,91d), **razz** (131b), **vaza** (114a)

- - AZ Agaz (193), **Ahaz** (86d), **Boaz** (135d)

A - - Z Agaz (193), **Ahaz** (86d)

BA - - Baal (142b), **baas** (97c), **baba** (108d,120c,166c,171a), **babe, Babi** (116c), **babu** (77a), **baby, Bach** (35c), **back** (75d,76d,159d), **Badb** (82b), **bade, baff** (69d), **baft** (14a,53b), **baga** (171b), **bago** (13d), **bahi** (60c), **baho** (122a), **baht** (146a), **bail** (43c), **bain** (61a), **bait** (15d,51a,94d,167b), **baju** (84a), **baka** (52b), **bake** (139a), **baku** (26d,157b,168c), **Bala** (26c,66a), **bald** (16c), **bale** (24b,74a), **balk** (118c,146a,156d), **ball, balm** (110a,172c), **Balt** (93a), **balu** (104b, 159a,181d), **Bana** (67a), **banc** (61a,85c), **band** (72a,157c), **bane** (74a,106b,120b,139a), **bang** (75d,105d,148a), **bani** (190), **bank** (18a,58c), **bans, bant** (43c), **bara** (188), **barb** (20b,57d,78b,117d, 120a,b,124b), **bard** (12d,120a), **bare** (43d,157c), **bari** (37c,79c), **Bari** (83d), **bark** (115c), **barm** (185b), **barn** (156d), **baro** (71a,122c), **barr** (49b), **Bart** (96b), **baru** (168c), **base** (6a,43b,44b,51c,60c,79b,94b, 122b), **bash, bask** (94d), **bass** (57b,c,177a), **bast** (16c,56a,117b, 184a), **Bast** (27b), **bata** (30a,142d), **bate** (43c,91b,100d), **bath, Bath** (50d,151c), **batt** (37c), **batz** (190), **baud** (162d), **baul** (18b), **Baum** (9c,112c), **bave** (61d,146c), **bawl, bawn** (181a), **baya** (179b), **Baya** (191)

- BA - abas (61c), **Ibad** (191), **Iban** (47c), **oban** (190)

- - BA Abba (20a,55a,161c), **alba** (98a,181a), **Alba** (151d), **amba** (161a), anba (36d), arba (135d,171a), baba (108d,120c,166c,171a), boba (29d), buba (170a), caba (184c), ceba (169b), cuba (189), Cuba (180b), Egba (191), Elba (105d), ezba (188), Faba, haba (151d), isba (135c), juba (106b), koba (11a), kuba (26d,189), Luba (191), Maba (103a,168d), Nuba (108c), peba (12d), Peba (193), Raba, reba (144a), Reba (18d,86c), saba (56a,117a), Saba (143d), Seba (18c,39d), Toba (80c), tuba (105a,137d), ueba (188)

B - - A baba (108d,120c,166c,171a), baga (171b), baka (52b), Bala (26c, 66a), Bana (67a), bara (188), bata (30a,142d), baya (179b), Baya (191), Beda (101d), bega (188), Beja (6c,191), beka (189), bela (12a), Bela (18b,48c), bema (28d,31a,114b,119b,125b,137a), bena, (176a), Bera (86d), Besa (68b,119c), beta (71a,91c,141d), biga (171d), bija (168c), bina (77a), bisa (11a), biwa (93d,168c), Bixa (145d), blaa, boba (29d), boca (152b,c), boga (57d,180b), bola (16a, 179b), boma (7d), bona (89d,183c), Bona, bora (181d,182b), bosa (12a), bota (189), boza (12a), brea (100b), buba (170a), buda (83d), buna (161c), bura (182b)

- BB - Abba (20a,55a,161c), abbe (32b,63b,123b), Abby (183d)

- - BB bibb (97c,146b), Cobb (9c), dubb (161c), hobb (124b), hubb (118b), jibb, lobb (23b,94c,163a)

B - - B Badb (82b), barb (20b,57d,78b,117d,120a,b,124b), bibb (97c, 146b), blab (162b), bleb (20c,23d,67c), blob, blub, Bodb (82b), bomb (144a), boob (146d), brab (113b), brob (153c), bulb (37a, 172c)

- BC - ABC's (57a)

B - - C banc (61a,85c), bloc (173a), Bosc (115c)

B - - D bald (16c), band (72a,157c), bard (12d,120a), baud (162d), bead (17a,122a,146b), Beld (155b), bend (39d,171b), bind (33b,165c), biod (59d,79c), bird, bled, bold (41a), bond (92a,101c,141d,143b, 159d,165c), bord (100b), brad (54d,67c,105b), bred (23c,48c,127c), bund (49c,66c,90c), Byrd (9c,120b)

BE - - bead (17a,122a,146b), beak (19a), beal (139d), beam, bean (91b, 142a,175a), bear (27a,50b,113c,155a), beat (58c,87b,131a,164d, 165b,180d), beau, beck (107c), Beda (101d), Bede (48c,50c,101d, 175b), beef, been (149a), beer (18c), bees (185b), beet (175a), bega (188), behn (137d), Beid (155b), Beja (6c,191), beka (189), bela (12a), Bela (18b,48c,78d), Beli (23c), bell (24c,39d), Bell (162d), belt (16a,31a), bema (28d,31a,114b,119b,125b,137a), bena (176a), bend (39d,171b), bene (18a,83c,90a,106d,122a,180a), beng (43a), beni (116a,142d), Beni (191), beno (113b,117a), bent (80b), benu (49a), Bera (86d), berg (79b), berm (25d,90d,145c), Bern (160d), Bert (96b), Besa (68b,119c), Bess (76c,183d), best (41d, 159c,160a), beta (71a,91c,141d), bete (61a,107c), beth (91c), Beth (8c,183d), bevy (38a,58c)

- BE - abed (130c), Abel (7a,25b), abet (8b,15b,50a,59b,75d,81c,141d, 159d), Eben (96a), Eber (51a,75c,99d), ibex (67d,68a), obex (22d), obey (35c,75c), Obed (135d), uber (66b)

- - BE abbe (32b,63b,123b), albe (133a), babe, Bube (180b), cube (66b, 150a), dobe (159b,c,172b), Elbe (108a), gabe (162a), gibe (8a,42c, 84d,100d,138c,144c,149b), gybe (144c), Habe (191), Hebe (39c,

277

69c,186b), **imbe** (37a,56a,133d), **jibe** (8a,33b,35d,37b,42c,100d, 138c,144c,149b), **jube** (28d), **kibe, Kobe** (78a), **lobe** (90c,134b), **lube** (110a), **ribe** (139a), **robe** (65b), **rube** (37d,135d,185d), **Rube** (96b), **sabe, tobe** (7d,137b), **tube** (118b,158a)

B - - E babe, bade, bake (139a), bale (24b,74a), bane (74a,106b,120b, 139a), bare (43d,157c), base (6a,43b,44b,51c,60c,79b,94b,122b), bate (43c,91b,100d), bave (61d,146c), Bede (48c,50c,101d,175b), bene (18a,83c,90a,106d,122a,180a), bete (61a,107c), bice (20d, 117d), Bice (27b), bide (47c,50b,130a,158b), bike, bile (30c), bine (145b,156a,171c,176b), bise (182a), bite (29d,156b), bize (182a), blae (93b), blue (33c,98c,102c,150d,173a), boce (23b,52a,57b), bode (14c,60a,110b,121b), bole (31d,32a,169b), bone, bore (14c, 25b,46a,116a,165c,179b), bose (163c), brae (76d,139a,c,140b, 148c), bree (139a), Brie (29c), Bube (180b), bure (61b), byee (189), byre (38a)

- BF - Abfa (76b)

B - - F baff (69d), beef, biff, buff (134c,161d)

B - - G bang (75d,105d,148a), beng (43a), berg (79b), bing, bong, borg (40d), brag (21a,175a), brig (72b,106a,144d), bung (119d,156d), burg (22b,73c)

BH - - Bhar (191), bhat (80c), bhel (126d), Bhil (191), b'hoy (134b), bhut (67a)

- - BH Cobh (37a)

B - - H Bach (35c), bash, bath, Bath (50d,151c), beth (91c), Beth (8c, 183d), bikh (120b), binh (189), bish (120b), blah, booh (52c), bosh, both, bruh (95a), bukh (122a), bush

BI - - bias (43b,123a), bibb (97c,146b), bibi (87d), bice (20d,117d), Bice (27b), bide (47c,50b,130a,158b,162a,177b), bien (63a,140c,179a, 180a), bier (33b,66b), biff, biga (171d), bija (168c), bike, bikh (120b), bile (30c), bilk (29b,41c,42a), bill (17b,147a), Bill (96b), bilo (131b), bina (77a), bind (33b,165c), bine (145b,156a,171c, 176b), bing, binh (189), Bini (191), binn (22c), bino (113b,117a), biod (59d,79c), bion (117b), bios (92a), bird, birl (93c,131a,153c), birn (31d,139a), birr (180d), bisa (11a), bise (182a), bish (120b), bisk (120b,151a), bite (29d,156b), biti (20b), bito (7d,57d,168c), bitt (54d,175c), biur (35a), biwa (93d,168c), Bixa (145d), bize (182a), bizz

- BI - Abia (18d,137a), Abib (102a,b), Abie (96b,107a), abir (129a), ibid (80a,117a,137a), ibis (48d,49a,177b), ibit (117a), obia (55d), obit (41b,64c), Ubii (191)

- - BI Albi (58a), ambi (34a,122c), Babi (116c), bibi (87d), Bubi (180b), cubi (188), gabi (162a), gobi, Gobi (42d), kobi (84b), mabi (58d), rabi (38d,74a), Rabi (14b,117b), sebi (34b), tabi (84c,149d), Tybi (102a), Wabi (192), Yobi

B - - I Babi (116c), bahi (60c), Bali, bani (190), bari (79c), Bari (37c, 83d), Beli (23c), beni (116a,142d), Beni (191), bibi (87d), Bini (191), biti (20b), Boii (191), Boni (63b), Bori (110d,150c), Bubi (180b), Bugi (191), buri (56b)

- - BK nabk (30d,164d), nubk (30d,164d), Sobk (38d)

278

B - - K   **back** (75d,76d,159d), **balk** (118c,146a,156d), **bank** (18a,58c), **bark** (115c), **bask** (94d), **beak** (19a), **beck** (107c), **bilk** (29b,41c,42a), **bisk** (120b,151a), **bock** (17c,90d,144a), **bonk** (190), **book, bosk** (164b), **bowk** (155d), **buck, bukk** (122a), **bulk** (97b), **bunk, busk** (17b,37b,55d,161b)

BL - -   **blaa, blab** (162b), **blae** (93b), **blah, blas** (6c,49c), **Blas** (67b), **blat** (25b), **blay** (57d), **bleb** (20c,23d,67c), **bled, blet** (64a), **bleu** (61b), **blew, blob, bloc** (173a), **blot, blow, blub, blue** (33c,98c,102c,150d, 173a), **blup, blur, blut** (66b)

- BL -   **able** (26b,35b,126a,147c), **ably** (147c)

B - - L   **baal** (142b), **bail** (43c), **ball, baul** (18b), **bawl, beal** (139d), **bell** (24c,39d), **Bell** (162d), **bhel** (126d), **Bhil** (191), **bill** (17b,147a), **Bill** (96b), **birl** (93c,131a,153c), **boil, boll** (119b,d), **bool** (39d), **bowl, bual** (182c), **buhl** (81a), **bull** (113c), **burl** (87c,169a)

B - - M   **balm** (110a,172c), **barm** (185b), **Baum** (9c,112c), **beam, berm** (25d, 90d,145c), **boom** (152d), **Bram** (96a), **brim**

B - - N   **bain** (61a), **barn** (156d), **bawn** (181a), **bean** (91b,142a,175a), **been** (149a), **behn** (137d), **Bern** (160d), **bien** (63a,140c,179a,180a), **binn** (22c), **bion** (117b), **birn** (31d,139a), **Bonn** (17d), **boon** (18b,20c, 55a), **born, bran** (23c,39a,70b,72a,79c), **Bran** (23c,50c), **bren** (72d, 95a), **brin** (32c,54c,146c), **bunn** (25b), **burn**

BO - -   **boar** (77c,117c,160c,181c), **boat** (27b,106a), **Boaz** (135d), **boba** (29d,) **bobo** (112c,168c), **boca** (152b,c), **boce** (23b,52a,57b), **bock** (17c,90d,144a), **Bodb** (82b), **bode** (14c,60a,110b,121b), **Bodo** (88c), **body** (72a), **Boer** (151a), **boga** (57d,180b), **bogo** (117a,168c), **Bogo** (191), **bogy** (153a), **boho** (117a,179d), **Bohr** (14b,40d,138c), **Boil** (191), **boil, bois** (62b,63a,183d), **bojo** (117a), **boko** (52b), **bola** (16a, 179b), **bold** (41a), **bole** (31d,32a,169b), **boll** (119b,d), **bolo** (87a, 179b), **bolt** (13b,54d,58b,132d,160a), **boma** (7d), **bomb** (144a), **bona** (89d), **Bona** (183c), **bond** (92a,101c,141d,143b,159d,165c), **bone, bong, Boni** (63b), **bonk** (190), **Bonn** (17d), **bony** (147c), **Bony** (96b), **boob** (146d), **booh** (52c), **book, bool** (39d), **boom** (152d), **boon** (18b,20c,55a), **boor** (47a,135d,172c), **boot** (128d), **bora** (181d, 182b), **bord** (100b), **bore** (14c,25b,46a,116a,165c,179b), **borg** (40d), **Bori** (110d,150c), **born, boro** (154b), **Boro** (193), **Bors** (70b,134b), **bort** (43b), **Bort** (134b), **bosa** (12a), **Bosc** (115c), **bose** (163c), **bosh, bosk** (164b), **boss** (49d,157d), **bota** (189), **both, Boto** (192), **bott** (32a,88d), **bout** (36c), **bouw** (188), **bowk** (155d), **bowl, boxy, boza** (12a), **bozo** (55b)

- BO -   **aboo** (17a), **Abot** (100c), **Abou** (48b,55a), **abox** (22d), **eboe** (28b, 110a,168c,169b), **Eboe, ebon** (20b), **oboe** (74b,104d,105a,182a, 184a), **obol** (29b,110a)

- - BO   **albo** (34d,181a), **ambo** (125b,128b), **bobo** (112c,168c), **bubo** (112c), **Egbo** (141d), **Gobo** (84d), **hobo** (168a,174b), **jobo** (77c), **lobo** (165d,183c), **nabo** (117a), **Nebo** (68c,102d,103d,183a), **umbo** (22b), **zobo** (186b)

B - - O   **bago** (13d), **baho** (122a), **baro** (71a,122c), **beno** (113b,117a), **bilo** (131b), **bino** (113b,117a), **bito** (7d,52d,168c), **bobo** (112c,168c), **Bodo** (88c), **bogo** (117a,168c), **Bogo** (191), **boho** (117a,179d), **bojo** (117a), **boko** (52b), **bolo** (87a,179b), **boro** (154b), **Boro** (193), **Boto**

(192), **bozo** (55b), **broo** (139a), **bubo** (112c), **Bufo** (166c), **Buto** (142d), **buyo** (18b), **bygo** (114c)

B - - P   **blup, bump**

BR - -   **brab** (113b), **brad** (54d,67c,105b), **brae** (76d,139a,c,140b,148c), **brag** (21a,175a), **Bram** (96a), **bran** (23c,39a,70b,72a,79c), **Bran** (23c,50c), **bras** (61a), **brat, bray, brea** (100b), **bred** (23c,48c,127c), **bree** (139a), **bren** (72d,95a), **Brer** (172b), **Bres, brew** (35d), **brey** (194), **Brie** (29c), **brig** (72b,106a,144d), **brim, brin** (32c,54c,146c), **brit** (76c), **brob** (153c), **broo** (139a), **brow, bruh** (95a), **brut** (182c), **Brut** (23c)

- BR -   **abra** (26b), **Abra, abri** (61c,62c,144b), **Ebro** (132a), **obra** (152d, 184c)

B - - R   **barr** (49b), **bear** (27a,50b,113c,155a), **beer** (18c), **Bhar** (191), **bier** (33b,66b), **birr** (180d), **biur** (35a), **blur, boar** (77c,117c,160c,181c), **Boer** (151a), **Bohr** (14b,40d,138c), **boor** (47a,135d,172c), **Brer** (172b), **buhr** (180d), **burr** (123b)

- BS -   **Absi** (191)

- - BS   **dibs** (70c), **Lubs** (94c), **nibs** (116c), **nobs** (38c,87a)

B - - S   **baas** (97c), **bans, bass** (57b,c,177a), **bees** (185b), **Bess** (76c,183d), **bias** (43b,123a), **bios** (92a), **blas** (6c,49c), **Blas** (67b), **bois** (62b, 63a,183d), **Bors** (70b,134b), **boss** (49d,157d), **bras** (61a), **Bres, buss** (87a,148c)

- - BT   **debt** (91d,109b)

B - - T   **baft** (14a,53b), **baht** (146a), **bait** (15d,51a,94d,167b), **Bait** (93a), **bant** (43c), **Bart** (96b), **bast** (16c,56a,117b,184a), **Bast** (27b), **batt** (37c), **beat** (58c,87b,131a,164d,165b,180d), **beet** (175a), **belt** (16a, 31a), **bent** (80b), **Bert** (96b), **best** (41d,159c,160a), **bhat** (80c), **bhut** (67a), **bitt** (54d,175c), **blat** (25b), **blet** (64a), **blot, blut** (66b), **boat** (27b,106a), **bolt** (13b,54d,58b,132d,160a), **boot** (128d), **bort** (43b), **Bort** (134b), **bott** (32a,88d), **bout** (36c), **brat, brit** (76c), **brut** (182c), **Brut** (23c), **bult** (76d), **bunt** (15d,180c), **bust, butt** (27a,77b,127d,162a,182b)

BU - -   **bual** (182c), **buba** (170a), **Bube** (180b), **Bubi** (180b), **bubo** (112c), **buck, buda** (83d), **buff** (134c,161d), **Bufo** (166c), **Bugi** (191), **buhl** (81a), **buhr** (180d), **bukh** (122a), **bukk** (122a), **bulb** (37a,172c), **bulk** (97b), **bull** (113c), **bult** (76d), **bump, buna** (161c), **bund** (49c,66c,90c), **bung** (119d,156d), **bunk, bunn** (25b), **bunt** (15d, 180c), **buoy** (28d,58c), **bure** (61b), **burg** (22b,73c), **buri** (56b), **burl** (87c,169a), **burn, burr** (123b), **bury** (81d), **bush, busk** (17b,37b,55d,161b), **buss** (87a,148c), **bust, busy, Buto** (142d), **butt** (27a,77b,127d,162a,182b), **buxy** (115b), **buyo** (18b) **buzz**

- BU -   **abut** (22a,167c), **ebur** (89c)

- - BU   **babu** (77a), **kobu** (84b), **Nabu** (68c,183a), **tabu** (59d,111d), **Tibu** (191), **zebu** (22d,80d,112c)

B - - U   **babu** (77a), **baju** (84a), **baku** (26d,157b,168c), **balu** (104b,159a, 181d), **baru** (168c), **beau, benu** (49a), **bleu** (61b)

B - - W   **blew, blow, bouw** (188), **brew** (35d), **brow**

BY - -   byee, (189), bygo (114c), Byrd (9c,120b), byre (38a)

- - BY   Abby (183d), baby, doby (159b,c), gaby (59c,146d), goby (57d), kiby (29a), ruby (20a,65d,179c), toby (8c,85c,104b), Toby (96b, 125c)

B - - Y   baby, bevy (38a,58c), b'hoy (134b), blay (57d), body (72a), bogy (153a), bony (147c), Bony (96b), boxy, bray, brey (194), buoy (28d,58c), bury (81d), busy, buxy (115b)

B - - Z   batz (190), bizz, Boaz (135d), buzz

CA - -   caam (93d), caba (184c), Caca (67a), caco (73b), cade (25c,27a,76c, 85d,116d), Cade (50c), cadi (12a,103a,171a), cady (69d), Caen, cafe, cage (36a), cagy (178b), caid (35a,151d,152b), cain (169c), Cain (6a,7a,50d,88a,104c,143a), caja (152a), caji (180b), cake, caky, cale (72d), calf, calk (78c,109a,141c,178d), call (145c,159b, 176d), calm (8d,11d,112b,118d,126c,d,172b,173d), calo (72d), calp (92b), calx (23c,75c,112c), came (182b), Came (192), camp (163b), Cana (57a,64b,100c), cane (17b,128a,156a,159a,177d), Cane, cang (184a), cano (152a), cant (28d,81b,84d,90c,109b,136c,165d,166a), capa (152a,166d), cape (75a,96c,124b,161a), caph (91c), Capp (27a), cara (83a), Cara (48b,183c), card (33d,114d), care (11b, 14c,35d,150a,184d), cark (26d,184d), carl (115c,135d), Carl (96a), carn (156c), caro (83a), Caro (183d), carp (27d,38d,40c,55a,56c, 57a), carr (120d,140a), cart (171d,175a,177b), casa (152b), case (22c,36c,81c,91a,108c), cash (101c), cask, Caso (82d) cass (140c, 177a), Cass (147a), cast (165b,167c), cata (122c), cate (165c), Cato (132d,133b), Catt (9d), cauk (139b), caul (16d,74d), caup, caur (139a), cava (116a,175b), cave (27d), cavy (72b,120d,132c, 157b), cawk (133c), cayo, caza, cazi (103a), cazy (103a)

- CA -   ecad (73a,119b), ical (158c), scab (80b,107d,157c), scad (31a,57a, 78b,88d,137c), scan (52b,93d,98a,116d,128b,c,140d), scar (31a, 184d), scat (26b,67a,d,126c,169c)

- - CA   acca (53b,d), Alca (14c,128b), arca (9a,22c,29d,115a,130a), Arca (101b), Auca (192), boca (152b,c), Caca (67a), coca (29d,33a,105d, 113a), cuca (33a,105d), deca (34d,122d), Ecca (66a), esca (11c, 44a,70c), Inca (14b,30a), jaca (84a), juca (27a), mica (82c,100b, 146c), onca (189), orca (86b), paca (132c,154a), peca (190), pica (66b,95b,172c), puca (68a), raca (19a,59c,130b,184d), Teca (192), unca (49a), Ynca (193), yuca (27a)

C - - A   caba (184c), Caca (67a), caja (152a), Cana (57a,64b,100c), capa (152a,166d), cara (83a), Cara (48b,183c), casa (152b), cata (122c), cava (116a,175b), caza, ceba (169b), cela (62d), cena (88d,133a), cepa (110c), cera (152d,161d,179a), chaa (162b), chia (136d), cima (83b,c), Civa (56d), coca (29d,33a,105d,113a), coda (32c,35d,55d, 56c), coja (103b,166b), cola (25b,108d,149d,168c), coma (91c, 157d,170c,172b), copa (88b,113c), cora (65d), Cora (42b,69c,80c, 116b,124d,172b,183c), cota (117a), coxa (77b), crea (92c,151d), cuba (189), Cuba (180b), cuca (33a,105d), Cuna (193), cura (152c), cuya (39b), cyma (101a,b)

C - - B   chab (184a), chib (167a), chob (23c), chub (40c,154c), club (39c), Cobb (9c), comb (38c), crab (39b,144b,181b), crib (96b,120d), curb (130c,146b)

- CC - acca (53b,d), **Ecca** (66a), **ecce** (17d,89a,c)

C - - C chic (148d), circ (31a), cric (131c), croc (13a,74a)

C - - D caid (35a,151d,152b), **card** (33d,114d), **Chad** (158b), **chid, Chud** (191), **clad** (46a,82a), **clod** (22a,45b,157d), **coed, cold** (65d), **cond** (156a), **cord** (39b,131a), **curd** (99d)

CE - - ceba (169b), cede (67b,70c,129d,160a,168b,185d), ceil (92c,112a), cela (62d), cell (39b), celt (30c,123a,156c,167b,179b), **Celt** (10a, 180a,b), cena (88d,133a), cene (34c), cens (115b), cent (36d), cepa (110c), cepe (48c), cera (152d,161d,179a), cere (19a,114b,149d, 179a), cern (41c), cero (57b,c,d,180b), cess (91d,94c,162b), cest (18a,67b), cete (180b,c), ceto (34a), **Ceyx** (73b)

- CE - Acer (96c), icer

- - CE ance (158b,c,d), bice (20d,117d), **Bice** (27b), boce (23b,52a,57b), dace (57a,b), dice (65a), duce (29d), ecce (17d,89a,c), ence (158c), esce (158d), face (159d,176c), lace (58b,179c), luce (58c,117d), **Luce** (7b,35a), mace (49d,108d,153b,154d,161a,178a), mice, nice (54d,119c,130c), **Nice** (98c), once (60b,79b), pace (64b,98a,153b, 156a,170b,177d), pice (190), puce (33c,d,52a), race (116a,153b, 154b), **Rice** (46a), sice (71d,147b), syce (71d), tace (13a,155d), tice (9a,38c,51a,185d), vice (31d,158a), voce (83c,177a)

C - - E cade (25c,27a,76c,85d,116d), **Cade** (50c), cafe, cage (36a), cake, cale (72d), came (182b), **Came** (192), cane (17b,128a,156a,159a, 177d), **Cane, cape** (75a,96c,124b,161a), care (11b,14c,35d,150a, 184d), case (22c,36c,81c,91a,108c), cate (165c), cave (27d), cede (67b,70c,129d,160a,168b,185d), cene (34c), cepe (48c), cere (19a, 114b,149d,179a), cete (180b,c), chee (189), cine (104b,152c), cise (147b), cite (15a,98d,126d,159b), cive (110c), clee (19a,129a), **Cloe** (183c), clue, code (21c,31a,40c,161c), coke (32d,64a), cole (25a), **Cole, come, cone** (66b,150a,157c), cope (12b,26b,36c,65b, 157d,176a), core (28b,51c,75b,81b), cose (29b), cote (19b,143d, 144a,b), cove (17a,73d,107d), coze (29b), **Cree** (192), cube (66b, 150a), cuke (39b), cure (123b,d), cute (39c), cyke (40c), cyme (58d, 69c)

C - - F calf, chef, clef (104d,105a), coif (73a), cuff (148a), cuif (139a,d, 140c)

C - - G cang (184a), chug (53a), clog (30c,145b), coag (45d,118a,163b), crag (132c), crig (20d)

CH - - chaa (162b), chab (184a), **Chad** (158b), chai (72d), cham (20a,29d), **Cham** (8c) chan (26c,130c), chap (55b), char (24d,138c,170b), chat (9b,19c,161c), chaw (97c), chay (48a,128d), chee (189), chef, chek (59c), **Chen** (149b), cher (61b), chew (97c), chez (14b,61a), chia (136d), chib (167a), chic (148d), chid, ch'ih (188), chil, chin, **Chin** (30b), chip (69d), chir (29b,116d), chit (67b,98c,108b,116c, 177c), chiv (87a), chob (23c), chol (118d), **Chol** (192), chop (98a), chor (164b), chou (61b), **Chou** (30b), chow (45a), choy (48a,128d), chub (40c,154c), **Chud** (191), chug (53a), chum (38d), **Chun** (30c), chut!

- CH - ache (79a,112d,185b), acht (66c), achy, echo (130b,d), **Echo** (105d), icho (67b), ichu (10b,70d), ocha (189), tcha (162c), tche (13d,30b, 105a), tchi, **Tchi, tchu**

- - CH   **aich** (9a), **arch** (29d,38b,39d,123d,132c), **bach, Bach** (35c), **each, etch, Foch** (63b), **hoch** (52c,66c), **Hoch, inch, itch, Koch** (66d), **lech** (102b), **loch** (88a,139d), **much, nach, ouch, rich, Roch** (136c), **sech** (97c), **such** (146d), **Tech, Vach** (153b), **Zach** (96b)

C - - H   **caph** (91c), **Caph, cash** (101c), **ch'ih** (188), **Cobh** (37a), **cosh** (35a, 97c), **cush** (101c), **Cush** (51d,73c)

CI - -   **cima** (83b,c), **cine** (104b,152c), **cinq** (61d), **cion** (42d,70b,145b, 148b,154b,156a), **cipo** (91d), **circ** (31a), **cirl** (24c), **cise** (147b), **cist** (22c,29d,156c), **cite** (15a,98d,126d,159b), **cito** (89d,126c), **cits, city, Civa** (56d), **cive** (110c)

- CI -   **acid** (151a,162a), **Acis** (64b), **Scio**

- - CI   **asci** (154a), **deci** (163b), **foci** (28b), **fuci** (132c), **loci** (66b,118c), **Pici** (19c,184a), **unci** (31d)

C - - I   **cadi** (12a,103a,171a), **Cadi, caji** (180b), **cazi** (103a), **chai** (72d), **coli, Coni, Cori** (138c), **cubi** (188)

- - CK   **back** (75d,76d,159d), **beck** (107c), **bock** (17c,90d,144a), **buck, cock** (19a,29a,55a,133d,136d,161d,174b), **deck** (13b,41c, 144d), **dick** (43a,55b), **Dick** (96b), **dock** (40a,117c,144d,179d), **duck** (26b,53b,179c), **hack** (40a,77c,184d), **heck** (100a), **hick** (185d), **hock** (91a,115b,182b,c), **huck** (167d), **jack** (26c,58a,127c), **Jack** (96b), **jock** (96b), **Jock, juck** (114c), **kick, lack** (178a), **lick, lock** (54d), **luck** (28d), **mack, mick** (82c), **mock** (131b,162b), **muck, neck** (83a), **nick** (30c,108b), **nock** (13b,108b), **pack** (24b,140d), **peck** (24d), **pick, puck** (44b,68a,77c,100c), **Puck** (99d,143b), **rack** (32c,64b), **reck** (26d,75c), **rick** (74d,117d), **rock** (160b), **ruck** (39a, 185a), **sack** (43d,118a,119d,182b), **seck** (173d), **sick, sock** (157c, 182a), **suck, tack** (28d,37d,54d), **teck** (128b), **tick** (12b,20d,97c), **tock** (7d,19b), **tuck** (156b), **wick**

C - - K   **calk** (78c,109a,141c,178d), **cark** (26d,184d), **cask, cauk** (139b), **cawk** (133c), **chek** (59c), **coak** (45d,118a,163b), **cock** (19a,29a, 55a,133d,136d), **conk** (41c,108a,156d,157c), **cook** (137b), **cork** (119d), **cusk** (57b)

CL - -   **clad** (46a,82a), **clam** (20b,101b), **clan** (169c), **clap** (58b), **claw** (29c, 105b,161d,173a), **clay, Clay** (9d), **clee** (19a,129a), **clef** (104d,105a), **clem** (56b,158b), **Cleo** (126b), **clew** (16a,33a,77b,136b,164d), **Clim** (12b), **Clio** (104d), **clip** (54d,143d), **clod** (22a,45b,157d), **Cloe** (183c), **clog** (30c,145b), **clop, clot** (32d,94d), **clou** (62b), **clow** (58c,148c), **cloy** (61b,137c,159d), **club** (39c), **clue, Clym** (12b)

- CL -   **acle** (13d,82c,115d)

C - - L   **call** (145c,159b,176d), **carl** (115c,135d), **Carl** (96a), **caul** (16d,74d), **ceil** (92c,112a), **cell** (39b), **chil, chol** (118d), **Chol** (192), **cirl** (24c), **coal** (49c,64a), **coel** (39b), **coil** (39d,171c,185a), **cool** (25c,107d), **cowl** (101d), **cral, cull** (117c), **curl** (38d,73b,93b,131d)

- CM -   **acme** (39c,115c,186b)

C - - M   **caam** (93d), **calm** (8d,11d,112b,118d,126c,d,172b), **cham** (20a,29d), **Cham** (8c), **chum** (38d), **clam** (20b,101b), **clem** (56b,158b), **Clim** (12b), **Clym** (12b), **coom** (32d,150c,178d), **corm** (24b,38d,156a), **cram** (157d), **Crom, culm** (11a,32d,70d,145a,156a)

CN - -   **Cnut** (40d,50c)

283

- CN -   acne (147c)

C - - N   Caen, cain (169c), Cain (6a,7a,50d,88a,104c,143a), carn (156c), cern (41c), chan (26c,130c), Chen (149b), chin, Chin (30b), Chun (30c), cion (42d,70b,145b,148b,154b,156a), clan (169c), Coan (37b), coin (19b,37a,100c,101c,179d), conn (43d,156a), coon (121c), corn (39d,95c,123a), coyn (37a), cran (160c), crin (146c), cyan

CO - -   coag (45d,118a,163b), coak (45d,118a,163b), coal (49c,64a), Coan (37b), coat (160a), coax (180c), Cobb (9c), Cobh (37a), coca (29d, 33a,105d,113a), cock (19a,29a,55a,133d,136d,161d,174b), coco, (113a), coda (32c,35d,56c), code (21c,31a,40c,161c), codo (188), coed, coel (39b), coho (136d), coif (73a), coil (39d,171c,185a), coin (19b,37a,100c,101c,179d), coir (33a,37a,56a,133d), Coix (70d,85b), coja (103b,166b), coke (32d,64a), coky, cola (25b,108d,149d,168c), cold (65d), cole (25a), Cole, coli, colp (28a,148b), colt (78c,131a, 185d,186b), Colt, coly (104a), coma (91c,157d,170c,172b), comb (38c), come, Como, cond (156a), cone (66b,150a,157c), Coni, conk (41c,108a,156d,157c), conn (43d,156a), cony (127a), cook (137b), cool (25c,107d), coom (32d,150c,178d), coon (121c), coop, Coos, (192), coot (19b,46d,72b,138d,141a,146d,157d), copa (88b,113c), cope (12b,26b,36c,65b,157d,176a), copt (48d), copy, cora (65d), Cora (42b,69c,80c,116b,124d,172b,183c), cord (39b,139a), core (28b,51c,75b,81b), Cori (138c), cork (119d), corm (24b,38d,156a), corn (39d,95c,123a), cose (29b), cosh (35a,97c), coso (152c), coss (98a), cost (29a), cosy (149c), cota (117a), cote (19b,143d,144a,b), coto (16c,90b), Coty (63c), coup (20d,97c,157b,c,162d), cous (38a), cove (17a,73d,107d), cowl (101d), coxa (77b) coyn (37a), coyo (15a,30c), coze (29b), cozy (149c)

- CO -   acon (62c,140d), acor (6d), icon (79d,92b,136a), scob (42a), scon (162c), scop (120a), scot (14a,162b), Scot (64b,132c), scow (21a, 58b)

- - CO   alco (45b), caco (73b), coco (113a), Duco, fico (169d), loco (38b, 119b,120b), mico (97a), paco (9b,146d), peco (162b), pico (65a, 152c), poco (83b,93a), saco (189), soco (22d), Teco (192), toco (19b,167c), unco (140c), Waco

C - - O   caco (73b), calo (72d), cano (152a), caro (83a), Caro (183d), Caso (82d), Cato (132d,133b), cayo, cero (57b,c,d,180b), ceto (34a), cipo (91d), cito (89d,126c), Cleo (126b), Clio (104d), coco, (113a), codo (188), coho (136d), Como, coso (152d), coto (16c,90b), coyo (15a,30c)

C - - P   calp (92b), camp (163b), Capp (27a), carp (27d,38d,40c,55a,56c, 57a), caup, chap (55b), chip (69d), chop (98a), clap (58b), clip (54d,143d), clop, colp (28a,148b), coop, coup (20d,97c,157b,c, 162d), crop (38b), cusp (38c,78b,119a,120a,b)

C - - Q   cinq (61d)

CR - -   crab (39b,144b,181b), crag (132c), cral, cram (157d), cran (160c), craw (38d,72c,156c), Crax (19b,39d), crea (92c,151d), Cree (192), crew (72a,106a), Crex (37a), crib (96b,120d), cric (131c), crig (20d), crin (146c), cris (40b,95d), croc (13a,74a), Crom, crop (38b), crow (19a), crus (91a,143c), crux (39a,151b)

- CR -   acre (39b,56a,88b), **Acre, ecru** (17d,23d,172b), **ocra** (72c,175a)

C - - R   carr (120d,140a), **caur** (139a), **char** (24d,138c,170b), **cher** (61b), **chir** (29b,116d), **chor** (164b), **coir** (33a,37a,56a,133d), **cuir** (45c,62a), **curr** (104c), **Czar** (42d,49d,60b,135c)

- - CS   ABC's (57a), **pacs** (94c)

C - - S   cass (140c,177a), **Cass** (147a), **cens** (115b), **cess** (91d,94c,162b), **cits, Coos** (192), **coss** (98a), **cous** (38a), **cris** (40b,95d), **crus** (91a, 143c), **cuss**

- CT -   acta (41d,123d,128d,164c), **acth** (13b), **acto** (152b), **Acts, actu** (7a, 89a), **ecto** (34c,122d), **octa** (122c), **octo** (34a,89b,122c)

- - CT   duct (170c), **fact** (7a,128b), **lact** (34c), **pact** (8a), **Pict** (23c,47d), **rect** (117b), **sect** (42b,54a,114c), **tact** (43c,d,116a)

C - - T   cant (28d,81b,84d,90c,109b,136c,165d,166a), **cart** (171d,175a, 177b), **cast** (165b,167c), **Catt** (9d), **celt** (30c,82c,123a,156c,167b, 179b), **Celt** (10a,180a,b), **cent** (36d), **cest** (18a,67b), **chat** (9b,19c, 161c), **chit** (67b,98c,108b,116c,177c), **chut!**, **cist** (22c,29d,156c), **clot** (32d,94d), **coat** (160a), **colt** (78c,131a,185d,186b), **Colt** (131a), **coot** (19b,46d,72b,138d,141a,146d,157d), **Copt** (48d), **cost** (29a), **cult** (141d,161c), **curt** (145b,c), **cyst**

CU - -   cuba (189), **Cuba** (180b), **cube** (66b,150a), **cubi** (188), **cuca** (33a, 105d), **cuff** (148a), **cuif** (139a,d,140c), **cuir** (45c,62a), **cuke** (39b), **cull** (117c), **culm** (11a,32d,70d,145a,156a), **cult** (141d,161c), **Cuna** (193), **cura** (152c), **curb** (130c,146b), **curd** (99d), **cure** (123b), **curl** (38d,73b,93b,131d), **curr** (104c), **curt** (145b,c), **cush** (101c), **Cush** (51d,73c), **cusk** (57b), **cusp** (38c,78b,119a,120a,b), **cuss, cute** (39c), **cuvy** (141a), **cuya** (39b)

- CU -   acus (89d,118a), **scud** (32c,126c,135b,160c), **scum** (129b), **scup** (57a,121b), **scur** (78b), **scut** (145c,161b)

- - CU   jacu (19a,151b), **jocu** (45b,57a)

C - - U   chou (61b), **Chou** (30b), **clou** (62b)

C - - V   chiv (87a)

C - - W   chaw (97c), **chew** (97c), **chow** (45a), **claw** (29c,105b,161d,173a), **clew** (16a,33a,77b,136b,164d), **clow** (58c,148c), **craw** (38d,72c, 156c), **crew** (72a,106a), **crow** (19a)

C - - X   calx (23c,75c,112c), **Ceyx** (73b), **coax** (180c), **Coix** (70d,85b), **Crax** (19b,39d), **Crex** (37a), **crux** (39a,151b)

CY - -   cyan, **cyke** (40c), **cyma** (101a,b), **cyme** (58d,69c), **cyst**

- CY -   acyl (6d)

- - CY   ancy (158c), **lacy, Lucy** (183c), **racy** (153b)

C - - Y   cady (69d), **cagy** (178b), **caky, cavy** (72b,120d,132c,157b), **cazy** (103a), **chay** (48a,128d), **choy** (48a,128d), **city, clay, Clay** (9d), **cloy** (61b,137c,159d), **coky, coly** (104a), **cony** (127a), **copy, cosy** (149c), **Coty** (63c), **cozy** (149c), **cuvy** (141a)

CZ - -   czar (42d,49d,60b,135c)

C - - Z   chez (14b,61a)

DA - -   dace (57a,b), **Dada** (13b,63a,157d), **dado** (41c,111c,115c, 177d), **daer** (22b), **daez, daff** (125d), **daft** (59c), **dagg** (118c), **dagh**

(76d), **Dago, Dail** (49a,82b,c), **dain** (188), **dais** (119b), **dale** (43c, 128a,174b), **dali** (168c,169b), **dama** (65d,152b), **dame** (67b,87c, 166b), **damn, damp** (101a), **Dana** (28a,96a,171d), **Dane** (85d,107d, 138a), **dang, dank** (40b,101a), **dans** (62a), **Danu** (28a), **Dara** (18d), **Dard, dare** (28d,41b,42a,74d,175b), **Dare** (57a), **dari** (38a,70b), **dark** (47a,67d,109b,160b), **darn** (130b), **darr** (163c), **dart** (13b,88a, 100c,120b,153a,160c), **dash** (125c,162d), **dasi** (77a), **data** (54a), **date** (64a,153a), **dato** (95c,102c,117a), **datu** (95c,102c,117a), **daub** (148d), **dauk** (95c), **Daur** (139b), **dauw** (24c), **Dave** (96b), **Davy** (96b,136b), **dawk** (95c), **dawm** (190), **dawn** (14d,41b), **Daye** (123d), **days, Daza** (191), **daze** (157d), **dazy**

- **DA -**   **adad** (52c,56a), **Adad** (68c,157a,182a), **Adah** (25b,51b), **Adam** (26b,96a,111c), **adan** (102d), **Adar** (85c,102a), **adat** (90b,95d), **Edam** (29c), **Edar** (18d), **Idas** (27b,71c), **odah** (170d), **odal** (48a,88b,112c), **Odax** (132c), **udad** (143d,144a,181c), **udal** (76b, 88b,131c)

- - **DA**   **adda** (147d), **Adda** (68c,119d), **Aida** (110d,175c), **alda** (152b), **Alda** (110d,150c), **anda** (23a,168c), **Beda** (101d), **Buda** (83d), **coda** (32c,35d,56c), **Dada** (13b,63a,157d), **Edda** (76b,79b,107d), **Erda** (23d,41a,47d,68d,69a,131d,177b), **Juda, kada** (188), **Leda** (27b, 75d,120c,153a,171d,186b), **Lida** (183c), **meda** (110a), **nuda** (39b), **peda** (114d,144b), **rada** (135c,172a), **Roda** (107b), **sida** (37a, 126c,170a), **soda** (19a,149d,181a), **Teda** (191), **Toda** (45d,76d), **Veda** (77a,b), **Vida** (183c)

D - - A   **Dada** (13b,63a,157d), **dama** (65d,152b), **Dana** (28a,96a,171d), **Dara** (18d), **data** (54a), **Daza** (191), **deca** (34d,122d), **depa** (188), **dera** (34c), **deva** (23d,42a,b,56d,77a), **dewa, dika** (23a), **Disa** (111a), **dita** (117a), **diva** (110d,123c), **dola** (189), **dona** (83d,121c,151d), **dopa** (117d), **dora** (70b), **Dora** (36d,41a,43b), **dosa** (74b), **doxa** (48b), **draa** (188), **Duma** (135c), **dura** (153c), **dyna** (34c)

- - **DB**   **Badb** (82b), **Bodb** (82b), **Medb**

D - - B   **daub** (148d), **dieb** (84a), **doab** (157c), **doob** (18b), **doub** (18b), **drab** (23d,29c,33d,46d,53b,d), **drib** (46b), **drub** (17b,39c), **duab** (157c), **dubb** (161c), **dumb** (153b)

D - - C   **disc** (31b), **douc** (101d)

DD - -   **DDSC** (42a)

- **DD -**   **adda** (147a), **Adda** (68c,119d,157a,182a), **Addu** (68c,157a,182a), **Addy** (183d), **Edda** (76b,79b), **eddo** (162a), **eddy** (37d, 39d,160d, 180d), **odds** (28d,172d)

- - **DD**   **dodd** (139c,140d), **gedd** (140a), **Ladd** (143c), **ludd** (23c), **mudd** (188), **Nudd** (23c), **Redd** (153a), **Ridd** (94a), **rodd** (38d), **rudd** (26d, 57a,b), **sadd** (33a,40b,58c,107b), **sudd** (40b,58c,107b), **wadd** (109c)

D - - D   **dard, dead, deed** (7a,52d,91a,166c,168b), **diad** (113a), **dord** (42c), **dowd** (143b), **duad** (113a,171d), **dyad** (113a)

DE - -   **dead, deaf, deal** (11d,16c,36c,44c,81a,168b), **dean** (33c,109d), **dear, debt** (91d,109b), **deca** (34d,122d), **deci** (163b), **deck** (13b, 41c,144d), **dedo** (188), **deed** (7a,52d,91a,166c,168b), **deem** (36b, 85c,164c), **deep** (124a), **deer** (28c,135a,154d) **defi** (61b), **deft** (147c), **defy** (28d), **degu** (132c), **deil** (139b), **dein** (66d), **dele** (26a, 49c,51b,53a,110b,123d,124c,130a,145c,161b), **dell** (43c,174b),

deme (71b,c,167d), **demi** (34b,122c), **demo** (122d), **demy** (113d), **dene** (137a), **Dene** (192), **dens** (90a,167b), **dent** (42c,77d), **deny** (36d,43d,129b), **depa** (188), **dera** (34c), **dere** (74a,79c), **derm** (147c,158d), **desi** (85d), **desk, deul** (77b), **deus** (68a,89b), **Deva** (23d,42a,b,56d,77a), **Devi** (147b,153b), **dewa, dewy** (101a)

- DE -   **aden** (34b), **Aden, Ader** (18d), **Ades** (73a), **edel** (66c), **Eden** (6b,50d, 107c,113d,123c), **Eder, EDES** (71c), **idea** (54c,108c,124a,164d), **idee** (61d), **idem** (89d,164a), **Iden** (76a), **ideo** (34b,d), **ides** (41a, b,133a), **odea** (105a,164a), **odel** (48a,112c), **Oder** (132a)

- - DE   **aide** (7b,14a,75d), **Ande** (193), **Aude, bade, Bede** (48c,50c,101d, 175b), **bide** (47c,50b,130a,158b,162a), **bode** (14c,60a,110b,121b), **cade** (25c,27a,76c,85d,116d), **Cade** (50c), **cede** (67b,70c,129d, 160a,168b,185d), **code** (21c,31a,40c,161c), **Dode** (96b), **dude** (40d), **eide** (119c), **fade** (181d,183b), **fide, gade, Gide** (63a), **hade** (66a, 148c,173c), **hide** (53a), **hyde** (188), **Hyde** (45a), **inde, jade** (33c, 65d,71d,166a), **Jude** (11c,96a), **kade** (144a), **lade** (24c,26d,43c,93b, 100a,132a,139d,161b,178d), **lode** (42c,99a,111b,175b), **made, Mede** (10a,b,13c), **mide** (110a), **mode** (54d,96b,157d,179a), **nide** (23c,72a,106c,116d), **node** (35c,85b,87c,94d,120a,124d,160c), **nude** (16c), **onde** (63a,178d), **rede** (37c,81d,138d), **ride** (46b,85c), **rode** (46c), **rude** (134b,172b), **sade** (91d), **side** (13d,22a,b,54a,58a,89a, 161b), **tide** (39d,75d,109c,141c,159d), **Tide, tode** (80a,148a), **unde** (179a), **urde** (86b), **vade** (42c,67d,89b), **vide** (89d,126a,142a), **wade, wide** (133d)

D - - E   **dace** (57a,b), **dale** (43c,128a,174b), **dame** (67b,87c,166b), **Dane** (85d,107d,138a), **dare** (28d,41b,42a,74d,175b), **Dare** (57a), **date** (64a,153a), **Dave** (96b), **Daye** (123d), **daze** (157d), **dele** (26a,49c, 51b,53a,110b,123d,124c,130a,145c,161b), **deme** (71b,c,167d), **dene** (137a), **Dene** (192), **dere** (74a,79c), **dice** (65a), **dike** (49c, 91d), **Dike** (78a), **dime, dine, dire** (45d,55a,104a,163c), **dite** (150b), **dive** (42b,74b,119d), **dobe** (159b,c,172b), **Dode** (96b), **doge** (95b), **dole** (44c,118c,121c,129d), **Dole** (74c), **dome** (39c,133c,155d), **done, dope** (46c,105d), **dore** (61d,67b,69d,117d), **Dore** (50d,63a,b), **dose** (123a), **dote** (17a,90b,94b,97a,112a,139d,165d), **dove** (19a, 117d), **doze** (148a), **dree** (139b,140c,158b,172c), **duce** (29d), **dude** (40d), **duff** (125b), **duke** (107c), **dune** (137a), **dupe** (27c,41c, 72c,160c), **duse** (83c), **dyke** (49c,91d), **dyne** (59d)

D - - F   **daff** (125d), **deaf, doff** (130a,161b), **duff** (125b)

- DG -   **edge** (22a,96d,131c,143c,146b), **edgy** (106c)

D - - G   **dagg** (118c), **dang, ding** (130b), **Doeg** (137c), **dong, drag** (74a, 125b), **dreg, drug** (105d)

DH - -   **dhak** (48a,169a), **dhal** (12b), **dhan** (124c), **dhao** (24c), **Dhar, dhaw** (125a), **dhow** (88d,111c,175d)

- - DH   **sadh** (77a), **Sadh, yodh** (91d)

D - - H   **dagh** (76d), **Dagh, dash** (125c,162d), **dish, doth, drah** (188)

DI - -   **diad** (113a), **dial** (25c), **dian** (46c,130d,170b), **Dian** (68d,69a,c, 102b), **Diau** (192), **dibs** (70c), **dice** (65a), **dick** (43a,55b), **Dick** (96b), **dido** (11b,26c,65a,122a), **Dido** (27a,172c), **dieb** (84a), **diem** (89b,116a), **dier, dies** (41b,89b), **diet** (14a,54c,84c,91b,176a), **Dieu** (61d), **dika** (23a), **dike** (49c,91d), **Dike** (78a), **dill** (13a,117c), **dilo**

287

(120d,168c), **dime, dine, ding** (130b), **dino** (34b), **dint** (48c,59d, 122a), **Dion** (96a,152a), **dipt, dire** (45d,55a,104a,163c), **dirk** (40b), **dirt, Disa** (111a), **disc** (31b), **dish, disk** (31b), **diss** (98b), **dita** (117a), **dite** (150b), **diva** (110d,123c), **dive** (42b,74b,119d), **divi, dixi**

- DI -   **Adib** (155b, **adit** (51a,100a,114d), **edit** (20d,49d,123a,129a,131a), **idic** (79b), **idio** (34b,c), **odic** (79c,120a), **Odin** (7c,29d,63c,68c,175d, 183b), **odio** (83b), **udic** (108a)

- - DI   **Andi** (27d), **cadi** (12a,103a), **kadi** (103a,171a), **Lodi** (105d), **ludi** (133b), **Madi** (174a), **medi** (34c), **Midi** (151b), **nidi** (106c), **nodi** (35c,87c), **padi** (131b), **pedi** (34b), **rodi** (98c), **sidi** (103b), **wadi** (46c,106a,109a,128a,132a)

D - - I   **dali** (168c,169b), **dari** (38a,70b), **dasi** (77a), **deci** (163b), **defi** (61b), **demi** (34b,122c), **desi** (85d), **Devi** (147b,153b), **divi, dixi, doni** (21a,28c,168a), **drei** (66d,165a)

- DJ -   **Idjo** (191)

- - DJ   **hadj** (98b,118a)

D - - K   **dank** (40b,101a), **dark** (47a,67d,109b,160b), **dauk** (95c), **dawk** (95c), **deck** (13b,41c,144d), **desk, dhak** (48a,169a), **dick** (43a,55b), **Dick** (96b), **dirk** (40b), **disk** (31b), **dock** (40a,117c,144d,179d), **dook** (184a), **duck** (26b,53b,179c), **dunk** (43c,79d), **dusk** (171c), **Dyak** (22b)

- DL -   **idle** (174b,c,178c), **idly**

D - - L   **Dail** (49a,82b,c), **deal** (11d,16c,36c,44c,81a,168b), **dell** (139b), **dell** (43c,174b), **deul** (77b), **dhal** (12b), **dial** (25c), **dill** (13a,117c), **doll** (125c), **dowl, dual** (45c,171d), **duel, dull** (21a,32c,173a), **Dull** (94b)

- DM -   **admi** (65d)

D - - M   **dawm** (190), **deem** (36b,85c,164c), **derm** (147c,158d), **diem** (89b, 116a), **doom** (42d,55a,134c), **dorm, doum** (168c), **dram** (46b,110c, 121d,148c), **drum** (105a), **duim** (188)

- DN -   **Edna** (183c)

D - - N   **dain** (188), **darn, damn, dawn** (14d,41b), **dean** (33c,109d), **dein** (66d), **dhan** (124c), **dian** (46c,130d,170b), **Dian** (68d,69a,c,102b), **Dion** (96a,152a), **Domn** (135a), **doon** (140b,168c), **dorn** (164d), **down** (149d), **duan** (64b)

DO - -   **doab** (157c), **doat** (17a,94b,112a,165d), **dobe** (159b,c,172b), **doby** (159b,c), **dock** (40a,117c,144d,179d), **dodd** (139c,140c), **Dode** (96b), **dodo** (19b), **Doeg** (137c), **doer** (8a,116b), **does, doff** (130a,161b), **doge** (95b,175b), **dogy** (46d,103c), **doit** (47a,169d,180d), **Doko** (191), **dola** (189), **dole** (44c,118c,121c,129d), **Dole** (74c), **doli, doll** (125c), **dolt** (20c,59c,157d), **dome** (39c,133c,155d), **Domn** (135a), **domy, dona** (83d,121c,151d), **done, dong, doni** (21a,28c, 168a), **don't, doob** (18b), **dook** (184a), **doom** (42d,55a,134d), **doon** (140b,168c), **door** (51a,121b), **dopa** (117d), **dope** (46c,105d), **dopp** (43c), **dora** (70b), **Dora** (36d,41a,43b,183c,d), **dord** (42c), **dore** (61d,67b,69d,117d), **Dore** (50d,63a,b), **dorm, dorn** (164d), **dorp** (73c,176b), **dorr** (32b), **dory** (21b,58b,144c), **dosa** (74b), **dose** (123a), **doss** (17c), **dost, dote** (17a,90b,94b,97a,112a,139d,165d),

288

doth, Doto (141b), **doty** (43d), **doub** (18b), **douc** (101d), **doum** (168c), **dour** (67d,159a), **dove** (19a,117d), **dowd** (143b), **dowl, down** (149d), **doxa** (48b), **doxy** (129d), **doze** (148a), **dozy**

- DO - **ador** (153b), **Edom** (18c,51b,79b,82c,84a), **idol** (48c,54c,55a,75b, 79d,112d,130b,184d), **odor** (138b,156a)

- - DO **Bodo** (88c), **codo** (188), **dado** (41c,111c,115c,177d), **dedo** (188), **dido** (11b,26c,65a,122a), **Dido** (27a,172c), **dodo** (19b), **eddo** (162a), **endo** (34d,122d,183b), **fado** (121c), **Jodo** (113d), **judo** (84b,85c, 142b), **Lido** (83d,175b), **ludo** (65a,112b), **mado** (14d,57a,170b), **ordo** (22a,30d,122a,171a), **pedo** (34b), **redo** (165c), **sado** (26d, 84d), **todo** (22b,24d,35b,64c,156b), **undo** (11a,93d), **Yedo** (166d)

D - - O **dado** (41c,111c,115c,177d), **Dago, dato** (95c,102c,117a), **dedo** (188), **demo** (122d), **dhao** (24c), **dido** (11b,26c,65a,122a), **Dido** (27a,172c), **dilo** (120d,168c), **dino** (34b), **dodo** (19b), **Doko** (191), **Doto** (141b), **Duco, duro** (190)

D - - P **damp** (101a), **deep** (124a), **dopp** (43c), **dorp** (73c,176b), **drap** (61b, c,62a), **drip, drop** (43d,54b,100b,114c,168b), **dump**

DR - - **draa** (188), **drab** (23d,29c,33d,46d,53b,d), **drag** (74a,125b), **drah** (188), **dram** (46b,110c,121d,148c), **drap** (61b,c,62a), **drat** (100a), **Drau, draw** (42c,53a,92b,117c,121c,167d), **dray** (27a,154c,177b), **dree** (139b,140c,158b,172c), **dreg, drei** (66d,165a), **drew, drey** (154c), **drib** (46b), **Drin, drip, drop** (43d,54b,100b,114c,168b), **drub** (17b,39c), **drug** (105d), **drum** (105a), **drun** (132b)

- DR - **adry** (164c)

- - DR **sadr** (94a), **Sadr** (155b)

D - - R **daer** (22b), **darr** (163c), **Daur** (139b), **dear, deer** (28c,135a,154d), **Dhar, dier, doer** (8a,116b), **door** (51a,121b), **dorr** (32b), **dour** (67d, 159a), **duar, Duhr** (155b), **durr** (70b), **dyer**

- DS - **DDSC** (42a)

- - DS **duds** (32c,166d), **Eads** (23b,24b,50b,82a), **odds** (28d,172d), **suds** (59a)

D - - S **dais** (119b), **dans** (62a), **days, dens** (90a,167b), **deus** (68a,89b), **dibs** (70c), **dies** (41b,89b), **diss** (98b), **does, doss** (17c), **duds** (32c,166d), **Duns, Dyas** (66a)

D - - T **daft** (59c), **dart** (13b,88a,100c,120b,153a,160c), **debt** (91d,109b), **deft** (147c), **dent** (42c,77d), **diet** (14a,54c,84c,91b,176a), **dint** (48c,59d,122a), **dipt, dirt, doat** (17a,94b,112a,165d), **doit** (47a, 169d,180d), **dolt** (20c,59c,157d), **don't, dost, drat** (100a), **Duat** (172d), **duct** (170c), **duet** (104d,171d), **duit** (190), **Duit** (192), **dunt, dust**

DU - - **duab** (157c), **duad** (113a,171d), **dual** (45c,171d), **duan** (64b), **duar, Duat** (172d), **dubb** (161c), **duce** (29d), **duck** (26b,53b,179c), **Duco, duct** (170c), **dude** (40d), **duds** (32c,166d), **duel, duet** (104d,171d), **duff** (125b), **Dufy** (63a), **Duhr** (155b), **duim** (188), **duit** (190), **Duit** (192), **duke** (107c), **duku** (95d,168c), **dull** (21a,32c,173a), **Dull** (94b), **Duma** (135c), **dumb** (153b), **dump, dune** (137a), **dunk** (43c, 79d), **Duns, dunt, dupe** (27c,41c,72c,160c), **dura** (153c), **duro** (190), **durr** (70b), **duse** (83c), **dusk** (171c), **dust, duty** (109b,162b)

- DU - **idun** (107d), **odum** (168c,180a)

- - DU   **Addu** (68c,157a,182a), **Jadu** (95a), **Kadu** (191), **kudu** (11a), **ordu** (170d), **pudu** (41d), **Urdu** (77b), **widu** (102d), **wudu** (102d)

D - - U   **Danu** (28a), **datu** (95c,102c,117a), **degu** (132c), **Diau** (192), **Dieu** (61d), **Drau**, **duku** (95d,168c)

D - - W   **dauw** (24c), **dhaw** (125a), **dhow** (88d,111c,175d), **draw** (42c,53a, 92b,117c,121c,167d), **drew**

DY - -   **dyad** (113a), **Dyak** (22b), **Dyas** (66a), **dyer**, **dyke** (49c,91d), **dyna** (34c), **dyne** (59d,173b)

- DY -   **idyl** (114d), **Idyo** (191), **odyl** (59d,79c)

- - DY   **Addy** (183d), **Andy** (96b), **body** (72a), **cady** (69d), **eddy** (37d,39d, 160d,180d), **fady**, **jady**, **Judy** (125c,183d), **lady**, **sidy** (123b), **tidy** (106a,111b), **tody** (19b,d,59a,166a), **undy** (179a), **urdy** (86b), **wady** (109a,128a,132a)

D - - Y   **Davy** (96b,136b), **dazy**, **defy** (28d), **demy** (113d), **deny** (36d,43d, 129b), **dewy** (101a), **doby** (159b,c), **dogy** (46d,103c), **domy**, **dory** (21b,58b,144c), **doty** (43d), **doxy** (129d), **dozy**, **dray** (27a,154c, 177b), **drey** (154c), **Dufy** (63a), **duty** (109b,162b)

- DZ -   **adze** (40c,167a), **Idzo** (191)

- - DZ   **Lodz**

D - - Z   **Daez**

EA - -   **each**, **Eads** (23b,24b,50b,82a), **eard** (139b), **earl** (107c,166b), **earn** (42d,64b,99a), **ease** (7c,8d,35a,100d,129d,130b,c,150c), **east**, **East** (111b), **easy** (54a,146d,149d,172b) **eats**, **eaux** (178c), **eave** (133c),

- EA -   **bead** (17a,122a,146b), **beak** (19a), **beal** (139d), **beam**, **bean** (91b, 142a,175a), **bear** (27a,50b,113c,155a), **beat** (58c,87b,131a,164d, 165b,180d), **beau**, **dead**, **deaf**, **deal** (11d,16c,36c,44c,81a,168b), **dean** (33c,109d), **dear**, **feak** (39d,171c), **fear** (113c,155a), **feat** (7a, 52d), **geal** (47d,163c), **gean** (29c), **gear** (32c,112a,167b), **geat** (77d, 101a), **Geat** (138a), **head** (29b), **heaf** (144a), **heal**, **heap** (117d), **hear** (75b,c,92d), **heat** (37c), **jean** (37c), **Jean** (183c), **keal** (25a), **lead** (35d,43d,72b,74d,81a), **leaf** (55c,73c,119b), **Leah** (19a,84a,87b, 183c), **leak** (110c), **leal** (54b,94c,139d), **lean** (128a,148b,152d, 164b,166a), **leap** (26c), **lear** (139d), **Lear** (37a,143b), **mead** (46a, 78a,97d,99b), **Mead** (78a), **meal** (72a,130b), **mean** (15a,42b,146c, 156b), **meat** (59b), **neaf** (58a,73c), **Neal, neap** (165c,167a,177b), **near** (11d,32c,107b), **neat** (165c,169d), **peag** (144a,178a), **peal** (98b), **peak** (9a,38c,159b,186b), **peal** (131c,d), **pean** (64c,150b), **pear** (64a), **peat** (64a,175a), **read** (116d,157d), **real** (7a), **ream** (18c,37d,50d,113d,171c), **reap** (7a,40a,74a), **rear** (15b,23a,b,24a, 51b,76d,127c), **seah** (188), **seal** (10c,d,54d,64c,96a,118b,128a), **seam** (85b,d,160a,176d,185a), **Sean** (85b,96a), **sear** (23d,27d,72d, 138c), **seat** (98c,156b), **teak** (41a,48a,168c), **teal** (19b,20d,46c,d), **team** (38c,72a,113a), **tean** (140c,167a), **tear** (67c,87b,130a), **veal**, **weak** (55b), **weal** (124d,157c,180c,d), **wean** (8d,42d), **wear** (50b), **yeah, Yean** (88a), **year, yeas** (177c), **zeal** (12c,55d)

- - EA   **Alea** (14b,31c,167d), **area** (37d,38a,44c,53a,93b,110d,127d, 138c,168a,186d), **asea** (39b,177c), **brea** (100b), **crea** (92c,151d), **evea** (82a), **Evea** (95a), **flea** (81b), **Frea, Gaea** (47d,69a), **idea** (54c, 108c,124a,164d), **Itea** (145d,160c,181d), **odea** (105a,164a), **olea**

(170b), **Olea** (110b), **Otea** (71a,82d), **oxea** (153d), **plea** (51a,52d, 122a,130b), **rhea** (37a,56a,111d,133d), **Rhea** (19b,68d,87c,103c, 186b), **shea** (25a,168c,d), **Thea** (162c), **uvea** (53c,82b)

E - - A   **Ecca** (66a), **Edda** (76b,79b,107d,136b), **Edna** (183c), **Egba** (191), **Ekka** (26d), **Elba** (105d), **Elia** (88a,115d), **ella** (152c, 158c), **Ella** (183c), **Elsa** (70a,93c,110d,177b,183c), **Emma** (183c), **Enna** (146a), **epha** (75c), **Erda** (23d,41a,47d,68d,69a,131d,177b), **eria** (13d,146d), **Erma** (183c), **Erua** (103c), **esca** (11c,44a,70c), **esta** (152d,164c), **etna** (75b,153c,157a,175d,177a,c), **Etta** (183c), **evea** (82a,95a), **eyra** (181d), **ezba** (188), **Ezra** (96a)

EB - -   **Eben** (96a), **Eber** (51a,75c,99d), **Ebro** (132a), **eboe** (28b,110a,168c, 169b), **Eboe, ebon** (20b), **ebur** (89c)

- EB -   **ceba** (169b), **debt** (91d,109b), **Hebe** (39c,69c,186b), **Nebo** (68c, 102d,103d,183a), **peba** (12d), **Peba** (193), **Reba** (18d,86c,144a), **Seba** (18c,39d), **sebi** (34b), **ueba** (188), **zebu** (22d,80d,112c)

- - EB   **bleb** (20c,23d,67c), **dieb** (84a), **pleb** (10d,35b,180b), **Sleb** (12a), **sweb** (160d), **theb** (188)

EC - -   **ecad** (73a,119b), **Ecca** (66a), **ecce** (17d,89a,c), **echo** (130b,d), **Echo** (105d), **ecru** (17d,23d,172b), **ecto** (34c,122d)

- EC -   **beck** (107c), **deca** (34d,122d), **deci** (163b), **deck** (13b,41c,144d), **heck** (100a), **lech** (102b), **neck** (83a), **peca** (190), **peck** (24d), **peco** (162c), **reck** (26d,75c), **rect** (117b), **sech** (97c), **seck** (173d), **sect** (42b,54a,114c), **teca, Teca** (192), **Tech, teck** (128b), **Teco** (192)

- - EC   **alec** (10a,57c,d,76c), **Alec** (137a), **avec** (63a,183a), **haec** (90a, 164c), **spec**

E - - C   **epic** (76b,120a), **eric** (115b), **Eric** (71d,96a,107d,138a,164a,176b), **eruc** (37a,56a)

ED - -   **Edam** (29c), **Edar** (18d), **Edda** (76b,79b,107d,136b), **eddo** (162a), **eddy** (37d,39d,160d,180d), **edel** (66c), **Eden** (6b,50d,107c,113d, 123c), **Eder, Edes** (71c), **edge** (22a,96d,131c,143c,146b), **edgy** (106c), **edit** (20d,49d,123a,129a,131a), **Edna** (183c), **Edom** (18c, 51b,79b,82c,84a)

- ED -   **Beda** (101d), **Bede** (48c,50c,101d,175b), **cede** (67b,70c,129d,160a, 168b,185d), **dedo** (188), **gedd** (140a), **Leda** (27b,75d,120c,153a, 171d,186b), **meda** (110a), **Medb, Mede** (10a,b,13c), **medi** (34c), **peda** (114d,144b), **pedi** (34b), **pedo** (34b), **redd** (153a), **rede** (37c, 81d,138d), **redo** (165c), **Teda** (191), **Veda** (77a,b), **Yedo** (166d)

- - ED   **abed** (130c), **aged** (110a), **bled, bred** (23c,48c,127c), **coed, deed** (7a,52d,91a,166c,168b), **feed** (108c), **fled, Fred** (96b), **gled** (19a, 52a,87a), **heed** (14c,75b,109b), **hued, lied** (66d,150b), **meed** (128c, 131a), **Moed** (100c), **need** (42b,52d,87b,122a,178a), **Obed** (135d), **pied** (96c,103c,114b,117c,154a,174d), **reed** (16a,70d,97b,105a, 111b,118b,144b), **Reed** (163a), **roed, seed** (70b,111c,112c,119a, 151b,154a), **shed** (27a,90c,101b,144b), **sled** (40a), **sned** (93d,125a, 140a), **sped, syed** (103b), **tied, toed, used** (6d,73a), **weed**

E - - D   **eard** (139b), **ecad** (73a,119b), **egad** (100a,109a), **eild** (138d,140a), **elod** (49b,59d,79c), **emyd** (163c,167c), **Enid** (13b,25d,66b,163a, 183c)

EE - -   **eely** (185a), **eery** (172b,180a)

291

- EE - beef, been (149a), beer (18c), bees (185b), beet (175a), deed (7a, 52d,166c,168b), deem (36b,85c,164c), deep (124a), deer (28c, 135a,154d), feed (108c), feel (72a,142c), fees (128c), Geez (6c, 51d), heed (14c,75b,109b), heel, Heep (41a,43b), heer (47a,184b, 185b), jeel, jeep, jeer (138c,162b), keef (75d), keek (154c), keel (128d,134d,144c,d), keen (15a,88a,177b), keep (123a,130d), keet (72b), leek (58b,76a,110c,177d), leer (9d,58a,67c,93d,112a,148c), lees (46a,142a), leet (26a,38a,139d), meed (128c,131a), meek (93d,99d), meer, meet (11d,13d,36a,50a,81d,142d), need (42b, 52d,87b,122a,178a), neem (96d,168c,169a), neep (140c,171b), neer (14b,86b,108b), peek (93d), peel (53a,114a), peen (73c), peep (93d,115c), peer (51a,107c), peet (64a), reed (16a,70d,97b,105a, 111b,118b,144b), Reed (163a), reef (129a,137a,145a), reek (49d, 53c,64a,148d,149a), reel (21b,40b,d,153c,154a,c,d,180d), reem (18d), seed (70b,111c,112c,119a,151b,154a), seek (141c), seel (20c,32c,143b), seem (11c), seen, seep (110c,116a,154b), seer (60a,124c,150c), teel (142d), teem (6b,121d), teen (139b,c,140b, 158d), teer (25b,69d), Tees (108a), veer (28d,144c,171b), weed week, weel (16d,57d,140d,180d), weep (39b,88a,104a), weet (19d)

- - EE agee (13d,15c,38d), ajee (15c,139a), akee (168c), alee (15c,75d, 144b,157a,182a), bree (139a), byee (189), chee (189), clee (19a, 129a), Cree (192), dree (139b,140c,158b,172c), epee (55c,160d), flee, free (44a,70d,131b), ghee (24d), glee (99a,150b), idee (61d), inee (120b), Klee (113a), knee (85b), ogee (40c,101a,b,120b), pree (139d), Rhee (87c), shee (82b), skee (149c), slee (140b,148c), smee (19b,46c,d,118b,119d,141b,181b), Smee (116d), snee (40a, b,43d,87a), Spee (66d,70b), thee (124b), tree (11d,37a,66a,184b), twee, tyee (29d), usee, whee

E - - E ease (7c,8d,35a,100d,129d,130b,c,150c), eave (133c), eboe (28b, 110a,168c,169b), Eboe, ecce (17d,89a,c), edge (22a,96d,131c, 143c,146b), elde (119c), eine (66c), Eire (82b), Elbe (108a), elle (62b,c), else (18b,79b,111d), ence (158c), enne (34c), ense (139b, 158c), ente (70b,151d), epee (55c,160d), Erie (82c,87d), erne (19c, d,47b,54b,141a) Erse (28a,64b,82b), esce (158d), esne (10c,45b, 142c,148a,164d), esse (7a,18a,52d,89a,90a,159a,166c), este (152b, d,164c), Este (55c,83c,112d), etre (61a,c,62d,166c), ette (158a,c,d), euge (180a), evoe (15b,130d,181c), eyre (23c,31b,85c), Eyre

EF - - Efik (191)

- EF - defi (61b), deft (147c), defy (28d), heft (179d), Heft, jefe (152a), jeff (133d), left (42c), reft (32a,42c,44d,167b), teff (6c), weft (39a,165a,184b)

- - EF alef (91c), atef (39a,48d), beef, chef, clef (104d,105a), elef (91c), fief (55d), keef (75d), kief (75d), lief (181d), reef (129a,137a, 145a), tref (172b)

E - - F elef (91c), Enif (155b)

EG - - egad (100a,109a), Egba (191), Egbo (141d), Eger (49a), eggs (112a), eggy (185d), Egil (107d), egis (14b,d,115a,124d,144b,154a,161a), egol (11b)

- EG - bega (188), degu (132c), hegh, mega (34b,c), pega (57a,130a, 158b), Pegu (24c,102a,127d), sego (24b,25a,92b,174c), tegg (143d,

171d), **vega** (110d,152c), **Vega** (155b), **Wega** (155b), **Wegg** (111d), yegg (24c)

- - EG   **areg** (116a,137a), **Areg, Doeg** (137c), **dreg, Gheg** (8c), **skeg** (7d, 86a,144d,157d,184a), **sneg** (139b), **waeg** (19b,72c,87a)

EH - -   **eheu** (52c)

- EH -   **behn** (137d), **Hehe** (191), **jehu** (46b), **Jehu** (18c), **lehr** (67c,112a), **peho** (19b,102c,106d), **sehr** (66d), **tehr** (27c,68a)

- - EH   **okeh** (8d,37b)

E - - H   **each, Elah** (18c,86d), **Esth** (16a,51d), **Etah** (51c,71d), **etch, eyah** (95b,108d,111c)

EI - -   **eide** (119c), **eild** (138d,140a), **eine** (66c) **Eire** (82b)

- EI -   **Beid** (155b), **ceil** (92c,112a), **deil** (139b), **dein** (66d), **feis** (82b), **gein** (67d), **heii** (74b), **hein** (52c,61c), **heir, keif** (75d), **keir** (20c, 174d), **Leif** (107d), **Leir, mein** (30b), **nein** (66c), **meio** (188), **Neil** (96a), **reim** (112c), **rein** (29b,130c), **reis** (26c,29d,75a,103b), **seid** (103b), **Seid** (42d,101a,171a), **Seik** (77b), **Seim** (120c), **sein** (146c), **seip** (110c), **Seir** (51b,94a,103d), **seis** (147b,152c), **seit** (189), **Teig** (96a), **teil** (92b,c,168c), **veil** (74d,76c), **vein** (20d,157b), **weir** (40b,57d), **zein**

- - EI   **drei** (66d,165a), **kuei** (44a), **kwei** (44a), **Omei** (24a), **quei** (189), **vlei** (38c,160a)

E - - I   **Ekoi** (191), **Enki** (15b), **equi** (122d), **etui** (27a,29b,62c,106b,148d, 166d,174b)

EJ - -   **ejoo** (55b,168c)

- EJ -   **Beja** (6c,191), **Nejd, reja** (152b), **Sejm** (120c), **teju** (151b)

EK - -   **Ekka** (26d), **Ekoi** (191)

- EK -   **beka** (189), **feke, Peke** (45a,148d), **Reki** (16a), **weka** (58c,106d, 107a,127b), **weki** (55c), **Zeke** (96b)

- - EK   **chek** (59c), **esek** (18d), **hoek** (39d), **keek** (154c), **leek** (58b,76a, 110c,177d), **meek** (93d,99d), **peek** (93d,115c), **reek** (49d,53c, 64a,148d,149a), **seek** (141c), **trek** (85c,93c,99d,168b)

E - - K   **Efik** (191), **esek** (18d)

EL - -   **Elah** (18c,86d), **Elam** (18d,37d,82a,116c,144b), **elan** (12c,41a,50d, 62a,153c,177a,186b), **ELAS** (71c), **Elba** (105d), **Elbe** (108a), **elef** (91c), **Elia** (88a,115d), **Elis** (22c,37d,71b,107c), **ella** (152c,158c, **Ella** (183c), **elle** (62b,c), **elmy, elod** (49b,59d,79c), **Elon** (18c,51b, 108a), **Elsa** (70a,93c,110d,177b,183c), **else** (18b,79b,111d), **Elul** (102b)

- EL -   **bela** (12a), **Bela** (18b,48c,78d), **Beli** (23c), **bell** (24c,39d), **Bell** (162d), **belt** (16a,31a), **cela** (62d), **cell** (39b), **celt** (30c,82c,123a, 156c,167b,179b), **Celt** (10a,180a,b), **dele** (26a,49c,51b,53a,110b, 123d,124c,130a,145c,161b), **dell** (43c,174b), **eely** (185a), **fell** (40a, 58b,76c,115d,147d), **fels** (190), **felt, geld** (162b), **gelt** (101c), **Heła** (93c), **held, helm** (144d,165d), **help** (14a), **kela** (189), **keld** (154b), **kelp** (82a,141c), **Kelt** (180b), **Lely** (47a), **mele** (74b,150b), **melt, Nell** (110a,183d), **pela** (30c), **Pele** (69c,74c), **pelf** (131b), **pelo** (83b), **pelt** (53a), **pelu** (30a,106d,168c), **rely** (16b,170b), **self** (48d,80d), **sell** (97a,115c,175b), **tela** (22d,98c,121b,166a,179c), **tele** (34b,

122c), **teli** (94b), **tell** (105d,129c,154b), **Tell** (160d), **vela** (98c 136b,149d), **Vela** (36b,c), **veld** (151a), **velo** (175b), **weld** (47c,85b, 173c), **Welf** (67a), **welk** (65c,96d,141b), **well, welt** (36d,131b, 145a,b,177b,d), **yell** (145c), **yelp, yelt** (151b)

- - EL **Abel** (7a,25b), **bhel** (126d), **coel** (39b), **duel, edel** (66c), **esel** (66b), **ezel** (47a,85d), **feel** (72a,142c), **fuel** (65c), **Gael** (28a,96c,138d), **goel** (15a,75c), **heel, Jael** (147b), **jeel, Joel** (96a), **keel** (128d,134d, 144c,d), **kiel** (128d,134d), **Kiel** (25d), **koel** (19a,b,39b), **nael** (189), **noel** (26d,150b), **Noel** (30d,96a), **odel** (48a,112c), **Orel, peel** (53a, 114a), **reel** (21b,40b,d,153c,154a,c,d,180d), **Riel** (129a), **ryel** (190), **seel** (20c,32c,143b), **tael** (91d,179d), **teel** (142d), **tuel, weel** (16d, 57d,140d,180d), **wiel** (140d,180d)

E - - L **earl** (107c), **edel** (66c), **Egil** (107d), **egol** (11b), **Elul** (102b), **Emil** (96a), **enol** (29c,158b), **eral** (51a), **esel** (66b), **etal** (89a), **evil** (79c, 95d,147a,181a,185c), **ezel** (47a,85d)

EM - - **Emer** (39b,183c), **emeu** (111d), **Emil** (96a), **Emim** (67a,100d), **emir** (12a,103a,b,123c,134d,135a,171a), **emit** (43d,49a,53c,58d,83a, 142c), **Emma** (183c), **emyd** (163c,167c), **Emys** (167c,171b)

- EM - **bema** (28d,31a,114b,119b,125b,137a), **deme** (71b,c,167d), **demi** (34b,122c), **demo** (122d), **demy** (113d), **feme** (181b), **hemi** (122c), **hemo** (34a,122b), **hemp** (26a,37a,56a,133d), **kemp** (139b), **memo** (108b), **Nema** (34d,48c,134b,164d,176c), **nemo** (34b), **Nemo** (56a, 85c), **Remi** (10b), **Rems, seme** (45c,138b,151b,154b,155c,157b), **semi** (34b,80b,122c,d), **tema** (12a,164a), **Tema, xema** (72c), **Xema** (12c), **zeme** (55d,161b,180b), **zemi** (55d,161b,180b)

- - EM **ahem, alem** (98b,155a,170d,171a), **asem** (9a,49a,69c), **clem** (56b, 158b), **deem** (36b,85c,164c), **diem** (89b,116a), **haem** (122b), **idem** (89d,164a), **item** (6d,13b,42d,51a,90d,92d,107a,113d,114c), **Khem** (113c), **neem** (96d,168c,169a), **poem** (51a), **reem** (18d), **riem** (76c, 112c,157c,164d), **seem** (11c), **Shem** (107c), **stem** (29b,125a,154d, 155a,156d), **teem** (6b,121d), **them** (124b)

E - - M **edam** (29c), **Edom** (18c,51b,79b,82c,84a), **Elam** (18d,37d,82a,116c, 144b), **Emim** (67a,100d), **enam** (70c,77a), **Enam** (85c), **etym** (133d), **exam**

EN - - **enam** (70c,77a,85c), **ence** (158c), **endo** (34d,122d,183b), **Enid** (13b,25d,66b,163a,183c), **Enif** (155b), **enin** (20d), **Enki** (15b), **Enna** (146a), **enne** (34c), **enol** (29c,158b), **Enon** (18c,d), **Enos** (7a,18d,52a, 70c,96a,143a), **enow** (50d,123a,158b), **ense** (139b,158c), **enso** (34d,183b), **ente** (70b,151d), **ento** (34b,d,183b), **envy** (41b), **Enyo** (12c,69c,178a), **Enzu** (102b)

- EN - **bena** (176a), **bend** (39d,171b), **bene** (18a,83c,90a,106d,122a, 180a), **beng** (43a), **beni** (116a,142d), **Beni** (191), **beno** (113b,117a), **bent** (80b), **benu** (49a), **cena** (88d,133a), **cene** (34c), **cens** (115b), **cent** (36d), **dene** (137a), **Dene** (192), **dens** (90a,167b), **dent** (42c, 77d), **deny** (36d,43d,129c), **fend** (114b,178b), **gena** (29b), **gene** (54a,76b), **Gene** (96b), **gens** (42d,132d), **gent, genu** (6b,18a,87a, 89c), **hens** (121d), **Jena** (105d,165b), **keno, Kent** (90d), **lena** (56d), **Lena** (36b), **lend** (6d,79d), **lene** (36b,149a,172b), **leno** (37c, 53b), **lens** (67c,95b,111a,129b,162d), **lent** (54d), **Lent** (115d,141c), **mend** (130b), **mene** (19a,73d,108d,185c), **Ment** (54b,164a), **menu**

(19a,27a), **Menu, nene** (19b,74c), **pend, pene, pent** (36a), **rena** (25b,132c), **rend** (32a,159c,162c,185a), **Reni** (83d), **Reno, rent** (58a,91b,138b,153d,162c,167c), **send** (42c,44b,95c,121c,130a, 144c,168b), **senn** (76b), **Sens** (63b), **sent, tend** (26d,80b,93d,100a), **tene** (34d,131b), **teng** (188), **tent** (26b,115a), **vena** (90a,175a), **vend** (97a,115c,142b), **Vend** (10b,148a), **vent** (8b,11b,110d,112a), **wend** (67d,123d), **Wend** (10b,148a), **went** (42c), **xeno** (34d), **yeni** (19b,161d), **Zend, Zeno** (71b), **zenu** (143d)

- - EN **aden** (34b), **Aden, alen** (40d,138a), **amen** (14a,80b,94a,137a,149c, 175c,184b), **Amen** (86d,127d,164a), **aten** (150a,159b), **been** (149a), **bien** (63a,140c,179a,180a), **bren** (72d,95a), **Caen, Chen** (149b), **Eben** (96a), **Eden** (6b,50d,107c,113d,123c), **even** (51a,58b,79d,91d, 149a,173a), **glen** (43c), **hien** (30b), **hoen** (189), **Iden** (76a), **Iren** (127c), **Iten** (192), **keen** (15a,88a,177b), **lien** (65c,91a,124c), **mien** (11c,17b,26d,44c,96b), **omen** (14c,59d,60a,121c,123a,146b), **open** (26a,60d,81a,109b,112c,125b,172b,173c), **oven** (15d,78c,86b), **Owen** (96a,183c), **oxen** (10c), **peen** (73c), **pien** (13b), **rien** (62b), **seen, Shen** (68a), **sken** (164a), **sten** (72c,95a), **teen** (139b,c,140b, 158d), **then, tien** (147d), **T-men** (168b), **when** (180d), **wren** (19b,c), **Wren** (50b)

E - - N **earn** (42d,64b,99a), **Eben** (96a), **ebon** (20b), **Eden** (6b,50d,107c, 113d,123c), **elan** (12c,41a,50d,62a,153c,177a,186b), **Elon** (18c, 51b), **enin** (20d), **Enon** (18c,d), **Eoan** (41a,85b), **Eoin** (85b), **Erin** (82b), **Eton** (33b,50c,84a), **Evan** (96a), **even** (51a,58b,79d,91d, 149a,173a), **Ewan**

EO - - **Eoan** (41a,85b), **Eoin** (85b)

- EO - **feod** (55d), **Leon** (96a), **meou, meow, neon** (65c), **peon** (28c,59c, 99c), **Teos** (82a)

- - EO **areo** (34c), **Ateo** (120d), **Cleo** (126b), **ideo** (34b,d,164d), **oleo** (34c), **skeo** (57d)

E - - O **Ebro** (132a), **echo** (130b,d), **Echo** (105d), **ecto** (34c,122d), **eddo** (162a), **Egbo** (141d), **ejoo** (55b,168c), **endo** (34d,122d,183b), **enso** (34d,183b), **ento** (34b,d,183b), **Enyo** (12c,69c,178a), **ergo** (164b)

EP - - **epee** (55c,160d), **epha** (75c), **epic** (76b,120a), **epos** (51a,76b,120a)

- EP - **cepa** (110c), **cepe** (48c), **depa** (188), **kepi** (99d), **kept, Nepa** (106b, 178c), **pepo** (39b,64a,70a,98c,125c,154c), **repp** (53b,131a), **seps** (93b,142d), **sept** (31d,82b,143a,149c), **Sept** (45b), **Veps** (191), **wept**

- - EP **deep** (124a), **Heep** (41a,43b), **jeep, keep** (123a,130d), **neep** (140c, 171b), **peep** (93d,115c), **prep** (138b), **seep** (110c,116a,154b), **skep** (16d,17c,77c), **step** (70b,112b,177b,d), **weep** (39b,88a,104a)

EQ - - **equi** (122d)

ER - - **eral** (51a), **erat** (89c), **Erda** (23d,41a,47d,68d,69a,131d,177b), **erer** (17d,150c), **ergo** (164b), **eria** (13d,146b), **eric** (115b), **Eric** (71d, 96a,107d,138a,164a,176b), **Erie** (82c,87d), **Erin** (82b), **Eris** (12c, 68d,109c), **Erma** (183c), **erne** (19c,d,47b,54b,141a), **Eros** (11c, 39c,68b,97c,182d), **Erse** (28a,64b,82b), **erst** (60b), **Erua** (103c), **eruc** (37a,56a), **eryx** (137a)

- ER - **aera** (8a), **aeri** (34a), **aero** (8b,34a,b,58c,59a), **aery** (47b,51d,106c), **Bera** (86d), **berg** (79b), **berm** (25d,90d,145c), **Bern** (160d), **Bert**

(96b), **cera** (152d,161d,179a), **cere** (19a,114b,149d,179a), **cern** (41c), **cero** (57b,c,d, 180b), **dera** (34c), **dere** (74a,79c), **derm** 147c,158d), **eery** (172b,180a), **fern** (142a), **feru** (37a,56a,133d), **gerb** (56d,143d), **Gerd** (63c), **Gere** (183c), **Geri** (183c), **germ** (17d, 99c,134d), **Hera** (69c,85d,110b,126b,186b,d), **herb** (58b,158b), **herd** (39a,46c,72a), **here, herl** (16b,59a), **hero** (42b,124d,137b), **Hero** (90c), **Herr** (66c), **hers** (124c), **jerk** (153a), **kerb** (146b), **kere** (75c,128b), **kerf** (40a,108b), **keri** (75c,128b), **kern** (59c,172a), **Kern** (132b), **Kerr, Lero** (82d), **lerp** (51d,141d), **mere** (16c,22b, 62a,78b,87d,96c,110c,120d,146d,148b), **merl** (20b), **mero** (72a), **Meru** (77a,103d), **Nera** (165b), **Neri, Nero** (8a,126d,133a,172c), **Pera** (60a), **pere** (61c,63b), **peri** (54b,116b,c,122b), **perk** (84d, 93a), **perm** (49b,97d), **pern** (78a), **pero** (152a), **pert** (80a,93a,137c, 154b), **Peru, qere** (75c), **qeri** (75c), **sera** (11b,20d,59a,83a,180d), **Serb** (15d,148a,186c), **sere** (24d,46a,46c,138c,183b), **Sere** (158b), **serf** (21d,148a), **seri** (18b), **Seri** (192), **sero** (34d,88d,164b,178d), **Sert** (151d), **tera** (23d,84c), **term** (92b,105b,142b,166b), **tern** (19b, 32d,72c,94a,138c,141a,160a), **terp** (12b,123a), **vera** (140c,151b, 175c), **Vera** (183c), **verb** (7a,114b,184b), **verd** (71d), **veri** (28b), **vert** (71d,166a,171b), **very** (149c), **were** (139b), **werf** (54d), **werl** (15c,27c), **wert, zero** (31a,84c,108c), **Zero** (118d)

- - **ER** **Acer** (96c) **Ader** (18d), **afer** (48a,182b), **ager** (47c,56a,89b,c,131d, 133b), **amer** (61b), **aner** (18d,96b), **aper** (32d), **Aser** (84a), **Ater** (18c), **Auer** (79a), **aver** (7c,14a,15c,41c,95c,140d,155c,160b, 184c), **beer** (18c), **bier** (33b,66b), **Boer** (151a), **Brer** (172b), **cher** (61b), **daer** (22b), **deer** (28c,135a,154d), **dier, doer** (8a,116b), **dyer, Eber** (51a,75c,99d), **Eder, Eger** (49a), **Emer** (39b,183c), **erer** (17d, 150c), **eser, euer** (66d), **ever** (9b,14b,80b), **ewer** (84c,85c,118c, 181b), **eyer, gier** (47b), **goer, heer** (47a, 184b, 185b), **hier** (63a, 185d), **Hier** (141a), **hoer, icer, Imer, Iser** (49a), **iter** (22d,76c,85c, 89c,114d,132a,b,133a,b), **jeer** (138c,162b), **kier** (20c,174d), **leer** (9d,58a,67c,93d,112a,148c), **meer, neer** (14b,86b,108b), **Oder** (132a), **omer** (51a,75c), **oner** (20d,53a,75c,162d,173a,d), **oser** (61b), **over** (6b,38c,80a,114d,130a), **oxer** (55c), **oyer** (38a,75b,119c), **peer** (51a,93d,107c), **pier** (23a,88b,180c), **rier** (180b), **roer** (72d), **ruer, saer** (163a), **seer** (60a,124c,150c), **sher** (65d,165c), **sier** (57a,118b), **ster** (158c,d), **suer** (124d), **teer** (25b,69d), **tier** (118a,134b), **tyer, uber** (66b), **user** (49d), **veer** (28d,144c,171b), **vier** (66c), **waer** (40b), **Ymer** (67a,131c), **Yser**

E - - R **Eber** (51a,75c,99d), **ebur** (89c), **Edar** (18d), **Eder, Eger** (49a), **Emer** (39b,183c,), **emir** (12a,103a,b,123c,171a), **erer** (17d,150c), **eser, euer** (66d), **ever** (9b,14b,80b), **ewer** (84d,85c,118c,181b), **eyer**

ES - - **Esau** (82c,84a,128c), **Esay, esca** (11c,44a,70c), **esce** (158d), **esek** (18d), **esel** (66b), **eser, esne** (10c,45b,142c,148a,164d), **Esop** (53b, 54a), **esox** (57b), **espy** (44a,142a), **esse** (7a,18a,52d,89a,90a,159a, 166c), **esta** (152d,164c), **este** (152b,d,164c), **Este** (55c,83c,d,112d), **Esth** (16a,51d), **Esus**

- **ES -** **aesc** (12d,64d), **Besa** (68b,119c), **Bess** (76c,183d), **best** (41d,159c, 160a), **cess** (91d,94c,162b), **cest** (18a,67b), **desi** (85d), **desk, euer** (66d), **fess** (23c,51b), **fest, gest** (7c,41d,52d,133c), **hest** (35a), **jess** (157a), **jest** (169c), **Jesu, less** (100c,108b,141d), **lest** (59d,163d), mesa (49b,76d,119b,161a), mese (71c), mesh (50d,106c), mess (22b,44b,77c,85d,104d,165c,173d), ness (26b,75a,124b), nest (38b, 74b,130d,149c,160b), oese (15d,119c), pesa (190), peso (99c), pest (108c,116b,118d,170a), rese (127b), resh (91d), rest (15d,91b, 104d,105a,115a,b,130a,b,161b), sesi (20b,57a,149b), sess (149c, 162b), Tesa (80c), Tess (73d,164c,183d), test (26a,51c,144a,169c, 170c), vest (32c,177b), West (9c,50b,109b), Yeso (72d), zest (55d, 72d)

- - ES   Ades (73a), Ames (9c,82a), anes (110c,140a), Ares (49b,51b,68c, 76a,97a,105c,110b,178a,186d), ates (160c), Aves (19d), bees ⟨185b), Bres, dies (41b,89b), does, EDES (71c), fees (128c), Ghes (193), gres (156d), ides (41a,b,133a), Ives (9c,90b), lees (46a, 142a), ones (116a), oyes (38a,39b,75b), pres (62b), spes, Spes (69a,78a), Tees (108a), tres (19a,52b,63a,152d,165a,175c), uses (18a), wies (185a)

E - - S   Eads (23b,24b,50b,82a), eats, EDES (71c), eggs (112a), egis (14b, d,115a,124d,144b,154a,161a), ELAS (71c), Elis (22c,37d,71b, 107c), Emys (167c,171b), Enns, Enos (7a,18d,52a,70c,96a,143a), epos (51a,76b,120a), Eris (12c,68d,109c), Eros (11c,39c,68b,97c, 182d), Esus, etes (177c), eyas (106c,173a)

ET - -   Etah (51c,71d), etal (89a), etat (62d), etch, etes (177c), etna (75b, 153c,157a,175d,177a,c), Eton (33b,50c,84a), etre (61a,c,62d,166c), Etta (183c), ette (158a,c,d), etui (27a,29b,62c,106b,148d,166d, 174b), etym (133d)

- ET -   Aeta (94d,95d,100a,106b,117a), beta (71a,91c,141d), bete (61a,107c), beth (91c), Beth (8c,183d), cete (180b,c), ceto (34a), fete (55d,129b), geta (84b,145a), gett (44d), Heth (77c), jete (16a), Jeth (102a), keta (45a), Keta, Ketu (48b), lete, Leti (82d), Leto (11c), Lett (16a,90a,93a), meta (132d,133a), Meta, mete (9a, 11d,22b,44c,45b,98a,121c), nete (71c,108b,163d), neti (164a), nett, pete (136b), Pete (96b), peto (57a,177b), Peto (76a), rete (106c,119c), seta (23b,27c,73a,b,123b,153c), seth (98d), Seth (7a, 52b,68a,b,96a,98d), seti (34a), Seti (116d), sett (115a,156d), tete (61d,73b,74d), teth (91d), veta (104a), veto (94a,124a), Veto, weta (93c), yeta (84c), zeta (71b,91c)

- - ET   abet (8b,15b,50a,59b,75d,81c,141d,159d), Ahet (49a,102a), anet (43c), Apet (97c), aret (128c), beet (175a), blet (64a), diet (14a, 54c,84c,91b,176a), duet (104d,171d), evet (48d,107a,136c,169d), fret (28c,35b,111c,184d), keet (72b), khet (188), laet (60d), leet (26a,38a), meet (11d,13d,36a,50a,81d,142d), oket (189), peet (64a), piet (29b,95b), plet (135d), poet (49b), pret (188), pyet (95b), spet (16c,57a,142c), stet (91b,123d,124c), suet (54d), tret (9a,178b,179d), voet (188), weet (19d), whet (143c,156b)

E - - T   east, East (111b), edit (20d,49d,123a,129a,131a), emit (43d,49a, 53c,58d,83a,142c), erat (89c), erst (60b), etat (62d), evet (48d, 107a,136c,169d), exit (114d), eyot (82d)

EU - -   euer (66d), euge (180a)

- EU -   deul (77b), deus (68a,89b), feud (55d,126b,175d), Geum (76b), jeux (61d), meum (27a,89c), Meum, neue (66c), peur (61c), Zeus (135a)

- - EU bleu (61b), Dieu (61d), eheu (52c), emeu (111d), lieu (118c,155d)

E - -U ecru (17d,23d,172b), eheu (52c), emeu (111d), Enzu (102b), Esau (82c,84a,128c)

EV - - Evan (96a), even (51a,58b,79d,91d,149a,173a), evea (82a,95a), ever (9b,14b,80b), evet (48d,107a,136c,169d), evil (79c,95d,147a, 181a,185c), evoe (15b,130d,181c)

- EV - bevy (38a,58c), Deva (23d,42a,b,56d,77a), Devi (147b,153b), hevi (111d), Leve (62a), Levi (84a,90c), levo (91a), levy (14a, 162b), Neva (91b,132a), neve (56d,67c,70c,149b), peva (12d), pevy (91d,94c), reve (61c,104d), revs (131a), seve (63a,182c)

- - EV Kiev, Stev (155b)

EW - - Ewan, ewer (84d,85c,118c,181b), ewry (133c)

- EW - dewa, dewy (101a), hewn, mewl (180d), mews (154c), news (165c), newt (48d,136c,169d), sewn, Tewa (193)

- - EW anew (7c), blew, brew (35d), chew (97c), clew (16a,33a,77b,136b, 164d), crew (72a,106a), drew, flew, grew, knew, Llew (40c), phew (52c), plew (17c), shew (44c), skew (148a,160c,171c), slew (160a), smew (19b,46d,99a,137d), spew (35a,49a), stew (21c,44b,184d), thew (104c), view (93d,138b), whew

E - - W enow (50d,123a,158b)

EX - - exam, exit (114d)

- EX - next (106a), sext (26b,111b,147b), text (21c,140d)

- - EX Amex (184d), apex (39c,76c,115c,118b,159b,166a,167b), Crex (37a), faex (46a), flex (18a), ibex (67d,68a), ilex (77d), obex (22d), plex (60b), spex, Ulex (153c)

E - - X eaux (178c), eryx (137a), esox (57b)

EY - - eyah (95b,108d,111c), eyas (106c,173a), eyer, eyey (74b), eyot (82d), eyra (181d), eyre (23c,31b,85c), Eyre, eyry (47b,106c)

- EY - Ceyx (73b), teyl (92b,c,168c)

- - EY ahey (52c), akey (189), brey (194), drey (154c), eyey (74b), fley (63d), Frey (7c,68b,124d), grey (33c), hoey (114c), joey (86a,185d), Joey (96b,109c), obey (35c,75c), prey (119d,176a), roey (103d), skey (185d), sley (179b), Spey, they (124b), trey (26c,165a), Urey (14b,107c,138c), whey (100a)

E - - Y easy (54a), eddy (37d,39d,160d,180d), edgy (106c), eely (185a), eery (172b,180a), eggy (185d), elmy, envy (41b), esay, espy (44a, 142a), ewry (133c), eyey (74b), eyry (47b,106c)

EZ - - ezba (188), ezel (47a,85d), Ezra (96a)

- - EZ chez (14b,61a), daez, Geez (6c,51d), Inez (45c,183c), juez (152b), knez (123c), oyez (38a,39b,75b)

FA - - Faam (111a), Faba, face (159d,176c), fact (7a,128b), fade (181d, 183b), fado (121c), fady, faex (46a), fail, fain (42d,67c,183b), fair (17a,55d), fait (6d,61b), fake (123a,143c), faky, fala (129b), fall (46b,141c), falx (133b), Fama (135a), fame (130a), famn (188), fana, fane (30d,137a,162d), fang (167b), fano (51d,96b,113c,d), faon (33c,55a), fard (112d) fare (43c,59b,67d,123b), farl (138c, 140b), farm (165d), faro (65a), fash (140c,176a), fass (189), fast (56d,126c,141d,160c,173a,d), fate (42d,52a,87a,94a), faun (56a,

68b,137c,161a,184a), **favi** (138a,165d), **fawn** (33c), **faze** (43d)

- FA - afar (44c), **Afar** (6c)

- - FA **Abfa** (76b), **alfa** (70d), **gufa** (21b,99a), **Kafa** (6c), **kufa** (21b,99a), **Offa** (163d), **sofa** (44d), **tufa** (121b,177a), **Urfa** (99a)

F - - A **Faba, fala** (129b), **Fama** (135a), **fana, flea** (81b), **fora** (133a), **Frea, Fria, fuga**

F - - B **flub** (22b), **frab** (138c), **frib** (43d)

F - - C **fisc** (52c,134c), **floc** (149a)

- - FD **Wafd** (49a)

F - -D **fard** (112d), **feed** (108c), **fend** (114b,178b), **feod** (55d), **feud** (55d, 126b,175b), **find** (44a), **fled, fold, fond** (7c,94b), **food** (109a,176b), **ford** (177b), **foud** (54d,144b), **Fred** (96b), **Fuad** (54d), **fund** (6d, 101c,130c), **fyrd** (110a)

FE - - **feak** (39d,171c), **fear** (113c,155a), **feat** (7a,52d), **feed** (108c), **feel** (72a,142c), **fees** (128c), **feis** (82b), **feke, fell** (40a,58b,76c,115d, 147d), **fels** (190), **felt, feme** (181b), **fend** (114b,178b), **feod** (55d), **fern** (142a), **feru** (37a,56a,133d), **fess** (23c,51b), **fest, fete** (55d, 129b), **feud** (55d,126b,175b)

- FE - **afer** (48a,182b)

- - FE **cafe, fife** (59a,105a), **jefe** (152a), **life** (19a,177a), **nife** (37a), **orfe** (57a,b,185c), **rife** (6b,c,39d,123b), **safe** (141d,157d,174d), **wife** (154a)

F - - E **face** (159d,176c), **fade** (181d,183b), **fake** (123a,143c), **fame** (130a), **fane** (30d,137a,162d), **fare** (43c,59b,67d,123b), **fate** (42d,52a,87a, 94a), **faze** (43d), **feke, feme** (181b), **fete** (55d,129b), **fide, fife** (59a,105a), **fike** (139c), **file** (13a,127d), **fine** (49b,50a,104b,115d, 159a), **fire** (13a,43d,44b), **five flee, floe** (79b), **flue** (8b,30a), **fore** (63d,174b), **free** (44a,70d,131b), **froe** (32a,167a,179d), **fume** (129a, 149a,157a), **fuse** (98c), **fute** (51c), **fuze** (98c), **fyke** (15d)

- FF - **affy** (18b), **offa, Offa** (163d), **offs** (38c)

- - FF **baff** (69d), **biff, buff** (134c,161d), **cuff** (148a), **daff** (125d), **doff** 130a,161b), **duff** (125b), **gaff** (57c,d,152d,153a), **goff** (32d), **guff**, **huff** (58a), **jeff** (133d), **Jeff, jiff** (101c), **kiff** (88c), **koff** (47a), **luff** (136b), **miff** (44c), **moff** (53b,146c), **muff, piff** (24b), **puff** (180d), **raff** (75b), **riff** (131d), **Riff** (18b,102c), **ruff** (19b,33b,63d, 137a), **teff** (6c), **tiff** (126b), **toff** (40d), **tuff** (121b,177a)

F - - F **fief** (55d)

F - - G **fang** (167b), **flag** (16b,50d,82b,88c,115a,155a), **flog** (180d), **Fong** (40b), **frog** (10a,17a,126d), **Fung** (191)

F - - H **fash** (140c,176a), **fish, Foch** (63b)

FI - - **fiat** (35a,41d,48c,111b,137a), **Fiat** (83c), **fico** (169d), **fide, fief** (55d), **fife** (59a,105a), **fike** (139c), **file** (13a,127d), **fili, fill** (109b), **film** (164b), **filo, fils** (62d,150b), **find** (44a), **fine** (49b,50a,104b, 115d,159a), **fink** (19a,56c,157c), **Finn** (107d), **Fiot** (191), **fire** (13a,43d,44b), **firm** (154c,173d), **firn** (67c,70c,106c,149b), **fisc** (52c,134c), **fish, fisk** (24d,52c,134c), **fist** (80c), **five**

- FI - **Efik** (191), **ifil** (117a,168c)

- - FI **defi** (61b), **Safi** (191), **sufi** (103a,116c)

F - - I   favi (138a,165d), **fill, foci** (28b), **fuci** (132c), **fuji** (84b), **Fuji** (84d)

F - - J   Funj

F - - K   feak (39d,171c), **fink** (19a,56c,157c), **fisk** (24d,52c,134c), **flak** (11a), **folk** (116a,169c), **fork, fulk** (173a), **funk** (63d,113c)

FL - -   flag (16b,50d,82b,88c,115a,155a), **flak** (11a), **flam** (169c), **flan** (39d,40a,114d), **flap** (17b,59a,104a,118d,161a,182d), **flat** (41b, 124b,173a), **flaw, flax, flay** (147c,157c), **flea** (81b), **fled, flee, flew, flex** (18a), **fley** (63d), **flip** (167c), **flit** (41a), **flix, floc** (149a), **floe** (79b), **flog** (180d), **flop** (54a), **flot** (173a), **flow** (157b), **flub** (22b), **flue** (8b,30a), **flux** (28d,58d)

F - - L   fail, fall (46b,141c), **farl** (138c,140b), **feel** (72a,142c), **fell** (40a, 58b,76c,115d,147d), **fill** (109b), **foal** (78c), **foil** (15d,55c,165b), **fool** (24a,41c,47a,146d), **foul** (173a), **fowl, fuel** (65c), **full** (7b, 130b), **furl** (132d)

F - - M   Faam (111a), **farm** (165d), **film** (164b), **firm** (154c,173d), **flam** (169c), **foam** (63d,154b), **form** (54d,143c), **frim** (58d), **from**

F - - N   fain (42d,67c,183b), **famn** (188), **faon** (33c,55a), **faun** (56a,68b, 137c,161a,184a), **fawn** (33c), **fern** (142a), **Finn** (107d), **firn** (67c, 70c,106c,149b), **flan** (39d,40a,114d), **fohn** (182b)

FO - -   foal (78c), **foam** (63d,154b), **Foch** (63b), **foci** (28b), **fogy, fohn** (182b), **foil** (15d,55c,165b), **fold, folk** (116a,169c), **fond** (7c,94b), **Fong** (40b), **fono** (137a), **fons** (60c), **font** (16b,171d,172a), **food** (109a,176b), **fool** (24a,41c,47a,146d), **foot** (115a), **fora** (133a), **ford** (177b), **fore** (63d,174b), **fork, form** (54d,143c), **fort** (63d, 157d), **foss** (44d,100d), **foud** (54d,144b), **foul** (173a), **four** (26c), **fowl, foxy** (38b,39c,181d)

- - FO   Bufo (166c)

F - - O   fado (121c), **fano** (51d,96b,113c,d), **faro** (65a), **fico** (169d), **filo, fono** (137a)

F - - P   flap (17b,59a,104a,118d,161a,182d), **flip** (167c), **flop** (54a), **frap** (45d,165c)

FR - -   frab (138c), **frap** (45d,165c), **frat, frau** (181b), **fray** (56b,60d), **Frea, Fred** (96b), **free** (44a,70d,131b), **fret** (28c,35b,111c,184d), **Frey** (7c,68b,124d), **Fria, frib** (43d), **frim** (58d), **frit** (64c,67c), **friz** (39d), **froe** (32a,167a,179d), **frog** (10a,17a,126d), **from, frot** (28c), **frow** (47a,167a)

- FR -   Afra (183c)

F - - R   fair (17a,55d), **fear** (113c,155a), **four** (26c)

- - FS   offs (38c)

F - - S   fass (189), **fees** (128c), **feis** (82b), **fels** (190), **fess** (23c,51b), **fils** (62d,150b), **fons** (60c), **foss** (44d,100d), **fuss** (22b,35b)

- - FT   baft (14a,53b), **daft** (59c), **deft** (147c), **gift** (123a), **haft** (76d), **heft** (179d), **Heft, left** (42c), **lift** (49b), **loft** (14c,69d,104b,178b), **raft** (27b,33c,58c,75b), **reft** (32a,42c,44d,167b), **rift** (30c,32a,58a, 110d), **sift** (140d,142c,146b), **soft** (48b,95d,99d,163a), **Taft** (29d), **tuft** (24b,32d,38c), **waft** (20d,58c), **weft** (39a,165a,184b), **yuft** (135c)

F - - T fact (7a,128b), fait (6d,61b), fast (56d,126c,141d,160c,173a,d), feat (7a,52d), felt, fest, Fiat (83c), fiat (35a,41d,48c,111b,137a), Fiot (191), fist (80c), flat (41b,124b,173a), flit (41a), flot (173a), font (16b,171d,172a), foot (115a), fort (63d,157d), frat, fret (28c, 35b,111c,184d), frit (64c,67c), frot (28c), fust (105c,143b)

FU - - Fuad (54d), fuci (132c), fuel (65c), fuga, fugu (84b), fuji (84b), Fuji (84d), fulk (173a), full (7b,130b), fume (129a,149a,157a), fumy, fund (6d,101c,130c), Fung (191), funk (63d,113c), furl (132d), fury (157a), fuse (98c), fuss (22b,35b), fust (105c,143b), fute (51c), fuze (98c), fuzz (45d)

F - - U feru (37a,56a,133d), frau (181b), fugu (84b)

F - - W flaw, flew, flow (157b), frow (47a,167a)

F - - X faex (46a), falx (133b), flax, flex (18a), flix, flux (28d,58d)

FY - - fyke (15d), fyrd (110a)

- - FY affy (18b), defy (28d), Dufy (63a)

F - - Y fady, faky, flay (147c,157c), fley (63d), fogy, foxy (38b,39c,181d), fray (56b,60d), Frey (7c,68b,124d), fumy, fury (157a)

F - - Z friz (39d), fuzz (45d)

GA - - gaal (23b,174d), gabe (162a), gabi (162a), gaby (59c,146d), gade Gaea (47d,69a), Gael (28a,96c,138d), gaff (57c,d,152d,153a), gage (28d,98a,119c,d), gagl (160b), Gaia (47d,69a), gail (23b, 174d), Gail (183d), gain (7a,b,124a,181d), gait (96b,179a), gajo (107c), gala (55d), Gala (191), gale (181d), gali (6c), gall (19a, 28c,29b,82c,160c,176a), galt, Gama (121c), game (64d,154a), gamp (172a), gane (185b), gang (38c), Gano (132d), gaol (123d), Gaol (164a), Gaon (85b), gape (185b), gapo (60a), gapy, gara (190), garb (32c,46a), gare (61b,c,62c,127c,184b), Garm (178c), garn (67d,185b), Garo (88c), Gary, gash (40a), gasp (113c), gata (143c), gate (51a,121b), Gath (117a), gaub (116c), gaud (169d), gaue (67a), Gaul (10a,60d,63c), gaup, gaur (112c,181c), gaus (67a), gaut (88b,103d,132a), gave, gawd (169c), gawk (146d), gawp, Gaza (117a), gaze, gazi, gazy

- GA - Agag (18c,86c,137a), agal (17c,36d), Agao (6c,73c), agar (7d,28c, 39c,103c,141c), Agau (73c), Agaz (193), egad (100a,109a), ngai (48a,159c), ngan, ogam (82b,c), Sgau (88c)

- - GA alga (141b,c), baga (171b), bega (188), biga (171d), boga (57d, 180b), fuga (56a,105a), giga (56a,105a), goga (24a), hoga (144b), inga (145d, 170a), Jaga (191), juga (27a), mega (34b,c), muga (13d, 33a,55b,127c), Naga (24c,77a,88c,176d), Olga (135c,183c), paga (117a), pega (57a,130a,158b), raga (56d,105a), riga (118b), ruga (59b,185a), saga (79b,91a,138a,157a,161b,c,168a), Saga, soga (70d,152b), Soga (191), toga (132d,133a,b), vega (152c), Vega (155b), Wega (155b), yoga (10b,13c,77a), Yuga (76d), zyga (134b)

G - - A Gaea (47d,69a), Gaia (47d,69a), gala (55d), Gala (191), Gama (121c), gara (190), gata (143c), Gaza (117a), gena (29b), geta (84b, 145a), giga (56a, 105a), gila (93b), Gita, Gjoa (144d), glia (106c), goga (24a), gola (27b,40c,70c,157a), Goma (191), Gona (106d), gora (81c), Goya (151d), gufa (21b,99a),

Guha (191), **gula** (90a,101a,165b), **guna** (106a,137b)

- GB -   **Egba** (191), **Egbo** (141d)

G - - B   **garb** (32c,46a), **gaub** (116c), **gerb** (56d,143d), **glib** (58d,149a,177c), **glub**, **grab** (105b,142a,149b), **grub** (88d), **guib** (11a)

G - - D   **gaud** (169d), **gawd** (169c), **gedd** (140a), **geld** (162b), **Gerd** (63c), **gild** (14a,49c,69c,98b), **gird** (32c,50a,123a,160a), **glad** (85c), **gled** (19a,52a,87a), **goad** (80b,154b), **gold, Gond, good, grad** (28b), **grid** (17a,70d,119b,156d)

GE - -   **çeal** (47d,163c), **gean** (29c), **gear** (32c,112a,167b), **geat** (77d,101a), **Geat** (138a), **gedd** (140a), **Geez** (6c,51d), **gein** (67d), **geld** (162b), **gelt** (101c), **gena** (29b), **gene** (54a,76b), **Gene** (96b), **gens** (42d, 132d), **gent, genu** (6b,18a,87a,89c), **gerb** (56d,143d), **Gerd** (63c), **Gere** (183c), **Geri** (183c), **germ** (17d,99c,134d), **gest** (7c,41d,52d, 133c), **geta** (84b,145a), **gett** (44d), **Geum** (76b)

- GE -   **aged** (110a), **agee** (13d,15c,38d), **ager** (47c,56a,89b,c,131d,133b), **Eger** (49a), **ogee** (101a,b,120b)

- - GE   **ange** (61a), **auge** (123c,132b), **cage** (36a), **doge** (95b,175b), **edge** (22a,96d,131c,143c,146b), **euge** (180a), **gage** (28d,98a,119c,d), **huge, Inge** (24d,67d,117c,119c), **kuge** (84c), **loge** (164a), **luge** (148a), **mage** (95b), **page** (51b,59b,142d,159b), **rage** (10c,30c,157a, 161d), **sage** (13a,90d,100c,141c,145c,180b,183a), **tige** (118a), **urge** (42d,46b,79d,80a,b,81c,124a,150a), **wage** (27a,115b), **yage** (23a)

G - - E   **gabe** (162a), **gade, gage** (28d,98a,119c,d), **gale** (181d), **game** (64d, 154a), **gane** (185b), **gape** (185b), **gare** (61b,c,62c,127c, 184b), **gate** (51a,121b), **gaue** (67a), **gave, gaze, gene** (54a,76b), **Gene** (96b), **ghee** (24d), **gibe** (8a,42c,84d,100d,138c,144c,149b), **Gide** (63a), **gime** (77d), **gite** (62a,118d), **give** (79d,123a), **glee** (99a, 150b), **glue** (7b,156a), **gone** (6b,15c,42c,44c,114d), **gore** (115d, 117c,154c,169c), **guze** (128d), **gybe** (144c), **gyle** (23b,174d), **gyne** (34b,55b,183c), **gyre** (31b,171b), **gyve** (55d,143b)

· G - - F   **gaff** (57c,d,152d,153a), **goaf** (104b), **goff** (32d), **golf** (154a), **goof, Graf** (37c,66b,67a,107c,186b), **guff, gulf** (6c)

- GG -   **eggs** (112a), **eggy** (185d)

- - GG   **dagg** (118c), **hagg, hogg** (144a), **jagg, magg** (95b), **migg** (96c), **nogg** (48d), **tegg** (143d,171d), **vugg** (28a,66a,132b), **Wegg** (111d), **wigg, yegg** (24c)

G - - G   **gang** (38c), **Gheg** (8c), **glug, gong, grig** (38c,70d,93a), **grog** (92d, 153d)

GH - -   **ghat** (32d,88b,103d,132a), **ghee** (24d), **Gheg** (8c), **Ghes** (193), **ghor** (174b), **ghos** (30b), **Ghuz** (171a)

- GH -   **agha** (35a,171a)

- - GH   **dagh** (76d), **hegh, high, Hugh** (96a), **Lugh** (28b), **Magh** (102a), **nigh** (106a), **ough, pugh, sigh, vugh** (28a,66a,136b), **yogh** (10c, 185a)

G - - H   **gash** (40a), **Gath** (117a), **gish** (102c), **gosh, Goth** (16c), **gush** (35a, 154c)

GI - -   **gibe** (8a,42c,84d,100d,138c,144c,149b), **Gide** (63a), **gier** (47b),

302

gift (123a), **giga** (56a,105a), **gila** (93b), **gild** (14a,49c,69c,98b), **gill** (22d), **gilo** (48a), **gilt** (69c,77c,151b,185d), **gime** (77d), **gimp** (169d), **gink** (48b), **gird** (32c,50a,123a,160a), **girl**, **giro** (38c,83c, 167c), **girt** (50a), **gish** (102c), **gist** (95c,118c), **Gita**, **gite** (62a, 118d), **give** (79d,123a)

- GI -   **Agib** (12a,42d), **agio** (52c,60a,101c,123a), **Agis** (86d), **Egil** (107d), **egis** (14b,d,115a,124d,144b,154a,161a)

- - GI   **Bugi** (191), **hagi** (84b), **jogi** (76d), **magi** (123c), **Magi** (95b,116c, 183a), **ragi** (28b), **sugi** (84b), **vagi** (38b), **yogi** (76d)

G - - I   **gabi** (162a), **gali** (6c), **gazi**, **Geri** (183c), **goai** (106d,168c), **gobi, Gobi** (42d), **goli** (105c), **Guti**, **gyri** (22d,131b)

GJ - -   **Gjoa** (144d)

G - - J   **gunj** (70c)

G - - K   **gawk** (146d), **gink** (48b), **gowk** (146d)

GL - -   **glad** (85c), **gled** (19a,52a,87a), **glee** (99a,150b), **glen** (43c), **glia** (106c), **glib** (58d,149a,177c), **glim**, **glis** (45c), **glom** (155d,160d, 178c), **glow** (144c), **glub**, **glue** (7b,156a), **glug**, **glum** (102c,159a), **glut** (52c,70a,137c,159d)

- GL -   **agla** (7a), **iglu** (51c,149b), **ogle** (9d,53c,91a,93d,148c)

- - GL   **gagl** (160b)

G - - L   **gaal** (23b,174d), **Gael** (28a,96c,138d), **gagl** (160b), **gail** (23b,174d), **Gail** (183d), **gall** (19a,28c,29b,82c,160c,176a), **gaol** (123d), **Gaol** (164a), **Gaul** (10a,60d,63c), **geal** (47d,163c), **gill** (22d), **girl**, **goal** (8b,109b,120b,125d), **goel** (15a,75c), **Goll, goul** (102a), **gowl** (102a, 140d,185b), **gull** (32d,41c,42a,72c,99b,141a)

G - - M   **Garm** (178c), **germ** (99c,134d), **Geum** (76b), **glim, glom** (155d, 160d,178c), **glum** (102c,159a), **gram** (29d,99b,148d,160d,180a), **Gram, grim** (156a), **grum** (102c), **Guam**

GN - -   **gnar** (72a), **gnat** (59a,81b,99c), **gnaw** (20a,107a,178b)

- GN -   **agni** (88a,89c), **Agni** (56d,68b)

- - GN   **sign** (121c,146c)

G - - N   **gain** (7a,b,124a,181d), **Gaon** (85b), **garn** (67d,185b), **gean** (29c), **gein** (67d), **glen** (43c), **Goan, goon** (157c,163c), **gown, gran, grin, guan** (151b), **Gwyn** (40c,50b)

GO - -   **goad** (80b,154b), **goaf** (104b), **goai** (106d,168c), **goal** (8b,109b, 120b,125d), **Goan, goat** (135a), **gobi, Gobi** (42d), **gobo** (84d), **goby** (57d), **goel** (15a,75c), **goer, goff** (32d), **goga** (24a), **gogo** (16b,24a, 149c), **Gogo** (191), **gola** (27b,40c,70c,157a), **gold, golf** (154a) **goli** (105c), **Goll, Golo** (191), **Goma** (191), **Gona** (106d), **Gond, gone** (6b,15c,42c,44c,114d), **gong, good, goof, goon** (157c,163c), **Goop** (107d), **goor, gora** (81c), **gore** (115d,117c,154c,169c), **gory, gosh, Goth** (16c,163d), **goul** (102a), **gour** (112c,181c), **gout, gowk** (146d), **gowl** (102a,140d,185b), **gown**, **Goya** (151d)

- GO -   **agog** (47b,52c,86b), **agon** (12c,36c,41b,55d),71b), **egol** (11b), **Igor** (135d), **Ogor** (170d)

- - GO   **ango** (171a), **Argo** (12c,36b,c), **bago** (13d), **bogo** (117a, 168c), **Bogo** (191), **bygo** (114c), **Dago, ergo** (164b), **gogo** (16b,24a,

149c), **Gogo** (191), **Hugo** (63a,96a), **Iago** (54b,111d,143c), **kago** (113a), **Iago** (83b,152b), **mogo** (74b), **Pogo** (121c), **sago** (54c, 59b,113b,125b,155c), **sego** (24b,25a,92b,174c), **upgo** (13c), **zogo** (136a)

G - - O   gajo (107c), **Gajo, Gano** (132d), **gapo** (60a), **Garo** (88c), **gilo** (48a), **giro** (38c,83c,167c), **gobo** (84d), **gogo** (16b,24a,149c), **Gogo** (191), **Golo** (191), **grao** (189), **guao** (168c,169b), **Gulo** (183c), **gyro** (34d)

- GP -   **Ogpu** (135d)

G - - P   gamp (172a), **gasp** (113c), **gaup, gawp, gimp** (169d), **Goop** (107d), **gulp** (46a,79d,160a), **Gump** (43b), **grip** (159a)

GR - -   grab (105b,142a,149b), **grad** (28b), **Graf** (37c,66b,67a,107c,186b), **gram** (29d,99b,148d,160d,180a), **grao** (189), **gras** (78b), **gray** (33c, 77c), **Gray** (50c), **gres** (156d), **grew, grey** (33c), **grid** (17a,70d, 119b,156d), **grig** (38c,70d,93a), **grim** (156a), **grin, grip** (159a), **gris** (61d), **grit** (137a,b), **grog** (92d,153d), **gros** (47a,53d,146c), **Gros** (63a), **grot** (27d), **grow** (154b), **grub** (43c,88d), **grum** (102c), **Grus** (36b,c,38b)

- GR -   agra (26d,34d), **Agra** (161b), **agri** (89b), **agro** (149d), **ogre** (67a, 102a)

G - - R   gaur (112c,181c), **gear** (32c,167b), **Ghor** (174b), **gier** (47b), **gnar** (72a), **goer, goor, gour** (112c,181c) **guar** (46c,59d), **guhr** (47d)

- - GS   eggs (112a), **togs** (32c)

G - - S   gaus (67a), **gens** (42d,132d), **Gens, Ghes** (193), **ghos** (30b), **glis** (45c), **Glis, gras** (78b), **gres** (156d), **gris** (61d), **gros** (47a,53d,146c), **Gros** (63a), **Grus** (36b,c,38b), **gyps, Gyps** (71d)

- - GT   togt (77c), **Vogt**

G - - T   gait (96b,179a), **galt, gaut** (88b,103d,132a), **geat** (77d,101a), **Geat** (138a), **gelt** (101c), **gent, gest** (7c,41d,52d,133c), **gett** (44d), **ghat** (32d,88b,103d,132a), **gift** (123a), **gilt** (69c,77c,151b), **girt** (50a), **gist** (95c,118c), **glut** (52c,70a,137c,159d), **gnat** (59a,81b,99c), **goat** (135d), **grit** (137a,b), **grot** (27d), **gust**

GU - -   Guam, guan (151b), **guao** (168c,169b), **guar** (46c,59d), **gufa** (21b, 99a), **guff, gugu, Guha** (191), **guhr** (47d), **guib** (11a), **gula** (90a, 101a,165b), **gulf** (6c), **gull** (32d,41c,42a,72c,99b,141a), **Gulo** (183c), **gulp** (46a,79d,160a), **Gump** (43b), **guna** (106a,137b), **gunj** (70c), **guru** (77b), **gush** (35a,154c), **gust, Guti, guze** (128d)

- GU -   agua (152d,166c,178c), **ague** (30a,55d,95c), **ogum** (82b)

- - GU   degu (132c), **fugu** (84b), **gugu, kagu** (106c), **Pegu** (24c,102a,127d)

G - - U   genu (6b,18a,87a,89c), **gugu, guru** (77b)

GW - -   Gwyn (40c,50b)

G - - W   glow (144c), **gnaw** (20a,107a,178b), **grew, grow** (154b)

GY - -   gybe (144c), **gyle** (23b,174d), **gyne** (34b,55b,183c), **gyps, Gyps** (71d), **gyre** (31b,171b), **gyri** (22d,131b), **gyro** (34d), **gyve** (55d, 143b)

- - GY   algy, **Algy** (96b), **bogy** (153a), **cagy** (178b), **dogy** (46d,103c), **edgy** (106c), **eggy** (185d), **fogy, logy** (46d), **Nagy** (78d), **orgy** (26d,130d, 137c), **pogy** (57a,88a,98d,103c), **sagy**

G - - Y   gaby (59c,146d), Gaby, gapy, Gary, gazy, goby (57d), gory, gray (33c,77c), Gray (50c), grey (33c)

G - - Z   Geez (6c,51d), Ghuz (171a)

HA - -   Haab (97d), haaf (57d), haak (57b,178a), haar (139c), haba (151d), Habe (191), hack (40a,77c,184d) hade (66a,148c,173c), hadj (98b,118a), haec (90a,164c), haem (122b), haft (76d), hagg, hagi (84b), haha (55c,159c), haik (57b,65b,108a), hail (6d,15a,71d), hair (56b,164d), haje (33a,48d), hake (57a,b), hakh (46d), hako (115b), haku (86d), hala (112b), hale (125b), Hale (9d,131a), half (101a), hall (37b,114d), halm, halo (14d,31b,92a,107b,131d), Hals (47a), halt (13b,28a,38d,156d), hami (78a), hand (60c,114c,115d,184c), hang (160a), hank (147c), Hano (125b), Hans (66d,96a), hant (67a), Hapi (66a,107b,136a), hapu (106d), Harb (191), hard (109b), hare (91b,132c), hark (92d), harl (16b,56b,59a), harm (40b,81a), harp (105a,129a), hart (41d,154d), hase (74d) hash, hasp (31d, 54d,153c), hast, hate (6a,43a), hath, Hati (48d), haul (27b,45d), have, hawk (19c,115c), hayz, haze (100c,174d), hazy (174b)

- HA -   Ahab (18c,26c,85b,86d,100d,116a,180b), Ahaz (86d), Bhar (191), bhat (80c), chaa (162b), chab (184a), Chad (158b), chai (72d), cham (20a,29d), Cham (8c), chan (26c,130c), chap (55b), char (24d,26c, 170b), chat (9b,19c,161c), chaw (97c), chay (48a,128d), dhak (48a, 169a), dhal (12b), dhan (124c), dhao (24c), Dhar, dhaw (125a), ghat (32d,88b,103d,132a), khan (7c,26c,81b,93d,116c,123c,130c, 166c), khar (189), khas (153a), khat (105d), Phad (155b), shad (27d,57a,b,c), shag (73b,105b,161d,166d), shah (116c), sham (41c, 55b,60d,80a,123a,b,146d), Shan (13c,80d,88c,101d), shap, shat (87d), shaw (164b), Shaw (50c,53d), shay (110c), Thai (146a), than (35b), thar (68a,76d), that (42b,124b,129c), thaw, wham (157c), what (129c), whau (107a,168c)

- - HA   agha (35a,171a), Akha (86a,c), Asha (191), Azha (155b), epha (75c), Guha (191), haha (55c,159c), Isha (174a), kaha (123d), maha (28c,88c,136d), moha (42b,83d), ocha (189), paha (67b), poha (74c), saha, taha (179b), tcha (162c), Usha (16a,150c),

H - - A   haba (151d), Haba, haha (55c,159c), hala (112b), Hela (93c), Hera (69c,85d,110b,126b,186b,d), hila (53c), Hima (191), hoga (144b), hoja (166b), hola (74c,152b), hora (22a,40b), Hova (95a), Hoya (14d), Hsia (30b,47c), huia (19a,106d), hula (74b), Hupa (192), hura (20a,137a), Hura, Hyla (10a,166d,169b)

H - - B   Haab (97d), Harb (191), herb (58b,158b), hobb (124b), hubb (118b)

H - - C   haec (90a,164c)

H - - D   hand (60c,114c,115d,184c), hard (109b), head (29d), heed (14c, 75b,109b), held, herd (39a,46c,72a), Hild, hind (15b,41d,45a), hold (95c,124c,130d), hood (38a,74d), hued

HE - -   head (29d), heaf (144a), heal, heap (117d), hear (75b,c,92d), heat, Hebe (39c,69c,186b), heck (100a), heed (14c,75b,109b), heel, Heep (41a,43b), heer (47a,184b,185b), heft (179d), Heft, hegh, Hehe (191), heil (74b), hein (52c,61c), heir, Hela (93c), held, helm (144d,165d), help (14a), hemi (122c), hemo (34a,122b), hemp (26a, 37a,56a,133d), hens (121d), Hera (69c,85d,110b),126b,186b,d), herb (58b,158b), herd (39a,46c,72a), here, herl (16b,59a), hero

305

(42b,124d,137b), **Hero** (90c), **Herr** (66c), **hers** (124c), **hest** (35a), **Heth** (77c), **hevi** (111d), **hewn**

- HE -   **ahem, Ahet** (49a,102a), **ahey** (52c), **bhel** (126d), **chee** (189), **chef, chek** (59c), **Chen** (149b), **cher** (61b), **chew** (97c), **chez** (14b,61a), **eheu** (52c), **ghee** (24d), **Gheg** (8c), **Ghes** (193), **Hehe** (191), **Khem** (113c), **khet** (188), **phew** (52c), **rhea** (37a,56a,111d), **Rhea** (19b,68d, 87c,103c,186b), **Rhee** (87c), **shea** (25a,168c,d), **shed** (27a,90c,101b, 144b), **shee** (82b), **Shem** (107c), **Shen** (68a), **sher** (65d,165c), **shew** (44c), **Thea** (162c), **theb** (188), **thee** (124b), **them** (124b), **then, thew** (104c), **they** (124b), **whee, when** (180d), **whet** (143c,156b), **whew, whey** (100a)

- - HE   **ache** (79a,112d,185b), **Hehe** (191), **Hohe** (192), **tche** (13d,30b,105a)

H - - E   **Habe** (191), **hade** (66a,148c,173c), **haje** (33a,48d), **hake** (57a,b), **hale** (125b), **Hale** (9d,131a), **hare** (91b,132c), **hase** (74d), **hate** (6a, 43a), **have, haze** (100c,174d), **Hebe** (39c,69c,186b), **Hehe** (191), **here, hide** (53a), **hike, hipe** (185a), **hire** (49d,50b,91b,130a), **hive** (17c), **Hohe** (192), **hole** (6c,11b,110d,118c,147a), **home, hone** (110a,143c,180d), **hope** (13d,52d), **hose** (156c), **hove** (92a,157d), **howe** (77d), **Howe** (17a,82a), **huge, hule** (23a,134c), **Hume** (50c), **huse** (180c), **hyde** (188), **Hyde** (45a), **hyke, hyle** (97c), **hype** (185a)

H - - F   **haaf** (57d), **half** (101a), **heaf** (144a), **hoof** (173a), **huff** (58a)

H - - G   **hagg, hang** (160a), **hing** (13c), **hogg** (144a), **hong** (30b), **hung**

- - HH   **sahh** (188)

H - - H   **hakh** (46d), **hash, hath, hegh, Heth** (77c), **high, hish, hoch,** (52c, 66c), **Hoch, hoth, Hoth** (20c), **Hugh** (96a), **hunh?, hush** (17b,146c)

HI - -   **hick** (185d), **hide** (53a), **hien** (30b), **hier** (63a,185d), **high, hike, hiku** (57a,106d,138a), **hila** (53c), **Hild, hill, hilo** (74c), **hilt** (73c), **Hima** (191), **hind** (15b,41d,45a), **hing** (13c), **hino** (106d,168c), **hint** (9a,39c,159a), **hipe** (185a), **hire** (49d,50b,91b,130a), **hiro, hish, hiss** (146a), **hist** (25c,93d), **hive** (17c)

- HI -   **Ahir** (27b), **Bhil** (191), **chia** (136d), **chib** (167a), **chic** (148d), **chid, ch'ih** (188), **chil, chin, Chin** (30b), **chip** (69d), **chir** (29b,116d), **chit** (67b,98c,108b,116c,177c), **chiv** (87a), **jhil, ohia** (74c,168c), **Ohio, Phil** (96b), **phit** (24b), **phiz** (54a), **Rhin, shih** (189), **Shik** (171a), **shim** (91d,144c,162a,179d), **shin** (91a,d,140b,143c), **ship, shir** (36d, 65d,165c), **thin** (43b,c,148b), **this** (42b,124b), **Whig, whim** (26c, 54c,108c), **whin** (64c,70a,132b,181d), **whip** (58c,88d), **whir** (25c, 181a), **whit** (166c), **whiz** (25c)

- - HI   **bahi** (60c), **Bahi, pahi** (21b,26a), **tchi, Tchi, tshi, Tshi** (69c)

H - - I   **hagi** (84b), **hami** (78a), **Hapi** (66a,107b,136a), **Hati** (48d), **heli** (74b), **hemi** (122c), **hevi** (111d), **Holi** (77a), **hopi** (33c), **Hopi** (12c, 102c,125b), **hoti**

H - - J   **hadj** (98b,118a)

H - - K   **haak** (57b,178a), **hack** (40a,77c,184d), **haik** (57b,65b,108a), **hank** (147c), **hark** (92d), **hawk** (19c,115c), **heck** (100a), **hick** (185d), **hock** (91a,115b,182b,c), **hoek** (39d), **honk** (70a), **hook** (27b,39d), **howk** (139b), **huck** (167d), **hulk** (144d,173d), **hunk, husk** (53a,78d, 142a)

HL - -   **Hler** (141a)

- - HL buhl (81a), kohl (53c), kuhl (53c)

H - - L hail (6d,15a,71d), hall (37b,114d), harl (16b 56b,59a), haul (27b, 45d), heal, heel, herl (16b,59a), hill, howl (39b), hull (141d,142a, 144c,d), hurl (167c)

H - - M haem (122b), halm, harm (40b,81a), helm (144d,165d), holm (77d, 82d,109a)

- HN - ohne (66d,183b)

- - HN behn (137d), fohn (182b), John (11c,96a,121a,186b)

H - - N hein (52c,61c), hewn, hien (30b), hoen (189), hoon (190), horn (11a, 105a,170b,182a), hymn (150c)

HO - - hoar (63d,71a,181a), hoax (41c,122a), hobb (124b), hobo (168a, 174b), hoch (52c,66c), hock (91a,115b,182b,c), hoek (39d), hoen (189), hoer, hoey (114c), hoga (144b), hogg (144a), Hohe (192), hoja (166b), hoju (84b), hola (74c,152b), hold (95c,124c,130d), hole (6c,11b,110d,118c,147a), Holi (77a), holm (77d,82d,109a), holt (36d,119b,184b), holy, home, homo (122d), homy (38b), hone (110a,143c,180d), hong (30b), honk (70a), hood (38a,74d), hoof (173a), hook (27b,39d), hoon (190), hoop (181b), hoot (112c), hope (13d,52d), hopi (33c), Hopi (12c,102c,125b), hops (17c), hora (22a, 40b), horn (11a,105a,170b,182a), hors (62b), hose (156c), host (13a,51d,104c), Hoth (20c), hoti, hour, Hova (95a), hove (92a, 157d), howe (77d), Howe (17a,82a), howk (139b), howl (39b), Hoya (14d)

- HO - Ahom (88c), ahoy (106a), b'hoy (134b), chob (23c), chol (118d), Chol (192), chop (98a), chor (164b), chou (61b), Chou (30b), chow (45a), choy (48a,128c), dhow (88d,111c,175d), Ghor (174b), ghos (30b), khot', mhor (180b), ohoy (106a), phon (94a), phoo, phos, phot (173b), rhob (64a,85c), Shoa (6c), shod, shoe (166a), shoo (46b,67a,138b), shop, shoq (169a), shor (136d), Shor (162b), shot (9d,43d,90c,174d), shou (41d), show (42b,44c,96b), thob (128a), Thor (7c,68c,99c,100c,109c,165b), Thos (84a,181c), thou (124b), whoa (156d), whom (42b), whoo

- - HO baho (122a), boho (117a,179d), coho (136d), echo (130b,d), Echo (105d), icho (67b), kiho (82a), moho (19a,78a), otho (133a), paho (122a), peho (19b,102c,106d), Saho (6c), soho!, Soho (93c), toho (79a)

H - - O hako (115b), halo (14d,31b,92a,107b,131d), Hano (125b), hemo (34a,122b), hero (42b,124d,137b), Hero (90c), hilo (74c), hino (106d,168c), hiro, hobo (168a,174b), homo (168a,174b), Hugo (63a,96a), huso (180c), hypo (117b)

H - - P harp (105a,129a), hasp (31d,54d,153c), heap (117d), Heep (41a, 43b), help (14a), hemp (26a,37a,56a,133d), hoop (181b), hump (124d)

- HR - Shri (17c,166c)

- - HR Bohr (14b,40d,138c), buhr (180d), Duhr (155b), guhr (47d), lehr (67c,112a), mahr (103a), mohr (65d), rohr (72d), Ruhr, sehr (66d), tahr (68a,76d), tehr (27c,68a)

H - - R haar (139c), hair (56b,164d), hear (75b,c,92d), heer (47a,184b, 185b), heir, Herr (66c), hier (63a,185d), Hier (141a), hoar (63d,

       71a,181a), **hoer, hour**

HS - - **Hsia** (30b,47c)

H - - S **Hals** (47a), **Hans** (66d,96a), **hens** (121d), **hers** (124c), **hiss** (146a), **hops** (17c), **hors** (62b), **hyps**

- - HT **acht** (66c), **baht** (146a)

H - - T **haft** (76d), **halt** (13b,28a,38d,156d), **hant** (67a), **hart** (41d,154d), **hast, heat, heft** (179d), **Heft, hest** (35a), **hilt** (73c), **hint** (9a,39c, 159a), **hist** (25c,93d), **holt** (36d,119b,184b), **hoot** (112c), **host** (13a, 51d,104c), **hunt** (141c), **hurt**

HU - - **hubb** (118b), **huck** (167d), **hued, huff** (58a), **huge, Hugh** (96a), **Hugo** (63a,96a), **huia** (19a,106d), **hula** (74b), **hule** (23a,134c), **hulk** (144d,173d), **hull** (141d,142a,144c,d), **hulu** (55b), **Hume** (50c), **hump** (124d), **hung, hunh?, hunk, hunt** (141c), **Hupa** (192), **hura** (20a,137a), **Hura, hurl** (167c), **hurt, huse** (180c), **hush** (17b,146c), **husk** (53a,78d,142a), **huso** (180c), **huzz**

- HU - **ahum, bhut** (67a), **chub** (40c,154c), **Chud** (191), **chug** (53a), **chum,** (38d), **Chun** (30c), **chut!, Ghuz** (171a), **jhum, Phud** (110b), **phut** (24b), **Phut** (110b), **rhum** (8c), **Rhus** (159a), **shul** (161a), **shun** (15a, 51b,52a), **shut, thud, thug** (65a), **thus** (149c), **whun** (64c,70a)

- - HU **ichu** (10b,70d), **jehu** (46b), **Jehu** (18c), **kahu** (14d), **Oahu, Rahu** (42b,48b), **sahu** (153d), **tchu**

H - - U **haku** (86d), **hapu** (106d), **hiku** (57a,106d,138a), **hoju** (84b), **hulu** (55b)

- HV - **IHVH** (159d), **JHVH** (159d), **YHVH** (159d)

- HW - **JHWH** (159d), **YHWH** (159d)

H - - X **hoax** (41c,122c)

HY - - **hyde** (188), **Hyde** (45a), **hyke, Hyla** (10a,166d,169b), **hyle** (97c), **hymn** (150c), **hype** (185a), **hypo** (117b), **hyps**

- HY - **whyo** (59d,65a)

- - HY **achy, ashy** (113a,178a)

H - - Y **hazy** (174b), **hoey** (114c), **holy, homy** (38b)

H - - Z **Hayz, huzz**

IA - - **Iago** (54b,111d,143c), **Ialu** (48d), **Iamb** (59c)

- IA - **bias** (43b,123a), **diad** (113a), **dial** (25c), **dian** (46c,130d,170b), **Dian** (68d,69a,c,102b), **Diau** (192), **fiat** (35a,41d,48c,111b,137a), **Fiat** (83c), **kiak** (51c), **Liam** (181d), **liar** (98d), **Lias** (66a), **miam** (14d), **mian** (97c,147b,166b), **Miao** (30a,b), **mias** (111a), **Mias, miau** (27b,99b), **miaw** (27b,99b), **Nias** (82d), **Piaf** (63c), **piat** (11a), **piay** (98b), **rial** (190), **siak** (72d), **sial** (112a), **Siam** (163d,181a), **Tiam, tiao, tiar** (39a,75a,121a), **vial** (148c)

- - IA **Abia** (18d,137a), **akia** (74c), **amia** (22c,170d), **apia** (121b), **aria** (8b,98c,150a,c), **Asia** (48a), **chia** (136d), **Elia** (88a,115d), **eria** (13d, 146d), **Fria, Gaia** (47d,69a), **glia** (106c), **Hsia** (30b,47c), **huia** (19a, 106d), **ilia** (21d,77b,115d), **inia** (9b,109b), **Inia** (28c,45b), **ixia** (37a), **Maia** (76b,109a,153b,155b,177c), **Naia** (33a), **obia** (55d), **ohia** (74c, 168c), **okia** (190), **raia** (107d), **Raia** (147b), **Soia, tsia** (162c), **Uria** (14c,16d)

308

I - - A **idea** (54c,108c,124a,164d), **ijma** (103b), **ikra** (27d), **ilia** (21d,77b, 115d), **Inca** (14b,30a), **inga** (145d), **inia** (9b,109b), **Inia** (28c,45b), **Inka** (193), **lola, lona** (28a,82d), **iota** (71a,85c,91c,114c,166c,176a, 180d), **Iowa** (193), **Irra** (68c,178a), **isba** (135c), **Isha** (174a), **Itea** (145d,160c,181d), **Itza** (192), **ixia** (37a)

IB - - **Ibad** (191), **Iban** (47c), **ibex** (67d,68a), **ibid** (80a,117a,137a), **ibis** (48d,49a,177b), **ibit** (117a)

- IB - **bibb** (97c,146b), **bibi** (87d), **dibs** (70c), **gibe** (8a,42c,84d,100d,138c, 144c,149b), **jibb, jibe** (8a,33b,35d,37b,42c,100d,138c,144c,149b), **kibe, kiby** (29a), **nibs** (116c), **ribe** (139a), **Tibu** (191)

- - IB **Abib** (102a,b), **Adib** (155b), **Agib** (12a,42d), **chib** (167a), **crib** (96b, 120d), **drib** (46b), **frib** (43d), **glib** (58d,149a,177c), **guib** (11a), **snib** (54d,93c), **stib** (19b,47a,137a)

I - - B **iamb** (59c)

IC - - **ical** (158c), **icer, icho** (67b), **ichu** (10b,70d), **icon** (79d,92b,136a)

- IC - **aich** (9a), **bice** (20d,117d), **Bice** (27b), **dice** (65a), **dick** (43a,55b), **Dick** (96b), **fico** (169d), **hick** (185d), **kick, lick, mica** (82c,100b, 146c), **mice, mick** (82c), **mico** (97a), **nice** (54d,119c,130c), **Nice** (98c), **nick** (30c,108b), **pica** (66b,95b,172c), **pice** (190), **Pici** (19c, 184a), **pick, pico** (65a,152c), **Pict** (23c,47d), **rice, Rice** (46a), **rich, rick** (74d,117d,154d), **sice** (71d,147b), **sick, tice** (9a,38c,51a,185d), **tick** (12b,20d,97c), **vice** (31d,158a), **wick**

- - IC **amic** (9d), **chic** (148d) **cric** (131c), **epic** (76b,120a), **eric** (115b), **Eric** (71d,96a,107d,138a,164a,176b), **idic** (79b), **laic** (32b,90b,107d, 124a,141d), **odic** (79c,120a), **olic** (158b), **otic** (14c,d,47b), **saic** (86b, 91d,175d), **Udic** (108a), **Uvic** (70c)

I - - C **idic** (79b)

ID - - **Idas** (27b,71c), **idea** (54c,108c,124a,164d), **idee** (61d), **idem** (89d, 164a), **Iden** (76a), **ideo** (34b,d,164d), **ides** (41a,b,133a), **idic** (79b), **idio** (34b,c), **Idjo** (191), **idle** (174b,c,178c), **idly, idol** (48c,54c,55a 75b,79d,112d,130b,184d), **Idun** (107d), **idyl** (114d), **Idyo** (191), **Idzo** (191)

- ID - **Aida** (110d,175c), **aide** (7b,14a,75d), **bide** (47c,50b,130a,158b, 162a,177b), **dido** (11b,26c,65a,122a), **Dido** (27a,172c), **eide** (119c), **fide, Gide** (63a) **hide** (53a), **Lida** (183c), **Lido** (83d,175b), **mide** (110a), **Midi** (151b), **nide** (23c,72a,106c,116d), **nidi** (106c), **Ridd** (94a), **ride** (46b,85c), **sida** (37a,126c,170a), **side** (13d,22a,b,54a, 58a,89a,161b), **sidi** (103b,166b), **sidy** (123b), **tide** (39d,75d,109c, 141c,159d), **tidy** (106a,111b), **Vida** (183c), **vide** (89d,126a,142a), **wide** (133d), **widu** (102d)

- - ID **acid** (151a,162a), **amid** (9d,50a), **arid** (46c,85a), **avid** (47b,71a, 186b), **Beid** (155b), **caid** (35a,151d,152b), **chid, Enid** (13b,25d,66b, 163a,183c), **grid** (17a,70d,119b,156d), **ibid** (80a,117a,137a), **imid** (29c), **irid** (38d,67c), **kaid** (29d,66a), **laid, maid** (45b,142d), **naid** (63c), **olid** (55d,60c,148d,157d), **ooid** (48d), **Ovid** (132d,133b), **oxid** (112c), **paid** (129c), **qaid** (35a), **quid** (39b,166b), **raid** (59d,80c), **said** (174c), **Said** (42d,101a,121b), **seid** (103b), **Seid** (42d,101a, 171a), **skid** (148b), **slid, uvid** (101a), **void** (11a,49d,108d), **zoid**

I - - D **Ibad** (191), **ibid** (80a,117a,137a), **imid** (29c), **Irad** (18d), **irid** (38d, 67c)

- IE - bien (63a,140c,179a,180a), bier (33b,66b), dieb (84a), diem (89b, 116a), dier, dies (41b,89b), diet (14a,54c,84c,91b,176a), Dieu (61d), fief (55d), gier (47b), hien (30b), hier (63a,185d), kief (75d), kiel (128d,134d), Kiel (25d), kier (20c,174d), Kiev, lied (66d,150b), lief (181d), lien (65c,91a,124c), lieu (118c,155d), mien (11c,17b, 26d,44c,96b), pied (96c,103c,114b,117c,154a,174d), pien (13b), pier (23a,88b,180c), piet (29b,95b), Riel (129a), riem (76c,112c, 157c,164d), rien (62b), rier (180b), sier (57a,118b), tied, tien (147d), tier (118a,134b), vier (66c), view (93d,138b), wiel (140d, 180d), wies (185a)

- - IE Abie (96b,107a), Amie (61d), Brie (29c), Erie (82c,87d), Okie (99d), Opie (50c), plie (32c,59b), soie (62c), unie (173a)

I - - E idee (61d), idle (174b,c,178c), ille (89b,d,163d), imbe (37a,56a, 133d), inde, inee (120b), Inge (24d,67d,117c,119c), inre (35d,80a), lole (52a,76b,123c), lone (24b,88d,94d), ipse (44d,89c), Irae (43c), isle (8b,53c,81d,82d,86b,88a), ixle (56a)

IF - - ifil (117a,168c)

- IF - biff, fife (59a,105a), gift (123a), jiff (101c), kiff (88c), life (19a,177a), lift (49b), miff (44c), nife (37a), piff (24b), rife (6b,c, 39d,123b), riff (131d), Riff (18b,102c), rift (30c,32a,58a,110d), sift (140d,142c,146b), tiff (126b), wife (154a)

- - IF alif (12b), arif (127d), coif (73a), cuif (139a,d,140c), Enif (155b), kaif (88c), keif (75d), Leif (107d), luif, naif (74b,105d), waif (157b)

IG - - iglu (51c,149b), Igor (135d)

- IG - biga (171d), giga (56a,105a), high, migg (96c), nigh (106a), riga (118b), Riga, sigh, sign (121c,146c), tige (118a), wigg

- - IG brig (72b,106a,144d), crig (20d), grig (38c,70d,93a), prig (112a, 116c), snig (45d), swig (46a,72c), Teig (96a), trig (106a,148d,154b, 169d), twig, Whig

I - - G ilog (132a,161b)

IH - - IHVH (159d)

- IH - kiho (82a)

- - IH ch'ih (188), shih (189)

I - - H IHVH (159d), inch, itch, Ivah (18d)

II - - iiwi (19a,74b)

- II - Ilin (188), Riis (9d)

- - II alii (74c,134c), apii (74c), Boii (191), helii (74b), Ubii (191)

I - - I iiwi (19a,74b), immi (189), impi (86a), Inti (159b), Ioni (192)

IJ - - ijma (103b)

- IJ - bija (168c), Ilja (57a,90d,173a)

IK - - ikat (53b,159a), ikmo (18b), ikon (79d,136a), ikra (27d)

- IK - bike, bikh (120b), dika (23a), dike (49c,91d), Dike (78a), fike (139c), hike, hiku (57a,106d,138a), kiki (27b), kiku (30d), like (13c,37d,146d), mike, Mike (96b), Nike (69c,100c,182d), pika (93a,128a,132c), pike (57a,b,76c,120b,153a), piki (95c), piky,

310

rikk (49a), **sika** (41d,84b), **Sikh** (77b), **tike** (29d), **Tiki** (120c)

- - IK **Atik** (155b), **Efik** (191), **haik** (57b,65b,108a), **kaik** (96c), **naik, raik** (188,189), **Seik** (77b), **Shik** (171a)

I - - K **Irak** (99a,d), **irok** (55b)

IL - - **ilex** (77d), **ilia** (21d,77b,115d), **ille** (89b,d,163d), **ills** (170a), **ilog** (132a,161b), **ilot** (82d), **ilus** (88d,170b)

- IL - **aile** (62b,63a,182c,d), **bile** (30c), **bilk** (29b,41c,42a), **bill** (17b,147a), **Bill, bilo** (131b), **dill** (13a,117c), **dilo** (120d,168c), **eild** (138d,140a), **file** (13a,127d), **fili, fill** (109b), **film** (164b), **filo, fils** (62d,150b), **gila** (93b), **gild** (14a,49c,69c,98b), **gill** (22d), **gilo** (48a), **gilt** (69c,77c,151b,185d), **hila** (53c), **Hild, hill, hilo** (74c), **hilt** (73c), **Jill** (183d), **jilt, kile** (189), **kill** (38c), **kiln** (15d,112a), **kilo** (99b, 122d), **kilt, Lila** (183c), **lill** (15d,118a), **lilt** (93a,131a,147a), **lily, mila** (188), **mild** (32a,66a), **mile** (64c), **milk, mill** (126c), **milo** (70b, 87c,150d), **Milo, milt** (153d), **nile** (33c,71d), **Nile** (106b), **nill** (173d), **oily** (110b,172c), **pile** (45d,75b,117c), **pili** (34b,108d), **pill, pily, rile** (10c,d,82c,125a,156b,176a), **rill** (23c,102b,132a,148d,157b), **rily** (176a), **silk** (53b,179c), **sill** (45c,76c,165a,182b), **silo** (59a, 156d), **silt** (104b), **tile** (31d,56d,72b,95b,133c,163c), **till** (39c,101c, 173d), **tilt** (26b,d,166a), **vila** (54b), **vile** (16c,56c), **vili** (54b), **Vili** (109c), **vill** (176b), **vily** (54b), **wild** (38b,173d), **wile** (13b,41c,157b, 169c), **wilk** (65c,96d,141b), **will** (18b,43a,163c,177c), **wilt** (46b), **wily** (13b,38b,39c)

- - IL **amil** (45a,48a,185c), **anil** (47c,80d,180b), **aril** (142a), **axil** (10c), **bail** (43c), **Bhil** (191), **boil, ceil** (92c,112a), **chil, coil** (39d,171c, 185a), **Dail** (49a,82b,c), **deil** (139b), **Egil** (107d), **Emil** (96a), **evil** (79c,95d,147a,181a,185c), **fail, foil** (15d,55c,165b), **gail** (23b, 174d), **Gail** (183d), **hail** (6d,15a,71d), **ifil** (117a,168c), **ipil** (117a, 168c,169a), **Ixil** (192), **jail** (123d), **jhil, kail** (8c,22a,25a,79b), **mail** (12d,99b,121c), **moil** (46c,184c), **nail** (31d,54d,141d,161d,173a), **Neil** (96a), **noil** (87c,178b), **pail Phil** (96b), **rail** (16b,19b,c,37a,97b, 138c,150c,177b), **roil** (44c,104b,156b,170d,176a), **sail** (144c,185a), **skil** (57a), **soil** (154d,159a,163c), **tail** (11d,27d,59b,143b), **teil** (92b, c,168c), **toil** (46c,184c), **vail** (94b,124a,174b), **veil** (74d,76c), **wail** (39b,88a), **ypil** (117a,168c)

I - - L **ical** (158c), **idol** (48c,54c,55a,75b,79d,112d,130b,184d), **idyl** (114d), **ifil** (117a,168c), **ipil** (117a,168c,169a), **itol** (158b), **Ixil** (192)

IM - - **imam** (25c,102d,103a), **imbe** (37a,56a,133d), **Imer, imid** (29c), **immi** (189), **impi** (86a)

- IM - **cima** (83b,c), **dime, gime** (77d), **gimp** (169d), **Hima** (191), **lima** (17b,152b,174d), **Lima** (31b), **limb** (12d,22d), **lime** (25b,27d,31b, 33c,102d,168c), **limn** (45d,121c), **limp** (58a,81a,177d), **limu** (141c), **limy** (176d), **mima** (185d), **mime** (24a,71b,85a,100a), **Mime** (131d, 148d), **mimi** (14d), **Mimi** (87b,110d,125b,183d), **nimb** (31b, 73b,92a,107b,131d), **oime** (8b), **pima** (37c), **Pima** (192), **rima** (23a,30c,32a,58a,110d), **rime** (30c,36a,58a,63d,77c), **rimu** (79d,106d,129a,168c), **rimy** (63d), **sima** (132b) **sime** (101d), **Simi** (82d), **simp** (59c,146d), **time** (47a,131a), **Yima** (84a,116b,c), **Zimb** (6c)

- - IM Anim (18d), Akim (135d,191), alim (103b,162c), brim, Clim (12b), duim (188), Emim (67a,100d), frim (58d), glim, grim (156a), maim (43d,81a,105c), prim (156b), Seim (120c), shim (91d,144c,162a, 179d), skim (67c), slim (148b,160a), swim (58c), trim (40a,106a, 154b,160a,165c,169d), urim (18d,23a,110a), whim (26c,54c,108c), zaim (170d)

I - - M idem (89d,164a), imam (25c,102d,103a), item (6d,13b,42d,51a, 90d,92d,107a,113d,114c)

IN - - inar (65b), Inca (14b,30a), inch, inde, inee (120b), Inez (45c,183c), inga (145d,170a), Inge (24d,67d,117c,119c), inia (9b,109b), Inia (28c,45b), Inka (193), inky (20b), inly, inre (35d,80a), inro (84b,c, 106c), Inti (159b), into (123a,183b)

- IN - aine (49b,62c), Aine (142c), Aino (84a,c), aint, Ainu (84a,c), bina (77a), bind (33b,165c), bine (145b,156a,171c,176b), bing, binh (189), Bini (191), binn (22c), bino (113b,117a), cine (104b, 152c), cinq (61d), dine, ding (130b), dino (34b), dint (48c,59d, 122a), fine (49b,50a,104b,115d,159a), fink (19a,56c,157c), Finn (107d), gink (48b), hind (15b,41d,45a), hing (13c), hino (106d, 168c), hint (9a,39c,159a), jink (42b,103b,153c), jinx (78a), kina (126d), kind (150d,153a,174d), kine (38a,112c), king (26c, 29c), kink (38b,171c), kino (27c,34c,47c,72c,98b,161d,168c), lina (188), Lina (183d), line (12b,22b,36d,38a,126c,134b,157b,158b, 162d,175c), ling (24c,57a,b,75b,178c), link (36a,81d,85b), Linn (120d,140a,c,168c,178d), lino, lint (46a,58d), liny (157b), Linz (40d), mina (10b,70b,71d), Mina (23a,183d), mind (75c,81d,93d, 109b), mine (69c,79d,111b,124c), Ming (30b,c), mink (176d), mino (84c), mint (13a,33b,58b,76a), minx (116c), miny, nina (152a), Nina (26c,33d,68d,183d), nine (26c,104d), nino (152a), pina (35d,118b), pine (36a,52a,88c,93c,168c,d,169a), ping, pink (26d,33c,60c,138a), pino (152c), pint (67b), piny, rind (53a, 115c), Rind (109c,174b), rine (44d,75d,135c), ring (50a), rink (147c,154a), sina (46c), Sina (102d,103d), Sind, sine (64c,66b,90a, 97c,126a,163b,169d,183b), sing (26d,178a), sinh (97c), sink (41c, 43c,46b,158a), sino (34a), Tina (183d), tind (86b), tine (11b,124b, 167b), ting (166a), Ting (30c), Tino (136d), tint (33c,d,114d), tiny (100c,148c), vina (77a,105a), vine (32b), vino (92d,182b), vint (26c,182c), viny, wind (33b,39d,171c,185a), wine, wing (10d,58c, 59a,118b,d), wink (107a), winy (176c), Xina (183d), zinc (21a), zing

- - IN akin (8b,92b,129c), alin (188), amin (9d), Asin (102a), ayin (91c), bain (61a), brin (32c,54c,146c), cain (169c), Cain (6a,7a,50d,88a, 104c,143c), chin, Chin (30b), coin (19b,37a,100c,101c,179d), crin (146c), dain (188), dein (66d), Drin, enin (20d), Eoin (85b), Erin (82b), fain (42d,67c,183b), gain (7a,b,124a), gein (67d), grin, hein (52c,61c), Jain (77b), join (36a,173c), Kain, lain, liin (188), loin (98a), main (29d,35d,123d), mein (30b), nein (66c), Odin (7c, 29d,63c,68c,175d,183b), pain (7c), rain (121d,162d), rein (130c), Rhin, ruin (42d), sain (20c,38a,48a), sein (146c), shin (91a,d,140b, 143c), skin (53a,76c,115c,d), spin (131a,180d), tain (166a), thin (43b,c,148b), trin (169d), Tsin (30b), twin (45c,171d), vain (81a), vein (20d,157b), wain (177b), Wain, whin (64c,70a,132b,181d),

zaln (41a), **zeln**

I - - N **Iban** (47c), **icon** (79d,92b,136a), **Iden** (76a), **Idun** (107d), **ikon** (79d,136a), **Iran** (6a,48c,116b), **Iren** (127c), **iron** (55c,d,69d,81a, 97b,143b,149a,173d,179c), **Iten** (192), **Ivan** (40c,85b,96a)

IO - - **Iola, Iole** (52a,76b,123c), **Iona** (28a,82d), **Ione** (24b,88d,94d), **Ioni** (192), **iota** (71a,85c,91c,114c,166c,176a,180d), **Iowa** (193)

- IO - **biod** (79c,59d), **bion** (117b), **bios** (92a), **cion** (42d,70b,145b,148b, 154b,156a), **Dion** (96a,152a), **Fiot** (191), **lion** (55b,86c), **niog** (33a,168c), **niou** (188), **pion** (43c,52b), **piot** (95b), **riot** (44c, 111d,170c,173d), **siol** (82c), **sion** (125c,158c), **Sion** (75b,c,83a,157d), **tion** (158b), **Tiou** (192), **viol** (105a), **Zion** (75b,c,83a,157d)

- - IO **agio** (52c,60a,101c,123a), **apio** (125b), **Clio** (104d), **idio** (34b,c), **meio** (188), **moio** (188), **naio** (107a,168c), **noio** (107c,163c), **odio** (83b), **Ohio, olio** (44b,77c,98c,100d,121d), **Scio, skio** (57d), **trio** (104d,165a,169c), **Unio** (105c)

I - - O **Iago** (54b,111d,143c), **icho** (67b), **ideo** (34b,d,164d), **idio** (34b,c), **Idjo** (191), **Idyo** (191), **Idzo** (191) **ikmo** (18b) **inro** (84b,c,106c), **into** (123a), **ipso** (89c), **itmo** (18b)

IP - - **ipil** (117a,168c,169a), **ipse** (44d,89c), **ipso** (89c)

- IP - **aipi** (27a), **cipo** (91d), **dipt, hipe** (185a), **kipp, lipa** (54d), **nipa** (14b, 46b,48a,164a,168c), **pipa** (159d) **pipe** (105a,180d,182a), **pipi** (106d, 119d), **pipy** (145d), **ripa** (16b,131d), **ripe** (58a,97c,98c), **Sipe** (101a, 110c,140b), **tipe** (168b), **tipi** (181b), **wipe, Xipe** (15c), **Zipa** (29d), **zipp, Zips** (40c)

- - IP **atip** (14b,166a), **chip** (69d), **clip** (54d,143d), **drip, flip** (167c), **grip** (159a), **knip** (115c), **quip** (183a,b), **raip** (36d), **seip** (110c), **ship, skip** (110b,114c,147c), **slip** (67c,119a), **snip** (32b,40a), **trip** (85c), **whip** (58c,88d)

I - - Q **Iraq** (99a,d)

IR - - **Irad** (18d), **Irae** (43c), **Irak** (99a,d), **Iran** (6a,48c,116b), **Iraq** (99a,d), **Iras** (11b,32a), **Iren** (127c), **irid** (38d,67c), **iris** (53c,58a,111c), **Iris** (127c), **Irma** (96d), **irok** (55b), **iron** (55c,d,69d,81a,97b,143b,149a, 173d,179c), **Irra** (68c,178a), **irus** (109d)

- IR - **Aira** (70d), **aire** (82c), **Aire, airs** (123b), **airy** (176d,177a), **bird, birl** (93c,131a,153c), **birn** (31d,139a), **birr** (180d), **cirl** (24c), **circ** (31a), **dire** (45d,55a,104a,163c), **dirk** (40b), **dirt, Eire** (82b), **fire** (13a,43d,44b), **firm** (154c,173d), **firn** (67c,70c,106c,149b), **gird** (32c,50a,123a,160a), **girl, giro** (38c,83c,167c), **girt** (50a), **hire** (49d,50b,91b,130a), **hiro, kiri** (86a,87c,115a,168c), **kirk** (31a,139b), **lira** (28b,79a,170d), **lire** (62c), **Mira** (155b,174d), **mire** (21c,104b), **mirk** (41a,67d), **miro** (19a,106d,184a), **Miro** (113a, 151d), **miry, pirn** (21b,129a,179b), **Piro** (192), **pirr** (181a), **rire** (62a), **sire** (17d,55a,59d,124a,163b,166b), **siri** (18b), **tire** (15a,22a, 52d,55a,179b,180d), **tiro** (9b,17d,108c), **Vira** (191), **vire** (11a,13b), **wire, wiry** (147a,167c), **zira** (188)

- - IR **Abir** (129a), **Ahir** (27b), **amir** (7c,12a,103a,b,123c,170d), **chir** (29b,116d), **coir** (33a,37a,56a,133d), **cuir** (45c,62a), **emir** (12a, 103a,b,123c,134d,135a,171a), **fair** (17a,55d), **hair** (56b,164d), **heir, kair, keir** (20c,174d), **koir** (33a), **lair** (37c,42b), **Leir, loir** (45c),

Loir, Muir (8b,142c), **Nair** (45d), **noir** (61b,134b), **pair** (22d,37d, 85b,171d), **sair** (140b,150d), **Seir** (51b,94a,103d), **shir** (36d,65d, 165c), **skir, soir** (61c), **spir** (97c), **stir** (8a,13a,35b,78d,100d), **tair** (68a,76d), **vair** (64c,154c), **weir** (40b,57d), **whir** (25c,181a), **Ymir** (67a,131c)

I - - R **icer, Igor** (135d), **Imer, inar** (65b), **Isar** (41a,104c,132a), **Iser** (49a), **iter** (22d,76c,85c,89c,114d,132a,b,133a,b), **Iyar** (102b), **izar** (65b,103b), **Izar** (155b)

IS - - **Isar** (41a,104c,132a), **isba** (135c), **Iser** (49a), **Isha** (174a), **Isis** (68d, 78c,111d), **isle** (8b,53c,81d,82d,86b,88a), **ismy** (45a)

- IS - **bisa** (11a), **bise** (182a), **bish** (120b), **bisk** (120b,151a), **cise** (147b), **cist** (22c,29d,156c), **Disa** (111a), **disc** (31b), **dish, disk** (31b), **diss** (98b), **fisc** (52c,134c), **fish, fisk** (24d,52c,134c), **fist** (80c), **gish** (102c), **gist** (95c,118c), **hish, hiss** (146a), **hist** (25c,93d), **kish** (16d,70c), **Kish** (137c), **kiss** (148c), **kist** (29d,58a,139b), **Lisa** (183d), **lisp** (153b), **liss** (54b,58b,60c,129d,140a), **list** (26d,27b, 75b,83d,134a,138b,165d), **mise** (8a,10a,70c), **miss, mist** (46b,59b, 59b,174d), **Nish** (19d), **nisi** (90a,173c), **Oise, Pisa** (90c), **pise** (127d), **pish** (36c,107d), **pisk** (9c,19b), **piso** (189), **pist** (25c), **rise** (49d,80b,155a), **Rise** (110d,150c), **risk** (74d), **risp** (99a), **Riss** (66a), **sise** (62c,147b), **sish** (79b), **sisi** (121b), **sist** (139b), **visa** (114d), **vise** (31d,77d,114d), **viss** (189), **wise** (136b), **wish** (42d), **wisp** (148c), **wist** (87c)

- - IS **acis** (64b), **Agis** (86d), **anis** (55c), **Apis** (17c,24b,49a,125a,136a), **aris** (101b), **atis** (76d,102a), **avis** (89a), **Avis** (183c), **axis** (28b, 41d,77c,153c), **bois** (62b,63a,183d), **Bois, cris** (40b,95d), **dais** (119b), **egis** (14b,d,115a,124d,144b,154a,161a), **Elis** (22c,37d, 71b,107c), **Eris** (12c,68d,109c), **feis** (82b), **glis** (45c), **gris** (61d), **ibis** (48d,49a,177b), **iris** (53c,58a,111c), **Iris** (127c), **kris** (40b,95d), **Isis** (68d,78c,111d), **itis** (158c), **Lais** (17c), **Lois** (165d,183c), **mais** (61b), **nais** (63c,132a), **Otis** (9c,d,24d,82a,111a), **Ovis** (143d), **pais** (37d), **rais** (26c,29d,75a,103b), **Rais** (106b), **reis** (26c,29d,75a, 103b), **Riis** (9d), **sais** (48d,71d), **seis** (147b,152c), **this** (42b,124b), **tris** (122d), **unis** (91b), **Upis** (13b)

I - - S **ibis** (48d,49a,177b), **Ibis, Idas** (27b,71c), **ides** (41a,b,133a), **ills** (170a), **Ilus** (88d,170b), **Iras** (11b,32a), **iris** (53c,58a,111c), **Iris** (127c), **Irus** (109d), **Isis** (68d,78c,111d), **Itys** (163b), **Ives** (9c,90b)

IT - - **itch, Itea** (145d,160c,181d), **item** (6d,13b,42d,51a,90d,92d,107a, 113d,114c), **Iten** (192), **iter** (22d,76c,85c,89c,114d,132a,b,133a,b), **itis** (158c), **itmo** (18b), **itol** (158b), **Itys** (163b), **Itza** (192)

- IT - **bite** (29d,156b), **biti** (20b), **bito** (7d,57d,168c), **bitt** (54d,175c), **cite** (15a,98d,126d,159b), **cito** (89d,126c), **cits, city, dita** (117a), **dite** (150b), **Gita, gite** (62a,118d), **jiti, kite** (19c,49a,74c,d), **kith** (63c), **lite** (158c,d), **lith** (34d,156c), **liti** (60d), **litz** (127b), **mite** (12b,81b,82a,114a,c,148c,d,181b), **mitt** (56c), **mitu** (39d), **mity, nito** (55c), **pita** (9c,28b,56a,83a), **pith** (37a,51c,67b,95c,97a, 119b,126d), **pitt** (50d), **Pitt** (155d), **pito** (9c,28b,83a), **pity** (35b), **rita, Rita** (37b,78d,183c), **rite** (93a,131d), **Sita** (127d), **site** (93b), **sito** (34b), **titi** (20d,102a,145d,168d,181b), **Tito** (186c), **vita** (89c, 92a), **vite** (62b), **viti** (17ob), **with** (10b)

314

- - IT adit (51a,100a,114d), alit (44b,143a), amit (94a), bait (15d,51a, 94d,167b), brit (76c), chit (67b,98c,108b,116c,177c), doit (47a, 169d,180d), duit (190), Duit (192), edit (20d,49d,123a,129a,131a), emit (43d,49a,53c,58d,83a,142c), exit (114d), fait (6d,61b), flit (41a), frit (64c,67c), gait (96b,179a), grit (137a,b), ibit (117a), knit (173c,179b), lait (62a), nuit (62b), obit (41b,64c), omit (49c, 52c,106b,114c,147d), phit (24b), quit (90d,130c), seit (189), skit (145c), slit (40a), spit (120a,132b,c), suit (38a,58a,91a,112a,119c, 137c), tait (14d), trit (34d,164c), twit (162b,c), unit (101c,110c, 147a), wait (26d,42b,92c,155d,162a), whit (166c), writ (91a), Yuit (51c)

I - - T ibit (117a), ikat (53b,159a), ilot (82d)

- IU - biur (35a), Niue (137d), Pius (121a)

I - - U lalu (48d), ichu (10b,70d), iglu (51c,149b)

IV - - Ivah (18d), Ivan (40c,85b,96a), Ives (9c,90b)

- IV - Civa (56d), cive (110c), diva (110d,123c), dive (42b,74b,119d), divi, five, give (79d,123a), hive (17c), jiva (77a), jive (160c), kiva (28c,125b), kive (174d), kivu (170c), live (47c), Livy (132d,133a), rive (32a,153d), siva (67a,120d), Siva (56d,77a), sive (146a), viva (93d), vive (93d), vivo (93a), wive (97a)

- - IV chiv (87a), skiv (151b)

- IW - Biwa (93d,168c), iiwi (19a,74b), kiwi (11d,19a,58c)

IX - - ixia (37a), Ixil (192), ixle (56a)

- IX - Bixa (145d), dixi, Mixe (192), mixy, pixy (154b)

- - IX Alix (183c), Coix (70d,85b), flix, noix (67c)

IY - - Iyar (102b)

- IY - kiyi (185d)

I - - Y idly, inky (20b), inly, ismy (45a)

IZ - - izar (65b,103b), Izar (155b)

- IZ - bize (182a), bizz, size, sizy (176d), sizz, tiza (172a), zizz (181a)

- - IZ friz (39d), phiz (54a), swiz (160c), whiz (25c)

I - - Z Inez (45c,183c)

JA - - jaca (84a), jack (26c,58a,127c), Jack (96b), jacu (19a,151b), jade (33c,65d,71d,166a), jadu (95a), jady, Jael (147b), Jaga (191), jagg, jail (123d), Jain (77b), jake (40d), Jake (96b), jako (71a), jama (103b), jamb (12d,45c,118a,146b,174a), jami (103b), jane (190), Jane (183c), jann (102d), jaob, jape (85a,b), jarl (40d,107d), jass (160d), jati (27b), jato (173b), jaun (113a), Java (33a), Jave (84d), jawy, jazz

- JA - ajar (110c), Ajax (71b,162d)

- - JA Beja (6c,191), bija (168c), caja (152a), coja (103b,166b), hoja (166b), lija (57a,90d,173a), maja (151c), Maja (153b), Naja (33a), puja (77a), raja (77a,123c), reja (152b), soja (151b)

J - - A jaca (84a), Jaca, Jaga (191), jama (103b), Java (33a), Jena (105d, 165b), jiva (77a), jota (151c), Jova (193), juba (106b), juca (27a), Juda, juga (27a), jula, jura, Juza (155b)

J - - B jamb (12d,45c,118a,146b,174a), jaob, jibb, Joab (41a)

- - JD   Nejd

J - - D   Joad (50c)

JE - -   jean (37c), Jean (183c), Jeel, jeep, jeer (138c,162b), jefe (152a), Jeff (133d), Jeff, jehu (46b), Jehu (18c), Jena (105d,165b), jerk (153a), jess (157a), jest (169c), Jesu, jete (16a), Jeth (102a), jeux (61d)

- JE -   ajee (15c,139a)

- - JE   haje (33a,48d), yaje (23a)

J - - E   jade (33c,65d,71d,166a), jake (40d), Jake (96b), jane (190), Jane (183c), jape (85a,b), Jave (84d), jefe (152a), jete (16a), jibe (8a, 33b,35d,37b,42c,100d,138c,144c,149b), jive (160c), joke (183a), Jole (29b), Jose (96a), Jove (85d), jube (28d), Jude (11c,96a), juke (114c), Jule (183d), June (183c), jupe (62b,84a), jure (90b), jute (37a,48a,56a,133d,136a), Jute

J - - F   jeff (133d), Jeff, jiff (101c)

J - - G   jagg, joug (138d), Jung (125a)

JH - -   Jhil, jhum, JHVH (159d), JHWH (159d)

J - - H   Jeth (102a), josh (85b), JHVH (159d), JHWH (159d)

JI - -   jibb, jibe (8a,33b,35d,37b,42c,100d,138c,144c,149b), jiff (101c), Jill (183d), jilt, jink, jinn (42b,103b,153c), jinx (78a), jiti, jiva (77a), jive (160c)

- - JI   caji (180b), Caji, fuji (84b), Fuji (84d), koji (185b), suji (180c)

J - - I   jami (103b), jati (27b), Jati, jiti, jogi (76d), joli (62b), joti

J - - K   jack (26c,58a,127c), Jack (96b), jerk (153a), jink, jock, Jock (96b), jonk, juck (114c), junk (30a,134c)

J - - L   Jael (147b), jail (123d), jarl (40d,107d), jeel, jhil, Jill (183d), Joel (96a), jowl (29b)

- JM -   ijma (103b)

- - JM   Sejm (120c)

J - - M   jhum, joom (39c)

J - - N   Jain (77b), jann, Jann (102d), jaun (113a), jean (37c), Jean (183c), jinn (42b,103b,153c), Joan (183c), John (11c,96a,121a,186b), join (36a,173c), juan (113a), Juan (96a)

JO - -   Joab (41a), Joad (50c), Joan (183c), joar (100a), jobo (77c), jock, Jock (96b), jocu (45b,57a), Jodo (113d), Joel (96a), joey (86a, 185d), Joey (96b,109c), jogi (76d), John (11c,96a,121a,186b), join (36a,173c), joke (183a), joky, jole (29b), joli (62b), jolt (143b), jonk, joom (39c), Jose (96a), josh (85b), joss (30b), Josy (183d), jota (151c), joti, joug (138d), Jova (193), Jove (85d), jowl 29b), Jozy

- JO -   ajog, ejoo (55b,168c), Gjoa (144d)

- - JO   bojo (117a), gajo (107c), Idjo (191), majo, mojo (177c), pajo (122a, rojo (129a,152c), tajo (152a,d)

J - - O   jako (71a), Jako, jato (173b), jobo (77c), Jodo (113d), judo (84b, 85c,142b), Juno (69c,85d,100c,126b)

J - - P   jeep, jump

J - - R jeer (162b), joar (100a), juar (100a)

J - - S jass (160d), jess (157a), joss (30b)

J - - T jest (169c), jilt, jolt (143b), just (51b,54b)

JU - - juan (113a), Juan (96a), juar (100a), juba (106b), jube (28d), juca (27a), juck (114c), Juda, Jude (11c,96a), judo (84b,85c,142b), Judy (125c,183d), juez (152b), juga (27a), juju (29b,55d), juke (114c), jula, Jule (183d), jump, June (183c), Jung (125a), junk (30a,134c), Juno (69c,85d,100c,126b), jupe (62b,84a), jura, Jura, jure (90b), jury (38a), just (51b,54b), jute (37a,48a,56a,133d, 136a), Jute, Juza (155b)

- - JU baju (84a), hoju (84b), juju (29b,55d), teju (151b)

J - - U jacu (19a,151b), jadu (95), jehu (46b), Jehu (18c), Jesu, jocu (45b,57a), juju (29b,55d)

J - - X jeux (61d), jinx (78a), jynx (78a), Jynx (184a)

JY - - jynx (78a), Jynx (184a)

J - - Y jady, jawy, joey (86a,185d), Joey (96b,109c), joky, Josy (183d), Jozy, Judy (125c,183d), July, jury (38a)

J - - Z jazz, juez (152b)

KA - - kaan (93d,116c), kaat (105d), kada (188), kade (144a), kadi (103a, 171a), Kadu (191), Kafa (6c), kago (113a), kagu (106c), kaha (123d), kahu (14d), kaid (29d,66a), kaif (88c) kaik (96c), kail (18c, 22a,25a,79b), Kain, kair, kaka (114b), kaki (84c,106d), kala (19a), kale (22a,25a,119b,175a), kali (26d,67c,136d,167a), Kali (147b), kalo (162a), Kama (56d), kame (67b,139b), Kami (68a,84b,88c, 107c,144c), kana (84d), Kane (74c), k'ang (30a), Kano (84c,177d), kant (28d), Kant (67a), kapa (74b), kaph (91d), Kapp, Kara (132a), Kari (14d), Karl (96a), karn (156c), karo (106d), kasa (48a), kasi (116b), kasm (189), Kate (143c,183d), kath (14a), Katy (183d), kaun (93d), kava (18c,116a), Kavi (84d), kawa (18c,116a), Kawi (84d), kawn (93d), kayo (87c), kazi (103a), kazy (103a)

- KA - Akal (56d), Akan (191), ikat (53b,159a), okay (8d), skag (7d, 46d), skat (181b), Skat (155b)

- - KA Akka (125d), Atka (11a), baka (52b), beka (189), dika (23a), Ekka (26d), Inka (193), kaka (114b), loka (173c,184c), pika (93a, 128a,132c), puka (107a,168c), roka (95a,168c,d), Saka (10a), sika (41d,84b), soka (20c), waka (26a), weka (58c,106d,107a,127b), Yaka (191)

K - - A kada (188), Kafa (6c), kaha (123d), kaka (114b), kala (19a), Kama (56d), kana (84d), kapa (74b), kara (132a), kasa (48a), kava (18c 116a), kawa (18c,116a), kela (189), keta (45a), kina (126d), kiva (28c,125b), koba (11a), kola (25b,84a,108d), Kola (135b,c,d), kona (74c), kora (19a,178c), kota (117a), Kota (45d), kuba (26d,189), kufa (21b,99a), kula (189), kusa

K - - B kerb (146b), knab (107a), knob (73c,107c,124d), knub (178b)

K - - D kaid (29d,66a), keld (154b), kind (150d,153a,174d), Kurd (48b, 82a)

KE - - keal (25a), keef (75d), keek (154c), keel (128d,134d,144c,d), keen (15a,88a,177b), keep (123a,130d), keet (72b), keif (75d), keir

317

(20c,174d), **kela** (189), **keld** (154b), **kelp** (82a,141c), **Kelt** (180b), **kemp** (139b), **keno, Kent** (90d), **kepi** (99d), **kept, kerb** (146b), **kere** (75c,128b), **kerf** (40a,108b), **keri** (75c,128b), **kern** (59c,172a), **Kern** (132b), **Kerr, keta** (45a), **Ketu** (48b)

- KE -   **akee** (168c), **akey** (189), **okeh** (8d,37b), **oket** (189), **skee** (149c), **skeg** (7d,86a,144d,157d,184a), **sken** (164a), **skeo** (57d), **skep** (16d,17c,77c), **skew** (148a,160c,171b,c), **skey** (185d)

- - KE   **bake** (139a), **bike, cake, coke** (32d,64a), **cuke** (39b), **cyke** (40c), **dike** (49c,91d), **Dike** (78a), **duke** (107c), **dyke** (49c,91d), **fake** (123a,143c), **feke, fike** (139c), **fyke** (15d), **hake** (57a,b), **hike, hyke!, jake** (40d), **Jake** (96b), **joke** (183a), **juke** (114c), **lake** (117d), **like** (13c,37d,146d), **Loke** (15d,68b), **luke, Luke** (52a, 96a), **make** (35b,36d,54a,123a), **mike, Mike** (96b), **moke** (45c, 157d), **Nike** (69c,100c,182d), **Peke** (45a,148d), **pike** (57a,b,76c, 120b,153a), **poke** (108c), **rake** (41b,44c,134b,140d), **roke** (174d, 175b), **sake** (84b,125d), **soke** (44c,85d), **syke** (194), **take, tike** (29d), **tuke** (26b,53b), **tyke** (29d), **wake** (134b,168a), **woke, yoke** (85b,92d,173c), **Zeke** (96b)

K - - E   **kade** (144a), **kale** (22a,25a,119b,175a), **kame** (67b,139b), **Kane** (74c), **Kate** (143c,183d), **kere** (75c,128b), **kibe kile** (189), **kine** (38a,112c), **kite** (19c,49a,74c,d), **kive** (174d), **Klee** (113a), **knee** (85b), **koae** (74b), **Kobe** (78a), **Kome** (71d), **kore** (107b) **Kore** (29a, 42b,116b,124d), **kuge** (84c), **Kure** (84c), **kyle** (57a,139c)

- - KF   **wakf** (103a), **wukf** (103a)

K - - F   **kaif** (88c), **keef** (75d), **keif** (75d), **kerf** (40a,108b), **kief** (75d), **kiff** (88c), **koff** (47a)

K - - G   **k'ang** (30a), **king** (26c,29c), **knag** (115d,139c), **krag** (131c), **kung** (125b)

KH - -   **khan** (7c,26c,81b,93d,116c,123c,130c,166c), **khar** (189), **khas** (153a), **khat** (105d), **Khem** (113c), **khet** (188), **khot**

- KH -   **Akha** (86a,c)

- - KH   **ankh** (38d,162b), **bikh** (120b), **bukh** (122a), **hakh** (46d), **lakh** (110c), **rukh** (53b,54a), **Sikh** (77b)

K - - H   **kaph** (91d), **kath** (14a), **kish** (16d,70c), **Kish** (137c), **kith** (63c), **Koch** (66d), **koph** (91d), **Kush, kyah** (19a)

KI - -   **kiak** (51c), **kibe, kiby** (29a), **kick, kief** (75d), **kiel** (128d,134d), **Kiel** (25d), **kier** (20c,174d), **Kiev, kiff** (88c), **kiho** (82a), **kiki** (27b), **kiku** (30d), **kile** (189), **kill** (38c), **kiln** (15d,112a), **kilo** (99b,122d), **kilt, kina** (126d), **kind** (150d,153a,174d), **kine** (38a,112c), **king** (26c,29c), **kink** (38b,171c), **kino** (27c,34c,47c,72c,98b,161d,168c), **kipp, kiri** (86a,87c,115a,168c), **kirk** (31a,139b), **kish** (16d,70c), **Kish** (137c), **kiss** (148c), **kist** (29d,58a,139b), **kite** (19c,49a,74c,d), **kith** (63c), **kiva** (28c,125b), **kive** (174d), **kivu** (170c), **kiwi** (11d, 19a,58c), **kiyi** (185d)

- KI -   **akia** (74c), **Akim** (135d,191), **akin** (8b,92b,129c), **okia** (190), **Okie** (99d), **skid** (148b), **skil** (57a), **skim** (67c), **skin** (53a,76c,115c, d), **skio** (57d), **skip** (110b,114c,147c), **skir, skit** (145c), **skiv** (151b)

- - KI   **Enki** (15b), **kaki** (84c,106d), **kiki** (27b), **Kuki** (191), **Loki** (7c,15d, 68b), **maki** (91b), **moki** (127b), **piki** (95c), **Reki** (16a), **saki** (39c,

318

84b,102a), **Tiki** (120c), **weki** (55c), **yaki** (193)

K - - I   **kadi** (103a,171a), **kaki** (84c,106d), **kali** (26d,67c,136d,167a), **Kali** (147b), **Kami** (68a,84b,88c,107c,144c), **Kari** (14d), **kasi** (116b), **Kavi** (84d), **Kawi** (84d), **kazi** (103a), **kepi** (99d), **keri** (75c,128b), **kiki** (27b), **kiri** (86a,87c,115a,168c), **kiwi** (11d,19a,58c), **kiyi** (185d), **kobi** (84b), **koji** (185b), **Koli** (27b), **Komi** (191), **kopi** (107a, 168c), **Kopi** (172a), **kori** (7d,77a), **kuei** (44a), **Kuki** (191), **Kuli** (27b), **Kuri** (191), **kwei** (44a)

- KK -   **Akka** (125d), **Ekka** (26d)

- - KK   **bukk** (122a), **rikk** (49a)

K - - K   **kaik** (96c), **kiak** (51c), **keek** (154c), **kick, kink** (38b,171c), **kirk** (31a,139b), **konk** (41c), **kunk** (188), **kurk** (31a,139b), **kyak** (51c)

KL - -   **klam** (189), **Klee** (113a), **klom** (189), **klop** (150d)

K - - L   **kail** (18c,22a,25a,79b), **Karl** (96a), **keal** (25a), **keel** (128d,134d, 144c,d), **kiel** (128d,134d), **Kiel** (25d), **kill** (38c), **koel** (19a,b,39b), **kohl** (53c), **kral, kuhl** (53c)

- KM -   **ikmo** (18b)

K - - M   **kasm** (189), **Khem** (113c), **klam** (189), **klom** (189)

KN - -   **Knab** (107a), **knag** (115d,139c), **knap** (76d,107a,139b,159b,166a, 170c,185b), **knar** (87c,134b), **knee** (85b), **knew, knez** (123c), **knip** (115c), **knit** (173c,179b), **knob** (73c,107c,124d), **knop** (124b,170c, 185b), **knor** (87c), **knot** (43c,99d,107c,124d,137b), **knub** (178b), **knur** (67d,87c,107c), **knut, Knut** (40d,50c,96a)

K - - N   **kaan** (93d,116c), **Kain, karn** (156c), **kaun** (93d), **kawn** (93d), **keen** (15a,88a,177b), **kern** (172a), **Kern** (132b), **khan** (7c,26c,81b,93d, 116c,123c,130c,166c), **kiln** (15d,112a), **kran** (190), **kuan** (30b), **Kuan** (30c), **kwan** (30b)

KO - -   **koae** (74b), **koba** (11a), **Kobe** (78a), **kobi** (84b), **kobu** (84b), **Koch** (66d), **koel** (19a,b,39b), **koff** (47a), **kohl** (53c), **koir** (33a), **koji** (185b), **koko** (106d,114b), **Koko** (93d,186c), **koku** (189), **kola** (25b,84a,108d,168c), **Kola** (135b,c,d), **Koli** (27b), **kolo** (59b,135c), **Kome** (71d), **Komi** (191), **kona** (74c), **konk** (41c), **koop** (16c), **koph** (91d), **kopi** (107a,168c), **Kopi** (172a), **kora** (19a,178c), **Kora, kore** (107b), **Kore** (29a,42b,116b,124d), **kori** (7d,77a), **koso** (6c,80d), **Koso** (192,193), **koss** (188), **kota** (117a), **Kota** (45d), **koto** (84b), **kozo** (113d,168c)

- KO -   **akov** (189), **Ekoi** (191), **ikon** (79d,136a)

- - KO   **boko** (52b), **Doko** (191), **hako** (115b), **jako** (71a), **koko** (106d,114b), **Koko** (93d,186c), **mako** (18a,19a,20d,143c,168c,182c), **moko** (96c), **toko** (30c)

K - - O   **kago** (113a), **kalo** (162a), **Kano** (84c,177d), **karo** (106d), **kayo** (87c), **keno, kiho** (82a), **kilo** (99b,122d), **kino** (27c,34c,47c,72c, 98b,161d,168c), **koko** (106d,114b), **Koko** (93d,186c), **kolo** (59b, 135c), **koso** (6c,80d), **Koso** (192,193), **koto** (84b), **kozo** (113d,168c), **Kroo** (191)

K - - P   **Kapp, keep** (123a,130d), **kelp** '82a,141c), **kemp** (139b), **kipp, klop** (150d), **knap** (76d,107a,139b,159b,166a,170c,185b), **knip** (115c), **knop** (124b,170c,185b), **koop** (16c)

KR - - krag (131c), kral, kran (190), kras (76d), kris (40b,95d), Kroo (191)

- KR - akra (176a), Akra (191), ikra (27d), okra (72c,175a), okro (72c, 175a)

- - KR Askr (107d)

K - - R kair, keir (20c,174d), Kerr, khar (189), kier (20c,174d), knar (87c,134b), knor (87c), knur (67d,87c,107c), koir (33a), Kuar (102a), kyar (33a)

- - KS oaks (154d)

K - - S khas (153a), kiss (148c), koss (188), kras (76d), kris (40b,95d), kvas (135c)

- - KT takt (105a,163a)

K - - T kaat (105d), kant (28d), Kant (67a), keet (72b), Kelt (180b), Kent (90d), kept, khat (105d), khet (188), khot, kilt, kist (29d,58a, 139b), knit (173c,179b), knot (43c,99d,107c,124d,137b), knut, Knut (40d,50c,96a), kyat (189)

KU - - Kuan (30c), kuan (30b), Kuar (102a), kuba (26d,189), kudu (11a), kuei (44a), kufa (21b,99a), kuge (84c), kuhl (53c), Kuki (191), kuku (19a,106d), kula (189), Kuli (27b), kung (125b), kunk (188), Kurd (48b,82a), Kure (84c), Kuri (191), kurk (31a,139b), kusa, Kush

- KU - akua (120d), skua (19b,72c,84a,141a)

- - KU baku (26d,157b,168c), duku (95d,168c), ḥaku (86d), hiku (57a, 106d,138a), kiku (30d), koku (189), kuku (19a,106d), Maku (192), poku (11a), puku (11a), Suku (191), Taku (80c)

K - - U Kadu (191), kagu (106c), kahu (14d), Ketu (48b), kiku (30d), kivu (170c), kobu (84b), koku (189), kudu (11a), kuku (19a,106d)

KV - - kvas (135c)

- KV - NKVD (135d)

K - - V Kiev

KW - - kwan (30b), kwei (44a)

K - - W knew, know

KY - - kyah (19a), kyak (51c), kyar (33a), kyat (189), kyle (57a,139c)

- KY - Skye (163c), skyr (21d,151a), skyt (138c,140b)

- - KY alky, caky, coky, faky, inky (20b), joky, laky, oaky, piky, poky (148c), taky, waky

K - - Y Katy (183d), kazy (103a), kiby (29a)

K - - Z knez (123c)

LA - - laap (51d,91b,141d), lace (58b,179c), lack (178a), lact (34c), lacy, Ladd (143c), lade (24c,26d,43c,93b,100a,132a,139d,161b,178d), lady, laet (60d), lago (83b,152b), laic (32b,90b,107d,124a,141d), laid, lain, lair (37c,42b), Lais (17c), lait (62a), lake (117d), lakh (110c), laky, lala (129b), lalo (16b,34d,153a), Lalo (35c), lama (23d,24a,91d,165b), lamb, Lamb (49c), lame (38d,43d,73b), lamp (92a,94c), lana (58a,66a,90a,184b), land (44a,163c), lane (134b, 157b), lank (148b,164b), lant, lanx (133a,b), Laos (80d,129c), Lapp (108a), Lara (25c), lard (54d,61a,71a,110a), lari (78a,101c),

320

Lari (72c), **lark** (19a,63d,177b), **larp** (51d), **Lars** (51d,121b), **lash** (58c,87b,165c,180d), **Lasi** (191), **lass** (95b), **last** (36c,50b,145a, 174c), **lata** (85d,95d), **late** (128c), **lath** (157c), **latu** (190), **laud** (122a), **laun** (146b), **lava** (101c,132b,151a,177a), **lave** (16d,178b), **lawn** (20a,37c,53b,92c), **laze** (79b), **Laze** (191), **Lazi** (191), **lazo** (88d,128b,133d), **lazy**

- LA -   **alae** (182d), **alai** (171a), **Alai** (135c), **alan** (45a,79a,183c), **Alan,** **alar** (15c,145c,182d), **alas** (52c,136b,183b), **alat** (136d), **alay** 5c), **blaa, blab** (162b), **blae** (93b), **blah, blas** (6c,49c), **Blas** (~7b), **blat** (25b), **blay** (57d), **clad** (46a,82a), **clam** (20b,101b), **clan** (169c), **clap** (58b), **claw** (29c,105b,161d,173a), **Clay** (9d), **Elah** (18c,86d), **elan** (12c,41a,50d,62a,153c,177a,186b), **Elam** (18d,37d, 82a,116c,144b), **ELAS** (71c), **flag** (16b,50d,82b,88c,115a,155a), **flak** (11a), **flam** (169c), **flan** (39d,40a,114d), **flap** (17b,59a,104a, 118d,161a,182d), **flat** (41b,124d,173a), **flaw, flax, flay** (147c,157c), **glad** (85c), **klam** (189), **Olaf** (108a,176b), **olam** (51a,d,75c,81a), **Olan** (115c), **Olax** (52b), **olay** (113b), **plan** (99b,124a,138b), **plap** (54b), **plat** (22b,96c,114a,119c,133d), **play** (63d,154a), **slab** (148b), **slag** (46c,99a,138c,148d,177a), **slam** (180d,182d), **slap** (24a,128c, 148c), **slat** (58b,89a,117c,184a), **Slav** (13c,40c,48b,52a,120b,135b), **slaw, slay, Ulam** (67b), **ulan** (27d,88a)

- - LA   **agla** (7a), **alla** (6d), **amla** (48a,161d,168c,169a), **aula** (66c,73b), **Bala** (26c,66a), **bela** (12a), **Bela** (18b,48c,78d), **bola** (16a,179b), **cela** (62d), **cola** (25b,108d,149d,168c), **dola** (189), **ella** (152c, 158c), **Ella** (183c), **fala** (129b), **gala** (55d), **Gala** (191), **gila** (93b), **gola** (27b,40c,70c,157a), **gula** (90a,101a,165b), **hala** (112b), **Hela** (93c), **hila** (53c), **hola** (74c,152b), **hula** (74b), **Hyla** (10a,166d, 169b), **Iola, jula, kala** (19a), **kela** (189), **kola** (25b,84a,108d,168c), **Kola** (135b,c,d), **kula** (189), **lala** (129b), **Lila** (183c), **Lola** (27d,97b), **mala** (89c,90a,94b,97d,109d,185c), **mela** (34a,129d), **mila** (188), **Mola** (159c), **Nala** (77a), **Nola, olla** (36d,44b,84d,113b,121d, 151d,152c,181b), **pala** (189), **Pala** (88b), **pela** (30c), **Pola,** **pyla** (22d), **sala** (50c,152a,b,c), **Sala** (50c), **sola** (9a,48a,74b,118c, 154a,167b), **Sula** (65a), **tala** (16d,113a,168c,d), **tela** (22d,98c, 121b,166a,179c), **tola** (48a,80d,180a), **Tola** (85b), **tula** (9a), **Tula,** **upla, vela** (98c,136b,149d), **Vela** (36b,c), **vila** (54b), **vola** (89d), **Zola** (63a)

L - - A   **lala** (129b), **lama** (23d,24a,91d,165b), **lana** (58a,66a,90a,184b), **Lara** (25c), **lata** (85d,95d), **lava** (101c,132b,151a,177a), **Leda** (27b, 75d,120c,153a,171d,186b), **lena** (56d), **Lena** (36b), **Lida** (183c), **lija** (57a,90d,173a), **Lila** (183c), **lima** (17b,152b,174d), **Lima** (31b), **lina** (188), **Lina** (183d), **lipa** (54d), **lira** (28b,79a,170d), **Lisa** (183d), **loka** (173c,184c), **Lola** (27d,97b), **loma** (58b,63d), **lora** (146b,149b, 151c,169b), **Lora** (183c), **lota** (24c,121d,178d), **Lota, Iowa** (19a), **Luba** (191), **luna** (103c), **Luna** (102b), **lura** (22d,82a), **lyra, Lyra** (36b,74a)

- LB -   **alba** (98b,181a), **Alba** (151d), **albe** (133a), **Albi** (58a), **albo** (34d, 181a), **Elba** (105d), **Elbe** (108a)

- - LB   **bulb** (37a,172c)

L - - B   **lamb, Lamb** (49c), **limb** (12d,22d), **lobb** (23b,94c,163a)

- LC -   **Alca** (14c,128b), **alco** (45b)

- - LC   **talc** (28d,63b,99c,100b,122a,149c)

L - - C   **laic** (32b,90b,107d,124a,141d)

- LD -   **Alda** (110d,150c), **alda** (152b)

- - LD   **bald** (16c), **bold** (41a), **cold** (65d), **eild** (138d,140a), **fold, geld** (162b), **gild** (14a,49c,69c,98b), **gold, held, Hild, hold** (95c,124c, 130d), **Keld** (154b), **meld** (26a,41c,99a,118b), **mild** (32a,66a), **mold** (54d,143c), **sold, suld** (188), **told** (129c), **veld** (151a), **weld** (47c, 85b,173c), **wild** (38b,173d), **wold** (47c,60a,118d,174a,184a)

L - - D   **Ladd** (143c), **laid, land** (44a,163c), **lard** (54d,61a,71a,110a), **laud** (122a), **lead** (35d,43d,72b,74d,81a), **lend** (6d,79d), **lied** (66d,150b), **load** (24c,26d,161b), **lood** (189) **lord** (107c), **loud** (156a), **Ludd** (23c)

LE - -   **lead** (35d,43d,72b,74d,81a), **leaf** (55c,73c,119b), **Leah** (19a,84a, 87b,183c), **leak** (110c), **leal** (54b,94c,139d), **lean** (128a,148b,152d, 164b,166a), **leap** (26c), **lear** (139d), **Lear** (37a,143b), **lech** 102b), **Leda** (27b,75d,120c,153a,171d,186b), **leek** (58b,76a,110c,177d), **leer** (9d,58a,67c,93d,112a,148c), **lees** (46a,142a), **leet** (26a, 38a,139d), **left** (42c), **lehr** (67c,112a) **Leif** (107d), **Leir, Lely** (47a), **lena** (56d), **Lena** (36b), **lend** (6d,79d), **lene** (36b,149a, 172b), **leno** (37c,53b), **lens** (67c,95b,111a,129b,162d), **lent** (54d), **Lent** (115d,141c), **Leon** (96a), **Lero** (82d), **lerp** (51d,141d), **less** (100c,108b,141d), **lest** (59d,163d), **lete, Leti** (82d), **Leto** (11c), **Lett** (16a,90a,93a), **leve** (62a), **Levi** (84a,90c), **levo** (91a), **levy** (14a, 162b)

- LE -   **Alea** (14b,31c,167d), **alec** (10a,57c,d,76c,137c), **alee** (15c,75d, 144b,157a,182a), **alef** (91c), **alem** (98b,155a,170d,171a), **alen** (40d, 138a), **bleb** (20c,23d,67c), **bled, blet** (64a), **bleu** (61b), **blew, clee** (19a,129a), **clef** (104d,105a), **clem** (56b,158b), **clew** (16a,33a,77b, 136b,164d), **elef** (91c), **flea** (81b), **fled, flee, flew, flex** (18a), **fley** (63d), **gled** (19a,52a,87a), **glee** (99a,150b), **glen** (43c), **Hler** (141a), **ilex** (77d), **Klee** (113a), **Lleu** (40c), **Llew** (40c), **olea** (170b), **Olea** (110b), **oleo** (34c), **plea** (51a,52d,122a,130b), **pleb** (10d,35b,180b), **plet** (135d), **plew** (17c), **plex** (60b), **Sleb** (12a), **sled** (40a), **slee** (140b,148c), **slew** (160a), **sley** (179b), **Ulex** (153c), **vlei** (38c, 160a), **vley** (160a)

- - LE   **able** (26b,35b,126a,147c), **acle** (13d,82c,115d), **aile** (62b,63a,182c, d), **Alle** (14c), **atle** (136d,161d,169b), **axle** (153c,180c), **bale** (24b, 74a), **bile** (30c), **bole** (31d,32a,169b), **cale** (72d), **cole** (25a), **Cole, dale** (43c,128a,174b), **dele** (26a,49c,51b,53a,110b,123d,124c,130a, 145c,161b), **dole** (44c,118c,121c,129d), **Dole** (74c), **elle** (62b,c), **file** (13a,127d), **gale** (181d), **gyle** (23b,174d), **hale** (125b), **Hale** (9d,131a), **hole** (6c,11b,110d,118c,147a), **hule** (23a,134c), **hyle** (97c), **idle** (174b,c,178c), **ille** (89b,d,163d), **iole** (52a,76b,123c), **isle** (8b,53c,81d,82d,86b,88a), **ixle** (56a), **jole** (29b), **Jule** (183d), **kale** (22a,25a,119b,175a), **kile** (189), **kyle** (57a,139c), **male** (154d), **Male** (45d), **mele** (74b,150b), **mile** (64c), **mole** (19d,23a,24d,85a, 117c,155c), **Mole** (88c), **mule** (45b,148b,153c,180b), **nile** (33c, 71d), **Nile** (106b), **ogle** (9d,53c,91a,93d,148c), **orle** (17b,56b,76a, 144b,177a), **pale** (113a,117c,178a), **Pele** (69c,74c), **pile** (45d,75b, 117c), **pole** (132c,143b,177b,184a), **Pole** (52a), **pule** (180d), **pyle** (34b), **Pyle** (9c,178a), **rale** (7c,23a,29d,41b), **rile** (10c,d,82c,125a,

156b,176a), **role** (114b), **rule** (11b,26b,90b), **sale** (14c,61c,62b,c,
168b), **sole** (52c,57a,b,58b,d,110c,115d,150a), **tale** (91a,185b), **tele**
(34b,122c), **tile** (31d,56d,72b,95b,133c,163c), **tole** (9a,51a,99b,
163a), **tule** (24b,27c), **vale** (54c,128a,174b), **Vale** (7c,109c), **vile**
(16c,56c), **vole** (97d,104a), **wale** (70b,131b,157c,163d,179a,180a,
c,d), **wile** (13b,41c,157b,169c), **Yale** (173c), **Yule** (30d)

L - - E   **lace** (58b,179c), **lade** (24c,26d,43c,93b,100a,132a,139d,161b),
178d), **lake** (117d), **lame** (38d,43d,73b), **lane** (134b,157b), **late**
(128c), **lave** (16d,178d), **laze** (79b), **Laze** (191), lene(36b,149a,
172b), **lete**, **leve** (62a), **life** (19a,177a), **like** (13c,37d,146d), **lime**
(25b,27d,31b,33c,102d,168c), **line** (12b,22b,36d,38a,126c,134b,
157b,158b,162d,175c), **lire** (62c), **lite** (158c,d), **live** (47c), **lobe**
(90c,134b), **lode** (42c,99a,111b,175b), **loge** (164a), **Loke** (15d,68b),
Lome, lone (150a), **lope** (48b,64b,d), **lore** (77c,87c,90d,151c,183a),
lose (60a,100c), **lote** (24c,94a), **love** (163a), **lube** (110a), **luce**
(58c,117d), **Luce** (7b,35a), **luge** (148a), **luke, Luke** (52a,96a), **lune**
(38c,73b,74d), **lupe** (19a,64a), **lure** (41c,51a,54b,163a), **lute** (11c,
28b,84d,105a,131d), **luxe** (61c,62d,159c), **lyre** (11c,81c,105a,111c),
lyse

- LF -   **alfa** (70d)

- - LF   **calf, golf** (154a), **gulf** (6c), **half** (101a), **pelf** (22a,56c,131b), **self**
(48d,80d), **Welf** (67a), **wolf**

L - - F   **leaf** (55c,73c,119b), **Leif** (107d), **lief** (181d), **loaf** (49b,94b), **loof**
(144c,153d), **luff** (136b), **luif**

- LG -   **alga** (141b,c), **Algy** (96b), **Olga** (135c,183c)

L - - G   **ling** (24c,57a,b,75b,178c), **long** (38b,185b), **lung, lurg** (96d,141b,
184d)

L - - H   **lakh** (110c), **lash** (58c,87b,165c,180d), **lath** (157c), **Leah** (19a,84a,
87b,183c), **lech** (102b), **lith** (34d,156c), **loch** (88a,139d), **losh**
(178b), **loth** (15a,173d), **Lugh** (28b), **lush** (94d)

LI - -   **Liam** (181d), **liar** (98d), **Lias** (66a), **lick, Lida** (183c), **Lido** (83d,
175b), **lied** (66d,150b), **lief** (181d), **lien** (65c,91a,124c), **lieu** (118c,
155d), **life** (19a,177a), **lift** (49b), **liin** (188), **lija** (57a,90d,173a),
like (13c,37d,146d), **Lila** (183c), **lill** (15d,118a), **lilt** (93a,131a,
147a), **lily, lima** (17b,152b,174d), **Lima** (31b), **limb** (12d,22d),
lime (25b,27d,31b,33c,102d,168c), **limn** (45d,121c), **limp**
(58a,81a,177d), **limu** (141c), **limy** (176d), **lina** (188), **Lina**
(183d), **line** (12b,22b,36d,38a,126c,134b,157b,158b,162d,175c),
ling (24c,57a,b,75b,178c), **link** (36a,81d,85b), **linn** (120d,140a,c,
168c,178d), **lino, lint** (46a,58d), **liny** (157b), **Linz** (40d), **lion** (55b,
86c), **lipa** (54d), **lira** (28b,79a,170d), **lire** (62c), **Lisa** (183d), **lisp**
153b), **liss** (54b,58b,60c,129d,140a), **list** (26d,27b,75b,83d,134a,
138b,165d), **lite** (158c,d), **lith** (34d,156c), **liti** (60d), **litz** (127b),
live (47c), **Livy** (132d,133a)

- LI -   **alia** (89d), **alif** (12b), **alii** (74c,134c), **alim** (103b,162c) **alin** (188),
alit (44b,143a), **Alix** (183c), **Clim** (12b), **Clio** (104d), **clip** (54d,
143d), **Elia** (88a,115d), **Elis** (22c,37d,71b,107c), **flip** (167c), **flit**
(41a), **flix, glia** (106c), **glib** (58d,149a,177c), **glim, glis** (45c), **ilia**
(21d,77b,115d), **ille** (89b,d), **olic** (158b), **olid** (55d,60c,148d,157d),
olio (44b,77c,98c,100d,121d), **plie** (32c,59b), **slid, slim** (148b,

160a), **slip** (67c,119a), **slit** (40a)

- - LI   **amli** (48a,161d,168c,169a), **Atli** (14c,72b,79a,107d), **Bali, Beli** (23c), **coli, dali** (168c,169b), **doli, fili, gali** (6c), **goli** (105c), **Holi** (77a), **joli** (62b), **kali** (26d,67c,136d,167a), **Kali** (147b), **Koli** (27b, **Kuli** (27b), **mali** (27b), **pali** (122b), **Pali** (23d,24a,137b,175a), **pili** (34b,108d), **puli** (45a,78d), **soli** (12c,110c), **tali** (189), **teli** (94b), **vali** (171a,176a), **Vali** (7c,109c), **vili** (54b), **Vili** (109c), **wali** (171a), **yali** (171a)

L - -I   **Lari** (72c), **lari** (78a,101c), **Lasi** (191), **Lazi** (191), **Leti** (82d), **Levi** (84a,90c), **liti** (60d), **loci** (66b,118c), **Lodi** (105d), **Loki** (7c,15d, 68b), **lori** (91b), **Loti** (63a,176a), **ludi** (133b), **Luri** (191)

- LK -   **alky**

- - LK   **balk** (118c,146a,156d), **bilk** (29b,41c,42a), **bulk** (97b), **calk** (78c, 109a,141c,178d), **folk** (116a,169c), **fulk** (173a), **hulk** (144d,173d), **milk, mulk** (60d), **polk** (37c), **pulk** (37c,88d), **silk** (53b,179c), **sulk** (159a), **talk, volk** (66c,105d,116a), **Volk, walk, welk** (65c,96d, 141b), **yolk**

L - - K   **lack** (178a), **lank** (148b,164b), **lark** (19a,63d,177b), **leak** (110c), **leek** (58b,76a,110c,177d), **lick, link** (36a,81d,85b), **lock** (54d), **lonk** (143d), **look** (11c,53c,142a), **luck** (28d), **lurk** (92a, 147d)

LL - -   **llyn** (120d,140a), **Lleu** (40c), **Llew** (40c)

- LL -   **alla** (6d), **Alle** (14c), **allo** (34c), **ally** (14a,35c,d,173c), **ella** (152c, 158c), **Ella** (183c), **elle** (62b,c), **ille** (89b,d,163d), **ills** (170a), **olla** (36d,44b,84d,113b,121d,151d,152c,181b), **ullo** (6a,144a), **Ullr** (146b,164d)

- - LL   **ball, bell** (24c,39d), **Bell** (162d), **bill** (17b,147a), **Bill** (96b), **boll** (119b,d), **bull** (113c), **call** (145c,159b,176d), **cell** (39b), **cull** (117c), **dell** (43c,174b), **dill** (13a,117c), **doll** (125c), **dull** (21a,32c,173a), **Dull** (94b), **fall** (46b,141c), **fell** (40a,58b,76c,115d,147d), **fill** (109b), **full** (7b,130b), **gall** (19a,28c,29b,82c,160c,176a), **gill** (22d), **Goll, gull** (32d,41c,42a,72c,99b,141a), **hall** (37b,114d), **hill** (109b), **hull** (141d,142a,144c,d), **Jill** (183d), **kill** (38c), **lill** (15d,118a), **loll** (94b,128c), **lull** (126d,150c), **mall** (95d,124b,143b), **mill** (126c), **moll, Moll** (183d), **mull** (53b,135a,164c), **Nell** (110a,183d), **nill** (173d), **Noll** (96b,110b), **null** (108c,177a), **pall** (32d,81b,112a), **pill, poll** (74d,160a,177c), **pull** (45d,167d), **rill** (23c,102b,132a,148d, 157b), **roll** (134a,160b), **rull** (170b), **sell** (97a,115c,175b), **sill** (45c, 76c,165a,182b), **tall** (118d), **tell** (105d,129c,154b), **Tell** (160d), **till** (39c,101c,173d), **toll** (131c), **vill** (176b), **wall, well, will** (18b,43a, 163c,177c), **yell** (145c)

L - - L   **leal** (54b,94c,139d), **lill** (15d,118a), **loll** (94b,128c), **lull** (25c,126d,150c)

- LM -   **alma** (40d,53d,146d,147a), **Alma** (38d,183c), **alme** (40d,147a), **alms** (29a), **elmy, ulme** (49c)

- - LM   **balm** (110a,172c), **calm** (8d,11d,112b,118d,126c,d,172b,173d), **culm** (11a,32d,70d,145a,156a), **film** (164b), **halm, helm** (144d, 165d), **holm** (77d,82d,109a), **malm** (32a,92b), **palm** (59b,168a,169b)

L - - M   **Liam** (181d), **loam** (47d), **loom** (11c,146b,179b), **lyam** (139a)

- LN -   **ulna** (21d,39b)

- - LN   **kiln** (15d,112a), **vuln** (184d)

L - - N   **Lain, laun** (146b), **lawn** (20a,37c,53b,92c), **lean** (128a,148b,152d, 164b,166a), **Leon** (96a), **lien** (65c,91a,124c), **liin** (188), **limn** (45d, 121c), **linn** (120d,140a,c,168c,178d), **lion** (55b,86c), **llyn** (120d, 140a), **loan, loin** (40a,98a), **loon** (19a,b,c,157d,179c), **lorn** (42d, 60b), **loun** (19a,b), **lown** (157d)

LO - -   **load** (24c,26d,161b), **loaf** (79b,94b), **loam** (47d,150a), **loan, lobb** (23b,94c,163a), **lobe** (90c,134b), **lobo** (165d,183c), **loch** (88a,139d), **loci** (66b,118c), **lock** (54d), **loco** (38b,119b,120b), **lode** (42c,99a, 111b,175b), **Lodi** (105d), **Lodz, loft** (14c,69d,104b,178b), **loge** (164a), **logy** (46d), **loin** (40a,98a), **loir** (45c), **Loir, Lois** (165d,183c), **loka** (173c,184c), **Loke** (7c,15d,68b), **Loki** (7c,15d,68b), **Lola** (27d, 97b), **loll** (94b,128c), **Lolo** (27d,30a), **loma** (58b,63d), **Lome, lone** (150a), **long** (38b,185b), **Lonk** (143d), **lood** (189), **loof** (144c,153d) **look** (11c,53c,142a), **loom** (11c,146b,179b), **loon** (19a,b,c,157d, 179c), **loop** (31b,107d), **Loos, loot** (22a,118a,119d,136a,153d), **lope** (48b,64b,d), **lora** (146b,149b,151c,169b), **Lora** (183c), **lord** (107c), **lore** (77c,87c,90d,151c,183a), **lori** (91b), **lorn** (42d,60b), **loro** (19a,114b), **lory** (19a,114a), **lose** (60a,100c), **losh** (178b), **loss** (42c,123d,178b), **lost, iota** (24c,121d,178d), **lote** (24c,94a), **loth** (15a,173d), **Loti** (63a,176a), **loto** (65a,121d,178d), **lots, loud** (156a), **loun** (19a,b), **loup** (61d,62a,90c,139d), **Loup** (193), **lour** (13d,63d), **lout** (15c,22a,24b,45b,109a,157d), **love** (163a), **lowa** (19a), **lown** (157d), **lowp** (90c,139d)

- LO -   **alod** (51c,55d,88a,124c), **aloe** (7d,20a,76a,b,92b,98b,119b,158b, 167a,183d), **alop** (13d,46b,93d), **alow** (18a,172c), **blob, bloc** (173a), **blot, blow, clod** (22a,45b,157d), **Cloe** (183c), **clog** (30c,145b), **clop, clot** (32d,94d), **clou** (62b), **clow** (58c,148c), **cloy** (61b,137c, 159d), **elod** (49b,59d,79c), **Elon** (18c,51b,108a), **floc** (149a), **floe** (79b), **flog** (180d), **flop** (54a), **flot** (173a), **flow** (157b), **glom** (155d, 160d,178c), **glow** (144c), **ilog** (132a,161b), **ilot** (82d), **klom** (189), **klop** (150d), **Olor** (160a,b), **plod** (170b), **plop** (54b), **plot** (25a,36b, 118d,138b), **plow** (39c,165d), **ploy** (43c), **slob** (173d), **sloe** (14a,20b, 64a,119d,181c), **sloo** (160a), **slop, slot** (10d, 11b,41d,110d,167d,168a,181b), **slow** (43c)

- - LO   **allo** (34c), **bilo** (131b), **bolo** (87a), **calo** (72d), **dilo** (120d,168c), **filo, gilo** (48a), **Golo** (191), **Gulo** (183c), **halo** (14d,31b,92a), **hilo** (74c), **kalo** (162a), **kilo** (99b,122d), **kolo** (59b,135c), **lalo** (16b,34d), **Lalo** (35c), **Lolo** (27d,30a), **malo** (23a,74c,152a), **milo** (70b,87c), **Milo, nolo** (42a), **orlo** (56b,119c), **Oslo, palo** (152c), **pelo** (83b), **polo** (154a), **Polo** (175b), **ralo** (188), **silo** (59a), **solo** (12c,89a,110c), **ullo** (6a,144a), **velo** (175b)

L - - O   **lago** (83b,152b), **lalo** (16b,34d), **Lalo** (35c), **lazo** (88d,128b,133d), **leno** (37c,53b), **Lero** (82d), **Leto** (11c), **levo** (91a), **Lido** (83d,175b), **lino, lobo** (165d,183c), **loco** (38b,119b,120b), **Lolo** (27d,30a), **loro** (19a,114b), **loto** (65a,121d), **ludo** (65a,112b)

- LP -   **Alph** (132a), **Alps** (85d), **olpe** (90d,182c)

- - LP   **calp** (92b), **colp** (28a,148b), **gulp** (46a,79d,160a), **help** (14a), **kelp** (82a,141c), **palp** (11a,55b,58b,167c), **pulp, salp** (148d), **yelp**

L - - P laap (51d,91b,141d), lamp (92a,94c), Lapp (108a), larp (51d), leap (26c), lerp (51d,141d), limp (58a,81a,177d), lisp (153b), loop (31b,107d), loup (61d,62a,90c,139d), Loup (193), lowp (90c,139d), lump (45a,160c)

- - LR Ullr (146b,164d)

L - - R lair (37c,42b), lear (139d), Lear (37a,143b), leer (9d,58a,67c,93d, 112a,148c), lehr (67c,112a), Leir, liar (98d), loir (45c), Loir, lour (13d,63d)

- LS - also (10b,18b,80a), Elsa (70a,93c,110d,177b,183c), else (18b,79b, 111d)

- - LS fels (190), fils (62d,150b), Hals (47a), ills (170a)

L - - S Lais (17c), Laos (80d,129c), Lars (51d,121b), lass (95b), lees (46a, 142a), lens (95b,111a,129b,162d), less (100c,108b,141d), Lias (66a), liss (54b,58b,60c,129d,140a) Lois (165d,183c), Loos, loss (42c,123d,178b), lots, Lubs (94c), Lyas (66a)

- LT - alta (89c,152d), alto (152b,176c,177a)

- - LT Balt (93a), belt (16a,31a), bolt (13b,54d,58b,132d,160a), bult (76d), celt (30c,82c,123a,156c,167b,179b), Celt (10a,180a,b), colt (78c,131a,185d,186b), Colt, cult (141d,161c), dolt (20c,59c,157d), felt, galt, gelt (101c), gilt (69c,77c,151d,185d), halt (13b,28a,38d, 156d), hilt (73c), holt (36d,119b,184b), jilt, jolt (143b), Kelt (180b), kilt, lilt (93a,131a,147a), malt (17c), melt, milt (153d), molt (27a, 143d) pelt (53a), salt (35d,105b,123a,136c,141c,149d), silt (104b, 142a), tilt (26b,d,166a), tolt, volt (49b,78c), Walt (96b), welt (36d,131b,145a,b,177b,d), wilt (46b), yelt (151b)

L - - T lact (34c), laet (60d), lait (62a), lant, last (36c,50b,145a,174c), leet (26a,38a,139d), left (42c), lent (54d), Lent (115d,141c), lest (59d, 163d), Lett (16a,90a,93a), lift (49b), lilt (93a,131a,147a), lint (46a, 58d), list (26d,27b,75b,83d,134a,138b,165d), loft (14c,69d,104b, 178b), loot (22a,118a,119d,136a,153d), lost, lout (15c,22a,24b,45b, 109a,157d), lust (41b)

LU - - Luba (191), lube (110a), Lubs (94c), luce (58c,117d), Luce (7b,35a), luck (28d), lucy, Lucy (183c), Ludd (23c), ludi (133b), ludo (65a, 112b), luff (136b), luge (148a), Lugh (28b), luif, luke, Luke (52a, 96a), lull (25c,126d,150c), lulu (19a,57b,112c), Lulu (183d), lump (45a,160c), luna (103c), Luna (102b), lune (38c,73b,74d), lung, luny (38b), lupe (19a,64a), lura (22d,82a), lure (41c,51a,54b,163a), lurg (96d,141b,184d), Luri (191), lurk (92a,147d), lush (94d), lust (41b), lute (11c,28b,84d,105a,131d), luxe (61c,62d,159c)

- LU - alum (14a,45c), Alur (191), blub, blue (33c,98c,102c,150d,173a), blup, blur, blut (66b), club (39c), clue, Elul (102b), flub (22b), flue (8b,30a), flux (28d,58d), glub, glue (7b,156a), glug, glum (102c, 159a), glut (52c,70a,137c,159d), Ilus (88d,170b), plug (156d,184d), plum, plup, plus (10b,102c) slub (171c), slue (97b,148b,160a), slug (46b,99b,157c), slum, slur (44b,124c,148b,168a), ulua (57a,74c), Ulua (141b)

- - LU Aalu (6b,48d), aulu (74c,168c), balu (104b,159a,181d), hulu (55b), lalu (48d), iglu (51c,149b), lulu (19a,57b,112c), Lulu (183d), pelu (30a,106d,168c), pulu (74c), Sulu (102c), tolu (16a), Tulu (45d), zulu (171d,175d), Zulu (86a)

L - - U latu (190), lieu (118c,155d), limu (141c), Lleu (40c), lulu (19a,57b, 112c), Lulu (183d)

- LV - Alva (151d), Ulva (141b)

LW - - Lwow

L - - W Llew (40c), Lwow

- - LX calx (23c,75c,112c), falx (133b)

L - - X lanx (133a,b), lynx (26c,181d), Lynx (36b)

LY - - lyam (139a), Lyas (66a), lynx (26c,181d), Lynx (36b), Lyra (36b, 74a), lyre (11c,81c,105a,111c), lyse

- LY - Alya (155b,c), Alys (183c), Clym (12b), Ilyn (120d,140a)

- - LY ably (147c), ally (14a,35c,d,173c), coly (104a), eely (185a), holy, idly, inly, July, Lely (47a), lily, moly (76a,181c), oily (110b, 172c), only (24d,52c,98d,147a,150a), Orly (8b), paly (194), pily, poly (34c,76b), puly, rely (16b,170b), rily (176a), ugly, vily (54b), wily (13b,38b,39c)

L - - Y Lacy, lady, laky, lazy, Lely (47a), levy (14a,162b), lily, limy (176d), liny (157b), livy (132d,133a), logy (46d), lory (19a,114a), lucy, Lucy (183c), luny (38b)

L - - Z Linz (40d), litz (127b), Lodz

MA - - maal (188), ma'am (95a,166b), maar (177a), Maas (132a), Maat (69a,b,85d), Maba (103a,168d), mabi (58d), mace (49d,108d,153b, 154d,161a,178a), mack, made, Madi (174a), mado (14d,57a,170b), mage (95b), magg (95b), Magh (102a), magi (123c), Magi (95b, 116c,183a), maha (28c,88c,136d), mahr (103a), Maia (76b,109a, 153b,155b,177c), maid (45b,142d), mail (12d,99b,121c), maim (43d,81a,105c), main (29d,35d,123d), mais (61b), maja (151c), Maja (153b), majo, make (35b,36d,54a,123a), maki (91b), mako (18a,19a,20d,143c,168c,182c), Maku (192), mala (89b,c,90a,94b, 97d,109d,185c), male (154d), Male (45d), mali (27b), mall (95d, 124b,143b), malm (32a,92b), malo (23a,74c,152a), malt (17c), mama, Mama (116d), mamo (19a,74b), mana (30a,120d,122a, 159c), mand (28b), mane, mani (115c), mann (189), Mann (9c, 48c,185c), mano (71d,73d,74b,83b), Mans (30a), Manu (10a,76d, 77a,b), Manx (27b,28a,82d), many (108d), mapo (68a,148d), mara (114d), Mara (24a,d,105b,107b), marc (70c), Marc (96a) mare (78b), Mare (108b), mari (61d), Mari (16a), mark (146b,155a), Mark (52a, 96a), marl (32a,42c,55d), maro (144d), Mars (68c,118d,119a,129a, 178a), mart (49d,97a), Mart (96b,183d), maru (84c,144d), Mary (50c,126b,183c), masa (37a), mash (39b,156c), mask (44a,45c), mass (8a,24b,35b,142d), mast (17c,108d,120b,144d,152d), masu (57a,84c), mate (18c,35b,41d,113a,154a,162c), math (77a), Matt, maty (80c), maud (53d,71a,136d,143c), Maud (181a,183c), Maui (120d), maul (73c,96b), maun (139d), maya (77a,179b), Maya (23d, 186c), Mayo (193), maze (87b,157d)

- MA - amah (95b,108d,111c), amar (189), imam (25c,102d,103a), Oman (159a), omao (165c), omar (103b), Omar (48c,51b,116c,163b), Xmas

- - MA alma (40d,53d,146d,147a), Alma (38d,183c), amma (6a), atma (150d), bema (28d,31a,114b,119b,125b,137a), boma (7d),

cima (83b,c), **coma** (91c,157d,170c,172b), **cyma** (101a,b), **dama** (65d,152b), **Duma** (135c), **Emma** (183c), **Erma** (183c), **Fama** (135a), **Gama** (121c), **Goma** (191), **Hima** (191), **ijma** (103b), **Irma** (96d), **jama** (103b), **Kama** (56d), **lama** (23d,24a,91d,165b), **lima** (17b,152b,174d), **Lima** (31b), **loma** (58b,63d), **mama, Mama** (116d), **mima** (185d), **Nama** (78c), **Nema** (34d,48c,134b,164d,176c), **Numa** (133a), **pima** (37c), **Pima** (192), **puma** (27b,37c,55b,103d), **Rama** (77a,80b,176d), **rima** (23a,30c,32a,58a,110d), **Roma** (83c,d), **sama** (105c,169d), **sima** (132b), **soma** (10c,21c,34a,48a,81d,136b), **Tama** (192), **tema** (12a,164a), **Toma** (191), **xema** (72c), **Xema** (12c), **Yama** (57a,68a), **Yima** (84a,116b,c), **Yuma, Zama** (73d, 141d)

M - - A   **Maba** (103a,168d), **maha** (28c,88c,136d), **Maia** (76b,109a,153b, 155b,177c), **maja** (151c), **Maja** (153b), **mala** (89b,c,90a,94b,97d, 109d,185c), **mama, Mama** (116d), **mana** (30a,120d,122a,159c), **mara** (114d), **Mara** (24a,d,105b,107b), **masa** (37a), **maya** (77a, 179b), **Maya** (23d,186c), **meda** (110a), **mega** (34b,c), **mela** (34a, 129d), **mesa** (49b,76d,119b,161a), **meta** (132d,133a), **Meta, mica** (82c,100b,146c), **mila** (188), **mima** (185d), **mina** (10b,70b,71d, 179d), **Mina** (23a,183d), **mira** (174d), **Mira** (155b), **moha** (42b, 83d), **Mola** (159c), **mona** (72b,101d), **mora** (42b,65a,72b,83d,99b, 153a,161a), **mota** (103a), **moxa** (27d,30c), **muga, mura** (84d), **Mura** (192), **Musa** (16a), **muta** (28d,103a), **myna** (19a,c,70b), **Myra** (10a, 31b,183c), **myxa** (168c,169a)

- MB -   **amba** (161a), **ambi** (34a,122c), **ambo** (125b,128b), **imbe** (37a,56a, 133d), **umbo** (22b)

- - MB   **bomb** (144a), **comb** (38c), **dumb** (153b), **iamb** (59c), **jamb** (12d, 45c,118a,146b,174a), **lamb, Lamb** (49c), **limb** (12d,22d), **nimb** (31b,73b,92a,107b,131d), **numb, rumb** (120b), **tomb, Zimb** (6c)

M - - B   **medb, Moab** (18d,85a,86d,94a)

M - - C   **marc** (70c), **Marc** (96a)

M - - D   **maid** (45b,142d), **mand** (28b), **maud** (53d,71a,136d,143c), **Maud** (181a,183c), **mead** (46a,78a,97d,99b), **Mead** (78a), **meed** (128c, 131a), **meld** (26a,41c,99a,118b), **mend** (130b), **mild** (32a,66a), **mind** (75c,81d,93d,109b), **Moed** (100c), **mold** (54d,143c), **mood** (44c), **mudd** (188), **mund** (124d)

ME - -   **mead** (46a,78a,97d,99b), **Mead** (78a), **meal** (72a,130b), **mean** (15a, 42b,146c,156b), **meat** (59b), **meda** (110a), **Medb, Mede** (10a,b,13c), **medi** (34c), **meed** (128c,131a), **meek** (93d,99d), **meer, meet** (11d, 13d,36a,50a,81d,142d), **mega** (34b,c), **mein** (30b), **meio** (188), **mela** (34a,129d), **meld** (26a,41c,99a,118b), **mele** (74b,150b), **melt, memo** (108b), **mend** (130b), **mene** (19a,73d,108d,185c), **Ment** (54b,164a), **menu** (19a,27a), **Menu, meou, meow, mere** (16c,22b, 62a,78b,87d,96c,110c,120d,146d,148b), **meri** (20b), **mero** (72a), **Meru** (77a,103d), **mesa** (49b,76d,119b,161a), **mese** (71c), **mesh** (50d,106c), **mess** (22b,44b,77c,85d,104b,165c,173d), **meta** (132d, 133a), **Meta, mete** (9a,11d,22b,44c,45b,98a,121c), **meum** (27a, 89c), **Meum, mewl** (180d), **mews** (154c)

- ME -   **amen** (14a,80b,94a,137a,149c,175c,184b), **Amen** (86d,127d,159b, 164a), **amer** (61b), **Ames** (9c,82a), **Amex** (184d), **Emer** (39b,183c),

328

emeu (111d), **Imer, Omei** (24a), **omen** (14c,59d,60a,121c,123a, 146b), **omer** (51a,75c), **smee** (19b,46c,d,118b,119d,141b,181b), **Smee** (116d), **smew** (19b,46d,99a,137d), **T-men** (168b), **Ymer** (67a, 131c)

- - ME acme (39c,115c,186b), **alme** (40d), **arme** (63a,179b), **came** (182b), **Came** (192), **come, cyme** (58d,69c), **dame** (67b,87c,166b), **deme** (71b,c,167d), **dime, dome** (39c,133c,155d), **fame** (130a) **feme** (181b), **fume** (129a,149a,157a), **game** (64d,154a), **gime** (77d), **home, Hume** (50c), **kame** (67b,139b), **Kome** (71d), **lame** (38d,43d, 73b), **lime** (25b,27d,31b,102d,168c), **Lome, mime** (24a,71b,85a, 100a), **Mime** (131d,148d), **name** (8a,11b,d,25c,46c,107c,130b,157d, 163b,166b), **nome** (71c,163b), **Nome, oime** (8b), **pome** (11d), **Pume** (137d,175b,185b), **rame** (22d), **rime** (30c,36a,58a,63d,77c), **Rome** (31c,51d), **ryme** (178d), **same** (44d,79b), **seme** (45c,138b,151b, 154b,155c,157b), **sime** (101d), **some** (114b,121c,126a), **tame** (45a, 66a), **Tame, time** (47a,131a), **tome** (21d,177c), **ulme** (49c), **zeme** (55d,161b,180b), **zyme** (55c)

M - - E mace (49d,108d,153b,154d,161a,178a), **made, mage** (95b), **make** (35b,36d,54a,123a), **male** (154d), **Male** (45d), **mane, mare** (78b), **Mare** (108b), **mate** (18c,35b,41d,113a,154a,162c), **maze** (87b, 157d), **Mede** (10a,b,13c), **mele** (74b,150b), **mene** (19a,73d,108d, 185c), **mere** (16c,22b,62a,78b,87d,96c,110c,120d,146d,148b), **mese** (71c), **mete** (9a,11d,22b,44c,45b,98a,121c), **mice, mide** (110a), **mike, Mike** (96b), **mile** (64c), **mime** (24a,71b,85a,100a), **Mime** (131d,148d), **mine** (69c,79d,111b,124c), **mire** (21c,104b), **mise** (8a, 10a,70c), **mite** (12b,81b,82a,114a,c,148c,d,181b), **Mixe** (192), **mode** (54d,96b,157d,179a), **moke** (45c,157d), **mole** (19d,23a,24d,85a, 117c,155c), **Mole** (88c), **mope** (92d,159a), **more** (71a), **More** (50b), **Mose** (96b), **mote** (114c,153a), **moue** (61d,62b), **move, mule** (45b, 148b,153c,180b), **mure** (177d), **muse** (65b,93d,120d,164c), **Muse** (68d), **mute** (146c,153b)

M - - F miff (44c), **moff** (53b,146c), **muff**

M - - G magg (95b), **migg** (96c), **Ming** (30b,c), **morg** (188), **mung** (70d)

MH - - mhor (180b)

- - MH samh (56b)

M - - H Magh (102a), **mash** (39b,156c), **math** (77a), **mesh** (50d,106c), **moth, Moth** (112d), **much, mush** (97d), **muth** (188), **myth** (8b,91a)

MI - - miam (14d), **mian** (97c,147b,166b), **Miao** (30a,b), **mias** (111a), **miau** (27b,99b), **miaw** (27b,99b), **mica** (82c,100b,146c), **mice, mick** (82c), **mico** (97a), **mide** (110a), **Midi** (151b), **mien** (11c, 17b,26d,44c,96b), **miff** (44c), **migg** (96c), **mike, Mike** (96b), **mila** (188), **mild** (32a,66a), **mile** (64c), **milk, mill** (126c), **milo** (70b,87c, 150d), **Milo, milt** (153d), **mima** (185d), **mime** (24a,71b,85a,100a), **Mime** (131d,148d), **mimi** (14d), **Mimi** (87b,110d,125b,183d), **mina** (10b,70b,71d,179d), **Mina** (23a,183d), **mind** (75c,81d,93d,109b), **mine** (69c,79d,111b,124c), **ming** (30b,c), **mink** (176d), **mino** (84c), **mint** (13a,33b,58b,76a), **minx** (116c), **miny, Mira** (155b,174d), **mire** (21c,104b), **mirk** (41a,67d), **miro** (19a,106d,184a), **Miro** (113a, 151d), **miry, mise** (8a,10a,70c), **miss, mist** (46b,59b,174d), **mite** (12b,81b,82a,114a,c,148c,d,181b), **mitt** (56c), **mitu** (39d), **mity, Mixe** (192), **mixy**

- MI -   amia (22c,170d), amic (9d), amid (9d,50a), amie (61d), amil (45a, 48a,185c), amin (9d), amir (7c,12a,103a,b,123c,170d), amit (94a), Emil (96a), Emim (67a,100d), emir (12a,103a,b,123c,134d,135a, 171a), emit (43d,49a,53c,58d,83a,142c), imid (29c), omit (49c, 52c,106b,114c,147d)

- - MI   admi (65d), ammi (98c), demi (34b,122c), hami (78a), hemi (122c), immi (189), jami (103b), kami (68a,84b), Kami (88c,107c,144c), Komi (191), mimi (14d), Mimi (87b,110d,125b,183d), rami (22d), Remi (10b), romi (72d), semi (34b,80b,122c,d), Simi (82d), zemi (55d,161b,180b)

M - - I   Mabi (58d), Madi (174a), magi (123c), Magi (95b,116c,183a), maki (91b), mali (27b), mani (115c), mari (61d), Mari (16a), Maui (120d), medi (34c), Midi (151b), mimi (14d), Mimi (87b,110d,125b,183d), moki (127b), Moki

M - - J   munj (70d)

M - - K   Mack, mark (146b,155a), Mark (52a,96a), mask (44a,45c), meek (93d,99d), mick (82c), milk, mink (176d), mirk (41a,67d), mock (131b,162b), monk (28b,63c,129d), mosk (97b,103b), muck, mulk (60d), murk (41a,67d), musk (116b)

- ML -   amla (48a,161d,168c,169a), amli (48a,161d,168c,169a)

M - - L   maal (188), mail (12d,99b,121c), mall (95d,124b,143b), marl (32a, 42c,55d), maul (73c,96b), meal (72a,130b), merl (20b), mewl (180d), mill (126c), moil (46c,184c), moll, Moll (183d), mull (53b, 135a,164c)

- MM -   amma (6a), ammi (98c), ammo (9d), ammu (9d), Emma (183c), immi (189)

M - - M   ma'am (95a,166b), maim (43d,81a,105c), malm (32a,92b), meum (27a,89c), Meum, miam (14d)

- MN -   omni (34a)

- - MN   damn, Domn (135a), famn (188), hymn (150c), limn (45d,121c)

M - - N   main (29d,35d,123d), mann (189), Mann (9c,48c,185c), maun (139d), mean (15a,42b,146c,156b), mein (30b), mian (97c,147b, 166b), mien (11c,17b,26d,44c,96b), moan, moon (40b,132c,137c), morn, mown

MO - -   Moab (18d,85a,86d,94a), moan, moat (44d), mock (131b,162b), mode (54d,96b,157d,179a), Moed (100c), moff (53b,146c), mogo (74b), moha (42b,83d), moho (19a,78a), mohr (65d), moil (46c, 184c), moio (188), mojo (177c), moke (45c,157d), moki (127b), moko (96c), Mola (159c), mold (54d,143c), mole (19d,23a,24d,85a, 117c,155c), Mole (88c), moll, Moll (183d), molt (27a,143d), moly (76a,181c), mona (72b,101d), monk (28b,63c,129d), mono (34c, 78d,122d,147a), Mono (193), mons (89c), Mons (184d), mont (62b), mood (44c), moon (40b,132c,137c), moor (10a,75b,137b,141d, 178b), Moor (102c,d,111d), moot (41b,44c), mope (92d,159a), mora (42b,65a,72b,83d,99b,153a,161a), more (71a), More (50b), morg (188), morn, moro (19a,56c), Moro (100a,103a,117a,159a), Mors (41b), mort (41b,47a,78b,136d), Mose (96b), mosk (97b,103b), moss (91d,104c,114a,170c), most, mosy (67d), mota (103a), mote (114c,153a), moth, Moth (112d), moto (104b), moue (61d,62b), move, mown, moxa (27d,30c), **Moxo** (192), **mozo** (152b)

-MO- amoi (62a), amok (18b,63c), **Amon** (86d,96b,127d,159b,164a), amor (152b), **Amor** (39c,68b), **Amos** (96a,144b), **Amoy** (88c)

--MO ammo (9d), atmo (34d,174d), **Como, demo** (122d), **hemo** (34a, 122b), **homo** (122d), **ikmo** (18b), **itmo** (18b), **mamo** (19a,b,74b), **memo** (108b), **nemo** (34b), **Nemo** (56a,85c), **Pomo** (192), **Sumo**

M--O mado (14d,57a,170b), **majo, mako** (18a,19a,20d,143c,168c,182c), **malo** (23a,74c,152a), **mamo** (19a,74b), **mano** (71d,73d,74b,83b), **mapo** (68a,148d), **maro** (144d), **Mayo** (193), **meio** (188), **memo** (108b), **mero** (72a), **Miao** (30a,b), **mico** (97a), **milo** (70b,87c, 150d), **Milo, mino** (84c), **miro** (19a,106d,184a), **Miro** (113a,151d), **mogo,** (74b), **moho** (19a,78a), **moio** (188), **mojo** (177c), **moko** (96c), **mono** (34c,78d,122d,147a), **Mono** (193), **moro** (19a,56c), **Moro** (100a,103a,117a,159a), **moto** (104b), **Moxo** (192), **mozo** (152b), **Muso** (192), **Muzo** (192), **myxo**

-MP- impi (86a), **umph**

--MP bump, camp (163b), **damp** (101a), **dump, gamp** (172a), **gimp** (169d), **Gump** (43b), **hemp** (26a,37a,56a,133d), **hump** (124d), **jump, kemp** (139b), **lamp** (92a,94c), **limp** (58a,81a,177d), **lump** (45a, 160c), **mump** (29b,153d), **pomp** (111d,112d), **pump, ramp** (65a, 80b,127b,148b), **romp** (63d), **rump, samp** (70b,77d,121b), **simp** (59c,146d), **sump** (28c,45d,100b), **tamp** (46b,112b,121d), **tump** (60a,76d,103d), **tymp** (20c), **vamp** (80a,145a)

M--P mump (29b,153d)

-MR- amra (77c), **Omri** (18c,86d)

M--R maar (177a), **mahr** (103a), **meer, mhor** (180b), **mohr** (65d), **moor** (10a,75b,137b,141d,178b), **Moor** (102c,d,111d), **Muir** (8b, 142c), **murr** (72b,128b)

-MS- Omsk

--MS alms (29a), **arms, Rems**

M--S Maas (132a), **Mais** (61b), **Mans** (30a), **Mars** (68c,118d,119a,129a, 178a), **mass** (8a,24b,35b,142d), **mess** (22b,44b,77c,85d,104b,165c, 173d), **mews** (154c), **mias** (111a), **miss, mons** (89c), **Mons** (184d), **Mors** (41b), **moss** (91d,104c,114a,170c), **muss** (135b,173d)

M--T Maat (69a,b,85d), **malt** (17c), **mart** (49d,97a), **Mart** (96b,183d), **mast** (17c,108d,120b,144d,152d), **Matt, meat** (59b), **meet** (11d,13d,36a,50a,81d,142d), **melt, Ment** (54b,164a), **milt** (153d), **mint** (13a,33b,58b,76a), **mist** (46b,59b,174d), **mitt** (56c), **moat** (44d), **molt** (27a,143d), **mont** (62b), **moot** (41b,44c), **mort** (41b,47a, 78b,136d), **most, must** (70c,101a,106d,157d,182c), **mutt** (39c, 101d), **myst** (71c,123b)

MU-- Muav (66a), **much, muck, mudd** (188), **muff, muga, Muir** (8b, 142c), **mule** (45b,148b,153c,180c), **mulk** (60d), **mull** (53b,135a, 164c), **mump** (29b,153d), **mund** (124d), **mung** (70d), **munj** (70d), **mura** (84d), **Mura** (192), **mure** (177d), **murk** (41a,67d), **murr** (72b, 128b), **Musa** (16a), **muse** (65b,93d,120d,164c), **Muse** (68d), **mush** (97d), **musk** (116b), **Muso** (192), **muss** (135b,173d), **must** (70c,101a, 106d,157d,182c), **muta** (28d,103a), **mute** (146c,153b), **muth** (188), **mutt** (39c,101d), **Muzo** (192)

- MU - Amun (86d,127d,159b,164a), **smug, smur** (32c,46b,100c), **smut** (32d,44a,119a,150c)

- - MU ammu (9d), **Atmu** (143a,159b), limu (141c), rimu (79d, 106d,129a, 168c)

M - - U **Maku** (192), **Manu** (10a,76d,77a,b), **maru** (84c,144d), **masu** (57a, 84c), **menu** (19a,27a), **Menu, meou, Meru** (77a,103d), **miau** (99b), **mitu** (39d), **Mitu**

M - - V Muav (66a)

M - - W meow, miaw (27b,99b)

M - - X Manx (27b,28a,82d), minx (116c)

MY - - myna (19a,c,70b), **Myra** (10a,31b,183c), **myst** (71c,123b), **myth** (8b,91a), **myxa** (168c,169a), **myxo**

- MY - amyl (155c), emyd (163c,167c), **Emys** (167c,171b)

- - MY army (78c), demy (113d), **domy, elmy, fumy, homy** (38b), **ismy** (45a), limy (176d), rimy (63d)

M - - Y many (108d), **Mary** (50c,126b,183c), **maty** (80c), **miny, miry, mity, mixy, moly** (76a,181c), **mosy** (67d)

NA - - **Naab, naam** (44c,150b), **nabk** (30d,164d), **nabo** (117a), **Nabu** (68c, 183a), **nach, nael** (189), **naga** (13d,33a,55b,127c), **Naga** (24c,77a, 88c,176d), **Nagy** (78d), **Naia** (33a), **naid** (63c), **naif** (74b,105d), **naik, nail** (31d,54d,141d,161d,173a), **naio** (107a,168c), **Nair** (45d), **nais** (63c,132a), **Naja** (33a), **Nala** (77a), **Nama** (78c), **name** (8a, 11b,25c,46c,107c,130b,157d,163b,166b), **nana** (118b), **Nana** (15c, 105d,116d,186d), **nane** (139d), **naos** (28a,71c,137a,163a), **Naos** (155b), **napa** (25c,67d,90d), **Napa** (182c), **nape** (15b,108c,d), **napu** (29d,80d), **nard** (13a,97c,102b,110a,153c), **Nare** (93c), **nark** (81a, 156d), **nary** (108b), **nase** (26b,75a,124b), **Nash** (9c), **nasi** (34c,108a, 115a), **Nast** (9c,27a), **nata** (47c), **Nata** (15c), **Nate** (22b), **Nath** (155c), **Nato** (6a,8d), **natr** (189), **Natt** (107b), **naut** (141b), **nave** (30d,31a,78d,114b,180c), **navy** (33c,58b), **naze** (26b,124b), **Nazi**

- NA - anai (163b,181a), **Anak** (67a), **anam** (159a,168c), **Anam, anan** (49a,159a,180c), **Anas** (46c,d), **Anat** (138c,147d), **Anax** (43c, 120c) **anay** (72b,163b,181a), **enam** (70c,77a), **Enam** (85c), **gnar** (72a), **gnat** (59a,81b,99c), **gnaw** (20a,107a,178b), **inar** (65b), **knab** (107a), **knag** (139c), **knap** (76d,107a,139b,159b,166a,170c,185b), **knar** (87c,134b), **Onan** (18c,85c), **snab** (23c,139a), **snag** (11b, 27b,35c,87c,124b,166a), **snap** (23a,36d,38b,48b,54d,56c,58c,149d), **unal** (147a), **unau** (148c,171d)

- - NA anna (190), **Anna** (110c,166d), **arna** (24a,181b), **Bana** (67a), **bena** (176a), **bina** (77a), **bona** (89d), **Bona** (183c), **buna** (161c), **Cana** (57a,64b,100c), **cena** (88d,133a), **Cuna** (193), **Dana** (28a,96a, 171d), **dona** (83d,121c,151d), **dyna** (34c), **Edna** (183c), **Enna** (146a), **etna** (75b,153c,157a,175d,177a,c), **fana, gena** (29b), **Gona** (106d), **guna** (106a,137b), **Iona** (28a,82d), **Jena** (105d,165b), **kana** (84d), **kina** (126d), **kona** (74c), **Iana** (58a,66a,90a,184b), **Iena** (56d), **Lena** (36b), **lina** (188), **Lina** (183d), **luna** (103c), **Luna** (102b), **mana** (30a,120d,122a,159c), **mina** (10b,70b,71d,179d), **Mina** (23a, 183d), **mona** (72b,101d), **myna** (19a,c,70b), **nana** (118b), **Nana** (15c,105d,116d,186d), **nina** (152a), **Nina** (26c,33d,68d,183d),

nona (89b,107b), **Nona** (69a,114a,183c), **orna** (169d,182c), **Pana, pina** (35d,118b), **puna** (10b,33b,104a,119b,182a), **rana** (77a,123c), **Rana** (63d), **rena** (132c), **sana** (56a,166d), **Sana** (185d), **sina** (46c), **Sina** (102d,103d), **tana** (159a), **Tana** (87d), **Tina** (183d), **tuna** (57a, b,123b,170d), **ulna** (21d,39b), **urna** (133a), **vena** (90a,175a), **vina** (77a,105a), **Xina** (183d), **Yana** (192,193), **zona** (144c,186d)

N - - A **naga** (13d,33a,55b,127c), **Naga** (24c,77a,88c,176d), **Naia** (33a), **Naja** (33a), **Nala** (77a), **Nama** (78c), **nana** (118b), **Nana** (15c,105d, 116d,186d), **napa** (25c,67d,90d), **Napa** (182c), **nata** (47c), **Nata** (15c), **nema** (34d,48c,134b,164d,176c), **Nepa** (106b,178c), **Nera** (165b), **Neva** (91b,132a), **Nina** (26c,33d,68d,183d), **nipa** (14b, 46b,48a,164a,168c), **Nola, nona** (89b,107b), **Nona** (69a,114a,183c), **Nora** (79b,107a,164c,183c), **nota** (15c,89c), **nova** (20c,106d,155c, 174d), **noxa, Nuba** (108c), **Nuda** (39b), **Numa** (133a)

- NB - **anba** (36d)

N - - B **Naab, nimb** (31b,73b,92a,107b,131d), **numb**

- NC - **ance** (158b,c,d), **ancy** (158c), **ence** (158c), **Inca** (14b,30a), **inch, onca** (189), **once** (60b,79b), **unca** (49a), **unci** (31d), **unco** (140c), **Ynca** (193)

- - NC **banc** (61a,85c), **zinc** (21a)

- ND - **anda** (23a,168c), **Ande** (193), **Andi** (27d), **Andy** (96b), **endo** (34d, 122d,183b), **inde, onde** (63a,178d), **unde** (179a), **undo** (11a,93d), **undy** (179a)

- - ND **Arnd** (67a), **band** (72a,157c), **bend** (39d,171b), **bind** (33b,165c), **bond** (92a,101c,141d,143b,159d,165c), **bund** (49c,66c,90c), **cond** (156a), **fend** (114b,178b), **find** (44a), **fond** (7c,94b), **fund** (6d,101c, 130c), **Gond, hand** (60c,114c,115d,184c), **hind** (15b,41d,45a), **kind** (150d,153a,174d), **land** (44a,163c), **lend** (6d,79d), **mand** (28b), **mend** (130b), **mind** (75c,81d,93d,109b), **mund** (124d), **pend, pond, pund** (189), **rand** (16d,22a,131b,145a,b), **Rand** (69c), **rend** (32a, 159c,162c,185a), **rind** (53a,115c), **Rind** (109c,174b), **rynd** (100a), **sand** (71d,146c), **send** (42c,44b,95c,121c,130a,144c,168b), **Sind, tend** (26d,80b,93a,100a), **tind** (86b), **tund** (121d), **vend** (97a,115c, 142b), **Vend** (10b,148a), **wand** (120b,132c,156a), **wend** (67d,123d), **Wend** (10b,148a), **wind** (33b,39d,171c,185a), **yond** (164d), **Zend**

N - - D **naid** (63c), **nard** (13a,97c,102b,110a,153c), **need** (42b,52d,87b, 122a,178a), **Nejd, NKVD** (135d), **Nudd** (23c)

NE - - **neaf** (58a,73c), **Neal, neap** (165c,167a,177b), **near** (11d,32c,107b), **neat** (165c,169d), **Nebo** (68c,102d,103d,183a), **neck** (83a), **need** (42b,52d,87b,122a,178a), **neem** (96d,168c,169a), **neep** (140c, 171b), **neer** (14b,86b,108b), **Neil** (96a), **nein** (66c), **Nejd, Nell** (110a, 183d), **nema** (34d,48c,134b,164d,176c), **nemo** (34b), **Nemo** (56a,85c), **nene** (19b,74c), **neon** (65c), **Nepa** (106b,178c), **Nera** (165b), **Neri, Nero** (8a,126d,133a,150b,172c), **ness** (26b,75a,124b), **nest** (38b,74b,130d,149c,160b), **nete** (71c,108b,163d), **neti** (164a), **nett, neue** (66c), **Neva** (91b,132a), **neve** (56d,67c,70c,149b), **news** (165c), **newt** (48d),136c,169d), **next** (106a)

- NE - **Aner** (18d,96b), **anes** (110c,140a), **anet** (43c), **anew** (7c), **inee** (120b), **Inez** (45c,183c), **knee** (85b), **knew, knez** (123c), **oner** (20d, 53a,75c,162d,173a,d), **ones** (116a), **sned** (93d,125a,140a), **snee**

(40a,43d,87a), **sneg** (139b)

- - NE acne (147c), aine (49b,62c,142c), **Anne** (50c,84a,143b,183c), **a-one** (52b,167b), **Arne** (35c,50c,134d), aune (188), bane (74a,106b,120b, 139a), bene (18a,83c,90a,106d,122a,180a), bine (145b,156a,171c, 176b), bone, cane (17b,128a,156a,159a,177d), **Cane, cene** (34c), cine (104b,152c), cone (66b,150a,157c), **Dane** (85d,107d,138a), dene (137a), **Dene** (192), dine, done, dune (137a), dyne (59d,173b), eine (66c), enne (34c), erne (19c,d,47b,54b,141a), esne (10c, 45b,142c,148a,164d), fane (30d,137a,162d), fine (49b,50a,104b, 115d,159a), gane (185b), gene (54a), **Gene** (96b), gone (6b,15c,42c, 44c,114d), gyne (34b,55b,183c), hone (110a,143c,180d), **Ione** (24b,88d,94d), jane (190), **Jane** (183c), **June** (183c), kane (74c), kine (38a,112c), lane (134b,157b), lene (36b,149a,172b), line (12b, 22b,36d,38a,126c,134b,157b,158b,162d,175c), **Ione** (150a), lune (38c,73b,74d), mane, mine (69c,79d,111b,124c), mene (19a,73d, 108d,185c), nene (19b,74c), nine (26c,104d), none (108b), ohne (66d,183b), orne (169d,182c), **Orne** (25b), pane (113c,155a,b), pene, pine (36a,52a,88c,93c,168c,d,169a), pone (37a,85b), rine (44d,75d, 135c), rone (127c,164b), rune (9b,67a,94a,95a,105c,107d,120a, 141d,163d), sane (128a), sine (64c,66b,90a,97c,126a,163b,169d, 183b), syne (140b,147a), **Tane** (120d), tene (34d,131b), tine (11b, 124b,167b), tone (6c,118c,150d), tune (8b,12c,98c), tyne, **Tyne** (108a), vane (179b,182a), vine (32b), wane (41c,43c), wine, zone (44c,50a,160a)

N - - E name (8a,11b,d,25c,46c,107c,130b,157d,163b), nane (139d), nape (15b,108c,d), **Nare** (93c), nase (26b,75a,124b), **Nate** (22b), nave (30d,31a,78d,114b,180c), naze (26b,124b), nene (19b,74c), nete (71c,108b,163d), neue (66c), neve (56d,67c,70c,149b), nice (54d, 119c,130c), **Nice** (98c), nide (23c,72a,106c,116d), nife (37a), **Nike** (69c,100c,182d), nile (33c,71d), **Nile** (106b), nine (26c,104d), **Niue** (137d), node (35c,85b,87c,94d,120a,124d,160c), nome (71c,163b), **Nome, none** (108b), **Nore** (163d), nose (118d,125a,149b), note (98c,109b,124b,128d,130a,177c), nove (83b), noze (75a), nude (16c,172d), **Nupe** (191)

N - - F naif (74b,105d), neaf (58a,73c)

NG - - ngai (48a,159c), ngan

- NG - ange (61a), ango (171a), inga (145d,170a), **Inge** (24d,67d,117c 119c)

- - NG bang (75d,105d,148a), beng (43a), bing, bong, bung (119d,156d), cang (184a), dang, ding (130b), dong, fang (167b), **Fong** (40b), **Fung** (191), gang (38c), gong, hang (160a), hing (13c), hong (30b), hung, **Jung** (125a), k'ang (30a), king (26c,29c), kung (125b), ling (24c,57a,b,75b,178c), long (38b), lung, **Ming** (30b,c), mung (70d), pang (165b), ping, pong, pung (22c,148b), **Qung** (191), rang, ring (50a), **Rong** (88c), rung (28c,39a), sang, sing (26d,178a), song (12c,170c), sung, **Sung** (30b), tang (30b,58b,186b), teng (188), ting (166a), **Ting** (30c), tong (30a,c), tung (110a,168c), uang (131a), vang (72d,134a,140b), wang (189), wing (10d,58c,59a, 118b,d), wong (56a), yang (30b,70a), zing

N - - G niog (33a,168c), nogg (48d)

334

- - NH binh (189), **hunh?, sinh** (97c), **tanh** (97c)

N - - H Nach, Nash (9c), Nath (155c), nigh (106a), Nish (19d), Noah (88a, 99b)

NI - - Nias (82d), nibs (116c), nice (54d,119c,130c), Nice (98c), nick (30c,108b), nide (23c,72a,106c,116d), nidi (106c), nife (37a), nigh (106a), Nike (69c,100c,182d), nile (33c,71d), Nile (106b), nill (173d), nimb (31b,73b,92a,107b,131d), nina (152a), Nina (26c, 33d,68d,183d), nine (26c,104d), nino (152a), niog (33a,168c), niou (188), nipa (14b,46b,48a,164a,168c), Nish (19d), nisi (90a, 173c), nito (55c), Niue (137d)

- NI - anil (47c,80d,180b), Anim (18d), anis (55c), Enid (13b,25d,66b, 163a,183c), Enif (155b), enin (20d), inia (9b,109b), Inia (28c,45b), knip (115c), knit (173c,179b), snib (54d,93c), snig (45d), snip (32b,40a), unie (173a), Unio (105c), unis (91b), unit (101c,110c, 147a)

- - NI Aani (45a,48d), agni (88a,89c), Agni (56d,68b), arni (24a,181b), bani (190), beni (116a,142d), Beni (191), Bini (191), Boni (63b), Coni, doni (21a,28c,168a), Ioni (192), mani (115c), omni (34a), Pani (120c), rani (72d,77b,123c,127c), Reni (83d), yeni (19b,161d), Zuni (125b)

N - - I nasi (34c,108a,115a), Nazi, Neri, neti (164a), ngai (48a,159c), nidi (106c), nisi (90a,173c), nodi (35c,87c), nori (8c,141c)

- - NJ Funj, gunj (70c), munj (70d)

NK - - NKVD (135d)

- NK - ankh (38d,162b), Enki (15b), Inka (193), inky (20b)

- - NK bank (18a,58c), bonk (190), bunk, conk (41c,108a,156d,157c), dank (40b,101a), dunk (43c,79d), fink (19a,56c,157c), funk (63d, 113c), gink (48b), hank (147c), honk (70a), hunk, jink, jonk, junk (30a,134c), kink (38b,171c), konk (41c), kunk (188), lank (148b, 164b), link (36a,81d,85b), lonk (143d), mink (176d), monk (28b, 63c,129d), pank (189), pink (26d,33c,60c,138a), punk (9b,166a, 167c), rank (31d,55d,70b,92c,94d,157c), rink (147c,154a), sank, sink (41c,43c,46b,158a), sunk, tank (175a,d), tonk (173c), wink (107a), yank, Yank

N - - K nabk (30d,164d), naik, nark (81a,156d), neck (83a), nick (30c, 108b), nock (13b,108b), nook (37a,130d), nubk (30d,164d)

- NL - inly, only (24d,52c,98d,147a,150a)

N - - L nael (189), nail (31d,54d,141d,161d,173a), Neal, Neil (96a), Nell (110a,183d), nill (173d), noel (26d,150b) Noel (30d,96a), noil (87c, 178b), Noll (96b,110b), noyl (87c), null (108c,177a), nurl (33b,87c)

N - - M naam (44c,105b), Naam, neem (96d,168c,169a), norm (15a,115a, 128a,155a)

- NN - Anna (110c,166d,183c), anna (190), Anne (50c,84a,143b,183c), Enna (146a), enne (34c), Enns

- - NN binn (22c), Bonn (17d), bunn (25b), conn (43d,156a), Finn (107d), Jann (102d), jinn (42b,103b,153c), linn (120d,140a,c,168c,178d), mann (189), Mann (9c,48c,185c), rann (175c), senn (76b), sunn (56a), wynn (165d)

N - - N nein (66c), neon (65c), ngan, noon, Norn (69a,163d,174b), noun (114b,158a)

NO - - Noah (88a,99b), nobs (38c,87a), nock (13b,108b), node (35c,85b, 87c,94d,120a,124d,160c), nodi (35c,87c), noel (26d,150b), Noel (30d,96a), noes (177c), nogg (48d), noil (87c,178b), noio (107c, 163c), noir (61b,134b), noix (67c), Nola, Noll (96b,110b), nolo (42a), nome (71c,163b), Nome, nona (89b,107b), Nona (69a,114a, 183c), none (108b), nono (83b), nook (37a,130d), noon, Nora (79b, 107a,164c,183c), Nore (163d), nori (8c,141c), norm (15a,115a, 128a,155a), Norn (69a,163d,174b), nose (118d,125a,149b), Nosu (27d), nosy, nota (15c,89c), note (98c,109b,124b,128d,130a,177c), Nott (107b), noun (114b,158a), noup (124b), nous (81d,100a, 128b), nova (20c,106d,155c,174d), nove (83b), nowt (106a,139a), nowy (194), noxa, noyl (87c), noze (75a)

- NO - anoa (28a,60a,112c,181c), anon (7d,14d,79d,80b,123a,145c,150c, 164a), enol (29c,158b), Enon (18c,d), Enos (7a,18d,52a,70c,96a, 143a), enow (50d,123a,158b), knob (73c), knop (124b,170c,185b), knor (87c), knot (43c,99d,107c,124d,137b), know, snob (159c), snod (169d), snow

- - NO Aino (84a,c), Arno (27a), asno (151d), beno (113b,117a), cano (152a), dino (34b), fano (51d,96b,113c,d), fono (137a), Gano (132d), Hano (125b), hino (106d,168c), Juno (69c,85d,100c,126b), Kano (84c,177d), keno (161d,168c), kino (27c,34c,47c,72c,98b), leno (37c,53b), lino, mano (71d,73d,74b,83b), mino (84c), mono 34c,78d,122d,147a), Mono (193), nino (152a), nono (83b), pino (152c), puno (182a), Reno, sano (152b), sino (34a), Tano (192), Tino (136d), tuno (28b,168c), vino (92d,182b), xeno (34d), Zeno (71b)

N - - O nabo (117a), naio (107a,168c), Nato (6a,8d), Nebo (68c,102d,103d, 183a), nemo (34b), Nemo (56a,85c), Nero (8a,126d,133a,150b, 172c), nino (152a), nito (55c), noio (107c,163c), nolo (42a), nono (83b)

N - - P neap (165c,167a,177b), neep (140c,171b), noup (124b)

- - NQ cinq (61d)

- NR - inre (35d,80a), inro (84b,c,106c)

N - - R Nair (45d), natr (189), near (11d,32c,107b), neer (14b,86b,108b), noir (61b,134b), nurr (67d)

- NS - ansa (73c,93d,137c), anse (61d), ansu (11d), ense (139b,158c), enso 34d,183b)

- - NS bans, cens (115b), dans (62a), dens (90a,167b), Duns, Enns, fons (60c), gens (42d,132d), Hans (66d,96a), hens (121d), lens (67c, 95b,111a,129b,162d), Mans (30a), mons (89c), Mons (184d), oons (100a,186d), Pons (13d,63c,110d,150c), sans (63a,183b), Sens (63b), sons (98d,109d), Vans (107d)

N - - S nais (63c,132a), naos (28a,71c,137a,163a), Naos (155b), ness (26b, 75a,124b), news (165c), Nias (82d), nibs (116c), nobs (38c,87a), noes (177c), nous (81d,100a,128b)

- NT - anta (83d,117c,d,121a), Anta (164a), ante (87a,89a,115b,120b, 122b,125d,154d), anti (7d,111a,122b), Anti (193), ente (70b,151d),

ento (34b,d,183b), **Inti** (159b), **into** (123a,183b), **onto** (76a,174a), **unto** (166c), **untz** (189)

- - NT   **aint, arn't, aunt** (129c), **bant** (43c), **bent** (80b), **bunt** (15d,180c), **cant** (28d,81b,84d,90c,109b,136c,165d,166a), **cent** (36d), **dent** (42c,77d), **dint** (48c,59d,122a), **dont, dunt, font** (16b,171d,172a), **gent, hant** (67a), **hint** (9a,39c,159a), **hunt** (141c), **kant** (28d), **Kant** (67a), **Kent** (90d), **lant, lent** (54d), **Lent** (115d,141c), **lint** (46a,58d), **Ment** (54b,164a), **mint** (13a,33b,58b,76a), **mont** (62b), **oont** (25d), **pant, pent** (36a), **pint** (67b), **pont** (55d,61b), **punt** (21a,58b), **rant** (41c,127b,128a,161d), **rent** (58a,77c,91b,138b, 153d,162c,167c), **runt** (47a,172d), **sent, tent** (26b,115a), **tint** (33c, d,114d), **vent** (8b,11b,110d,112a), **vint** (26c,182c), **want** (41b, (38b,74b,106b,122a), **went** (42c), **wont** (6d,40a,73a,174c)

N - - T   **Nast** (9c,27a), **Natt** (107b), **naut** (141b), **neat** (165c,169d), **nest** (38b,74b,130d,149c,160b), **nett, newt** (48d,136c,169d), **next** (106a), **Nott** (107b), **nowt** (106a,139a), **nuit** (62b)

NU - -   **Nuba** (108c), **nubk** (30d,164d), **nuda** (39b), **Nudd** (23c), **nude** (16c, 172d), **nuit** (62b), **null** (108c,177a), **Numa** (133a), **numb, Nupe** (191), **nurl** (33b,87c), **nurr** (67d)

- NU -   **Cnut** (40d,50c), **knub** (178b), **knur** (67d,87c,107c), **knut, Knut** (40d,50c,96a), **onus** (24c,93b,109b), **snub** (128c,148b), **snug** (35a, 38b,165c), **Snug** (99d), **snup** (149b)

- - NU   **Ainu** (84a,c), **benu** (49a), **Danu** (28a), **genu** (6b,18a,87a,89c), **Manu** (10a,76d,77a,b), **menu** (19a,27a), **Menu, tunu** (28b), **zenu** (143d)

N - - U   **Nabu** (68c,183a), **napu** (29d,80d), **niou** (188), **Nosu** (27d)
- NV -   **envy** (41b)
- - NX   **jinx** (78a), **jynx** (78a), **Jynx** (184a), **lanx** (133a,b), **lynx** (26c,181d), **Lynx** (36b), **Manx** (27b,28a,82d), **minx** (116c), **Yunx** (184a)

N - - X   **noix** (67c)
- NY -   **Enyo** (12c,69c,178a), **onym** (162c), **onyx** (25d,28d,65d,142b), **Pnyx** (71c)

- - NY   **bony** (147c), **Bony** (96b), **cony** (127a), **deny** (36d,43d,129b), **liny** (157b), **luny** (38b), **many** (108d), **miny, piny, pony, puny** (55b, 179a), **tiny** (100c,148c), **tony, Tony** (96b), **tuny, viny, wany, winy** (176c), **zany** (24a,32d,59c)

N - - Y   **Nagy** (78d), **nary** (108b), **navy** (33c,58b), **nosy, nowy** (194)
- NZ -   **anzu** (11d), **Enzu** (102b), **onza** (189), **unze** (189)
- - NZ   **Linz** (40d)
OA - -   **Oahu, oaks** (154d), **oaky, oary, oast** (15d,86b,112a), **oath** (119c, 150a)

- OA -   **boar** (77c,117c,160c,181c), **boat** (27b,106a), **Boaz** (135d), **coag** (45d,118a,163b), **coak** (45d,118a,163b), **coal** (49c,64a), **Coan** (37b), **coat** (160a), **coax** (180c), **doab** (157c), **doat** (17a,94b,112a,165d), **Eoan** (41a,85b), **foal** (78c), **foam** (63d,154b), **goad** (80b,154b), **goaf** (104b), **goai** (106d,168c), **goal** (8b,109b,120b,125d), **Goan, goat** (135a), **hoar** (63d,71a,181a), **hoax** (41c,122a), **Joab** (41c,122a), **Joad** (50c), **Joan** (183c), **joar** (100a), **koae** (74b), **load** (24c,26d,161b), **loaf** (79b,94b), **loam** (47d,150a), **loan, Moab** (18d,85a,86d,94a),

337

moan, moat (44d), **Noah** (88a,99b), **road** (37d,164d), **roam** (178a), **roan** (78b,c,114c,128d,144a,181a), **roar** (145c), **soak** (46c,137c), **soap, soar** (59a), **toad** (10a,17a,63d,126d), **woad** (20d,47c), **Zoar, Zoas** (20b)

- - OA   **anoa** (28a,60a,112c,181c), **Aroa** (175b), **Gjoa** (144d), **pooa** (76a, 125b), **proa** (21b,26a,95c,d), **Shoa** (6c) **stoa** (33c,121a,c), **tooa** (17c), **whoa** (156d)

O - - A   **obia** (55d), **obra** (152d,184c), **ocha** (189), **ocra** (72c,175a), **octa** (122c), **odea** (105d,164a), **Offa** (163d), **ohia** (74c,168c), **okia** (190), **okra** (72c,175a), **olea** (170b), **Olea** (110b), **Olga** (135c,183c), **olla** (36d,44b,84d,113b,121d,151d,152c,181b), **onca** (189), **onza** (189), **orca** (86b), **orna** (169d,182c), **orra** (139c,d,140a), **ossa** (21d), **Ossa** (103d,110b,164b), **Otea** (71a,82d), **otra** (152c), **oxea** (153d)

OB - -   **oban** (190), **Obed** (135d), **obex** (22d), **obey** (35c,75c), **obia** (55d), **obit** (41b,64c), **oboe** (74b,104d,105a,182a,184a), **obol** (29b,110a), **obra** (152d,184c)

- OB -   **boba** (29d), **bobo** (112c,168c), **Cobb** (9c), **Cobh** (37a), **dobe** (159b, c,172b), **doby** (159b,c), **gobi, Gobi** (42d), **gobo** (84d), **goby** (57d), **hobb** (124b), **hobo** (168a,174b), **jobo** (77c), **Koba** (11a), **Kobe** (78a), **kobi** (84b), **kobu** (84b), **lobb** (23b,94c,163a), **lobe** (90c, 134b), **lobo** (165d,183c), **nobs** (38c,87a), **robe** (65b), **Sobk** (38d), **Toba** (80c), **tobe** (7d,137b), **toby** (8c,85c,104b), **Toby** (96b,125c), **Yobi, zobo** (186b)

- - OB   **blob, boob** (146d), **brob** (153c), **chob** (23c), **doob** (18b), **jaob, knob** (73c,107c,124d), **rhob** (64a,85c), **scob** (42a), **slob** (173d), **snob** (159c), **swob** (102b), **thob** (128a)

OC - -   **ocha** (189), **ocra** (72c,175a), **octa** (122c), **octo** (34a,89b,122c)

- OC -   **boca** (152b,c), **boce** (23b,52a,57b), **bock** (17c,90d,144a), **coca** (29d, 33a,105d,113a), **cock** (19a,29a,55a,133d,136d,161d,174b), **coco, dock** (40a,117c,144d,179d), **Foch** (63b), **foci** (28b), **hoch** (52c, 66c), **hock** (91a,115b,182b,c), **jock, Jock** (96b), **jocu** (45b,57a), **Koch** (66d), **loch** (88a,139d), **loci** (66b,118c), **lock** (54d), **loco** (38b, 119b,120b), **mock** (131b,162b), **nock** (13b,108b), **poco** (83b,93a), **Roch** (136c), **rock** (160b), **sock** (157c,182a), **soco** (22d), **tock** (7d, 19b), **toco** (19b,167c), **voce** (83c,177a)

- - OC   **bloc** (173a), **croc** (13a,74a), **floc** (149a)

O - - C   **odic** (79c,120a), **olic** (158b), **otic** (14c,d,47b)

OD - -   **odah** (170d), **odal** (48a,88b,112c), **Odax** (132c), **odds** (28d,172d), **Odea** (105a,164a), **odel** (48a,112c), **Oder** (132a), **odic** (79c,120a), **Odin** (7c,29d,63c,68c,175d,183b), **odio** (83b), **odor** (138b,156a), **odum** (168c,180a), **odyl** (59d,79c)

- OD -   **Bodb** (82b), **bode** (14c,60a,110b,121b), **Bodo** (88c), **body** (72a), **coda** (32c,35d,56c), **code** (21c,31a,40c,161c), **codo** (188), **dodd** (139c,140c), **Dode** (96b), **dodo** (19b), **Jodo** (113d), **lode** (42c,99a,111b,175b), **Lodi** (105d), **Lodz** (132c), **mode** (54d,96b,157d, 179a), **node** (35c,85b,87c,94d,120a,124d,160c), **nodi** (35c,87c), **Roda** (107b), **rodd** (38d), **rode** (46c), **rodi** (98c), **soda** (19a,149d, 181a), **Toda** (45d,76d), **tode** (80a,148a), **todo** (22b,24d,35b,64c, 156b), **tody** (19b,d,59a,166a), **yodh** (91d)

- - OD   **alod** (51c,55d,88a,124c), **apod** (59d), **Arod** (86c), **biod** (59d,79c),

338

clod (22a,45b,157d), **elod** (49b,59d,79c), **feod** (55d), **food** (109a, 176b), **good, hood** (38a,74d), **lood** (189), **mood** (44c), **plod** (170b, 177d), **pood** (189), **prod** (67d,80b,106b,120b), **quod** (123d), **rood** (38d,39a,88b), **shod, snod** (169d), **stod** (40d,67d), **trod, wood**

O - - D   **obed** (135d), **olid** (55d,60c,148d,157d), **ooid** (48d), **oord** (190), **orad** (104a), **Ovid** (132d,133b), **oxid** (112c)

OE - -   **oese** (15d,119c)

- OE -   **Boer** (151a), **coed, coel** (39b), **Doeg** (137c), **doer** (8a,116b), **does, goel** (15a,75c), **goer, hoek** (39d), **hoen** (189), **hoer, hoey** (114c), **Joel** (96a), **joey** (86a,185d), **Joey** (96b,109c), **koel** (19a,b,39b), **Moed** (100c), **noel** (26d,150b), **Noel** (30d,96a), **noes** (177c), **poem** (51a), **poet** (49b), **roed, roer** (72d), **roey** (103d), **toed, voet** (188)

- - OE   **aloe** (7d,20a,76a,b,92b,98b,119b,158b,167a,183d), **Cloe** (183c), **eboe** (28b,110a,168c,169b), **evoe** (15b,130d,181c), **floe** (79b), **froe** (32a,167a,179d), **oboe** (74b,104d,105a,182a,184a), **Otoe** (147b), **shoe** (166a), **sloe** (14a,20b,64a,119d,181c)

O - - E   **oboe** (74b,104d,105a,182a,184a), **oese** (15d,119c), **ogee** (40c,101a, b,120b), **ogle** (9d,53c,91a,93d,148c), **ogre** (67a,102a), **ohne** (66d, 183b), **Oime** (8b), **Oise, Okie** (99d), **olpe** (90d,182c), **once** (60b, 79b), **onde** (63a,178d), **ooze** (53c,104b,116a), **orfe** (57a,b,185c), **orle** (17b,56b,76a,144b,177a), **orne** (169d,182c), **Orne** (25b), **oste** (21d,83b), **Otoe** (147b), **Ouse** (132a,185d), **owse**

OF - -   **Offa** (163d), **offs** (38c)

- OF -   **doff** (130a,161b), **goff** (32d), **koff** (47a), **loft** (14c,69d,104b, 178b), **moff** (53b,146c), **sofa** (44d), **soft** (48b,95d,99d,163a), **toff** (40d)

- - OF   **Azof** (20b,135d), **goof, hoof** (173a), **loof** (144c,153d), **poof, roof** (78d), **stof** (135c), **woof** (39a,163d,165a,179d)

O - -F   **Olaf** (108a,176b)

OG - -   **ogam** (82b,c), **ogee** (40c,101a,b,120b), **ogle** (9d,53c,91a,93d,148c), **Ogor** (170d), **Ogpu** (135d), **ogre** (67a,102a), **ogum** (82b)

- OG -   **boga** (57d,180b), **bogo** (117a,168c), **Bogo** (191), **bogy** (153a), **doge** (95b,175b), **dogy** (46d,103c), **fogy, goga** (24a), **gogo** (16b,24a, 149c), **Gogo** (191), **hoga** (144b), **hogg** (144a), **jogi** (76d), **loge** (164a), **logy** (46d), **mogo** (74b), **nogg** (48d), **Pogo** (121c), **pogy** (57a,88a,98d,103c), **soga** (70d,152b), **Soga** (191), **toga** (132d,133a, b), **togs** (32c), **togt** (77c), **Vogt, yoga** (10b,13c,77a), **yogh** (10c, 185a), **yogi** (76d), **zogo** (136a)

- - OG   **agog** (47b,52c,86b), **ajog, clog** (30c,145b), **flog** (180d), **frog** (10a, 17a,126d), **grog** (92d,153d), **ilog** (132a, 161b), **niog** (33a,168c), **slog** (157c,170b,177d), **stog** (155a), **voog** (28a,66a,132b)

OH - -   **ohia** (74c,168c), **Ohio, ohne** (66d,183b), **ohoy** (106a)

- OH -   **boho** (117a,179d), **Bohr** (14b,40d,138c), **coho** (136d), **fohn** (182b), **Hohe** (192), **John** (11c,96a,121a,186b), **kohl** (53c), **moha** (42b,83d), **moho** (19a,78a), **mohr** (65d), **poha** (74c), **rohr** (72d), **soho!, Soho** (93c), **toho** (79a)

- - OH   **booh** (52c), **pooh** (22b,107d)

O - - H   **oath** (119c,150a), **odah** (170d), **okeh** (8d,37b), **opah** (23b,57a,b, 86d), **ouch!, ough**

OI - -   oily (110b,172c), oime (8b), Oise

- OI -   Boii (191), boil, bois (62b,63a,183d), coif (73a), coil (39d,171c, 185a), coin (19b,37a,100c,101c,179d), coir (33a,37a,56a,133d), Coix (70d,85b), doit (47a,169d,180d), Eoin (85b), foil (15d,55c, 165b), join (36a,173c), koir (33a), loin (40a,98a), loir (45c), Loir, Lois (165d,183c), moil (46c,184c), moio (188), noil (87c,178b), noio (107c,163c), noir (61b,134b), noix (67c), ooid (48d), roil (44c, 104b,156b,170d,176a), Soia, soie (62c), soil (154d,159a,163c), soir (61c), toil (46c,184c), void (11a,49d,108d,174b), zoid

- - OI   amoi (62a), Ekoi (191)

O - - I   Omei (24a), omni (34a), Omri (18c,86d)

- OJ -   bojo (117a), coja (103b,166b), hoja (166b), hoju (84b), koji (185b), mojo (177c), rojo (129a,152c), soja (151b)

OK - -   okay (8d), okeh (8d,37b), oket (189), okia (190), Okie (99d), okra (72c,175a), okro (72c,175a)

- OK -   boko (52b), coke (32d,64a), coky, Doko (191), joke (183a), joky, koko (106d,114b), Koko (93d,186c), koku (189), loka (173c,184c), Loke (15d,68b), Loki (7c,15d,68b), moke (45c,157d), moki (127b), Moki, moko (96c), poke (108c), poku (11a), poky (148c), roka (95a,168c,d), roke (174d,175b), soka (20c), soke (44c,85d), toko (30c), woke, yoke (85b,92d,173c)

- - OK   amok (18b,63c), asok (13d), book, cook (137b), dook (184a), hook (27b,39d), irok (55b), look (11c,53c,142a), nook (37a,130d), pook (68a), rook (19b,29c,39a), sook (22a,25c,97a), took

O - - K   Omsk

OL - -   Olaf (108a,176b), olam (51a,d,75c,81a), Olan (115c), Olax (52b), olay (113b), Olea (110b,170b), oleo (34c), Olga (135c,183c), olic (158b), olid (55d,60c,148d,157d), olio (44b,77c,98c,100d,121d), olla (36d,44b,84d,113b,121d,151d,152c,181b), Olor (160a,b), olpe (90d,182c)

- OL -   bola (16a), bold (41a), bole (31d,32a,169b), boll (119b,d), bolo (87a,179b), bolt (13b,54d,58b,132d,160a), cola (25b,108d,149d, 168c), cold (65d), cole (25a), Cole, coli, colp (28a,148b), colt (78c, 131a,185d,186b), Colt, coly (104a), dola (189), dole (44c,118c, 121c,129d), Dole (74c), doli, doll (125c), dolt (20c,59c,157d), fold folk (116a,169c), gola (27b,40c,70c,157a), gold, golf (154a), goli (105c), Goll, Golo (191), hola (74c,152b), hold (95c,124c,130d), hole (6c,11b,110d,118c,147a), Holi (77a), holm (77d,82d,109a), holt (36d,119b,184b), holy, lola, lole (52a,76b,123c), jole (29b), joli (62b), jolt (143b), kola (25b,84a,108d,168c), Kola (135b,c,d), Koli (27b), kolo (59b,135c), Lola (27d,97b), loll (94b,128c), Lolo (27d,30a), Mola (159c), mold (54d,143c), mole (19d,23a,24d,85a, 117c,155c), Mole (88c), moll, Moll (183d), molt (27a,143d), moly (76a,181c), Nola, Noll (96b,110b), nolo (42a), Pola, pole (132c,143b,177b,184a), Pole (52a), polk (37c), poll (74d,160a, 177c), polo (154a), Polo (175b), poly (34c,76b), role (114b), roll (134a,160b), sola (9a,48a,74b,118c,154a,167b), sold, sole (52c, 57a,b,58b,d,110c,115d,150a), soli (12c,110c), solo (12c,89a,110c), tola (48a,80d), Tola (85b,180a), told (129c), tole (9a,51a,99b,163a), toll (131c), tolt, tolu (16a), vola (89d,150a), vole (97d,104a,148a,

340

149b), **volk** (66c,105d,116a,184c), **Volk, volt** (49b,78c,173b), **wold** (47c,60a,118d,174a,184a), **wolf, yolk, Zola** (63a)

- - OL   **bool** (39d), **chol** (118d), **Chol** (192), **cool** (25c,107d), **egol** (11b), **enol** (29c,158b), **fool** (24a,41c,47a,146d), **gaol** (123d), **Gaol** (164a), **idol** (48c,54c,55a,75b,79d,112d,130b,184d), **itol** (158b), **obol** (29b, 110a), **pool** (65a,119d,120d), **siol** (82c), **tool** (27c), **viol** (105a), **wool** (58b,179c)

O - - L   **obol** (29b,110a), **odal** (48a,88b,112c), **odel** (48a,112c), **odyl** (59d, 79c), **opal** (20a,65d,67b,82b), **oral** (114a,153d,174c,175c), **Orel, oval** (48d,49c), **oxyl** (112c)

OM - -   **Oman** (159a), **omao** (165b), **omar** (103b), **Omar** (48c,51b,116c, 163b), **Omei** (24a), **omen** (14c,59d,60a,121c,123a,146b), **omer** (51a,75c), **omit** (49c,52c,106b,114c,147d), **omni** (34a), **Omri** (18c, 86d), **Omsk**

- OM -   **boma** (7d), **bomb** (144a), **coma** (91c,157d,170c,172b), **comb** (38c), **come, Como, dome** (39c,133c,155d), **Domn** (135a), **domy, Goma** (191), **home, homo** (122d), **homy** (38b), **Kome** (71d), **Komi** (191), **loma** (58b,63d), **Lome, nome** (71c,163b), **Nome, pome** (11d), **Pomo** (192), **pomp** (111d,112d), **Roma** (83c,d), **Rome** (31c,51d), **romi** (72d), **romp** (63d), **soma** (10c,21c,34a,48a,81d,136b), **some** (114b, 121c,126a), **Toma** (191), **tomb, tome** (21d,177c)

- - OM   **Ahom** (88c), **asom** (18d), **atom** (101c,114c,180d), **boom** (152d), **coom** (32d,150c,178d), **Crom, doom** (42d,55a,134d), **Edom** (18c, 51b,79b,82c,84a), **from, glom** (155d,160d,178c), **joom** (39c), **klom** (189), **loom** (11c,146b,179b), **room** (28d), **stom** (34c), **toom** (139b), **whom** (42b), **zoom**

O - - M   **odum** (168c,180a), **ogam** (82b,c), **ogum** (82b), **olam** (51a,d,75c, 81a), **onym** (162c), **ovum** (48d)

ON - -   **Onan** (18c,85c), **onca** (189), **once** (60b,79b), **onde** (63a,178d), **oner** (20d,53a,75c,162d,173a,d), **ones** (116a), **only** (24d,52c,98d, 147a,150a), **onto** (76a,174a), **onus** (24c,93b,109b), **onym** (162c), **onyx** (25d,28d,65d,142b), **onza** (189)

- ON -   **a-one** (52b,167b), **bona** (89d), **Bona** (183c), **bond** (92a,101c,141d, 143b,159d,165c), **bone, bong, Boni** (63b), **bonk** (190), **Bonn** (17d), **bony** (147c), **Bony** (96b), **cond** (156a), **cone** (66b,150a,157c), **Coni, conk** (41c,108a,156d,157c), **conn** (43d,156a), **cony** (127a), **dona** (83d,121c,151d), **done, dong, doni** (21a,28c,168a), **don't, fond** (7c,94b), **Fong** (40b), **fono** (137a), **fons** (60c), **font** (16b,171d,172a), **Gona** (106d), **Gond, gone** (6b,15c,42c,44c,114d), **gong, hone** (110a, 143c,180d), **hong** (30b), **honk** (70a), **Iona** (28a,82d), **Ione** (24b, 88d,94d), **Ioni** (192), **jonk, kona** (74c), **konk** (41c), **lone** (150a), **long** (38b,185b), **lonk** (143d), **mona** (72b,101d), **monk** (28b,63c, 129d), **mono** (34c,78d,122d,147a), **Mono** (193), **mons** (89c), **Mons** (184d), **mont** (62b), **nona** (89b,107b), **Nona** (69a,183c), **none** (108b), **nono** (83b), **oons** (100a,186d), **oont** (25d), **pond, pone** (37a,85b), **pong, Pons** (13d,63c,110d,150c), **pont** (55d,61b), **pony, rone** (127c,164b), **Rong** (88c), **song** (12c,170c), **sons** (98d,109d), **tone** (6c,118c), **tong** (30a,c), **tonk** (173c), **tony, Tony** (96b), **wong** (56a), **wont** (6d,40a,73a), **yond** (164d), **zona** (144c,186d), **zone** (44c,50a,160a)

ᴸ - ON   acon (62c,140d), **agon** (12c,36c,41b,55d,71b), **Amon** (86d,96b, 127d,159b,164a), **anon** (7d,14d,79d,80b,123a,145c,150c,164a), **aton** (150a,159b), **Avon** (143b), axon (106c,153c), **azon** (127b), **bion** (117b), **boon** (18b,20c,55a), **cion** (42d,70b,145b,148b,154b, 156a), **coon** (121c), **Dion** (96a,152a), **doon** (140b,168c), **ebon** (20b), **Elon** (18c,51b,108a), **Enon** (18c,d), **Eton** (33b,50c,84a), **faon** (33c, 55a), **Gaon** (85b), **goon** (157c,163c), **hoon** (190), **icon** (79d,92b, 136a), **ikon** (79d,136a), **iron** (55c,d,69d,81a,97b,143b,149a,173d, 179c), **Leon** (96a), **lion** (55b,86c), **loon** (19a,b,c,157d,179c), **moon** (40b,132c,137c), **neon** (65c), **paon** (115b), **peon** (28c,59c,99c), **phon** (94a), **pion** (43c,52b), **poon** (97c), **roon** (41a,168b), **scon** (162c), **sion** (125c,158c), **Sion** (75b,c,83a,157d), **soon** (123a), **tion** (158b), **toon** (80c,95b,168c), **tron** (180a), **upon** (6b), **woon** (24c), **Zion** (75b,c,83a,157d) **zoon** (43a)

O - - N   oban (190), **Odin** (7c,29d,63c,68c,175d,183b), **Olan** (115c), **Oman** (159a), **omen** (14c,59d,60a,121c,123a,146b), **onan** (18c), **Onan** (85c), **open** (26a,60d,81a,109b,112c,125b,172b,173c), **Oran, oven** (15d,78c,86b), **Owen** (96a,183c), **oxan** (65c), **oxen** (10c)

OO - -   ooid (48d), **oons** (100a,186d), **oont** (25d), **oord** (190), **ooze** (53c, 104b,116a), **oozy** (148b)

- OO -   boob (146d), **booh** (52c), **book, bool** (39d), **boom** (152d), **boon** (18b,20c,55a), **boor** (47a,135d,172c), **boot** (128d), **cook** (137b), **cool** (25c,107d), **coom** (32d,150c,178d), **coon** (121c), **coop, Coos** (192), **coot** (19b,46d,72b,138d,141a,146d,157d), **doob** (18b), **dook** (184a), **doom** (42d,55a,134d), **doon** (140b,168c), **door** (51a,121b), **food** (109a,176b), **fool** (24a,41c,47a,146d), **foot** (115a), **good, goof, goon** (157c,163c), **Goop** (107d), **goor, hood** (38a,74d), **hoof** (173a), **hook** (27b,39d), **hoon** (190), **hoop** (181b), **hoot** (112c), **joom** (39c), **koop** (16c), **lood** (189), **loof** (144c,153d), **look** (11c,53c,142a), **loom** (11c,146b,179b), **loon** (19a,b,c,157d,179c), **loop** (31b,107d), **Loos, loot** (22a,118a,119d,153d), **mood** (44c), **moon** (40b,132c, 137c), **moor** (10a,75b,137b,141d,178b), **Moor** (102c,d,111d), **moot** (41b,44c), **nook** (37a,130d), **noon, pooa** (76a,125b), **pood** (189), **poof, pooh** (22b,107d), **pook** (68a), **pool** (65a,119d,120d), **poon** (97c), **poop** (41c), **poor** (33a), **poot!, rood** (38d,39a,88b), **roof** (78d), **rook** (19b,29c,39a), **room** (28d), **roon** (41a,168b), **root** (53a), **Roos** (67a), **sook** (22a,25c,97a), **soon** (123a,145c), **soot** (20b, 26c,88a), **tooa** (17c), **took, tool** (27c), **toom** (139b), **toon** (80c, 95b,168c), **toot, voog** (28a,66a,132b), **wood, woof** (39a,163d, 165a,179d), **wool** (58b,179c), **woon** (24c), **yoop, zoon** (43a)

- - OO   aboo (17a), **aroo** (80c,82b), **broo** (139a), **ejoo** (55b,168c), **Kroo** (191), **phoo, shoo** (46b,67a,138b), **sloo** (160a), **whoo**

O - - O   octo (34a,89b,122c), **odio** (83b), **Ohio, okro** (72c,175a), **oleo** (34c), **olio** (44b,77c,98c,100d,121d), **omao** (165b), **onto** (76a,174a), **ordo** (22a,30d,122a,171a), **orlo** (56b,119c), **Oslo, otho** (133a), **otro** (151d), **otto** (58d,116b,134a), **Otto** (14c,66d,67a,96a)

OP - -   opah (23b,57a,b,86d), **opal** (20a,65d,67b,82b), **open** (26a,60d, 81a,109b,112c,125b,172b,173c), **Opie** (50c), **opus** (35c,105a,184c)

- OP -   copa (88b,113c), **cope** (12b,26b,36c,65b,157d,176a), **Copt** (48d),

copy, dopa (117d), **dope** (46c,105d), **dopp** (43c), **hope** (13d,52d), **hopi** (33c), **Hopi** (12c,102c,125b), **hops** (17c), **koph** (91d), **kopi** (107a,168c), **Kopi** (172a), **lope** (48b,64b,d), **mope** (92d,159a), **pope** (20a,30d,31c,120d), **qoph** (91d), **rope** (36d,88d,128b), **ropy** (157c, 176d), **soph, Sopt** (45b), **tope** (24a,46b,57a,143c,151a), **toph** (75c), **topi** (37a,75a,118c), **tops** (159c)

- - OP **alop** (13d,46b,93d)¦ **asop** (180b), **atop** (112a,174a), **chop** (98a), **clop, coop, crop** (38b), **drop** (43d,54b,100b,114c,168b), **Esop** (53b,54a), **flop** (54a), **Goop** (107d), **hoop** (181b), **klop** (150d), **knop** (124b,170c,185b), **koop** (16c), **loop** (31b,107d), **plop** (54b), **poop** (41c), **prop** (159d), **scop** (120a), **shop, slop, stop** (73b,111b), **swop** (168a), **trop** (62d,167a), **yoop**

- - OQ **shoq** (169a)

OR - - **orad** (104a), **oral** (114a,153d,174c,175c), **Oran, oras** (40d), **orca** (86b), **ordo** (22a,30d,122a,171a), **ordu** (170d), **Orel, orfe** (57a,b, 185c), **orgy** (26d,130d,137c), **orle** (17b,56b,76a,144b,177a), **orlo** (56b,119c), **Orly** (8b), **orna** (169d,182c), **orne** (169d,182c), **Orne** (25b), **orra** (139c,d,140a), **orts** (60d), **oryx** (11a)

- OR - **bora** (181d,182b), **bord** (100b), **bore** (14c,25b,46a,116a,165c, 179b), **borg** (40d), **Bori** (110d,150c), **born, boro** (154b), **Boro** (193), **Bors** (70b,134b), **bort** (43b), **Bort** (134b), **cora** (65d), **Cora** (42b, 69c,80c,116b,124d,172b,183c), **cord** (39b,131a), **core** (28b,51c, 75b,81b), **cork** (119d), **Cori** (138c), **corm** (24b,38d,156a), **corn** (39d,95c,123a), **dora** (70b), **Dora** (36d,41a,43b,183c,d), **dord** (42c), **dore** (61d,67b,69d,117d), **Dore** (50d,63a,b), **dorm, dorn** (164d), **dorp** (73c,176b), **dorr** (32b), **dory** (21b,58b,144c), **fora** (133a), **ford** (177b), **fore** (63d,174b), **fork, form** (54d,143c), **fort** (63d,157d), **gora** (81c), **gore** (115d,117c,154c,169c), **gory, hora** (22a,40b), **horn** (11a,105a,170b,182a), **hors** (62b), **kora** (178c), **Kora, kore** (107b), **Kore** (29a,42b,116b,124d), **kori** (7d,77a), **lora** (146b,149b,151c,169b), **Lora** (183c), **lord** (107c), **lore** (77c,87c, 90d,151c,183a), **lori** (91b), **lorn** (42d,60b), **loro** (19a,114b), **lory** (19a,114a), **mora** (42b,65a,72b,83d,99b,153a,161a), **more** (71a), **More** (50b), **morg** (188), **morn, moro** (19a,56c), **Moro** (100a,103a, 117a,159a), **Mors** (41b), **mort** (41b,47a,78b,136d), **Nora** (79b, 107a,164c,183c), **Nore** (163d), **nori** (8c,141c), **norm** (15a,115a, 128a,155a), **Norn** (69a,163d,174b), **oord** (190), **pore** (59d,110d, 111c,120d,157d), **pork, Poro** (141d), **port** (73d,136b,140c,170c,d, 182b,c), **Rori** (16b), **sora** (19b,c,127b), **sorb** (11d,103d,134b,142d), **Sorb** (148a,180a), **sore** (23d,142c), **sori** (55c,64a), **sorn** (139a,d), **sors** (44d,89b), **sort** (31d,39c,70b,86b,153a), **sory** (176d), **tora** (11a,44d,74a,75c,85c,90b,102d,115d), **tore, tori** (101b), **torn** (130a), **toro** (38a,107a,152a,168c), **torp** (54c), **tort** (31c,91a,185c), **Tory** (23c,36b,94c,172a), **word** (124b,165c), **wore, work** (64c,76b), **worm, worn** (143b), **wort** (76a,95d,121d), **yore** (10b,69d,93c,110b, 165d), **york** (38c), **York** (50b,c)

- - OR **acor** (6d), **ador** (153b), **amor** (152b), **Amor** (39c,68b), **asor** (75c, 105a), **boor** (47a,135d,172c), **chor** (164b), **door** (51a,121b), **Ghor** (174b), **goor, Igor** (135d), **knor** (87c), **mhor** (180b), **moor** (10a, 75b,137b,141d,178b), **Moor** (102c,d,111d), **odor** (138b,156a), **Ogor** (170b), **Olor** (160a,b), **poor** (33a), **shor** (136d), **Shor** (162b), **Thor**

343

(7c,68c,99c,100c,109c,165b), **utor** (90a,166c)

O - - R **Oder** (132a), **odor** (138b,156a), **Ogor** (170d), **Olor** (160a,b), **omar** (103b), **Omar** (48c,51b,116c), **omer** (51a,75c), **oner** (20d,53a,75c, 162d,173a,d), **osar** (51b,67b,131b), **oser** (61b), **over** (6b,38c,80a, 114d), **oxer** (55c), **oyer** (38a,75b,119c)

OS - - **osar** (51b,67b,131b), **oser** (61b), **Oslo**, **ossa** (21d) **Ossa** (103d,110b, 164b), **oste** (21d,83b)

- OS - **bosa** (12a), **Bosa, Bosc** (115c), **bose** (163c), **bosh, bosk** (164b), **boss** (49d,157d), **cosh** (35a,97c), **cose** (29b), **coso** (152c), **coss** (98a), **cost** (29a), **cosy** (149c), **dosa** (74b), **dose** (123a), **doss** (17c), **dost, foss** (44d,100d), **gosh, hose** (156c), **host** (13a,51d,104c), **Jose** (96a), **josh** (85b), **joss** (30b), **Josy** (183d), **koso** (6c,80d), **Koso** (192,193), **koss** (188), **lose** (60a,100c), **losh** (178b), **loss** (42c,123d, 178b), **lost, Mose** (96b), **mosk** (97b,103b), **moss** (91d,104c,114a, 170c), **most, mosy** (67d), **nose** (118d,125a,149b), **Nosu** (27d), **nosy, pose** (14c,15d), **posh** (49b,148c), **post** (89a,95c,155d), **Rosa** (58d, 134a,145d,183c), **rose** (33c), **Rose** (6a,50c,183c), **ross** (16c,161d), **Ross** (50c), **rosy** (21a,111a), **sosh** (81d), **soso** (99c,114c,166d), **tosh** (106a), **Tosk** (8c), **toss** (24a,132d, **Xosa** (86a)

- - OS **Amos** (96a,144b), **bios** (92a), **Coos** (192), **Enos** (7a,18d,52a,70c, 96a,143a), **epos** (51a,76b,120a), **Eros** (11c,39c,68b,97c,182d), **ghos** (30b), **gros** (47a,53d,146c), **Gros** (63a), **Laos** (80d,129c), **Loos, naos** (28a,71c,137a,163a), **Naos** (155b), **phos, Taos** (192), **Teos** (82a), **Thos** (84a,181c)

O - - S **oaks** (154d), **odds** (28d,172d), **offs** (38c), **ones** (116a), **onus** (24c, 93b,109b), **oons** (100a,186d), **opus** (35c,105a,184c), **oras** (40d), **orts** (60d), **Otis** (9c,d,24d,82a,111a), **Otus** (67a), **ours** (124c), **Ovis** (143d), **oyes** (38a,39b,75b)

OT - - **Otea** (71a,82d), **Otho** (133a), **otic** (14c,d,47b), **Otis** (9c,d,24d,82a, 111a), **Otoe** (147b), **otra** (152c), **otro** (151d), **otto** (58d,116b,134a), **Otto** (14c,66d,67a,96a), **Otus** (67a)

- OT - **bota** (189), **both, Boto** (192), **bott** (32a,88d), **cota** (117a), **cote** (19b,143d,144a,b), **coto** (16c,90b), **Coty** (63c), **dote** (17a,90b,94b, 97a,112a,139d,165d), **doth, Doto** (141b), **doty** (43d), **Goth** (16c, 163d), **Hoth** (20c), **hoti, iota** (71a,85c,91c,114c,166c,176a,180d), **jota** (151c), **joti, kota** (117a), **Kota** (45d), **koto** (84b), **lota** (24c, 121d,178d), **loth** (15a,173d), **lote** (24c,94a), **Loti** (63a,176a), **loto** (65a,121d,178d), **lots, mota** (103a), **mote** (114c,153a), **moth, Moth** (112d), **moto** (104b), **nota** (15c,89c), **note** (98c,109b,124b, 128d,130a,177c), **Nott** (107b), **pott** (113d), **rota** (27c,30d,38a,79a, 92d,133a,134a,b,180c), **rote** (130b,134b,143a,159d), **roti** (62c), **rotl** (103b,111c), **roto** (30a,122d,127b,152c,171b), **sote** (150c), **tota** (71d), **tote** (27a,73c), **toto** (8d,15a,34d,89a,181a), **toty** (87b), **vota** (133b), **vote** (60b), **Vote** (56d), **Voth** (191), **Voto** (192), **Wote** (191)

- - OT **Abot** (100c), **blot, boot** (128d), **clot** (32d,94d), **coot** (19b,46d,72b, 138d,141a,146d,157d), **eyot** (82d), **Fiot** (191), **flot** (173a), **foot** (115a), **frot** (28c), **grot** (27d), **hoot** (112c), **ilot** (82d), **khot, knot** (43c,99d,107c,124d,137b), **loot** (22a,118a,119d,136a,153d), **moot** (41b,44c), **phot** (173b), **piot** (95b), **plot** (25a,36b,118d,138b), **poot!**, **riot** (44c,111d,170c,173d), **root** (53a), **ryot** (115c), **scot** (14a,

344

162b), **Scot** (64b,132c), **shot** (9d,43d,90c,174d), **slot** (10d,11b,41d, 110d,167d,168a,181b), **soot** (20b,26c,88a), **spot** (93b,118c,154d, 162a), **stot** (154d,155d,157d,179b,186a), **swot, toot, trot** (85b, 93d,112d)

O - - T   oast (15d,86b,112a), obit (41b,64c), oket (189), omit (49c,52c, 106b,114c,147d), oont (25d), oust (44c,49a,52b,125d)

OU - -   ouch!, ough!, ours (124c), Ouse (132a,185d), oust (44c,49a,52b, 125d)

- OU -   Aoul (191), bout (36c), bouw (188), coup (20d,97c,157b,c,162d), cous (38a), doub (18b), douc (101d), doum (168c), dour (67d, 159a), foud (54d,144b), foul (173a), four (26c), goul (102a), gour (112c,181c), gout, hour, joug (138d), loud (156a), loun (19a,b), loup (61d,62a,90c,139d), Loup (193), lour (13d,63d), lout (15c, 22a,24b,45b,109a,157d), moue (61d,62b), noun (114b,158a), noup (124b), nous (81d,100a,128b), pouf, poul (190), pour (162d), pous (188), pout (159a), roud (57a,b), roue (41b,44c,127c,134b), roup (44a,121d), rout (41d,44b,46b), souf (146b), souk (22a,97a), soul (10d,125a,153c,176d), soup, sour, sous (62d,172c), toug (171a), toup (95d), tour (31b,85c), tout (61a,127a), youp (185d), your (124c)

- - OU   Abou (48b,55a), chou (61b), Chou (30b), clou (62b), meou, niou (188), shou (41d), thou (124b), Tiou (192), Yaou (30c)

O - - U   Oahu, Ogpu (135d), ordu (170d)

OV - -   oval (48d,49c,127a), oven (15d,78c,86b), over (6b,38c,80a,114d, 130a), Ovid (132d,133b), Ovis (143d), ovum (48d)

- OV -   cove (17a,73d,107d), dove (19a,117d), Hova (95a), hove (92a, 157d), Jova (193), Jove (85d), love (163a), move, nova (20c,106d, 155c,174d), nove (83b), rove (127d,132b,178a), wove, Xova (193)

- - OV   akov (189), Azov (20b)

OW - -   Owen (96a,183c), owse

- OW -   bowk (155d), bowl, cowl (101d), dowd (143b), dowl, down (149d), fowl, gowk (146d), gowl (102a,140d,185b), gown, howe (77d), Howe (17a,82a), howl (39b), howk (139b), Iowa (193), jowl (29b), lowa (19a), lown (157d), lowp (90c,139d), mown, nowt (106a,139a), nowy (194), powe, rowy (157b), town (73c), towy (58b), yowl, yowt (139c)

- - OW   alow (18a,172c), arow (92c,158b), avow (6d,36a,41c,112c), blow, brow, chow (45a), clow (58c,148c), crow (19a), dhow (88d,111c, 175d), enow (50d,123a,158b), flow (157b), frow (47a,167a), glow (144c), grow (154b), know, Lwow, meow, plow (39c,165d), prow (21b,22c,144d,156a), scow (21a,58b), show (42b,44c,96b), slow (43c), snow, stow (112b), swow (100a), trow (18a,21a,159d,164c, 170b)

OX - -   oxan (65c), oxea (153d), oxen (10c), oxer (55c), oxid (112c), oxyl (112c)

- OX -   boxy, coxa (77b), doxa (48b), doxy (129d), foxy (38b,39c,181d), moxa (27d,30c), Moxo (192), noxa, Roxy (183d), toxa (153d)

- - OX   abox (22d), esox (57b)

O - - X   obex (22d), Odax (132c), Olax (52b), onyx (25d,28d,65d,142b),

345

oryx (11a)

OY - - oyer (38a,75b,119c), oyes (38a,39b,75b), oyez (38a,39b,75b)

- OY - coyn (37a), coyo (15a,30c), Goya (151d), Hoya (14d), noyl (87c), soya (151b)

- - OY ahoy (106a), Amoy (88c), b'hoy (134b), buoy (28d,58c), choy (48a,128d), cloy (61b,137c,159d), ohoy (106a), ploy (43c), troy (161c,180a), Troy

O - - Y oaky, oary, obey (35c,75c), ohoy (106a), oily (110b,172c), okay (8d), olay (113b), only (24d,52c,98d,147a,150a), oozy (148b), orgy (26d,130d,137c), Orly (8b)

- OZ - boza (12a), bozo (55b), coze (29b), cozy (149c), doze (148a), dozy, Jozy, kozo (113d,168c), mozo (152b), noze (75a), ooze (53c, 104b,116a), oozy (148b)

O - - Z oyez (38a,39b,75b)

PA - - paal (188), paar (28c), paca (132c,154a), pace (64b,98a,153b,156a, 170b,177d), pack (24b,140d), paco (9b,146d), pacs (94c), pact (8a), padi (131b), paga (117a), page (51b,59b,142d,159b), paha (67b), pahi (21b,26a), paho (122a), paid (129c), pail, pain (7c), pair (22d,37d,85b,171d), pais (37d), pajo (122a), pala (189), Pala (88b), pale (113a,117c,178a), pali (122b), Pali (23d,24a,137b,175a), pall (32d,81b,112a), palm (59b,168c,169b), palo (152c), palp (11a,55b, 58b,167c), paly (194), Pana, pane (113c,155a,b), pang (165b), Pani (120c), pank (189), pant, paon (115b), papa, pape (19b,113a), para (134c,170d), Para (18a,51d), parc (62b,112c), pard (27b, 91b), pare (115c,129a), pari (34a,180a), park, parr (136d,137a, 147c), pars (89d), part (44d,60d,121c,159c), paru (57a), pasa (46a,127c,152c), pasi (94b), pass (110b,155c), past (25c,69d,165d), pata (32c,160d), pate (39a,74d), path (132a,134b), pato (46d), patu (179b), paul, Paul (96a), paun (18b), paut (140a), pave (85a), pavo (115b), Pavo (36b,c), pavy (115b), pawa (189), pawl (43a, 95a), pawn (29c,119c)

- PA - Apap (102a), apar (12d), opah (23b,57a,b,86d), opal (20a,65d,67b, 82b), spad (105b), Spad (118d), spae (139c), span (23b,107b,113a, 128b,162c), spar (22c,24c,64b,97b,100b,144d), spat (112c,126b, 134b), upas (84d,120b,168c,d)

- - PA arpa (83b), capa (152a,166d), cepa (110c), copa (88b,113c), depa (188), dopa (117d), Hupa (192), kapa (74b), lipa (54d), napa (25c, 67d,90d), Napa (182c), Nepa, 106b,178c), nipa (14b,46b,48a,164a, 168c), papa, pipa (159d), pupa (30d,81b,c), ripa (16b,131d), ropa (152a), rupa (60b), sapa (70c), supa (168c), tapa (16c,32c,53b, 56a,74b,104b,112b,113d,120d), yapa (113b), Zipa (29d)

P - - A paca (132c,154a), paga (117a), paha (67b), pala (189), Pala (88b), Pana, papa, para (134c,170d), Para (18a,51d), pasa (46a, 127c,152c), pata (32c,160d), pawa (189), peba (12d), Peba (193), peca (190), peda (114d,144b), pega (57a,130a), pela (30c), Pera (60a), pesa (190), peva (12d), pica (66b,95b,172c), pika (93a,128a, 132c), pima (37c), Pima (192), pina (35d,118b), pipa (159d), Pisa (90c), pita (9c,28b,56a,83a), plea (51a,52d,122a,130b), poha (74c), pola, pooa (76a,125b), proa (21b,26a,95c,d), puca (68a),

puja (77a), **puka** (107a,168c), **puma** (27b,37c,55b,103d), **puna** (10b,33b,104a,119b,182a), **pupa** (30d,81b,c), **Puya** (118b), **pyla** (22d)

P - - B   **pleb** (10d,35b,180b)

P - - C   **parc** (62b,112c)

P - - D   **paid** (129c), **pard** (27b,91b), **pend, Phad** (155b), **Phud** (110b), **pied** (96c,103c,114b,117c,154a,174d), **plod** (170b,177d), **pond, pood** (189), **prod** (67d,80b,106b,120b), **pund** (189), **puud** (189)

PE - -   **peag** (144a,178a), **peai** (98b), **peak** (9a,38c,159b,186b), **peal** (131c,d), **pean** (64c,150b), **pear** (64a), **peat** (64a,175a), **peba** (12d), **Peba** (193), **peca** (190), **peck** (24d), **peco** (162b), **peda** (114d,144b), **pedi** (34b), **pedo** (34b), **peek** (93d,115c), **peel** (53a,114a), **peen** (73c), **peep** (93d,115c), **peer** (51a,93d,107c), **peet** (64a), **pega** (57a,130a,158b), **Pegu** (24c,102a,127d), **peho** (19b,102c,106d), **Peke** (45a,148d), **pela** (30c), **Pele** (69c,74c), **pelf** (22a,56c,131b), **pelo** (83b), **pelt** (53a), **pelu** (30a,106d,168c), **pend, pene, pent** (36a), **peon** (28c,59c,99c), **pepo** (39b,64a,70a,98c,125c,154c), **Pera** (60a), **pere** (61c,63b), **peri** (54b,116b,c,122b), **perk** (84d,93a), **perm** (49b,97d), **pern** (78a), **pero** (152a), **pert** (80a,93a,137c,154b), **Peru, pesa** (190), **peso** (99c), **pest** (108c,116b,118d,170a), **pete** (136b), **Pete** (96b), **peto** (57a,177b), **Peto** (76a), **peur** (61c), **peva** (12d), **pevy** (91d,94c)

- PE -   **aper** (32d), **Apet** (97c), **apex** (39c,76c,115c,118b,159b,166a,167b), **epee** (55c,160d), **open** (26a,60d,81a,109b,112c,125b,172b,173c), **spec, sped, Spee** (66d,70b), **spes, Spes** (69a,78a), **spet** (16c,57a, 142c), **spew** (35a,49a), **spex, Spey**

- - PE   **cape** (75a,96c,124b,161a), **cepe** (48c), **cope** (12b,26b,36c,65b,157d, 176a), **dope** (46c,105d), **dupe** (27c,41c,72c,160c), **gape** (185b), **hipe** (185a), **hope** (13d), **hype** (185a), **jape** (85a,b), **jupe** (62b, 84a), **lope** (48b,64b,d), **lupe** (19a,64a), **mope** (92d), **nape** (15b,108c,d), **Nupe** (191), **olpe** (90d), **pape** (19b,113a), **pipe** (105a,180d,182a), **pope** (20a,30d,31c,120d), **ripe** (58a,97c,98c), **rope** (36d,88d,128b), **rype** (19b,125a), **sipe** (101a,110c,140b), **supe** (53a,154d), **sype** (110c), **tape** (16a,19a,128d), **tipe** (168b), **tope** (24a,46b,57a,143c, 151a), **type** (31d,115a,155a), **wipe, Xipe** (15c)

P - - E   **pace** (64b,98a,153b,156a,170b,177d), **page** (51b,59b,142d,159b), **pale** (113a,117c,178a), **pane** (113c,155a,b), **pape** (19b,113a), **pare** (115c,129a), **pate** (39a,74d), **pave** (85a), **Peke** (45a,148d), **Pele** (69c,74c), **pene, pere** (61c,63b), **pete** (136b), **Pete** (96b), **pice** (190), **pike** (57a,b,76c,120b,153a), **pile** (45d,75b,117c), **pine** (36a, 52a,88c,93c,168c,d,169a), **pipe** (105a,180d,182a), **pise** (127d), **plie** (32c,59b), **poke** (108c), **pole** (132c,143b,177b,184a), **Pole** (52a), **pome** (11d), **pone** (37a,85b), **pope** (20a,30d,31c, 120d), **pore** (59d,110d,111c,120d,157d), **pose** (14c,15d), **powe, pree** (139d), **puce** (33c,d,52a), **pule** (180d), **pume** (137b), **Pume** (175b,185b), **pure** (29b,172b,173c), **pyle** (34b), **Pyle** (9c,178a), **pyre** (64c)

P - - F   **pelf** (22a,56c,131b), **Piaf** (63c), **piff** (24b), **poor, pouf, puff** (180d)

- PG -   **upgo** (13c)

P - - G   **pang** (165b), **peag** (144a,178a), **ping, plug** (156d,184d), **pong,**

prig (112a,116c), **pung** (22c,148b)

PH - -   **Phad** (155b), **phew** (52c), **Phil** (96b), **phit** (24b), **phiz** (54a), **phon** (94a), **phoo, phos, phot** (173b), **Phud** (110b), **phut** (24b), **Phut** (110b)

- PH -   **epha** (75c)

- - PH   **Alph** (132a), **caph** (91c), **kaph** (91d), **koph** (91d), **qoph** (91d), **soph, toph** (75c), **umph**

P - - H   **path** (132a,134b), **pish** (36c,107d), **pith** (37a,51c,67b,95c,97a, 119b,126d), **pooh** (22b,107d), **posh** (49b,148c), **prah** (21b, 26a,95c,d), **Ptah** (48d,98c), **pugh!, push** (145c)

PI - -   **Piaf** (63c), **piat** (11a), **piay** (98b), **pica** (66b,95b,172c), **pice** (190), **Pici** (19c,184a), **pick, pico** (65a,152c), **Pict** (23c,47d), **pied** (96c, 103c,114b,117c,154a,174d), **pien** (13b), **pier** (23a,88b,180c), **piet** (29b,95b), **piff** (24b), **pika** (93a,128a,132c), **pike** (57a,b,76c,120b, 153a), **piki** (95c), **piky, pile** (45d,75b,117c), **pili** (34b,108d), **pill, pily, pima** (37c), **Pima** (192), **pina** (35d,118b), **pine** (36a,52a,88c, 93c,168c,d,169a), **ping, pink** (26d,33c,60c,138a), **pino** (152c), **pint** (67b), **piny, pion** (43c,52b), **piot** (95b), **pipa** (159d), **pipe** (105a, 180d,182a), **pipi** (106d,119d), **pipy** (145d), **pirn** (21b,129a,179b), **Piro** (192), **pirr** (181a), **Pisa** (90c), **pise** (127d), **pish** (36c,107d), **pisk** (9c, 19b), **piso** (189), **pist** (25c), **pita** (9c,28b,56a,83a), **pith** (37a, 51c,67b,95c,97a,119b,126d), **pito** (9c,28b,83a), **Pitt** (50d,155d), **pity** (35b), **Pius** (121a), **pixy** (154b)

- PI -   **apia** (121b), **apii** (74c), **apio** (125b), **Apis** (17c,24b,49a,125a,136a), **epic** (76b,120a), **ipil** (117a,168c,169a), **Opie** (50c), **spin** (131a, 180d), **spir** (97c), **spit** (120a,132b,c), **Upis** (13b), **ypil** (117a,168c)

- - PI   **aipi** (27a), **Hapi** (66a,107b,136a), **Hopi** (12c,102c,125b), **hopi** (33c), **impi** (86a), **kepi** (99d), **kopi** (107a,168c), **Kopi** (172a), **pipi** (106d,119d), **tipi** (181b), **topi** (37a,75a,118c), **Tupi** (192)

P - - I   **padi** (131b), **pahi** (21b,26a), **pali** (122b), **Pali,** (23d,24a,137b,175a), **Pani** (120c), **pari** (34a,180a), **pasi** (94b), **peai** (98b), **pedi** (34b), **peri** (54b,116b,c,122b), **Pici** (19c,184a), **piki** (95c), **pili** (34b, 108d), **pipi** (106d,119d), **puli** (45a,78d), **puri** (80d)

P - - K   **pack** (24b,140d), **pank** (189), **park, peak** (9a,38c,159b,186b), **peck** (24d), **peek** (93d,115c), **perk** (84d,93a), **pick, pink** (26d,33c,60c, 138a), **pisk** (9c,19b), **polk** (37c), **pook** (68a), **pork, puck** (44b,68a, 77c,100c), **Puck** (99d,143b), **pulk** (37c,88d), **punk** (9b,166a,167c)

PL - -   **plan** (99b,124a,138b), **plap** (54b), **plat** (22d,96c,114a,119c,133d), **play** (63d,154a), **plea** (51a,52d,122a,130b), **pleb** (10d,35b,180b), **plet** (135d), **plew** (17c), **plex** (60b), **plie** (32c,59b), **plod** (170b, 177d), **plop** (54b), **plot** (25a,36b,118d,138b), **plow** (39c,165d), **ploy** (43c), **plug** (156d,184d), **plum, plup, plus** (10b,102c)

- PL -   **upla**

P - - L   **paal** (188), **pail, pall** (32d,81b,112a), **paul, Paul** (96a), **pawl** (43a, 95a), **peal** (131c,d), **peel** (53a,114a), **Phil** (96b), **pill, poll** (74d, 160a,177c), **pool** (65a,119d,120d), **poul** (190), **pull** (45d,167d), **purl** (87c,104c), **pyal** (175c)

P - - M   **palm** (59b,168c,169b), **perm** (49b,97d), **plum, poem** (51a), **pram** (15a), **prim** (156b)

348

PN - - Pnyx (71c)

P - - N pain (7c), paon (115b), paun (18b), pawn (29c,119c), pean (64c, 150b), peen (73c), peon (28c,59c,99c), pern (78a), phon (94a), pien (13b), pion (43c,52b), pirn (21b,129a,179b), plan (99b,124a, 138b), poon (97c)

PO - - poco (83b,93a), poem (51a), poet (49b), Pogo (121c), pogy (57a, 88a,98d,103c), poha (74c), poke (108c), poku (11a), poky (148c), pola, pole (132c,143b,177b,184a), Pole (52a), polk (37c), poll (74d,160a,177c), polo (154a), Polo (175b), poly (34c,76b), pome (11d), Pomo (192), pomp (111d,112d), pond, pone (37a,85b), pong, Pons (13d,63c,110d,150c), pont (55d,61b), pony, pooa (76a,125b), pood (189), poof, pooh (22b,107d), pook (68a), pool (65a,119d, 120d), poon (97c), poop (41c), poor (33a), poot!, pope (20a,30d, 31c,120d), pore (59d,110d,111c,120d,157d), pork, Poro (141d), port (73d,136b,140c,170c,d,182b,c), pose (14c,15d), posh (49b, 148c), post (89a,95c,155d), pott (113d), pouf, poul (190), pour (162d), pous (188), pout (159a), powe

- PO - apod (59d), epos (51a,76b,120a), spot (93b,118c,154d,162a), upon (6b)

- - PO cipo (91d), gapo (60a), hypo (117b), mapo (68a,148d), pepo (39b, 64a,70a,98c,125c,154c), sapo (149c,166d), typo (35c,51b)

P - - O paco (9b,146d), paho (122a), pajo (122a), palo (152c), pato (46d), pavo (115b), Pavo (36b,c), peco (162b), pedo (34b), peho (19b, 102c,106d), pelo (83b), pepo (39b,64a,70a,98c,125c,154c), pero (152a), peso (99c), peto (57a,177b), Peto (76a), phoo, pico (65a, 152c), pino (152c), Piro (192), piso (189), pito (9c,28b,83a), poco (83b,93a), Pogo (121c), polo (154a), Polo (175b), Pomo (192), Poro (141d), prao (21b,26a,95c,d), puno (182a), pyro

- - PP Capp (27a), dopp (43c), kapp, kipp, Lapp (108a), repp (53b,131a), typp (185b), wapp (54b,133d,145d), Yapp (22a), zipp

P - - P palp (11a,55b,58b), peep (93d,115c), plap (54b), p'op (54b), plup, pomp (111d,112d), poop (41c), prep (138b), prop (159d), pulp, pump

PR - - prah (21b,26a,95c,d), pram (15a), prao (21b,26a,95c,d), prau (21b, 26a,95c,d), pray (18b,51a,159d), pree (139d), prep (138b), pres (62b), pret (188), prey (119d,176a), prig (112a,116c), prim (156b), proa (21b,26a,95c,d), prod (67d,80b,106b,120b), prop (159d), prow (21b,22c,144d,156a), prut!, Prut (41a)

- PR - spry (7a,107b)

P - - R paar (28c), pair (22d,37d,85b,171d), parr (136d,137a,147c), pear (64a), peer (51a,93d,107c), peur (61c), pier (23a,88b,180c), pirr (181a), poor (33a), pour (162d), purr (104c)

- PS - apse (9b,20a,31a,128c,130a,142b,175a), Apsu (29a), ipse (44d, 89c), ipso (89c)

- - PS Alps (85d), gyps, Gyps (71d), hops (17c), hyps, seps (93b,142d), tops (159c), Veps (191), Zips (40c)

P - - S pacs (94c), pais (37d), pars (89d), pass (110b,155c), phos, Pius (121a), plus (10b,102c), Pons (13d,63c,110d,150c), pous (188), pres (62b), puss

PT - -   Ptah (48d,98c)

- - PT   Copt (48d), dipt, kept, rapt (6c,27a,50d), sept (31d,82b,143a,149c), Sept (45b), Sopt (45b), wept

P - - T   pact (8a), pant, part (44d,60d,121c,159c), past (25c,69d,165d), paut (140a), peat (64a,175a), peet (64a), pelt (53a), pent (36a), pert (80a,93a,137c,154b), pest (108c,116b,118d,170a), phit (24b), phot (173b), phut (24b), Phut (110b), piat (11a), Pict (23c, 47d), piet (29b,95b), pint (67b), piot (95b), pist (25c), Pitt (50d, 155d), plat (22d,96c,114a,119c,133d), plet (135d), plot (25a,36b, 118d,138b), poet (49b), pont (55d,61b), poot!, port (73d,136b, 140c,170c,d,182b,c), post (89a,95c,155d), pott (113d), pout (159a), pret (188), prut!, Prut (41a), punt (21a,58b), putt (69d), pyat (95b), pyet (95b)

PU - -   puca (68a), puce (33c,d,52a), puck (44b,68a,77c,100c), Puck (99d,143b), pudu (41d), puff (180d), pugh!, puja (77a), puka (107a,168c), puku (11a), pule (180d), puli (45a,78d), pulk (37c, 88d), pull (45d,167d), pulp, pulu (74c), puly, puma (27b,37c,55b, 103d), pume (137b), Pume (175b,185b), pump, puna (10b,33b, 104a,119b,182a), pund (189), pung (22c,148b), punk (9b,166a, 167c), puno (182a), punt (21a,58b), puny (55b,179a), pupa (30d, 81b,c), pure (29b,172b,173c), puri (80d), purl (87c,104c), purr (104c), Puru (192), push (145c), puss, putt (69d), puud (189), puxy, Puya (118b)

- PU -   Apus (36b,c), opus (35c,105a,184c), spud (121d,151c), spun, spur (10d,67d,167d,168a,181b), sput (21c)

- - PU   hapu (106d), napu (29d,80d), Ogpu (135d), tapu

P - - U   paru (57a), patu (179b), Pegu (24c,102a,127d), pelu (30a,106d, 168c), Peru, poku (11a), prau (21b,26a,95c,d), pudu (41d), puku (11a), pulu (74c), Puru (192)

P - - W   phew (52c), plew (17c), plow (39c,165d), prow (21b,22c,144d, 156a)

P - - X   plex (60b), Pnyx (71c)

PY - -   pyal (175c), pyat (95b), pyet (95b), pyla (22d), pyle (34b), Pyle (9c,178a), pyre (64c), pyro

- - PY   copy, espy (44a,142a), gapy, pipy (145d), ropy (157c,176d), typy

P - - Y   paly (194), pavy (115b), pevy (91d,94c), piay (98b), piky, pily, piny, pipy (145d), pity (35b), pixy (154b), play (63d,154a), ploy (43c), pogy (57a,88a,98d,103c), poky (148c), poly (34c,76b), pony, pray (18b,51a,159d), prey (119d,176a), puly, puny (55b,179a), puxy

P - - Z   phiz (54a)

QA - -   Qaid (35a)

Q - - D   Qaid (35a), quad (33c,172a), quid (39b,166d), quod (123d)

QE - -   qere (75c), qeri (75c)

Q - - E   qere (75c), quae (176b)

- - QF   waqf (103a)

Q - - G   quag (21c,102c), Qung (191)

Q - - H   qoph (91d)

Q - - I   qeri (75c), quai (88b,117c,180c), quei (189)

Q - - N   quan (190)

QO - -   qoph (91d)

Q - - P   quip (183a,b)

Q - - S   quas (135c)

Q - - T   quit (90d,130c)

QU - -   quad (33c,172a), quae (176b), quag (21c,102c), quai (88b,117c, 180c), quan (190), quas (135c), quay (88b,117c,180c), quei (189), quid (39b,166d), quip (183a,b), quit (90d,130c), quiz, Qung (191), quod (123d)

- QU -   aqua (90a,178c), equi (122d)

Q - - Y   quay (88b,117c,180c)

Q - - Z   quiz

RA - -   raab (32d), raad (14a,49b,151a,165b), raas (91b), Raba, rabi (38d, 74a), Rabi (14b,117b), raca (19a,59c,130b,184d), race (116a,153b, 154b,169c), rack (32c,64b), racy (153b), rada (135c,172a), rade (138d), raff (75b), raft (27b,33c,58c,75b), raga (56d,105a), rage (10c,30c,157a,161d), ragi (28b), Rahu (42b,48b), Raia (107d,147b), raid (59d,80c), raik (188,189), rail (16b,19b,c,37a,97b,138c,150c, 177b), rain (121d,162d), raip (36d), rais (26c,29d,75a,103b), Rais (106b), raja (77a,123c), rake (41b,44c,134b,140d), rale (7c,23a, 29d,41b), ralo (188), Rama (77a,80b,176d), rame (22d), rami (22d), ramp (65a,80b,127b,148b), rana (77a,123c), Rana (63d), rand (16d,22a,131b,145a,b), Rand (69c), rang, rani (72d,77b,123c,127c), rank (31d,55d,70b,92c,94d,157d), rann (175c), rant (41c,127b, 128a,161d), rapt (6c,27a,50d), rara (119a), rare (138b,164b,172b, 173d), rasa (51c), rase (42b,91d), rash (75a), rasp (56b,70d,140d), rata (29d,56b,89d,96c,106d,120c,168c), rate (11d,14a,31d,36b,51d, 52a,70b,85c,112b,123b,127d,128a,138c,143a,174b), rath (29a, 76d,162d), rati (189), rats, rave,(41c,157a,161d), ravi (61b), Ravi (16b), raya (19b,23c,76d,107d), raze (42b,91d) razz (131b)

- RA -   Arab (30a,78b,c,106a,107c,157b,160c,185d), arad (13a,c,84a), arah (52c), Aral (135d), Aram (18d,50c,105c,144b,161c), Aran (18c,48c,64d,82d,174c), arar (137a,168c), Aras, brab (113b), brad (54d,67c,105b), brae (76d,139a,c,140b,148c), brag (21a,175a), Bram (96a), bran (23c,39a,70b,72a,79c), Bran (23c,50c), bras (61a), brat, bray, crab (39b,144b,181b), crag (132c), cral, cram (157d), cran (160c), craw (38d,72c,156c), Crax (19b,39d), draa, drab (23d,29c,33d,46d,53d), drag (74a,125b), drah (188), dram (46b,110c,121d,148c), drap (61b,c,62a), drat (100a), Drau, draw (42c,53a,92b,117c,121c,167d), dray (27a,154c), eral (51a), erat (89c), frab (138c), frap (45d,165c), frat, frau (181b), fray (56b,60d), grab (105b,142a,149b), grad (28b), Graf (37c,66b,67a, 107c,186b), gram (29d,99b,148d,160d,180a), grao (189), gras (78b), gray (33c,77c), Gray (50c), Irad (18d), Irae (43c), Irak (99a,d), Iran (6a,48c,116b), Iraq (99a,d), Iras (11b,32a), krag (131c), kral, kran (190), kras (76d), orad (104a), oral (114a,153d, 174c,175c), Oran, oras (40d), prah (21b,26a,95c,d), pram (15a), prao (21b,26a,95c,d), prau (21b,26a,95c,d), pray (18b,51a,159d), tram (170a), tran (7a), trap (27b,67b,132b,149b), tray (128c,136d,

351

142d,143c), **ural, Ural** (135c), **uran** (101d), **Wraf, wrap** (32b,51a)

- - RA   **abra** (26b), **Abra, aera** (8a), **Afra** (183c), **agra** (26d,34d), **Agra** (161b), **Aira** (70d), **akra** (176a), **Akra** (191), **amra** (77c), **arra** (47d, 52c,82b), **aura** (44c,49c,66a,96b,158a,170d,177c), **bara** (188), **Bera** (86d), **bora** (181d,182b), **bura** (182b), **cara** (83a), **Cara** (48b, 183c), **cora** (65d), **Cora** (42b,69c,80c,116b,124d,172b,183c), **cura** (152c), **Dara** (18d), **dera** (34c), **dora** (70b), **Dora** (36d,41a,43b, 183c,d), **dura** (153c), **eyra** (181d), **Ezra** (96a), **fora** (133a), **gara** (190), **gora** (81c), **Hera** (69c,85d,110b,126b,186b,d), **hora** (22a,40b), **hura** (20a,137a), **Hura, ikra** (27d), **Irra** (68c, 178a), **jura, Jura, Kara** (132a), **kora** (19a,178c), **Kora, Lara** (25c), **lira** (28b,79a,170d), **lora** (146b,149b,151c,169b), **Lora** (183c), **lura** (22d,82a), **Lyra** (36b,74a), **mara** (114d), **Mara** (24a,d,105b,107b), **mira** (174d), **Mira** (155b), **mora** (42b,65a,72b,83d,99b,153a,161a), **mura** (84d), **Mura** (192), **Myra** (10a,31b,183c), **Nera** (165b), **Nora** (79b,107a,164c,183c), **ocra** (72c,175a), **okra** (72c,175a), **orra** (139c,d,140a), **otra** (152c), **para** (134c,170d), **Para** (18a,51d), **Pera** (60a), **Sara** (24d,183c), **sera** (11b,20d,59a,83a,180d), **sora** (19b,c, 127b), **sura** (87c,113b,166d), **Syra, tara** (22a,55c,113a,168c), **Tara** (82b,c,138b), **tera** (23d,84c), **tora** (11a,44d,74a,75c,85c,90b,102d, 115d), **vara** (151d), **vera** (140c,151b,175c), **Vera** (183c) **Vira** (191), **zira** (188)

R - - A   **Raba, raca** (19a,59c,130b,184d), **rada** (135c,172a), **raga** (56d,105a), **Raia** (107d,147b), **raja** (77a,123c), **Rama** (77a,176d), **rana** (77a,123c), **Rana** (63d), **rara** (119a), **rasa** (51c), **rata** (29d,56b,89d), 96c,106d,120c,168c), **raya** (19b,23c,76d,107d), **reba** (144a), **Reba** (18d,86c), **rede** (37c,81d), **reja** (152b), **rena** (25b,132c), **rhea** (37a, 56a,111d,133d), **Rhea** (19b,68d,87c,103c,186b), **riga** (118b), **Riga, rima** (23a,30c,32a,58a,110d), **ripa** (16b,131d), **rita, Rita** (37b, 78d,183c,), **Roda** (107b), **roka** (95a,168c,d), **Roma** (83c,d), **ropa** (152a), **Rosa** (58d,134a,145d,183c), **rota** (27c,30d,38a,79a,92d, 133a,134a,b,180c), **ruga** (59b,185a), **rupa** (60b), **rusa, Rusa** (41d, 136d), **Ruta** (76b,134d)

- RB -   **arba** (135d,171a)

- - RB   **barb** (20b,57d,78b,117d,120a,b,124b), **curb** (130c,146b), **garb** (32c,46a), **gerb** (56d,143d), **Harb** (191), **herb** (58b,158b), **kerb** (146b), **Serb** (15d,148a,186c), **sorb** (11d,103d,134b,142d), **Sorb** (148a,180a), **verb** (7a,114b,184b)

R - - B   **raab** (32d), **rhob** (64a,85c), **rumb** (120b)

- RC -   **arca** (9a,22c,29d,115a,130a), **Arca** (101b), **arch** (29d,38b,39d,123d, 132c), **orca** (86b)

- - RC   **circ** (31a), **marc** (70c), **Marc** (96a), **parc** (62b,112c)

- RD -   **Erda** (23d,41a,47d,68d,69a,131d,177b), **ordo** (22a,30d,122a,171a), **ordu** (170d), **urde** (86b), **Urdu** (77b), **urdy** (86b)

- - RD   **bard** (12d,120a), **bird, bord** (100b), **Byrd** (9c,120b), **card** (33d,114d), **cord** (39b,131a), **curd** (99d), **Dard, dord** (42c), **eard** (139b), **fard** (112d), **ford** (177b), **fyrd** (110a), **Gerd** (63c), **gird** (32c,50a,123a,160d), **hard** (109b), **herd** (39a,46c,72a), **Kurd** (48b, 82a), **lard** (54d,61a,71a,110a), **lord** (107c), **nard** (13a,97c,102b, 110a,153c), **oord** (190), **pard** (27b,91b), **sard** (26d,28d,65d,111a),

352

142b,156d), **Sard, surd** (82c,177a), **verd** (71d), **ward** (31c,55c,86b), **word** (124b,165c), **Wurd, Wyrd** (107d), **yard** (152d)

R - - D **raad** (14a,49b,151a,165b), **Raad** (151a), **raid** (59d,80c), **rand** (16d, 22a,131b,145a,b), **Rand** (69c), **read** (116d,157d), **redd** (153a), **reed** (16a,70d,97b,105a,111b,118b,144b), **Reed** (163a), **rend** (32a,159c, 162c,185a), **Ridd** (94a), **rind** (53a,115c), **Rind** (109c,174b), **road** (37d,164d), **rodd** (38d), **roed, rood** (38d,39a,88b), **roud** (57a,b), **rudd** (26d,57a,b), **rynd** (100a)

RE - - **read** (116d,157d), **real** (7a), **ream** (18c,37d,50d,113d,171c), **reap** (7a,40a,74a), **rear** (15b,23a,b,24a,51b,76d,127c), **reba** (144a), **Reba** (18d,86c), **reck** (26d,75c), **rect** (117b), **redd** (153a), **rede** (37c, 81d,138d), **redo** (165c), **reed** (16a,70d,97b,105a,111b,118b,144b), **Reed** (163a), **reef** (129a,137a,145a), **reek** (49d,53c,64a,148d,149a), **reel** (21b,40b,d,153c,154a,c,d,180d), **reem** (18d), **reft** (32a,42c, 44d,167b), **reim** (112c), **rein** (29b,130c), **reis** (26c,29d,75a,103b), **reja** (152b), **Reki** (16a), **rely** (16b,170b), **Remi** (10b), **Rems, rena** (25b,132c), **rend** (32a,159c,162c,185a), **Reni** (83d), **Reno, rent** (58a,77c,91b,138b,153d,162c,167c), **repp** (53b,131a), **rese** (127b), **resh** (91d), **rest** (15d,91b,104d,105a,115a,b,130a,b,161b), **rete** (106c,119c), **reve** (61c,104d), **revs** (131a)

- RE - **area** (37d,38a,44c,53a,93b,110d,127d,138c,168a,186d), **areg** (116a, 137a), **areo** (34c), **Ares** (49b,51b,68c,76a,97a,105c,110b), **aret** (128c), **brea** (100b), **bred** (23c,48c,127c), **bree** (139a), **bren** (72d, 95a), **Brer** (172b), **Bres, brew** (35d), **brey** (194), **crea** (92c), **Cree** (192), **crew** (72a,106a), **Crex** (37a), **dree** (139b,140c,158b,172c), **drei** (66d,165a), **dreg, drew, drey** (154c), **erer**, (17d,150c), **Frea, Fred** (96b), **free** (44a,70d,131b), **fret** (28c,35b,111c,184d), **Frey** (7c, 68b,124d), **gres** (156d), **grew, grey** (33d), **Iren** (127c), **Orel, pree** (139d), **prep** (138b), **pres** (62b), **pret** (188), **prey** (119d), **tree** (11d, 37a,66a,184b), **tref** (172b), **trek** (85c,93c,99d,168b), **tres** (19a,52b, 63a,152d,165a,175c), **tret** (9a,178b,179d), **trey** (26c,165a), **Urey** (107c,138c), **wren** (19b,c), **Wren** (50b)

- - RE **Aare, acre** (39b,56a,88b), **Acre, aire** (82c), **Aire, bare** (43d,157c), **bore** (14c,25b,46a,116a,165c,179b), **bure** (61b), **byre** (38a), **care** (11b,14c,35d,150a,184d), **cere** (19a,149d,179a), **core** (28b,51c, 75b,81b), **cure** (123b), **dare** (28d,41b,42a,74d,175b), **Dare** (57a), **dere** (74a,79c), **dire** (45d,55a,104a,163c), **dore** (61d,67b,69d, 117d), **Dore** (50d,63a,b), **Eire** (82b), **etre** (61a,c,62d,166c), **eyre** (23c,31b,85c), **Eyre, fare** (43c,59b,67d,123b), **fire** (13a,43d, 44b), **fore** (63d,174b), **gare** (61b,c,62c,127c), **Gere** (183c), **gore** (115d,117c,154c,169c), **gyre** (31b,171b), **hare** (91b,132c), **here, hire** (49d,50b,91b,130a), **inre** (35d,80a), **jure** (90b), **kere** (75c, 128b), **kore** (107b), **Kore** (29a,42b,116b,124d), **Kure** (84c), **lire** (62c), **lore** (77c,87c,90d,151c,183a), **lure** (41c,51a,54b,163a), **lyre** (11c,81d,105a,111c), **mare** (78b), **Mare** (108b), **mere** (16c,22b,62a, 78b,87d,96c,110c,120d,146d,148b), **mire** (21c,104b), **more** (71a), **More** (50b), **mure** (177d), **Nare** (93c), **Nore** (163d), **ogre** (67a,102a), **pare** (115c,129a), **pere** (61c,63b), **pore** (59d,110d,111c,120d,157d), **pure** (29b,172b,173c), **pyre** (64c), **qere** (75c), **rare** (138b,164b, 172b,173d), **rire** (62a), **sere** (24d,46a,c,138c,183b), **Sere** (158b), **sire** (17d,55a,59d,124a,163b,166b), **sore** (23d,142c), **sure** (173d), **tare** (9a,18d,41a,176a,179d), **tire** (15a,22a,52d,55a,179b,180d),

tore, tyre (15a), **Tyre** (31b,90d,117b), **vare** (179b), **vire** (11a,13b), **ware** (27d,35a), **were** (139b), **wire, wore, yare** (96b,124b,128b), **yore** (10b,69d,93c,110b,165d)

R - - E **race** (116a,153b,154b,169c), **rade** (138d), **rage** (10c,30c,157a, 161d), **rake** (41b,44c,134b,140d), **rale** (7c,23a,29d,41b), **rame** (22d), **rare** (138b,164b,172b,173d), **rase** (42b,d,91d), **rate** 11d,14a,31d,36b,51d,52a,70b,85c,112b,123b,127d,128a,138c,143a, 174b), **rave** (41c,157a,161d), **raze** (42b,d,91d), **rede** (37c,81d,138d), **rese** (127b), **rete** (106c,119c), **reve** (61c,104d), **ribe** (139a), **Rice** (46a), **ride** (46b,85c), **rife** (6b,c,39d,123b), **rile** (10c,d,82c,125a, 156b,176a), **rime** (30c,36a,58a,63d,77c), **rine** (44d,75d,135c), **ripe** (58a,97c,98c), **rire** (62a), **rise** (49d,80b,155a), **Rise** (110d,150c), **rite** (93a,131d), **rive** (32a,153d), **robe** (65b), **rode** (46c), **role** (114b), **Rome** (31c,51d), **rone** (127c,164b), **rope** (36d,88d,128b), **rose** (33c), **Rose** (6a,50c,183c), **rote** (130b,134b,143a,159d), **roue** (41b,44c,127c,134b), **rove** (127d,132b,178a), **rube** (37d,135d, 185d), **Rube** (96b), **rude** (134b,172b), **rule** (11b,26b,90b), **rune** (9b,67a,94a,95a,105c,107d,120a,141d,163d), **ruse** (13b,77c,157b, 169c), **rute** (188), **ryme** (178d), **rype** (19b,125a)

- RF - **orfe** (57a,b,185c), **Urfa** (99a)

- - RF **kerf** (40a,108b), **serf** (21d,148a), **surf** (23a), **turf** (115c,149d, 160b), **warf, werf** (54d), **zarf** (39c,155a)

R - - F **raff** (75b), **reef** (129a,137a,145a), **riff** (131d), **Riff** (18b,102c), **roof** (78d), **ruff** (19b,33b,63d,137a)

- RG - **Argo** (12c,36b,c), **ergo** (164b), **orgy** (26d,130d,137c), **urge** (42d, 46b,79d,80a,b,81c,124a,150a)

- - RG **berg** (79b), **borg** (40d), **burg** (22b,73c), **lurg** (96d,141b,184d), **morg** (188), **Sarg** (96d,125c)

R - - G **rang, ring** (50a), **Rong** (88c), **rung** (28c,39a)

RH - - **rhea** (37a,56a,111d,133d), **Rhea** (19b,68d,87c,103c,186b), **Rhee** (87c), **Rhin, rhob** (64a,85c), **rhum** (8c), **Rhus** (159a)

R - - H **rash** (75a), **rath** (29a,76d,162d), **resh** (91d), **rich, Roch** (136c), **rukh** (53b,54a), **rush, ruth** (35b,118c), **Ruth** (105b,183c)

RI - - **rial** (190), **ribe** (139a), **rice, Rice** (46a), **rich, rick** (74d,117d,154d), **Ridd** (94a), **ride** (46b,85c), **Riel** (129a), **riem** (76c,112c,157c,164d), **rien** (62b), **rier** (180b), **rife** (6b,c,39d,123b), **riff** (131d), **Riff** (18b, 102c), **rift** (30c,32a,58a,110d), **riga** (118b), **Riga, Riis** (9d), **rikk** (49a), **rile** (10c,d,82c,125a,156b,176a), **rill** (23c102b,132a,148d, 157b), **rily** (176a), **rima** (23a,30c,32a,58a,110d), **rime** (30c,36a,58a, 63d,77c), **rimu** (79d,106d,129a,168c), **rimy** (63d), **rind** (53a,115c), **Rind** (109c,174b), **rine** (44d,75d,135c), **ring** (50a), **rink** (147c, 154a), **riot** (44c,111d,170c,173d), **ripa** (16b,131d), **ripe** (58a,97c, 98c), **rire** (62a), **rise** (49d,80b,155a), **Rise** (110d,150c), **risk** (74d), **risp** (99a), **Riss** (66a), **rita, Rita** (37b,78d,183c), **rite** (93a,131d), **rive** (32a,153d)

- RI - **aria** (8b,98c,150a,c,170c), **arid** (46c,85a), **arif** (127d), **aril** (142a), **aris** (101b), **Brie** (29c), **brig** (72b,106a,144d), **brim, brin** (32c,54c,146c), **brit** (76c), **crib** (96b,120d), **cric** (131c), **crig** (20d), **crin** (146c), **cris** (40b,95d), **drib** (46b), **Drin, drip, eria** (13d,146d), **eric** (115b), **Eric** (71d,96a,107d,138a,164a,176b), **Erie** (82c,87d),

354

Erin (82b), **Eris** (12c,68d,109c), **Fria, frib** (43d), **frim** (58d), **frit** (64c,67c), **friz** (39d), **grid** (17a,70d,119b,156d), **grig** (38c,70d, 93a), **grim** (156a), **grin, grip** (159a), **gris** (61d), **grit** (137a,b), **irid** (38d,67c), **iris** (53c,58a,111c) **Iris** (127c), **kris** (40b,95d), **prig** (112a, 116c), **prim** (156b), **trig** (106a,148d,154b,169d), **trim** (40a,106a, 154b,160a,165c,169d), **trin** (169d), **trio** (104d,165a,169c), **trip** (85c), **tris** (122d), **trit** (34d,164c), **Uria** (14c,16d), **urim** (18d,23a, 110a), **writ** (91a)

- - RI   **abri** (61c,62c,144b), **aeri** (34a), **agri** (89b), **Atri, auri** (34a), **bari** (37c,79c), **Bari** (83d), **Bori** (110d,150c), **buri** (56b), **Cori** (138c), **dari** (38a,70b), **Geri** (183c), **gyri** (22d,131b), **kari** (14d), **keri** (75c,128b), **kiri** (86a,87c,115a,168c), **kori** (7d,77a), **Kuri** (191), **lari** (78a,101c), **Lari** (72c), **lori** (91b), **Luri** (191), **mari** (61d), **Mari** (16a), **Neri, nori** (8c,141c), **Omri** (18c,86d), **pari** (34a, 180a), **peri** (54b,116b,c,122b), **puri** (80d), **qeri** (75c), **Rori** (16b), **sari** (48b,65b,77b), **seri** (18b), **Seri** (192), **Shri** (17c,166c), **siri** (18b), **sori** (55c,64a), **Tari** (47d,69a), **tori** (101b), **Turi** (191), **vari** (34d,91b,134d,174d), **veri** (28b), **weri** (15c,27c)

R - - I   **rabi** (38d,74a), **Rabi** (14b,117b), **ragi** (28b), **rami** (22d), **rani** (72d, 77b,123c,127c), **rati** (189), **ravi** (61b), **Ravi** (16b), **Reki** (16a), **Remi** (10b), **Reni** (83d), **rodi** (98c), **romi** (72d), **Rori** (16b), **roti** (62c)

- - RK   **bark** (115c), **cark** (26d,184d), **cork** (119d), **dark** (47a,67d,109b, 160b), **dirk** (40b), **fork, hark** (92d), **jerk** (153a), **kirk** (31a,139b), **kurk** (31a,139b), **lark** (19a,63d), **lurk** (92a,147d), **mark** (146b, 155a), **Mark** (52a,96a), **mirk** (41a,67d), **murk** (41a,67d), **nark** (81a, 156d), **park, perk** (84d,93a), **pork, Sark** (28d), **Turk** (101d,102d, 106a,111d), **work** (64c,76b), **yark** (22c), **york** (38c), **York** (50b,c)

R - - K   **rack** (32c,64b), **raik** (188,189), **rank** (31d,55d,70b,92c,94d,157d), **reck** (26d,75c), **reek** (49d,53c,64a,148d,149a), **rick** (74d,117d, 154d), **rikk** (49a), **rink** (147c,154a), **risk** (74d), **rock** (160b), **rook** (19b,29c,39a), **ruck** (39a,185a), **rusk** (23a)

- RL -   **orle** (17b,56b,76a,144b,177a), **orlo** (56b,119c), **Orly** (8b)

- - RL   **birl** (93c,131a,153c), **burl** (87c,169a), **carl** (115c,135d), **Carl** (96a), **cirl** (24c), **curl** (38d,73b,93b,131d), **earl** (107c), **farl** (138c,140b), **furl** (132d), **girl, harl** (16b,56b,59a), **herl** (16b,59a), **hurl** (167c), **jarl** (40d,107d), **Karl** (96a), **marl** (32a,42c,55d), **merl** (20b), **nurl** (33b,87c), **purl** (87c,104c), **yarl** (40d,107d)

R - - L   **rail** (16b,19b,c,37a,97b,138c,150c,177b), **real** (7a), **reel** (21b,40b,d, 153c,154a,c,d,180d), **rial** (190), **Riel** (129a), **riil** (23c,102b,132a, 148d,157b), **roil** (44c,104b,156b,170d,176a), **roll** (134a,160b), **rotl** (103b,111c), **rull** (170b), **ryal** (110a,190), **ryel** (190)

- RM -   **arme** (63a,179b), **arms, army** (78c), **Erma** (183c), **Irma** (96d)

- - RM   **barm** (185b), **berm** (25d,90d,145c), **corm** (24b,38d,156a), **derm** (147c,158d), **dorm, farm** (165d), **firm** (154c,173d), **form** (54d, 143c), **Garm** (178c), **germ** (17d,99c,134d), **harm** (40b,81a), **norm** (15a,115a,128a,155a), **perm** (49b,97d), **term** (92b,105b,142b,166b), **turm** (132d), **warm** (7c,75b,163b), **worm, wurm** (67c)

R - -M   **ream** (18c,37d,50d,113d,171c), **reem** (18d), **reim** (112c), **rhum** (8c), **riem** (76c,112c,157c,164d), **roam** (178a), **room** (28d)

- RN -   **arna** (24a,181b), **Arnd** (67a), **Arne** (35c,50c,134d), **arni** (24a,181b),

Arno (27a), **arn't, erne** (19c,d,47b,54b,141a), **orna** (169d,182c), **orne** (169d,182c), **Orne** (25b), **urna** (133a)

- - RN   **barn** (156d), **Bern,** 160d), **birn** (31d), **born, burn, carn** (156c), **cern** (41c), **corn** (39d,95c,123a), **darn** (130b), **dorn** (164d), **earn** (42d, 64b,99a), **fern** (142a), **firn** (67c,70c,106c,149b), **garn** (67d,185b), **horn** (11a,105a,170b,182a), **karn** (156c), **kern** (59c,172a), **Kern** (132b), **lorn** (42d,60b), **morn, Norn** (69a,163d,174b), **pern** (78a), **pirn** (21b,129a,179b), **sorn** (139a,d), **tarn** (87d,103d,120d), **tern** (19b,32d,72c,94a,138c,141b,160a), **torn** (130a), **turn** (28d,131a, 175a), **warn** (7b), **worn** (143b), **yarn** (154b,161b,184b)

R - - N   **rain** (121d,162d), **rann** (175c), **rein** (29b,130c), **Rhin, rien** (62b), **roan** (78b,c,114c,128d,144a,181a), **roon** (41a,168b), **ruin** (42d)

RO - -   **road** (37d,164d), **roam** (178a), **roan** (78b,c,114c,128d,144a, 181a), **roar** (145c), **robe** (65b), **Roch** (136c), **rock** (160b), **Roda** (107b), **rodd** (38d), **rode** (46c), **rodi** (98c), **roed, roer** (72d), **roey** (103d), **rohr** (72d), **roil** (44c,104b,156b,170d,176a), **rojo** (129a, 152c), **roka** (95a,168c,d), **roke** (174d,175b), **role** (114b), **roll** (134a, 160b), **Roma** (83c), **Rome** (31c,51d), **romi** (72d), **romp** (63d), **rone** (127c, 164b), **Rong** (88c), **rood** (38d,39a,88b), **roof** (78d), **rook** (19b,29c,39a), **room** (28d), **roon** (41a,168b), **Roos** (67a), **root** (53a), **ropa** (152a), **rope** (36d,88d,128b), **ropy** (157c,176d), **Rori** (16b), **Rosa** (58d,134a,145d,183c), **rose** (33c), **Rose** (6a,50c,183c), **ross** (16c,161d), **Ross** (50c), **rosy** (21a,111a), **rota** (27c,30d,38a,79a,92d, 133a,134a,b,180c), **rote** (130b,134b,143a,159d), **roti** (62c), **rotl** (103b,111c), **roto** (30a,122d,127b,152c,171b), **roud** (57a,b), **roue** (41b,44c,127c,134b), **roup** (44a,121d), **rout** (41d,44b,46b), **rove** (127d,132b,178a), **rowy** (157b), **Roxy** (183d)

- RO -   **Aroa** (175b), **Arod** (86c), **aroo** (80c,82b), **arow** (92c,158b), **brob** (153c), **broo** (139a), **brow, croc** (13a,74a), **Crom, crop** (38b), **crow** (19a), **drop** (43d,54b,100b,114c,168b), **Eros** (11c,39c,68b,97c,182d), **froe** (32a,167a,179d), **frog** (10a,17a,126d), **from, frot** (28c), **frow** (47a,167a), **grog** (92d,153d), **gros** (47a,53d), **Gros** (63a), **grot** (27d), **grow** (154b), **irok** (55b), **iron** (55c,d,69d,81a,97b,143b, 149a,173d,179c), **Kroo** (191), **proa** (21b,26a,95c,d), **prod** (67d,80b, 106b,120b), **prop** (159d), **prow** (21b,22c,144d,156a), **trod, tron** (140d,180a), **trop** (62d,167a), **trot** (85b,93d,112d), **trow** (18a,21a, 159d,164c,170b), **troy** (161c,180a)

- - RO   **aero** (8b,34a,b,58c,59a), **agro** (149d), **arro** (52c), **baro** (71a,122c), **boro** (154b), **Boro** (193), **caro** (83a), **Caro** (183d), **cero** (57b,c,d, 180b), **duro** (190), **Ebro** (132a), **faro** (65a), **Garo** (88c), **giro** (38c, 167c), **gyro** (34d), **hero** (42b,124d,137b), **Hero** (90c), **hiro, inro** (84b,c,106c), **karo** (106d), **Lero** (82d), **loro** (19a,114b), **maro** (144d), **mero** (72a), **miro** (19a,106d,184a), **Miro** (113a,151d), **moro** (19a,56c), **Moro** (100a,103a,117a,159a), **Nero** (8a,126d,133a,150b, 172c), **okro** (72c,175a), **otro** (151d), **pero** (152a), **Piro** (192), **Poro** (141d), **pyro, sero** (34d,88d,164b,178d), **taro** (13c,48c,49b,64b, 112b,120a,133d,155c,170a,c), **tiro** (9b,17d,108c), **toro** (38a,107a, 152a,168c), **tyro** (9b,17d,108c), **zero** (31a,84c,108c), **Zero** (118d)

R - - O   **ralo** (188), **redo** (165c), **Reno, rojo** (129a), **roto** (30a,122d,127b)

- RP -   **arpa** (83b)

- - RP   **carp** (27d,38d,40c,55a,56c,57a), **dorp** (73c,176b), **harp** (105a,129a),

larp (51d), **lerp** (51d,141d), **tarp** (26b,178d), **terp** (12b,123a), **torp** (54c), **turp**, **warp** (36c,165a,171c), **zarp** (120c)

R - - P   **raip** (36d), **ramp** (65a,80b,127b,148b), **rasp** (56b,70d,140d), **reap** (7a,40a,74a), **repp** (53b,131a), **risp** (99a), **romp** (63d), **roup** (44a, 121d), **rump**

- RR -   **arra** (47d,52c,82b), **arro** (52c), **Irra** (178a), **orra** (139c,d,140a)

- - RR   **barr** (49b), **birr** (180d), **burr** (123b), **carr** (120d,140a), **curr** (104c), **darr** (163c), **dorr** (32b), **durr** (70b), **Herr** (66c), **Kerr, murr** (72b,128b), **nurr** (67d), **parr** (136d,137a,147c), **pirr** (181a), **purr** (104c), **turr** (24d,105a), **Tyrr** (68c,109c,163d,178a), **yarr** (72a)

R - - R   **rear** (15b,23a,b,24a,51b,76d,127c), **rier** (180b), **roar** (145c), **roer** (72d), **rohr** (72d), **ruer, Ruhr**

- RS -   **Erse** (28a,64b,82b), **erst** (60b), **Ursa** (17b,36b,43d)

- - RS   **airs** (123b), **Bors** (70b,134b), **hers** (124c), **hors** (62b), **Lars** (51d, 121b), **Mars** (68c,118d,119a,129a,178a), **Mors** (41b), **ours** (124c), **pars** (89d), **sors** (44d,89b)

R - - S   **raas** (91b), **rais** (26c,29d,75a,103b), **Rais** (106b), **rats, reis** (26c, 29d,75a,103b), **Rems, revs** (131a), **Rhus** (159a), **Riis** (9d), **Riss** (66a), **Roos** (67a), **ross** (16c,161d), **Ross** (50c), **Russ** (135b)

- RT -   **Arta** (72b), **arto** (34a), **arts** (138c), **arty, orts** (60d), **Urth** (68d, 107d,163d)

- - RT   **Bart** (96b), **Bert** (96b), **bort** (43b), **Bort** (134b), **cart** (171d,175a, 177b), **curt** (145b,c), **dart** (13b,88a,100c,120b,153a,160c), **dirt, fort** (63d,157d), **girt** (50a), **hart** (41d,154d), **hurt, mart** (49d,97a), **Mart** (96b,183d), **mort** (41b,47a,78b,136d), **part** (44d,60d,121c, 159c), **pert** (80a,93a,137c,154b), **port** (73d,136b,140c,170c,d,182b, c), **Sart** (82b,103b,170d), **Sert** (151d), **sort** (31d,39c,70b,86b,153a), **tart** (114d), **tort** (31c,91a,185c), **vert** (71d,166a,171b), **wart** (124d), **wert, wort** (76a,95d,121d), **yurt** (101d)

R - - T   **raft** (27b,33c,58c,75b), **rant** (41c,127d,128a,161d), **rapt** (6c,27a, 50d), **rect** (117b), **reft** (32a,42c,44d,167b), **rent** (58a,77c,91b,138b, 153d,162c,167c), **rest** (15d,91b,104d,105a,115a,b,130a,b,161b), **rift** (30c,32a,58a,110d), **riot** (44c,111d,170c,173d), **root** (53a), **rout** (41d,44b,46b), **runt** (47a,172b), **rust** (37b,112c,119a), **ryot** (115c)

RU - -   **ruay** (189), **rube** (37d,135d,185d), **Rube** (96b), **ruby** (20a,65d, 179c), **ruck** (39a,185a), **rudd** (26d,57a,b), **rude** (134b,172b), **ruer ruff** (19b,33b,63d,137a), **ruga** (59b,185a), **Ruhr, ruin** (42d), **rukh** (53b,54a), **rule** (11b,26b,90b), **rull** (170b), **rumb** (120b), **rump, rune** (9b,67a,94a,95a,105c,107d,120a,141d,163d), **rung** (28c,39a), **runt** (47a,172d), **rupa** (60b), **ruru** (19b,102c,106d), **rusa, Rusa** (41d, 136d), **ruse** (13b,77c,157b,169c), **rush, rusk** (23a), **Russ** (135b), **rust** (37b,112c,119a), **Ruta** (76b,134d), **rute** (188), **ruth** (35b,118c), **Ruth** (105b,183c)

- RU -   **arui** (11b,143d,144a,181c), **arum** (13a,39b,58d,92b,155c), **Arum** (66a), **bruh** (95a), **brut** (182c), **Brut** (23c), **crus** (91a,143c), **crux** (39a,151b), **drub** (17b,39c) **drug** (105d), **drum** (105a), **drun** (132b), **erua** (103c), **eruc** (37a,56a), **grub** (43c,88d), **grum** (102c), **Grus** (36b,c,38b), **irus** (109d), **prut!, Prut** (41a), **true** (7a,8d,37b,54b, 94c,149c), **urus** (14d,53a,112c)

- - RU Aaru (6b,48d), **baru** (168c), **ecru** (17d,23d,172b), **feru** (37a,56a, 133d), **guru** (77b), **maru** (84c,144d), **Meru** (77a,103d), **paru** (57a), **Peru, Puru** (192), **ruru** (19b,102c,106d), **Yaru** (48d)

R - - U Rahu (42b,48b), **rimu** (79d,106d,129a,168c), **ruru** (19b,102c,106d)

- RV - urva (38b)

RY - - ryal (110a,190), **ryel** (190), **ryme** (178d), **rynd** (100a), **ryot** (115c), **rype** (19b,125a)

- RY - Arya (80d), **eryx** (137a), **oryx** (11a), **tryp** (114a)

- - RY adry (164c), **aery** (47b,51d,106c), **airy** (177a,176d), **atry** (141b), **awry** (13d,38d,171c), **bury** (81d), **dory** (21b,58b,144c), **eery** (172b, 180a), **ewry** (133c), **eyry** (47b,106c), **fury** (157a), **Gary, gory, jury** (38a), **lory** (19a,114a), **Mary** (50c,126b,183c), **miry, nary** (108b), **oary, sory** (176d), **spry** (7a,107b), **Tory** (23c,36b,94c,172a), **vary** (28d,43c), **very** (149c), **wary** (27d,176b), **wiry** (147a,167c)

R - - Y racy (153b), **rely** (16b,170b), **rily** (176a), **rimy** (63d), **roey** (103d), **ropy** (157c,176d), **rosy** (21a,111a), **rowy** (157b), **Roxy** (183d), **ruay** (189), **ruby** (20a,65d,179c)

R - - Z razz (131b)

SA - - Saad (12b), **saah** (188), **saal** (66c,73b), **Saan** (24d), **Saar** (63b,102d, 132a), **saba** (56a,117a), **Saba** (143d), **sabe, sack** (43d,118a,119d, 182b), **saco** (189), **sadd** (33a,40b,58c,107b), **sade** (91d), **sadh** (77a), **sado** (26d,84d), **sadr** (94a), **Sadr** (155b), **saer** (163a), **safe** (141d,157d,174d), **Safi** (191), **saga** (79b,91a,138a,157a,161b,c, 168a), **Saga, sage** (13a,90d,100c,141c,145c,180b,183a), **sago** (54c, 59b,113b,125b,155c), **sagy, saha, sahh** (188), **Saho** (6c), **sahu** (153d), **saic** (86b,91d,175d), **said** (174c), **Said** (42d,101a,121b), **sail** (144c,185a), **sain** (20c,38d,48a), **sair** (140b,150d), **sais** (48d, 71d), **Saka** (10a), **sake** (84b,125d), **saki** (39c,84b,102a), **sala** (152a, b,c), **Sala** (50c), **sale** (14c,61c,62b,c,168b), **salp** (109c,148d), **salt** (35d,105b,123a,136c,141c,149d), **sama** (105c,169d), **same** (44d, 79b), **samh** (56b), **samp** (70b,77d,121b), **sana** (56a,166d), **Sana** (185d), **sand** (71d,146c), **sane** (128a), **sang, sank, sano** (152b), **sans** (63a,183b), **sapa** (70c), **sapo** (149c,166d), **Sara** (24d,183c), **sard** (26d,28d,65d,111a,142b,156d), **Sard, Sarg** (96d,125c), **sari** (48b,65b,77b), **Sark** (28d), **Sart** (82b,103b,170d), **sasa** (55c), **sash** (18a,45c,67b,182b), **sass, sate** (32d,52c,67d,70d,137c,159d), **sati, Sati** (49a,126b,147b), **Sauk** (192), **saul** (48a,168c), **Saul** (18c,86d, 115a), **saum** (189), **save** (52b,110c,123a,173c), **sawk** (188), **sawn saxe** (20d,33c), **saya** (117a)

- SA - asak (13d,168c,169a), **asar** (67b), **Esau** (82c,84a,128c), **Esay, Isar** (41a,104c,132a), **osar** (51b,67b,131b), **tsar** (42d,49d,60b,135c), **usar** (8d,16c), **Usas** (68d)

- - SA ansa (73c,93d,137c), **Ausa, Besa** (68b,119c), **bisa** (11a), **bosa** (12a), **casa** (152b), **Disa** (111a), **dosa** (74b), **Elsa** (70a,93c,110d, 177b,183c), **kasa** (48a), **kusa, Lisa** (183d), **masa** (37a), **mesa** (49b, 76d,119b,161a), **Musa** (16a), **ossa** (21d), **Ossa** (103d,110b,164b), **pasa** (46a,127c,152c), **pesa** (190), **Pisa** (90c), **rasa** (51c), **Rosa** (58d,134a,145d,183c), **rusa, Rusa** (41d,136d), **sasa** (55c), **Susa** (49a), **Tesa** (80c), **Ursa** (17b,36b,43d), **vasa** (46d,114a,160b,175d), **Vasa, visa** (114d), **Xosa** (86a)

S - - A   saba (56a,117a), **Saba** (143d), saga (79b,91a,138a,157a,161b,c, 168a), saha, **Saka** (10a), sala (152a,b,c), **Sala** (50c), sama (105c, 169d), sana (56a,166d), **Sana** (185d), sapa (70c), **Sara** (24d,183c), sasa (55c), saya (117a), **Seba** (18c,39d), sera (11b,20d,59a,83a, 180d), seta (23b,27c,73a,b,123b,153c), shea (25a,168c,d), **Shoa** (6c), sida (37a,126c,170a), sika (41d,84b), sima (132b), sina (46c), **Sina** (102d,103d), **Sita** (127d), siva (67a,120d), **Siva** (56d,77a), skua (19b,72c,84a,141a), soda (19a,149d,181a), sofa (44d), soga (70d,152b), **Soga** (191), **Soia, soja** (151b), soka (20c), sola (9a,48a, 74b,118c,154a,167b), soma (10c,21c,34a,48a,81d,136b), sora (19b, c,127b), soya (151b), stoa (33c,121a,c), **Sula** (65a), supa (168c), sura (87c,113b,166d), **Susa** (49a), **Syra**

- SB -   isba (135c)

S - - B   scab (80b,107d,157c), scob (42a), **Serb** (15d,148a,186c), slab (148b), **Sleb** (12a), slob (173d), slub (171c), snab (23c,139a), snib (54d,93c), snob (159c), snub (128c,148b), sorb (11d,103d,134b, 142d), **Sorb** (148a,180a), stab (14c,87a,117c), stib (19b,47a,137a), stub (156c), swab (102b), sweb (160d), swob (102b)

SC - -   scab (80b,107d,157c), scad (31a,57a,78b,88d,137c), scan (52b,93d, 98a,116d,128b,c,140d), scar (31a,184d), scat (26b,67a,d,126c, 169c), **Scio, scob** (42a), scon (162c), scop (120a), scot (14a,162b), **Scot** (64b,132c), scow (21a,58b), scud (32c,126c,135b,160c), scum (129b), scup (57a,121b), scur (78b), scut (145c,161b)

- SC -   asci (154a), esca (11c,44a,70c), esce (158d)

- - SC   aesc (12d,64d), **Bosc** (115c), **DDSC** (42a), disc (31b), fisc (52c,134c)

S - - C   saic (86b,91d,175d), spec

S - - D   **Saad** (12b), sadd (33a,40b,58c,107b), said (174c), **Said** (42d,101a, 121b), sand (71d,146c), sard (26d,28d,65d,111a,142b,156d), **Sard, scad** (31a,57a,78b,137c), scud (32c,126c,135b,160c), seed (70b, 111c,112c,119a,151b,154a), seid (103b), **Seid** 42d,101a, 171a), send (42c,44b,95c,121c,130a,144c,168b), shad (27d,57a, b,c), shed (27a,90c,101b,144b), shod, **Sind,** skid (148b), sled (40a), slid, sned (93d,125a), snod (169d), sold, spad (105b), **Spad** (118d), sped, spud (121d,151c), stad (151b,167d,176b), stod (40d,67d), stud (22b,25a,42d,54d,111c,143a,174a), sudd (40b,58c,107b), suld (188), surd (82c,177a), swad (94d), syed (103b), syud (103b)

SE - -   seah (188), seal (10c,d,54d,64c,96a,118b,128a), seam (85b,d,160a, 176d,185a), **Sean** (85b,96a), sear (23d,27d,72d,138c), seat (98c, 156b), **Seba** (18c,39d), sebi (34b), sech (97c), seck (173d), sect (42b,54a,114c), seed (70b,111c,112c,119a,151b,154a), seek (141c), seel (20c,32c,143b), seem (11c), seen, seep (110c,116a, 154b), seer (60a,124c,150c), sego (24b.25a,92b,174c), sehr (66d), seid (103b), **Seid** (42d,101a,171a), **Seik** (77b), **Seim** (120c), sein (146c), seip (110c), **Seir** (51b,94a,103d), seis (147b,152c), seit (189), **Sejm** (120c), self (48d,80d), sell (97a,115c,175b), seme (45c, 138b,151b,154b,155c,157b), semi (34b,80b,122c,d), send (42c, 44b,95c,121c,130a,144c,168b), senn (76b), **Sens** (63b), sent, seps, (93b,142d), sept (31d,82b,143a,149c), **Sept** (45b), sera (11b,20d, 59a,83a,180d), **Serb** (15d,148a,186c), sere (24d,46a,c,138c,183b), **Sere** (158b), serf (21d,148a), seri (18b), **Seri** (192), sero (34d,88d,

359

164b,178d), **Sert** (151d), **sesi** (20b,57a,149b), **sess** (149c,162b), **seta** (23b,27c,73a,b,123b,153c), **seth** (98d), **Seth** (7a,52b,68a,b,96a, 98d), **seti** (34a), **Seti** (116d), **sett** (115a,156d), **seve** (63a,182c), **sewn, sext** (26b,111b,147b)

- SE -   **asea** (39b,177c), **asem** (9a,49a,69c), **Aser** (84a), **esek** (18d), **esel** (66b), **eser, Iser** (49a), **oser** (61b), **used** (6d,73a), **usee, user** (49d), **uses** (18a), **yser**

- - SE   **anse** (61d), **apse** (9b,20a,31a,128c,130a,142b,175a), **asse** (25a, 60d,74a), **base** (6a,43b,44b,51c,60c,79b,94b,122b), **bise** (182a), **bose** (163c), **case** (22c,36c,81c,91a,108c), **cise** (147b), **cose** (29b), **dose** (123a), **duse** (83c), **ease** (7c,8d,35a,100d,129d,130b,c,150c), **else** (18b,79b,111d), **ense** (139b,158c), **Erse** (28a,64b,82b), **esse** (7a,18a,52d,89a,90a,159a,166c), **fuse** (98c), **hase** (74d), **hose** (156c), **huse** (180c), **ipse** (44d,89c), **Jose** (96a), **lose** (60a,100c), **lyse, mese** (71c), **mise** (8a,10a,70c), **Mose** (96b), **muse** (65b,93d, 120d,164c), **Muse** (68d), **nase** (26b,75a,124b), **nose** (118d,125a, 149b), **oese** (15d,119c), **Oise, Ouse** (132a,185d), **owse, pise** (127d), **pose** (14c,15d), **rase** (42b,d,91d), **rese** (127b), **rise** (49d,80b,155a), **Rise** (110d,150c), **rose** (33c), **Rose** (6a,50c,183c), **ruse** (13b,77c, 157b,169c), **sise** (62c,147b), **vase, vise** (31d,77d,114d), **wise** (136b)

S - - E   **sabe, sade** (91d), **safe** (141d,157d,174d), **sage** (13a,90d,100c,141c, 145c,180b,183a), **sake** (84b,125d), **sale** (14c,61c,62b,c,168b), **same** (44d,79b), **sane** (128a), **sate** (32d,52c,67d,70d,137c,159d), **save** (52b,110c,123a,173c), **saxe** (20d,33c), **seme** (45c,138b,151b,154b, 155c,157b), **sere** (24d,46a,c,138c,183c), **Sere** (158b), **seve** (63a, 182c), **shee** (82b), **shoe** (166a), **sice** (71d,147b), **side** (13d,22a,b, 54a,58a,89a,161b), **sine** (101d), **sine** (64c,66b,90a,97c,126a,163b, 169d,183b), **sipe** (101a,110c,140b), **sire** (17d,55a,59d,124a,163b, 166b), **sise** (62c,147b), **site** (93b), **sive** (146a), **size, skee** (149c), **Skye** (163c), **slee** (140b,148c), **sloe** (14a,20b,64a,119d,181c), **slue** (97b,148b,160a), **smee** (19b,46c,d,118b,119d,141b,181b), **Smee** (116d), **snee** (40a,b,43d,87a), **soie** (62c), **soke** (44c,85d), **sole** (52c, 57a,b,58b,d,110c,115d,150a), **some** (114b,121c,126a), **sore** (23d, 142c), **sote** (150c), **spae** (139c), **Spee** (66d,70b), **supe** (53a,154d), **sure** (173d), **syce** (71d), **syke** (194), **syne** (140b,147a), **sype** (110c)

S - - F   **self** (48d,80d), **serf** (21d,148a), **souf** (146b), **stof** (135c), **surf** (23a)

SG - -   **Sgau** (88c)

S - - G   **sang, Sarg** (96d,125c), **shag** (73b,105b,161d,166d), **sing** (26d,178a), **skag** (7d,46d), **skeg** (7d,86a,144d,157d,184a), **slag** (46c,99a,138c, 148d,177a), **slog** (157c,170b,177d), **slug** (46b,99b,157c), **smug, snag** (11b,27b,35c,87c,124b,166a), **sneg** (139b), **snig** (45d), **snug** (35a,38b,165c), **Snug** (99d), **song** (12c,170c), **stag** (65a,98d), **stog** (155a), **sung, Sung** (30b), **swag** (22a,156c), **swig** (46a,72c)

SH - -   **shad** (27d,57a,b,c), **shag** (73b,105b,161d,166d), **shah** (116c), **sham** (41c,55b,60d,80a,123a,b,146d), **Shan** (13c,80d,88c,101d), **shap, shat** (87d), **shaw** (164b), **Shaw** (50c,53b), **shay** (110c), **shea** (25a, 168c,d), **shed** (27a,90c,101b,144b), **shee** (82b), **Shem** (107c), **Shen** (68a), **sher** (65d,165c), **shet, shew** (44c), **shih** (189), **Shik** (171a), **shim** (91d,144c,162a,179d), **shin** (91a,d,140b,143c), **ship, shir** (36d, 65d,165c), **Shoa** (6c), **shod, shoe** (166a), **shoo** (46b,67a,138b), **shop, shoq** (169a), **shor** (136d), **Shor** (162b), **shot** (9d,43d,90c,174d), **shou**

(41d), **show** (42b,44c,96b), **Shri** (17c,166c), **shul** (161a), **shun** (15a, 51b,52a), **shut**

- **SH -**   **Asha** (191), **ashy** (113a,178a), **Isha** (174a), **Tshi** (69c), **Usha** (16a, 150c)

- - **SH**   **bash, bish** (120b), **bosh, bush, cash** (101c), **cosh** (35a,97c), **cush** (101c), **Cush** (51d,73c), **dash** (125c,162d), **dish, fash** (140c,176a), **fish, gash** (40a), **gish** (102c), **gosh, gush** (35a,154c), **hash, hish, hush** (17b,146c), **josh** (85b), **kish** (16d,70c), **Kish** (137c), **Kush lash** (58c,87b,165c,180d), **losh** (178b), **lush** (94d), **mash** (39b, 156c), **mesh** (50d,106c), **mush** (97d), **Nash** (9c), **Nish** (19d), **pish** (36c,107d), **posh** (49b,148c), **push** (145c), **rash** (75a), **resh** (91d), **rush, sash** (18a,45c,67b,182b), **sish** (79b), **sosh** (81d), **tash** (154d), **tosh** (106a), **tush** (167b), **wash, wish** (42d)

S - - H   **saah** (188), **sadh** (77a), **sahh** (188), **samh** (56b), **sash** (18a,45c,67b, 182b), **seah** (188), **sech** (97c), **seth** (98d), **Seth** (7a,52b,68a,b,96a, 98d), **shah** (116c), **shih** (189), **sigh, Sikh** (77b), **sinh** (97c), **sish** (79b), **soph, sosh** (81d), **such** (146d)

SI - -   **siak** (72d), **sial** (112a), **Siam** (163d,181a), **sice** (71d,147b), **sick, sida** (37a,126c,170a), **side** (13d,22a,b,54a,58a,89a,161b), **sidi** (103b, 166b), **sidy** (123b), **sier** (57a,118b), **sift** (140d,142c,146b), **sigh, sign** (121c,146c), **sika** (41d,84b), **Sikh** (77b), **silk** (53b,179c), **sill** (45c,76c,165a,182b), **silo** (59a,156d), **silt** (104b,142a), **sima** (132b), **sime** (101d), **Simi** (82d), **simp** (59c,146d), **sina** (46c), **Sina** (102d, 103d), **Sind, sine** (64c,66b,90a,97a,126a,163b,169d,183b), **sing** (26d,178a), **sinh** (97c), **sink** (41c,43c,46b,158a) **sino** (34a), **siol** (82c), **sion** (125c,158c), **Sion** (75b,c,83a,157d), **sipe** (101a,110c, 140b), **sire** (17d,55a,59d,124a,163b,166b), **siri** (18b), **sise** (62c, 147b), **sish** (79b), **sisi** (121b), **siss, sist** (139b), **Sita** (127d), **site** (93b), **sito** (34b), **siva** (67a,120d), **Siva** (56d,77a), **Sive** (146a), **size, sizy** (176d), **sizz**

- SI -   **Asia** (48a), **Asin** (102a), **Hsia** (30b,47c), **Isis** (68d,78c,111d), **tsia** (162c), **Tsin** (30b)

- - SI   **Absi** (191), **assi** (77d), **dasi** (77a), **desi** (85d), **kasi** (116b), **Lasi** (191), **nasi** (34c,108a,115a), **nisi** (90a,173c), **pasi** (94b), **sesi** (20b,57a), **sisi** (121b), **susi** (53b,d)

S - - I   **Safi** (191), **saki** (39c,84b,102a), **sari** (48b,65b,77b), **sati, Sati** (49a, 126b,147b), **sebi** (34b), **semi** (34b,80b,122c,d), **seri** (18b), **Seri** (192), **sesi** (20b,57a,149b), **seti** (34a), **Seti** (116d), **Shri** (17c,166c), **sidi** (103b,166b), **Simi** (82d), **siri** (18b), **sisi** (121b), **soli** (12c,110c), **sori** (55c,64a), **sufi** (103a,116c), **sugi** (84b), **suji** (180c), **susi** (53b,d)

SK - -   **skag** (7d,46d), **skat** (181b), **Skat** (155b), **skee** (149c), **skeg** (7d,86a, 144d,157d,184a), **sken** (164a), **skeo** (57d), **skep** (16d,17c,77c), **skew** (148a,160c,171b,c), **skey** (185d), **skid** (148b), **skil** (57a), **skim** (67c), **skin** (53a,76c,115c,d), **skio** (57d), **skip** (110b,114c,147c), **skir, skit** (145c), **skiv** (151b), **skua** (19b,72c,84a,141a), **Skye** (163c), **skyr** (21d,151a), **skyt** (138c,140b)

- SK -   **Askr** (107d)

- - SK   **bask** (94d), **bisk** (120b,151a), **bosk** (164b), **busk** (17b,37b,55d, 161b), **cask, cusk** (57b), **desk, disk** (31b), **dusk** (171c), **fisk** (24d,52c,134d), **husk** (53a,78d,142a), **mask** (44a,45c), **mosk** (97b,

103b), **musk** (116b), **Omsk, pisk** (9c,19b), **risk** (74d), **rusk** (23a), **task** (156b), **Tosk** (8c), **tusk** (167b)

S - - K   **sack** (43d,118a,119d,182b), **sank, Sark** (28d), **Sauk** (192), **sawk** (188), **seck** (173d), **seek** (141c), **Seik** (77b), **Shik** (171a), **siak** (72d), **sick, silk** (53b,179c), **sink** (41c,43c,46b,158a), **soak** (46c,137c), **Sobk** (38d), **sock** (157c,182a), **sook** (22a,25c,97a), **souk** (22a,97a), **suck, sulk** (159a), **sunk**

SL - -   **slab** (148b), **slag** (46c,99a,138c,148d,177a), **slam** (180d,182d), **slap** (24a,128c,148c), **slat** (58b,89a,117c,184a), **Slav** (13c,40c,48b,52a, 120b,135b), **slaw, slay, Sleb** (12a), **sled** (40a), **slee** (140b,148c), **slew** (160a), **sley** (179b), **slid, slim** (148b,160a), **slip** (67c,119a), **slit** (40a), **slob** (173d), **sloe** (14a,20b,64a,119d,181c), **slog** (157c,170b, 177d), **sloo** (160a), **slop, slot** (10d,11b,41d,110d,167d,168a,181b), **slow** (43c), **slub** (171c), **slue** (97b,148b,160a), **slug** (46b,99b,157c), **slum, slur** (44b,124c,148b,168a)

- SL -   **isle** (8b,53c,81d,82d,86b,88a), **Oslo**

S - - L   **saal** (66c,73b), **sail** (144c,185a), **saul** (48a,168c), **Saul** (18c,86d, 115a), **seal** (10c,d,54d,64c,96a,118b,128a), **seel** (20c,32c,143b), **sell** (97a,115c,175b), **shul** (161a), **sial** (112a), **sill** (45c,76c,165a, 182b) **siol** (82c), **skil** (57a), **soil** (154d,159a,163c), **soul** (10d,125a, 153c,176d)

SM - -   **smee** (19b,46c,d,118b,119d,141b,181b), **Smee** (116d), **smew** (19b, 46d,99a,137d), **smug, smur** (32c,46b,100c), **smut** (32d,44a,119a, 150c)

- SM -   **ismy** (45a)

- - SM   **kasm** (189)

S - - M   **saum** (189), **scum** (129b), **seam** (85b,d,160a,176d,185a), **seem** (11c), **Seim** (120c), **Sejm** (120c), **sham** (41c,55b,60d,80a,123a,b, 146d), **Shem** (107c), **shim** (91d,144c,162a,179d), **Siam** (163d,181a), **skim** (67c), **slam** (180d,182d), **slim** (148b,160a), **slum, stem** (29b, 125a,154d,155a,156d), **stom** (34c), **stum** (70c,105c,131a,173a), **swam, swim** (58c), **swum**

SN - -   **snab** (23c,139a), **snag** (11b,27b,35c,87c,124b,166a), **snap** (23a, 36d,38b,48b,54d,56c,58c,149d), **sned** (93d,125a,140a), **snee** (40a, b,43d,87a), **sneg** (139b), **snib** (54d,93c), **snig** (45d), **snip** (32b, 40a), **snob** (159c), **snod** (169d), **snow, snub** (128c,148b), **snug** (35a,38b,165c), **Snug** (99d), **snup** (149b)

- SN -   **asno** (151d), **esne** (10c,45b,142c,148a,164d)

S - - N   **Saan** (24d), **sain** (20c,38d,48a), **sawn, scan** (52b,93d,98a,116d, 128b,c,140d), **scon** (162c), **Sean** (85b,96a), **seen, sein** (146c), **senn** (76b), **sewn, Shan** (13c,80d,88c,101d), **Shen** (68a), **shin** (91a,d,140b, 143c), **shun** (15a,51b,52a), **sign** (121c,146c), **sion** (125c,158c), **Sion** (75b,c,83a,157d), **sken** (164a), **skin** (53a,76c,115c,d), **soon** (123a, 145c), **sorn** (139a,d), **span** (23b,107b,113a,128b,162c), **spin** (131a, 180d), **spun, sten** (72c,95a), **stun** (145a,157d), **sunn** (56a), **Svan** (27d), **swan** (19b,33a)

SO - -   **soak** (46c,137c), **soap, soar** (59a), **Sobk** (38d), **sock** (157c,182a), **soco** (22d), **soda** (19a,149d,181a), **sofa** (44d), **soft** (48b,95d,99d, 163a), **soga** (70d,152b), **Soga** (191), **soho!, Soho** (93c), **Soia, soie**

(62c), **soll** (154d,159a,163c), **soir** (61c), **soja** (151b), **soka** (20c), **soke** (44c,85d), **sola** (9a,48a,74b,118c,154a,167b), **sold, sole** (52c,57a,b, 58b,d,110c,115d,150a), **soli** (12c,110c), **solo** (12c,89a,110c), **soma** (10c,21c,34a,48a,81d,136b), some (114b,121c,126a), **song** (12c, 170c), **sons** (98d,109d), **sook** (22a,25c,97a), **soon** (123a,145c), **soot** (20b,26c,88a), **soph, Sopt** (45b), **sora** (19b,c,127b), **sorb** (11d,103d, 134b,142d), **Sorb** (148a,180a), **sore** (23d,142c), **sori** (55c,64a), **sorn** (139a,d), **sors** (44d,89b), **sort** (31d,39c,70b,86b,153a), **sory** (176d), **sosh** (81d), **soso** (99c,114c,166d), **sote** (150c), **souf** (146b), **souk** (22a,97a), **soul** (10d,125a,153c,176d), **soup, sour, sous** (62d,172c), **soya** (151b)

- **SO** - asok (13d), **asom** (18d), **asop** (180b), **asor** (75c,105a), **Esop** (53b, 54a), **esox** (57b)

- - **SO** also (10b,18b,80a), **Caso** (82d), **coso** (152c), **enso** (34d,183b), **huso** (180c), **ipso** (89c), **koso** (6c,80d), **Koso** (192,193), **Muso** (192), **peso** (99c), **piso** (189), **soso** (99c,114c,166d), **yeso** (72d)

S - - **O** saco (189), **sado** (26d,84d), **sago** (54c,59b,113b,125b,155c), **Saho** (6c), **sano** (152b), **sapo** (149c,166d), **Scio, sego** (24b,25a,92b,174c), **sero** (34d,88d,164b,178d), **shoo** (46b,67a,138b), **silo** (59a,156d), **sino** (34a), **sito** (34b), **skeo** (57d), **skio** (57d), **sloo** (160a), **soco** (22d), **soho!, Soho** (93c), **solo** (12c,89a,110c), **soso** (99c,114c,166d), **Sumo**

SP - - spad (105b), **Spad** (118d), **spae** (139c), **span** (23b,107b,113a,128b, 162c), **spar** (22c,24c,64b,97b,100b,144d), **spat** (112c,126b,134b), **spec, sped, Spee** (66d,70b), **spes, Spes** (69a,78a), **spet** (16c,57a, 142c), **spew** (35a,49a), **spex, spey, spin** (131a,180d), **spir** (97c), **spit** (120a,132b,c), **spot** (93b,118c,154d,162a), **spry** (7a,107b), **spud** (121d,151c), **spun, spur** (10d,67d,167d,168a,181b), **sput** (21c)

- **SP** - espy (44a,142a)

- - **SP** cusp (38c,78b,119a,120a,b), **gasp** (113c), **hasp** (31d,54d,153c), **lisp** (153b), **rasp** (56b,70d,140d), **risp** (99a), **wasp, wisp** (24b,148c)

S - - **P** salp (109c,148d), **samp** (70b,77d,121b), **scop** (120a), **scup** (57a, 121b), **seep** (110c,116a,154b), **seip** (110c), **shap, ship, shop, simp** (59c,146d), **skep** (16d,17c,77c), **skip** (110b,114c,147c), **slap** (24a, 128c,148c), **slip** (67c,119a), **slop, snap** (23a,36d,38b,48b,54d,56c, 58c,149d), **snip** (32b,40a), **snup** (149b), **soap, soup, step** (70b,112b, 177b,d), **stop** (73b,111b), **sump** (28c,45d,100b), **swap** (168a), **swop** (168a)

S - - **Q** shoq (169a)

S - - **R** Saar (63b,102d,132a), **sadr** (94a), **Sadr** (155b), **saer** (163a), **sair** (140b,150d), **scar** (31a,184d), **scur** (78b), **sear** (23d,27d,72d,138c), **seer** (60a,124c,150c), **sehr** (66d), **Seir** (51b,94a,103d), **sher** (65d, 165c), **shir** (36d,65d,165c), **shor** (136d), **Shor** (162b), **sier** (57a, 118b), **skir, skyr** (21d,151a), **slur** (44b,124c,148b,168a), **smur** (32c,46b,100c), **soar** (59a), **soir** (61c), **sour, spar** (22c,24c,64b,97b, 100b,144d), **spir** (97c), **spur** (10d,67d,167d,168a,181b), **star** (14a, 21c,94c,100c), **ster** (158c,d), **stir** (8a,13a,35b,78d,100d,104a), **suer** (124d)

- **SS** - asse (25a,60d,74a), **assi** (77d), **esse** (7a,18a,52d,89a,90a,159a, 166c), **ossa** (21d), **Ossa** (103d,110b,164b)

- - SS bass (57b,c,177a), Bess (76c,183d), boss (49d,157d), buss (87a, 148c), cass (140c,177a), Cass (147a), cess (91d,94c,162b), coss (98a), cuss, diss (98b), doss (17c), fass (189), fess (23c,51b), foss (44d,100d), fuss (22b,35b), hiss (146a), jass (160d), jess (157a), joss (30b), kiss (148c), koss (188), lass (95b), less (100c,108b,141d), liss (54b,58b,60c,129d,140a), loss (42c,123d,178b), mass (8a,24b, 35b,142d), mess (22b,44b,77c,85d,104b,165c,173d), miss, moss (91d,104c,114a,170c), muss (135b,173d), ness (26b,75a,124b), pass (110b,155c), puss, Riss (66a), ross (16c,161d), Ross (50c), Russ (135b), sass, sess (149c,162b), siss, Tass (107a,135d,151b), Tess (73d,164c,183d), toss (24a,132d), viss (189)

S - - S sais (48d,71d), sans (63a,183b), sass, seis (147b,152c), sens (63b), seps (93b,142d), sess (149c,162b), siss, sons (98d,109d), sors (44d, 89b), sous (62d,172c), spes, Spes (69a,78a), suds (59a)

ST - - stab (14c,87a,117c), stad (151b,167d,176b), stag (65a,98d), star (14a,21c,94c,100c), stat (72d), stay (72d,124c,130a,134a,162a), stem (29b,125a,154d,155a,156d), sten (72c,95a), step (70b,112b, 177b,d), ster (158c,d), stet (91b,123d,124c), stev (155b), stew (21c,44b,184d), stib (19b,47a,137a), stir (8a,13a,35b,78d,100d, 104a), stoa (33c,121a,c), stod (40d,67d), stof (135c), stog (155a), stom (34c), stop (73b,111b), stot (154d,155d,157d,179b,186a), stow (112b), stub (156c), stud (22b,25a,42d,54d,111c,143a,174a), stum (70c,105c,131a,173a), stun (145a,157d), Styx (29b,73a,105c)

-ST - asta (188), Asta (107a,164c), Asti (83d,182b), esta (152d,164c), este (152b,d,164c), Este (55c,83c,d,112d), Esth (16a,51d), oste (21d,83b)

- - ST bast (16c,56a,117b,184a), Bast (27b), best (41d,159c,160a), bust, cast (165b,167c), cest (18a,67b), dost, dust, east, East (111b), erst (60b), fast (56d,126c,141d,160c,173a,d), fest (80c), fist (80c), fust (105c,143b), gest (7c,41d,52d,133c), gist (95c,118c), gust, hast, hest (35a), hist (25c,93d), host (13a,51d,104c), jest (169c), just (51b,54b), kist (29d,58a,139b), last (36c,50b,145a,174c), lest (59d, 163d), list (26d,27b,75b,83d,134a,138b,165d), lost, lust (41b), mast (17c,108d,120b,144d,152d), mist (46b,59b,174d), most, must (70c,101a,106d,157d,182c), myst (71c,123b), Nast (9c,27a), nest (38b,74b,130d,149c,160b), oast (15d,86b,112a), oust (44c, 49a,52b,125d), past (25c,69d,165d), pest (108c,116b,118d,170a), pist (25c), post (89a,95c,155d), rest (15d,91b,104d,105a,115a,b, 130a,b,161b), rust (37b,112c,119a), sist (139b), test (26a,51c,144a, 169c,170c), vast (78d,79d), vest (32c,177b), wast, west, West (9c, 50b,109b), wist (87c), zest (55d,72d)

S - - T salt (35d,105b,123a,136c,141c,149d), Sart (82b,103b,170d), scat (26b,67a,d,126c,169c), scot (14a,162b), Scot (64b,132c), scut (145c,161b), seat (98c,156b), sect (42b,54a,114c), seit (189), sent, sept (31d,82b,143a,149c), Sept (45b), Sert (151d), sett (115a,156d), sext (26b,111b,147b), shat (87d), shot (9d,43d,90c, 174d), shut, sift (140d,142c,146b), silt (104b,142a), skat (181b), Skat (155b), skit (145c), skyt (138c,140b), slat (58b,89a,117c, 184a), slit (40a), slot (10d,11b,41d,110d,167d,168a,181b), smut (32d,44a,119a,150c), soft (48b,95d,99d,163a), soot (20b,26c,88a), Sopt (45b), sort (31d,39c,70b,86b,153a), spat (112c,126b,134b),

364

spet (16c,57a,142c), **spit** (120a,132b,c), **spot** (93b,118c,154d,162a), **sput** (21c), **stat** (72d), **stet** (91b,123d,124c), **stot** (154d,155d,157d, 179b,186a), **suet** (54d), **suit** (38a,58a,91a,112a,119c,137c), **swat** (15d,20d,32d,157c), **Swat** (103a), **swot**

SU - -   **such** (146d), **suck, sudd** (40b,58c,107b), **suds** (59a), **suer** (124d), **suet** (54d), **sufi** (103a,116c), **sugi** (84b), **suit** (38a,58a,91a,112a, 119c,137c), **suji** (180c), **Suku** (191), **Sula** (65a), **suld** (188), **sulk** (159a), **Sulu** (102c), **Sumo, sump** (28c,45d,100b), **sung, Sung** (30b), **sunk, sunn** (56a), **supa** (168c), **supe** (53a,154d), **sura** (87c,113b, 166d), **surd** (82c,177a), **sure** (173d), **surf** (23a), **Susa** (49a), **susi** (53b,d), **susu** (20c), **Susu** (191), **Susy** (183d)

- SU -   **Asur** (68c), **Esus, tsun** (30b), **Usun** (191)

- - SU   **ansu** (11d), **Apsu** (29a), **ausu** (168c,180b), **Jesu, masu** (57a,84c), **Nosu** (27d), **susu** (20c), **Susu** (191), **vasu** (106c), **Vasu** (176d)

S - - U   **sahu** (153d), **Sgau** (88c), **shou** (41d), **Suku** (191), **Sulu** (102c), **susu** (20c), **Susu** (191)

SV - -   **Svan** (27d)

S - - V   **skiv** (151b), **Slav** (13c,40c,48b,52a,120b,135b), **stev** (155b)

SW - -   **swab** (102b), **swad** (94d), **swag** (22a,156c), **swam, swan** (19b,33a), **swap** (168a), **swat** (15d,20d,32d,157c), **Swat** (103a), **sway** (104a), **sweb** (160d), **swig** (46a,72c), **swim** (58c), **swiz** (160c), **swob** (102b), **swop** (168a), **swot, swow** (100a), **swum**

S - - W   **scow** (21a,58b), **shaw** (164b), **Shaw** (50c,53b), **shew** (44c), **show** (42b,44c,96b), **skew** (148a,160c,171b,c), **slaw, slew** (160a), **slow** (43c), **smew** (19b,46d,99a,137d), **snow, spew** (35a,49a), **stew** (21c, 44b,184d), **stow** (112b), **swow** (100a)

S - - X   **spex, Styx** (29b,73a,105c)

SY - -   **syce** (71d), **syed** (103b), **syke** (194), **syne** (140b,147a), **sype** (110c), **Syra, syud** (103b)

- - SY   **busy, cosy** (149c), **easy** (54a,146d,149d,172b), **Josy** (183d), **mosy** (67d), **nosy, rosy** (21a,111a), **Susy** (183d)

S - - Y   **sagy, shay** (110c), **sidy** (123b), **sizy** (176d), **skey** (185d), **slay, sley** (179b), **sory** (176d), **Spey, spry** (7a,107b), **stay** (72d,124c,130a, 134a), **Susy** (183d), **sway** (104a)

S - - Z   **sizz, swiz** (160c)

TA - -   **Taal** (7d,88c,151a), **taar** (12b), **tabi** (84c,149d), **tabu** (59d,111d), **tace** (13a,155d), **tack** (28d,37d,54d), **tact** (43c,d,116a), **tael** (91d, 179d), **Taft** (29d), **taha** (179b), **tahr** (68a,76d), **tail** (11d,27d,59b, 143b), **tain** (166a), **tair** (68a,76d), **tait** (14d), **tajo** (152a,d), **take, takt** (105a,163a), **Taku** (80c), **taky, tala** (16d,113a,168c,d), **talc** (28d,63b,99c,100b,122a,149c), **tale** (91a,185b), **tali** (189), **talk, tall** (118d), **Tama** (192), **tame** (45a,b,66a), **Tame, tamp** (46b,112b, 121d,127d), **tana** (159a), **Tana** (87d), **Tane** (120d), **tang** (30b,58b, 186b), **tanh** (97c), **tank** (175a,d), **Tano** (192), **Taos** (192), **tapa** (16c, 32c,53b,56a,74b,104b,112b,113d,120d), **tape** (16a,19a,128d), **tapu, tara** (22a,55c,113a,168c), **Tara** (82b,c,138b), **tare** (9a,18d,41a, 176a,179d), **Tari** (47d,69a), **tarn** (87d,103d,120d), **taro** (13c,48c, 49b,64b,112b,120a,133d,155c,170a,c), **tarp** (26b,178d), **tart** (114d), **tash** (154d), **task** (156b), **Tass** (107a,135d,151b), **tate** (183a), **tatt**

(87c), **tatu** (12d), **Tatu, taun** (188), **taut** (163b,165c), **Tave** (183d), **Tavy** (183d), **tawa** (106d,168c), **taxi** (13a,125b), **taxo** (13a)

- TA - **atap** (113b), **atar** (58d,116b,134a), **Etah** (71d,51c), **etal** (89a), **etat** (62d), **Ptah** (48d,98c), **stab** (14c,87a,117c), **stad** (151b,167d,176b), **stag** (65a,98d), **star** (14a,21c,94c,100c), **stat** (72d), **stay** (72d,124c, 130a,134a,162a), **utac** (22d), **Utah** (180b), **utas** (49a,109c)

- - TA **acta** (41d,123d,128d,164c), **Aeta** (94d,95d,100a,106b,117a), **alta** (89c,152d), **anta** (83d,117c,d,121a), **Anta** (164a), **Arta** (72b), **asta** (188), **Asta** (107a,164c), **atta** (58d,90c,97d,160c,173d), **Atta** (94d,95d,100a,106b,117a), **bata** (30a,142d), **beta** (71a, 91c,141d), **bota** (189), **cata** (122c), **cota** (117a), **data** (54a), **dita** (117a), **esta** (152d,164c), **Etta** (183c), **gata** (143c), **geta** (84b,145a), **Gita, iota** (71a,85c,91c,114c,166c,176a,180d), **jota** (151c), **keta** (45a), **kota** (117a), **Kota** (45d), **lata** (85d, 95d), **lota** (24c,121d,178d), **Lota meta** (132d,133a), **Meta, mota** (103a), **muta** (28d,103a), **nata** (47c), **Nata** (15c), **nota** (15c, 89c), **octa** (122c), **pata** (32c,160d), **pita** (9c,28b,56a,83a), **rata** (29d,56b,89d,96c,106d,120c,168c), **rita, Rita** (37b,78d,183c), **rota** (27c,30d,38a,79a,92d,133a,134a,b,180c), **Ruta** (76b,134d), **seta** (23b,27c,73a,b,123b,153c), **Sita** (127d), **tota** (71d), **veta** (104a), **vita** (89c,92a), **vota** (133b), **weta** (93c), **yeta** (84c), **zeta** (71b,91c)

T - - A **taha** (179b), **tala** (16d,113a,168c,d), **Tama** (192), **tana** (159a), **Tana** (87d), **tapa** (16c,32c,53b,56a,74b,104b,112b,113d,120d), **tara** (22a, 55c,113a,168c), **Tara** (82b,c,138b), **tawa** (106d,168c), **tcha** (162c), **teca, Teca** (192), **Teda** (191), **tela** (22d,98c,121b,166a,179c), **tema** (12a,164a), **Tema, tera** (23d,84c), **tesa** (80c), **Tewa** (193), **Thea** (162c), **Tina** (183d), **tiza** (172a), **Toba** (80c), **Toda** (45d,76d), **toga** (132d,133a,b), **tola** (48a,80d,180a), **Tola** (85b), **Toma** (191), **tooa** (17c), **tora** (11a,44d,74a,75c,85c,90b,102d,115d), **tota** (71d), **toxa** (153d), **tsia** (162c), **tuba** (105a,137d), **tufa** (121b,177a), **tula** (9a), **Tula, tuna** (57a,b,123b), **tuza** (119d)

T - - B **theb** (188), **thob** (128a), **tomb**

TC - - **tcha** (162c), **tche** (13d,30b,105a), **tchi, Tchi, tchu**

- TC - **etch, itch**

T - - C **talc** (28d,63b,99c,100b,122a,149c)

T - - D **tend** (26d,80b,93d,100a), **thud, tied, tind** (86b), **toad** (10a,17a, 63d,126d), **toed, told** (129c), **trod, tund** (121d)

TE - - **teak** (41a,48a,168c), **teal** (19b,20d,46c,d), **team** (38c,72a,113a), **tean** (140c,167a), **tear** (67c,87b,130a), **teca, Teca** (192), **Tech, teck** (128b), **Teco** (192), **Teda** (191), **teel** (142d), **teem** (6b,121d), **teen** (139b,c,140b,158d), **teer** (25b,69d), **Tees** (108a), **teff** (6c), **tegg** (143d,171d), **tehr** (27c,68a), **Teig** (96a), **teil** (92b,c,168c), **teju** (151b), **tela** (22d,98c,121b,166a,179c), **tele** (34b,122c), **teli** (94b), **tell** (105d,129c,154b), **Tell** (160d), **tema** (12a,164a), **Tema, tend** (26d,80b,93d,100a), **tene** (34d,131b), **teng** (188), **tent** (26b), **115a), Teos** (82a), **tera** (23d,84c), **term** (92b,105b,142b,166b), **tern** (19b,32c,72c,94a,138c,141a,160a), **terp** (12b,123a), **tesa** (80c), **Tess** (73d,164c,183d), **test** (26a,51c,144a,169c,170c), **tete** (61d,73b,74d), **teth** (91d), **Tewa** (193), **text** (21c,140d), **teyl** (92b, c,168c)

- TE - atef (39a,48d), aten (150a,159b), **Ateo** (120d), **Ater** (18c), **ates** (160c), **Itea** (145d,160c,181d), item (6d,13b,42d,51a,90d,92d,107a, 113d,114c), **Iten** (192), **iter** (22d,76c,85c,89c,114d,132a,b,133a,b), **Otea** (71a,82d), **stem** (29b,125a,154d,155a,156d), **sten** (72c,95a), **step** (70b,112b,177b,d), **ster** (158c,d), **stet** (91b,123d,124c), **stev** (155b), **stew** (21c,44b,184d)

- - TE ante (87a,89a,115b,120b,122b,125d,154d), **bate** (43c,91b,100d), **bete** (61a,107c), **bite** (29d,156b), **cate** (165c), **cete** (180b,c), **cite** (15a,98d,126d,159b), **cote** (19b,143d,144a,b), **cute** (39c), **date** (64a,153a), **dite** (150b), **dote** (17a,90b,94b,97a,112a,139d,165d), **ente** (70b,151d), **este** (152b,d,164c), **Este** (55c,83c,d,112d), **ette** (158a,c,d), **fate** (42d,52a,87a,94a), **fete** (55d,129b), **fute** (51c), **gate** (51a,121b), **gite** (62a,118d), **hate** (6a,43a), **jete** (16a), **jute** (37a,48a,56a,133d,136a), **Jute, Kate** (143c,183d), **kite** (19c,49a, 74c,d), **late** (128c), **lete, lite** (158c,d), **lote** (24c,94a), **lute** (11c,28b, 84d,105a,131d), **mate** (18c,35b,41d,113a,154a,162c), **mete** (9a, 11d,22b,44c,45b,98a,121c), **mite** (12b,81b,82a,114a,c,148c,d,181b), **mote** (114c,153a), **mute** (146c,153b), **Nate** (22b), **nete** (71c,108b, 163d), **note** (98c,109b,124b,128d,130a,177c), **oste** (21d,83b), **pate** (39a,74d), **pete** (136b), **Pete, rate** (11d,14a,31d,36b,51d,52a,70b, 85c,112b,123b,127d,128a,138c,143a,174b), **rete** (106c,119c), **rite** (93a,131d), **rote** (130b,134b,143a,159d), **rute** (188), **sate** (32d,52c, 67d,70d,137c,159d), **site** (93b), **sote** (150c), **tate** (183a), **tete** (61d, 73b,74d), **tote** (27a,73c), **tute** (171b), **vite** (62b), **vote** (60b), **Vote** (56d), **Wate** (141a), **Wote** (191), **yate** (51d,168c)

T - - E tace (13a,155d), **take, tale** (91a,185b), **tame** (45a,b,66a), **Tame, Tane** (120d), **tape** (16a,19a,128d), **tare** (9a,18d,41a,176a,179d), **tate** (183a), **Tave** (183d), **tche** (13d,30b,105a), **tele** (34b,122c), **tene** (34d,131b), **tete** (61d,73b,74d), **thee** (124b), **tice** (9a,38c,51a, 185d), **tide** (39d,75d,109c,141c,159d), **tige** (118a), **tike** (29d), **tile** (31d,56d,72b,95b,133c,163c), **time** (47a,131a), **tine** (11b,124b, 167b), **tipe** (168b), **tire** (15a,22a,52d,55a,179b,180d), **tobe** (7d, 137b), **tode** (80a,148a), **tole** (9a,51a,99b,163a), **tome** (21d,177c), **tone** (6c,118c,150d), **tope** (24a,46b,57a,143c,151a), **tore, tote** (27a, 73c), **tree** (11d,37a,66a,184b), **true** (7a,8d,37b,54b,94c,149c), **tube** (118b,158a), **tuke** (26b,53b), **tule** (24b,27c), **tune** (8b,12c, 98c), **tute** (171b), **twee, tyee** (29d), **tyke** (29d), **tyne, Tyne** (108a), **type** (31d,115a,155a), **tyre** (15a), **Tyre** (31b,90d,117b)

T - - F teff (6c), **tiff** (126b), **toff** (40d), **tref** (172b), **tuff** (121b,177a), **turf** (115c,149d,160b)

T - - G tang (30b,58b,186b), **tegg** (143d,171d), **Teig** (96a), **teng** (188), **thug** (65a), **ting** (166a), **Ting** (30c), **tong** (30a,c,), **toug** (171a), **trig** (106a,148d,154b,169d), **tung** (110a,168c), **twig**

TH - - Thai (146a), **than** (35b), **thar** (68a,76d), **that** (42b,124b,129c), **thaw, Thea** (162c), **theb** (188), **thee** (124b), **them** (124b), **then, thew** (104c), **they** (124b), **thin** (43b,c,148b), **this** (42b,124b), **thob** (128a), **Thor** (7c,68c,99c,100c,109c,165b), **Thos** (84a,181c), **thou** (124b), **thud, thug** (65a), **thus** (149c)

- T H - Otho (133a)

- - T H acth (13b), **bath, Bath** (50d,151c), **beth** (91c), **Beth** (8c,183d), **both, doth, Esth** (16a,51d), **Gath** (117a), **Goth** (16c,163d), **hath,**

Heth (77c), Hoth (20c), Jeth (102a), kath (14a), kith (63c), lath (157c), lith (34d,156c), loth (15a,173d), math (77a), moth, Moth (112d), muth (188), myth (8b,91a), Nath (155c), oath (119c,150a), path (132a,134b), pith (37a,51c,67b,95c,97a,119b,126d), rath (76d,162d), ruth (35b,118c), Ruth (105b,183c), seth (98d), Seth (7a,52b,68a,b,96a,98d), teth (91d), Urth (68d,107d,163d), Voth (191), with (10b)

T - - H   tanh (97c), tash (154d), Tech, teth (91d), toph (75c), tosh (106a), tush (167b)

TI - -   Tiam, tiao, tiar (39a,75a,121a), Tibu (191), tice (9a,38c,51a,185d), tick (12b,20d,97c), tide (39d,75d,109c,141c,159d), tidy (106a, 111b), tied, tien (147d), tier (118a,134b), tiff (126b), tige (118a), tike (29d), Tiki (120c), tile (31d,56d,72b,95b,133c,163c), till (39c, 101c,173d), tilt (26b,d,166a), time (47a,131a), Tina (183d), tind (86b), tine (11b,124b,167b), ting (166a), Ting (30c), Tino (136d), tint (33c,d,114d), tiny (100c,148c), tion (158b), Tiou (192), tipe (168b), tipi (181b), tire (15a,22a,52d,55a,179b,180d), tiro (9b,17d, 108c), titi (20d,102a,145d,168d,181b), Tito (186c), tiza (172a)

- TI -   Atik (155b), atip (14b,166a), atis (76d,102a), itis (158c), otic (14c, d,47b), Otis (9c,d,24d,82a,111a), stib (19b,47a,137a), stir (8a, 13a,35b,78d,100d,104a)

- - TI   anti (7d,111a,122b), Anti (193), Asti (83d,182b), biti (20b), Guti, Hati (48d), hoti, Inti (159b), jati (27b), jiti, joti, Leti (82d), liti (60d), Loti (63a,176a), neti (164a), rati (189), roti (62c), sati, Sati (49a,126b,147b), seti (34a), Seti (116d), titi (20d,102a,145d,168d, 181b), viti (176b), yati (76d), zati (21d)

T - - I   tabi (84c,149d) tali (189), Tari (47d,69a), taxi (13a,125b), tchi, Tchi, teli (94b), Thai (146a), Tiki (120c), tipi (181b), titi (20d,102a, 145d,168d,181b), topi (37a,75a,118c), tori (101b), tshi, Tshi (69c), Tupi (192), Turi (191), tuwi (117a,168c), Tybi (102a)

- TK -   Atka (11a)

T - - K   tack (28d,37d,54d), talk, tank (175a,d), task (156b), teak (41a, 48a,168c), teck (128b), tick (12b,20d,97c), tock (7d,19b),tonk (173c), took, Tosk (8c), trek (85c,93d,99d,168b), tuck (156b), Turk (101d,102d,106a,111d), tusk (167b)

- TL -   atle (136d,161d,169b), Atli (14c,72b,79a,107d)

- - TL   rotl (103b,111c)

T - - L   Taal (7d,88c,151a), tael (91d,179d), tail (11d,27d,59b,143b), tall (118d), teal (19b,20d,46c,d), teel (142d), teil (92b,c,168c), tell (105d,129c,154b), Tell (160d), teyl (92b,c,168c), till (39c,101c, 173d), toil (46c,184c), toll (131c), tool (27c), tuel

TM - -   T-men (168b)

- TM -   atma (150d), atmo (34d,174d), Atmu (143a,159b), itmo (18b)

T - - M   team (38c,72a,113a), teem (6b), term (92b,105b,142b,166b), them (124b), tiam, toom (139b), tram (170a), trim (40a,106a,154b, 160a,165c,169d), turm (132d)

- TN -   etna (75b,153c,157a,175d,177a,c)

T - - N   tain (166a), tarn (87d,103d,120d), taun (188), tean (140c,167a), teen (139b,c,140b,158d), tern (19b,32d,72c,94a,138c,141a,160a),

than (35b), **then, thin** (43b,c,148b), **tien** (147d), **tion** (158b), **T-men** (168b), **toon** (80c,95b,168c), **torn** (130a), **town** (73c), **tran** (7a), **trin** (169d), **tron** (140d,180a), **Tsin** (30b), **tsun** (30b), **tuan** (95d,147b,166c), **turn** (28d,131a,175a), **twin** (45c,171d)

TO - - **toad** (10a,17a,63d,126d), **Toba** (80c), **tobe** (7d,137b), **toby** (8c, 85c,104b), **Toby** (96b,125c), **tock** (7d,19b), **toco** (19b,167c), **Toda** (45d,76d), **tode** (80a,148a), **todo** (22b,24d,35b,64c,156b), **tody** (19b,d,59a,166a), **toed, toff** (40d), **toga** (132d,133a,b), **togs** (32c), **togt** (77c), **toho** (79a), **toil** (46c,184c), **toko** (30c), **tola** (48a,80d,180a), **Tola** (85b), **told** (129c), **tole** (9a,51a,99b,163a), **toll** (131c), **tolt, tolu** (16a), **Toma** (191), **tomb, tome** (21d,177c), **tone** (6c,118c,150d), **tong** (30a,c), **tonk** (173c), **tony, Tony** (96b), **tooa** (17c), **took, tool** (27c), **toom** (139b), **toon** (80c,95b,168c), **toot, tope** (24a,46b,57a,143c,151a), **toph** (75c), **topi** (37a,75a, 118c), **tops** (159c), **tora** (11a,44d,74a,75c,85c,90b,102d,115d), **tore, tori** (101b), **torn** (130a), **toro** (38a,107a,152a,168c), **torp** (54c), **tort** (31c,91a,185c), **Tory** (23c,36b,94c,172a), **tosh** (106a), **Tosk** (8c), **toss** (24a,132d), **tota** (71d), **tote** (27a,73c), **toto** (8d,15a,34d, 89a,181a), **toty** (87b), **toug** (171a), **toup** (95d), **tour** (31b,85c), **tout** (61a,127a), **town** (73c), **towy** (58b), **toxa** (153d)

- TO - **atom** (101c,114c,180d), **aton** (150a,159b), **atop** (112a,174a), **Eton** (33b,50c,84a), **itol** (158b), **Otoe** (147b), **stoa** (33c,121a,c), **stod** (40d,67d), **stof** (135c), **stog** (155a), **stom** (34c), **stop** (73b,111b), **stot** (154d,155d,157d,179b,186a), **stow** (112b), **utor** (90a,166c)

- - TO **acto** (152b), **alto** (152b,176c), **auto** (34d), **bito** (7d,57d,168c), **Boto** (192), **Buto** (142d), **Cato** (132d,133b), **ceto** (34a), **cito** (89d,126c), **coto** (16c,90b), **dato** (95c,102c,117a), **Doto** (141b), **ecto** (34c,122d), **ento** (34b,d), **into** (123a,183b) **jato** (173b), **koto** (84b), **Leto** (11c), **loto** (65a,121d,178d), **moto** (104b), **Nato** (6a,8d), **nito** (55c), **octo** (34a,89b,122c), **onto** (76a,174a), **otto** (58d,116b,134a), **Otto** (14c,66d,67a,96a), **pato** (46d), **peto** (57a,177b), **Peto** (76a), **pito** (9c,28b,83a), **roto** (30a,122d,127b,152c,171b), **sito** (34b), **Tito** (186c), **toto** (8d,15a,34d,89a,181a), **Tyto** (16c), **unto** (166c), **veto** (94a,124a), **Veto, Voto** (192)

T - - O **tajo** (152a,d), **Tano** (192), **taro** (13c,48c,49b,64b,112b,120a,133d, 155c,170a,c), **taxo** (13a), **Teco** (192), **tiao, Tino** (136d), **tiro** (9b, 17d,108c), **Tito** (186c), **toco** (19b,167c), **todo** (22b,24d,35b,64c, 156b), **toho** (79a), **toko** (30c), **toro** (38a,107a,152a,168c), **toto** (8d,15a,34d,89a,181a), **trio** (104d,165a,169c), **tuno** (28b,168c), **typo** (35c,51b,123d), **tyro** (9b,17d,108c), **Tyto** (16c)

T - - P **tamp** (46b,112b,121d,127d), **tarp** (26b,178d), **terp** (12b,123a), **torp** (54c), **toup** (95d), **trap** (27b,67b,132b,149b), **trip** (85c), **trop** (62d,167a), **tryp** (114a), **tump** (60a,76d,103d), **turp, tymp** (20c), **typp** (185b)

TR - - **tram** (170a), **tran** (7a), **trap** (27b,67b,132b149b), **tray** (128c, 136d,142d,143c), **tree** (11d,37a,66a,184b), **tref** (172b), **trek** (85c, 93c,99d,168b), **tres** (19a,52b,63a,152d,165a,175c), **tret** (9a,178b, 179d), **trey** (26c,165a), **trig** (106a,148d,154b,169d), **trim** (40a,106a,154b,160a,165c,169d), **trin** (169d), **trio** (104d,165a, 169c), **trip** (85c), **tris** (122d), **trit** (34d,164c), **trod, tron** (140d, 180a), **trop** (62d,167a), **trot** (85b,93d,112d), **trow** (18a,21a,159d,

164c,170b), **troy** (161c,180a), **Troy, true** (7a,8d,37b,54b,94c,149c), **tryp** (114a)

- TR -   **Atri, atry** (141b), **etre** (61a,c,62d,166c)

- - TR   **natr** (189)

T - - R   **taar** (12b), **tahr** (68a,76d), **tair** (68a,76d), **tear** (67c,87b,130a), **teer** (25b,69d), **tehr** (27c,68a), **thar** (68a,76d), **Thor** (7c,68c,99c, 100c,109c,165b), **tiar** (39a,75a,121a), **tier** (118a,134b), **tour** (31b, 85c), **tsar** (42d,49d,60b,135c), **turr** (24d,105a), **tyer, Tyrr** (68c, 109c,163d,178a), **tzar** (42d,49d,60b,135c)

TS - -   **tsar** (42d,49d,60b,135c), **tshi, Tshi** (69c), **tsia** (162c), **Tsin** (30b), **tsun** (30b)

- - TS   **Acts, arts** (138c), **cits, eats, lots, orts** (60d), **rats**

T - - S   **Taos** (192), **Tass** (107a,135d,151b), **Tees** (108a), **Teos** (82a), **Tess** (73d,164c,183d), **this** (42b,124b), **Thos** (84a,181c), **thus** (149c), **togs** (32c), **tops** (159c), **toss** (24a,132d), **tres** (19a,52b,63a,152d,165a, 175c), **tris** (122d)

- TT -   **atta** (58d,90c,97d,160c,173d), **Atta** (94d,95d,100a,106b,117a), **Attu, Etta** (183c), **ette** (158a,c,d), **otto** (58d,116b,134a), **Otto** (14c,66d,67a,96a)

- - TT   **batt** (37c), **bitt** (54d,175c), **bott** (32a,88d), **butt** (27a,77b,127d, 162a,182b), **Catt** (9d), **gett** (44d), **Lett** (16a,90a,93a), **Matt, mitt** (56c), **mutt** (39c,101d), **Natt** (107b), **nett, Nott** (107b), **Pitt** (50d,155d), **pott** (113d), **putt** (69d), **sett** (115a,156d), **tatt** (87c), **watt** (173b,177c), **Watt** (82a)

T - - T   **tact** (43c,d,116a), **Taft** (29d), **tait** (14d), **takt** (105a,163a), **tart** (114d), **tatt** (87c), **taut** (163b,165c), **tent** (26b,115a), **test** (26a, 51c,144a,169c,170c), **text** (21c,140d), **that** (42b,124b,129c), **tilt** (26b,d,166a), **tint** (33c,d,114d), **todt** (66b), **tolt, toot, tort** (31c,91a,185c), **tout** (61a,127a), **tret** (9a,178b,179d), **trit** (34d,164c), **trot** (85b,93d,112d), **tuft** (24b,32d,38c), **twit** (162b,c)

TU - -   **tuan** (95d,147b,166c), **tuba** (105a,137d), **tube** (118b,158a), **tuck** (156b), **tuel, tufa** (121b,177a), **tuff** (121b,177a), **tuft** (24b,32d, 38c), **tuke** (26b,53b), **tula** (9a), **Tula, tule** (24b,27c), **Tulu** (45d), **tump** (60a,76d,103d), **tuna** (57a,b,123b,170d), **tund** (121d), **tune** (8b,12c,98c), **tung** (110a,168c), **tuno** (28b,168c), **tunu** (28b), **tuny, Tupi** (192), **turf** (115c,149d,160b), **Turi** (191), **Turk** (101d,102d, 106a,111d), **turm** (132d), **turn** (28d,131a,175a), **turp, turr** (24d, 105a), **tush** (167b), **tusk** (167b), **tute** (171b), **tutu** (16a,106d,147d), **tuwi** (117a,168c), **tuza** (119d)

- TU -   **atua** (120d), **Atum** (143a,159b), **etui** (27a,29b,62c,106b,148d, 166d,174b), **Otus** (67a), **stub** (156c), **stud** (22b,25a,42d,54d,111c, 143a,174a), **stum** (70c,105c,131a,173a), **stun** (145a,157d), **Utug** (159b), **utum** (19b,112c)

- - TU   **actu** (7a,89a), **Attu, datu** (95c,102c,117a), **Ketu** (48b), **latu** (190), **mitu** (39d), **patu** (179b), **tatu** (12d), **Tatu, tutu** (16a,106d,147d), **yutu** (19b,166a)

T - - U   **tabu** (59d,111d), **Taku** (80c), **tapu, tatu** (12d), **Tatu, tchu, teju** (151b), **thou** (124b), **Tibu** (191), **Tiou** (192), **tolu** (16a), **Tulu** (45d), **tunu** (28b), **tutu** (16a,106d,147d)

TW - -   **twee, twig, twin** (45c,171d), **twit** (162b,c)

T - - W   **thaw, thew** (104c), **trow** (18a,21a,159d,164c,170b)

TY - -   **Tybi** (102a), **tyee** (29d), **tyer, tyke** (29d), **tymp** (20c), **tyne, Tyne** (108a), **type** (31d,115a,155a), **typo** (35c,51b,123d), **typp** (185b), **typy, tyre** (15a), **Tyre** (31b,90d,117b), **tyro** (9b,17d,108c), **Tyrr** (68c,109c,163d,178a), **Tyto** (16c)

- TY -   **etym** (133d), **Itys** (163b), **Styx** (29b,73a,105c)

- - TY   **arty, city, Coty** (63c), **doty** (43d), **duty** (109b,162b), **Katy** (183d), **maty** (80c), **mity, pity** (35b), **toty** (87b)

T - - Y   **taky, Tavy** (183d), **they** (124b), **tidy** (106a,111b), **tiny** (100c,148c), **toby** (8c,85c,104b), **Toby** (96b,125c), **tody** (19b,d,59a,166a), **tony, Tony** (96b), **tory, Tory** (23c,36b,94c,172a), **toty** (87b), **towy** (58b), **tray** (128c,136d,142d,143c), **trey** (26c,165a), **troy** (161c,180a), **Troy, tuny, typy**

TZ - -   **tzar** (42d,49d,60b,135c)

- TZ -   **Itza** (192)

- - TZ   **batz** (190), **litz** (127b), **untz** (189)

UA - -   **uang** (131a)

- UA -   **bual** (182c), **duab** (157c), **duad** (171d), **dual** (45c,171d), **duan** (64b), **duar, Duat** (172d), **Fuad** (54d), **Guam, guan** (151b), **guao** (168c,169b), **guar** (46c,59d), **juan** (113a), **Juan** (96a), **juar** (100a), **kuan** (30b), **Kuan** (30c), **Kuar** (102a), **Muav** (66a), **quad** (33c,172a), **quae** (176b), **quag** (21c,102c), **quai** (88b,117c,180c), **quan** (190), **quas** (135c), **quay** (88b,117c,180c), **ruay** (189), **tuan** (95d,147b, 166c), **yuan** (190), **Yuan** (30b,101d)

- - UA   **agua** (152d,166c,178c), **akua** (120d), **aqua** (90a,178c), **atua** (120d), **Erua** (103c), **skua** (19b,72c,84a,141a), **ulua** (57a,74c), **Ulua** (141b)

U - - A   **ueba** (188), **ulna** (21d,39b), **ulua** (57a,74c), **Ulua** (141b), **Ulva** (141b), **unca** (49a), **upla, Urfa** (99a), **Uria** (14c,16d), **urna** (133a), **Ursa** (17b,36b,43d), **urva** (38b), **Usha** (16a,150c), **uvea** (53c,82b)

UB - -   **uber** (66b), **Ubii** (191)

- UB -   **buba** (170a), **Bube** (180b), **Bubi** (180b), **Bubo** (112c), **cuba** (189), **Cuba** (180b), **cube** (66b,150a), **cubi** (188), **dubb** (161c), **hubb** (118b), **juba** (106b), **jube** (28d), **kuba** (26d,189), **Luba** (191), **lube** (110a), **Lubs** (94c), **Nuba** (108c), **nubk** (30d,164d), **rube** (37d, 135d,185d), **Rube** (96b), **ruby** (20a,65d,179c), **tuba** (105a,137d), **tube** (118b,158a)

- - UB   **blub, chub** (40c,154c), **club** (39c), **daub** (148d), **doub** (189), **drub** (17b,39c), **flub** (22b), **gaub** (116c), **glub, grub** (43c,88d), **knub** (178b), **slub** (171c), **snub** (128c,148b), **stub** (156c)

- UC -   **Auca** (192), **buck, cuca** (33a,105d), **duce** (29d), **duck** (26b,53b, 179c), **Duco, duct** (170c), **fuci** (132c), **huck** (167d), **juca** (27a), **juck** (114c), **luce** (58c,117d), **Luce** (7b,35a), **luck** (28d), **lucy, Lucy** (183c), **much, muck, ouch!, puca** (68a), **puce** (33c,d,52a), **puck** (44b,68a,77c,100c), **Puck** (99d,143b), **ruck** (39a,185a), **such** (146d), **suck, tuck** (156b), **yuca** (27a)

- - UC   **douc** (101d), **eruc** (37a,56a)

U - - C   **Udic** (108a), **Utac** (22d)

UD - -   udad (143d,144a,181c), udal (76b,88b,131c), Udic (108a)

- UD -   Aude, buda (83d), Buda, dude (40d), duds (32c,166d), Juda, Jude (11c,96a), judo (84b,85c,142b), Judy (125c,183d), kudu (11a), Ludd (23c), ludi (133b), ludo (65a,112b), mudd (188), nuda (39b), Nudd (23c), nude (16c,172d), pudu (41d), rudd (26d,57a,b), rude (134b,172b), sudd (40b,58c,107b), suds (59a), wudu (102d)

- - UD   baud (162d), Chud (191), feud (55d,126b,175b), foud (54d,144b), gaud (169d), laud (122a), loud (156a), maud (53d,71a,136d,143c), Maud (181a,183c), Phud (110b), puud (189), roud (57a,b), scud (32c,126c,135b,160c), spud (121d,151c), stud (22b,25a,42d,54d, 111c,143a,174a), syud (103b), thud

U - - D   udad (143d,144a,181c), used (6d,73a), uvid (101a)

UE - -   ueba (188)

- UE -   Auer (79a), duel, duet (104d,171d), euer (66d), fuel (65c), hued, juez (152b), kuei (44a), quei (189), ruer, suer (124d), suet (54d), tuel

- - UE   ague (30a,55d,95c), blue (33c,98c,102c,150d,173a), clue, flue (8b,30a), gaue (67a), glue (7b,156a), moue (61d,62b), neue (66c), Niue (137d), roue (41b,44c,127c,134b), slue (97b,148b,160a), true (7a,8d,37b,54b,94c,149c)

U - - E   ulme (49c), unde (179a), unie (173a), unze (189), urde (86b), urge (42d,46b,79d,80a,b,81c,150a), usee

- UF -   buff (134c,161d), Bufo (166c), cuff (148a), duff (125b), Dufy (63a), gufa (21b,99a), guff, huff (58a), kufa (21b,99a), luff (136b), muff, puff, (180d), ruff (19b,33b,63d,137a), sufi (103a, 116c), tufa (121b,177a), tuff (121b,177a), tuft (24b,32d,38c), yuft (135c)

- - UF   pouf, souf (146b)

UG - -   ugly

- UG -   auge (123c,132b), Bugi (191), euge (180a), fuga, fugu (84b), gugu, huge, Hugh (96a), Hugo (63a,96a), juga (27a), kuge (84c), luge (148a), Lugh (28b), muga, ough, pugh, ruga (59b,185a), sugi (84b), vugg (28a,66a,132b), vugh (28a,66a,132b), Yuga (76d)

- - UG   chug (53a), drug (105d), glug, joug (138d), plug (156d,184d), slug (46b,99b,157c), smug, snug (35a,38b,165c), Snug (99d), thug (65a), toug (171a), Utug (159b)

U - - G   uang (131a), Utug (159b)

- UH -   buhl (81a), buhr (180d), Duhr (155b), Guha (191), guhr (47d), kuhl (53c), Ruhr

- - UH   bruh (95a)

U - - H   umph, Urth (68d,107d,163d), Utah (180b)

- UI -   cuif (139a,d,140c), cuir (45c,62a), duim (188), duit (190), Duit (192), guib (11a), huia (19a,106d), luif, Muir (8b,142c), nuit (62b), quid (39b,166d), quip (183a,b), quit (90d,130c), quiz, ruin (42d), suit (38a,58a,91a,112a,119c,137c), Yuit (51c)

- - UI   arui (11b,143d,144a,181c), equi (122d), etui (27a,29b,62c,106b, 148d,166d,174b), Maui (120d)

U - - I   Ubii (191), unci (31d)

- UJ -   fuji (84b), Fuji (84d), juju (29b,55d), puja (77a), suji (180c)

- UK -   bukh (122a), bukk (122a), cuke (39b), duke (107c), duku (95d, 168c), juke (114c), Kuki (191), kuku (19a,106d), luke, Luke (52a,96a), puka (107a,168c), puku (11a), rukh (53b,54a), Suku (191), tuke (26b,53b), wukf (103a)

- - UK   cauk (139b), dauk (95c), Sauk (192), souk (22a,97a)

UL - -   Ulam (67b), ulan (27d,88a), Ulex (153c), ullo (6a,144a), Ullr (146b,164d), ulme (49c), ulna (21d,39b), ulua (57a,74c), Ulua (141b), Ulva (141b)

- UL -   aula (66c,73b), aulu (74c,168c), bulb 37a,172c), bulk (97b), bull (113c), bult (76d), cull (117c), culm (11a,32d,70d,145a,156a),. cult (141d,161c), dull (21a,32c,173a), Dull (94b), fulk (173a), full (7b, 130b), gula (90a,101a,165b), gulf (6c), gull (32d,41c,42a,72c,99b, 141a), Gulo (183c), gulp (46a,79d,160a), hula (74b) hule, (23a, 134c), hulk (144d,173d), hull (141d,142a,144c,d), hulu (55b), jula, Jule (183d), July, kula (189), Kuli (27b), lull (25c,126d,150c), lulu (19a,57b,112c), Lulu (183d), mule (45b,148b,153c,180b), mulk (60d), mull (53b,135a,164c), null (108c,177a), pule (180d), pulk (37c,88d), puli (45a,78d), pull (45d,167d), pulp, pulu (74c), puly, rule (11b,26b,90b), rull (170b), Sula (65a), suld (188), sulk (159a), Sulu (102c), tula (9a), Tula, tule (24b,27c), Tulu (45d), vuln (184d), Yule (30d), zulu (171d,175d), Zulu (86a)

- - UL   Aoul (191), azul (151d), baul (18b), caul (16d,74d), deul (77b), Elul (102b), foul (173a), Gaul (10a,60d,63c), goul (102a), haul (27b,45d), maul (73c,96b), paul, Paul (96a), poul (190), saul (48a, 168c), Saul (18c,86d,115a), shul (161a), soul (10d,125a,153c, 176d)

U - - L   udal (76b,88b,131c), unal (147a), Ural (135c), uval (70c)

UM - -   umbo (22b), umph

- UM -   bump, Duma (135c), dumb (153b), dump, fume (129a,149a,157a), fumy, Gump (43b), Hume (50c), hump (124d), jump, lump (45a, 160c), mump (29b,153d), Numa (133a), numb, puma (27b,37c,55b, 103d), Pume (137b,175b,185b), pump, rumb (120b), rump, Sumo, sump (28c,45d), tump (60a,76d,103d), Yuma

- - UM   ahum, alum (14a,45c), arum (13a,39b,58d,92b,155c), Arum (66a), Atum (143a,159b), Baum (9c,112c), chum (38d), doum (168c), drum (105a), Geum (76b), glum (102c,159a), grum (102c), jhum, meum (27a,89c), Meum, odum (168c,180a), ogum (82b), ovum (48d), plum, rhum (8c), saum (189), scum (129b), slum, stum (70c,105c,131a,173a), swum, Ulam (67b), utum (19b,112c)

U - - M   urim (18d,23a,110a), utum (19b,112c)

UN - -   unal (147a), unau (148c,171d), unca (49a), unci (31d), unco (140c), unde (179a), undo (11a,93d), undy (179a), unie (173a), Unio (105c), unis (91b), unit (101c,110c,147a), unto (166c), untz (189), unze (189)

- UN -   aune (188), aunt (129c), buna (161c), bund (49c,66c,90c), bung (119d,156d), bunk, bunn (25b), bunt (15d,180c), Cuna (193), dune (137a), dunk (43c,79d), Duns, dunt, fund (6d,101c,130c), Fung

(191), **Funj, funk** (63d,113c), **guna** (106a,137b), **gunj** (70c), **hung, hunh?, hunk, hunt** (141c), **June** (183c), **Jung** (125a), **junk** (30a, 134c), **Juno** (69c,85d,100c,126b), **kung** (125b), **kunk** (188), **luna** 103c), **Luna** (102b), **lune** (38c,73b,74d), **lung, luny** (38b), **mund** (124d), **mung** (70d), **munj** (70d), **paun** (18b), **puna** (10b,33b,104a, 119b,182a), **pund** (189), **pung** (22c,148b), **punk** (9b,166a,167c), **puno** (182a), **punt** (21a,58b), **puny** (55b,179a), **Qung** (191), **rune** (9b,67a,94a,105c,107d,120a,141d,163d), **rung** (28c,39a), **runt** (47a172d), **sung, Sung** (30b), **sunk, sunn** (56a), **tuna** (57a,b,123b, 170d), **tund** (121d), **tune** (8b,12c,98c), **tung** (110a,168c), **tuno** (28b,168c), **tunu** (28b), **tuny, Yunx** (184a), **Zuni** (125b)

- - UN **Amun** (86d,127d,159b,164a), **Chun** (30c), **drun** (132b), **faun** (56a, 68b,137c,161a,184a), **Idun** (107d), **jaun** (113a), **kaun** (93d), **laun** (146b), **loun** (19a,b), **maun** (139d), **noun** (114b,158a), **paun** (18b), **shun** (15a,51b,52a), **spun, stun** (145a,157d), **taun** (188), **tsun** (30b), **Usun** (191), **whun** (64c,70a)

U - - N ulan (27d,88a), upon (6b), uran (101d), Usun (191), uzan (189)

- UO - buoy (28d,58c), quod (123d)

U - - O **ullo** (6a,144a), **umbo** (22b), **unco** (140c), **undo** (11a,93d), **Unio** (105c), **unto** (166c), **upgo** (13c)

UP - - upas (84d,120b,168c,d), upgo (13c), Upis (13b), upla, upon (6b)

- UP - **dupe** (27c,41c,72c,160c), **Hupa** (192), **jupe** (62b,84a), **lupe** (19a, 64a), **Nupe** (191), **pupa** (30d,81b,c), **rupa** (60b), **supa** (168c), **supe** (53a,154d), **Tupi** (192)

- - UP **blup, caup, coup** (20d,97c,157b,c,162d), **gaup, loup** (61d,62a,90c, 139d), **Loup** (193), **noup** (124b), **plup, roup** (44a,121d), **scup** (57a, 121b), **snup** (149b), **soup, toup** (95d), **yaup, youp** (185d)

UR - - **Ural** (135c), **uran** (101d), **urde** (86b), **Urdu** (77b), **urdy** (86b), **Urey** (17b,36b,43d), **Urth** (68d,107d,163d), **urus** (14d,53a,112c), **urva** 150a), **Uria** (14c,16d), **urim** (18d,23a,110a), **urna** (133a), **Ursa** (17b,36b,43d), **Urth** (68d,107d,163d), **urus** (14d,53a,112c), **urva** (38b)

- UR - aura (44c,49c,66a,96b,158a,170d,177c), auri (34a), bura (182b), bure (61b), burg (22b,73c), buri (56b), burl (87c,169a), burn, burr (123b), bury (81d), cura (152c), curb (130c,146b), curd (99d), cure (123b), curl (38d,73b,131d), curr (104c), curt (145b,c), dura (153c), duro (190), durr (70b), furl (132d), fury (157a), guru (77b), hura (20a,137a), Hura, hurl (167c), hurt, jura, Jura, jure (90b), jury (38a), Kurd (48b,82d), Kure (84c), Kuri (191), kurk (31a,139b), lura (22d,82a), lure (41c,51a,54b,163a), lurg (96d,141b,184d), Luri (191), lurk (92a,147d), mura (84d), Mura (192), mure (177d), murk (41a,67d), murr (72b,128b), nurl (33b,87c), nurr (67d), ours (124c), pure (29b,172b,173c), puri (80d), purl (87c,104c), purr (104c), Puru (192), ruru (19b,102c,106d), sura (87c,113b,166d), surd (82c,177a), sure (173d), surf (23a), turf (115c,149d,160b), Turi (191), Turk (101d,102d,106a,111d), turm (132d), turn (28d, 131a,175a), turp, turr (24d,105a), Wurd, wurm (67c), yurt (101d)

- - UR **Alur** (191), **Asur** (68c), **biur** (35a), **blur, caur** (139a), **Daur** (139b), **dour** (67d,159a), **ebur** (89c), **four** (26c), **gaur** (112c,181c), **gour** (112c,181c), **hour, knur** (67d,87c,107c), **lour** (13d,63d), **peur** (61c),

374

pour (162d), **scur** (78b), **slur** (44b,124c,148b,168a), **smur** (32c,46b, 100c), **sour**, **spur** (10d,67d,167d,168a,181b), **tour** (31b,85c), **your** (124c)

U - - R   **uber** (66b), **Ullr** (146b,164d), **usar** (8d,16c), **user** (49d), **utor** (90a, 166c)

US - -   **usar** (8d,16c), **Usas** (68d), **used** (6d,73a), **usee**, **user** (49d), **uses** (18a), **Usha** (16a,150c), **Usun** (191)

- US -   **Ausa**, **ausu** (168c,180b), **bush**, **busk** (17b,37b,55d,161b), **buss** (87a,148c), **bust**, **busy**, **cush** (101c), **Cush** (51d,73c), **cusk** (57b), **cusp** (38c,78b,119a,120a,b), **cuss**, **duse** (83c), **dusk** (171c), **dust**, **fuse** (98c), **fuss** (22b,35b), **fust** (105c,143b), **gush** (35a,154c), **gust**, **huse** (180c), **hush** (17b,146c), **husk** (53a,78d,142a), **huso** (180c), **just** (51b,54b), **kusa**, **Kush**, **lush** (94d), **lust** (41b), **Musa** (16a), **muse** (65b,93d,120d,164c), **Muse** (68d), **mush** (97d), **musk** (116b), **Muso** (192), **muss** (135b,173d), **must** (70c,101a,106d,157d,182c), **Ouse** (132a,185d), **oust** (44c,49a,52b,125d), **push**, (145c) **puss**, **rusa**, **Rusa** (41d,136d), **ruse** (13b,77c,157b,169c), **rush**, **rusk** (23a), **Russ** (135b), **rust** (37b,112c,119a), **Susa** (49a), **susi** (53b,d), **susu** (20c), **Susu** (191), **Susy** (183d), **tush** (167b), **tusk** (167b),

- - US   **acus** (89d,118a), **Apus** (36b,c), **avus** (89b), **cous** (38a), **crus** (91a, 143c), **deus** (68a,89b), **Esus**, **gaus** (67a), **Grus** (36b,c,38b), **Ilus** (88d,170b), **irus** (109d), **nous** (81d,100a,128b), **onus** (24c,93b,109b), **opus** (35c,105a,184c), **Otus** (67a), **Pius** (121a), **plus** (10b, 102c), **pous** (188), **Rhus** (159a), **sous** (62d,172c), **thus** (149c), **urus** (14d,53a,112c), **Zeus** (135a)

U - - S   **unis** (91b), **upas** (84d,120b,168c,d), **Upis** (13b), **urus** (14d,53a, 112c), **uses** (18a), **Usas** (68d), **utas** (49a,109c)

UT - -   **utac** (22d), **Utah** (180b), **utas** (49a,109c), **utor** (90a,166c), **Utug** (159b), **utum** (19b,112c)

- UT -   **auto** (34d), **Buto** (142d), **butt** (27a,77b,127d,162a,182b), **cute** (39c), **duty** (109b,162b), **fute** (51c), **Guti**, **jute** (37a,48a,56a,133d, 136a), **Jute**, **lute** (11c,28b,84d,105a,131d), **muta** (28d,103a), **mute** (146c,153b), **muth** (188), **mutt** (39c,101d), **putt** (69d), **Ruta** (76b, 134d), **rute** (188), **ruth** (35b,118c), **Ruth** (105b,183c), **tute** (171b), **tutu** (16a,106d,147d), **yutu** (19b,166a)

- - UT   **abut** (22a,167c), **bhut** (67a), **blut** (66b), **bout** (36c), **brut** (182c), **Brut** (23c), **chut!**, **Cnut** (40d,50c), **gaut** (88b,103d,132a), **glut** (52c,70a,137c,159d), **gout**, **knut**, **Knut** (40d,50c,96a), **lout** (15c, 22a,24b,45b,109a,157d), **naut** (141b), **paut** (140a), **phut** (24b), **Phut** (110b), **pout** (159a), **prut!**, **Prut** (41a), **rout** (41d,44b,46b), **scut** (145c,161b), **shut**, **smut** (32d,44a,119a,150c), **sput** (21c), **taut** (163b,165c), **tout** (61a,127a)

U - - T   **unit** (101c,110c,147a)

- UU -   **puud** (189)

U - - U   **unau** (148c,171d), **Urdu** (77b)

UV - -   **uval** (70c), **uvea** (53c,82b), **uvic** (70c), **uvid** (101a)

- UV -   **cuvy** (141a)

- UW -   **tuwi** (117a,168c)

- - UW   **bouw** (188), **dauw** (24c)

- UX -   **buxy** (115b), **luxe** (61c,62d,159c), **puxy**

- - UX   **crux** (39a,151b), **eaux** (178c), **flux** (28d,58d), **jeux** (61d), **Vaux** (63b)

U - - X   **Ulex** (153c)

- UY -   **buyo** (18b), **cuya** (39b), **Puya** (118b)

U - - Y   **ugly, undy** (179a), **urdy** (86b), **Urey** (14b,107c,138c)

UZ - -   **uzan** (189)

- UZ -   **auzu** (168c,180b), **buzz, fuze** (98c), **fuzz** (45d), **guze** (128d), **huzz, Juza** (155b), **Muzo** (192), **tuza** (119d), **wuzu** (102d), **zuza** (189)

- - UZ   **Ghuz** (171a)

U - - Z   **untz** (189)

VA - -   **Vach** (153b), **vade** (42c,67d,89b), **vagi** (38b), **vail** (94b,124a,174b), **vain** (81a), **vair** (64c,154c), **vale** (54c,128a,174b), **Vale** (7c,109c), **vali** (171a,176a), **Vali** (7c,109c), **vamp** (80a,145a), **vane** (179b, 182a), **vang** (72d,134a,140b), **Vans** (107d), **vara** (151d), **vare** 179b), **vari** (34d,91b,134d,174d), **vary** (28d,43c), **vasa** (46d,114a, 160b,175d), **Vasa, vase, vast** (78d,79d), **vasu** (106c), **Vasu** (176d), **Vaux** (63b), **Vayu** (68c,182a), **vaza** (114a)

- VA -   **aval** (70c), **Avar** (27d,108a), **Evan** (96a), **Ivah** (18d), **Ivan** (40c, 85b,96a), **kvas** (135c), **oval** (48d,49c,127a), **Svan** (27d), **uval** (70c)

- - VA   **Alva** (151d), **cava** (116a,175b), **Civa** (56d), **deva** (23d,42a,42b, 56d,77a), **diva** (100d,123c), **Hova** (95a), **Java** (33a), **jiva** (77a), **Jova** (193), **kava** (18c,116a), **kiva** (28c,125b), **lava** (101c,151a, 177a), **Neva** (91b,132a), **nova** (20c,106d,155c,174d), **peva** (12d), **siva** (67a), **Siva** (56d,77a), **Ulva** (141b), **urva** (38b), **viva** (93d), **Xova** (193), **yava**

V - - A   **vara** (151d), **vasa** (46d,114a,160b,175d), **Vasa, vaza** (114a), **Veda** (77a,b), **vega** (110d,152c), **Vega** (155b), **vela** (98c,136b,149d), **Vela** (36b,c), **vena** (90a,175a), **vera** (140c,151b,175c), **Vera** (183c), **veta** (104a), **Vida** (183c), **vila** (54b), **vina** (77a,105a), **Vira** (191), **visa** (114d), **vita** (89c,92a), **viva** (93d), **vola** (89d,150a), **vota** (133b)

V - - B   **verb** (7a,114b,184b)

- - VD   **NKVD** (135d)

V - - D   **veld** (151a), **vend** (97a,115c,142b), **Vend** (10b,148a), **verd** (71d), **void** (11a,49d,108d,174b)

VE - -   **veal, Veda** (77a,b), **veer** (28d,144c,171b), **vega** (110d,152c), **Vega** (155b), **veil** (74d,76c), **vein** (20d,157b), **vela** (98c,136b,149d), **Vela** (36b,c), **veld** (151a), **velo** (175b), **vena** (90a,175a), **vend** (97a, 115c,142b), **Vend** (10b,148a), **vent** (8b,11b,110d,112a), **Veps** (191), **vera** (140c,151b,175c), **Vera** (183c), **verb** (7a,114b,184b), **verd** (71d), **veri** (28b), **vert** (71d,166a,171b), **very** (149c), **vest** (32c, 177b), **veta** (104a), **veto** (94a,124a), **Veto**

- VE -   **avec** (63a,183a), **aver** (7c,14a,15c,41c,95c,140d,155c,160b,184c), **Aves** (19d), **evea** (82a,95a), **even** (51a,58b,79d,91d,149a,173a), **ever** (9b,14b,80b), **evet** (48d,107a,136c,169d), **Ives** (9c,90b), **oven** (15d,78c,86b), **over** (6b,38c,80a,114d,130a), **uvea** (53c,82b)

- - VE   **bave** (61d,146c), **cave** (27d), **cive** (110c), **cove** (17a,73d,107d),

Dave (96b), **dive** (42b,74b,119d), **dove** (19a,117d), **eave** (133c), **five**, **gave**, **give** (79d,123a), **gyve** (55d,143b), **have** (92a), **hive** (17c), **hove** (92a), **Jave** (84d), **jive** (160c), **jove** (85d), **kive** (174d), **lave** (16d,178b), **leve** (62a), **live** (47c), **love** (163a), **move**, **nave** (30d,31a,78d,114b,180c), **neve** (56d,67c,70c,149b), **nove** (83b), **pave** (85a), **rave** (41c,157a,161d), **reve** (61c,104d), **rive** (32a,153d), **rove** (127d,132b,178a), **save** (52b,110c,123a,173c), **seve** (63a, 182c), **sive** (146a), **Tave** (183d), **vive** (93d), **wave** (19a,59a,111c, 131d,160c,172d), **wive** (97a), **wove**

V - - E   **vade** (42c,67d,89b), **vale** (54c,128a,174b), **Vale** (7c,109c), **vane** (179b,182a), **vare** (179b), **vase**, **vice** (31d,158a), **vide** (89d,126a, 142a), **vile** (16c,56c), **vine** (32b), **vire** (11a,13b), **vise** (31d,77d, 114d), **vite** (62b), **vive** (93d), **voce** (83c,177a), **vole** (97d,104a, 148a,149b), **vote** (60b), **Vote** (56d)

V - - G   **vang** (72d,134a,140b), **voog** (28a,66a,132b), **vugg** (28a,66a,132b)

- - VH   **IHVH** (159d), **JHVH** (159d), **YHVH** (159d)

V - - H   **Vach** (153b), **Voth** (191), **vugh** (28a,66a,132b)

VI - -   **vial** (148c), **vice** (31d,158a), **Vida** (183c), **vide** (89d,126a,142a), **vier** (66c), **view** (93d,138b), **vila** (54b), **vile** (16c,56c), **vili** (54b), **Vili** (109c), **vill** (176b), **vily** (54b), **vina** (77a,105a), **vine** (32b), **vino** (92d,182b), **vint** (26c,182c), **viny**, **viol** (105a), **Vira** (191), **vire** (11a,13b), **visa** (114d), **vise** (31d,77d,114d), **viss** (189), **vita** (89c, 92a), **vite** (62b), **viti** (176b), **viva** (93d), **vive** (93d), **vivo** (93a)

- VI -   **avid** (47b,71a,186b), **avis** (89a), **Avis** (183c), **evil** (79c,95d,147a, 181a,185c), **Ovid** (132d,133b), **Ovis** (143d), **uvic** (70c), **uvid** (101a)

- - VI   **Devi** (147b,153b), **divi**, **favi** (138a,165d), **hevi** (111d), **Kavi** (84d), **Levi** (84a,90c), **ravi** (61b), **Ravi** (16b)

V - - I   **vagi** (38b), **vali** (171a,176a), **Vali** (7c,109c), **vari** (34d,91b,134d, 174d), **veri** (28b), **vili** (54b), **Vili** (109c), **viti** (176b), **vlei** (38c,160a)

V - - K   **volk** (66c,105d,116a,184c)

VL - -   **vlei** (38c,160a), **vley** (160a)

V - - L   **vail** (94b,124a,174b), **veal**, **veil**, (74d,76c), **vial** (148c), **vill** (176b), **viol** (105a)

V - - N   **vain** (81a), **vein** (20d,157b), **vuln** (184d)

VO - -   **voce** (83c,177a), **voet** (188), **Vogt**, **void** (11a,49d,108d,174b), **vola** (89d,150a), **vole** (97d,104a,148a,149b), **volk** (66c,105d,116a,184c), **volt** (49b,78c,173b), **voog** (28a,66a,132b), **vota** (133b), **vote** (60b), **Vote** (56d), **Voth** (191), **Voto** (192)

- VO -   **Avon** (143b), **Avow** (6d,36a,41c,112c), **evoe** (15b,130d,181c)

- - VO   **levo** (91a), **pavo** (115b), **Pavo** (36b,c), **vivo** (93a)

V - - O   **velo** (175b), **veto** (94a,124a), **Veto**, **vino** (92d,182b), **vivo** (93a), **Voto** (192)

V - - P   **vamp** (80a,145a)

V - - R   **vair** (64c,154c), **veer** (28d,144c,171b), **vier** (66c)

- - VS   **revs** (131a)

V - - S   **Vans** (107d), **Veps** (191), **viss** (189)

V - - T   **vast** (78d,79d), **vent** (8b,11b,110d,112a), **vert** (71d,166a,171b),

vest (32c,177b), **vint** (26c,182c), **voet** (188), **Vogt, volt** (49b,78c, 173b)

VU - - **vugg** (28a,66a,132b), **vugh** (28a,66a,132b), **vuln** (184d)

- VU - **avus** (89b), **ovum** (48d)

- - VU **kivu** (170c)

V - - U **vasu** (106c), **Vasu** (176d), **Vayu** (68c,182a)

V - - W **view** (93d,138b)

V - - X **Vaux** (63b)

- - VY **bevy** (38a,58c), **cavy** (72b,120d,132c,157b), **cuvy** (141a), **Davy** (96b,136b), **envy** (41b), **levy** (14a,162b), **Livy** (132d,133a), **navy** (33c,58b), **pavy** (115b), **pevy** (91d,94c), **Tavy** (183d), **wavy** (147b, 172d)

V - - Y **vary** (28d,43c), **very** (149c), **vily** (54b), **viny, vley** (160a)

WA - - **Waac, waag** (71d,101d), **Wabi** (192), **Waco, wadd** (109c), **wade, wadi** (46c,106a,109a,128a,132a), **wady** (109a,128a,132a), **waeg** (19b,72c,87a), **waer** (40b), **Wafd** (49a), **waft** (20d,58c), **wage** (27a, 115b), **waif** (157b), **wail** (39b,88a), **wain** (177b), **Wain, wait** (26d, 42b,92c,155d,162a), **waka** (26a), **wake** (134b,168a), **wakf** (103a), **waky, wale** (70b,131b,157c,163d,179a,180a,c,d), **wali** (171a), **walk, wall, Walt** (96b), **wand** (120b,132c,156a), **wane** (41c,43c), **wang** (189), **want** (41b,42d,87b,106b,122a), **wany, wapp** (54b,133d, 145d), **waqf** (103a), **ward** (31c,55c,86b), **ware** (27d,35a), **warf, warm** (7c,75b,163b), **warn** (7b), **warp** (36c,165a,171c), **wart** (124d), **wary** (27d,176b), **wash, wasp, wast, Wate** (141a), **watt** (173b, 177c), **Watt** (82a), **wave** (19a,59a,111c,131d,160c,172d), **wavy** (147b,172d), **waxy** (119c,149d), **ways**

- WA - **Awan** (191), **away** (6b,69d,76a,109d,111d), **Ewan, kwan** (30b), **swab** (102b), **swad** (94d), **swag** (22a,156c), **swam, swan** (19b,33a), **swap** (168a), **swat** (15d,20d,32d,157c), **Swat** (103a), **sway** (104a)

- - WA **biwa** (93d,168c), **dewa, Iowa** (193), **kawa** (18c,116a), **lowa** (19a), **pawa** (189), **tawa** (160d,168c), **Tewa** (193)

W - - A **waka** (26a), **Wega** (155b), **weka** (58c,106d,107a,127b), **weta** (93c), **whoa** (156d)

W - - C **Waac**

- - WD **dowd** (143b), **gawd** (169c)

W - - D **wadd** (109c), **Wafd** (49a), **wand** (120b,132c,156a), **ward** (31c,55c, 86b), **week, weld** (47c,85b,173c), **wend** (67d,123d), **Wend** (10b, 148a), **wild** (38b,173d), **wind** (33b,39d,171c,185a), **woad** (20d,47c), **wold** (47c,60a,118d,174a,184a), **wood, word** (124b,165c), **Wurd, Wyrd** (107d)

WE - - **weak** (55b), **weal** (124d,157c,180c,d), **wean** (8d,42d), **wear** (50b), **weed, week, weel** (16d,57d,140d,180d), **weep** (39b,88a,104a), **weet** (19d), **weft** (39a,165a,184b), **Wega** (155b), **Wegg** (111d), **weir** '40b,57d), **weka** (58c,106d,107a,127b), **weki** (55c), **weld** (47c,85b, 173c), **Welf** (67a), **welk** (65c,96d,141b), **well welt** (36d,131b,145a, b,177b,d), **wend** (67d,123d), **Wend** (10b,148a), **went** (42c), **wept, were** (139b), **werf** (54d), **weri** (15c,27c), **wert, west, West** (9c,50b, 109b), **weta** (93c)

378

- **WE -**   **ewer** (84d,85c,118c,181b), **kwei** (44a), **Owen** (96a,183c), **sweb** (160d), **twee**

- - **WE**   **howe** (77d), **Howe** (17a,82a), **powe**

W - - E   **wade, wage** (27a,115b), **wake** (134b,168a), **wale** (70b,131b,157c, 163d,179a,180a,c,d), **wane** (41c,43c), **ware** (27d,35a), **Wate** (141a), **wave** (19a,59a,111c,131d,160c,172d), **were** (139b), **whee, wide** (133d), **wife** (154a), **wile** (13b,41c,157b,169c), **wine, wipe, wire, wise** (136b), **wive** (97a), **woke, wore, Wote** (191), **wove**

W - - F   **waif** (157b), **wakf** (103a), **waqf** (103a), **warf, Welf** (67a), **werf** (54d), **wolf, woof** (39a,163d,165a,179d), **Wraf, wukf** (103a)

W - - G   **waag** (71d,101d), **waeg** (19b,72c,87a), **wang** (189), **Wegg** (111d), **Whig wigg, wing** (10d,58c,59a,118b,d), **wong** (56a)

WH - -   **wham** (157c), **what** (129c), **whau** (107a,168c), **wheel, when** (180d), **whet** (143c,156b), **whew, whey** (100a), **Whig, whim** (26c, 54c,108c), **whin** (64c,70a,132b,181d), **whip** (58c,88d), **whir** (25c, 181a), **whit** (166c), **whiz** (25c), **whoa** (156d), **whom** (42b), **whool, whun** (64c,70a), **whyo** (59d,65a)

- - **WH**   **JHWH** (159d), **YHWH** (159c)

W - - H   **wash, wish** (42d), **with** (10b)

WI - -   **wick, wide** (133d), **widu** (102d), **wiel** (140d,180d), **wies** (185a), **wife** (154a), **wigg, wild** (38b,173d), **wile** (13b,41c,157b,169c), **wilk** (65c,96d,141b), **will** (18b,43a,163c,177c), **wilt** (46b), **wily** (13b,38b,39c), **wind** (33b,39d,171c,185a), **wine, wing** (10d,58c, 59a,118b,d), **wink** (107a), **winy** (176c), **wipe, wire, wiry** (147a, 167c), **wise** (136b), **wish** (42d), **wisp** (24b,148c), **wist** (87c), **with** (10b), **wive** (97a)

- **WI -**   **swig** (46a,72c), **swim** (58c), **swiz** (160c), **twig, twin** (45c,171d), **twit** (162b,c)

- - **WI**   **iiwi** (19a,74b), **Kawi** (84d), **kiwi** (11d,19a,58c), **tuwi** (117a,168c)

W - - I   **Wabi** (192), **wadi** (46c,106a,109a,128a,132a), **wali** (171a), **weki** (55c), **weri** (15c,27c)

- - **WK**   **bowk** (155d), **cawk** (133c), **dawk** (95c), **gawk** (146d), **gowk** (146d), **hawk** (19c,115c), **sawk** (188)

W - - K   **walk, weak** (55b), **week, welk** (65c,96d,141b), **wick, wilk** (65c, 96d,141b), **wink** (107a), **work** (64c,76b)

- - **WL**   **bawl, bowl, cowl** (101d), **dowl, fowl, gowl** (102a,140d,185b), **howl** (39b), **jowl** (29b), **mewl** (180d), **pawl** (43a,95a), **yawl** (136b,171d, 175d), **yowl**

W - - L   **wail** (39b,88a), **wall, weal** (124d,157c,180c,d), **weel** (16d,57d,140d, 180d), **well, wiel** (140d,180d), **will** (18b,43a,163c,177c), **wool** (58b, 179c)

- - **WM**   **dawm** (190)

W - - M   **warm** (7c,75b,163b), **wham** (157c), **whim** (26c,54c,108c), **whom** (42b), **worm, wurm** (67c),

- - **WN**   **bawn** (181a), **dawn** (14d,41b), **down** (149d), **fawn** (33c), **gown, hewn, kawn** (93d), **lawn** (20a,37c,53b,92c), **lown** (157d), **mown, pawn** (29c,119c), **sawn, sewn, town** (73c), **yawn**

W - - N   **wain** (177b), **Wain, warn** (7b), **wean** (8d,42d), **when** (180d), **whin**

379

(64c,70a,132b,181d), **whun** (64c,70a), **woon** (24c), **worn** (143b), **wren** (19b,c), **Wren** (50b), **wynn** (165d)

WO - -   **woad** (20d,47c), **woke, wold** (47c,60a,118d,174a,184a), **wolf, wong** (56a), **wont** (6d,40a,73a,174c), **wood woof** (39a,163d,165a, 179d), **wool** (58b,179c), **woon** (24c), **word** (124b,165c), **wore, work** (64c,76b), **worm, worn** (143b), **wort** (76a,95d,121d), **Wote** (191), **wove**

- WO -   **Lwow, swob** (102b), **swop** (168a), **swot, swow** (100a)

W - - O   **Waco, whoo, whyo** (59d,65a)

- - WP   **gawp, lowp** (90c,139d), **yawp**

W - - P   **wapp** (54b,133d,145d), **warp** (36c,165a,171c), **wasp, weep** (39b, 88a,104a), **whip** (58c,88d), **wisp** (24b,148c), **wrap** (32b,51a)

WR - -   **Wraf, wrap** (32b,51a), **wren** (19b,c), **Wren** (50b), **writ** (91a)

- WR -   **awry** (13d,38d,171c), **ewry** (133c)

W - - R   **waer** (40b), **wear** (50b), **weir** (40b,57d), **whir** (25c,181a)

- WS -   **owse**

- - WS   **mews** (154c), **news** (165c)

W - - S   **ways, wies** (185a)

- - WT   **newt** (48d,136c,169d), **nowt** (106a,139a), **yowt** (139c)

W - - T   **waft** (20d,58c), **wait** (26d,42b,92c,155d,162a), **Walt** (96b), **want** (41b,42d,87b,106b,122a), **wart** (124d), **wast, watt** (173b,177c), **Watt** (82a), **weet** (19d), **weft** (39a,165a,184b), **welt** (36d,131b, 145a,b,177b,d), **went** (42c), **wept, wert, west, West** (9c,50b,109b), **what** (129c), **whet** (143c,156b), **whit** (166c), **wilt** (46b), **wist** (87c), **wont** (6d,40a,73a,174c), **wort** (76a,95d,121d), **writ** (91a)

WU - -   **wudu** (102d), **wukf** (103a), **Wurd, wurm** (67c), **wuzu** (102d)

- WU -   **swum**

W - - U   **whau** (107a,168c), **widu** (102d), **wudu** (102d), **wuzu** (102d)

W - - W   **whew!**

WY - -   **wynn** (165d), **Wyrd** (107d)

- WY -   **Gwyn** (40c,50b)

- - WY   **dewy** (101a), **jawy, nowy** (194), **rowy** (157b), **towy** (58b)

W - - Y   **wady** (109a,128a,132a), **waky, wany, wary** (27d,176b), **wavy** (147b,172d), **waxy** (119c,149d), **whey** (100a), **wily** (13b,38b,39c), **winy** (176c), **wiry** (147a,167c)

W - - Z   **whiz** (25c)

- XA -   **axal** (120b), **exam, oxan** (65c)

- - XA   **Bixa** (145d), **coxa** (77b), **doxa** (48b), **moxa** (27d,30c), **myxa** (168c, 169a), **noxa, toxa** (153d)

X - - A   **xema** (72c), **Xema** (12c), **Xina** (183d), **Xosa** (86a), **Xova** (193)

XE - -   **xema** (72c), **Xema** (12c), **xeno** (34d)

- XE -   **oxea** (153d), **oxen** (10c), **oxer** (55c)

- - XE   **luxe** (61c,62d,159c), **Mixe** (192), **saxe** (20d,33c)

X - - E   **Xipe** (15c)

XI - -   **Xina** (183d), **Xipe** (15c)

- XI -   axil (10c), **axis** (28b,41d,77c,153c), **exit** (114d), **ixia** (37a), **Ixil** (192), **oxid** (112c)

- - XI   **dixi, taxi** (13a,125b)

- XL -   **axle** (153c,180c), **ixle** (56a)

XM - -   **Xmas**

XO - -   **Xosa** (86a), **Xova** (193)

- XO -   **axon** (106c,153c)

- - XO   **Moxo** (192), **myxo, taxo** (13a)

X - - O   **xeno** (34d), **xylo** (35a,183d)

X - - S   **Xmas**

- - XT   **next** (106a), **sext** (26b,111b,147b), **text** (21c,140d)

XY - -   **xylo** (35a,183d)

- XY -   **oxyl** (112c)

- - XY   **boxy, buxy** (115b), **doxy** (129d), **foxy** (38b,39c,181d), **mixy, pixy** (154b), **puxy, Roxy** (183d), **waxy** (119c,149d)

YA - -   **yage** (23a), **yaje** (23a), **Yaka** (191), **Yaki** (193), **Yale** (173c), **yali** (171a), **Yama** (57a,68a), **Yana** (192,193), **yang** (30b,70a), **yank, Yank, Yaou** (30c), **yapa** (113b), **Yapp** (22a), **yard** (152d), **yare** (96b,124b,128b), **yark** (22c), **yarl** (40d,107d), **yarn** (154b,161b, 184b), **yarr** (72a), **Yaru** (48d), **yate** (51d,168c), **yati** (76d), **yaup, yava, yawl** (136b,171d,175d), **yawn, yawp, yaya** (113c,168c)

- YA -   ayah (108d), **cyan, dyad** (113a), **Dyak** (22b), **Dyas** (66a), **eyah** (95b, 108d,111c), **eyas** (106c,173a), **Iyar** (102b), **kyah** (19a), **kyak** (51c), **kyar** (33a), **kyat** (189), **Iyam** (139a), **Lyas** (66a), **pyal** (175c), **pyat** (95b), **ryal** (110a,190)

- - YA   **Alya** (155b,c), **Arya** (80d), **baya** (179b), **Baya** (191), **cuya** (39b), **Goya** (151d), **Hoya** (14d), **maya** (77a,179b), **Maya** (23d,186c), **Puya** (118b), **raya** (19b,23c,76d,107d), **saya** (117a), **soya** (151b), **yaya** (113c,168c)

Y - - A   **Yaka** (191), **Yama** (57a,68a), **Yana** (192,193), **yapa** (113b), **yava, yaya** (113c,168c), **yeta** (84c), **Yima** (84a,116b,c), **Ynca** (193), **yoga** (10b,13c,77a), **yuca** (27a), **Yuga** (76d), **Yuma**

- YB -   **gybe** (144c), **Tybi** (102a)

- YC -   **syce** (71d)

- YD -   **hyde** (188), **Hyde** (45a)

- - YD   **emyd** (163c,167c)

Y - - D   **yard** (152d), **yond** (164d)

YE - -   **yeah, yean** (88a), **year, yeas** (177c), **Yedo** (166d), **yegg** (24c), **yell** (145c), **yelp, yelt** (151b), **yeni** (19b,161d), **yeso** (72d), **yeta** (84c)

- YE -   **ayes** (177c), **byee** (189), **dyer, eyer, eyey** (74b), **oyer** (38a,75b, 119c), **oyes** (38a,39b,75b), **oyez** (38a,39b,75b), **pyet** (95b), **ryel** (190), **syed** (103b), **tyee** (29d), **tyer**

- - YE   **Daye** (123d), **Skye** (163c)

Y - - E   **yage** (23a), **yaje** (23a), **Yale** (173c), **yare** (96b,124b,128b), **yate** (51d,168c), **yoke** (85b,92d,173c), **yore** (10b,69d,93c,110b,165d), **Yule** (30d)

381

- YG - bygo (114c), zyga (134b)

Y - - G yang (30b,70a), yegg (24c)

YH - - YHVH (159d), YHWH (159d)

Y - - H yeah, YHVH (159d), YHWH (159d), yodh (91d), yogh (10c,185a)

YI - - Yima (84a,116b,c)

- YI - ayin (91c)

- - YI kiyi (185d)

Y - - I Yaki (193), yali (171a), yati (76d), yeni (19b,161d), Yobi, yogi (76d)

- YK - cyke (40c), dyke (49c,91d), fyke (15d), hyke!, syke (194), tyke (29d)

Y - - K yank, Yank, yark (22c), yolk, york (38c), York (50b,c)

- YL - gyle (23b,174d), Hyla (10a,166d,169b), hyle (97c), kyle (57a, 139c), pyla (22d), pyle (34b), Pyle (9c,178a), Xylo (35a,183d)

- - YL acyl (6d), amyl (155c), idyl (114d), noyl (87c), odyl (59d,79c), oxyl (112c), teyl (92b,c,168c)

Y - - L yarl (40d,107d), yawl (136b,171d,175d), yell (145c), yowl, ypil (117a,168c)

YM - - Ymer (67a,131c), Ymir (67a,131c)

- YM - cyma (101a,b), cyme (58d,69c), hymn (150c), ryme (178d), tymp (20c), zyme (55c)

- - YM clym (12b), etym (133d), onym (162c)

YN - - Ynca (193)

- YN - dyna (34c), dyne (59d,173b), gyne (34b,55b,183c), jynx (78a), Jynx (184a), lynx (26c,181d), Lynx (36b), myna (19a,c,70b), rynd (100a), syne (140b,147a), tyne, Tyne (108a), wynn (165d)

- - YN coyn (37a), Gwyn (40c,50b), llyn (120d,140a)

Y - - N yarn (154b,161b,184b), yawn, yean (88a), yuan (190), Yuan (30b, 101d)

YO - - Yobi, yodh (91d), yoga (10b,13c,77a), yogh (10c,185a), yogi (76d), yoke (85b,92d,173c), yolk, yond (164d), yoop, yore (10b,69d,93c, 110b,165d), york (38c), York (50b,c), youp (185d), your (124c), yowl, yowt (139c)

- YO - eyot (82d), ryot (115c)

- - YO buyo (18b), cayo, coyo (15a,30c), Enyo (12c,69c,178a), Idyo (191), kayo (87c), Mayo (193), whyo (59d,65a)

Y - - O Yedo (166d), yeso (72d)

YP - - ypil (117a,168c)

- YP - gyps, Gyps (71d), hype (185a), hypo (117b), hyps, rype (19b,125a), sype (110c), type (31d,115a,155a), typo (35c,51b), typp (185b), typy

- - YP tryp (114a)

Y - - P Yapp (22a), yaup, yawp, yelp, yoop, youp (185d)

- YR - Byrd (9c,120b), byre (38a), eyra (181d), eyre (23c,31b,85c), Eyre, eyry (47b,106c), fyrd (110a), gyre (31b,171b), gyri (22d,

131b), **gyro** (34d), **Lyra** (36b,74a), **lyre** (11c,81c,105a,111c), **Myra** (10a,31b,183c), **pyre** (64c), **pyro, Syra, tyre** (15a), **Tyre** (31b,90d, 117b), **tyro** (9b,17d,108c), **Tyrr** (68c,109c,163d,178a), **Wyrd** (107d)

- - YR skyr (21d,151a)

Y - - R yarr (72a), year, Ymer (67a,131c), Ymir (67a,131c), your (124c), Yser

YS - - Yser

- YS - cyst, lyse, myst (71c,123b)

- - YS Alys (183c), Emys (167c,171b), days, Itys (163b), ways

Y - - S yeas (177c)

- YT - myth (8b,91a), Tyto (16c)

- - YT skyt (138c,140b)

Y - - T yelt (151b), yowt (139c), yuft (135c), Yuit (51c), yurt (101d)

YU - - yuan (190), Yuan (30b,101d), yuca (27a), yuft (135c), Yuga (76d), Yuit (51c), Yule (30d), Yuma, Yunx (184a), yurt (101d), yutu (19b,166a)

- YU - syud (103b)

- - YU Vayu (68c,182a)

Y - - U Yaou (30c), Yaru (48d), yutu (19b,166a)

- YV - gyve (55d,143b)

- YX - myxa (168c,169a), myxo

- - YX Ceyx (73b), eryx (137a), onyx (25d,28d,65d,142b), oryx (11a), Pnyx (71c), Styx (29b,73a,105c)

Y - - X Yunx (184a)

- - YZ hayz

ZA - - Zach (96b), zaim (170d), zain (41a), Zama (73d,141d), zany (24a, 32d,59c), zarf (39c,155a), zarp (120c), zati (21d)

- ZA - Azam (166c), azan (102d), czar (42d,49d,60b,135c), izar (65b, 103b), Izar (155b), tzar (42d,49d,60b,135c), Uzan (189)

- - ZA boza (12a), caza, Daza (191), Gaza (117a), Itza (192), Juza (155b), onza (189), tiza (172a), tuza (119d), vaza (114a), zuza (189)

Z - - A Zama (73d,141d), zeta (71b,91c), Zipa (29d), zira (188), Zola (63a), zona (144c,186d), zuza (189), zyga (134b)

- ZB - ezba (188)

Z - - B Zimb (6c)

Z - - C zinc (21a)

Z - - D Zend, zoid

ZE - - zeal (12c,55d), zebu (22d,80d,112c), zein, Zeke (96b), zeme (55d,161b,180b), zemi (55d,161b,180b), Zend, Zeno (71b), zenu (143d), zero (31a,84c,108c), Zero (118d), zest (55d,72d), zeta (71b,91c), Zeus (135a)

- ZE - ezel (47a,85d)

- - ZE adze (40c,167a), bize (182a), coze (29b), daze (157d), doze (148a), faze (43d), fuze (98c), gaze, guze (128d), haze (100c,174d), laze (79b), Laze (191), maze (87b,157d), naze (26b,124b), noze (75a),

ooze (53c,104b,116a), **raze** (42b,d,91d), **size, unze** (189)

Z - - E   **Zeke** (96b), **zeme** (55d,161b,180b), **zone** (44c,50a,160a), **zyme** (55c)

Z - - F   **zarf** (39c,155a)

Z - - G   **zing**

- ZH -   **Azha** (155b)

Z - - H   **Zach** (96b)

ZI - -   **Zimb** (6c), **zinc** (21a), **zing, Zion** (75b,c,83a,157d), **Zipa** (29d), **zipp, Zips** (40c), **zira** (188), **zizz** (181a)

- - ZI   **cazi** (103a), **gazi, kazi** (103a), **Lazi** (191), **Nazi**

Z - - I   **zati** (21d), **zemi** (55d,161b,180b), **Zuni** (125b)

Z - - L   **zeal** (12c,55d)

Z - - M   **zaim** (170d), **zoom**

Z - - N   **zain** (41a), **zein, Zion** (75b,c,83a,157d), **zoon** (43a)

ZO - -   **Zoar, Zoas** (20b), **zobo** (186b), **zodi, zogo** (136a), **zoid, Zola** (63a), **zona** (144c,186d), **zone** (44c,50a,160a), **zoom, zoon** (43a)

- ZO -   **Azof** (20b,135d), **azon** (127b), **Azov** (20b,135d), **mozo** (152b), **Muzo** (192)

- - ZO   **bozo** (55b), **Idzo** (191), **kozo** (113d,168c), **lazo** (88d,128b,133d)

Z - - O   **Zeno** (71b), **zero** (31a,84c,108c), **Zero** (118d), **zobo** (186b), **zogo** (136a)

Z - - P   **zarp** (120c), **zipp**

- ZR -   **Ezra** (96a)

Z - - R   **Zoar**

Z - - S   **Zeus** (135a), **Zips** (40c), **Zoas** (20b)

Z - - T   **zest** (55d,72d)

ZU - -   **zulu** (171d,175d), **Zulu** (86a), **Zuni** (125b), **zuza** (189)

- ZU -   **azul** (151d)

- - ZU   **anzu** (11d), **auzu** (168c,180b), **Enzu** (102b), **wuzu** (102d)

Z - - U   **zebu** (22d,80d,112c), **zenu** (143d), **zulu** (171d,175d), **Zulu** (86a)

ZY - -   **zyga** (134b), **zyme** (55c)

- - ZY   **cazy** (103a), **cozy** (149c), **dazy, dozy, gazy, hazy** (174b), **Jozy, kazy** (103a), **lazy, oozy** (148b), **sizy** (176d)

Z - - Y   **zany** (24a,32d,59c)

- - ZZ   **bizz, buzz, fuzz** (45d), **huzz, jazz, razz** (131b), **sizz, zizz** (181a)

Z - - Z   **zizz** (181a)